Anthony Wood, Andrew Clark

The life and times of Anthony Wood, antiquary, of Oxford

1623-1695

Volume IV: Addenda

Anthony Wood, Andrew Clark

The life and times of Anthony Wood, antiquary, of Oxford 1623-1695
Volume IV: Addenda

ISBN/EAN: 9783741103902

Manufactured in Europe, USA, Canada, Australia, Japa

Cover: Foto ©Thomas Meinert / pixelio.de

Manufactured and distributed by brebook publishing software
(www.brebook.com)

Anthony Wood, Andrew Clark

The life and times of Anthony Wood, antiquary, of Oxford

1623-1695

Oxford Historical Society

VOL XXX

LIFE AND TIMES

OF

ANTHONY WOOD

The Life and Times of

Anthony Wood, antiquary,

of Oxford, 1632–1695,

described by Himself

COLLECTED FROM

HIS DIARIES AND OTHER PAPERS

BY

ANDREW CLARK, M.A.

LINCOLN COLLEGE, OXFORD

VOLUME IV: ADDENDA

WITH ILLUSTRATIONS

Oxford

PRINTED FOR THE OXFORD HISTORICAL SOCIETY

AT THE CLARENDON PRESS

1895

PREFACE.

IN this volume I have brought together certain documents and notes which seemed to me to serve naturally as appendixes to Wood's autobiographical remains.

By prescription of former editions, some of the documents connected with Wood's trial for libel, 1692–1693, had acquired a right to a place in Wood's Life. To these I was able to add other documents of the set, recently brought to light by the Keeper of the Archives, and not inferior in value or interest to those hitherto published. Nor did I think it right, on account of the triviality of some of the records, to leave out any document connected with the case. So far as I know, this is the only suit in the University Court, in which anything approaching to a complete set of documents is preserved; and, therefore, apart from its connexion with Wood's life, it is the one case in which we have set before us the procedure of the *Curia Cancellarii*.

The Catalogue of MS. Authorities was finished, after a fashion, in 1889, and sent to press on January 14, 1890, with a view to then printing it. It has since been added to and re-written. During the years in which it has lain by me in MS., I have found that it has supplied answers to many questions raised by others as well as myself; and therefore I have some warrant for supposing that, in spite of its imperfections, it will prove of service to students. Further search among MSS. bearing on Oxford would have improved it at many points; but in such further search I can take no part, since my new duties have removed me far from Oxford and from all libraries.

As regards the Additional Notes, I intended, at first, to give only such necessary corrections as had been suggested to me since the publication of the other three volumes. But having been led to peruse the account-books of the University in connexion with the seventeenth-century repairs of S. Mary's steeple, and finding that they contained accurate details on numerous points mentioned by Wood, I resolved to make full use of this source of information, so far as it threw light on Wood's Life and Times.

In the present volume I have to acknowledge very special obligations to the Rev. T. Vere Bayne, Keeper of the Archives of the University, and to Falconer Madan, Esq., Fellow of Brasenose College.

I have also to thank J. K. Hudson, Esq., B.A., of Wadham College, for kind help towards the Catalogue of MS. Authorities.

ANDREW CLARK.

ADDENDUM.

The old oath-book of the Tailors' Company, a charter of the Cordwainers' Company, and other documents relating to the trade-gilds are in the possession of F. P. Morrell, Esq., and were exhibited at the Loan Exhibition, Nov. 7 and 8, 1894, of the Oxford Architectural and Historical Society.—See *infra,* p. 187.

CONTENTS.

III. CATALOGUE OF WOOD'S MS. AUTHORITIES, pp. 87–312.

PLATES.

WOOD'S TRIAL FOR LIBEL ; AND EXPULSION FROM THE UNIVERSITY.

WOOD was prosecuted in the Vice-Chancellor's Court by Henry, second earl of Clarendon, for a libel on his father Edward Hyde, first earl, contained in the second volume of the *Athenae Oxonienses* (published in July 1692), where Wood had put down in print the freely-expressed opinion of the day that at the Restoration Lord Chancellor Hyde had received money from office-seekers. It seems strange to us that Wood in his defence took the narrow technical position that it could not be proved that he had written the words complained of, instead of urging that a dead man could not prosecute for libel and that Lord Clarendon had died in exile, avoiding impeachment on this very charge among others.

In the *Acta Curiae Cancellarii Oxon.*, the register of proceedings in the Vice-Chancellor's Court, only a bare outline of the suit is given. The most material papers, such as the case submitted by the prosecution, the defence put in, the questions asked of witnesses, the evidence tendered by them, the verdict given, were written on loose sheets and never entered in the register. Copies of some of these loose sheets, containing part of the cases for the prosecution and the defence, and the sentence, came into a bookseller's hands and were printed (circ. 1700 ?) on four folio pages. They were reprinted by Edmund Curll in ' *Miscellanies on several curious subjects*: now first publish'd from their originals,' 8vo, Lond. 1714: and have since appeared in successive editions of Wood's Life. The present Keeper of the Archives, the Rev. T. Vere Bayne, in the course of his work in arranging the ' indigesta moles' of papers in the Archives, has collected and had bound together [1] the scattered papers connected with Wood's trial. From

[1] the volume is marked ' Arch. Univ. Oxon. W. P. γ. 26.'

these and from the *Acta Curiae Canc. Oxon.* I am able, by his kindness, to add here a fuller and more intelligible set of documents concerning this case than it has hitherto been possible to give. It must, however, be noted that several important documents are still missing. These gaps are indicated as they occur.

Several of the documents here printed have in themselves few points of interest; but I thought that the suit deserved reproduction in its entirety, as a specimen of procedure in the University court.

I. The opening of the case.

11 Nov. 1692[1]; Officium domini contra Anthonium à Wood, Univ. Oxon., in Artibus Magistrum, in negotio reformationis morum, praesertim ob libellum sive libellos famosos ab eo compositos et scriptos et publicatos[4], promotum per honoratissimum virum ac dominum Henricum comitem de Clarendon.

Smith[5].

Quibus[2], &c., comparuit Johannes Smith[3], Ll. Bac., unus procuratorum generalium curiae Cancellarii Univ. Oxon., et exhibuit procuratorium suum in scriptis factum pro dicto honoratissimo viro ac domino Henrico comite de Clarendon, et fecit se partem pro eodem; necnon allegavit dictum Anthonium à Wood diligenter quaesitum fuisse 9° die[6] instantis Novembris, sed

non inventum, per Andream Skinner, mandatarium curiae praedictae, de veritate allegationis juratum. Unde dominus ad peticionem dicti Smith decrevit dictum à Wood personaliter citandum fore in proximum[7], si &c., alioquin viis et modis.

II. Lord Clarendon gives caution to carry on the suit.

Stipulacio[8]: 15 Novembr.[9], 1692. Decimo quinto die Novembris anno Domini 1692 venerabilis vir Gulielmus Levett, S.T.P. et aulae B^tae M. Magd. (principalis), stipulacionem interposuit juxta formam registri in summa decem librarum pro honoratissimo viro ac domino Henrico comite de Clarendon de lite sua persequenda expensisque solvendis casu quo in negotio seu causa contra Antonium à Wood succubuerit, coram me Jos. Woodward, registrario.

III. Wood gives caution for payment of expenses.

Stipulacio. Novemb. 18[10], 1692, sedente curia, Anthonius à Wood, Universitatis Oxon. in Artibus Magister, et Benjamin Wood, Coll. Novi in Universitate Oxon.

[1] Friday.

[2] sc. die et hora. The court sat between 1 and 3 p.m. in the Apodyterium.

[3] John Smith B.C.L. (S. John's) 23 Nov. 1686.

[4] the terms of the Statute (*Laudian Code*, Tit. xv. sect. 8) are—'Siquis aliquid scripto composuerit unde alicujus existimatio et fama laedi possit, vel aliquid ejusmodi . . . quoquo modo in vulgus sparserit aut disseminaverit, tanquam pacis perturbator banniatur.'

[5] i. e. the name of Lord Clarendon's proctor, John Smith.

[6] Wednesday.

[7] sc. diem ; i. e. Friday 18 Nov., the court meeting weekly on Friday afternoon: vol. iii. p. 407.

[8] i. e. security.

[9] Tuesday.

[10] Friday: vol. iii. p. 407.

socius, ejus fidejussor, conjunctim et divisim et in solid. se, haeredes, executores et administratores suos ⟨obligaverunt⟩ et eorum uterque se sic obligavit illustrissimo domino Jacobo duci &c. de Ormond et Universitatis Oxon. praedictae cancellario et successoribus ejus in quadraginta libris bonae et legalis monetae solvendis ad usum honoratissimi viri ac domini Henrici comitis de Clarendon pro et de comparendo in judicio et usque ad sententiam permanendo necnon de judicat. expensisque solvendis in negotio per dictum dominum Henrici comitis de Clarendon promotum contra dictum Anthonium à Wood.

IV. Wood appears and articles are exhibited against him.

⟨Friday⟩ 18 Nov. 1692[1]: officium domini promotum &c. contra Anthonium à Wood.   Smith[2].

Emanaverat decretum viis et modis contra dictum Anthonium à Wood.

Quibus[3] &c., reducto decreto viis et modis praedicto personaliter per Thomam Rogers mandatarium hujus curiae juxta certificatorium et desuper juratum, personaliter comparuit dictus Anthonius à Wood et stipulationem interposuit ut supra. In cujus praesentia Smith dedit articulos[4] in scriptis conceptos quos dominus ad ejus peticionem admisit quatenus &c. Necnon ad peticionem dicti à Wood assignavit ei ad respondendum in proximum &c. Tunc ad ulteriorem peticionem dicti Smith dominus judicialiter monuit dictum Anth. à Wood ad personaliter comparendum de die in diem usque ad sententiam in hoc negocio.

V. The articles[5] against Wood: 'exhibit. Friday 18 Nov. 1692.'

In Dei nomine, Amen. Nos Henricus Aldrich, S.T.P. vice-cancellarius universitatis Oxon. legitime constitutus tibi Antonio à Wood universitatis praedictae in artibus magistro, omnia et singula subscripta et subsequentia, articulos, capitula, sive interrogatoria morum et excessuum tuorum reformationem, praesertim libellum sive libellos famosos a te scriptos compositos et publicatos concernentes sive tangentes ex officio nostro ad promotionem honoratissimi viri et domini Henrici Comitis de Clarendon, damus, objicimus, ministramus et articulamur, planum, plenum et fidele responsum in scriptis in quantum de jure teneris respondere, dari et fieri requirentes. Et objicimus et articulamur conjunctim et divisim et de quolibet prout sequitur.

I. Imprimis Tibi praefato Antonio à Wood objicimus et articulamur, quod

---

[1] the record of each day's proceedings in a suit in the court falls into three parts; thus, here, there is *first*, a marginal note of the suit; *second*, (here beginning at 'Emanaverat') a memorandum of what had been ordered on the preceding court-day; *third*, (beginning with 'Quibus') a statement of what was done in court on the given day.

[2] see note 5, p. 2.

[3] see note 2, p. 2.

[4] these articles follow.

[5] these articles are taken from the official copy in the Archives of the University. There were some clerical errors in the paper, which the Court on 20 Jan. 169⅔ (see the paper in Arch. Univ. Oxon. W. P. γ. 26. fol. 7) allowed John Smith, proctor for Lord Clarendon, to amend. These corrections are inserted in the text here. The amending hand has also made some interlinear additions, here inclosed in square brackets, intended chiefly to render easier the proof of publication.

omnes et singuli, qui aliquid scripto composuerunt, aut quoquo modo in vulgus sparserunt aut disseminaverunt, aut publicaverunt, unde viri alicujus (praesertim magistratûs) sive vivi, sive mortui, existimatio et fama laedi possit, sunt de jure communi debitè corrigendi et puniendi, et speciatim ex statuto hujus universitatis, TIT. *De moribus conformandis*, § *De famosis libellis cohibendis* : omnes et singuli libellos famosos, sive componentes, sive disseminantes et publicantes, sunt tanquam pacis perturbatores banniendi. Et objicimus et articulamur ut supra, &c.

II. Item, Tibi objicimus et articulamur, quod mensibus Martii, Aprilis, Maii, Junii, Julii, Augusti, Septembris, Octobris, Novembris, Decembris, Januarii, Februarii, annorum Domini 1690, 1691 ; mensibusque Martii, Aprilis, Maii, Junii, Julii, Augusti, Septembris, Octobris, et Novembris, Anni instantis 1692 ; eorumve mensium et annorum pluribus uno sive aliquo, Tu librum quendam praetensum, cui titulus praetensus, ATHENÆ[1] OXONIENSES; AN EXACT HISTORY OF ALL THE WRITERS AND BISHOPS WHO HAVE HAD THEIR EDUCATION IN THE MOST ANCIENT AND FAMOUS UNIVERSITY OF OXFORD, FROM THE FIFTEENTH YEAR OF KING HENRY VII, ANNO DOMINI 1500, TO THE END OF THE YEAR 1690, REPRESENTING THE BIRTH, FORTUNE, PREFERMENT, AND DEATH OF ALL THOSE AUTHORS AND PRELATES, THE GREAT ACCIDENTS OF THEIR LIVES, AND THE FATE AND CHARACTERS OF THEIR WRITINGS[2] : TO WHICH ARE ADDED, THE FASTI OR ANNALS OF THE SAID UNIVERSITY FOR THE SAME TIME. THE SECOND VOLUME : reverâ autem libellum famosum seu potius libellos famosos, inferius deductos, in se continentem ; charitate semota, et ex odii fomite, infra praecinctum universitatis praedictae malitiose scripto composuisti et scripsisti, seu saltem scribi, ac deinceps typis mandari et imprimi mandasti et curasti et fecisti ; aut bibliopolae aut bibliopolis quibusdam [vendidisti[3], aut cum iisdem] ut imprimerentur, contraxisti, copiasque dicti praetensi libri sic impressi, ac libellos sive libellum famosum in se continentem falsitates, infra praecinctum universitatis praedictae, et loca vicina, et latè circumvicina ejusdem sparsisti, disseminasti et publicasti, saltem spargi, disseminari, et publicari fecisti et procurasti ; quarum copiarum una praesentibus annexa est (eamque et omnes et singulas sententias et clausulas ejusdem, pro hic exhibitis, insertis, lectis, et repetitis pars promovens habet et haberi petit, quatenus ex parte sua, et officii in ea parte nostri faciunt, et non aliter, neque alio modo). Et objicimus et articulamur, &c. ut supra.

III. Item, Magis speciatim tibi objicimus et articulamur quod infra tempus in proximo praecedenti articulo mentionatum, et inter alia in dicto libro, sic, ut praemittitur, composito, scripto, impresso et publicato, contenta, charitate semotâ, et ex odii fomite (infra universitatem Oxoniensem praedictam, et loca vicina, ac circumvicina ejusdem) malitiose scripto composuisti, scripsisti, seu saltem scribi, ac deinceps typis mandari et imprimi mandasti, procurasti ac fecisti ; aut bibliopolae aut bibliopolis quibusdam [vendidisti, aut cum iisdem] ut imprimerentur contraxisti, impressaque infra praecinctum universitatis praedictae sparsisti, disseminasti [seu saltem spargi, disseminari] et publicari fecisti et procurasti (unde honoratissimi viri ac domini Edvardi Hyde militis, nuper Comitis de Clarendon, regni Angliae [Domini] Cancellarii, necnon Cancellarii hujus universitatis, et patris naturalis et legitimi partis hujus promoventis defuncti existimatio et fama laedi possit) libellum famosum, sive verba haec Anglicana sequentia, viz. *After the*

---

[1] ' Fasti,' in the first hand : altered to ' Athenae ' by the second.

[2] ' lives,' in the first hand : altered to ' writeings ' by the second ; see note 5.

p. 3.

[3] words inserted by the second hand ; see p. 3.

restauration of King Charles the 2d it was expected by all, that he (quendam Davidem Jenkins, unum e judicibus regis in partibus Walliæ australibus, virum meritissimum, innuendo) *should be made one of the judges in Westminster hall; and so he* (eundem Davidem innuendo) *might have been, would he have given money to the then Lord Chancellor,* (praefatum honoratissimum virum ac dominum Edvardum Hyde militem, nuper Comitem de Clarendon, regnique Angliae [Dominum] Cancellarium, necnon Cancellarium hujus universitatis, patremque naturalem ac legitimum partis hujus promoventis defunctum innuendo) *but our author* (praefatum Davidem Jenkins innuendo) *scorning such an act, after all his sufferings, he retired to his estate in Glamorganshire*: prout in dictae copiae hic exhibitae columnis 220, et 221, continentur; aut iis similia in effectu (quam quidem copiam, et omnes et singulas sententias et clausulas ejusdem pro hic exhibitis, insertis, lectis et repetitis, pars promovens habet et haberi petit, quatenus pro parte sua, et officii in ea parte nostri faciunt, et non aliter neque alio modo). Et objicimus et articulamur, &c. ut supra.

IV. Item, Magis speciatim tibi objicimus et articulamur, quod infra tempus et loca superius in secundo articulo mentionata in dicto praetenso libro, sic ut praemittitur, composito, scripto, impresso, et publicato; ex odii fomite, charitate semota, malitiose scripto composuisti, scripsisti, seu saltem scribi, ac deinceps typis mandari, et imprimi mandasti, procurasti et fecisti, aut bibliopolae aut bibliopolis quibusdam [vendidisti, aut saltem cum iisdem] ut imprimerentur, contraxisti, impressaque sparsisti, disseminasti et publicasti [; seu saltem spargi, disseminari, et publicari fecisti et procurasti] (unde etiam praefati honoratissimi viri ac domini Edvardi Hyde militis, nuper Comitis de Clarendon, regni Angliae Domini Cancellarii, necnon hujus universitatis Cancellarii, et patris naturalis et legitimi partis hujus promoventis defuncti existimatio et fama laedi possit) libellum famosum, sive verba haec Anglicana sequentia, aut iis similia in effectu, viz. *After the restoration of K. Charles the 2d, he* (quendam Johannem Glinn, hominem —ut tibi placet—inidoneum, innuendo) *was made his* (innuendo, regis) *eldest serjeant at law, by the corrupt dealing of the then lord chancellor* (praefatum honoratissimum virum ac dominum Edvardum Hyde militem, nuper Comitem de Clarendon, regni Angliae Dominum Cancellarium, necnon Cancellarium hujus universitatis, patremque naturalem et legitimum hujus partis promoventis defuncti innuendo) prout in copiae praedictae exhibitae columnâ 269 continentur, (quam quidem copiam, et omnes et singulas sententias et clausulas ejusdem pro hic lectis et insertis pars promovens habet et haberi petit, quatenus pro parte sua et officii in hac parte nostri faciunt, et non aliter neque alio modo). Et objicimus et articulamur, &c. ut supra.

V. Item, Tibi objicimus et articulamur, de quibuslibet aliis verbis, sententiis, et clausulis in et per totum dictum librum tuum praetensum, cujus copia hic, ut praemittitur, exhibita est, sparsis et contentis, ad existimationis sive famae praefati honoratissimi viri Edvardi Hyde militis, nuper Comitis de Clarendon, laesionem sive diminutionem quomodolibet sonantibus (quam quidem copiam et omnes et singulas sententias et clausulas ejusdem pro hic lectis et insertis, pars promovens habet et haberi petit; quatenus pro parte sua et officii in hac parte nostri faciunt, et non aliter neque alio modo). Et objicimus et articulamur, &c. ut supra.

VI. Item, Tibi objicimus et articulamur, quod tempus reditus sive restaurationis Caroli 2di regis erat mense Maii, anno Domini 1660, hocque fuit et est notorium, publicum et manifestum. Et objicimus et articulamur, &c. ut supra.

VII. Item, Tibi objicimus et articulamur, quod praefatus David Jenkins, mense Decembris, anno Domini 1663, et praefatus Johannes Glynn, mense Novembris, anno Domini 1666, ex hac vita decesserunt; haecque fuisse et esse vera tu praefatus

Antonius à Wood novisti et noscis, intelligisti et intelligis, prout columnis 222 et 270 dicti libri tui praetensi, cujus copia hic, ut praemittitur, exhibita est (quam quidem copiam et omnes et singulas sententias et clausulas ejusdem pro hic lectis et insertis pars promovens habet et haberi petit, quatenus pro parte sua et officii in hac parte nostri faciunt, et non aliter neque alio modo) liquet et apparet. Et objicimus et articulamur, &c. ut supra.

VIII. Item, Tibi objicimus, et articulamur, quod praefatus honoratissimus vir Edvardus Hyde miles, et Comes de Clarendon, erat Dominus Cancellarius Angliae unicus, et e consiliariis regiis unus, toto ac omni tempore, a tempore reditûs sive restaurationis Caroli 2di Regis praedicti, necnon Cancellarius hujus universitatis, a mense Junii, seu saltem Novembris, anno Domini 1660 usque ad annum Domini 1667. Haecque fuerunt et sunt vera, notoria, publica, ac pariter manifesta. Et objicimus et articulamur, &c. ut supra.

IX. Item, Tibi Antonio à Wood objicimus et articulamur, quod es in artibus magister, et persona privilegiata hujus universitatis Oxoniensis, et tam ejus intuitu, quam ratione criminum superius deductorum infra praecinctum dictae universitatis, ut praemittitur, commissorum et perpetratorum, jurisdictioni hujus curiae in hac causa subditus et subjectus. Et objicimus et articulamur, &c. ut supra.

X. Item, Tibi objicimus et articulamur, quod omnia et singula praemissa fuerunt, et sunt vera, publica, notoria, pariter et manifesta, deque omnibus et quolibet eorum laboravit et laborat in praesenti publica vox et fama. Et objicimus et articulamur, &c. ut supra.

[Unde facta fide, &c.]

VI. Wood enters a plea of not guilty.

⟨Friday⟩ 25 Nov. 1692: officium domini promotum contra Anth. à Wood. Smith[1].

Dictus Antho. à Wood habet ad respondendum articulis contra eum datis et admissis in hunc diem.

Quibus &c. personaliter comparuit dictus Anth. à Wood juxta monicionem ultimi diei juridici et Smith[1] petiit responsum suum dictis articulis contra eum datis et admissis dictusque à Wood respondet negative eisdem, anima contestandi litem. Unde dominus ad petitionem Smith judicialiter monuit dictum à Wood ad dandum responsa sua in scriptis praedictis articulis quatenus de jure teneatur respondere eisdem in proximum. Tunc dictus Antho. à Wood constituit Tho. Wood et Jo. Cooke LLegum respective Bac. in ejus procuratores conjunctim et divisim juxta formam registri, quod procuratorium Cooke statim acceptavit fecitque se partem pro eodem.

VII. Wood's plea of not guilty.

Responsa[2] personalia Antonii Wood, de Oxon., gen., facta quibusdam praetensis articulis, exhibitis contra eum ad instantiam ac promotionem honoratissimi viri domini Henrici comitis de Clarendon 18° die Novembris 1692, sequuntur.

1. ad 1mum articulum respondet et dicit quod non credit eundem esse verum in aliquo, referendo se ad jus.

2. ad 2ndum articulum et ad praetensi libri sive libelli copiam exhibitam respondet et dicit quod quoad sua facta negat, quoad aliena non credit eundem esse verum in aliquo.

---

[1] see note 5, p. 2.   [2] from Arch. Univ. Oxon. W. P. γ. 26. fol. 4.

3. ad 3^{ium} articulum et ad praetensi libri sive libelli copiam exhibitam respondet et dicit quod quoad sua facta negat, quoad aliena non credit eundem esse verum in aliquo.

4, 5. ad 4^{tum} et 5^{tum} articulos et ad praetensi libri sive libelli copiam exhibitam respondet et dicit quod quoad sua facta negat, quoad aliena non credit eosdem esse veros in aliquo.

6. ad 6^{tum} articulum respondet et dicit quod credit eundem esse verum.

7, 8. ad 7^{mum} et 8^{vum} articulos respondet et dicit quod quoad sua facta negat, quoad aliena non credit eosdem esse veros.

9. ad 9^{num} articulum respondet et dicit that about 20 years agoe he was a master of arts of the University of Oxon, et aliter non credit eundem esse verum in aliquo.

10. ad 10^{mum} articulum respondet et dicit quod credit credita et negat negata, et aliter quoad reliqua non credit eundem esse verum in aliquo.

ANTHONY WOOD.

Repetit. et recognit.
coram Georgio Gardiner,
     assessore.

VIII. Wood disputes the validity of the articles against him.

⟨Friday⟩ 2 Dec. 1692: officium domini promotum contra A. Wood. Smith[1]. Wood, Cooke[2].   Judicialiter *monitus est dictus* Anth. à Wood ad dandum responsa sua in scriptis articulis in hoc negotio contra eum datis et admissis in hunc diem.

Quibus, &c., comparuit Tho. Wood LL^m. Bac. et acceptavit procuratorium suum alias in hoc negotio sibi per dictum à Wood concessum et factum fecitque se partem pro eodem; necnon allegavit dictos articulos ex parte honoratissimi domini Henrici comitis de Clarendon in hoc negotio datos fuisse ac esse nimis generales ineptos et inconcludentes in jure, ideoque petiit eos rejici. Unde dominus assignavit ad audiendum voluntatem suam desuper in proximum &c., necnon ad informandum eum in camera sua infra Coll. Omn. Animarum situata die Jovis proximo hora prima pomeridiana ejusdem diei, in praesentia Smith. Tunc facta trina praeconizatione pro dicto Antho. à Wood eoque non comparente, dominus, ad peticionem Smith accusantis ejus contumaciam in non dando responsa sua in scriptis dictis articulis juxta monitionem ei judicialiter factam, pronunciavit eum contumacem in hac parte sed reservavit ejus poenam in proximum &c., et continuavit monicionem &c. in eundem diem.

IX. The Court pronounces the articles valid.

⟨Friday⟩ 9 Dec.[3] 1692: officium domini promotum &c. contra Antho. à Wood. Smith. Wood, Cooke.   Dictus à Wood monitus est in hunc diem, in non dando responsa sua in scriptis articulis contra eum datis et admissis in hoc negotio juxta monitionem &c. Ad audiendum voluntatem domini &c. in eundem diem.

Quibus &c. habitis informacionibus juxta assignationem judicis ultimo die juridico factam dominus ad peticionem Smith declaravit exceptiones per Tho.

---

[1] John Smith, Lord Chancellor's proctor.

[2] Thomas Wood, John Cooke, Anthony Wood's proctors: vol. iii. p. 410.

[3] vol. iii. p. 411.

Wood factas contra articulos in hoc negotio ex parte honoratissimi promotoris officii sui non esse peremptorias, ideoque pronunciavit pro validitate articulorum praedictorum. Necnon ad ulteriorem peticionem Smith condemnavit à Wood in expensis informacionum praedictarum.

Tunc facta trina praeconizacione pro dicto à Wood eoque non comparente, dominus ad peticionem Smith, accusantis ejus contumaciam in non dando responsa sua in scriptis articulis praedictis juxta monicionem ei judicialiter factam, pronunciavit eum in hac parte contumacem, et in poenam contumaciae suae hujusmodi decrevit dictum à Wood arrestandum fore. Necnon continuavit dictam monitionem in proximum diem juridicum ex tunc sequentem. A quibus gravaminibus omnibus et singulis Thomas Wood et Cooke, procuratores à Wood praedicti, (salva reverentia judicis) protestati sunt de appellando ad judices delegatos venerabilis domus Congregationis Universitatis Oxon.

X. Wood fails to appear.

⟨Friday⟩ 16 Dec. 1692: officium domini promotum &c. contra Anth. A Wood. Smith. Wood, Cooke.

Continuatur monicio contra dictum à Wood. Emanaverat warrantum, &c. Quibus &c. facta trina praeconizacione pro dicto Antho. à Wood eoque non comparente, dominus ad peticionem Smith, accusantis ejus contumaciam, pronunciavit eum contumacem in non dando responsa sua in scriptis articulis contra eum datis et admissis juxta monicionem &c. Necnon continuavit monicionem in pr ximum, Wood dissentiente.

XI. A form of apology suggested by Wood, in hopes that Clarendon will withdraw the case.

Those things [1] that are excepted against the ATHENAE ET FASTI OXON. are not of the author's invention but what he found in letters sent to him from persons of knowne reputation [2], of which he is ready at any time to take his oath in any court of judicature. Which letters being at larg written he for his owne security did curtaile and contract them to what they now are without mentioning the name of the person. Yet notwithstanding this they are excepted against! If the earl of

[1] from the draft in Wood's hand in MS. Tanner 456 a fol. 66. On the same sheet are jottings, (1) of an excuse for the statements in the *Athenae*— 'several things put in at London by other hands,' (2) of the reason why a public apology was inconvenient—'submission if publick, no body will hereafter communicate records or letters to him.'

[2] among them John Aubrey, who communicated to Wood this note on David Jenkins (MS. Aubr. 8 fol. 27 a): —'JUDGE JENKINS, prisoner in the Tower of London, Windsore, &c., ...

yeares, for his loyaltie. He would have taken it kindly to have been made one of the judges in Westminster hall; but would give no money for it, *so the Lord Chancellor (Hyde) never preferred him.*—He was of very great courage; rode in the lord Gerard's army in Pembrokeshire, in the forlorne-hope, with his long rapier drawne, holding it on end. Obiit December 3. A. D. 1663; sepult. at Cowbridge church (in the south aisle) in Glamorganshire. No remembrance yet (1682) sett up for him.'

Clarendon will please to put an end to this process the author will faithfully promise to correct and amend all things, as his lordship will think fit, in his *Appendix* or *3d vol. of writers* which is almost ready for the press.

XII. Wood[1] complains that the terms of settlement offered by Clarendon are unsuitable.

'That[2] submission be read publicly in the Vice-chancellor's court and afterwards registered in the common register there.' If[3] it be put in the public Gazet it will (1) be a meanes to bring other people on the author[4] for other things mention'd in the book, and (2dly) deter the generality of people to send letters hereafter to the author[5] to carry on the next work—so that it will not be only a ruin to the author but to his studies. He hath been at great charg already to pay the common taxes, and if the same taxes goe forward the author must be forced to sell the best part of his books.

Pray let Dr. Bouchier and the noble earl of Clarendon know these things and desire them not to be an occasion of the author's ruin who only devotes himself to the public good, and studies, and (if possibly) to offend no man.

To make a submission (such as Dr. Bouchier shall think fit) in the next book to be published the author will faithfully promise to do it, but when that book will be published he cannot set a particular time, because (1) there must be many letters sent abroad, and as many answers to receive; (2) the book must goe through the licenser's hands, who perhaps may keep it a quarter of a yeare or more; (3) it must go through the bookseller's hands who is to be at the charg of printing it, who will be sure to communicate it to his friends for approbation: and (lastly) it must goe through the printers' hands and how long they will be in printing of it the author cannot assigne.

The licenser, bookseller, and printer of the ATHENAE ET FASTI OXON. did take great liberty to put in and out many things in the said book

---

[1] this paper, in Wood's hand, in MS. Tanner 456 a fol. 67, seems to be a draft of the terms he asked Henry Dodwell (on 16 Jan. 169⅞) to obtain from Clarendon: see *infra*, p. 26.

[2] the first sentence is what Clarendon had suggested Wood should do to secure the withdrawal of the case.

[3] Wood's objections to Clarendon's suggestion begin here. The connexion is—'If the apology be made publicly in open court, then it will get into the newspapers, and then it will (1) be &c.'

[4] 'on the author' is substituted for 'on my back.'

[5] 'the author' is substituted for 'me.'

either to please themselves, their friends, or to spite others, to the great injury of the author (being then in Oxon), as it hath since appeared.

Nothing done in this[1].

XIII. Wood gives his answers to the articles.

⟨Friday[2]⟩ 20 Jan. 169⅔: officium domini promotum &c. contra Anth. à Wood. Smith. Wood, Cooke.   Emanaverat warrantum contra dictum A. Wood, et monicio contra eum in hunc diem.

Quibus &c., facta trina praeconizacione pro dicto Anth. A. Wood eoque non comparente, dominus ad peticionem Smith, accusantis ejus contumaciam, pronunciavit eum contumacem in non dando responsa sua in scriptis articulis contra eum datis et admissis juxta monicionem &c. et continuavit dictam monicionem in proximum.

Tunc Wood et Cooke dederunt responsa dicti Anth. à Wood in scriptis facta articulis praedictis in praesentia Smith accept. eorundem quatenus &c., necnon allegantis juxta actum per eum datum super filo hujus termini remanentis. Unde dominus decrevit prout per dictum actum seu all⟨egaci⟩onem petitur.

XIV. Wood's answers to the articles.

Responsa[3] personalia Antonii Wood, de Oxon., gen., facta quibusdam praetensis articulis exhibitis contra eum in curia cancellarii Univ. Oxon., ad instantiam et promotionem honoratissimi viri domini Henrici comitis de Clarendon 18° die Novembris 1692, sequuntur : —

1. ad primum articulum respondet et dicit quod non credit eundem esse verum in aliquo:

'and particularly this respondent answereth and saith that he believes the statute of the University to be mis-recited as comprehending every person that writes or publishes a libell, whereas in truth it refers only to students and schollars within the University of Oxon or att the most to priviledged persons libelling or publishing libells against persons of the same character or against others living within the said University to the disturbance of the publick peace of the said University.'

2. ad 2ndum articulum respondet et dicit quod quatenus de jure tenetur respondere non credit eundem aut aliquam eorum partem esse verum in aliquo.

3. ad 3ium articulum respondet et dicit quod quatenus de jure tenetur respondere non credit eundem aut aliquam eorum partem esse verum in aliquo.

4, 5. ad 4tum et 5tum articulum respondet et dicit quod quatenus de jure tenetur respondere non credit eosdem aut aliquam eorum partem esse veros in aliquo.

6. ad 6tum articulum respondet et dicit quod credit eundem esse verum.

7. ad 7mum articulum respondet et dicit quod quatenus de jure tenetur respondere non credit eundem aut aliquam eorum partem esse verum in aliquo.

8. ad 8vum articulum respondet et dicit quod quatenus de jure tenetur respondere non credit eundem aut aliquam eorum partem esse verum in aliquo.

9. ad 9num articulum respondet et dicit :

'that he was and is a master of Arts but denies that he is a priviledged person

---

[1] note added by Wood later, when the apology he proposed was not entertained.

[2] vol. iii. p. 413.

[3] from Arch. Univ. Oxon. W. P. γ. fol. 8.

of the University of Oxon or that he is in this cause subject to the jurisdiction of this court, for that he has not lived in any collegiat manner nor had commons chamber or lodging in any colledge or hall these 20 years or upwards; and that if he has done any act which may be interpreted a submission to this court he does declare that he was forced to it thro fear of imprisonment : '

et aliter non credit eundem esse verum in aliquo.

10. ad 10^{mum} respondet et dicit quod quatenus de jure tenetur respondere non credit eundem aut aliquam eorum partem esse verum in aliquo.

ANTHONY WOOD[1].

Jan. 20, 1692[2]; repetit.
et recognit. coram me Georgio Gardiner,
       assess.

XV. The Court takes Wood's answers into consideration.

⟨Friday⟩ 27 Jan. 169⅔: officium domini promotum &c. contra Anth. A. Wood. Smith, Lloyd. Wood, Cooke. Emanaverat warrantum contra dictum A. Wood et continuatur monicio contra eum in hunc diem. Ultimo die juridico Wood et Cooke dederunt responsa &c. dicti à Wood facta articulis &c.

Quibus &c. comparuit Lloyd LL^m. Bac., procuratorum generalium hujus curiae unus, et exhibuit procuratorium suum in scriptis factum et concessum per honoratissimum dominum Henricum comitem de Clarendon promotorem &c., fecitque se partem pro eodem domino Henrico.

Tunc Smith et dictus Lloyd allegaverunt dictum Anth. à Wood nec plene nec plane respondisse articulis contra eum ex parte dicti honoratissimi domini Henrici comitis de Clarendon in hoc negocio datis et admissis. Unde dominus assignavit ad audiendum voluntatem suam in proximum &c. Necnon ad informandum eum in camera sua situata infra Coll. Omn. Animarum die Mercurii proximo sequente inter horas primam et secundam pomeridianas ejusdem diei, in praesentia Wood dissentientis.

Tunc facta trina praeconizacione pro dicto à Wood eoque non comparente, dominus ad peticionem Smith et Lloyd, accusantium ejus contumaciam, pronunciavit eum contumacem &c. et continuavit monicionem in proximum &c.

XVI. The Court orders Wood to send in fuller answers.

⟨Friday⟩ 3 Feb. 169⅔: officium domini promotum &c. contra Anth. à Wood. Smith, Lloyd. Cooke, Wood. Continuatur monicio contra dictum à Wood in hunc diem. Ad audiendum voluntatem domini super responsis dicti à Wood in eundem diem.

Quibus &c., habitis informacionibus juxta assignationem judicis, dominus declaravit et pronunciavit dictum Anth. à Wood nec plene nec plane respondisse articulis contra eum ex parte honoratissimi domini Henrici comitis de Clarendon in hoc negocio datis et admissis, necnon ad peticionem Smith et Lloyd decrevit pro responsis plenioribus dicti à Wood articulis praedictis, et condemnavit eum in expensis praedictarum informacionum, Wood et Cooke dissentientibus.

Tunc facta trina praeconizacione pro dicto Anth. à Wood eoque non comparente, dominus ad peticionem Smith et Lloyd, accusantium ejus contumaciam, pronunciavit eum contumacem &c. et continuavit dictam monicionem in proximum &c.

---

[1] autograph signature.   [2] i. e. 169⅔.

XVII. Wood submits fuller answers to the articles: and Clarendon submits an allegation.

⟨Friday[1]⟩ 10 Feb. 169⅔ : officium domini promotum &c. contra Anth. à Wood. Smith, Lloyd. Cooke, Wood.

Continuatur monicio contra dictum à Wood in hunc diem. Ultimo die juridico dominus decrevit pro responsis plenioribus dicti à Wood.

Quibus, &c., Wood et Cooke dederunt responsa pleniora dicti à Wood in scriptis conceptis facta articulis articulorum contra eum ex parte honoratissimi domini Henrici comitis de Clarendon in hoc negocio datis et admissis, in praesentia Smith et Lloyd accept. eorundem responsorum quatenus &c.,

et dantium allegacionem cum epistola sive praefacione necnon libro in folio cui titulus est *Historia et Antiquitates Universitatis Oxoniensis* ex parte dicti honoratissimi domini Henrici comitis de Clarendon quam dominus ad eorum peticionem admisit quatenus &c., Wood et Cooke dissentientibus.

Tunc facta trina praeconizacione pro dicto à Wood eoque non comparente, dominus ad peticionem Smith et Lloyd, accusantium ejus contumaciam, pronunciavit eum contumacem &c. et continuavit monicionem suam in proximum.

XVIII. Wood's fuller answers to the articles.

⟨These answers have not been found.⟩

XIX. Clarendon's allegation.

ALLEGATIO[2].
Exhibita Februarii 10ᵐᵒ 169⅔.

Officium Domini promotum per Honoratissimum Dominum Henricum Comitem de Clarendon contra Antonium à Wood Universitatis Oxon. A.M. ob libellum sive libellos famosos ab eo scriptos compositos et publicatos.

Quo die Smith et Lloyd nomine procuratorio et ut procuratores legitimi Honoratissimi Domini Domini Henrici Comitis de Clarendon omnibus melioribus via modo et Juris forma, &c. necnon ad omnem et quemcunque Juris effectum exinde quovismodo sequi valentem allegant et in his scriptis in jure proponunt conjunctim, divisim, articulatim prout sequitur, vizt.

1. Imprimis, That Mr. Anthony à Wood, the Defendant in the cause, before and during the time of printing the ATHENAE OXONIENSES and FASTI OXONIENSES VOLUME THE SECOND, exhibited in this Cause and within the time in the second Article of the Articles given in and admitted in this cause mentioned, did shew the same or many sheets or att least some one sheet thereof written with his own hand to divers or att least to some one person of this university and within the precincts thereof, and did own the same to have been composed in writing by him the said Mr. à Wood. Et ponunt ut supra.

2. Item, That the said Mr. à Wood did within the precincts of this university correct all or att least some of the first printed sheets or proof sheets of the said ATHENAE OXONIENSES and FASTI OXONIENSES VOLUME THE SECOND, as they

---

[1] vol. iii. p. 415.
[2] from the official copy in the University Archives (W. P. γ. 26. fol. 9). There is a copy in MS. Ballard xiv. fol. 27.

were first composed or sett att the presse, more especially those sheets which contain columne the two hundreth twenty first, and columne the two hundreth sixty ninth, in order to their being printed off and published as now they appear and are. Et ponunt ut supra.

3. Item, That the said Mr. Anthony à Wood was and is the author of and did compose in writing in English a certain book, (now extant in Latin and printed in folio) to which the title is HISTORIA ET ANTIQUITATES UNIVERSITATIS OXO-NIENSIS DUOBUS VOLUMINIBUS COMPREHENSAE, *Oxonii, e Theatro Sheldoniano,* MDCLXXIV, one copy[1] whereof is hereunto annexed, and as author of the said book did sell the same and did receive the summe of an hundred, sixty, fifty, fourty pounds as a price or gratuity for the same (ponunt tamen de qualibet alia summa, &c.). And did cause a draught of his coat of armes to bee placed in divers or att least one capital letter of the printed copyes of the said book, more particularly in the capital letter C before an epistle or preface of the said book (haecque fuerunt et sunt notoria publica pariter et manifesta et de et supra praemissis laborat publica vox et fama) quem quidem librum et epistolam sive prefacionem pars haec promovens hic exhibet et pro hic lecta et inserta habet et haberi petit, et vult quatenus, &c. Et ponunt ut supra.

4. Item, That since the said ATHENAE OXONIENSES ET FASTI OXONIENSES VOLUME THE SECOND were printed published and disseminated in such words as now they appear and are, the said Mr. à Wood hath given and distributed to and among divers persons of and within the said university copyes of the same; and to such persons, and others who before had the said ATHENAE ET FASTI OXONIENSES, hath given copyes in print of a certain epistle or preface composed in writing and printed or caused to bee printed by him the said Mr. à Wood, in the top whereof is placed his intended picture and in the capital letter whereof C, is placed his coat of arms; one copye whereof is hereunto annexed sic incipiens; ' *To the reader,*' et sic terminans, ' *he submits them and himself, Ab Æd. pat. in vic. S. J. Bapt. in antiq. et nob. civ. Bellos.* 5 *Jun.* 1691 ' (quae quidem pro hic lectis inspectis exhibitis et repetitis, quatenus, &c.) and bearing behaving and owning himself as the author of the said ATHENÆ ET FASTI OXONIENSES, did in perpetuall memory that he was the author thereof desire and direct the persons to whom he gave the said copyes to fasten them before the two volumes of the said ATHENÆ ET FASTI OXONIENSES as they now are published. And the said Mr. à Wood

---

[1] the copy of ATHENAE OXON. VOLUME THE SECOND, which was burnt by sentence of the court, was I suppose that put in by Lord Clarendon. Clarendon, while leaving the other documents connected with the case in the possession of the registrar of the court, thought it worth while to get an order for the return to him of the copy he had put in of HIST. ET ANTIQ. UNIV. OXON. I transcribe the original order in the University Archives (W. P. γ. 26. fol. 41):—

' Whereas in a matter of office promoted in the Chancellor's court of the University of Oxon by the right honourable the earl of Clarendon against Anthony à Wood, Mr. of Arts, in which matter or cause a book entitled HIST. ET ANTIQ. UNIV. OXON. was exhibited to prove the intention of the said earl of Clarendon, and the matter being ended by sentence, it is hereby ordered and decreed that the book aforesaid may be delivered by the register of the court aforesaid to Mr. John Smith or to Mr. Nathaniel Lloyd late proctors to the aforesaid right honourable Henry earl of Clarendon. In witness hereof I have hereunto sett my hand this 5th day of August 1693.

Geo. Gardiner, assess.'

had discourse with all or some of them concerning the painter's and the engraver's error in making the said picture no more like him the said Mr. à Wood. Et ponunt ut supra.

5. Item, That the coat of arms described and expressed in the said capital letter C in the next foregoing portion mentioned is the coat of armes used and claimed as particularly belonging to the family of à Wood *alias* Wood, late and now inhabiting and living within the parish of St. John Baptist scituate and being within the university and city of Oxford, and the males of the said family or some of them have the said coat engraven in the seals wherewith they usually seal their deeds and letters, and the said coat of armes is the same with that expressed and described in the capital letter C before that epistle or preface mentioned in the third portion of this matter (prout collatione habita, &c.). Quas quidem epistolas sive prefaciones pro hic lectis, insertis, invocatis, inspectis, et exhibitis, &c. And that the said Mr. Anthony à Wood is a more than ordinary retired and reserved person. Et ponunt ut supra.

6. Item, That the unfrequent and lesse usual abbreviations sett down att the end of the said epistle or preface, viz. *Ab Æd. Pat. in vic. S. J. Bapt. in antiq. et nob. civ. Bellos.* in the use and understanding of scholars are thus extended and doe import and signifye as followeth, viz. that the said epistle or preface to which the said abbreviations are subjoyn'd was dated *ab aedibus paternis* (of the writer) *in vico Sancti Johannis Baptistae in antiqua et nobili civitate Bellositi* : and that Bellositum is, in the opinion of antiquaries and other learned men, one of the ancient names of this place which wee now call Oxford. Et ponunt ut supra.

7. That the said Anthony à Wood in the month of June 1691 did and still doth live and inhabitte in a certain house scituate within the said parish of St. John Baptist in the university and city of Oxford which said house was accounted and esteemed to bee the house of the said Anthony à Wood's father deceased, and wherein his said father in his life time did live inhabit and abide. Et ponunt ut supra.

8. Item, That during the space of one—two—three years last past, there hath not been any person save the said Mr. Anthony à Wood who hath lived in the house of his ancestors within the said parish of St. John Baptist, who hath claimed or used the said coat of arms to himself and family appropriate and hath sufficient knowledge in the matters delivered in the said ATHENAE ET FASTI OXONIENSES and hath lived so retired a life as the author of the said ATHENAE ET FASTI is described in the said epistle or preface to doe (quam quidem epistolam et praefationem, &c.). Et ponunt ut supra.

9. Item, That within the space of five—ten—fifteen—twenty years last past, (ponunt tamen de quolibet alio annorum numero) the said Mr. Anthony à Wood and he only hath had and made a general inspection and search into all the registers of matriculation and of the acts of convocations and congregations of this university from the year of our Lord fifteen hundred to the year sixteen hundred and ninety, and took extracts of the same in order as he said to the writing of some book; and hath since given the Registrary of the said convocation one or more copyes of the said two volumes of ATHENAE ET FASTI OXONIENSES (in recompence for the paines he sustained during the said search) the second volume whereof agreeth in all things with that annexed to the Articles in this Cause, more particularly conteineth the infamous libells mentioned in the third and fourth Articles of the said Articles. Et ponunt ut supra.

10. Item, that the said Mr. Anthony à Wood on the sixth day of July in the

year of our Lord sixteen hundred fifty two, was admitted to and took the degree
of batchelaur of arts in this university: and on the fourteenth day of December in
the year of our Lord sixteen hundred fifty five was admitted to and took the degree
of master of arts in this said university according to the common and ordinary
course and form of the statutes concerning both those degrees: and took the oaths
requisite to the same: and from and after his said admission to the said degree of
batchelaur of arts, or att least of master of arts, to the time of the commencement
of this suite hath resided and continued the course of his studyes within the
precincts of this said university and worne an academicall habitt, and hath
continued to keep his bed, clothes, books and other necessary utensills within the
precincts of this said university, and hath not ceased to have a right to frequent
the public assemblies of the said university, and so much the said Mr. Anthony
à Wood hath published and declared. Hocque fuit et est notorium, &c. Et
ponunt ut supra.

11. Item, That since the said Anthony à Wood hath lived in the said house in
St. John's parish aforesaid, when and as oft as priviledged persons of this university
have been taxed and assessed by the pole or otherwise, apart from other persons
inhabiting within the precincts thereof and by persons of their own body, the said
Anthony hath also been taxed and assessed by the assessors of the said university.
Et ponunt ut supra.

12. Item, Quod premissa omnia et singula fuerunt et sunt publica notoria pariter
et manifesta et de et super premissis laborat publica vox et fama, &c.

[Unde facta fide, &c.]

XX. The Court fines Wood for delaying the case, and orders proof of the articles and allegation.

⟨Friday⟩ 17 Feb. 169¾: officium domini &c. contra Anth. à Wood.

Smith, Lloyd.   Wood, Cooke.

Continuatur monicio contra dictum à Wood in hunc diem. Ultimo die juridicǫ Wood et Cooke dederunt responsa pleniora dicti à Wood, et Smith et Lloyd dederunt allegacionem &c.

Quibus &c. dominus ad peticionem Smith et Lloyd decrevit dictum à Wood
citandum et in judicium evocandum fore in proximum ad dandum responsa sua in
scriptis posicionibus allegacionis alias in hoc negotio ex parte honoratissimi domini
domini Henrici comitis de Clarendon datis et admissis quatenus de jure teneatur
respondere eisdem.

Tunc facta trina praeconizacione pro dicto Anth. à Wood eoque non comparente,
dominus, ad peticionem Smith et Lloyd accusantium ejus contumaciam, pronunciavit eum contumacem &c et continuavit monicionem suam in proximum;

necnon ad ulteriorem peticionem Smith et Lloyd condemnavit eum in expensis
contumaciae suae sive retardati processus et assignavit eis ad offerendam billam
expensarum dictae contumaciae sive retardati processus taxari in proximum, in
praesentia Wood et Cooke dissentientium.

Insuperque dominus ad peticionem Smith et Lloyd assignavit eis tres dies juridicos
ex tunc sequentes ad probandum articulos et allegacionem in materiam per eos
datam ex parte dicti honoratissimi promotoris in hoc negocio et monuit Wood et
Cooke ad exhibendum quamcunque materiam defensivam si quam habuerint pro
dicto à Wood in proximum &c.

XXI.   Clarendon offers fourteen witnesses: Wood sends in an allegation, and obtains leave to interrogate Clarendon's witnesses.

⟨Friday⟩ 3 Martii 169⅚: officium domini promotum &c. contra Anth. à Wood.

Smith, Lloyd.   Wood, Cooke.

Primus dies probationis Smith et Lloyd. Emanaverat decretum pro responsis dicti à Wood fiendis posicionibus allegationis contra eum datae et admissae. Continuatur monicio contra dictum à Wood in hunc diem. Smith et Lloyd habent ad offerendum billam expensarum contumaciae sive retardati processus in eundem diem.

Quibus &c. reducto decreto praedicto executo juxta certificatorium in dorso ejusdem per Andream Skinner mandatarium hujus curiae de veritate ejusdem juratum, dominus ad peticionem Smith et Lloyd decrevit dictum à Wood citandum et in judicium evocandum fore in proximum &c. per decretum viis et modis pro responsis suis &c.

Factaque trina praeconizacione pro dicto à Wood eoque non comparente, dominus ad peticionem dictorum Smith et Lloyd, accusantium ejus contumaciam, pronunciavit eum contumacem et continuavit monicionem &c. in proximum.

Tunc dictus Smith obtulit billam expensarum contumaciae sive retardati processus contra à Wood quam dominus recepit et taxavit ad summam 2*li.* et 5*s* praeter &c., et decrevit à Wood monendum fore ad solvendum expensas taxatas citra proximum juridicum diem ex tunc sequentem, facta fide per dictum Smith clientem suum exposuisse vel expositurum esse summam taxatam.

Tunc Smith et Lloyd super posicionibus articulorum et allegacionis per eos ex parte honoratissimi domini Henrici comitis de Clarendon in hoc negocio dat. et admiss. produxerunt in testes venerabiles viros Gulielmum Levett S.T.P.; Rad. Bathurst, Ric. Lydall, M.DD.; et Jos. Pullen, Ben. Cooper, et Geo. Cooper, in Artibus Magistros; Hen. Clements, Jo. Hall, Ric^um Davis, Dan. Porter jun., Mich. Burgersh, Ric^um Hawkins, Gualt. Combes, et Jos. Jackson: quos dominus ad eorum peticionem admisit et juramento ad sancti Dei evangelia per eos corporaliter tacta et deosculata oneravit de plane, plene, et fideliter deponendo totam et meram veritatem quam in hac parte super articulis et allegacione in hoc negocio ex parte officii dat. et admiss. noverint aut eorum quilibet noverit, omnibus amore odio &c. spretis et postpositis, et monuit eos ad subeundum eorum in hac parte examen citra proximum secundum diem juridicum ex tunc proxime futurum, in praesentia Wood, procuratoris dicti à Wood, dissentientis et protestantis de dicendo contra deposiciones et personas dictorum testium si et quatenus nitantur deponere contra intentionem domini sui, et ex sua peticione habentis ei per dominum assignatum pro interrogatoriis testibus praedictis ministrandis citra diem Martis proximum vel quandocunque ante eorum examen.

Tunc Wood ex parte dicti Anth. à Wood dedit allegacionem quam dominus ad ejus peticionem admisit quatenus &c. in praesentia Smith et Lloyd dissentientium &c.

XXII.   Wood's allegation.

Martii 3º 169⅚: officium[1] domini promotum per honoratissimum dominum

Quo die Wood et Cook, nomine procuratorio, ac ut procuratores legitimi

---

[1] from Arch. Univ. Oxon. W. P. γ. 26. fol. 14.

dominum Henricum comitem de Clarendon contra Antonium Wood de Oxon
ob libellum sive libellos famosos ab eo
scriptos compositos et publicatos.

dicti Antonii Wood, omnibus meliori-
bus via, modo et juris forma, &c.
necnon ad omnem et quemcunque juris
effectum exinde quovis modo sequi
valentem, dicunt allegant, et in his
scriptis in jure proponunt, conjunctim, divisim, articulatim prout sequitur : viz.

1. *Imprimis,* This party proponent doth alledge that in the 14th year[1] of King Charles the Second there was and is att present now in force an act of parliament, entituled, *An Act for preventing the frequent abuses in printing seditious, treasonable and unlicensed books and pamphletts, and for regulating of printing and printing-presses.* In which statute or act of parliament, amongst other things, it was, and is enacted ; THAT no private person or persons whatsoever shall att any time print, or cause to be printed, any book whatsoever, unless the same book, together with all matters and things thereunto annexed, be first enter'd in the book of the register of the company of Stationers of London : And unless the same book or pamphletts, and all matters and things thereunto annexed, and therewith to be imprinted, shall be first lawfully licensed and authorized to be printed by such person and persons only, as are constituted and appointed to license the same, according to the direction and meaning of the said act. *Quod quidem statutum pars proponens hic invocat, et pro hic lecto et inserto habet et haberi petit, et vult, quatenus fecit pro parte sua et non aliter, &c. Et ponit ut supra.*

2. *Item,* That the book entituled ATHENAE OXONIENSES VOLUME THE SECOND, exhibited by the party promovent in this cause the 18th day of November 1692, with the preface and table, and other matters and things thereunto annexed, was first enter'd in the book of the register of the company of Stationers of London, according to the abovesaid act of parliament ; and that the abovesaid book, together with all matters and things thereunto annexed, was lawfully licensed and authorized to be printed, by one or both of the principall secretaries of state, or by their, or one of their appointments, according to the abovesaid act of parliament. *Quod quidem statutum pars proponens hic invocat, et pro hic lect. et insert. habet et haberi petit quatenus,* &c. *Et ponit ut supra.*

3. *Item,* More particularly, that one Mr. Fraser[2] was appointed and constituted supervisor or licenser of all books of profane history, by one, or both of the principall secretaries of state, in the year 1690, 1691, and 1692 (*ponit tamen pars proponens de aliquo alio annorum numero, pluribus sive uno*) and was in the time aforesaid generally so reputed and taken ; and that the said Fraser, so constituted and appointed as abovesaid, supervised and licensed the printing of the abovesaid book, entituled ATHENAE OXONIENSES VOLUME THE SECOND, exhibited by the party promovent in this cause 18th of November 1692 ; and that if there is, or are, any passages in the abovesaid book contrary to good manners, the government, or governours of the church and state, or reflecting upon any person or persons, the aforesaid licenser, or the principal secretary of state, by whose appointment the said licenser did act, was, and is only answerable for them, as by the meaning and intent of the abovecited act of parliament, does, and may more fully appear. *Ad quod quidem statutum pars proponens se refert,* &c. *Et ponit ut supra.*

4. *Item,* This proponent doth farther allege, that the abovesaid book, entituled ATHENAE OXONIENSES VOLUME THE SECOND, exhibited in this cause into the court, the 18th of November 1692, by the party promovent in this cause, was, and is printed for Mr. Thomas Bennett, bookseller in London, and published in London and (? not) within the university of Oxford, by the said Mr. Thomas Bennett,

[1] 1662.　　　　[2] James Frazer.

bookseller in London, and was received publickly by most or some of the book-sellers of the university of Oxford aforesaid from the said Mr. Bennett only. And, by vertue of the said publication only, the said book has been since the said publication, and is now att present, publickly to be sold, and permitted to be publickly sold in the said booksellers' shops, and from them, the said booksellers, to be dispers'd amongst the schollars and students of the said university, without the consent or order of Mr. Anthony Wood above-mention'd. *Et ponit ut supra.*

5. *Item,* That before the printing and publication in print of the aforesaid book, entituled ATHENAE OXONIENSES VOLUME THE SECOND, exhibited into this court by the party promovent in this cause, the aforesaid Mr. Thomas Bennett of London, bookseller, had the original papers of the author in writing in his custody, or in the custody of some others by his order, by the space of two years immediately before the printing of the aforesaid book, entituled ATHENAE OXONIENSES VOLUME THE SECOND and exhibited as aforesaid (*ponit tamen pars proponens de quolibet alio temporis spatio,*) &c. *Et ponit ut supra.*

6. *Item,* That the aforesaid Mr. Thomas Bennett, or some others by his order and consent, during the time in the precedent article deduced, altered the abovesaid original papers of the pretended author, by blotting out severall passages and lines in the said originall papers, by inserting many new characters of persons, and many pages and lines different from the originall papers, and that these alterations are printed without the consent or knowledg of Mr. Anthony Wood aforesaid. *Et ponit ut supra.*

7. *Item,* That James Harrington of the Inner Temple of London, esq. inserted the Introduction to the book entituled ATHENAE OXONIENSES VOLUME THE SECOND, exhibited as aforesaid, and also had the originall papers of the pretended author of the aforesaid book in his custody, and altered the aforesaid originall papers, by inserting many characters, pages, lines and sentences; and that the said alterations were and are printed in the aforesaid book, entituled ATHENAE OXONIENSES VOLUME THE SECOND, exhibited as aforesaid, without the knowledg and consent of Mr. Anthony Wood above-mention'd. *Et ponit ut supra.*

8. *Item,* That Mr. Fraser above-mentioned had the originall papers of the pretended author of the book, entituled ATHENAE OXONIENSES VOLUME THE SECOND, exhibited as aforesaid, in his custody and keeping, and altered the afore-said originall papers, inserting many new characters, pages, lines and sentences; and that the said alterations were and are printed in the aforesaid book, entituled ATHENAE OXONIENSES VOLUME THE SECOND, without the knowledge and consent of Mr. Anthony Wood above-mentioned. *Et ponit ut supra.*

9. *Item,* That the most reverend father in God now lord archbishop of Canterbury[1] had the originall papers, or some of the original papers, of the pretended author of the book, entituled ATHENAE OXONIENSES VOLUME THE SECOND exhibited as aforesaid, in his custody and keeping, and altered the aforesaid originall papers, inserting or blotting out many pages, lines, or sentences; and that the said alterations were and are printed in the aforesaid book, entituled ATHENAE OXONIENSES VOLUME THE SECOND, without the knowledg or consent of Mr. Wood aforesaid. *Et ponit ut supra.*

10. *Item,* That the right honourable Henry earl of Clarendon, the party promovent in this cause, had the originall papers, or some of the original papers, of the pretended author of the book, entituled ATHENAE OXONIENSES VOLUME THE

[1] John Tillotson.

SECOND, exhibited as aforesaid, in his custody and keeping, and altered the aforesaid originall papers, by razing out many lines, sentences, and words or inserting many lines, sentences and words relating to the character or characters of Edward late earl of Clarendon, without the knowledge or consent of Mr. Wood. *Et ponit ut supra.*

11. *Item*, That the clauses and sentences mentioned in the third and fourth articles of the articles exhibited in this cause, (*ad quos quidem articulos pars se refert*, &c.) and pretending to be reflecting and libellous upon Edward late earl of Clarendon, were and are inserted by some one of the persons above mentioned, or by the printer or printers of the said book, without the knowledg and consent of the said Mr. Anthony Wood. *Et ponit ut supra.*

12. *Item*, That during the time of printing the said book, entituled ATHENAE OXONIENSES VOLUME THE SECOND, exhibited as aforesaid, the author of the aforesaid book was absent and distant several miles from the printing-press all the time the said book was printing, *prout ex clausula circa principium dicti libri in excusatione erratorum typographicorum adducta plenius liquet et apparet. Ad quem librum et ad clausulas praedictas pars proponens se refert et pro hic lectis et insertis habet et haberi petit quatenus*, &c. *Et ponit ut supra.*

13. *Item*, This proponent doth farther allege, that between the time of the restauration of king Charles the Second and the year of our Lord 1667, (the time deduced and objected in the 8th article of certain articles exhibited in this cause) there were other lord chancellours, besides the right honourable Edward earl of Clarendon, deceased ; and particularly, the author or authors of the book, entituled ATHENAE OXONIENSES VOLUME THE SECOND, exhibited as aforesaid, were of that opinion, as appears by column 228 of the ATHENAE OXONIENSES VOLUME THE SECOND, and page 804 of the FASTI OXONIENSES annexed to the said book, and exhibited as aforesaid ; *ad quam quidem columnam et paginam dictorum librorum pars proponens se refert, et pro hic lect. habet et haberi petit quatenus*, &c. *Et ponit ut supra.*

14. *Item*, That the pretended libellous words objected in the 4th article of certain articles exhibited in this cause, did, and do refer to L'isle, chancellor or commissioner of the great seal, and not to the lord chancellor Hyde, as is falsly suggested in the aforesaid articles, *prout ex verbis antecedentibus dictam clausulam in dicto articulo objectam in columna libri exhibiti 269, facta collatione cum sententiis ad dictum L'isle referentibus in columna 228 dicti libri, intitulati* ATHENAE OXONIENSES VOLUME THE SECOND, *plenius liquet et apparet, ad quae quidem omnia pars proponens se refert et pro hic lect. habet quatenus*, &c. *Et ponit*, &c.

15. *Item*, That the copies in print of a certain Epistle or Preface composed in writing, and pretended to be printed by Mr. Wood the defendant, with his pretended picture and coat of arms, were printed and delivered with directions to be inserted before the preface only of the first volume of ATHENAE ET FASTI OXONIENSES, *prout ex dicta epistola ex parte partis promoventis in hac curia exhibita plenius liquet*, &c. *ad quam epistolam pars se refert et pro hic lect. habet quatenus*, &c. And this proponent doth farther alledge, that the first volume of ATHENAE OXONIENSES was printed and published by the space of two years before the second volume of ATHENAE OXONIENSES exhibited as aforesaid. *Ponit tamen pars de quolibet alio temporis spatio minori*, &c. *Et ponit ut supra.*

16. That the said Mr. Antony Wood hath not had any chamber, lodging, or diet, or any right to any lodging or diet, in any colledg or hall within the university of Oxon for these twenty years last, (*ponit tamen pars de quolibet alio temporis spatio majori*), &c. neither has he had any name in any buttery-book of any colledge or hall for the time aforesaid (*ponit tamen pars*, &c.) neither hath he

frequented any publick assemblies of the said university as a member thereof, or had any right to frequent the same, as a member thereof, for the time aforesaid; and that for the time aforesaid the said Mr. Anthony Wood has been reputed and taken to have forsaken all title or interest as a member of the said university. *Ponit tamen pars de alio temporis spatio majori,* &c.   *Et ponit ut supra.*

17. *Item, quod praemissa omnia sunt vera,* &c.

Unde facta fide de jure in hac parte requisita petit pars proponens jus et justitiam, &c.

XXIII. Clarendon gives new caution.

Stipulacio [1]. Decimo die [2] Martii anno D^{ni} (stilo Angliae) 1692 (i. e. $\frac{2}{1}$), Gul. Creed, M. Bac. et Coll. Corporis Xti in Universitate Oxon. socius, stipulacionem interposuit juxta formam registri in summam decem librarum pro honoratissimo viro domino Henrico comite de Clarendon de lite sua persequenda expensisque solvendis casu quo in negocio contra Anthonium à Wood succubuerit.

XXIV. Wood sends in his answers to the allegation, and his interrogatories to Clarendon's witnesses.

⟨Friday⟩ 10 Martii 169$\frac{2}{1}$: officium domini promotum, &c. contra Anth. à Wood.

Smith, Lloyd.   Wood, Cooke.

Secundus dies probacionis Smith et Lloyd. Emanaverat decretum viis et modis contra dictum Anth. à Wood pro responsis suis personalibus fiendis posicionibus allegacionis &c., et monicio ad solvendum expensas retardati processus. Ultimo die juridico Wood dedit allegacionem ex parte dicti à Wood.

Quibus &c., reducto decreto praedicto, Wood dedit responsa à Wood facta posicionibus allegacionis alias in hoc negocio ex parte honoratissimi domini Henrici comitis de Clarendon datae et admissae in scriptis conceptis in praesentia Smith et Lloyd, accept. eorundem quatenus, &c.

Tunc reducta monicione contra dictum à Wood ad solvendum expensis contumaciae sive retardati processus executa juxta certificatorium in dorso ejusdem per Andream Skinner mandatarium hujus curiae de veritate ejusdem juratum, dominus ad peticionem Smith et Lloyd decrevit monicionem viis et modis contra dictum à Wood ad solvendum dictas expensas.

Factaque trina praeconizacione pro dicto à Wood eoque non comparente, dominus ad peticionem Smith et Lloyd, accusantium ejus contumaciam, pronunciavit eum contumacem et in poenam contumaciae suae hujusmodi continuavit monitionem suam contra dictum à Wood in proximum, &c.

Necnon ad ulteriorem peticionem dictorum Smith et Lloyd decrevit interrogatoria, ex parte dicti à Wood ministrata, examinanda et inspicienda fore per eum ante examen testium super eisdem.

XXV. Wood's answers to the allegation.

Responsa [3] personalia Antonii Wood de Oxon. gen. facta quibusdam positionibus

---

[1] Dr. Levett, Lord Clarendon's original 'stipulator' (*supra*, p. 2), had withdrawn his name, perhaps with a view to his being called as a witness. This is commented upon by Wood's

proctor, *infra*, p. 22.

[2] Friday.

[3] from the original paper in Arch. Univ. Oxon. W. P. γ. 26. fol. 12.

cujusdam praetensae allegationis datae et exhibitae contra eum decimo Februarii
169⅔, sequuntur :—

1, 2, 3, ad 1^{mam} 2^{am} et 3^{am} positiones respondet et dicit quod quoad sua facta
negat quoad aliena non credit easdem aut aliquam earundem partem esse veras in
aliquo.

4, 5, 6,
7, 8, 9,   } ⟨the same formula is repeated.⟩
10, 11, 12

ANTH. WOOD [1].

Repetit. et recognit.
coram me G. Gardiner [2], assess.

XXVI. Wood's interrogatories to Clarendon's witnesses.

Interrogatoria [3] ministranda testibus productis ex parte honoratissimi viri domini
domini Henrici comitis de Clarendon super articulis et allegatione exhibitis in Curia
Cancellarii Oxoniensis contra Antonium Wood de Oxon. sequuntur.

1. Inprimis exposito cuilibet testi crimine et paena perjurii, interrogetur

'What advantage he proposeth to himself on the behalf of my Lord Clarendon
for deposing in this cause? Which party does he favour most and if it were in his
power would he not give the cause to my Lord Clarendon?'

Et fiet conjunctim et divisim.

2. Item interrogetur quilibet,

'Whether he does not know that severall lines, sentences or words have been
inserted into the book entituled ATHENAE OXONIENSES VOLUME THE 2d, by
one or more persons without the direction or consent of Mr. Anthony Wood?
Whether att least he hath not heard such a report? Whether he does not believe
that report to be true?'

Et fiet ut supra.

3. Item interrogetur quilibet,

'Whether he is acquainted with the stile of Mr. Anthony Wood's compositions
in English? If so, whether the two first leaves of ATHENAE OXONIENSES VOLUME
THE SECOND (videlicet, the introduction), and the last page (videlicet, the character
of Sir George Makenzie) are not of different stiles from the stile of Mr. Wood?
Whether he hath not heard and doth not beleive that the introduction was inserted
into the said volume without the consent or knowledge of Mr. Wood aforesaid?'

Et fiet ut supra.

4. Item interrogetur quilibet,

'Whether the Epistle with the pretended picture and Coat of Arms of Mr. Wood
were not printed and delivered with directions to be putt before the preface of the
first volume of ATHENAE OXONIENSES without any mention made of the second
volume? Whether the first volume was not published in print a year and an half
(more or less) before the publicacion of the second volume?'

Et fiet ut supra.

5. Item interrogetur quilibet,

'Whether the book entituled ATHENAE OXONIENSES VOLUME THE SECOND
has not been sold since the publicacion and is not att present to be sold publickly
in the booksellers' shops in this University without any interruption or molestacion
from the authority of the said University? Whether the said book was and is not

---

[1] autograph signature.   [3] from the original paper in Arch.
[2] the assessor's autograph signature.   Univ. Oxon. W. P. γ. 26. fol. 29.

deposited in the publick library of this University by the said authority? In severall Colledge libraries in the said University? Whether the printing of the said book according to the title of it was not encouraged by subscription in a publick manner by the late and present vicechancellour with other reverend and learned members of this University?'

Et fiet ut supra.

6. Item interrogetur quilibet,

'Whether Mr. Anthony Wood hath wore an academicall habitt (videlicet, a statutable Master of Arts' gown) for seven years last past? Whether Mr. Anthony Wood hath had any chamber, lodging, diett or commons, or a right to any lodging, chamber, or commons in any Colledge or Hall, or had any name in the buttery book of any Colledge or Hall within the University of Oxon for these twenty years last past? (interrogetur tamen de quolibet alio temporis spatio minori.) Whether he hath frequented the Convocations or Congregations of the said University for the time aforesaid, or for the time aforesaid hath he been reputed to have a vote or right of being present in the said assemblies?' (Interrogetur tamen de quolibet alio temporis spatio minori.)

Et fiet ut supra.

7. Item interrogetur reverendus vir Doctor Levett,

'*Whether he was not stipulator for my lord Clarendon in this cause? in what penalty? What was the inducement that he substracted his stipulation?* If he is not chaplain to my lord Clarendon? If he has not sollicited in this cause on the behalf of my lord Clarendon? Whether he has not sought for witnesses on the behalf of my lord Clarendon? Whether he did not examine Dr. Bathurst, Dr. Lydall, Mr. Davis, Mr. Hall, Mr. Clements, Mr. Burghers and others, one or more of them, in reference to their being evidences against Mr. Anthony Wood, and desire them or some of them to appear as witnesses against him?'

Et fiet ut supra.

8. Item interrogetur Dr. Levett and Mr. Pullen,

'whether they have not heard my lord Clarendon, the party promovent in this cause, confess and declare that he corrected and altered severall or one of the originall papers of the author of ATHENAE OXONIÉNSES VOLUME THE SECOND? Whether he did not own and confess also that he blotted out or inserted severall sentences or words in the originall papers relating to the character or characters of my Lord Chancellour Hyde deceased in the book entituled ATHENAE OXONIENSES VOLUME THE SECOND? Whether my lord Clarendon did not likewise own that he privately received the originall paper or papers from Mr. Fraser the licenser of the said book?'

Et fiet ut supra.

9. Item interrogetur Benjaminus Cooper et Georgius Cooper,

'whether Mr. Peers the beadle, deceased, and others within these twenty years last past have not made a generall inspection into the Matriculacion Book and Registries of this University in order to the writing some book or books? Whether there were not one or more Chancellours (besides my Lord Chancellor Hyde) between the restauracion of King Charles the second and the year of our Lord 1667?'

Et fiet ut supra.

Reddat etiam quilibet testis veras et concludentes causas suae scientiae: alioquin protestatur pars de nullitate examinacionis, &c.

XXVII. Evidence of six of Clarendon's witnesses.

⟨The sheets containing the evidence of Dr. William Levett, Dr. Ralph Bathurst, Dr. Richard Lydall, Josias Pullen, M.A., Benjamin Cooper the registrar of the University, and George Cooper (apparently Benjamin's assistant or deputy), have not been found. It was stated in court on Friday, 17 March, that their evidence had been taken.⟩

XXVIII. Clarendon's other witnesses are ordered to give evidence: Clarendon puts in a second allegation and two letters: Wood is ordered to give answers to this second allegation and fuller answers to the first allegation. Clarendon and Henry Dodwell are summoned to give evidence.

⟨Friday⟩ 17 March 169⅔: officium domini promotum, &c. contra Anth. à Wood. Smith, Lloyd. Wood, Cooke. Ultimus dies probationis Smith et Lloyd. Continuatur monicio contra dictum à Wood in hunc diem. Non emanaverat monicio viis et modis contra eum ad solvendum expensas contumaciae suae, &c. Dr. Bathurst, Dr. Levett, Dr. Lydall, Mr. Pullen, Mr. Cooper sen. et Mr. Cooper jun., testes, &c. examen subierunt. Hen. Clements, Jo. Hall, Ric. Davis, Mich. Burghers, Dan. Porter jun., Ric. Hawkins, Gualterus Combes, et Jos. Jackson, testes ex parte officii producti admissi et jurati non subierunt examen.

Quibus &c., facta trina praeconizacione pro dictis Hen. Clements, Johanne Hall, Ric. Davis, Mich. Burghers, Dan. Porter, Ric. Hawkins, Gualt. Combes, et Jos. Jackson, testibus productis admissis et juratis, sed non examinatis, dominus ad peticionem Smith et Lloyd, accusantium eorum contumacias in non subeundo eorum examen juxta monicionem eis judicialiter factam, pronunciavit eos contumaces sed reservavit eorum poenas in proximum, &c.

Tunc dicti Smith et Lloyd allegaverunt expensas contumaciae sive retardati processus à Wood solutas esse;

et in subsidium probacionis contentorum in articulis et allegacione per eos in hoc negocio ex parte officii datis et admissis, dederunt allegationem cum duabus litteris eidem annexis quam dominus ad eorum peticionem admisit quatenus, &c.;

necnon decrevit pro responsis dicti à Wood faciendis posicionibus ejusdem, Wood dissentiente.

Tunc dicti Smith et Lloyd allegaverunt Anth. à Wood nec plene nec plane respondisse 5, 6, et 7 posicionibus allegacionis alias in hoc negocio ex parte officii datis et admissis. Unde dominus ad eorum peticionem decrevit pro responsis plenioribus dicti à Wood in proximum, &c.,

in praesentia Wood dissentientis et allegantis se posse relevari ab onere probandi ex responsis personalibus honoratissimi promotoris hujus negotii. Unde dominus ad ejus peticionem decrevit honoratissimum comitem de Clarendon citandum fore in proximum pro responsis suis personalibus faciendis posicionibus allegationis ex parte dicti à Wood in hoc negocio datis et admissis, in praesentia Smith et Lloyd dissentientium, &c.,

necnon allegantium Hen. Dodwell A.M esse testem eis necessarium ad probandum intencionem eodem deductam in praedicta allegacione, sed, oblatis ei viaticis et expensis, ad hoc tribunal venire recusat, unde dominus ad eorum peticionem decrevit eum compellendum fore in proximum, &c.

XXIX. Clarendon's second allegation, with two letters written by Wood.

Officium[1] Domini promotum per honoratissimum dominum dominum Henricum comitem de Clarendon contra Antonium à Wood infra Universitatem Oxon. in Artibus Magistrum in quodam negotio reformationis morum, et exhibit. 17 Martii 169⅔. Quibus &c., Smith et Lloyd nomine procuratorum ac ut procuratores legitimi domini Henrici comitis de Clarendon omnibus melioribus via modo et juris forma quibus melius et efficacius de jure potuit et potest necnon ad omnem et quemcunque juris effectum exinde quovis modo sequi valentem, in subsidium probationis articulorum originalium et allegationis 10ᵐᵒ die Februarii 169⅔ exhibit., dicunt allegant et in his scriptis in jure proponunt conjunctim divisim et articulatim prout sequitur: vizt.

1. *Imprimis*, that a certain letter exhibited with this allegation, incipiens *May itt please your lordship* et sic terminans *Your most humble servant A. Wood*, was and is the proper handwriting of Mr. Anthony à Wood, the defendant, and that he wrote and subscribed the same with his proper hand and name; and the same, so written and subscribed and sealed with his own seal bearing his owne coat of arms, did direct for and send the same as his proper letter to *the right honourable Henry earl of Clarendon att Swallowfeild near Reading Berkshire*, prout collatione habita ad responsa personalia aliasque scripturas manu propria dicti à Wood scriptas et subscriptas necnon ad insignia gentilitia dicti à Wood in hoc negotio mentionata et exhibita plenius liquet et apparet: quas quidem litteras una cum sigillo iisdem annexo[2] pars haec proponens hic exhibet et pro hic lectis, inspectis et exhibitis habet et haberi petit et vult quatenus, &c., et ponit ut supra.

2. *Item*, that one other letter exhibited also with this allegation, sic incipiens *Good Mr. Dodwell* et sic terminans *Your humble servant A. Wood*, was and is the proper handwriting of the said Mr. Anthony à Wood the defendant, and that he wrote and subscribed the same with his proper hand and name and the same so written and subscribed did direct for and send the same to *his worthy friend Mr. Henry Dodwell* as his proper letter, prout collatione habita ⟨&c., as before⟩; quas quidem litteras ⟨&c., as before⟩.

3. *Item*, quod praemissa omnia et singula fuerunt et sunt vera, notoria pariter et manifesta.

Unde facta fide de jure in hac parte requisita petit pars ista proponens jus et justitiam sibi et parti suae fieri et denuntiari cum effectu, &c.

[1] from Arch. Univ. Oxon. W. P. γ. 26. fol. 18.

[2] the letter is given below: the seal is now broken off.

⟨Copies of the letters annexed to the preceding :—⟩

I. ANTHONY WOOD TO HENRY EARL OF CLARENDON[1].

May it please your Lordship.

Had I had the happiness to have knowne that you were in Oxon last Octob. I would have waited upon ⟨you⟩, to have satisfied you as to the matter now in hand ; but I knew nothing of your being here till you were gone.—Soon after there was a sute commenced against me in your name for one or two passages mention'd in the second vol. of ATH. ET FASTI OXON. concerning your father ; at which the generallity of scholars (especially those that understand the common law) did wonder, considering that in the said passages was no mention made of *Edward,* or of *Hyde* or of *Clarendon.* However in complyance to your lordship (tho I am no privileged man and so consequently not subject to the court of the chancellor of Oxon) I did appear and stipulate, thinking to be favourablely used. But so it is that I having been coarsly treated as yet, and in all probability worse hereafter. I have hitherto suffered in divers respects—(1) As to the loss of my pretious time and hindrance of my public studies ; for since the commenceing of the said sute I have done nothing relating thereunto ; but, for the diversion of my thoughts arising from my hard usage, I have kept such company that I delight not in. (2) As to the loss of the reward which I expected from the Universitie for the dedication of ATH. ET FASTI OXON. of which tho I had a promise, yet now they refuse it. (3) By the payment of considerable summs of money due, as fees to legists &c.

Dr. Bouchier also tells my proctor that I must also pay such fees as he thinks fit, that will satisfy such legists that you have employed ; and under that notion he will get what he pleases from me, and so consequently ruin me. In order to the payment of these moneys, I have sold certaine antient manuscripts, which I intended for the University, and am now about to sell other books ; and if I should pay double taxes, as I have been several times threatned to doe, unless I take the oathes, I must be forced to sell all I have.

Your Lordship hath the reputation of a learned man, and of one who is a lover of learning and scholars ; and therefore if your Lordship (who is also one of the chief officers of this university) should deal otherwise but favourablely with one who is a zealous pretender to learning, and hath spent all his time, even from his youth, in doing honour to the University of Oxon, may, under favour, sound but ill in the eares of posterity.

I do here send to your honour the epistle which was to be put before the ATH. ET FASTI OXON. but by the unworthy dealing of the bookseller it was refused to be printed—If your Lordship please to have another copie of it to be put before your book (which I presume you have) I shall put it into the hands of Dr. Levet that he might convey it to you (inclosed in a book or parcel) unrumpled. There were printed here last Octob. 200 and odd of the said epistles, and this is the fifth that I have yet dispersed ; and no more are to be dispersed till an end of this controversie be made. The printer who printed them tells me that he can add at the end of the same epistle 8 or 10 lines ; and therefore if your Lordship think fit, or only say the word, that the retraction which I sent to Mr. Dodwell and he imparted to you at Magd. Hall shall be put at the end of the said 200 copies, it shall be forthwith done, and I will, by bond given, see that every book of the said

[1] from the original (Wood's holo-graph) in the Archives (W. P. γ. 26. fol. 13). In MS. Tanner 456. fol. 37, 38 are Wood's two first drafts of this letter, much scored out and corrected.

ATH. ET FASTI OXON. which are in the public and college libraries, shall have a copie of it put into each book. This being just and equitable, there need not, I presume, any recantation be made or registred; for if any be registred, or knowne to be registred, I shall never be at rest, but continually be troubled by presbyterians and fanaticks for every little triviall thing. So leaving these things to your lordship's consideration

I remaine
Your most humble servant
A. WOOD.

From my Lodging neare Merton Coll., 16 Feb. 1692 [1].

For the right honora-
ble Henry earl of

Paid 4*d*	Clarendon at
[to [2] Maidinghead	Swallowfield
to be sent to the	neare
Post Office in	Reading
Reading].	Berkshire.

II. ANTHONY WOOD TO HENRY DODWELL [3].

Good Mr. Dodwell

I desire that you would be pleased to represent to his lordship the earl of Clarendon, that I offer to insert this following advertisement in my next volume of ATH. ET FASTI OXON. for his lordship's satisfaction.

'Whereas in the second volume of ATH. ET FASTI OXON. particularly in pag. 221 and p. 269 there are several reflections upon *the then Lord Chancellour*, the author upon further enquiry does find that he has been imposed upon by the persons that gave him those accounts. Wherefore he desires the reader to take notice that he does recall those expressions, there being no just grounds for any such insinuations.'

This would be accepted, but Dr. Bouchier out of a severe and rigid temper proposes that I should come publickly into the Vicechancellour's court and pray that this my submission may be accepted and registred, and that I should there pay his lordship's charges and give my oath that I will publish within a certaine time the aforesaid advertisement.

This additional satisfaction seemes very unreasonable to me, that I cannot comply with it. (1) Because it containes a double punishment, viz. a publick submission in court, registred to all posterity (to which the law can only force me, if upon a hearing I am cast,) and a publick recantation in print. (2) Because it will invite other persons to sue me for what I have said of the phanaticks their ancestors, (to which I was obliged as a faithful historian) against whome I can have little or no defence, if I consent to such a judicial act and confession. (3) Thirdly, it ties me to a limited time to publish my third vol., which I cannot fairly promise, because the bookseller, the licenser and printer, will have their owne time.

Pray intercede with his lordship that he would not leave the method of my giving satisfaction to any lawyer, or to Dr. Bouchier especially, for that I have

---

[1] i. e. 169$\frac{2}{3}$.

[2] the words in square brackets are added by another hand, probably some one in the post office.

[3] from the original (Wood's holo- graph) in the University Archives (W. P. γ. 26. fol. 5). Wood's first draft of the letter is in MS. Ballard XIV. fol. 24.

reason to expect from him (tho I have never offended him in word or action) the most cruel usuage.

I am willing the Advertisement should be first published in the *Terme Catalogue* of books, (which will come out in the latter end of this next terme) under the title of ATHENAE ET FASTI OXON. which shall be put therein, wherein I 'le promise to repeate the same in my third vol. provided this may be look'd upon as my owne act and not seem forced from me by law as a convict libeller.

Upon this proposal I hope his lordship will admit me to his favour, and not think I am unadviseable, if I am not content to be registred in a University for a libeller, for whose honour, reputation and glory I have laboured from my youth and spent all that I have gotten.

As for the charges of the sute, I am scarce in a capacitie to pay mine owne, For during the raigne of this present king I have paid all taxes, and am now in paying the quarterly tax of 1*li*. 1*s od*: And if I pay double taxes, which I have been several times threatned to doe, I must be forced to leave Oxon and my public studies, and betake myself to an obscure or meane employment in the country—so wishing you all health and happiness
I remaine
Your humble servant
A. WOOD.

Jan. 16, 1692.

> Pray Sir keep this paper private [1],
>   and let no body see it, but his
>   lordship, if you think fit.
>   For his worthy Friend
>   Mr. Henry Dodwell.

[1] the first sentence of the following letter will show by what gross violation of promise the preceding letter marked 'private' was yet produced against Wood in court. It is found in MS. Ballard XXXIV. fol. 4, endorsed by Wood:—' Mr. Dodwell's letter to me, 18 Jan. 1692.'

Sir,

I have shewn your letter to my lord Clarendon, and left it in his hands, that he might consider it at leisure, upon his promise that he would keep it to himself. What he desires farther is that you would own in open court, and get it registred, that you are sorry for having been made an instrument by the misinformation of others for aspersing his ffather's memory. His lordship's desires herein are so very just and becoming him that I do not see how you can as a good Christian refuse complyance. You can pretend no informations in this whole matter but what may very probably fayl you. And if you should engage yourself by this precedent to make the like amends for all like cases, without any compulsion, onely on being convicted of your mistakes, as it would be very much for the advantage of your soul, so it will add not detract from the credit of your other collections. Your ingenuity will very much recommend your better informations. If I may therefore be so bold as to advise you, I should think it your best way to perform what is desired, and for other things to cast yourself upon his lordship's generosity. I give this as my own advise, not by any suggestion from his lordship. His lordship has perhaps more proof then you are aware of. But I would rather have you do what you think fit as a good man and as a Christian, then upon any account of fear. I am

Your affectionate friend and
humble servant,
HENRY DODWELL.

Jan. 18 169⅔.

ffor my honoured ffriend Mr. Anthony Wood.

XXX. Evidence of one of Clarendon's witnesses.

⟨The evidence of John Hall, stated in court (on 24 March) to have been taken, is missing.⟩

XXXI. Evidence of seven of Clarendon's witnesses [1].

HENRICUS CLEMENTS de Universitate Oxon. bibliopola, in qua Universitate Oxon. moram traxit 26 annos ultimos elapsos, oriundus apud Abingdon in comitatu Berks, aetatis circiter 47 annos, testis productus, admissus, et juratus super propositis in hoc negocio ex parte officii datis et admissis, examinatus vero 21º die [2] Martii anno Domini (stilo Angliae) 1692 [3], dicit et deponit prout sequitur (viz[t]).

2. Ad secundam posicionem articulorum praedictorum et ad copiam 'ATHENAE ET FASTI OXONIENSES' annexam et repetitam dicit et deponit

that 'in the moneths of July, August, September, or October last past, and after the publicacion of the first and second volumes of the book entituled ATHENAE ET FASTI OXONIENSES, the articulate Mr. Anthony à Wood came to this deponent in the Schooles within the University of Oxon articulate and asked him to buy of him some of his books, meaneing the ATHENAE ET FASTI OXONIENSES, desireing this deponent, if he wanted any of them, to deale with him for them rather then to have them from Mr. Bennett, who printed the said book':

et aliter nescit deponere.

3. Ad 3 posicionem et ad copiam exhibitam et repetitam dicit et deponit

that 'he hath read the life and character of David Jenkyns in the columnes 220 and 221 of the articulate second volume of the ATHENAE ET FASTI OXONIENSES, and finds the authour of them to have defamed the memory of the articulate Edward, earl of Clarendon, late Lord Chancellour of England and [4] this University, and father of the present Henry, earl of Clarendon, by writeing or causing the said character to be printed':

et aliter nescit deponere.

4. Ad 4 posicionem dictorum articulorum et ad copiam exhibitam et repetitam dicit et deponit

that 'he hath read the life or character of John Glynne in the articulate 269 columne of the articulate second volume of the ATHENAE ET FASTI OXONIENSES, and finds the author thereof in some part of the character of John Glynne to have defamed the memory of the articulate Edward, earl of Clarendon, late Lord Chancellour of England and of this University of Oxon, and father of the present Henry, earl of Clarendon, by writeing and causeing the said character to be printed':

et aliter nescit deponere.

10. Ad 10 proposicionem articulorum praedictorum dicit et deponit quod praedeposita per eum sunt vera, and further saith

that 'there was and is a public fame and report that Mr. Anth. à Wood was and is the author of the book entituled ATHENAE ET FASTI OXONIENSES, which fame and report this deponent beleives was and is true, because the said Mr. Anth. à Wood offered to sell some of them to this deponent, as he hath deposed':

et aliter nescit deponere.

---

[1] from Arch. Univ. Oxon. W. P. γ. 26. fol. 20 sqq.   [2] Tuesday.
[3] i. e. 169¾.   [4] Chancellor of.

Super reliquis posicionibus dictorum articulorum non examinatur e direccione procuratorum eum producentium.

Praedictus Henricus Clements super allegacionem—

1. Ad primam posicionem dictae allegacionis dicit et deponit quod nescit deponere.

4. Ad 4 posicionem dictae allegacionis et ad praefacionem exhibitam et repetitam dicit et deponit

that 'since the second volume of the ATHENAE ET FASTI OXONIENSES articulate were printed and published, as they now appeare, the articulate Mr. Anth. à Wood, when he offered this deponent to sell him some of his ATHENAE ET FASTI OXONIENSES, as he hath before deposed, said he had printed a preface to them and offered to sell this deponent 26 of those prefaces articulate for six pence each, telling him (this deponent) that the prefaces were to be placed according to the direction printed on the bottom of them' :

et aliter nescit deponere.

5. Ad 5 posicionem dictae allegacionis et ad prefaciones annexas et repetitas dicit et deponit

that 'the articulate Mr. Anthony à Wood lives in the house articulate, and that the Coat of Armes expressed in the capital lettre C in the next foregoing posicion mentioned is the same Coat of Armes described in the capital lettre C before the epistle or preface mencioned in the 3ᵈ posicion of this matter, as appeares by collateing them. And further this deponent says that the articulate Mr. Anthony à Wood is a more then ordinary retired and reserved person' :

et aliter nescit deponere.

Super reliquis posicionibus dictae allegacionis non examinatur e direccione procuratorum eum producentium.

Praedictus Henricus Clements ad interrogatoria—

1. Satisfactus est et ulterius respondet

that 'he is not known to the lord Clarendon; is acquainted with Mr. Wood; but if it were in his power to determine this matter he would doe it according to justice' :

et aliter respondet negative.

2. Ad 2 interrogatorium respondet quod nescit respondere.

3. Ad primam partem 3 interrogatorii respondet negative ideoque residuum non concernit eum.

4. Ad 4 interrogatorium respondet quod refert se ad praedeposita et ulterius respondet

that 'the first volume of the ATHENAE OXONIENSES interrogate was published in print about a year and an halfe before the second volume' :

et aliter nescit respondere.

5. Ad 5 interrogatorium respondet

that 'he hath sold severall of the interrogate ATHENAE ET FASTI OXONIENSES since the publicacion thereof and att present hath them to be sold; that he was never molested for selling of them; that he subscribed to Mr. Bennett that printed the ATHENAE ET FASTI OXONIENSES for about 24 of them which he received first and last' :

et aliter nescit respondere.

6. Non examinatur ad 6 e direccione judicis.

7, 8, et 9 interrogatoria non concernunt eum.

HENRY CLEMENTS[1].

Repetitum et recognitum coram
    G. Gardiner, assessore.

[1] autograph signature.

MICHAEL BURGHERS de Oxonia, ingraver, ubi moram traxit circiter 20 annos ultimos elapsos, natus apud Amsterdam, aetatis circiter 40 annos, testis productus admissus et juratus super propositis in hoc negocio ex parte officii datis et admissis, examinatus vero 22 die[1] Martii anno Domini (stilo Angliae) 1692[2], dicit et deponit prout sequitur, viz[6].

10. Ad 10 posicionem articulorum praedictorum dicit et deponit quod nescit deponere.

Super reliquis posicionibus dictorum articulorum non examinatur e direccione procuratorum eum producentium.

Praedictus Michael Burghers ad allegacionem.

4. Ad 4 posicionem dictae allegacionis et ad praefacionem annexam dicit et deponit

that 'he (this deponent) by the order and desire of Mr. Anthony à Wood did take a draught from his face of the picture or face before the preface articulate now shewed to this deponent at his examinacion and did afterwards engrave the same face or picture in copper for the articulate Mr. à Wood's picture or face, who told this deponent that *his friend was displeased because it was no more like him* (the articulate Mr. Anthony à Wood); but doth not remember the time when':

et aliter nescit deponere.

5. Ad 5 posicionem dictae allegacionis et ad praefaciones annexas dicit et deponit

that 'the Coate of Armes expressed in the capitall letter C in the next foregoeing posicion mencioned is the same Coat of Armes with that expressed in the capitall letter C before the epistle or preface mencioned in the third posicion of this matter, and that this deponent made some small alteracions in the copper plate therof, which he received from the articulate Mr. Anthony à Wood, who then lived in the house articulate:'

et aliter nescit deponere.

Super reliquis posicionibus dictae allegacionis non examinatur e direccione procuratorum eum producentium.

Praedictus Michael Burghers ad interrogatoria.

1. Satisfactus est et ulterius respondet

that 'he equally favours the parties litigant and wishes that justice and right may take place; that he expects only his necessary charges for losse of time in being a witnesse in this cause':

et aliter nescit respondere.

2. Ad 2 interrogatorium respondet quod nescit respondere.

3. Ad primam partem 3 interrogatorii respondet negative ideoque residuum non concernit eum.

4. Ad 4 interrogatorium respondet quod nescit respondere.

5. Ad 5 interrogatorium respondet quod nescit respondere.

6. Non examinatur ad 6 interrogatorium e direccione judicis.

7, 8, et 9 interrogatoria non concernunt eum.

MICHAEL BURGHERS[3].

Repetitum et recognitum
coram G. Gardiner[4], assessore.

RICARDUS DAVIS de Universitate Oxon bibliopola, natus apud Oxoniam, aetatis 75, testis productus admissus et juratus super propositis in hoc negocio ex

---

[1] Wednesday.
[2] i. e. 169¾.

[3] autograph signature.
[4] autograph signature.

parte officii datis et admissis, examinatus vero 22° die[1] Martii 169⅔ dicit et deponit prout sequitur (vizᵗ)

10. Ad 10 posicionem dictorum articulorum dicit et deponit

that 'there was and is a publick fame and report that Mr. Anth. à Wood was and is the author of the second volume of the ATHENAE ET FASTI OXONIENSES':

et aliter nescit deponere.

Praedictus Ricardus Davis super allegacionem.

3. Ad 3 posicionem allegacionis et ad librum et praefacionem annex. et repetit. dicit et deponit quod nescit deponere.

6. Ad 6 posicionem dictae allegacionis nescit deponere.

Super reliquis posicionibus dictae allegacionis non examinatur e direccione procuratorum eum producentium.

Praedictus Ricardus Davis ad interrogatoria.

1. Satisfactus est et ulterius respondet

that 'he hath noe concerne with either of the parties interrogate':

et aliter respondet negative.

2. Ad 2 interrogatorium respondet quod nescit respondere.

3. Ad primam partem 3 interrogatorii respondet negative ideoque residuum non concernit eum.

4. Ad 4 interrogatorium respondet quod nescit respondere.

5. Ad 5 interrogatorium respondet quod nescit respondere.

6. non examinatur ad 6 e direccione judicis.

7, 8, et 9 non concernunt eum.

Repetitum et recognitum coram [2]

RIC. DAVIS[3].

RICARDUS HAWKINS de civitate Oxon, alderman, ubi moram traxit circiter 70 annos ultimos elapsos, ætatis circiter 82 annos, testis productus, admissus et juratus super propositis in hoc negocio ex parte officii datis et admissis, examinatus vero 23 die[4] Martii, anno Domini 169⅔, dicit et deponit prout sequitur (vizᵗ)

Super posicionibus dictorum articulorum non examinatur e direccione procuratorum eum producentium.

5. Ad 5 posicionem dictae allegacionis dicit et deponit

that 'the Coat of Armes described in the capital lettre C in the next foregoing posicion mencioned hath been drawne by him (this deponent), (but without a Crest, as he remembers) for the articulate Mr. Anth. à Wood and for others of his family[5], but whether the right leg of the woolfe was passant or guardant he doth not remember; and does beleive that the males of the ffamily of the Woods articulate doe use the Coat of Armes articulate engraven on their seales with their proper distinctions: and further this deponent says that the said Coat of Armes is the same with that expressed in the capitall letter C before the epistle or preface mencioned in the 3ᵈ. posicion of this matter, haveing compared the same at his examinacion':

et aliter nescit deponere.

---

[1] Wednesday.

[2] the assessor has not added his signature. A marginal direction is put at the beginning of Davis' evidence—'you need not copy, Mr. Davis not being repeated.'

[3] autograph signature.

[4] Thursday.

[5] 'others of his family' is substituted for 'his late brother, under-sheriffe of Oxon.'

Super reliquis posicionibus dictae allegacionis non examinatur e direccione procuratorum eum producentium.

Praedictus Ricardus Hawkins ad interrogatoria.
Satisfactus est et ulterius respondet
that 'he hath nothing to doe in the cause but wishes that right may take
place':
et aliter respondet negative.
2. Ad 2 interrogatorium respondet quod nescit respondere.
3. Ad 3 interrogatorium respondet negative.
4. Ad 4 interrogatorium nescit respondere.
5. Ad 5 interrogatorium respondet quod nescit respondere.
6. Non examinatur ad 6 e direccione judicis.
7, 8, et 9 non concernunt eum.

RICHARD HAWKINS[1].

Repetitum et recognitum coram
    Geo. Gardiner[2], assessore.

GUALTERUS COMBES de Universitate Oxon. tonsor, ubi moram fecit circiter
40 annos ultimos elapsos, oriundus apud Milton in comitatu Berks, aetatis circiter
60 annos, testis productus, admissus et juratus super propositis in hoc negocio datis
et admissis, examinatus vero 23° die[3] Martii anno Domini 169⅔, dicit et deponit
prout sequitur, vizt.
Super articulis in hoc negocio datis et admissis non examinatur e direccione procuratorum eum producentium.

7. Ad 7 posicionem dictae allegacionis dicit et deponit
that 'he hath of late frequently seen the articulate Mr. Anthony Wood *alias*
à Wood goe in to and out of the house articulate, which was and is esteemed the
house of his ancestours; that this deponent knew the articulate à Wood's ffather
very well and remembers that in his life time he lived and inhabited in the house
articulate in the parish articulate':
et aliter nescit deponere.

Super reliquis posicionibus dictae allegacionis non examinatur e direccione procuratorum eum producentium.

Praedictus Gualterus Combes ad interrogatoria.
1. Ad 1 partem interrogatorii satisfactus est et ulterius respondet
that 'he knows the interrogate Mr. Wood but doth not know the lord Clarendon,
and if it were in his power to determine this cause he would give it according to
justice':
et aliter respondet negative.
2. Ad 2 interrogatorium respondet quod nescit respondere.
3. Ad 3 interrogatorium respondet
that 'he understands not the question, nor does he know of any books the
interrogate Mr. Wood hath written or composed':
et aliter nescit respondere.
4. Ad 4 interrogatorium respondit quod nescit respondere.
5. Ad 5 interrogatorium respondet quod nescit respondere.

---

[1] autograph signature.   [2] autograph signature.
[3] Thursday.

6. Non examinatur ad 6 e direccione judicis.
7, 8, et 9 interrogatoria non concernunt eum.

WALTER COMBES [1].

Repetitum et recognitum
coram G. Gardiner [2] assessore.

DANIEL PORTER de Oxonia aurifaber, ibidemque natus, ubi moram fecit a nativitate sua, aetatis 29 annos, testis productus, admissus et juratus super propositis in hoc negocio ex parte officii datis et admissis, examinatus vero 23 die [3] Martii anno Domini 169⅔, dicit et deponit prout sequitur (vizt.)

Super articulis in hoc negocio datis et admissis non examinatur e direccione procuratorum eum producentium.

5. Ad 5 posicionem dictae allegacionis et ad praefaciones annexas et repetitas dicit et deponit

that 'he hath engraved the Coat of Armes expressed in the capitall lettre C. in the next foregoing posicion mencioned for severall of the articulate Mr. Anth. à Wood *alias* Wood's family; that the articulate Mr. Anthony à Wood now liveth in the house articulate in the parish articulate, where he remembers his brother called 'mouns^r. Wood' did also live and inhabit, and where one of his sonnes named Mr. Robert Wood now lives; and further this deponent says that about 5 or 6 yeares since the articulate Mr. Anthony à Wood *alias* Wood came to this deponent and bespoake a steel seale of him, and ordered the same Coat of Armes and Crest as are expressed in the two capitall lettres C. now shewed to this deponent at his examinacion to be engraven thereon and that the same Coat and Crest were engraven by this deponent's brother and delivered finished by this deponent to the articulate Mr. Anthony à Wood *alias* Wood; and also this deponent says that the Coat of Armes is the same with that expressed and described in the capitall lettre C. before the epistle or preface mencioned in the 3^d posicion of this allegacion, haveing compared them':

et aliter nescit deponere.

Super reliquis posicionibus dictae allegacionis non examinatur e direccione procuratorum eum producentium.

Praedictus Daniel Porter ad interrogatoria.
1. Satisfactus est et ulterius respondet

that 'he equally favours the parties litigant and wishes right and justice to take place':

et aliter respondet negative.

2. Ad 2 interrogatorium respondet quod nescit respondere.

3. Ad primam partem 3 interrogatorii respondet negative ideoque residuum non concernit eum.

4. Ad 4 interrogatorium respondet quod nescit respondere.

5. Ad 5 interrogatorium respondet quod nescit respondere.

6. Non examinatur ad 6 e direccione judicis.

7, 8, 9 non concernunt eum.

DANLL PORTER [4], *Junr*.

Repetitum et recognitum coram
    G. Gardiner [5], assessore.

---

[1] autograph signature.   [4] autograph signature.
[2] autograph signature.   [5] autograph signature.
[3] Thursday.

JOSEPHUS JACKSON coquus e Coll. Merton in Universitate Oxon. in parochia S. Jo. Bapt. ubi moram fecit circiter 19 annos ultimos elapsos, natus apud Yefley in com. Oxon., aetatis 48 annos, testis productus admissus et juratus super propositis in hoc negotio ex parte officii datis et admissis, examinatus vero 23° die [1] Martii Anno Domini 169⅔ dicit et deponit prout sequitur, vizt.

Super articulis in hoc negotio datis non examinatur e direccione procuratorum eum producentium.

7. Ad 7 posicionem dictae allegacionis dicit et deponit

that 'he beleives the articulate Anth. à Wood did live in the house articulate in the moneth of June articulate and that he still does live there; that the house articulate is esteemed and accounted to belong to the Woods, but the articulate Mr. Anth. à Wood's father died before this deponent knew the parish articulate':

et aliter nescit deponere.

Super reliquis posicionibus dictae allegacionis non examinatur e direccione procuratorum eum producentium.

Praefatus Jos. Jackson ad interrogatoria.

1. Satisfactus est et ulterius respondet

that 'he wishes that right may take place; that he is a stranger to the parties litigant':

et aliter respondet negative.

2, 3, 4, et 5 interrogatoria, respondet quod nescit respondere.

6. Non examinatur ad 6 e direccione judicis.

7, 8, et 9 interrogatoria non concernunt eum.

JOSEPH JACKSON [2].

Repetit. et recognit. coram
    G. Gardiner [3], assess.

XXXII. Formal proceedings.

⟨Friday⟩ 24 Martii 169⅔: officium domini promotum, &c. contra Anth. à Wood. Smith, Lloyd. Wood, Cooke. Jo. Hall, Hen. Clements, Mich. Burghers, Ric. Davis, Ric. Hawkins, Gualt. Combes, Dan. Porter, et Jos. Jackson examen subierunt. Ultimo die juridico Smith et Lloyd dederunt allegacionem cum duabus litteris annexis &c. Emanavit decretum pro responsis à Wood posicionibus dictae allegacionis et pro plenioribus responsis 5, 6, et 7 posicionibus allegacionis contra eum datae &c. Emanaverunt compulsorium contra Hen. Dodwell A.M. testem &c., et decretum pro responsis honoratissimi domini Henrici comitis de Clarendon faciendis posicionibus allegacionis ex parte à Wood datae et admissae.

Quibus &c., facta trina praeconizacione pro praedictis Ric. Hawkins, Ricardo Davis, et Gualtero Combes testibus ex parte officii productis admissis juratis et examinatis sed nondum repetitis, dominus ad peticionem Smith et Lloyd, accusantium eorum in hac parte contumacias, pronunciavit eos contumaces et in poena contumaciarum suarum hujusmodi decrevit eos arrestandos fore.

Tunc reducto decreto praedicto pro responsis à Wood faciendis posicionibus allegacionis cum litteris annexis et pro plenioribus suis responsis faciendis 5, 6, et 7° posicionibus allegacionis praedictae, executo per Andream Skinner mandatarium hujus curiae juxta certificatorium in dorso ejusdem desuper juratum, unde dominus

---

[1] Thursday.   [2] autograph signature.   [3] autograph signature.

ad peticionem dictorum Smith et Lloyd decrevit dictum Anth. à Wood personaliter citandum fore pro responsis suis ut praedicitur si &c. alioquin viis et modis in proximum, in praesentia Wood dissentientis.

Tunc reducto compulsorio praedicto contra Hen. Dodwell executo per Andream Skinner praedictum juxta certificatorium desuper juratum, dominus ad peticionem Smith et Lloyd decrevit dictum Hen. Dodwell personaliter citandum et compellendum fore si &c. alioquin per compulsorium viis et modis in proximum.

Tunc reducto decreto pro responsis honoratissimi domini Henrici comitis de Clarendon faciendis posicionibus allegacionis ex parte dicti Anth. à Wood in hoc negocio datis et admissis executo per Andream Skinner praedictum juxta certificatorium &c. desuper juratum, factaque trina praeconizacione pro praedicto honoratissimo domino Hen. comite de Clarendon eoque non comparente, Wood accusavit ejus in ea parte contumaciam, sed dominus reservavit ejus poenam in proximum &c.

XXXIII. Wood sends in fuller answers to Clarendon's first allegation, and his answers to Clarendon's second allegation. A commission issued to take Clarendon's answers to Wood's allegation.

(Friday) 31 March 1693: officium domini promotum &c. contra Anth. à Wood. Smith, Lloyd. Wood, Cooke. Non emanaverunt warranta contra Ric. Davis, Ric. Hawkins, et Gualt. Combes testes &c.

Emanaverunt decretum pro responsis et plenioribus responsis dicti à Wood, et compulsorium viis et modis contra Hen. Dodwell &c. Reservatus est honoratissimus dominus Hen. comes de Clarendon in hunc diem.

Quibus &c. reducto decreto pro responsis plenioribus et responsis Anth. à Wood, Wood et Cooke dederunt responsa pleniora dicti à Wood facta posicionibus allegacionis in hoc negotio ex parte officii primo loco datae, et responsa dicti à Wood facta posicionibus allegacionis cum 2^{abus} litteris annexis in scriptis concepta, in praesentia Smith et Lloyd acceptantium eorundem quatenus &c.

Tunc reducto compulsorio viis et modis contra dictum Hen. Dodwell A.M. testem &c. executum per Andream Skinner mandatarium hujus curiae juxta certificatorium desuper juratum; factaque 3^{ua} praeconizacione pro dicto Hen. Dodwell eoque non comparente, dominus, ad peticionem Smith et Lloyd accusantium ejus contumaciam in non comparendo juxta &c., pronunciavit eum contumacem in ea parte sed reservavit ejus poenam in proximum &c.

Tunc Smith et Lloyd allegaverunt honoratissimum dominum Hen. comitem de Clarendon in remotis partibus agere ita ut ad hoc tribunal commode venire non posset, quare petierunt commissionem emanare sub mutuae vicissitudinis obtentu venerabili viro Hen. Newton LL^m. Dri et reverendi in Xto patris domini Henrici episcopi London officiali principali pro recepcione repeticione et recognicione responsorum dicti honoratissimi domini Hen. comitis de Clarendon faciendorum posicionibus allegacionis alias in hoc negocio ex parte dicti Anth. à Wood datae et admissae. Dominus decrevit uti petitur et assignavit terminum pro transmissione dictae commissionis in vel citra primum diem juridicum termini Paschatis ex tunc proxime futuri, in praesentia Wood dissentientis.

XXXIV. Wood's fuller answers to Clarendon's first allegation.

Responsa [1] pleniora Antonii Wood de Oxon., gen., facta quibusdam posicionibus cujusdam praetensae allegacionis datis et exhibitis contra eum decimo Februarii 169$\frac{2}{3}$, sequuntur.

1. ad 1^{am} et 2^{dam} posiciones respondet et dicit quod negat easdem esse veras in aliquo.

3. ad 3^{am} posicionem, ad librum et epistolam sive praefationem invocatam, respondet et dicit quod negat eandem esse veram in aliquo.

4, 5. ad 4^m et 5^m posiciones et ad epistolas invocatas respondet et dicit quod negat easdem esse veras in aliquo.

6. ad 6^m posicionem respondet et dicit quod non credit eandem esse veram in aliquo.

7. ad 7^m respondet et dicit quod negat eandem esse veram in aliquo.

8. ad 8^m et ad epistolam invocatam respondet et dicit quod negat eandem esse veram in aliquo.

9, 10, 11. ad 9^m, 10^m, et 11^m posiciones respondet et dicit quod negat easdem esse veras in aliquo.

12. ad 12^m posicionem respondet et dicit quod credit credita et negat negata.

ANTHO. WOOD [2].

Martii 31°, 1693, repetit. et recognit. coram me
  Geo. Gardiner [3] assess.

XXXV. Wood's answers to Clarendon's second allegation.

Responsa [4] personalia Ant. Wood de Oxon., gen., facta quibusdam posicionibus cujusdam praetensae allegacionis datae et exhibitae contra eum 17° die Martii 1693 sequuntur.

1, 2, 3. ad 1^{mam} 2^{dam} et 3^{am} posiciones et ad epistolas cum sigillis invocatas et exhibitas respondet et dicit quod negat easdem aut aliquam earundem partem esse veras in aliquo.

ANTHONY WOOD [5].

Martii 31°, 1693, repetit. et recognit. coram me
  Geo. Gardiner [6], assess.

XXXVI. Clarendon sends in a third allegation: Clarendon asks evidence of experts in handwriting to be taken: Wood is ordered to give fuller answers to Clarendon's second allegation.

(Friday) 7 April 1693: officium domini promotum &c. contra Anth. à Wood. Lloyd. Wood, Cooke.

Non emanavit warrantum contra Ric. Davis testem productum admissum juratum et examinatum sed non repetitum. Poena Mri. Dodwell reservatur in hunc diem.

Quibus &c., Lloyd in subsidium probacionis contentorum in propositis in hoc

[1] from Arch. Univ. Oxon. W. P. γ. 26. fol. 27.
[2] autograph signature.
[3] autograph signature.
[4] from Arch. Univ. Oxon. W. P. γ. 26. fol. 28.
[5] autograph signature.
[6] autograph signature.

negocio ex parte officii dedit actum, seu allegacionem apud acta, cum schedula annexa, quam dominus ad ejus peticionem admisit, in praesentia Wood et Cooke dissentientium.

Tunc dictus Lloyd etiam in subsidium contentorum in propositis in hoc negocio ex parte officii dedit alteram allegacionem apud acta quam dominus admisit, et decrevit comparationem fieri juxta &c.

Necnon Geo. Cooper, Jac. Newlin, et Ffr. Clarke, peritos in arte scribendi, juramento oneravit de fideliter comparando respective exhibita et de referendo eorum judicium primo die juridico termini Paschatis ex tunc sequentis, ⟨in praesentia⟩ Wood et Cooke dissentientium.

Insuperque Lloyd allegavit quasdam materias (praesertim 2 literas) per Smith et eum in hoc negocio datas et admissas non inspectas fuisse per dictum Anth. à Wood tempore examinacionis ejus pro responsis &c. ; unde dominus ad ejus peticionem decrevit dictum à Wood examinandum fore coram eo per registrarium [1] hujus curiae pro responsis suis fiendis allegacioni cum 2 literis annexis citra proximum, ⟨in praesentia⟩ Wood et Cooke dissentientium.

XXXVII. Clarendon's third allegation.

Officium[2] domini promotum per honoratissimum dominum dominum Henricum comitem de Clarendon contra Ant. à Wood infra Universitatem Oxon. in Artibus Magistrum, in quodam negotio reformacionis morum &c., exhibitum Aprilis 7°. 1693.

Quibus &c. Smith et Lloyd nomine procuratorio ac ut procuratores legittimi domini domini Henrici comitis de Clarendon in subsidium probacionis articulorum originalium ac allegationis 10° die Februarii 169⅔ in hoc negotio datae et admissae exhibuerunt quandam chartulam typis impressam cui titulus *Proposalls for printing Athenae Oxonienses and Fasti Oxonienses both written by the famous Antiquary and Historiographer Anthony à Wood M.A. Author of the History and Antiquities of the University of Oxford*: Quam quidem chartulam praefati Smith et Lloyd allegaverunt fuisse et esse sparsam et publice disseminatam infra praecinctum Universitatis Oxon. Quam allegacionem fideliter positam, dicti Smith et Lloyd ponunt conjunctim et divisim et eandem admitti petunt una cum chartula annexa, et jus et justitiam &c.

Dominus admisit eandem allegacionem ad peticionem Lloyd, in praesentia Wood et Cooke dissentientium.

XXXVIII. Clarendon asks the evidence of experts in handwriting to be taken.

Officium[3] domini promotum per honoratissimum dominum dominum Henricum comitem de Clarendon contra Antonium à Wood infra universitatem Oxoniensem in Artibus Magistrum in quodam negotio reformacionis morum, &c., exhibitum Aprilis 7ᵐᵒ. 1693.

Quibus &c. Smith et Lloyd nomine procuratorio ac ut procuratores legitimi domini domini Henrici comitis de Clarendon in subsidium probacionis articulorum originalium et allegacionum, praecipue allegationis 17ᵐᵒ. Martii 169⅔ in hoc negotio datae et admissae allegaverunt nomen et cognomen Ant. à Wood in hoc negotio defendentis tribus [4]

---

[1] Joseph Woodward.
[2] from the official copy in Arch. Univ. Oxon. W. P. . 26. fol. 32.

[3] from the official copy in Arch. Univ. Oxon. W. P. γ. 26. fol. 31.
[4] *supra*, pp. 11, 21, 36.

responsis personalibus dicti à Wood in hoc negocio exhibitis, apposita et subscripta et pro sic appositis et subscriptis coram venerabili domino domino assessore recognita et recensita, fuisse et esse scripta et exarata propria manu dicti à Wood et ipsa et eadem manu cum qua quaedam literae originales in hoc negocio jam datae et exhibitae, scriptae et exaratae fuerunt et sunt: ideoque petierunt comparationem fieri inter nomen et cognomen dictis responsis apposita et subscripta et dictas literas originales, et peritos in arte scribendi elegi et juramento onerari de fideliter comparando praemissa, et de referendo eorum judicium stato die. Quam allegacionem ponunt conjunctim et divisim ac eandem admitti petunt, ac jus, &c. Dominus admisit dictam allegacionem ad peticionem Lloyd, in praesentia Wood et Cooke dissentientium.

XXXIX. Clarendon sends in answers to Wood's allegation: the Court takes these into consideration: Wood has leave to bring in witnesses.

⟨Friday⟩ 5 May 1693: officium domini promotum &c. contra Anth. à Wood. Smith, Lloyd. Wood, Cook.

Data sunt responsa honoratissimi domini Hen. comitis de Clarendon. Comparatores habent ad referendum judicium &c. in hunc diem. Non examinatus est dictus à Wood coram judice.

Quibus, &c., terminus ad referendum judicium comparatorum continuatur in proximum.

Dominus ad peticionem Smith et Lloyd publicavit dicta et deposiciones testium ex parte dicti honoratissimi promotoris hujus negocii productorum juratorum et examinatorum, decrevitque eis[1] copias deposicionum dictorum testium, in praesentia Wood et Cook dissentientium et allegantium responsa dicti honoratissimi domini Hen. comitis de Clarendon facta posicionibus cujusdam allegacionis ex parte dicti à Wood datae et admissae esse nec plene nec plane 3, 4, 5, 10, 11, 13, 14, et 15 posicionibus dictae allegacionis, nec de jure admittenda. Unde dominus assignavit ad audiendum voluntatem suam in proximum et ad informandum eum desuper in camera sua infra Coll. Omn. Animarum die Jovis proxime futuro hora prima pomeridiana ejusdem diei.

Tunc dominus ad peticionem Wood et Cook, decrevit eis 3 dies juridicos ex tunc sequentes ad probandum allegacionem alias per eos in hoc negocio ex parte dicti à Wood datae et admissae, ⟨in praesentia⟩ Smith et Lloyd dissentientium.

XL. Clarendon's answers to Wood's allegation.

Responsa[2] personalia honoratissimi viri ac domini domini Henrici comitis de Clarendon facta quibusdam posicionibus cujusdam pretensae allegacionis datae et exhibitae contra eum in Curia Cancellarii Universitatis Oxon. 3° Martii 169⅔ sequuntur, videlicet,

1. Ad primam posicionem praetensam sub protestacione de nimia generalitate, indebita specificatione, ineptitudine, iniquitate, et non concludentia ejusdem, et omnium et singulorum subsequentium, et hac protestacione sua sibi in omnibus semper salva, et pro repetita habita, respondet et dicit eandem esse positionem juris, et aliter censet se non teneri de jure respondere, referendo se ad jus.

2. Ad 2ᵈᵃᵐ posicionem praetensam respondet et dicit,

[1] MS. has 'eisque.'

[2] from the official copy in Arch. Univ. Oxon. W. P. γ. 26. fol. 35.

' that, saving his answers to the next following posicion, non credit eandem esse veram in aliquo.'

3. Ad 3ᵃᵐ posicionem praetensam respondet et credit

' that one Mr. Fraser was appointed supervisor or licencer of the books, and by one or both of the persons and in the years in this posicion sett forth, and was so reputed to bee, and as such did supervise the book herein mentioned, written by the defendent in this cause, and did alter and mend many unfitting and scandalous reflections in itt, and as much as in him lay did licence or give way to the printing thereof so altered and amended. And this respondent saith that the remaining part of this posicion is matter of undue inference in the law (to which he referreth himself),'

et aliter non credit eandem esse veram in aliquo.

4. Ad 4ᵗᵃᵐ posicionem praetensam respondet et dicit,

' that he beleiveth that the book in this posicion mencioned was printed for Mr. Bennett in this posicion mencioned, he having bought the manuscript of the said defendant. And that the said Mr. Bennett sold many copyes of the said book so printed in London, and to booksellers within the University of Oxford,'

et aliter non credit eandem esse veram in aliquo.

5. Ad 5ᵗᵃᵐ posicionem praetensam respondet et dicit,

' that he beleiveth that the defendant having sold one copye of the originall papers in writing to the said Mr. Bennett, the said Mr. Bennett had them in custodie of himself and others by his orders a time convenient for the supervising them immediatly before the printing of them, which he beleiveth was the space of one year and noe more,'

et aliter non credit eandem esse veram in aliquo.

6, 7, 8, 9. Ad 6ᵗᵃᵐ, 7ᵃᵐ, 8ᵃᵐ, 9ⁿᵃᵐ posiciones praetensas respondet et dicit, quod salvis praeresponsis suis ad 3ᵃᵐ et 5ᵗᵃᵐ posicionem, non credit easdem aut earundem aliquam esse veram in aliquo.

10. Ad 10ᵐᵃᵐ posicionem praetensam respondet et dicit,

' that Mr. Wood the defendant as author of the book articulate did communicate to this respondent one sheet only of the originall papers thereof in writing, to witt, that sheet wherein was contained the direct and particular account of Sir Edward Hyde, late Lord Chancellor of England and Earl of Clarendon, this respondent's father deceased, containing matters of his birth, accidents of his life, his writings and death, wherein this respondent finding many words, and sentences either not decently expressed, or not true, this respondent did return the said sheet unaltered to the said defendant, butt by his letter to the said Mr. Wood, did desire him that he would say nothing of his said father, saving giving an account of the place and time of his birth and death, and of his coming to the University, for that an account was already prepared of his life, or to that effect; for more certainty whereof this respondent referreth himself to the said letter, if the said defendant shall think fitt to exhibitt the same,'

et aliter salvis praeresponsis suis ad tertiam posicionem non credit eandem esse veram in aliquo.

11. Ad 11ᵐᵃᵐ posicionem praetensam respondet et dicit,

' that this posicion is criminous to himself (and to many other persons who are absent, and no way concerned in this cause) to which he conceiveth himself not bound by law to answer, referring himself to the law : yett nevertheless for the sake of justice, and that the author or authors, exhibitor, or exhibitors, of the infamous scandalls therein contained, may have no pretence of disadvantage in probation from this respondent's declining to answer, he answereth and saith

that as far as this posicion concerneth his own fact he utterly denyeth and abhorreth
the same, and as far as itt concerneth the fact of other persons, he utterly
disbeleiveth the same to bee true, or any part thereof, protesting, on his part,
that if the infamous matter sett forth against him in this posicion bee not proved
he will use the benefitt of the law.'

12. Ad 12^{mam} posicionem praetensam respondet et credit eandem esse veram.

13, 14. Ad 13^{am} et 14^{tam} posiciones praetensas et columnas in eisdem mentionatas
respondet et dicit quod non credit easdem aut earum alterutram esse veras in aliquo.

15. Ad 15^{tam} posicionem praetensam respondet et dicit,

'that he beleiveth that the epistle or preface herein mentioned was composed in
writing and procured to bee printed by the defendant in this cause together with
his intended picture and Coat of Armes and being so printed were delivered by
the said defendant Mr. Wood, and others by his appointment, with directions to
insert or fasten the same before his first volume of *Athenae Oxonienses*, butt not
before the said first volume onely, more particularly the said defendant sent one to
this respondent as by his letter to this respondent in this cause exhibited
(to which he referreth himself) may and doth appear. And this respondent
beleiveth that the said first volume was printed and published about the space
of one year, and no more, before the second volume articulate (yett for more
certainty he referreth himself to the title pages of both the said books and the
dates there sett down). And this respondent beleiveth neverthelesse, that the said
epistle or preface was printed and delivered to bee inserted as abovesaid, some
months after the printing and publication of both the said volumes, as by the said
letter written and sent to this respondent, and in this cause exhibited, may alsoe
and doth appear, to which he referreth himself,'

et aliter quoad factum suum negat quoad alienum non credit eandem esse veram
in aliquo.

16. Ad 16^{tam} posicionem praetensam respondet et dicit,

'that he beleiveth that about twenty years agoe, and no more, the defendant
Mr. Wood his father gave him the use of a chamber in his said father's house in
St. John Baptist parish within the University of Oxford, whereupon the defendant
to save chamber-rent and other charges, quitted his chamber and batteling in
Merton College and removed his bed and books to the chamber in his said father's
house, and hath from that time generally continued to lodge and dyett there, and
to wear an academicall habitt, and to frequent the publick library of the said
University, and to continue the course of his studys within the precincts of the said
University, as other students, though in a more than ordinary retired manner.
And this respondent beleiveth that the said Mr. Wood the defendant being deaf, by
reason thereof hath seldom frequented the publick assemblies of the said University,'

et aliter non credit eandem esse veram in aliquo.

17. Ad 17^{am} respondet et dicit, quod credit credita, et negat negata ; et aliter
negat eandem esse veram in aliquo.

CLARENDON [1].

> Aprilis die 18° 1693.
> Repetit. et recognit.
> coram Geo. Gardiner [2], assessore.

[Endorsed :—] Responsa personalia Honoratissimi
Domini Domini Comitis de Clarendon.

---

[1] autograph signature.   [2] autograph signature.

XLI. Clarendon's answers are again taken into consideration by the Court: the opinion of the experts in handwriting is given.

⟨Friday⟩ 12 May 1693: officium domini promotum contra Anth. à Wood. Smith, Lloyd. Wood, Cook. Non emanavit decretum contra dictum à Wood pro reponsis suis plenioribus &c. faciendis. Coram judice publicatae sunt deposiciones ex parte officii. Terminus ad referendum judicium comparatorum continuatur in hunc diem. Primus dies probationis Wood et Cooke. Ad audiendum voluntatem domini super responsis honoratissimi promotoris &c. in hunc diem.

Quibus &c. habitae sunt informaciones juxta &c. Unde dominus decrevit pro informacionibus ulterioribus super responsis honoratissimi promotoris ad allegacionem ex parte dicti à Wood datam et admissam die Mercurii proxime sequente inter horas primam et 2^{dam} pomeridianam ejusdem diei et ad audiendum voluntatem suam desuper in proximum.

Tunc Mr. Geo. Cooper, unus comparatorum &c., dedit judicium comparatorum in scriptis sub eorum chyrographis, in praesentia procuratorum hinc inde ;

et dominus ad peticionem Smith et Lloyd assignavit ad sententiandum primo in proximum &c., ⟨in praesentia⟩ Wood et Cooke dissentientium.

XLII. The evidence of the experts in handwriting.

We[1] whose names are subscribed, being sworne truly and faithfully to compare the hand writing of two letters and their respective subscriptions *A : Wood* annexed to an allegacion exhibited March the 17, 169¾, with the subscriptions *Anthony Wood* and *Antho : Wood*, to three personal answers given into the Chancellour's Court of the Universitie of Oxon at the promotion of the right honourable the earle of Clarendon, are upon due comparison made of the same induc'd to beleeve that the letters and subscriptions thereto *A. Wood* aforesaid are of the same hand writing with the words *Anthony Wood* subscribed to the personal answer exhibited January 20, 169¾. In witness whereof we have hereunto sett our hands the eighth day of April 1693.

GEO: COOPER
JAMES NEWLIN } Comparitors.
FRAN: CLARKE

XLIII. The Court pronounces Clarendon's answers sufficient: Wood's witnesses are to be summoned.

⟨Friday⟩ 19 May 1693: officium domini promotum contra Anth. à Wood. Smith, Lloyd. Cooke. 2^{dus} dies probationis Wood et Cooke. Non emanavit decretum contra à Wood pro responsis suis &c. Ad sententiendum primo in hunc diem ad peticionem Smith et Lloyd. Habitae sunt informaciones 2do loco.

Quibus &c., dominus pronunciavit responsa honoratissimi domini Hen. comitis de Clarendon facta posicionibus allegacionis in hoc negocio ex parte à Wood datae et admissae fuisse ac esse plena, sed decrevit computacionem faciendam expensarum informacionum.

Ad idem, in proximum ad peticionem Smith et Lloyd, in praesentia Cooke dissentientis et allegantis quosdam Anth. Peisley, Jo. Howell, Rob. Wood, Gul.

---

[1] from the official copy in Arch. Univ. Oxon. W. P. γ. 26. fol. 33.

Hackett, et Andream Adderly esse testes necessarios sibi ad probandum intencionem suam deductam in quadam allegacione ex parte dicti à Wood data et admissa in hoc negocio, sed oblatis eis viaticis et expensis ad hoc tribunal venire recusant. Unde dominus ad ejus peticionem decrevit eos compellendos fore in proximum &c., ⟨in praesentia⟩ Smith et Lloyd dissentientium.

XLIV. Wood gives 'fuller' answers to Clarendon's second allegation: Wood's witnesses are produced.

⟨Friday⟩ 26 May 1693: officium domini promotum contra Anth. à Wood. Smith, Lloyd. Cooke. Ultimus dies probacionis Wood et Cooke. Ad sententiandum primo in hunc diem. Emanaverat decretum pro responsis à Wood &c., et compulsorium contra 5 testes ex parte dicti à Wood.

Quibus &c., data sunt responsa personalia dicti à Wood in scriptis conceptis facta posicionibus cujusdam allegacionis ex parte honoratissimi domini promotoris coram domino assessore, ⟨in praesentia⟩ Smith et Lloyd acceptantium eorundem quatenus &c.

Tunc reducto compulsorio praedicto personaliter executo contra Jo. Howell, Rob. Wood, Guliel. Hackett, et Antho. Peisley testes ex parte dicti à Wood per Andr. Skinner mandatarium hujus curiae juxta certificatorium desuper juratum, comparuerunt praedicti Jo. Howell, Rob. Wood, et Gul. Hackett quos Cooke super posicionibus cujusdam allegacionis in hoc negocio ex parte dicti à Wood datae et admissae produxit in testes. Dominus eos admisit et juramento ad sancta Dei evangelia per eos corporaliter tacta et deosculata oneravit de bene et fideliter deponendo totam et meram veritatem quam in hac parte noverint, omnibus amore favore odio semotis, et judicialiter monuit eos ad subeundum eorum in hac parte examen citra proximum, in praesentia Smith et Lloyd dissentientium &c. et habentium terminum eis assignatum ad ministranda interrogatoria quandocunque ante examen.

Tunc facta 3ⁿᵃ praeconizacione praedicti Anth. Peisley eoque non comparente, dominus ad peticionem Cooke accusantis ejus contumaciam, pronunciavit eum in hac parte contumacem et in poenam contumaciae suae hujusmodi decrevit eum arrestandum fore.

Insuperque ad peticionem Smith et Lloyd assignavit ad sententiandum 2° in proximum et ad informandum eum super meritis hujus negocii aliquo die per eum designando et intimandum procuratoribus hinc inde, in praesentia Cooke dissentientis, et ex sua peticione habentis copias deposicionum ex parte officii ei decretas quandocunque &c.

XLV. Wood's 'fuller' answers to Clarendon's second allegation.

Responsa[1] personalia Antonii à Wood in Artibus Magistri facta positionibus cujusdam allegationis cum 2 litteris eidem annexis ex parte honoratissimi domini domini Henrici comitis de Clarendon propositis &c. contra eum in curia Cancellarii Universitatis Oxon., dat. et adm. 17 Martii 169⅔, sequuntur :—

1, 2, 3. ad 1ᵐᵃᵐ, 2ᵘᵈᵃᵐ et 3ⁱᵃᵐ positiones dictae allegationis et ad litteras eidem annexas et repetitas respondet et negat easdem esse veras in aliqua parte earundem.

ANTH. WOOD[2].

Rescript., repet., et recogn.
coram G. Gardiner[3], assess.

[1] from Arch. Univ. Oxon. W. P. γ. 26. fol. 19.

[2] autograph signature.

[3] autograph signature.

XLVI. Clarendon's interrogatories to Wood's witnesses.

These have not been found.

XLVII. Minutes of the evidence given by Wood's witnesses.

These have not been found.

XLVIII. Further examination of Wood's witnesses.

⟨Friday⟩ 23 Junii 1693: officium domini promotum contra Anth. à Wood. Smith, Lloyd.　Wood, Cook.　Ad sententiandum 2º in hunc diem ad peticionem Smith et Lloyd. Jo. Howell testis &c. examen subiit. Rob. Wood et Gul. Hackett examen non subierunt &c.　Non emanavit warrantum contra Anth. Peisley testem.

Quibus &c., nondum habitae sunt informaciones &c.

Tunc comparuit Anth. Peisley, et Wood super posicionibus allegacionis alias per eum et Cook in hoc negocio ex parte à Wood datae et admissae produxit eum in testem, quem dominus admisit et juramento ad sancta Dei evangelia per eum corporaliter tacta et deosculata oneravit de bene et fideliter deponendo totam et meram veritatem quam in hac parte noverit omnibus amore odio &c. semotis (facta prius fide per Thomam Wood se non producere eum in testem ex causa dilacionis) et monuit eum ad subeundum ejus examen citra proximum &c.

Tunc dictus Wood, salva examinacione dicti Peisley, publicavit dicta et deposiciones testium ex parte sua productorum &c. et dominus decrevit copias earundem depositionum, in praesentia Smith et Lloyd dissentientium, &c.　Unde dominus ad eorum peticionem assignavit ad idem in proximum &c., ⟨in praesentia⟩ Wood et Cooke dissentientium.

Tunc Smith et Lloyd allegaverunt Ben. Cooper, registrarium Universitatis Oxon. praesentem in judicio recepisse et habuisse copias libri entitulati ATHENAE ET FFASTI OXONIENSES a dicto Anth. A Wood.　Unde dominus ad peticionem dicti Smith et Lloyd monuit eum ad exhibendum et introducendum copias dicti libri coram eo tempore informacionum super meritis hujus negotii.

XLIX. The Court prepares to give its sentence.

⟨Friday⟩ 30 Junii 1693: officium domini promotum contra Anth. à Wood. Smith, Lloyd.　Cook.　Ad sententiandum 2ᵈᵒ in hunc diem. Anth. Peisley testis &c. examen subiit. Quibus &c., dominus ad peticionem Smith et Lloyd assignavit ad idem in proximum &c. et ad informandum eum super meritis hujus negotii in hospitio domini vicecancellarii vel camera ejus situata in Collegio Omnium Animarum in dicta Universitate decimo tertio die mensis Julii proxime futuro inter horas 8 et 9 antemeridianas ejusdem diei, in praesentia Cook dissentientis.

L. Wood procures a writ to stay proceedings.

⟨Friday⟩ 14 July 1693: officium domini promotum contra Ant. à Wood. Smith, Lloyd.　Wood, Cook.　Ad audiendum sententiam in hunc diem. Habitae sunt informaciones juxta &c. Quibus &c., Ric. Dodwell[1], attornatus, exhibuit breve regium vocatum *Habeas Corpus cum causa.*　Unde dominus ad deliberandum duxit in proximum.

---

[1] vol. iii. p. 428.

LI. The proceedings are still stayed.

⟨Wednesday⟩ 19 July 1693 : officium domini promotum &c. contra Antonium à Wood.

Quibus, &c., dominus iterum duxit ad deliberandum in proximum, &c.

LII. Sentence is given and Wood expelled from the University.

⟨Saturday[1]⟩ 29 Julii 1693 : officium domini &c. promotum contra Ant. à Wood.

Smith, Lloyd.   Wood.

Dominus duxit ad deliberandum in hunc diem.

Quibus &c., Smith et Lloyd exhibuerunt breve regium de procedendo. Unde dominus ad eorum peticionem decrevit procedendum fore.

Tunc Smith et Lloyd juxta assignaciones in retroactis hujus curiae dederunt sententiam in scriptis diffinitivam quam petierunt ferri, legi, et promulgari. Dominus dictam sententiam per Smith et Lloyd datam legit tulit et promulgavit in scriptis diffinitivam decernendo pronunciando declarando et condemnando prout in eadem continetur, in praesentia Wood petentis justitiam.

Super cujus proclamatione dicti Smith et Lloyd requisiverunt me Jos. Woodward registrarium de conficiendo eis unum vel plura instrumentum seu instrumenta publicum seu publica, praesentibus tunc et ibidem Nic. Vilett, LL^m. Bac., notario publico, et Gul. Bunbury, A.M., testibus fidedignis ad praemissa testificanda specialiter requisitis et rogatis.

Tunc dominus ad ulteriorem peticionem dictorum Smith et Lloyd decrevit dictum Ant. à Wood monendum fore ad solvendum summam 34*li.*, vizt., expensas dicti honoratissimi promotoris in hoc negocio factas in dicta sententia taxatas praedicto promotori vel procuratori seu procuratoribus ejus legitimis citra primum diem juridicum termini S^ti Michaelis ex tunc proxime futurum, in praesentia Wood procuratoris dicti à Wood dissentientis.

LIII. The sentence [2].

In Dei nomine, Amen. Auditis, visis, intellectis, ac plenariè et maturè discussis per nos Georgium Gardiner LL. doctorem, ac venerabilis et egregii viri Henrici Aldrich, S.T.P., et almae universitatis Oxoniensis cancellarii, assessorem seu deputatum legitime constitutum; meritis circumstantiis cujusdam negotii reformationis morum quod, coram nobis, in judicio inter honoratissimum dominum dominum Henricum comitem de Clarendon, partem officium nostrum promoventem ex una, et Antonium à Wood, Universitatis praedictae in Artibus Magistrum, partem contra quam hujusmodi negotium promovetur ex altera, partibus, aliquandiu vertebatur et adhuc vertitur, ac pendet indecisum, ritè et legitimè procedendum [3],

---

[1] vol. iii. p. 429.

[2] I have taken this from the printed copy (the original not being forthcoming), but have been able to correct it in several places by the next document. The printed copy contains many mistakes due to the ignorance of the transcriber, who has filled up wrongly the contractions of the original. In MS. Ballard 14. fol. 30 is a summary, in Wood's hand, of this sentence:—

'(1) 2 sheets of the *Athenae Oxon.* wherein are the things excepted against are to be publickly burnt; (2) expulsion; (3) condemnation in the charges (which I am not able to beare); (4) recantation in open court.'

[3] some lines do not construe for the reason stated in the preceding note.

partibusque praedictis eorum procuratores legitimos coram nobis in judicio ritè et legitimè comparantes ; parteque dicti honoratissimi viri ac domini Henrici comitis de Clarendon pro parte sua sententiam ferri et promulgari, parte vero dicti Antonii à Wood justitiam fieri pro parte sua instanter et respectivè postulantibus et petentibus, rimatoque primitus per nos toto et integro processu, ita dicto negotio facto, et diligenter recensito, servatisque per nos de jure in hac parte servandis, ad nostrae sententiae definitivae, sive nostri finalis decreti, in dicto negotio, prolationem sic diximus procedendum fore, et procedimus in hujusmodi qui sequitur modum, *viz.* Quia post acta deducta, allegata, exhibita, pariter ac probata, in hujusmodi negotio, comperimus, et luculenter invenimus partem ante dictam honoratissimi viri ac domini domini Henrici comitis de Clarendon deductam hujusmodi negotio datam, exhibitam, et penes registrarium hujus curiae remanentem, quorum quidem articulorum tenor sequitur, et est talis, *viz.* In Dei nomine, Amen. Nos Henricus Aldrich [1] .... ministramus et articulamur, &c. (quos quidem articulos pro hic lectis et insertis habemus et haberi volumus quatenus expedit) sufficienter et ad plenum, quoad inferius pronunciatum, fundasse ac probasse, nihilque effectuale ex parte aut per partem antedicti Antonii à Wood allegatum aut probatum fuisse aut esse quod intentionem antedicti domini domini Henrici comitis de Clarendon ex hac parte elideret, seu quovis modo enervaret. Idcirco nos Georgius Gardiner judex antedictus, Christi nomine primitus invocato, ac ipsum Deum solum oculis nostris praeponentes, de, ac cum concilio jurisperitorum, quibuscum in hac parte praedicta communicavimus, praefatum Antonium à Wood, intra tempus et loca in hoc negotio articulata, librum quendam praetensum, cujus titulus praetensus sic incipit, ' ATHENAE OXONIENSES : *An exact History of all the Writers and Bishops who have had their education in the most ancient and famous University of Oxford, from the* 15*th yeare of King Henry VII, Anno Domini* 1500, *to the end of the year* 1690, *representing the birth, fortune,* &c.,' et sic terminatur, ' *The second volume compleating the whole work*' : et inter alia in dicto libro contenta, libellos famosos in verba Anglicana sequentia, viz. columna 221, ' *After the restauration of King Charles II 'twas expected by all, that he*' (quendam Davidem Jenkins, unum e judicibus regiis in partibus Walliae australibus virum meritissimum, innuendo) ' *should be made one of the judges in Westminster hall ; and so he might have been, would he have given money to the then Lord Chancellour*' (honoratissimum virum ac dominum, dominum Edvardum Hyde, militem, nuper comitem de Clarendon, regnique Angliae dominum cancellarium, nec non cancellarium hujus universitatis, patremque naturalem et legitimum partis hoc negotium promoventis defunctum innuendo), et columna 269 ' *After the restauration of King Charles II he*' (innuendo quendam Johannem Glynn) ' *was made his*' (domini regis, innuendo) ' *eldest serjeant at law, by the corrupt dealing of the then Lord Chancellour*' (praefatum honoratissimum virum ac dominum dominum Edvardum Hyde, militem, nuper comitem de Clarendon, regni Angliae dominum cancellarium, necnon cancellarium hujus universitatis, patremque naturalem et legitimum partis hoc negotium promoventis defunctum, similiter innuendo) scripto composuisse et publicasse, unde praefati honoratissimi viri ac domini, domini Edvardi Hyde, reliquis additionibus suis ut praemittitur colendissimi, existimatio et fama laedi possit, pronunciamus : ideoque dictum Antonium à Wood, quo usque ob tantum morum suorum excessum recantationem (per nos aut alium judicem hujus curiae competentem approbandam) subscripserit, cautionem item sufficientem fidejussoriam de pace conservanda et quoad crimina objecta honestè in posterum se gerendo interposuerit, ex hac dicta universitate Oxoniensi tanquam pacis perturbatorem banniendum, et privilegiis

---

[1] I omit here words cited from *supra*, p. 3.

ejusdem universitatis exuendum fore decernimus, et etiam bannimus et exuimus, praemissaque instrumento publice affigendo denuncianda et publicanda declaramus : in criminis insuper tam infesti detestationem, dicti libri copiam, copiam etiam (omisso nomine magistri Johannis Cook procuratoris) allegationis[1] cujusdam intemperantis, famosae et scandalosae ex parte dicti Antonii à Wood datae in hoc negotio tertio die mensis Martii anno Domini 169⅔, nullatenus vero probatae, hora nona antemeridiana diei trigesimae primae mensis instantis Julii, viz. die Lunae proxime sequentis, in area Theatri Sheldoniani per hujus curiae mandatariorum unum flammis committendam et comburendam fore decernimus; dictumque Antonium à Wood in expensis legitimis ex parte dicti honorabilis viri ac domini domini Henrici comitis de Clarendon in hoc negotio factis condemnandum fore pronunciamus, decernimus et declaramus, prout condemnamus, quas (visa prius billa) taxamus ad summam triginta et quatuor librarum per hanc nostram sententiam definitivam sive hoc nostrum finale decretum; quam sive quod ferimus et promulgamus, ac etiam (cum in hujusmodi negotio appellatio non sit admittenda) executioni demandamus in his scriptis.

　　　　　Lectum per nos

29 Julii 1693.　　　　　　　　　　　　　GEORGIUM GARDINER, *Asses.*

LIV. Certificate of the sentence [2].

Henricus Aldrich S.T.P. necnon Universitatis Oxon. vicecancellarius omnibus ad quos praesentes literae pervenerint easque inspecturis salutem.　Cum venerabilis vir Georgius Gardiner LL[m]. D[r]. assessor noster in quodam negotio reformacionis morum promoto in curia Cancellarii Universitatis Oxon. per honoratissimum virum ac dominum Henricum comitem de Clarendon contra Antonium à Wood, dictae Universitatis Oxon. in Artibus magistrum, praesertim ob libellum sive libellos famosos ab eo compositos, scriptos et publicatos, rite et legitime procedens sententiam suam diffinitivam in scriptis contra dictum Antonium à Wood legerit, tulerit et promulgaverit in qua (inter alia) praefatum Antonium à Wood[3] . . . et publicanda declaraverit.

Nos igitur Henricus Aldrich vicecancellarius antedictus tenore praesentium eundem Antonium à Wood tanquam pacis perturbatorem, quousque ut praemittitur, bannitum ex hac dicta Universitate, et privilegiis ejusdem exutum denunciamus et declaramus per praesentes.

In quorum omnium et singulorum fidem sigillum officii Cancellariatus Universitatis Oxon. praesentibus apposuimus.

　　Datum apud Oxon.
vicesimo nono die mensis Julii
　　　anno domini 1693.

　　　　　　　Concordat cum parte sententiae judicis praedicti

　　　　　　　　　　　JOS. WOODWARD[4], registrarius.

LV. Entry of the sentence in the Proctors' Black Book.

This was done on Dec. 27, 1693 : see vol. iii. p. 438.

[1] see art. 11 on pp. 19, 39 *supra.*

[2] Clarendon asked for such a certificate, *supra*, p. 44.　This paper is from the original in Arch. Univ. Oxon. W. P. γ. 26. fol. 38 b.　It is endorsed 'Bannitio Antonii à Wood.'

[3] I omit here the words cited from the preceding document, *supra*, p. 45 (*sub fin.*), with merely the change of the verbs from first person plural to third person singular.

[4] autograph signature.

LVI. Wood's criticism [1] of the notice of the sentence in the London Gazette.

Whereas in the Gazet that was published on the 3 Aug. 1693 was mention made, by the appointment of Henry earl of Clarendon, of divers infamous libells against his father Edward late earl of Clarendon, Lord Chancellour of England &c., that had been published in the second vol. of *Athenae Oxonienses* without naming them or the particular page that they are mention'd (which were omitted, as it seems, because they would have seemed frivolous things) the reader therefore is desired to know that the said ' infamous libells,' as they are so called, are only two, namely, that in page 221 in the life of David Jenkyns, a most loyal judge and a great sufferer for his majestie's cause [2], running thus :—

' After the restoration of King Charles 2 'twas expected by all that he' (Jenkyns) ' should be made one of the judges in Westminster hall, and so he might have been *would he have given money to the then Lord Chancellour,*' &c.

which very words the author of the said *Athenae Oxon.* had from [3] the daughters and nephew of the said David Jenkyns. In which you see is no mention made of *Edward* or of *Hyde* or of *Clarendon*, nor that there was money given or money received.

The other libell (so called) is in page 269 in the life of sir John Glynne [4], an active man in the grand rebellion (which the long Parliament raised against King Charles I), a judge in Oliver's raigne and one of his lords or ' other house,' running thus :—

' After the restoration of King Charles II, he' (Glynne) ' was made his eldest Serjeant at Law *by the corrupt dealing of the then Lord Chancellour,*' &c. [5]

[1] from a paper by Wood in MS. Tanner 456 a, fol. 68: see vol. iii. p. 429.

[2] another draft of this has ' and the greatest sufferer for the king's cause of any person of his profession in his time.'

[3] also from John Aubrey, see Doble's *Hearne's Collections*, iii. 35.

[4] in another draft of this paper, a transcript of which is inserted in bp. Tanner's copy of the *Athenae* (MS. Top. Oxf. b. 8), Wood says :—' Sir John Glynne; a prime instrument in bringing the immortall Strafford to the block ; an enemy to archbishop Laud ; an enjoyer of the places of certain royalists ejected for their loyaltie ; made Recorder of London and Serjeant at Law by the long or rebellious parliament (and so consequently, being several times appointed an itinerant justice, fell many a noble and generous heart by his dismal sentence) ; made lord chief justice of the King's bench by Oliver ; and one of the other house, that is, the house of lords, made and created by that person.'

[5] in other drafts of this paper Wood adds here, either (a) ' whereas other suffering law(yers) that had more (claim) were put aside' ; or (b) ' whereas he should rather have had a halter, or at least excepted out of the Act of Oblivion ;' or (c) ' Can any man

in which words, or elswhere, is no mention made of *Edward* or of *Hyde* or of *Clarendon*.

But the reasons why the author should say so were (i) from the vulgar report that then flew abroad, especially among such royallists who by their great sufferings for the king's cause could not then get anything without money, several of whom yet living do report the same things to this day [1]; (ii) from the articles of high treason and hainous misdemeanours that were drawne up by the Parliament against the said Edward earl of Clarendon in the yeares 1663 and 1667, among which one runs thus :—

' *That he hath malitiously and contrary to law enrich'd himself and his creatures by the sale of offices,*' &c. After the articles which were drawne up in 1667, and intended to be prosecuted by the Parliament, were published and given in, the said Edward earl of Clarendon withdrew himself and fled into France to save his head : and about that time sending a petition and address to the House of Lords to apologise for himself against some of the said articles (which were printed in a book entit. *State Tracts* &c., anno 1689) they esteemed them such scandalous things that by order of the Parliament they were burnt by the hands of the common hangman before the gate of Gresham College, then the place of the Exchang, in the presence of the sheriffs of the city of London between the hours of twelve and one on the 12 day of December anno 1667, as it appeares in the Gazet that was published on the 16 of the said month and in the same yeare.

LVII. Wood complains that lord Clarendon has been too hard on him.

⟨I.⟩ Things [1] done by the authour to please his lordship Henry earl of Clarendon.

1. The author freely and readily communicated that part of the copy in the 2ᵈ. part of ATH. ET FAST. OXON. which concerned Edward earl of Clarendon his father before it went to the press. He blotted out many things, which if they had stood, there would have been no pretence to go to law.

2. He appeared in the vice-chancellour's court, which he might have refused, if he had so pleased, but because he had a mind to please the said earl, he therefore did appeare, thinking to obtain his favour, and now you see what the event is.

3. He sent a submission to the said earl, to have it put into the Term Catalogue, Gazet, &c. but he returned it to the court, to ruin the plea that the author's proctor put in to make the opposite party prove that he was author of the book.

think to ⟨the⟩ contrary but that he gave money for his place when he rather had deserved the halter or at least to be excepted from the oblivion.' MS. Tanner 456 a.

[1] see Doble's *Hearne's Collections*, i.

246, for the continuance of this report.

[2] from the original draft in Wood's hand prefixed to one of bp. Tanner's copies of the *Athenae* (MS. Top. Oxf. b. 9).

4. He sent a letter with a printed epistle to the said earl for an accommodation, and for putting an end to the controversie, but he return'd it to the court to ruin his cause. The epistle contain'd the character of the retir'd life of the author, which, one would think, would have mollified the court.

5. He dealt freely and generously with the said earl and his party for an accommodation &c. but his generosity was returnd upon him, to ruin his cause.

6. He speaks honorably of the said Henry earl of Clarendon in his 2ᵈ. vol. of ATH. ET FASTI OXON. p. 808, and of his father, p. 388.

7. He procured an *Habeas Corpus* to prolong the suit, that he might gain time to make his peace.

(8.) He denied the translation of the matter to Westm. Hall, purposely to please him.

(II.) Things done by Henry earl of Clarendon to ruin the author and his cause.

1. His dashing and scoring out of the original copies several matters relating to his father without any authority, which, if they had stood, he could not have pretence to go to law. He disarmes the author, then fights with him naked.—He takes away his papers, and then bids him plead.—He cuts out his tongue, and then bids him speake.

2. He endeavoured to set Sir William Glynn on his back.

3. He entertained two proctors contrary to the custome, purposely to put Mr. Wood to charg, knowing well that by his greatness and money he should overcome him—he got Dr. Levet to rake and scrape up witnesses to augment the charg, because every witness that is taken and sworn, money is to be given to the register, apparator, &c.

4. He return'd Mr. Wood's submission which he had sent to him, to ruin his cause, when his proctor put in a plea to make the opposite partie prove that he was author of ATH. ET FASTI OXON.

5. He recal'd a *Habeas Corpus,* in the time of vacation, contrary to all custome.

6. He very readily put his name into the Gazet for an infamous libeller, without naming the libells what they were.

And, after al this, the author is to submit for what he hath said, and be made a tool to recover the credit of a person that hath been banished 28 yeares and dead 20.

LVIII. Mock recantation[1] by Wood.

The submission[2] of Mr. A. Wood.

Whereas in the sentence which passed against Mr. Wood it is said that he shall continue banished till such time that he shall subscribe

[1] this paper has been sometimes taken seriously, as a submission made by Wood to obtain the recall of his sentence of expulsion. That sentence continued formally against him to his death, although (vol. iii. pp. 485, 491) he contended that the Act of Parliament overrode it. Dr. Bliss's remark that no *satisfecit* appears written over the entry in the Proctors' Black Book cannot, however, be cited as an argument that the sentence continued in force, because the practice of the proctors in cancelling the records of punishments inflicted by them was very irregular.

[2] from the original draft in Wood's hand in MS. Tanner. 456 a, fol. 65.

such a publick recantation as the judge of that court shall approve of, and which, upon his enquiry, he cannot yet learne what it is ; he himself has therefore, in the meane time, drawn up a forme which is this :—

Whereas I Anth. Wood, Mr. of Arts, have from my youth laboured in good letters for the honour of the most famous university of Oxford without any prospect of reward or preferment, I am sorry and much griev'd at heart, that I have fallen into the hands of most barbarous and rude people of our owne body, who have endeavoured to ruin me and my name, by making the second volume of Athenae et Fasti Oxon. a libell (which by the sentence of the assessor of the vice-chancellour's court, a civil law court, hath been burnt) and afterwards to banish me from the said university to the great abhorrence of the generality thereof, purposely to please the supercilious and tyrannical humour[1] of a certain lord, for 3 or 4 lines mention'd in the said second volume p. 221 and 269 concerning a person there mention'd without any name or title, who hath been banish'd from England Scotland and Ireland, for refusing to answer to divers articles of treason and misdemeanours, for about 28 years and dead about 18.　I say I am heartily sorry for these things,

witness my hand.

LIX. A decree requiring Wood to pay the costs of the suit.

(Friday) 20 Oct. 1693: officium domini promotum &c. contra Anth. à Wood.

Emanavit monicio contra dictum à Wood ad solvendum expensas &c. Quibus, &c.

LX. What lord Clarendon did with the money.

The[2] three statues[3] in the nitches in the gate of the Physick Garden were purchas'd with the fourty pounds that Ant. à Wood was fined[4] by the University for words which were judged to be reflecting upon Edward Hyde earl of Clarendon ; which money was laid out to that end by Dr. Aldrich dean of Xt. Ch. and then vicechancellor[5].

---

[1] substituted for 'the supercilious and capricious and domineering humour.'

[2] note by Thomas Hearne in MS. Rawl. C. 867, fol. 37 b. I have the greatest doubt whether this report (like many others circulated about Wood, shortly after his death) is not altogether baseless.

[3] 'on each side' of the gate of the Physic Garden 'are the statues of King Charles Ist and IId, and over all the earl of Danby's statue in busto, the founder of this garden.'—John Pointer's *Oxoniensis Academia*, Lond. 1749, p. 169.

[4] but see *supra*, p. 46; there was no fine, and the expenses were taxed at 34 *li*.

[5] Henry Aldrich's term of office as Vicechancellor ended on 4 Oct. 1695.

Vol. I, p. 13, note 2.—I feel sure that this missing volume is to be identified with MS. Aubrey 33. Having been re-bound, its press-mark was lost; it was then marked 'Ashm. 1820'; and afterwards put into the Aubrey set because of the autograph 'John Aubrey' on the second leaf. It was no doubt sent by Aubrey to Wood. Its size shows that it does not belong to the Aubrey set, the 32 volumes of which are arranged in diminishing sizes, while this added no. 33 is much bigger than the last volumes. Cp. Vol. III, p. 239, note 2.

Vol. I, p. 43, anno 1632. Since the completion of the text of the Diaries, I have had the privilege of perusing the yearly accounts of the Vicechancellor, and of the Proctors. I have taken from these a great many notes, as supplying exact information, often of a curious sort, on points mentioned by Wood. For symmetry's sake I have made these notes even in the earlier years, where Wood says nothing about University affairs. With these additions, this issue of Wood's Diaries may be regarded as giving a very full outline of Oxford affairs from 1632 to 1695.

    Comp. Vicecanc. for 1631–32 :—'for gloves given when the court was at Woodstocke, 22*li.* 10*s*; for a Bible to the clarke of the king's kitchin, 1*li.* 18*s*; for a payre of silver flaggons for the Communion (at St. Mary's), 28*li.* 10*s* 4*d.*'

Vol. I, p. 43, anno 1632.—At this time the Thames was navigable from London only as far as Burcot (see p. 53 *infra*). The University expended from time to time considerable sums of money towards extending the navigable portion as high up as Oxford. E.g. *Registrum Cistae Universitatis* :—6 Aug. 1632, the sum of 537*li.* 0*s* 2*d*, the balance of a legacy of 2000 marks by Sir Nicholas Kempe of London, was ordered by Convocation to be expended 'towards the making of the river navigable to the citie of Oxford'; 6 Aug. 1635, the sum of 129*li.* 13*s* 2*d*, the 'ultimate residue' of Kempe's legacy, was paid to Dr. John Tolson, commissioner 'pro aqua fluviali ducenda ad Universitatem et Civitatem Oxon.' *Comp. Vicecanc.* for 1637–38, 'to Dr. Pinke for makeing the river navigable, 60*li.* 6*s.*' *Comp. Vicecanc.* for 1658–59 :—'to Dr. ⟨Joshua⟩ Crosse to be imployed toward the water-workes for making the river of Thames navigable, 40*li.*' *Comp. Vicecanc.* for 1661–62 :—'to Mr. John Houghton to be imployed towards the maintayning of the water-workes for making the Thames navigable, 20*li.*' *Comp. Vicecanc.* for 1662–63 :—'to Mr. Wright towards the water-workes, 30*li.*'

Vol. I, p. 44, anno 1633.—*Comp. Vicecanc.* for 1632–1633 :—'for gloves to my Lord Treasurer's lady (the Countess of Portland), 1*li.*; for gloves to my Lord

Chamberlain (Philip Herbert, earl of Montgomery), 2*li.*; for gloves to baron Oxenstiern and Gustavus Horne, 3 *li.*, and for silver seales sett to the testimonialls of their being created Masters, 2*li.* 9*s*; for gloves to the Queen's almoner and a Doctor of Sorbon with him, 3*li.*'—'For the fees of the first charter, for printing, and bringing it doune, 25*li.* 10*s*; for the charges of the second charter, 40*li.* 11*s* 2*d*.'—'To the printer for copies of verses to the king upon his recovery, 4*li.*; to Mr. (Matthew) Crosse for his charges in carrying up those copies, 2*li.*'

Vol. I, p. 44, anno 1634.—*Comp. Vicecanc.* for 1633–34 :—' to Sir Henry Wooton's man who brought bookes to the Library, 1*li.*'—'For copies of the booke of verses on the King's retourne (from Scotland), 5*li.*; to Mr. (John) Thimble's charges in carrying up the verses, 3*li.* 12*s*.'—'For gloves when the king was at Woodstock, 25*li.*; to the waytors and to the trumpetters, 3*li.*; for a Bible to the clarke of the kichin, 1*li.* 10*s*.'—'For the last bookes of verses on the byrth of the duke of Yorke[1], 5*li.*; to Mr. Crosse for his charges in carrying up the last booke, 2*li.* 3*s* 10*d*.'—'For the paveing of St. Marie's, 67*li.* 5*s*; to the playsterer for whytyng the churche and mending many places, 9*li.*; to the glazier for St. Marie's, 37*li.* 2*s* 6*d*; to the two sextons of Christ Church for their paynes whyle St. Marie's was repayring, 1*li.*'—'For gloves given to a Bohemian baron, the baron of Kinsky, 1*li.* 2*s*.'

Vol. I, p. 45, line 3.—There is an account of the University's plea of exemption in Twyne XXIV. 578 : ' Memorandum that, in August 1634, two heralds of armes, Mr. (John) Philpott called Summerset and Mr. (William) Riley called Blewemantle, came to the Universitie of Oxon with commission to visit in the Universitie as well as in the towne conceringe matters of heraldrie and armes. And comminge to the Vicechanc. then beinge, Dr. (Robert) Pinke, Warden of Newe College, to shewe their commission (as they had done two or 3 dayes before to the judges in the Yeeld Hall at the Assizes then held, in their rich coates, to have their commission allowed) they alleadged that heretofore, in Mr. Dr. Humphrey's time [2] anno 1574, their predecessors had done the like and visited in the Universitie about reforminge of errors in heraldry, &c. But the Registers of the Universitie beinge perused specified no such matter.

And allthough these heraldes had in a manner procured a kinde of leave of the Lord Arch:bish. of Cant: then Chancellor [3] of the Universitie, to give some fayre waye to this their proceedinge, yet the Vicechancellor consultinge with the heds of houses, the matter did not relish very well unto them, that the said heralds should be suffered to keepe any such inquisition either within the Colledges (as they required) or within the precincts of the University.

Moreover there was sent to the vicechancellor a table of all the College armes blasoned in their proper collours and mettalls set forth by authoritie by Jo: Scott; and that the Colledges could not shewe the heraldes any other armes then them, there sett forth ; and so it would be needlesse for them to enquyre any further about it.

---

[1] the University had in the same way acknowledged the birth of Prince Charles; *Comp. Vicecanc.* for 1630–31 : —'to John Leichfeild towards the printing of the booke of verses for the prince, 2*li.* 10*s*.'

[2] Laurence Humphrey, Pres. of Magd. Coll., Vice-chancellor 1571–76. Twyne notes in the margin, 'Richard Lee, Portcullice, afterwardes Clarentieulx king of armes, pretended to have visited the Universitie at that time.'

[3] William Laud, Chancellor of Oxford, 1630–41.

The Vicechancellor was allso enformed of the Universitie's exemption by King Henry the 4th and King Henry the 8th's charter, 'a mareschallis regiis' &c. And that if the heraldes should happen to fine any priviledged person for any fault concerninge heraldry, yet the Universitie ought still to have the fine by King Henry the 8 his charter. And that the heraldes themselves, nowe duringe the time of their abode within the Universitie, were to be accounted priviledged men, by vertue of a composition betwixt the Universitie and the towne in 37° of King Henry the 6 ⟨1459⟩ in regard that they bringe a message lettres and commission to the whole Universitie; and therefore they were to be ordered by the Vicechancellor under whose jurisdiction they nowe were, and not he by them. —All which thinges beinge well considered, it would be little avayelable for the saide heraldes to proceede any farther in this their intended visitation in the Universitie.

And so after the Vicechancellor had entertayned them at a supper (whereat I was present) they tooke their leave and promised to make as fayre a report of their usage in the Universitie as they might, &c. And this was all that was then done in that businesse.

Here I had forgotten to procure of them the sight of that allegation which they produced for their visitation in Dr. Humphrey's time &c. in regard that we have no memorandum thereof.'

Vol. I, p. 45, anno 1635.—In this and the following years were built the New Convocation house with its vestry (Apodyterium), and the large west room of the Library (the Selden end) over them. The following are the payments in connexion with these buildings.

Comp. Vicecanc. pro Scholis for 1632–33 :—'to the king's controllour for his coach-hire and in other expences in comeing hither to give directions about the stairecase and for gloves, 9*li.*; to a surveyhour for drawing of modells and three severall journeys about the same businesse, 12*li.*' *Ibid.* for 1633–34, 'to Mayoe for his severall journeys about timber, 4*li.* 3*s*; given to the coopers that came about the bargain for timber, 6*s*; to Bromfield the carpenter, 7*li.* 8*s* 6*d*; to Hugh Davies, by consent of the delegates, 40*li.*; given to Mr. Mason, by consent of the delegates, 10*li.*; to Mr. Estcott for his journey to London about the building, 4*li.* 9*s*; to Mason towards his bargain for building the Library, 350*li.*'—*Comp. Vicecanc. pro Scholis* for 1633–34 :—'given to our counsell for drawing up the bargain for Exeter College, 1*li.* 2*s.*' *Comp. Vicecanc.* for 1634–35 :—'to the Rector and Fellows of Exeter Colledge for the land sold by them to the Universitie at the west end of the Library, 264*li.* 13*s* 4*d.*'—*Comp. Vicecanc. pro Scholis* for 1634–35 :—'to James Harrison for bringing the timber from Reding to Burcot and for bringing the deale boardes and tackle from London to Burcott, 34*li.* 8*s* 10*d*; to the said James for the use of John Ellis, wharfinger, at Reding for the wharfage there of the said timber and for three skidds to bring the timber upon, 1*li.* 3*s* 6*d*; to Anthony Jenings for bringing part of the timber and the ginne from Burcott to Oxford, 10*li.* 12*s* 2*d*; to Thomas Edgerlie for the carriage of 31 tunne and 2 feete of timber from Burcott to Oxford, 12*li.* 8*s*; to Stephen Rabbetts and John Wilkins in discharge of theire bill for carriage of timber and for 5 foote of timber over 48 tunne, 2*li.* 14*s*; to Stephen Rabbetts and John Wilkins in full payment for 48 tunne of timber, 85*li.* 16*s*; to Edward Bromfield, carpenter, in discharge of his bill of expences in travelling about the timber to the wood and to Burcott, 5*li.* 18*s*; to Edward Bromfield for his journeys about the timber and deales and for a ginne to loade the timber with at Burcott, 6*li.* 18*s* 9*d*; to William House in discharge of his bill for carriage of the deales from Burcott, for the wharfage of timber and deales there, and for pitch and other things used about the timber, 8*li*. 8*s* 10*d*; to Mr. Mayo and Edward Brumfield, carpenters, in full payment for their worke done about the partition in the Librarie, 3*li*. 4*s* 6*d*; for 70 long deale boardes chosen by Mr. Comptroller's appointment and for exchange of others, 45*li*.; for the gables and tackle for to drawe up the timber with, 10*li*.; to Mr. Mayo for 10 tunne and 48 foote of timber at 31*s* a tunne, 17*li*., and for the carriage of it to the Physick Gardens, 1*li*. 3*s*; to Mr. Richard Powell, esquire, for 20 loades and 48 foote of timber (50 foote being a loade) at 43*s* the loade, 45*li*. 1*s* 4*d*; to Thomas Halsey his man for sealing that timber, 6*s* 8*d*; to Thomas Mayo in part of payment for the carriage of timber from the Phisick Garden to the Scholes, 4*li*.; to Thomas Mayo and Edward Bromfield, carpenters, in part of payment for carpenters worke, 115*li*. 4*s*; to William Mason in discharge of his bill for carrying earth into the Convocation house and for stone and workemanship about the two vaults, 11*li*. 3*s*; to William Mason in part of payment for the stone work of the new building at the west end of the Librarie, 642*li*.; to Thomas Adams, smith, for ironworke done by him about the newe building, 134*li*. 6*s* 2½*d*; for 126 pigges of lead weighing 18 fothers, 5 hundred ⟨weight ?⟩ 3 quarters and 10 pounds, and for all charge about the same in bringing it home, 245*li*. 10*s* 2*d*.' *Comp. Vicecanc. pro Scholis* for 1635–36 :—'for timber bought of severall men, 18*li*. 2*s* 8*d*; to Mayo and Bromfield for materialls and worke about the old beame, 6*li*. 13*s* 4*d*; to Mayo for oaken boards for the roofe, 3*li*. 5*s*; to Mr. Leigh, timber merchant, for 500 deale boards and for carriage of them by water and land, 46*li*. 8*s* 6*d*; to William Mason for the ropes, poles, pullies, and makeing of strapps for the tackle, 9*s* 7*d*; to Mayo and Bromfield for the carriage of timber from the Physick Garden to the Schooles and afterwards into the new building, 10*li*. 15*s* 6*d*; to Bromfeild for a barrell of pitch and a sack of coales used in layeing the timber upon the walls, 1*li*. 11*s* 4*d*; to Mayo and Bromfeild for the carpenter's worke of the upper floore and the roofe, 76*li*.; prae manibus ⟨i. e. before-hand⟩ to Mayo and Bromfeild upon a reckoning towards the seats of the Convocation house, 10*li*.; to William Mason for the stone worke of the building at the west end of the Library, 408*li*.; for pease and straw to stopp the windowes and to labourers to stoppe it in, 11*s*; to William Mason for 14 great poles, 40 small poles, 9 beech poles, and 64 putlogges to scaffold with, 8*li*. 7*s*; to Adams, the smith, for ironworke about the roofe of the new building, 15*li*. 5*s* 7*d*; to Fletcher, the plumber, for casting and laying the University lead and for other newe lead used on the roofe, 140*li*. 15*s*; to Fletcher the glazier, for the glasse of the windowes of the upper roome of the new building. 12*li*. 2*s* 2*d*.' *Comp. Vicecanc. pro Scholis* for 1636–37 :—'to Thomas Adams, smith, for ironworke about the windowes in the new building at the west end of the Library, 21*li*. 14*s*; to James Fletcher for new glasse in the windowes of the new Convocation house and vestry, 12*li*. 6*s* 8*d*.' *Comp. Vicecanc. pro Scholis* for 1637–38 :—'to Jackson for building the wall neere the new Convocation house, 112*li*. 10*s*; for carrieing away rubbidge out of the court by the new Convocation house, 6*li*. 19*s* 10*d*; to Mr. Jackson for cleansing the yard by the new Convocation house, 1*li*.' *Comp. Vicecanc.* for 1637–38 : 'to Richardson for all materials and workmanship in the new Convocation house, 265*li*.; lent to Richardson upon his bonds for the materials that hee hath already provided for the west end of the Librarie and toward the workmanship thereof[1], 300*li*.; to ⟨Thomas⟩ Richardson for all materialls and workmanship

---

[1] this sum was taken out of the University Chest, 30 Dec. 1639, 'pro opere tabulato in parte occidentali Bibliothecae.'—*Reg. Cistae.*

in the entrance to the new Convocation house, to witt, for the paveing and for the frett-worke, 60*li.*' *Comp. Vicecanc. pro Scholis* for 1638–39;—'to Richardson for wainscot in the new Vestry, 73*li.* 18*s.*' *Comp. Vicecanc.* for 1639-40 :—'to Richardson for a deske for the Register in the Congregation house, 1*li.* 4*s*; to Mayo the carpenter for the Congregation house doore, 6*li.*; to the smith for ironworke about it, 3*li.* 7*s*; to Badger and Piddington for paveing the passage of the Congregation house and pitching the gutters, 32*li.* 10*s*; for painting the doore of the Congregation house, 1*li.*' *Comp. Vicecanc.* for 1640–41 :—'to Thomas Richardson in full of his bargaine of 1000*li.* for wainscotting the west end of the Library, 400*li.*[1]; to him more for new wainscott in the vestry adjoining to the Convocation house where the ⟨Vicechancellor's⟩ Court is now kept, 20*li.*; to Jackson the painter for worke in the west end of the Librarie, vizt. the inscriptions ⟨see vol. iii. p. 237, note 4⟩ of my Lord of Canterburie's guift, the Lord of Pembrooke's guift, and Sir Kenelm Digbie's guift, 6*li.*'—The balance in the University Chest in 1641 at the end of all this expenditure was 922*li.* 5*s* 2*d* (*Reg. Cistae*).

It may be of interest to tabulate in round figures the above expenditure on the Convocation house, Apodyterium, and Selden end of the Library.

I. For the site		264*li.*
II. For the fabric		2816
(i.) timber	260*li.*	
(ii.) lead	245	
(iii.) carpenter's work	200	
(iv.) plumber's work	140	
(v.) smith's work	175	
(vi.) glazier's bill	24	
(vii.) mason's bill	1420	
(viii.) commissions and minor payments to work-men, architects, agents, &c.	91	
(ix.) carriage of timber	96	
(x.) incidental work	165	
III. For the interior		1130
		Total 4210*li.*

Vol. I, pp. 45, 46, annis 1635, 1636.—*Comp. Vicecanc.* for 1635–36 :—'to the wayters when the court was at Woodstocke, 2*li.*; to ⟨Thomas⟩ Bland, the glover, for 8 paire of gloves bestowed then upon his majestie and the noblemen, 26*li.*'—'for the charges of his Majestie's commissioners[2] in their comminge downe to Oxforde, at Oxford, and in their returne, 30*li.* 4*s* 6*d*; to Mr. ⟨Brian⟩ Twine for his charges about the University charter, 309*li.* 17*s* 1*d*; to Mr. Twine for his charges about the heareings betweene the towne and the University and concerning ⟨Laud's projected⟩ metropoliticall Visitation, 45*li.* 17*s* 6*d*; to Mr. ⟨Matthew⟩ Crosse for the charges of the delegates that went to Hampton Court about the heareing concerning the said Visitation, 34*li.* 5*s* 6*d*; to Mr. ⟨Peter⟩ Turner of Merton Colledge for his charges in three journeys about

---

[1] towards this sum 300*li.* was taken out of the University chest on 25 Sept. 1640.—*Reg. Cistae.*

[2] Proctors' accounts for 1636–37 :—'pro expensis in itinere ad inducendum et reducendum commissionarios domini Regis cum afferrent *librum Statutorum* ad Universitatem, 2*li.* 10*s*.' This was on 21 June 1636, Wood's *Annals*, ii. 403.

the University statutes and for the confirmation of them, 40*li. os 6d.*'—'for copies of the bookes of verses on the birth of the lady Elizabeth[1], 12*li. 4s 6½d*; to Mr. Lichfield for his charges in carrying up the verses, 1*li. 19s 4d.*'—In this year or the beginning of the next the University must have been much disturbed by tumults[2]; the Proctors' account for 1635–36 contains an item 'pro punitione delinquentium, 4*li. 13s 4d*,' the ordinary charge under this head being about 5*s* or 6*s.*

Vol. I, p. 46, anno 1636.—*Comp. Vicecanc.* for 1636–37 :—'paid, by allowance of the Heads of Houses, to ⟨John Bancroft⟩ the Lord Bishop of Oxford for the poore of Whately, being visited, 10*li.*'—'To John Edgerlie for carrieing the University present to the Queene being at Richmund, 5*li.*'—'To Mr. Crosse for his expenses in his journey to London with the verses on the birth of the lady Anne[3], and for his horse-hire up and downe, 2*li. 11s 1d*; to Leonard Litchfield for copies of the said bookes of verses and to Mr. Badger for binding them up, 6*li. 9s 9d.*'—'To Mr. Litchfeild for his expenses in two journeys to the Court to carry letters to the Queene, 5*li.*'—'To Mr. Wright, the goldsmith, for 3 boxes wherein the seale of the University was sent to conferre the degree of Mr. of Arts on Christianus, lantgrave of Hassia, Ernestus, his brother, and Winandus a Polhelm, their counsellour, 2*li. 11s*; item, for ribon for labells, 3*s.*'

Vol. I, p. 46, l. 12.—*Comput. Vicecanc.* for 1636–37 :—'layd out in the two comedies att Christ Church (the third comedie for his majestie being acted at St. John's Colledge at the proper charge of his Grace) for the King's entertainment—843*li. 15s 6d*;' 'layd out more for the king's entertainment for gloves and for bookes for the King, Queene, Balsgrave, his brother, and other particulars,—77*li. 0s 4d*; for the pitching of Smith gate against the king's comeing, 5*li. 19s 6d.*'

Vol. I, p. 46, anno 1637.—*Comp. Vicecanc.* for 1637–38 :—'to Mr. Jackson 22*li.*, which, upon a review of the porch and wall at St. Marie's by Mr. Vicechancellor ⟨Richard Baylie⟩, Dr. ⟨Thomas⟩ Walker, and Dr. ⟨Peter⟩ Turner, was judged fit to bee given unto him beyond his bargaine (viz*t*. 230*li.* which summe was given by Dr. Morgan Owen for that worke); to Mayo, Ranckling, and Hawkins the painter for worke about the porch and gates, 18*li. 12s*; to Hobbs for lead used at St. Marie's, 13*li. 16s.*'—Proctors' accounts for 1636–37 :—' pro excubiis ad portas civitatis occasione pestis praeter et ultra recepta, 2*li. 14s.*'

Vol. I, p. 47, anno 1638. Coronation day, 2 February, was observed by bonfires. Proctors' accounts for 1637–38 :—'pro fasciculis in die inaugurationis regis nostri Caroli, 4*s*'; ibid. for 1638–39 :—' pro fascibus in quinto die Novembris et die inaugurationis Caroli regis, 8*s.*'

Vol. I, p. 47, annis 1638, 1639.—*Comp. Vicecanc.* for 1638–39 :—'for gloves given at Woodstock, when the king was there[4], 26*li. 10s*; to the waiters at the Court, 2*li.*; for a Bible for the clarke of the kitchin there, 1*li. 17s*; to the king's trumpeters, 1*li.*'—'To Short for assisting in viewing the priviledged men's armes[5], 10*s.*'—'To Leichfeild for printing our *Charisteria*, 1*li. 10s*; in expenses at the print-house, 7*s*; to Barnes for binding the *Charisteria* some in plush, some in

---

[1] died 8 Sept. 1650.

[2] cp. Proctors' accounts for 1640–41 : —' pro punitione delinquentium et sedatione tumultuum, 1*li. 9s 6d.*'

[3] daughter of Charles I, died young.

[4] in August 1638: Wood's *Annals*, ii. 417.

[5] war proclaimed against Scotland April 1639. Cp. vol. i. p. 54.

sattin, some in vellam, 36 bookes in all, and for plush for two of them, 3*li.* 19*s*;
to Mr. Dennis for silke strings for 36 bookes and sattin covers for six, 2*li.* 10*s*;
to Mr. Gayton for his charges in carryeing the verses to court, 2*li.* 10*s*.'—'For the
carriage of ⟨Laud⟩ our chancellor's MSS. from Lambeth hither, 4*li.* 16*s*; to
a porter for carryeing them to the Schooles, and two others for carryeing them
thence up to the closett, 8*s* 6*d*.'

Vol. I, p. 47, anno 1639.—*Comp. Vicecanc.* for 1639-40 :—'for the expences of the
Vicechancellor, Doctors, and others sent for to the Councell-table, 19*li.* 7*s* 10*d*.
To Barnes for binding 38 bookes of verses (30 in vellam, 6 in sattin, 2 in velvett)
and for the velvet, 4*li.* 6*s*; to Mr. Dennis for ribbon and sattin for the bookes,
2*li.* 16*s*; to Mr. Lichfield for printing verses, and 176 copies sent to Lambeth,
5*li.* 10*s*; to Mr. Gayton for his journey to court with the verses, 4*li.* 18*s*.'
Comp. Vicecanc. for 1640-41 : 'to Mr. Gaiton for Badger for binding verses
(due in Dr. Frewin's time), 17*s*.'

Vol. I, p. 49, anno 1641.—*Comp. Vicecanc.* for 1640-41 :—'the charges of
Mr. Vicechancellor in Januarie last [164$\frac{1}{2}$] and of the delegates in Febr. and March
att two severall heareings then before the Lords of Parliament in the case betwixt
the Universitie and the Cittie[1], 233 *li.* 6*s* 11*d*; to Mr. Holloway att Oxford for
draweing brevates of the cause, 2*li.*, and to his clearke for transcribeing the same,
1*li.*; and for transcribeing the cittie petition thrice, 6*s*; to William Ball for faire
writeing the last great charter, breifes att London against the citty, and divers
other things for the Universitie, 13*li.* 6*s* 8*d*.'—'For binding 50 bookes of
verses (2 in plush, 6 in sattin, and 42 in vellam, gilt and filletted) and for ribon
for strings, 5*li.*; to Mr. Dennis for sattin and plush for their covers, 3*li.* 2*s*; to
Mr. Lichfield for printing 159 copies, 4*li.* 17*s* 6*d*; for carrieing them up to London,
2*s*; Mr. Gaiton's charges at London in delivering them, 2*li.* 9*s* 4*d*.'—'to
Mr. ⟨Thomas⟩ Dennis of Exeter College for a sermon preached at St. Marie's,
Septr. 7mo, ex decreto praefectorum, 3*li.*'—*Comp. Vicecanc.* for 1641-42 :—'to
Mr. ⟨Leonard⟩ Bowman, mayor, toward the keeping of those that were sick of
the plague, 5*li.* 14*s*.'

   Comp. Vicecanc. for 1640-41 :—'to John Reyer for makeing the new clocke
at St. Marie's and quarter clock, 22*li.*; to Adams, Tomlins, Stripling, and Jeffes
for their severall workes done about the same and the clock-house, 7*li.* 9*s* 6*d*.'

Vol. I, p. 49, anno 1641.—*Comp. Vicecanc. pro Scholis* for 1640-41 :—'to Richard
Hawkins for painting the south diall on the Schooles, 3*li.*; to Mr. Jackson for
makeing the nest of the king's picture in the Librarie, 6*li.*'   The bust of Charles I,
in the niche here mentioned, is still *in situ* on the right hand of the arch leading
into Duke Humphrey.

Vol. I, p. 51, l. 21.—*Comp. Vicecanc.* for 1640-41 :—'to the charge of Mr. Vice-
chancellor's journey to London to prefer the petitions to his majestie and the
Parliament, 4*li.* 3*s* 8*d*.'

Vol. I, p. 51, l. 28.—Philip Herbert, 4th earl of Pembroke was then elected
Chancellor.—*Comp. Vicecanc.* for 1640-41 :—'charges of the journie to London
for admission of the new Chancellor; vizt. 14 Heades and Proctors, 42*li.*;
9 Maisters, 18*li.*; 5 beedles, register, and virger, 10*li.* 10*s*—70*li.* 10*s* :' 'for the
silver box for the seale ⟨of the Chancellor's patent⟩, 19*s* 4*d*.'

Vol. I, p. 51, anno 164$\frac{1}{2}$.—*Comp. Vicecanc.* for 1641-42 :—'given to the printer's
men at two severall times whilst they were printing the king's declarations, 5*s*;

---

[1] Proctors' accounts for 1640-41 :—   proctor, in the court at London against
'expences of Peter Allibond, lately   the citizens, 8*li.* 15*s*.'

to porters diverse times for bringing packetts from the king and parliament, 5*s*.'—Proctors' accounts for 1641–42 :—' Mr. Abraham Woodhead, junior proctor, sent for to parliament to give an account of certain things done in Congregation, 4*li*. 17*s* 8*d*.'

Vol. I, p. 52, anno 1642.—*Comp. Vicecanc.* for 1641–42 :—' to Mr. Lichfield, printer, for 280 bookes of verses, 7*li*. ; to Barnes for binding, 5*li*. 10*s* ; to Mr. Gayton for his charges and binding some verses in London and distributiug them, 4*li*. 15*s* ; to Mr. Vicechancellor for his expences for himselfe and 6 horses first to London and thence to Hampton Court to deliver some copies of verses, 10*li*. ; to Mr. ⟨Thomas⟩ Dennis, mercer, for plush and sattin to bind the bookes in, 4*li*.'—' To Dr. ⟨John⟩ Tolson for his charges for himselfe and men to London in University businesses, 5*li*. 18*s*.'—Proctors' accounts for 1641–42 :—' pro fascibus in die celebrandae pacificationis inter Anglos et Scotos, 4*s*.'

Vol. I, p. 52, anno 1642.—The University stock in the 'Cista Universitatis' was 922*li*. 4*s* 8*d* : on 11 July 1642 the sum of 860*li*. was taken out 'in usum serenissimi regis nostri Caroli juxta decretum Convocationis,' leaving the 'status cistae' at 62*li*. 4*s* 8*d*.   On 19 June 1644 the stock in the chest was only 29*li*. 15*s* 5*d* ; on 29 Apr. 1645 it had sunk to 9*s* 1*d*.—*Reg. Cistae.*

Vol. I, p. 64, l. 8 from foot.—On the occasion of this visit a present of gloves was made to lord Saye, which remained unpaid for till the surrender of Oxford again put the Puritan party into the ascendant. *Comp. Vicecanc.* for 1646–47 :—' for a paire of gloves bestowed on my Lord Say (1642), 1*li*. 15*s* ; for gloves at the Lent assizes, 164⅘, bestowed on my Lord Say, 1*li*. 6*s* 8*d*.'

Vol. I, p. 68, l. 1.—*Comp. Vicecanc.* for 1642–43 :—' to Mr. ⟨Richard⟩ Allestree of Ch. Ch. for his journey to know after what manner the University should receive the king, 13*s*.'

Vol. I, p. 69, l. 18.—*Comp. Vicecanc.* for 1641–42 :—' for 2 silver boxes for the prince and the duke to preserve the seales, 1*li*. 17*s* ; for vellam, ribband for labells, and wrighting the instruments of the prince his incorporation and the duke of Yorke his creation Master of Arts, 1*li*.'

Vol. I, p. 69, l. 5 from foot.—*Comp. Vicecanc.* for 1642–43 :—' in full dischardge of the carpenter's bill about stables, by his majestie's command, 2*li*. 9*s*.'

Vol. I, p. 71, l. 13.—Proctors' accounts for 1642–43 :—' Johanni Gelliver pro fasciculis ad extruendas pyras sexties, 1*li*. 4*s*.'

Vol. I, p. 76, l. 8.—In *Liber vetus Comput. Vicecanc.* p. 248, is a transcript of Prideaux' letter :—' I heare that exceptions are taken in my accounts—

(1) to the 40*li*. laid out for the Grecian.   This was done upon our chancellor's letter to the University, by command from his majesty whome the Grecian had petitioned.   I proposed it to the Heads of Houses diverse times to rayse a proportionable contribution to make up the like summe as my Lord's Grace of Canterbury gave him, but I found it hopelesse.   The man wanted, was importunate ; his majestie's command must not be neglected ; I saw noe other way but to doe as I did.'

(2) for the 15*li*. 11*s* 6*d* laid out in searching for the stoppage which cut off the water from Carfax conduit, he was forced to act at once, by popular clamour. He intended to levy the amount from the Colleges and private houses which were supplied from the conduit ⟨see Clark's Wood's City, i. 448⟩ but he had to leave Oxford before he could do this.

(3) ' for Mr. Wake's [1] 10*li.* hee is a fellow of a house, and there to answeare for him selfe. If he have overlashed, it is noe prodigality of mine. Hee is of ability and will acquitt mee.'

Vol. I, p. 77, l. 15.—The University Press during this year and next was kept very busy printing declarations, &c. *Comp. Vicecanc.* for 1641–42 :—'to Mr. Lichfeild for printing 300 protestations, 2*li.* 10*s* ; to Wilcocks for stitching 1500 of the printed protestations, 5*s* ; to Mr. Lichfeild for printing his Majestie's declarations, 40*li.* ; to the printer's men [2] when they were printing the King's declarations, 5*s* ; to Mr. Lichfeild for printing declarations and proclamations, 15*li.*' *Comp. Vicecanc.* for 1642–43 :—' to Mr. Leichfeild for 500 copies of the Parliament's ordinances and his majestie's declaration by way of answer, 1*s* 4*d* a hundred, 3*li.* 10*s* ; to Henry Hall for printing books for the University, 28*li.*'

Vol. I, p. 82, note 3.—Read *James* Stuart, *fourth* duke of Lennox.

Vol. I, p. 85, l. 6 from foot.—*Comp. Vicecanc.* for 1642–43 :—' to Mr. Recorder of London (Sir Thomas Gardiner) and Mr. Halloway our counsell touching the right the Vicechancellor hath to keep courts notwithstanding the Act of Parliament, 2*li.*'

Vol. I, p. 98, note 4.—In the Archives in vol. 2 of *Collectanea B. Twyne, Langbaine, &c.* is a copy of a proclamation, 22 Apr. 1643, requiring arms to be brought in to the magazine at New College; also the following certificate—' Rec. 24 Aprill 1643 into his Ma[ts] store of Briant Twine on birdging peece one Browne Bill.   THO : EASTBROOK.'

These ' Collectanea,' unbound in Wood's time, are probably cited by Wood in this note as 'loos paper'; and the 'king's letter' is probably this proclamation.

Vol. I, p. 102, l. 17.—*Comp. Vicecanc.* for 1642–43 :—' for the transcript of the Universitie's petition to his majestie, 2*s* 6*d* ; for 8 copyes of the case to the judges and our counsell, 8*s* ; to the Lord Chiefe Justice' man for a copy of the Commissioners' order about priviledged men, 2*s* ; to one of Secretary Nicholas his men for his paines taken in reference to our petition, 2*li.*, and to another of his men, 20*s* ; July 28, 1643, to Sir Thomas Gardiner our counsell in the case of our privileges betweene the Universitie and the towne, 2*li.* ; Aug. 12 and Aug. 15, to Sir Thomas Gardiner at the meeting before the Lords of the Counsell, 2*li.* ; to the doore-keeper at the hearinge, 10*s*.'

Vol. I, p. 103, l. 16.—*Comp. Vicecanc.* for 1642–43 :—' given to the printers of the verses among them, 5*s* ; to Leichfeild the printer for 150 copies of verses, 3*li.* 10*s* ; to bookbinder Barnes for binding of bookes of verses in sattin and vellam, for guilding and silk strings, 9*li.* 10*s*.'

Vol. I, p. 103, l. 24.—For this success there seems to have been a Thanksgiving day appointed. *Comp. Vicecanc.* for 1643–44 :—' for carrying a letter to Dr. (Thomas) Laurence (Master of Balliol) at Long Hanburrough, to preach the Thanksgiving sermon for the victory in the west, 2*s*.'

Vol. I, p. 103, August.—*Comp. Vicecanc.* for 1642–43 :—'to Mr. Gayton for his journey to Glocester to deliver a petition, 1*li.*'

---

[1] See vol. i. p. 76, ll. 12, 13. *Comp. Vicecanc.* for 1641–42 : ' to one Kinson for himselfe and horse in a journey to Yorke, 2*li.* ; to Mr. (George) Wake of Magd. Coll. for his journey to Yorke, in the University business, 5*li.*'

[2] this tip to the workmen for expedition in printing is a common entry in these accounts.

Vol. I, p. 104, October.—By warrant from the King, Philip Herbert earl of Pembroke was ejected from the Chancellorship, and William Seymour marquess of Hertford elected Chancellor on 24 Oct. and admitted 31 Oct. The marquess nominated George Digby, lord Digby, to be High Steward. *Comp. Vicecanc.* for 1642-43 :—' to my Lord our Chancellor's servants for attending his admission heere at Oxford, 1*li*.; for 2 silver boxes for the Chancellor and Steward to preserve the seales, 2*li*. 2*s* 6*d*.'

Vol. I, p. 104.—*Comp. Vicecanc.* for 1642-43 :—' to Dr. ⟨Henry⟩ Jänson and Mr. ⟨Gerard⟩ Langbane towards their journey to Nottingham upon University busynesse, 5*li*.' *Comp. Vicecanc.* for 1644-45 :—' to Mr. Langbane in full dischardge of the expences of Dr. Jänson and his journy to Nottingham upon the University occasions (beside the 5*li*. paid before to Dr. Jänson), 3*li*.'

Vol. I, p. 106, line 5 from foot.—See Ogle's *Royal Letters to Oxford*, p. 365.

Vol. I, p. 117, April.—*Comp. Vicecanc.* for 1645-46 :—' for a silver box for the seale, labells, vellam, and wrighting the governor's diploma, 1*li*. 2*s*.' Sir William Legge, governor of Oxford, was created M.A. 16 Apr. 1645.

Vol. I, p. 122, l. 6.—This is perhaps one of the successes for which there were bonfires this year.—*Comp. Vicecanc.* for 1645-46 :—' to John Gilliver for bonefires in the year 1645, 12*s*.'

Vol. I, p. 127, 1646.—Richard Finmore's statement of the accounts of Dr. Samuel Fell, Vicechancellor, dated 17 Nov. 1646, and tendered to the Delegates of the Vicechancellor's Accounts on 22 Oct. 1649 (*Liber Vetus Comp. Vicecanc.*, fol. 269) contains this entry ' paid Adams, the smith, part of his bill for swivells for the Library bookes, 13*li*. 7*s*.' The books in the Bodleian accessible to readers were still chained; see Twyne II 108 sqq.

Vol. I, p. 129, September.—*Comp. Vicecanc.* for 1645-46 :—' to John Hopkins for his journey up to London in the University business, 1*li*.; to John Hopkins for his journey up to London in the University business and his abode there from Aug. 18 to 2 Sept., 3*li*. 10*s*; to Dr. Gerard Langbaine and Mr. Brookes for their journeys to and from London in busines for the University and abode there from Aug. 11 to Sept. 18, 1646, 14*li*. 18*s* 11*d*.'

Vol. I, p. 132, July (?).—*Comp. Vicecanc.* for 1646-47 :—' to Mr. Leichfeild for printing 500 coppies of the manner of the King's comming from Holmby, 1*li*. 2*s*.'

Vol. I, p. 139, line 4.—In Twyne XXI 753 is this note :—' The saltinge of freshmen, which hath bene antiently and is yet at Oxford used at their first comminge, was perhaps borrowed or continued from this custome at Athens described in Gregory Nazianzen in oratione funebri D. magni Basilii.'

Vol. I, p. 141, anno 1648.—*Comp. Vicecanc.* for 1648-50 :—' to Mr. ⟨William⟩ Newhouse for journeys and service to the University, 13*li*.; to Mr. ⟨John⟩ Blagrave for expences to London when he carried uppe the University Charters and in recompence for the loss of his horse, 4*li*. 10*s*; to Mr. ⟨John⟩ Langley for horse and other particulars to London, 1*li*. 10*s* 10*d*; to Dr. Henry Wilkinson for attendance on University buissynesse at London, 2*li*. 10*s*; to Dr. ⟨Francis⟩ Cheynell for severall expences for orders and other things concerning the University, 4*li*. 5*s*.'

Vol. I, p. 142, l. 4.—*Comp. Vicecanc.* for 1652-53 :—' to Mr. Ralph Austin and Mr. John Langley, the Visitors' registrary and mandatary, for 12 weekes and 2 dayes service, by order of the Visitors, 5*li*. 4*s*.' *Comp. Vicecanc.* for 1653-54 :—' to Ralph Austin and John Langley, the Visitors' Registrary and mandatory, 23*li*. 12*s*.'

Vol. I, p. 142, l. 16.—*Comp. Vicecanc.* for 1648–50 :—' to Dr. Francis Cheynell for a large Bible in folio presented to the Chancellour when he was heere, and other things, 5*li.* 12*s* 6*d*.' See Wood's *Annals*, ii. 562, note 4.

Vol. I, p. 143, l. 15.—*Comp. Vicecanc.* for 1650–52 :—' for two silver flagons presented to Lieutenant Colonel Kelzey, late governor of Oxon, as an honorary at his departure, 23*li.* 17*s* 4*d*.'

Vol. I, p. 147, November.—The Protestant zeal of the victorious Puritan party is shown by an unusual item of expenditure in *Comp. Vicecanc.* for 1648–50 :— ' for bonfires and to ringers Nov. 5th, 1648, 13*s*.' Cp. vol. iii. pp. 169, 281.

Vol. I, p. 150, l. 16.—This led to a tedious and expensive suit at law. *Comp. Vicecanc.* for 1648–50 :—' to Dr. ⟨Gerard⟩ Langbaine for expences in the controversy betweene the University and the Citty, 6*li.* 3*s*; laid out in our first journey, stay at London for about six weeks, and charges in the suite betweene the University and Citty, 31*li.* 11*s* 5*d*; to Dr. Langbaine, by his particular bill for the same, 4*li.* 18*s*; laid out in our second journey to London about the difference between the University and Citty, 10*li.* 13*s*; to Mr. Peter Wilkins for sollicitinge the University buissynesses by order of Convocation, 5*li.*; laid out in the suite with the citty in Michaelmas Term [1649], 52*li.* 16*s* 8*d*; to Dr. ⟨Edmund⟩ Stanton for his journey to London about presentinge a petition from the University, 5*li.* 1*s* 8*d*; to proctor ⟨John⟩ Maudit for his and Mr. ⟨Samuel⟩ Brewen's expences in the same busynesse, 12*li.* 3*s* 2*d*; to Dr. ⟨John⟩ Mills for monyes laid out by him in the University busyness, 5*li.* 18*s* 4*d*; to Dr. Mills for charges in severall journeys, 5*li.*; to the warden of Wadham College ⟨John Wilkins⟩ for his charges in two journeys to London, 15*li.* 5*s*; for coach hire to London for the company who went thither in March 16$\frac{4}{9}$ severall times, 15*s* 6*d*; spent in the suite with the citty by those who were sent up Jan. 14th, 16$\frac{4}{9}$, 27*li.* 15*s* 8*d*; to Dr. Langbaine in particular for the same, 8*li.* 15*s* 1*d*; for counsellour's fees and other expences at the hearinge before the committee, Jan. 17, 16$\frac{4}{9}$, 7*li.* 13*s* 8*d*; to Dr. ⟨Joshua⟩ Crosse for two journeys to London, 4*li.* 10*s*; to Dr. Crosse in another journey, being a month at London, 6*li.*' *Comp. Vicecanc.* for 1650–52 :—' to Dr. Langbaine, Dr. ⟨Christopher⟩ Rogers, Dr. Crosse, and Mr. ⟨Thankful⟩ Owen of St. John's, for their charges at London from 25 Aug. till 6 Dec. 1650 attendinge the buissinesse of the difference betwixt the University and Citty, 20*li.*; for charges in defending the University privileges in the suite against Mr. Dennis, 5*li.*; to Mr. Deane of Christ Church ⟨John Owen⟩, for his, Dr. Staunton, Dr. Goddard, and Mr. ⟨Thankful⟩ Owen's charges in a journey to London, 14*li.* 7*s* 6*d*; to Dr. Wilkins for the same journey, 1*li.* 5*s*; to Mr. Humphrey Robinson, of London, stationer, for stitchinge 20 copies of the Universitye's answer to the towne petition and reasons, 1*s* 8*d*.' *Comp. Vicecanc.* for 1652–53 :—' to Mr. Charles Zinzan sollicitinge buissinesse att London for the University and Colledges, 40*li.*; to Mr. Vice-chancellor ⟨John Owen⟩, for charges of his journey to London and stay there for three weekes, 10*li.*; for the like journey, Aug. 20th [1653], 10*li.*; to Mr. proctor ⟨Philip⟩ Ward for the like at the same time, . . .' *Comp. Vicecanc.* for 1654–55 :—' to Dr. ⟨John⟩ Palmer for his journey to London and stay there about the suite in lawe betweene the University and Mr. Herne, 20*li.*; to Dr. ⟨John⟩ Wilkins for the like, 20*li.*; and more to him which he gave the doorekeepers of the Parliament house, 10*s*; to Dr. ⟨Henry⟩ Wilkinson of Ch. Ch. for his journey to London about the suite betweene the University and Mr. Herne, 6*li.*; to Mr. Hopkins for sollicitinge in Trinity terme and for fees, 6*li.* 0*s* 4*d*.'

Vol. I, p. 152, note 5.—*Comp. Vicecanc.* for 1648–50 :—' to Hall the printer for printing 250 coppies of the University answer to the city petition and articles, 3*li.* 12*s* 6*d.*'

Vol. I, p. 153, May 19, 1649.—*Comp. Vicecanc.* for 1649–50 :—' for the banquett in the library for entertainment of the Lord General ⟨Thomas, lord Fairfax⟩, Leivetenant General ⟨Oliver Cromwell⟩, and officers of the army when they came to the University, 20*li.* 10*s* ; to Mr. Bodicot for wine for the same entertainment, 5*li.* 1*s* 8*d* ; to the glover for gloves presented to the Lord Generall, Lievetenant Generall, and others, 10*li.*'

Vol. I, p. 155, l. 21.—*Comp. Vicecanc.* for 1648–50 :—' to the glover for gloves presented to Major-general Lambert and Coll. Ingolsby at the time when they quieted the troubles heere, 3*li.* ; to the vintner for wine when Major-general Lambert and other commanders were heere, 6*s* 5*d.*'

Vol. I, p. 157, note 5.—*Comp. Vicecanc.* for 1650–52 :—' to Mr. Charles Holloway for a fee and other charges for a search made in Kettle hall for goods of the University supposed to be there, 17*s* 2*d* ; to a messenger sent to Dr. Farmer and to one that brought foure bedel's staves and to another that brought the senior proctor's bookes and keyes, 7*s* 6*d* ; to Mr. Wilkins goldsmith for mending the bedell's staves severall times, 13*s* 2*d* ; more to him for a staffe for the superior bedell in arts, 33*li.* 10*s* ; to Mr. ⟨Richard⟩ Campion, ⟨Anthony⟩ Fido, ⟨John⟩ Langley senior, theire charges in severall journeys in prosecution of the suite against Mr. Gayton and Henry Davis late bedells and fees to the messengers, 9*li.*' *Comp. Vicecanc.* for 1660–61 :—' to Henry Davis in lieu of his charges when he was prosecuted by law for detaining his bedell's staffe after his ejectment in Dr. ⟨Daniel⟩ Greenwood's vicechancellorship, 5*li.*'

Vol. I, p. 160, (?) Dec. 1649.—*Comp. Vicecanc.* for 1648–50 :—' to Dr. ⟨Francis⟩ Cheynell for his journey and attendance carryinge up the University answers given in at first about the Engagement, 10*li.*'

Vol. I, p. 162, anno 1650.—Before this date part of the Schools seems to have showed signs of settling. *Comp. Vicecanc. pro Scholis,* for 1648–50 :—' to Mr. Jackson, mason, for building a buttresse at the north-west end of the Schooles, 49*li.* 9*s.*' For the doubts felt at this time about the security of the Schools fabric, cp. vol. i. p. 251, l. 23.

Vol. I, p. 166, 1 January 165¾, Oliver Cromwell was elected Chancellor.—*Comp. Vicecanc.* for 1650–52 :—' to Dr. ⟨Joshua⟩ Crosse and Mr. ⟨Philip⟩ Stephens of New Colledge for charges att London in procuringe an order permitting the election of a chancellor, 6*li.* 2*s* 6*d* ; to the ringers at the election of the chancellor, 5*s* ; to Dr. ⟨Joshua⟩ Crosse, Dr. ⟨Francis⟩ Barksdale, Mr. ⟨Philip⟩ Stephens of New Colledge and Mr. ⟨James⟩ Ward of Magdalen Colledge for theire owne, theire horses', and servants' charges in theire journey to the Chancellor in Scotland, 66*li.* 13*s* 4*d* ; more to Dr. Crosse in lieu of a horse that fayled in that journey, 5*li.* 16*s* 7*d* ; more to Thomas Langley for the losse he sustayned by the faylinge of his horse in that journey and his charges comminge home by sea, 12*li.* ; more to Dr. Crosse for S^r. ⟨John⟩ Hooke and Robert Selby, who attended those that were sent to the Chancellor in Scotland by order of the delegates, 4*li.* ; more to Mr. Wright, goldsmith, for a box for the seale of the patent sent to the Chancellor, 17*s* 6*d.*'

Vol. I, p. 170, line 16. See the text of the orders issued to the Governor of Oxford in Ogle's *Royal Letters to Oxford*, p. 370.

Vol. I, p. 170, l. 8 from foot.—*Comp. Vicecanc.* for 1650–52 :—' to Mr. Langley, junior, for his journey to the Chancellor at Chipping-Norton, 5*s* 3*d*; to a messenger sent to the Councell of State when the Scotch army was at Worcester, 2*li.* 18*s.*'

Vol. I, p. 175, l. 17.—*Comp. Vicecanc.* for 1650–52 :—'for takinge downe the organ at St. Marye's, 4*s*; to Mr. Lichfeild for printing edicts and declarations three severall times, 1*li.* 10*s*; to Thomas Maio for settinge up the scaffolds in St. Maryes at the Act (1652), 7*li.* 3*s* 5*d*; to Mr. Langley, senior, for bays for the pulpit att the Act, 6*s*; to John Wyld joyner for mendinge seates in St. Marye's broken at the Act, 3*s* 10*d.*'

Vol. I, p. 185, 1654 (?).—*Comp. Vicecanc.* for 1653–54 :—'to Thomas Robinson, bookeseller, for bookes presented to major-generall ⟨John⟩ Desborough and his lady, 2*li.* 1*s.*'

Vol. I, p. 186, l. 2.—Oliver Cromwell became Protector on 16 Dec. 1653, and the University soon after sent a deputation to congratulate him.—*Comp. Vicecanc.* for 1653–54 :—'to Dr. ⟨John⟩ Wilkins and proctor ⟨Philip⟩ Ward for their expences in a journey to London to congratulate the Lord Protector, 12*li.*'

Vol. I, p. 189, l. 13.—*Comp. Vicecanc.* for 1653–54 :—' to Leonard Lichfield for printing the booke of verses upon conclusion of the peace with the Dutch, 6*li.* 9*s* 6*d*; to the printers for expedition in that worke, 2*s* 6*d*; to Mr. ⟨Bernard⟩ Hore for his charges in carrying up those verses to London, 2*li.* 10*s.*'

Vol. I, p. 195, l. 12.—*Comp. Vicecanc.* for 1656–57 :—' to Edward Wyse, gun-smith, for pistolls delivered at the insurrection in the west, 1*li.* 17*s.*'   I suppose there were preparations for mustering University volunteers as in 1651 (see vol. i. p. 170 at foot).

Vol. I, p. 196, 1655.—In this year and the next considerable changes were made in S. Mary's Church.—*Comp. Vicecanc.* for 1655–56 :—' to John Wild, joyner, for the new pulpitt and towards the Doctors' seates, 35*li.*'   *Ibid.* for 1656–57 :— ' to Mr. Jackson, stone-cutter, for worke done about the pulpitt in St. Maries, 1*li.* 12*s*; to Thomas Adams, smith, for iron-worke about the same pulpitt, 3*li.* 16*s* 6*d*; to Sheppard, carpenter, for making the new gallery by the bellferry and for tymber and boords used thereabouts, 15*li.* 1*s.*'

Vol. I, p. 237, l. 15.—*Comp. Vicecanc. pro Scholis* for 1657–58 :—' to two men for removing the bookes from Dr. Langbaine's to the Archives, 2*s* 6*d.*'

Vol. I, p. 251, l. 11 from foot.—*Comp. Vicecanc.* for 1656–57 :—' to Sheppard, carpenter, for worke done at Smithgate, 6*s* 6*d*; to Thomas Adams, smith, for worke done about the post at Smith gate, 12*s.*'

Vol. I, p. 254, note 4.—*Comp. Vicecanc.* for 1577–78 :—' in denariis datis Rodolpho Agas pro descriptione Oxon., 20*li.*'

Vol. I, p. 259, note 7.—*Comp. Vicecanc.* for 1656–57 :—' to the ringers at the election of the Lord Richard Cromwell chancellor, 10*s*; to the Doctors, Masters, and bedles for their journey to London to the Convocation [1] for the admission of the said Lord chancellor, 55*li.* 11*s* 8*d*; to Mr. ⟨Anthony⟩ Fidoe for his journey to the Lord Richard Cromwell, 1*li.*'

Vol. I, p. 266, 1659.—*Comp. Vicecanc.* for 1659–60 :—' to proctor ⟨Thomas⟩ Wyatt for carting a lewd woman, 2*s* 6*d.*'

Vol. I, p. 266, 1659.—*Comp. Vicecanc.* for 1658–59 :—' for the copies of 2 patents

---

[1] held for this purpose, in accordance with the permission of the Statutes, *extra Universitatem*; Laudian Code, p. 163.

concerning the Colledge at Durham and for other fees to clerkes, 2*li.* 10*s*; to Mr. ⟨Anthony⟩ Fidoe for writing 4 copies of the Universitie petition and reasons against erecting a Universitie at Durham, 2*li.* 10*s*; to Dr. ⟨Daniel⟩ Greenwood and Dr. ⟨John⟩ Wallis for the charges of their journey to London for preventing the erecting of the Universitie at Durham, 16*li.*'

Vol. I, p. 276, note 1.—The extreme rarity of the tract I am about to mention will probably excuse the attaching of it to this accidental mention of Middleton-Stony. Mr. Madan has pointed out to me in Martinus Nijhoff's, of La Haye, 'Catalogue d' . . . Pièces historiques . . . du xvi° siècle' no. 59, which is :—

Dye descriptie eñ contrefeytinge vande twee kinderen die in Engelant (binnen den Dorp vā Middleton inder plaetsen) aen malcanderen geboren sijn den den derden dach Augusti. Anno MDLII acht Englesche mijlen vande universiteyt van Oxfoort—

Printed 1552, at Antwerp, by Hans van Liesuelt.

Vol. I, p. 314, l. 10.—*Comp. Vicecanc. pro Scholis* for 1660-61 :— 'to Mr. Jackson for scaffolding up to the Tower in the Schooles and repayring of the King's armes, 4*li.* 18*s* 6*d.*' *Comp. Vicecanc.* for 1660-61 :—'to William Bird for mending the king's and founder's armes over the Physick Garden gate, 1*li.* 1*s.*'

Vol. I, p. 316, l. 24.—*Comp. Vicecanc.* for 1659-60 :—'to the ringers at St. Marie's on the Thanksgiving day for his majestie's returne, 5*s.*'

Vol. I, p. 319, l. 3 from foot.—*Comp. Vicecanc.* for 1659-60 :—' expended in severall particulars in the University addresse to his majestie, 29*li.* 1*s* 1*d*; to 7 Doctors, two Proctors, 15 Masters, 5 bedells and the verger for their attendance in the Universitie addresse to his majestie, 73*li.* 10*s*; to Mrs. Litchfield for printing the verses (and severall occasional losses in that buisinesse, provided it be not taken into an example for the future), 20*li.*; given to the printers, 2*s* 6*d.*'

Vol. I, p. 328, l. 17.—*Comp. Vicecanc.* for 1660-61 :—'to Mr. Ballard for his attendance and paines as registrar to the Visitors, 10*li.*'

Vol. I, p. 332, l. 4 from foot.—*Comp. Vicecanc.* for 1660-61 :—'to Mr. Lichfield for paper to print the verses on the death of the duke of Glocester, 5*li.* 1*s* 8*d*; to Mr. ⟨Samuel⟩ Clarke sent to London with the said verses, 3*li.*; to John Barnes for binding the said verses sent to his majestie on the death of the duke of Glocester, 8*li.* 11*s* 10*d*; to the printers, 5*s.*'

Vol. I, p. 334, l. 2.—For this assault, George Hitchcock took them to law, and gave them an unpleasant time. *Comp. Vicecanc.* for 1660-61 :—'to Captaine Bacon for executing the Visitors' order against Mr. Hitchcock, 1*li.* : to a souldier at the same time, 2*s* 6*d*; given to Mr. ⟨Edward⟩ Astyn as a fee for the same, 10*s*; to the sergeant that arrested the Vicechancellor in London, 2*s*; to Captaine Bacon and Lieutenant Wade, by appointment of the Visitors, 3*li.*; to Captaine Bacon for the damage he received in being twice arrested by Mr. Hitchcock, by the same order, 6*li.*; to Sargeant Holloway for fees at severall times concerning Mr. Hitchcock's buisinesse, 2*li.* 17*s* 8*d*; to Mr. Astyn, attorney, in full discharge of all his bills relating to the suit against Mr. Hitchcock, 38*li.* 5*s*; to Dr. Lamplugh to consult with lawyers about an answer to Mr. Hitchcock's declaration, 2*li.*; to Dr. Lamplugh for his charges at London in Mr. Hitchcock's suit, 1*li.* 5*s*; to Mr. Baldwin for a fee in the same buisinesse, 1*li.*; to the Register for a journey to London to carry up King Henry VIII his charter in the suit with Mr. Hitchcock, 4*li.* 5*s.*' *Comp. Vicecanc.* for 1661-62 :—'to Mr. Astyn for charges in the suit against Mr. Hitchcock, 9*li.* 16*s* 2*d.*'

Vol. I, p. 337, l. 8.—*Comp. Vicecanc.* for 1660-61 :—'to 6 Doctors, 2 Proctors,

13 Masters, the Register. 5 bedells and the virgifer, sent to London for the admission of our Chancellor, 69*li*. 10*s*; tb Mr. ⟨William⟩ Ball for velame and writing the Lord Chancellor's diploma, 7*s* 6*d*; for a silver box and riband for the seal of the said diploma, 19*s* 6*d*; for coach-hire to London and given to the Lord Chancellor's servants, 5*s* 6*d*; for the carriage of the great chest to London and back againe to Oxon, wherein the habitts of the Doctors and Masters, &c., were put, 1*li*. 9*s* 4*d*; for the use of the said chest, &c., 5*s*.'

Vol. I, p. 350, l. 15.—*Comp. Vicecanc.* for 1660–61 :—' to Mr. Lichfield for printing verses on the death of the Princes⟨s⟩ of Orange, 6*li*. 10*s* ; to the printers, 5*s* ; to John Barnes for binding the said verses and for velvet, &c., 8*li*. 12*s* 10*d*; to Mr. ⟨Samuel⟩ Clark sent to London with the said verses and for a fortnight's stay there, 4*li*. 13*s* 8*d*.'

Vol. I, p. 371, l. 25.—*Comp. Vicecanc.* for 1660–61 :—' to sargeant Holloway for meeting the major and bailiffs in St. Marie's about taking the oath, 1*li*.'

Vol. I, p. 372, l. 32.—*Comp. Vicecanc.* for 1660–61 :—' to Dr. Yates for his expences in London in pursuance of the Universitie's petition to his majestie against the city, 20*li*. ; to Dr. Wallis for a journey to London and a fortnight's stay there about the citizens' refusing to take the annual oath, 5*li*. 8*s* ; to Dr. Wallis for a journey to London and seven weekes stay there in pursuance of the University's petition to his majestie, 15*li*. 9*s* : to the registrar for a journey to London about the same buisinesse, 2*li*. ; to the registrar and others for transcribing severall records relating to the petition of the Universitie to his majestie, 2*li*. 15*s*.' *Ibid.* for 1661–62 :—' to Dr. Yates for his charges in preferring the petition of the University to the King against the encroachments of the city, 28*li*. 14*s* 6*d*.'

Vol. I, p. 377, 1661.—In this, and some subsequent years, Oriel College repaired the chancel, &c., of S. Mary's. *Comp. Vicecanc.* for 1661–62 :—' given to Oriel College in consideration of their great cost in adorning the chancell of St. Marie's church, but not to be a precedent for the future, 10*li*.' *Comp. Vicecanc.* for 1664–65 :—' freely given to Oriel College, they having bin at a great charge in the repair of Adam Brome's chappell, 15*li*.'—Some work also was paid for by the University, *Comp. Vicecanc.* for 1661–62 :—' to Mr. Jackson, stone-cutter for work done at St. Marie's, 7*li*. 17*s* 7*d*.'

Vol. I, p. 379, l. 10, l. 15.—*Comp. Vicecanc.* for 1660–61 :—' to Mr. ⟨Henry⟩ Davis for a journey to London with two diplomas ⟨dated 1 Dec. 1660⟩ to the bishopps of Bristoll and Glocester for the degree of Dr. in Divinity, 1*li*. 10*s*.'

Vol. I, p. 381, last line.—*Comp. Vicecanc.* for 1660–61 :—' for two silver boxes and riband for two diplomas for the degree of Mr. of Arts granted to two of the Chancellor's sonnes, 2*li*. 3*s*.'

Vol. I, p. 384, l. 5 from foot.—*Comp. Vicecanc.* for 1660–61 :—' to Mr. Lichfield for printing programma's against disorders in Lent, &c., 1*li*. 4*s*.'

Vol. I, p. 399, l. 11.—*Comp. Vicecanc.* for 1660–61 :—' for ringing at St. Marie's on the Coronation day, 5*s*.'

Vol. I, p. 399, l. 5 from foot.—See the text of the Orders in Council then issued in Ogle's *Royal Letters to Oxford*, pp. 371–373.

Vol. I, p. 414, l. 4 from foot.—*Comp. Vicecanc.* for 1661–62 :—' paid and spent in the entertainment of the right honourable Edward earle of Clarendon our Lord Chancellor, 88*li*. 16*s* 7*d*; to Mr. Bland for gloves praesented to the Lord Chancellor, his countesse, the lord Cornbury, and the burgesse of the University, 19*li*. ; to Mr. Speed and Mr. Davis for their expences in a journey to Wickham to wait on the Lord Chancellor, 2*li*.'

Vol. I, p. 427, 1662.—In this year a large sum was spent (? on repairs) at the Schools. *Comp. Vicecanc. pro Scholis* for 1661–62 :—'to Jackson, the stone-cutter, as per bill to the 5th of Oct. 1662, 115*li*. 8*s* 9*d*.'

Vol. I, p. 429, note 4.—The 'twin volume' is MS. Twyne 21, in the Archives of the University.

Vol. I, p. 440, note 5.—*Comp. Vicecanc.* for 1661–62 :—' to Mr. Lichfield for printing the verses on the Queen's arivall called *Domiduca*, 18*li*. 16*s* ; to John Barnes for binding of the said verses and for stitching &c., 8*li*. 6*s* 6*d* ; to Mr. Davis the bedle for his expences when sent to London with the said verses, 3*l*. 12*s* 2*d* ; to Mr. Pawlin the mercer for velvett and sattin to cover the *Domi-duca's*, 6*li*. 10*s*.' *Ibid.* :—' paid to Holder for bonefires, &c., 1*li*. 12*s*,' probably refers to illuminations on the occasion of the royal wedding, not noticed by Wood.

Vol. I, p. 452, l. 10.—*Comp. Vicecanc.* for 1661–62 :—'paid to two Hungarians, by decrees of Convocation, 10*li*.'

Vol. I, p. 457, l. 2.—*Comp. Vicecanc.* for 1662–63 :—' to Mr. Davis for King Charles his workes neatly bound to be presented to the prince of Denmarke, 2*li*. 9*s*.'

Vol. I, p. 464, l. 14 from foot.—*Comp. Vicecanc.* for 1662–63 :—' to Mr. 〈William〉 Ball for velam, writing, and inserting the new statute for declamations into five bookes, 1*li*. 14*s*.' The five books would be, I suppose, the *Authenticus Liber* of the Laudian Code, and the books of the Vicechancellor, Senior and Junior Proctors, and the book for the use of the Esquire Bedell of Arts.

Vol. I, p. 465. The University Accounts for 1661–62 contain some interesting entries about the coinage, not noticed by Wood.—*Comp. Vicecanc.* for 1661–62 :—'paid for exchange of 31*li*. 7*s* 6*d* in Parliament coine, taken out of the University chest, 2*li*. 1*s*.'—*Comp. Vicecanc. pro Scholis* for 1661–62 :—' for exchange of 47*li*. 16*s* in Parliament coine taken out of 600*li*. put into the University chest, 2*li*. 5*s* 6*d* ; lost by brasse money, 16*s* ; for exchange of 33*li*. 4*s* 6*d* in Parliament coine taken out of 459*li*. 3*s* received from Dr. Hood and paid into the University chest, 1*li*. 11*s* 6*d* ; lost in brasse money, 11*s* 6*d*.'

Vol. I, p. 466, 1663.—*Comp. Vicecanc. pro Scholis* for 1662–63 :—' to 〈Thomas〉 Adams 〈the smith〉 for making a scheleton, 6*li*. ; to 〈John〉 Wild 〈the carpenter〉 for a case for the scheleton, 2*li*.'

Vol. I, p. 475, l. 4.—*Comp. Vicecanc.* for 1662–63 :—' for silver boxes &c., for the Lord Steward's patent and diploma, 2*li*. ; for riband for the Under-steward's seal, 1*s*.'

Vol. I, p. 490, l. 4.—Charles II had been expected to visit Oxford more than two years before ; *Comp. Vicecanc.* for 1660–61 :—' to proctor 〈Henry〉 Hawley as money paid by him in London for the University to make preparation for his majestie's entertainment at his intended comeing to Oxford, 50*li*.'

The items of expenditure at the present visit are thus given in the *Comp. Vice-canc.* for 1663–64 :—' to Mr. Richard Davis for a Bible presented to the King, 12*li*. 13*s* 6*d* ; to Mr. New for gloves presented to the king, queen, and royall family, Lord Chancellor, &c., (and for two pair of 10*li*. 15*s* price, not used but transmitted to the next Vice-chancellor against a like occasion, which could not be returned without losse), 60*li*. 10*s* ; to Mr. Richardson, confectioner, for the banquett, 266*li*. 10*s* ; to Mr. Jackson for salt meates bought by him at the same time, 3*li*. 1*s* 4*d* ; for Italian, High country, and French wine at the banquett, 6*li*. 16*s* ; for the loane and setting up of the " state " in the library, 3*li*. ; to Mr. Davis, the bedell, sent to London to procure things, 2*li*. 6*s* ; to Moore for his wagon sent on purpose to fetch things, 3*li*. 3*s* ; for bottles and glasses bought by Mr. Davis and Mris Dolben, 11*li.* 8*s*; for the use of linning and other necessaries, 3*s* 6*d*; to 12 men for attending at the banquett, 1*li.*; to Holder for gravelling of the Schoole Quadrangle, 15*s*; to Edward Prince for 2 dozen of torches at the king's entrance, 1*li.*; to Dr. ⟨John⟩ Lamphire to mend the street by Kettle Hall in that exigence, not to be a precedent for the future, by appoyntment of the delegates, 3*li.* 6*s* 6*d*; to Lichfield for printing the delegates' orders then, 13*s*; more to him for printing programma's at severall times, 1*li.* 3*s* 6*d*; to Holder for faggotts, ringers, &c., 1*li.* 2*s* 3*d*.' Besides the above expenditure out of the University moneys, other sums were spent on behalf of the University which had been raised by subscription. On 21 Oct. 1662 Dr. Walter Blandford paid in to the University chest 36*li.* 11*s* 3*d* 'pecuniam collectam ob expectatum adventum serenissimi regis et eidem usui reservatam'; which was taken out 18 Dec. 1663—*Reg. Cistae.* His 'sacred majesty' Charles II, like his father, was a 'sore saint' to the University.

Vol. I, p. 498, l. 11.—In MS. Rawl. Poet. 19 fol. 86ᵛ, 87 are 32 'Verses spoken to her Royall Highness the Dutches of York in New Colledge Chappell Oxon,' beginning—

> 'Madam! Forgive the zeal of him that dares
> Detayn you heer from your best welcome, prayers.'

Notwithstanding this pious exordium, they are conceived in a sufficiently blasphemous spirit of eulogy. I suppose they are verses spoken on this occasion.

Vol. I, p. 499, note 1.—In MS. Ballard 47 fol. 170 is 'Queen's College horn, a ballad to the tune of *King John and the Abbot of Canterbury*,' 22 stanzas of 4 lines.

Vol. II, p. 1, 1664.—In this year the University was engaged in getting possession of the exhibitions intended by John Craven, baron Craven of Ryton, who died in 1650. *Comp. Vicecanc.* for 1663–64 :—'to the principall of Jesus College ⟨Leoline Jenkins⟩ for his journey to London and attendance twice in the buisinesse of the lord Craven's exhibitioners, 9*li.*' *Comp. Vicecanc.* for 1664–65 :—'to Dr. ⟨Thomas⟩ Yates by the appoyntment of the delegates in the time of Dr. Blandford ⟨Vicechanc. 1662–64⟩ for the setling of the lord Craven's gift, 9*li.* 17*s* 6*d* : Memorandum that whereas the summe of 18*li.* 17*s* 6*d* is charged upon this and the last yeare's accompts, for setling the lord Craven's gift, Mr. Vicechancellor was desired to demand 20*s* per annum of each exhibitioner 'till the University be repayed the said summe.'

Vol. II, p. 1, anno 1664.—The University in this and the next two years was involved in litigation, because of disputes with the College of Physicians, London, and with the city of Oxford. *Comp. Vicecanc.* for 1663–64 :—'to the principall of Jesus College ⟨Leoline Jenkins⟩ for his journey to London and attendance there severall weekes in the physitians' buisinesse, 6*li.*; to Mr. Hopkins his severall disbursments for the University and for his journey to London about Thackwell, 12*li.* 3*s* 4*d*; to the principall of Jesus College for his journey to London and attendance there about the same buisinesse, 12*li.* 2*s* 6*d*; given by myselfe ⟨Walter Blandford, Vicechancellor⟩ to Sergeant ⟨John⟩ Maynard and Sergeant ⟨Charles⟩ Holloway for counsell in that buisinesse and to severall clerkes for copies of court rolls, 4*li.* 15*s*; to Dr. ⟨Leoline⟩ Jenkins for divers services done to the University, 30*li.*'—*Comp. Vicecanc.* for 1664–65 :—'to Dr. Jenkins for diverse services done for the University, 10*li*; to Dr. ⟨Thomas⟩ Yates, for his services done to the University in London, in a small piece of plate, by order of the delegates of the last Vicechancellor's accounts, 5*li.* 2*s*.' *Comp. Vicecanc.* for

1665-66 :—' to a piece of plate to Dr. ⟨Henry⟩ Deane for assisting the University upon severall occasions, 9*li.* 2*s* ; to the atturney for the charges of 3 termes about felons' goods, 7*li.* 8*s* ; to Sergeant ⟨Charles⟩ Holloway and to Mr. Richard Holloway at severall times in this cause, 5*li.* ; for transcribing severall writings imparted to our counsell upon that occasion, 6*s.*'

Vol. II, p. 14, l. 2 from foot.—*Comp. Vicecanc.* for 1663–64 :—' to the pro-Orator for his journey to London when he waited on my Lord of Canterbury with the University letter, 3*li.*'—Dr. John Fell was appointed treasurer for the work and at the end of the above *Computus* is entered his

'Account of moneys laid out upon the Theatre since July 7th 1664 to September 19, 1664.

	li.	*s*	*d*
Masons' bill July 9,	4	14	4
Masons' bill July 16,	10	13	3
Carpenters' bill July 16,	3	0	10
Quarrymen's bill July 16,	3	7	6
Masons' bill July 23,	11	5	8
Masons' bill July 30,	13	3	6
Masons' bill Aug. 6,	15	11	2
Masons' bill Aug. 13,	18	7	10
Masons' bill Aug. 20,	16	19	0
Masons' bill Aug. 27,	13	12	8
Masons' bill Sept. 3,	13	16	6
Masons' bill Sept. 10,	10	15	0
Masons' bill Sept. 17,	15	14	0
	151	12	0
Given by the Archbishop of Canterbury in part of 1000*li.*	200	0	0
Balance	48	8	0 '

Archbishop Sheldon subsequently took upon himself the whole cost of the building.

Dr. John Fell kept an exceedingly minute account of the expenditure on the Sheldonian, specifying the exact sums paid, the names of all the workmen, the amount of time they worked, the materials bought and the like. This shows that Sheldon laid out 12,239*li.* 4*s* 4*d* on the work. He also paid 'for two gold cupps presented to the Dean of Christ Church and Dr. Wren ⟨in recognition of their services, the former as treasurer, the latter as architect,⟩ 204*li.* 7*s* ; to Mr. ⟨David⟩ Loggan 10*li.*, (and to another that came with him, 40*s*,) who engraved the print of the Theatre ; to Mr. Logan who engraved the back part of the Theatre and presented his grace with it, 5*li.* ; for engrossing the booke of accompts, 10*li.*' This book of accounts of 'monies laid out in the building and adorning of the Theater in the University of Oxford at the sole expence' of Gilbert Sheldon, is now MS. Bodl. 898, having been 'given to the University of Oxford by Abraham Tucker, esq. of Belchworth Castle near Dorking in Surry A.D. 1760.'

Vol. II, p. 32, l. 16.—War had been declared against the Dutch, 22 Febr. Later on in this year a press-gang perhaps visited Oxford (cp. vol. iii. p. 388). *Comp. Vicecanc.* for 1665–66 :—' given to the watermen who were press'd here for his majestie's service, 3*li.*'

Vol. II, p. 38, l. 16.—*Comp. Vicecanc.* for 1664–65 :—' to Holder for three severall bonfires, 18*s.*' *Ibid.* for 1665–66 :—' to John Holder for severall bonfiers, 1*li.* 0*s* 6*d.*'

Vol. II, p. 40, l. 9 from foot.—*Comp. Vicecanc.* for 1665–66 :—'to Mr. ⟨Henry⟩ Davis, yeoman bedell of Divinity, for his warning and constant attending of the watch for 13 weekes during the time the members of the University served there, 5*li.*'

Vol. II, p. 40, l. 3 from foot.—Special forms of service were issued for this and similar specially appointed services (see p. 43, l. 4 from foot).—*Comp. Vicecanc.* for 1664–65 :—'to Richard Davis for service-bookes upon three severall occasions, 8*s* 8*d*.' *Ibid.* for 1665–66 :—'to Mr. Richard Davis for prayer-bookes on three severall occasions, 8*s* 8*d*.'

Vol. II, p. 44, note 6.—*Comp. Vicecanc.* for 1664–65 :—'to Leonard Lichfield for printing programma's, 12*s* 6*d*.' *Ibid.* for 1665–66 :—'to widow Lichfield for printing severall orders, 2*li.* 17*s*.'

Vol. II, p. 48, l. 23.—See the text of them in Ogle's *Royal Letters to Oxford*, p. 373.

Vol. II, p. 50, note 3.—*Comp. Vicecanc.* for 1646–47 :—'to Mr. Leichfeild for printing 1000 coppies of the *Reasons of the University*, 14*li.* 14*s* ; paid to Mr. Leichfeild for 30 coppies of the *Reasons of the University*, 10*s*.'

Vol. II, p. 61, l. 12.—It was a year or two before the University as a corporate body became liable to the tax. The first entry is *Comp. Vicecanc.* for 1669–70, 'ten fire-hearths for one year, viz. 7 in the little print house and 3 in the Theater, 1*li.*'

Vol. II, p. 62, l. 8.—*Comp. Vicecanc.* for 1665–66 :—'to the goldsmith for a silver box in which was inserted the diploma of colonell Strangewaye's degree, together with the parchment and writing of it, 1*li.* 1*s* 3*d*.'

Vol. II, p. 84, l. 8.—*Computus Vice-cancellarii* for 1666–67, 'to the tayler for publique patternes for gownes, 10*li.* 14*s*.'

Vol. II, p. 89, l. 17.—The University paid this tax.—*Comp. Vicecanc.* for 1666–67, 'the poll-bill for the University stock, 12*li.*'

Vol. II, p. 96, l. 16.—There was a movement for University volunteers during this war, no doubt when the news came of the presence of the Dutch fleet in the Thames in June 1667.—*Comp. Vicecanc.* for 1666–67, 'preparation for publique defence upon expectation of invasion, 66*li.* 8*s* 8*d*.'

Vol. II, p. 97, note 6.—In Twyne XXI p. 85 is a notice of trouble in connexion with football. 'The 26 of Febr. 1607 stilo veteri being Saturday, the schollers of Oxford at a match at football burned the fursesses of Bullington greene, contayninge 3 acres or thereabouts (some say 30 acres).'

Vol. II, p. 112, l. 6 from foot.—*Comp. Vicecanc.* for 1666–67, 'the diplomas for three Dutch divines, 3*li.* 4*s*.'

Vol. II, p. 120, l. 7.—This seems a fit place to bring together some notices of the formation of the 'Oxford Marbles' collection.—*Comp. Vicecanc.* for 1667–68, 'water carriage of the Arundell marbles, 4*li.* ; for the carriage of the Arundell marbles, 4*li.* 10*s* ; water carriage of the Latine inscriptions, 4*li.* 5*s* ; for the carriage of one marble left behind, 2*s* ; for cleansing the marbles, 7*li.*' *Ibid.* for 1668–69, 'to Simon White for a marble altar, 5*li.* ; to Mr. Walker for 5 marble inscriptions, 14*li.* ; for the carriage of marbles &c. by water, 7*li.* 16*s* ; to Mr. Bird for repairing and setting up the remainder of the marbles given by my Lord Howard and Mr. Selden, and 10*li.* in part for the two inscriptions intended for them, 24*li.* 0*s* 6*d* ; to Mr. Provost of Queen's College for a marble with a Greek inscription, 2*li*. 5*s* 6*d*.' *Ibid.* for 1671–72, 'for the carriage of the Tangier marble, 6*li*.; wharfage for the said marble, 1*s*; for removing the Tangier marble from Brooke's wharfe, 9*s* 3*d*; for transporting the great marble given by Mr. Dennington, 9*s*.' *Ibid.* for 1672–73, 'for setting up a marble, 2*s* 6*d*.' *Ibid.* for 1680–81, 'to Cully the boatman for carriage of marbles from London given by Mr. Wheeler, 14*s*.' *Ibid.* for 1682–83, 'to Rush the bargman for carriage of two altars of Dr. Lister's gift, 2*li*.' *Ibid.* for 1688–89, 'to Samuel Rush, bargman, for the carriage of two great marbles from London, 2*li*.; to Benjamin Cutler to pay for the carriage of marbles from the wharfe to the Theater, 6*s*.' *Ibid.* for 1690–91, 'for the carriage of the marble stone with an Arabick inscription, 1*li*. 6*s* 6*d*.' *Ibid.* for 1693–94, 'for the carriage of an image from Wales given to the Musaeum, 7*s*.' *Comp. Vicecanc.* for 1675–76, 'for the *Marmora Oxoniensia*, and some other bookes richly bound and presented to severall persons of quality, as by John Hall's bill, 30*li*. 10*s*.'

Vol. II, p. 128, note 3.—This litigation was costly.—*Comp. Vicecanc.* for 1667–68 :—'to Sergeant ⟨Charles⟩ Holloway ⟨University Council⟩ in Fish Line's case, 2*li*.,' and a further payment of 3*li*. : 'to Mr. Hodges, Mr. Puleston and the Proctor's man's charges to and in London, 5*li*. 10*s*; to Dr. Deane for his expences and services, 28*li*. 3*s* 2*d*; to Mr. Walker for money layd out by him and for services, 36*li*. 19*s* 6*d*; to Dr. Jenkins for money layd out by him and for services, 42*li*.; Mr. ⟨William⟩ Hopkin's the atturny's bill, 70*li*. 1*s*.'

Vol. II, p. 129, l. 5.—The suit about felons' goods was an expensive one: *Comp. Vicecanc.* for 1668–69, 'to Mr. Richard Holloway for councell at severall times in the cause about felons' goods, &c., 6*li*.; to Mr. Hopkins his severall bills about the suit in Chancery and upon a triall at the assizes here between the University and the Town for the goods of felons of themselves ⟨i. e. suicides⟩, 101*li*. 12*s* 6*d*.'—It will be found from these Additions that the goods of felons and (owing to the clemency of the University; see vol. ii. p. 503, note 3) of suicides brought in an insignificant amount. Richard Imings, *infra*, p. 75, is the only exception among suicides (felones de se); and of felons, the largest sum is *Comp. Vicecanc.* 1693–94, 'de bonis cujusdam felonis, 13*li*. 13*s* 6*d* '; against which we have to set such an entry as *Comp. Vicecanc.* for 1689–90, 'de bonis Ricardi Triplett, felonis, 2*s* 6*d*.'—Another point at issue between the University and City was the militia:—*Comp. Vicecanc.* for 1668–69, 'to Dr. Crosse for expences in the suit about the militia, 10*li*. 12*s* 6*d*.'

Vol. II, p. 129, l. 14.—*Comp. Vicecanc.* for 1667–68, 'printing the Lent programma's, 12*s*.'

Vol. II, p. 129, l. 13 from foot.—The Rev. R. B. Gardiner, F.S.A., sends me a very ingenious suggestion for this obscure passage, viz. 'that 1 ⟨i.e. one, some woman, cp. iii. 61⟩ had a kindnesse for me, but *she* had none.' So far as the MS. goes, this is altogether possible, the character being neither the distinctive I nor 1 which Wood often uses, but a hasty stroke which does duty indifferently for both.

Vol. II, p. 131, l. 2 from foot.—*Comp. Vicecanc.* for 1668–69, 'to Mr. Bird for the worke done in securing the vault of the Divinity Schole, making the new dore ⟨opposite the Theatre⟩, altering the professor's seat and the windowes, making a large sewer from the south side of the library round about the Convocation house into the sewer &c. 101*li*.; to Richard Frogley the carpenter for scaffolding within and without the Divinity Schole, and for worke done in newe laying the gutters over it, as also for worke about the printing house, 38*li*. 15*s* 11*d*; to Young the smith for cramps for the vault of the Divinity

Schole, and for the iron worke of the type over the professor's chair, 40*li.*;
to Bernard Rawlins for glazing work in all the Scholes and lead and work for
the new pipes and for cramps in and about the Divinity Schole, 107*li.* 13*s* 9*d*;
to Mr. Cleer, London, joyner, in part, for work done by him and his brother the
carver, in the Divinity Schole, 147*li.*' *Comp. Vicecanc.* for 1669–70, 'to Mr.
Hawkins for painting in the Divinity Schole, 19*li.* 12*s*; to Clere the joyner for
worke in the Divinity Schole, 60*li.*; to Edmund Smith for worke in the Divinity
Schole, 11*li.* 9*s.*'—Some changes were also made at St. Mary's: *Comp.
Vicecanc.* for 1668–69, 'for the dore and doreway into Adam Brome's chappell,
5*li.* 17*s.*'

Vol. II, p. 156, l. 1.—*Comp. Vicecanc.* for 1668–69: 'to Dr. Yerbury for his
expences in a journey to Salisbury when he was to attend the prince of Tuscany,
1*li.* 15*s*; to Mr. Sherwin for his journey to Cambridge, ⟨vol. ii. p. 155, line 4 from
foot⟩ he being sent to bring notice of the prince of Tuscany's intended journey
thither, 1*li.* 10*s*; for the King's works ⟨see vol. ii. p. 161, note 5⟩ and binding
them, being a present from the University to the prince of Tuscany, 4*li.* 5*s*; for
writing out the speeches and other entertainments of the prince, he desiring
to have copies of them, 1*li.* 10*s.*'—When Loggan's *Oxonia Illustrata* came out
a copy was sent to the prince. *Comp. Vicecanc.* for 1674–75, 'to Mr. Logan
for one of the Oxford Cutts in quires to be sent to the duke of Florence, 1*li.* 5*s*;
to Bartlett for the rich binding of the Oxford Antiquitys ⟨? Cutts⟩ for the duke
of Florence, 1*li.*' *Ibid.* for 1675–76, 'to Mr. Obadiah Walker for charges about
the duke of Florence his present and other things, 3*li.* 10*s* 10*d.*' See also
vol. ii. p. 323.—In July 1669 prince George of Denmark visited England and
the University sent him a present, not mentioned in Wood's Diary: *Comp.
Vicecanc.* for 1668–69, 'for binding a book to be presented to the prince of
Denmark, 16*s*; to Mr. James Allestree for King James his Workes presented
to the prince of Denmarke, 2*li.*'

Vol. II, p. 163, l. 23.—*Comp. Vicecanc.* for 1668–69, 'to the messinger who
brought the deed by which the Theater was given to the University, 2*li.*'

Vol. II, p. 165, l. 11.—*Comp. Vicecanc.* for 1668–69, 'for the messinger's expenses
to Worcester to bring hither the organ-maker against the Act, 14*s*; to the
organ-maker for his journey and worke in setting up the organ at the Act and
returning it, 12*li.*; to Robinson and the joyners for keeping the dores of the
Theater and St. Marie's at the Act, 2*li.* 19*s*; to Mr. Lowe for his expences at
the Act, 1*li.*'—Quaere, from whom this organ was borrowed? The passages
from Evelyn's Diary relating to this Act are printed in Quiller Couch's
Reminiscences of Oxford, pp. 29–32. It may be noted that the 'hedge of holly'
which Evelyn recommended was planted. *Comp. Vicecanc.* for 1670–71, 'paid
for hedging up the holly at the Theater, 13*s* 9*d.*' *Ibid.* for 1671–72, 'for
mending the hedge of the Theater, 7*s* 10*d.*'

Vol. II, p. 165, l. 12.—The following are the entries in the University accounts
which relate to the building of the Sheldonian. *Comp. Vicecanc.* for 1662–63 :
'to Bird for the modell of the new Theatre to be erected, estimated by Dr. Wren,
10*li.*; to the smith for his work about it and for expedition, 1*li.* 1*s*; for tenements and land purchased of alderman Wright, senior, 165*li.* 10*s*, of alderman
Wright, junior, 80*li.*, of John Newman, 98*li.*, of Marsh, tayler, 34*li.*, of Mrs.
Southam, 80*li.*; to the towne for renewing Mrs. Southam's lease, 12*li.* 11*s* 4*d*;
to the towne a fine for a lease of 1000 yeers, 100*li.*; to the towne officers and
counsell for fees upon the renewing of the lease of 1000 yeers, 10*li.* 0*s* 10*d*; to
Mr. Hopkins for drawing the assignations of the leases, 2*li.*' *Comp. Vicecanc.*

for 1663–64 :—' to Dr. Wren a present of plate for his paines about the modell of the Theater, by appoyntment of the delegates, 6*li.* 17*s* 6*d*; for sending the modell to London and bringing it back, 8*s* 6*d*; to Frogley for worke about clearing the Theater ground, 8*li.* 9*s*; to Sir George Stonehouse his wood-man for 1813 foot of timber at 9*d* a foot with 3*li.* 1*s* for his fee, 71*li.* 7*s* 9*d*; to Frogley for carriage of it, 15*li.* 10*s*; to John Boys for 2944 foot of timber and carriage at 12*d* per foot, 147*li.* 4*s*.' And see *supra*, p. 68.—In MS. Rawl. J. (fol.) 13, folios 25, 27, is a paper formerly CCCXCIV in some MS. of Wood's, not in Wood's handwriting, but dated by him ' die Veneris 9 Julii 1669,' containing (fol. 25) a programme of the exercises in the Act, and (fol. 27) the following account of the proceedings at the opening of the Theatre :—' On the Friday morning preceding the Act, a Convocation was called in the Theater; the cause of which being by the Vicechancellor ⟨John Fell⟩ declared to be the taking possession thereof and to receive that gift which was so large as to receive both the University and the whole assembly of strangers there so solemnly convened, he gave to the Register ⟨Benjamin Cooper⟩ the charter of donation, willing him to read it. Which being accordingly don, the Vicechancellor proceded to declare that the munificent founder had taken care to endow his benefaction and to that end had given the summe of 2000*li.* to be employed in buying lands, whose revenue might in all future times support the fabrick, and the surplusage to be applied to the encouragement of the learned presse there set up. The Vicechancellor having produced his Grace's letter which specified the aforesaid gift, he proceeded to signify to the University that, whereas they had bin for a long time wholy employed in receiving benefits, it would now be seasonable for them to make a returne at least of acknowledgement and thanks. After which he spake to the Orator (Robert South) to read the letter of thanks which he had prepared. Which the Orator having don, the Vicechancellor askt the suffrages of the house; and they approving what was written and ordering it to be sent, he again spake to the Orator that in the Universitie's name he should make a publick recognition of the benefits they had received. Upon which he proceeded to celebrate the benefaction in a copious oration. Which being ended, the degree of Master of Arts was given to several young noble men, students in the University; the ceremony of which being finisht, the Convocation was dismist.

In the afternoon the Theater being filled with strangers of all sorts and the several ranks of graduats and scholars (who were seated according to their respective conditions), at the entrance of the Vicechancellor and Doctors loud musick having solemnely sounded, and silence being made, the Superior Bedell in Law ⟨Samuel Clarke⟩ proclamed the opening of the Encenia in the following words . . .'—The rest of the paper is missing.

Vol. II, p. 168, l. 9 from foot.—*Comp. Vicecanc.* for 1668–69 : ' for a silver box for the seale of the Chancellor's patent, 1*li.* 5*s* ; for gold twist for the Chancellor's patent, 6*s*; to Mr. Ball for writing the chancellor's patent and entering the new statutes, 2*li.* 5*s* 10*d*; to the servants at Exeter house for their paines at the admission of the Chancellor, 1*li.* ; for the journey of the Vice-Chancellor, 8 Doctors, and the 2 proctors, at 3*li.*, 13 Masters at 2*li.* each, for the Register, five bedells, and the verger at 1*li.* 10*s* each, 69*li.* 10*s* ; for carriage of a trunk with the insignia and other necessaries for the University at the admission of the Chancellor, and for the carrier's stay in London a night extraordinary to bring them back, 1*li.* 10*s*.'

Vol. II, p. 171, l. 6 from foot.—*Comp. Vicecanc.* 1668–69, ' the charge of printing 500 copies of the verses on the Queen mother, and paper, 18*li.* 6*s*; the binders,

5*li.* 8*s*; the mercer's bill for velvett, sarsenett, and strings for the book on the Queen mother, 8*li.* 4*s*.'

Vol. II, p. 189, l. 2 from foot.—*Comp. Vicecanc.* for 1669–70, 'to Mr. Wood for his copie of the history of the University, by order of the delegats for printing, 100*li*.' In recompense for the work entailed by his carrying out the requests of the delegates, Wood received an additional payment of 50*li.* (see vol. ii. p. 296): *Comp. Vicecanc.* for 1674–75, 'to Mr. Anthony Wood upon the account of his booke, by order of the delegats, 50*li*.' The Press repaid the University the 100*li.*, but not the 50*li.* : *Comp. Vicecanc.* for 1673–74, 'recept. pro exemplari Historiae Universitatis, 100*li*.'

Vol. II, p. 198, note 2.—*Comp. Vicecanc.* for 1669–70, 'Barnes the bookebinder's bill for the verses, 10*li.* 18*s*; to Barnes for ⟨printing⟩ verse-books on Madam, 5*li.* 3*s* 6*d*; to Henry Hall for printing two sheets of the said verses, 13*s*; to Mr. Vicechancellor's servant for his journey with the verses on Madam, 3*li.* ; to Mr. Fifield for velvett for the verses, 13*li.* 11*s*; to John Holder for velvett for the verses, 1*li.* 19*s* 6*d*; given to the printers for their expedition in printing the verses upon the death of Madam, 5*s* ; to Nixon for stitching 24 bookes of verses, 4*s*.'

Vol. II, p. 207, l. 6.—*Comp. Vicecanc.* for 1670–71, 'for torches to attend the prince of Orange at his comeing to the University, 6*li.* 16*s* ; to the messenger that brought the expresse from my lord Arlington, 1*li.* 1*s* ; to the Register for two diplomas sent to the prince of Orange his chaplaines, 2*li.*' *Ibid.* for 1671–72, 'to Mr. Scott for the King's works presented to the prince of Orange, 8*li.* 10*s*.'

Vol. II, p. 214, l. 7.—*Comp. Vicecanc. pro Scholis* for 1639–40 :—'for repaireing the battlements of the Schooles blowne downe in the great wind, 1*li.* 1*s*.'

Vol. II, p. 218, l. 6.—*Comp. Vicecanc.* for 1672–73, 'to Mr. James for writing Dr. Gibbs his diploma and for vellam, 1*li.* 17*s* 6*d*; a silver box and gold twist for the seal, 2*li.* 4*s* 8*d*.'

Vol. II, p. 219, l. 5 from foot.—*Comp. Vicecanc.* for 1670–71, 'to Mr. Davis for his expences and journey to London with the verses on the dutchess of Yorke, 5*li.* 12*s* ; for sarcenett and stringes upon the same account, 5*li.* 5*s* ; to Mr. Barnes for binding the verses on the dutchess of Yorke 4*li.* 13*s*; Mr. Bennett's bill for printing ⟨ ? these verses⟩, 31*li.* 1*s*.'

Vol. II, p. 223, l. 10.—*Comp. Vicecanc.* for 1670–71, 'to Mr. Smith, organ-maker, 100*li.* ; for writing the conveiances of purchase, 2*li.* 10*s*; for painting the organ, 10*li.* ; paid the organ maker for his journey, 4*li.*; paid for carriage of the organ, 1*li.* 8*s* 6*d*.'

Vol. II, p. 225, l. 4.—*Comp. Vicecanc.* for 1670–71, 'to Mr. Lowe and the musick for their services at the Act, 5*li*.'

Vol. II, p. 241, l. 13 from foot.—*Comp. Vicecanc.* for 1671–72, 'given for the reliefe of those who were hurt by the fire at St. Aldat's and for a reward to those that laboured, 10*li*.'

Vol. II, p. 248, l. 6.—*Comp. Vicecanc.* for 1671–72, 'to John Hall for printing programma's and the ode for the Act, 1*li.* 2*s* 6*d*.'

Vol. II, p. 265, l. 6 from foot.—*Comp. Vicecanc.* for 1672–73, 'to the gentleman that presented the bookes given by the lord Fairfax, 10*li.* ; to two porters for removing of them, 2*s* ; to the porter for bringing Dr. Casaubon's MSS., 1*s*.'

Vol. II, p. 266, l. 12.—*Comp. Vicecanc.* for 1672–73, 'to Mr. Lowe and the musick for their service at the Act, 3*li.* 19*s* 4*d*; to Mr. Lock for composing the ode, 5*li*.'

Vol. II, p. 268, l. 10.—*Comp. Vicecanc.* for 1674-75, 'to Mr. Bernard for his journey to view Mr. Thayr's MSS., 1*li.* 16*s*.'

Vol. II, p. 275, note 2.—The true date seems to be 1664. *Comp. Vicecanc.* for 1663-64 : 'to one that presented the lady Newcastle's bookes, 10*s*,' i.e. to the messenger who brought the present to Oxford.

Vol. II, p. 280, l. 5 from foot.—His goods were nominally forfeit to the University. *Comp. Vicecanc.* for 1673-74, 'recept. de bonis cujusdam Dani, felonis de se, 2*s* 6*d*.'

Vol. II, p. 289, l. 3 from foot.—*Comp. Vicecanc.* for 1673-74, '17 copies of the History of the University of royall paper richly bound, 46*li.* 15*s* ; kept for the University's use 15 copies of royall paper, 30*li*.' Although the copies which Wood received were ordinary size (*ibid.* 'for 14 copies delivered to the author by Mr. Vicechancellor's order, 15*li.* 15*s* ") they were so numerous that Wood was very liberally treated.—Next year the University bought a large number of ordinary copies of the book, so as to have at hand to make presents of it : *Comp. Vicecanc.* for 1674-75, '100 copies of the History of the University, 100*li*.' In the same way with Loggan's *Oxonia Illustrata* (when, as I suspect, the stock began to run short) : *Comp. Vicecanc.* for 1688-89, 'to Mr. David Logan for 50 bookes of Cutts of the College and Halls, 50*li*.'

Vol. II, p. 307, l. 11 from foot.—*Comp. Vicecanc.* for 1677-78, 'for the defect in the collection of a gratuity for Dr. Fabricius, 4*li.* 12*s* 10*d*,' i.e. the University made up the sum collected from the Colleges to the sum promised. It is possible that he is the person mentioned in *Comp. Vicecanc.* for 1674-75, 'to a Palatinate gentleman recommended by Dr. Pocock, &c., 1*li*.'—Several other foreigners about this time had alms from the University : *Comp. Vicecanc.* for 1673-74, 'to a French gentleman recommended by the bishops of Oxford and Rochester, by consent of the heads of Houses, 2*li*.' *Ibid.* for 1674-75, 'to an Irishman recommended by the Chancellor, 1*li.* ; to an Armenian priest by consent of the heads of houses, 10*li.* ; to two Transylvanian scholars, 1*li.* 15*s*.' *Ibid.* for 1675-76, 'given to father Nicholas Wafions, a Greek priest, 1*li*.'

Vol. II, p. 312, note 4.—The Rev. J. T. Fowler suggests that the expression may be a reminiscence of the Prayer Book Versions of Psm. 141, verse 6.

Vol. II, p. 313, note 3.—In the life of Loggan in the Dict. Nat. Biograph. vol. xxxiv. p. 88, this note is misconstrued to mean that Loggan had a house in Holywell ; the reference is, of course, to the printer Lichfield.

Vol. II, p. 316, l. 21.—Dr. Marshall died 18 Apr. 1685 (vol. iii. p. 138). Some delay seems to have occurred in transferring the books to the Bodleian. *Comp. Vicecanc.* for 1689-90, 'to Dr. Marshall's servant for his paines about his master's bookes given to the University library, 5*s*.'

Vol. II, p. 323, l. 15.—*Comp. Vicecanc.* for 1675-76, 'contribution for the fire at Northampton to make up 450*li.* collection, 8*li.* 16*s* 6*d*.'

Vol. II, p. 323, note 9.—*Comp. Vicecanc.* for 1674-75, 'for the rich binding of severall Catalogues of the Library presented to his Majestie, duke of Yorke, Lord Treasurer, and other great persons, 15*li.* 8*s* 6*d* ; for sending two Catalogues to Hevelius and mounsieur Justellus, 6*s*.'—For Johannes Hevelius, see vol. i. p. 165 ; Macray's *Annals of the Bodleian*, p. 134. For Henry Justell, see Macray, l. c. p. 143. *Comp. Vicecanc.* for 1674-75, 'to Mr. James for writing Dr. Justellus his diploma and for velam, 1*li.* 10*s* 5*d* ; for a silver box and gold braid for the seale of the diploma, 1*li.* 7*s* ; paid for letters from mounsier

Justellus, 3*s* 6*d*; to Mr. Logan for one of the Oxford Cutts in quires to be sent to mounsier Justellus, 1*li.* 5*s*; to Bartlett for the rich binding of one of the Oxford Cutts for mounsier Justellus, 17*s* 6*d.*'

Vol. II, p. 341, l. 11.—His goods were forfeited to the University. *Comp. Vicecanc.* for 1675–76, 'recept. de pecuniis cujusdam scholaris Coll. Baliol., felonis de se, 1*li.*'

Vol. II, p. 344, l. 11.—*Comp. Vicecanc.* for 1675–76, 'to Robinson the mason for the stone, worke and setting up of 40 pinnacles about St. Marie's church at 2*li.* 10*s* per pinnacle, 100*li.*; more to him for anticks and other worke about Adam Brome's chappell, 5*li.* 2*s* 4*d*; to Thomas Wood for carving of anticks, &c., 4*li.* 14*s* 4*d.*'

Vol. II, p. 354, l. 4.—*Comp. Vicecanc.* for 1676–77, 'recept. de bonis et possessionibus Ricardi Imings, clerici, felonis de se, 314*li.* 3*s.*' This was one of the few cases in which the University retained more than a nominal part of the suicide's goods: after paying Imings' debts and the expenses of realising the estate, the University had a balance of a little over 120*li.* The items are : ' To William Symms of Ham in the county of Wilts for a debt due to him by bond from Mr. Imings, by decree of the delegates, 110*li.*; to Mr. Haslewood, apothecary, for a debt due to him by Mr. Imings, by the same order, 58*li.*; to Magd. Coll. for 1½ years rent for Mr. Imings' houses, 1*li.* 16*s*; to one for writing 16 large acquittances indented and sealed for two quarters' rent of Mr. Imings' houses, 5*s*; to Mr. Imings' 4 tenants according to what he constantly allowed them at Christmas, 5*s*; for a copy of the decree whereby Mr. Imings was judged felo de se, from the town-clerke, 1*s*; to Mr. Davis the bedell for his care and paines in the buisinesse of Mr. Imings, by order of the delegates, 15*li.*; to Mr. Cooper, Register of the University, for his paines in the business of Mr. Imings, 5*li.*'

Vol. II, p. 358, l. 6.—The University smoothed the way for this gift, and made some acknowledgement of it after the donor's death. *Comp. Vicecanc.* for 1675–76, 'presented to Mr. Francis Junius by consent of the delegats, 40*li.*' *Ibid.* for 1676–77, 'to Mr. Obadiah Walker for his expences to South-Leigh to bring Mr. Junius's books and MSS., 5*li.* 5*s* 10*d*; presented to Mr. Francis Junius by consent of the delegates, 40*li.*' *Ibid.* for 1678–79, 'paid Dr. Vossius at the delivery of the letters of Mr. Junius, the picture of Mr. Junius, and a mathematicall instrument, 100*li.*; to the rector of Lincolne College for his journey to Windsor and coach-hire, 5*li.* 13*s* 10*d*; to Dr. Allestree for carriage of Mr. Junius' letters, 1*li.* 6*s* 6*d*; a journey to London for the letters of Mr. Junius, 2*li.* 8*s.*' *Ibid.* for 1679–80, 'to Mr. ⟨Thomas⟩ Wood, stone-cutter, for Mr. Junius' monument, 20*li.*'

Vol. II, p. 358, l. 13.—The *Comp. Vicecanc.* for 1675–76 supplies us with the sums paid by the University: it is not stated whether the work was all on the interior, or whether any part was on the spire. ' To Mr. Bernard Smith for the organ at St. Marie's, 275*li.*; to Thomas Wood, stone-cutter, for laying the marble in St. Marie's church (which marble was the gift of Dr. Ralph Bathurst, vicechancellor), 87*li.* 19*s* 2*d*; to George Lowe for stone for paving in St. Marie's church, 11*li.* 17*s*; to Thomas Holding for 2257 foot of oaken bords used in St. Marie's, 18*li.*; to Robinson the mason for the reparations of St. Marie's church by severall bills, 176*li.* 0*s* 4*d*; to Frogley the carpenter for worke done similiter, 164*li.* 16*s* 2*d*; to Gardiner and Frogley for joyner's worke similiter, 107*li.* 0*s* 1*d*; to Job Dew the playsterer for worke done similiter, 28*li.* 11*s* 9*d.*'—Some of the work must have been on the steeple, because of the entry in *Comp. Vicecanc.* for

1676–77, 'to the parish of St. Marie's for hurt done to their chymes by the workmen, 2*li.* 10*s.*' Entries about the steeple are; *Comp. Vicecanc.* for 1666–67, 'to the churchwardens of St. Marie's,—a gift towards the repair of their steeple, 20*li.*' *Ibid.* for 1692–93, 'to St. Marie's parish towards the repairs of their steeple, 20*li.*'—There are several minor notices about repairs of the organ: and then these following. *Comp. Vicecanc.* for 1686–87, 'to Mr. Smith for repairing and adding new stops to the organ at St. Marie's, 26*li.* 17*s* 6*d*; to Thomas Minne for shashes and frames to the organ at St. Marie's, 5*li.* 5*s.*' *Ibid.* for 1690–91, 'to Mr. Smith for altering the organ at St. Marie's, 20*li.*' *Ibid.* for 1692–93, 'to Mr. Smith for altering the organ at St. Marie's, 40*li.*'

Vol. II, p. 358, note 5.—The note at the foot of the *Comp. Vicecanc.* for 1675–76 records the fact, but does not state the amount of Dr. Bathurst's gift. 'Memorandum that the marble for the pavement of St. Marie's church was given to the University at the sole cost and charge of Dr. Ralph Bathurst, vicechancellor.'

Vol. II, p. 363, l. 1.—See Macray's *Annals of the Bodleian*, p. 428. He had recently been a donor to the Bodleian. *Comp. Vicecanc.* for 1675–76, 'a gratuity to the duke of Newcastle's servant for a booke sent to the library, 1*li.* 1*s* 6*d.*'

Vol. II, p. 379, l. 2.—*Comp. Vicecanc.* for 1676–77, 'given to the archbishop of Samos by consent of the delegates, 10*li.*; to Mr. Rhodocanaces, the Grecian, by the same consent, 5*li.*'

Vol. II, p. 379, l. 4 from foot.—*Comp. Vicecanc.* for 1677–78, 'recept. pro bonis Bradshaw, scholaris C. C. C., felonis, 10*s.*'

Vol. II, p. 386, l. 3.—*Comp. Vicecanc.* for 1676–77, 'for entertainment of the Chancellor by severall bills approved by the delegates, 206*li.* 3*s* 3½*d*; for other expenses upon the same account brought in after the former were passed, 5*li.* 9*s.*'

Vol. II, p. 387, l. 13 from foot.—*Ibid.*, 'to 12 men at the Theater for attendance at the Chancellor's Act, 2*li.* 8*s*; to Mr. Lowe, the organist, for expenses at the Theater about the musick service at the same time, 10*s* 6*d*; to Mr. Lowe for the Act service, 3*li.*'

Vol. II, p. 387, l. 5 from foot.—*Ibid.*, 'for severall books richly bound and presented to the Chancellor and other persons of quality and also for the exercises of the Encaenia and Chancellor's Act, as by John Hall's bill appeareth, 29*li.* 13*s* 6*d.*'

Vol. II, p. 395, l. 2 from foot.—Among the Communion-plate of S. Michael's Church, Oxford, is a silver salver with the inscription :—

'Jan. 12, 1672.

The gift of James Deane to ye Parish-church of S^t. Michael's in Oxon to be kept by the Church-wardens for ye use of ye Parishoners at ye celebration of ye Holy Communion in that Church.'

Vol. II, p. 421, l. 8.—There were heavy expenses incurred in this suit. *Comp. Vicecanc.* for 1677–78, 'to Dr. Wallis for four bills, viz, in Mich. Hil. East. and Trin. terms, for feeing of counsell, journeys to London, &c. about the night-watch in the case of Barbor against Dodwell, 49*li.* 9*s*; to sergeant Richard Holloway, 2*li.*; to my owne (i. e. the Vicechancellor's) journey and men to London to prosecute the same cause against Dodwell in Trin. term 1678, 7*li.* 10*s* 4*d*; to Mr. Hopkins, the University solicitor, in Hil., East. and Trin. terms, in the same cause, 64*li.* 2*s* 3*d.*'

Vol. II, p. 424, l. 3.—*Comp. Vicecanc.* for 1678–79, 'given to the soldiers for helpe in quenching the fire that happened in the night at the request of the heads of houses, 5*li.*'—Another item in connexion with the troops is : *ibid.*, 'fire and candle for the soldiers the last winter, the city bearing the same proportion of charge, 9*li.* 10*s* 10*d.*'—The University volunteers seem to have been on the point of mustering : *ibid.*, ' for cleansing the University arms, 2*li.* 2*s* 6*d*; four barrells of gunpowder weighing sixty pound remaining to the use of the University, 2*li.* 13*s.*'

Vol. II, p. 451, note 9.—Insert 'stools' for 'shoots' in the text.

Vol. II, p. 483, l. 15.—*Comp. Vicecanc.* for 1679–80, 'to the under-sheriffe towards his extraordinary charges in hanging Thomas Hovell in chaines, 5*li.*'

Vol. II, p. 485, l. 13.—*Comp. Vicecanc.* for 1680–81, 'recept. pro lapidibus Aulae S*t* Edmundi venditis, 10*li.*' *Ibid.* 1681–82, 'recept. de lapidibus Collegio Novo venditis, 3*li.* 10*s.*'—These stones, I assume, were the materials of the old chapel, now pulled down.

Vol. II, p. 495, l. 10.—*Comp. Vicecanc.* for 1679–80, 'expended when the prince Palatine was in Oxford, 3*li.* 7*s* ; for a bible presented to him, 4*li.* 10*s.*'

Vol. II, p. 518, l. 8, and p. 520, line 1.—*Comp. Vicecanc.* for 1680–81, 'to the ringers when the duke of Hannover was here, 5*s* ; to the ringers when his majestie was here, 5*s* ; to Mr. Ingram for binding bookes presented to the king, queen, and duke of Hannover, 7*li.* 7*s* ; to Mr. Pitts for bookes presented to their majesties, duke of Hannover, &c., 10*li.*' See vol. ii. p. 528.

Vol. II, p. 550, l. 20.—Another copy of the verses in question is extant. In MS. Tanner 466, no. 64 is 'Libel on John Lambe, by Henry Thomas of Univ. Coll.'

Vol. II, p. 559, l. 13.—The rectory of Waddesdon was divided into three 'portions.' John Ellis in 1660 held the third portion ; on 14 Oct. 1661 he was appointed also to the first portion ; and, in addition, on 26 Oct. 1661, he was appointed to the second portion. He died 8 Nov. 1681.—Lipscomb's Buckinghamshire.

Vol. II, p. 564, l. 16.—*Comp. Vicecanc.* for 1660–61 :—' to Mr. Dolling, musick reader last year, 3*li.* ; to Mr. Torlesse, musick reader this year, 3*li.*' Edmund Dolling, M.A. Ch. Ch., 22 June 1658.

Vol. III, p. 4, l. 4.—His goods were forfeited to the University. *Comp. Vicecanc.* for 1681–82, 'recept. pro bonis Ricardi Souch, felonis de se, 2*li.*'

Vol. III, p. 10, l. 2 from foot.—This proposal seems to have been in prospect for some time. *Comp. Vicecanc.* for 1677–78, 'to sergeant Holloway for advice about the intended donation of a catechetick lecture, 2*li.*'

Vol. III, p. 11, l. 10 from foot.—One of these exiles seems to have settled in Oxford for some years and to have received help from the Colleges and the University. *Comp. Vicecanc.* for 1683–4, 'to make up M*nsr*. le Roy's collection from the University, 1*li.* 1*s.*' So also in 1685–86, 1687–88, and 1688–89. In 1689–90 the sum is 1*li.* 1*s* 6*d.*

Vol. III, p. 18, l. 11.—*Comp. Vicecanc.* for 1681–82, 'for bookes presented and other expenses when the Morocco ambassador was at Oxford, 20*li.* ; Logan's Cutts of the University, 2 copies, 2*li.* 8*s.*'

Vol. III, p. 25, l. 7 from foot.—*Comp. Vicecanc.* for 1681–82, 'to Sir Richard Holloway for a copy of the city of Oxon's charter, and for a copy of the plea of the city to the *Quo Warranto*, 5*li.* 14*s.*'

Vol. III, p. 39, l. 4.—*Comp. Vicecanc.* for 1682–83, 'to Cully the bargman for carriage of the goods in the Ashmolean Repository, 9*li.* 6*s.*'

Vol. III, p. 42, l. 14.—*Comp. Vicecanc.* for 1682–83, 'to Mr. Hugh Ellis, ⟨the University solicitor,⟩ for prosecuting the rioters, &c. 14*li.* 3*s* 8*d.*'

Vol. III, p. 46, l. 2 from foot.—In MS. Rawl. Poet. 19 are 25 lines spoken on this occasion before the Duchess of York and the Princess Anne, beginning :—

> 'These loyal tumults, this officious noise
> Does ill express our duty, well our joys'—

but the paper gives no indication of where the verses were spoken.

Vol. III, p. 52, l. 5 from foot.—*Comp. Vicecanc.* for 1682–1683, in 'entertainment of their royall highnesses, bookes presented to them, &c., 124*li.* 11*s* 6*d.*'

Vol. III, p. 54, l. 4 from foot.—It appears from the Vicechancellor's accounts that the Ashmolean had cost (in round figures) the University, when it was opened, 4530*li.*; viz. for site, 560*li.*; for structure, 3800*li.*; for the clerk of the works, 80*li.*; for fittings, 90*li.* The following are the items. *The site :—Comp. Vicecanc.* for 1678–79, 'for the lease of severall tenements near the Theater purchased for the building a roome for Dr. Ashmole's rarities, and the writings for it, 326*li.* 9*s* 6*d.*' *Ibid.* for 1681–82, 'to Dr. Bury for ground bought of Exeter College for Dr. Ashmole's Repository, 80*li.*; to the city of Oxford for the purchase of the ground whereon the Repository is built, 150*li.*; to Mr. sargeant Holloway for drawing up the writings for purchasing the fee simple of the ground where the Repository is built, 4*li.* 10*s.*' *The structure :—Comp. Vicecanc.* for 1678–79, 'spent in building Musaeum Ashmol., 467*li.* 10*s* 3*d.*' *Ibid.* for 1679–80, to Mr. ⟨Thomas⟩ Wood, ⟨stone-cutter,⟩ severall bills towards the building of the same, 1006*li.* 0*s* 11¾*d*; to Mr. ⟨Richard⟩ Frogley ⟨carpenter⟩ severall bills upon the same account, 216*li.* 13*s* 8*d*; to William Young for iron-worke about the same, 27*li.* 7*s* 7*d.*' *Ibid.* for 1680–81, 'to Young the smith for worke about the Repository, 13*li.* 7*s* 6*d*; to Mr. Wood by severall bills, 343*li.* 8*s* 2½*d*; to Frogley the carpenter, 71*li.* 8*s* 1*d*; to Bernard Rawlins for leading the Repository, 140*li.*; to removing rubbish from the Repository, 4*li.* 13*s* 3*d*; to John Dewe for work about the Repository, 1*li.* 1*s* 6*d*; to Mr. Wood for sawes and other utinsills about the Repository, 6*li.* 14*s* 7*d.*' *Ibid.* for 1681–82, 'to Young the smith for worke about the Repository, 53*li.* 3*s* 1*d*; to Mr. Wood, 440*li.* 5*s* 0½*d*; to Richard Frogley and William Longe, carpenters, 242*li.* 3*s* 3*d*; to Bernard Rawlins for lead for the Repository, 51*li.*; to Dew, the plaisterer, for worke there, 62*li.* 0*s* 7*d*; to Bernard Rawlins for glasing the Repository, 21*li.* 12*s*; to Wild the joyner for wainscott for Dr. Ashmole's Repository, 60*li.*; to Mr. Hawkins for painting the Repository, 4*li.* 16*s* 8*d.*' *Ibid.* for 1682–83, to Young, the smith, for casements, the iron gate, and other workes, 13*li.* 6*s* 8*d*; to Burrows the ironmonger for locks and bolts for the Repository, 39*li.* 11*s* 5*d*; to Mr. Wood the stonecutter, for worke done at the Laboratory, 106*li.* 17*s* 4*d*; to Thomas Robinson the mason for worke done there, 31*li.* 2*s* 4*d*; to Job Dew the plaisterer for worke done there, 1*li.* 16*s*; to William Longe and John White carpenters similiter, 23*li.* 14*s* 7*d*; to John Wild joyner for wainscott in the Repository, 110*li.*; to Bernard Rawlins for leading &c. similiter, 150*li.* 4*s* 8*d*; to Mr. Wood the stone-cutter for the stain'd marble chimney-piece and for pitching-worke before the Repository, 18*li.* 19*s* 6*d*; to Job Dew plaisterer for more worke similiter, 1*li.* 4*s* 7*d*; to John Wild for wainscott in the Repository, 10*li.*; to Bernard Rawlins for leading-worke similiter, 40*li.*; to John White carpenter, for worke in the Laboratory, 11*li.* 7*s* 6*d.*' *Ibid.* for

1683-84, 'to Bernard Rawlins for arrears for leading the Repository, 23*li*. 2*s* 6*d*.' *The clerk of the works* (Henry Davis, bailiff of the University) 'for overseeing the worke at Dr. Ashmole's Repository' in 1679-80, 30*li*.; in 1680-81, 20*li*., in 1681-82, 20*li*.; in 1682-83, 10*li*. *The fittings*:—*Comp. Vicecanc.* for 1682-83, 'to Mynne the joyner for a case of drawers for the Repository, 6*li*.; to Wild the joyner, for another case similiter, 6*li*.; for locks and keys for the Repository bought by Dr. Plott, 7*li*. 3*s* 8*d*; payd Dr. Plott what he had layd out for some vessells &c. for the laboratory 17*li*. 9*s*; to Mr. Christopher White for tin, copper, and iron vessells similiter, 44*li*. 17*s*.' *Ibid*. for 1683-84, 'to Minne the joyner for a cabinett, and other worke, &c., 11*li*. 1*s* 3*d*.'—*Comp. Vicecanc.* for 1689-90, 'payd Dr. Plott, for 3 cabinetts of drawers, 15*li*.'

Vol. III, p. 63, l. 18.—*Comp. Vicecanc.* for 1693-94, 'for a new coate to the bedle of beggers, 1*li*. 15*s* 9*d*.' *Ibid*. for 1695-96, 'a coate for the bedell of beggers, 2*li*.'

Vol. III, p. 64, l. 17.—*Comp. Vicecanc.* for 1682-83, 'expenses in writing the University censure and decree, &c. 3*li*. 4*s* 10*d*.'

Vol. III, p. 67, l. 16.—The charter of 3 James I (1605), as confirmed by the charter of 16 Charles II (1664). Ogle's *Royal Letters to Oxford*, pp. 228, 271.

Vol. III, p. 71, note. *For* 1684 *read* 1664.

Vol. III, p. 80, l. 1:—In MS. Rawl. E 8 fol. 58 is 'Mr. Foxe's sermon at my consecration.'

Vol. III, p. 84, l. 7 from foot.—There is a drawing of a 'monteith' in John Watney's 'Some Account of the Hospital of St. Thomas of Acon and of the plate of the Mercer's Company,' Lond. 1892, p. 230.

Vol. III, p. 86, l. 10.—This reservation in favour of the Crown was inserted in the new charter, issued 29 Sept. 1684; Ogle's *Royal Letters to Oxford*, p. 280.

Vol. III, p. 87, l. 4 from foot.—This legacy was considerable, but occasioned some trouble in realising. *Comp. Vicecanc.* for 1683-84, 'recept. pro parte legati dominae Meriton, 400*li*.; expens. to Mr. John Holloway for his paines in soliciting buisinesse about Mrs. Meriton's legacy, 5*li*. 7*s* 6*d*.' *Ibid*. for 1684-85, 'recept. pro parte legati dominae Meriton, 200*li*.; given to Mr. justice Holloway's servant at the receipt of Mrs. Meriton's legacy, 5*s*; paid Mr. Holloway for services done to the University about Mrs. Meriton's legacy, ordered by the delegates of last year, 5*li*. 7*s* 6*d*: paid to Mr. Holloway for his further pains in the buisinesse of Mrs. Meriton's legacy, 5*li*. 7*s* 6*d*.' *Ibid*. for 1685-86, 'recept. pro parte legati dominae Meriton, 46*li*. 18*s* 4*d*.' *Ibid*. for 1686-67, 'recept. pro proficuis legati dominae Meriton 2° Aprilis 1687 debit., 7*li*. 10*s*.' *Ibid*. for 1687-88, 'recept. pro residuo legati dominae Meriton, 80*li*.; et pro proficuis ejusdem, 5*li*.; expens. to Mr. John Holloway for his paines about Mrs. Meriton's legacy, 3*li*. 4*s* 6*d*.'

Vol. III, p. 90, note 5.—*Comp. Vicecanc.* for 1684-85, 'paid for a letter in the behalfe of Dr. Lister from the duke of Ormonde, 1*li*. 6*s* 6*d*; paid for a silver box for Dr. Lister's diploma, 17*s* 6*d*.' It was much later before Lister's books came to the University. *Comp. Vicecanc.* for 1694-95, 'for carriage of bookes from Dr. Lister, 2*s* 6*d*.' *Ibid*. for 1695-96, 'for carriage of Dr. Lister's bookes and trunks, 4*s* 6*d*.'

Vol. III, p. 95, l. 4.—*Comp. Vicecanc.* for 1684-85, 'paid Dr. Wallis for two journeys to London in the suit about printing, 23*li*. 13*s*; paid Dr. Wallis what he gave a counseller for advice in the buisinesse of the stationers, 1*li*. 1*s* 6*d*.'

Vol. III, p. 107, l. 2.—*Comp. Vicecanc.* for 1683-84, 'expended in waiting on the duke of Ormonde in coach hire, &c., 8*li*. 17*s* 6*d*.'

Vol. III, p. 112, l. 13.—See the text of it in Ogle's *Royal Letters to Oxford,* pp. 280–294. The University had taken steps to protect its own privileges; *Comp. Vicecanc.* for 1683–84, ' to Mr. attorney-general in the business of the city charter, 43*li.*' See vol. iii. p. 89, line 14 from foot.

Vol. III, p. 120, note 2.—*Comp. Vicecanc.* for 1674–75, ' towards the removing and rebuilding of Balliol College wall, by consent of the heads of houses, 10*li.*' *Ibid.* for 1575–76, ' to Baliol College towards their high-way and wall, by consent of the delegats, 10*li.*'

Vol. III, p. 133, l. 4.—*Comp. Vicecanc.* for 1684–85, 'the expenses in waiting on his Majestie with the address, 85*li.* 12*s* ; for binding the bookes of verses presented to their Majesties upon the death of his late Majestie, 11*li.* 16*s*; paid Mr. Nicholls of Ch. Ch. for writing two copies of the University address, 1*li.* ; paid John Hall, the printer, for the University verses and binding of statute-books, 16*li.* 2*s* 9*d.*'

Vol. III, p. 138, last line.—The Rev. J. T. Fowler suggests that ' winus quills ' is a corruption for ' wine of squills.' This was a common medicine for cough or cold, and an over-dose would cause vomiting.

Vol. III, p. 145, l. 4.—*Comput. Vicecanc.* for 1684–85 :—' paid for the carriage of arms from Windsor and Mr. Sherwin's journey, 13*li.* 12*s*; paid Mr. Bush for what he expended upon the gentlemen that guarded the armes from Windsor, 40*li.* 18*s*; paid Mr. George Thompson for what he paid the twelve men that guarded the ammunition from London, 13*li.* 7*s*; paid Moor the carrier for the carriage of the ammunition, 11*li.* ; paid Mr. Sherwin for his journey upon that account and expenses at the Tower and elswhere, 2*li.* 19*s* 6*d*; paid Upton and Scrivener, gunsmiths, for cleansing the armes, 10*li.* 0*s* 5*d* ; paid Mr. chancellor Alworth what he had given to the trumpeters of the University troope, 2*li.* 3*s*; to Hawkins the painter for worke in the Repository ⟨i. e. the Ashmolean⟩ and the 3ᵈ captain's colours, 5*li.* 17*s* 4*d*; paid Baker for two drums, 3*li.* ; paid my lord bishop of Oxford for what he laid out for 4 foot-colours, 7*li.* 3*s* 10*d*; paid Mr. Sherwin's bill for bringing in the armes to the Schooles, &c., 17*s* 6*d.*' *Comp. Vicecanc.* for 1685–86, ' paid for cleansing and carrying his Majesties armes and ammunition to Windsor, 36*li.* 14*s* 6*d*; given to Mr. Sherwin as a gratuity for his care about the armes, by order of the *stati delegati,* 10*li.*'—The ' bearing of arms ' of June–July 1685 thus cost the University over 150*li.*

Vol. III, p. 146, note 5.—I now conjecture that the ' pile or ' is a mistake, and that it should be a crown partly cut off by the canton.

Vol. III, p. 151, l. 7 from foot.—MS. Ballard 48 fol. 74 has a rough contemporary plan of the ground at Sedgemoor.

Vol. III, p. 177, l. 6, and note 1.—*For* 168⅘ *read* 168⅚.

Vol. III, p. 180, l. 1.—*Comp. Vicecanc.* for 1685–86, ' expended when Mr. Vice-chancellor and the doctors went to wait upon our Chancellor at Cornbury, 4*li.* 13*s.*'

Vol. III, p. 181, l. 8.—Notes of the family of Ellis from the registers of Waddesdon, Bucks, will be found in Bodl. MS. Top. Bucks. d. 2, fol. 29. Philip Ellis was bapt. 12 Sept. 1652; Welbore Ellis ⟨vol. iii. p. 331⟩ was born 10 Apr. and bapt. 14 Apr. 1661.

Vol. III, p. 189, l. 11.—*Comp. Vicecanc.* for 1685–86, ' recept. pro . . . Johannis Roswell . . . legato Principali et Magistris Aul. Magd., 20*li.*'

Vol. III, p. 202, l. 18.—It had been for some time decayed, and had been once or twice partially repaired. *Comp. Vicecanc.* for 1667–68, ' for wyer over the conduit at Carfax, 6*li.* 7*s.*' *Ibid.* for 1668–69, ' to Mr. Rawlins for glazing worke done at

St. Marie's and plummer's worke at the conduit, 6*li*. 14*s* 7*d*; the smith's bill for worke at St. Marie's and the conduit at Carfax, 2*li*. 10*s*.' *Ibid.* for 1673–74, 'to Thomas Robinson the mason for worke done about the conduit and for the carriage of 8 loads of stone, 13*li*. 16*s* 5*d*.' The extent of the present repairs is obvious both from the amount spent and the time taken in their execution. *Comp. Vicecanc.* for 1686–87, 'to Thomas Robinson, mason, severall bills for the conduit at Carfax, 110*li*. 1*s* 5*d*; to John White for worke at the conduit at Carfax, 3*li*. 18*s* 4*d*; to the smith for worke at the conduit, 5*li*. 19*s* 7*d*.' *Ibid.* for 1687–88, 'to Mr. Robinson, mason, ⟨Charles⟩ Cole, the plummer, Mr. Wood, stonecutter, Young, the smith, and John White, carpenter, severall bills about the conduit, 112*li*. 10*s* 10*d*.'

Vol. III, p. 214, l. 6 from foot.—*Comp. Vicecanc.* for 1686–87, 'to Eldrich for 3 coaches to goe twice to Cornbury to waite upon the Chancellor, 7*li*.; expended those two journies, 4*li*. 12*s*.'

Vol. III, p. 224, note 6.—*Comp. Vicecanc.* for 1687–88, 'to John Hall for printing severall orders about his Majestie's reception, 2*li*. 5*s*.'

Vol. III, p. 225, l. 1.—*Comp. Vicecanc.* for 1668–69, 'to Mr. Delgardno, who lived in the house now the little print-house, for relinquishing his interest, for his remove, and materialls left by him, 15*li*. 6*s* 6*d*.'

Vol. III, p. 225, l. 13.—In MS. Ballard 48 fol. 77 is 'The speech spoken in the councell chamber 16 Sept. 168[7] by William Wright, deputy-recorder, being the day on which the Right Hon. the earl of Abingdon took the place of High Steward.'

Vol. III, p. 227, l. 9.—*Comp. Vicecanc.* for 1687–88, 'to a messinger sent to Woodstock to give notice of the king's comeing, 5*s*; to a messinger sent to Windsor and Cyrencestre, 1*li*. 15*s*.'

Vol. III, p 234, l. 7.—*Comp. Vicecanc.* for 1687–88, 'for a bible and gloves presented to the king at his coming to the University, 21*li*. 15*s*; for Mr. Cutler's journey to London when he bought gloves for the king, 1*li*. 14*s* 6*d*.'

Vol. III, p. 236, l. 14 from foot.—*Comp. Vicecanc.* for 1687–88, 'for the whole charge of the banquett and entertainment which the University made for the king in the Library, 213*li*. 15*s* 5*d*; to the yeomen of the guard when the king was in Oxford, 10*li*. 15*s*.'

Vol. III, p. 269, l. 22.—*Comp. Vicecanc.* for 1687–88, 'to Dr. Halton for his journey to London, 2*li*. 10*s*; to Dr. Wallis for two journeys to London, 23*li*.; for Mr. Vicechancellor a journey to London and stay there 3 weeks, 10*li*. 10*s*.' *Ibid.* for 1688–89, 'to Dr. Wallis for his journey to London about the *Quo Warranto*, 8*li*.'

Vol. III, p. 272, l. 18.—*Comp. Vicecanc.* for 1687–88, 'to Mr. Hall for printing the verses upon the birth of the Prince of Wales, 30*li*. 13*s* 6*d*; to Mr. Cox for his journey to London with the said verses, 5*li*. 7*s*.'

Vol. III, p. 272, l. 2 from foot.—*Comp. Vicecanc.* for 1687–88, 'to Henry Edwards for a journey to the duke of Ormond in Dorsettshire, 2*li*. 2*s* 6*d*';—perhaps to announce to the young duke his election to the Chancellorship.

Vol. III, p. 275, l. 4.—*Comp. Vicecanc.* for 1687–88: 'for the journey of the Vice-Chancellor to London, 8 doctors, Mr. Finch (warden of All Souls Coll.) and the two Proctors at 3*li*. each, 12 Masters of Arts at 2*li*. each, and the Register and 5 bedells at 1*li*. 10*s* each, attending the admission of the duke of Ormond our Chancellor elect, 69*li*.; given to the duke of Ormond's servants at the same time, 21*li*. 10*s*; for a silver box for the seale of the Chancellor's patent and for velame, ribbon, and engrossing of the said patent, 1*li.* 16*s*; to Bartlett for carriage of the chest,&c., to London and back again when the Chancellor was installed, 1*li.* 10*s.*'

Vol. III, p. 277, 1. 3 from foot.—See the text of it in Ogle's *Royal Letters to Oxford*, pp. 295–314.

Vol. III, p. 278, 1. 22.—The University made preparations against attack. *Comp. Vicecanc.* for 1688–89, 'to Thomas Wells, gunsmith, for mending and cleansing the University armes, 6*li.* 2*s* 6*d*; to Thomas Wells, gunsmith, for matts to lay the University musquetts in, 1*li.* 1*s.*' *Ibid.* for 1689–90, 'to the gunsmith, 7*li.* 2*s* 6*d.*' The University had therefore an armoury of its own.

Vol. III, p. 279, 1. 2 from foot.—*Comp. Vicecanc.* for 1688–89, 'to the ringers at St. Marie's when the bishop of Winton came to towne, 10*s.*'

Vol. III, p. 287.—It is odd that Wood's Diary should be silent about the passing through Oxford of the Princess Anne and her husband Prince George of Denmark, and the entertainment provided for them by the University. See the references about it in Queen Anne in *Dict. Nat. Biograph.* The entries in the *Comp. Vicecanc.* for 1688–89 are as follows :—'for the entertainment of the Prince and Princess of Denmarke at Christ Church, 327*li.* 3*s* 2*d*; to Mr. Crosse for wood most of which was spent at Christ Church (in bonfires, probably) at the Prince's entertainment, 14*li.* 8*s*; to the innkeepers of the Eagle-and-Child and Greyhound for the Prince of Denmark's guards, 1*li.* 16*s.*'

Vol. III, p. 291, 1. 13.—*Comp. Vicecanc.* for 1688–89, 'for writing (i. e. a fair copy of) the University letter sent to the Prince of Orange, 2*s* 6*d*; to Henry Edwards for his journey to London with the said letter, 3*li.*; to Ferriman for his journey to Abingdon when the Prince of Orange was there, 5*s.*'

Vol. III, p. 299, 1. 1.—*Comp. Vicecanc.* for 1688–89, 'to the ringers at St. Marie's on the Thanksgiving day for the Prince and Princess of Orange, 10*s.*'

Vol. III, p. 301, note 5.—*Comp. Vicecanc.* for 1688–89; 'to the ringers at St. Marie's on Coronation day, 10*s*; to Mr. Goodson, organist, for his Theatre Music on the coronation day, 3*li.*; to Mr. Hall, printer, for printing and binding the verses on the King and Queen, 42*li.* 15*s*; to Henry Edwards for his journey to London with the University poeme, 2*li.* 5*s* 6*d*; for the journey of the Vice-Chancellor to London and 3 doctors at 3*li.* each, the two Proctors and 4 Masters of Arts at 2*li.* apiece, to wait on their majesties with the University poeme, 24*li.*' *Ibid.* 'to Mr. Hall, printer, for two large bibles of imperial paper, and for binding 8 bookes of (Loggan's) College Cutts, 19*li.* 10*s.*'—these no doubt were presented to 'their majesties' and courtiers at the same time.

Vol. III, p. 311, 1. 5.—Wood's papers and notes about Sir George Mackenzie are in MS. Ballard 48 fol. 64. Among them is a Latin life of Mackenzie written for Wood by some Scotch friend.

Vol. III, p. 322, 1. 4.—*Comp. Vicecanc.* for 1689–90, 'to Sir Thomas Clarges and Mr. Harrington about our bill in Parliament, 29*li.* 2*s* 6*d*: for Dr. Wallis his journey to London, 12*li.* 4*s* 6*d*; for Mr. Harrington's journey to London, his attendance, and stay there 6 weeks about our bill in Parliament, 15*li.*' *Ibid.* for 1690–91, 'to Mr. Harrington for his care and paines in soliciting our bill in Parliament severall weeks, 5*li.* 7*s* 6*d.*' *Ibid.* for 1691–92, 'to Mr. Harrington for soliciting our bill in Parliament, 5*li.* 7*s* 6*d.*' *Ibid.* for 1692–93, 'to Mr. Harrington for the prosecution of our bill in parliament, 30*li.*'

Vol. III, p. 326, note 3.—*Comp. Vicecanc.* for 1689–90: 'for a silver box for the seal of Dr. Walker's diploma, 1*li.* 3*s* 6*d.*'

Vol. III, p. 328, l. 27.—His goods were forfeit to the University. *Comp. Vice-canc.* 1689–90 'recept. de bonis . . . Goodere, felonis de se, 1*li.* 15*s.*'

Vol. III, p. 333, l. 8 from foot.—*Comp. Vicecanc.* for 1689–90, 'to the ringers at St. Marie's on July 8, (1690), 5*s.*'

Vol. III, p. 334, l. 7.—*Comp. Vicecanc.* for 1689–90 : 'for Mr. Ashmole's entertainment at the Musaeum, 84*li.* 11*s* 6*d.*' *Ibid.* for 1691–92, 'to Mr. Lloyd ⟨E. Lhuyd⟩, keeper of the Musaeum, for his journey to London, upon the account of Mr. Ashmole's legacy, 4*li.* ; for boxes and carriage of Mr. Ashmole's bookes from London to Oxford, 7*li.* 7*s* 6*d.*' *Ibid.* for 1692–93, 'to William Jones for making a catalogue of bookes in the Musaeum, 5*li.* ; for binding of bookes for the Musaeum, 5*li.* 18*s* 6*d.*' *Ibid.* for 1694–95, 'to Mr. Lloyd for his expenses to London in quest of a person suspected of having robbed the Musaeum, by order of the delegates, 4*li.* 10*s.*' *Ibid.* for 1695–96, 'to Mr. Lloyd for taking a Catalogue of the bookes in the Musaeum, 10*li.* 10*s,*' perhaps for the 1697 Catalogue of MSS.

Vol. III, p. 339, note 3.—*Comp. Vicecanc.* for 1690–91 : 'to the bookebinders for binding the verses printed upon the king's returne from Ireland, 23*li.* 15*s* ; to Mr. White for velvett to bind severall of the said bookes with gold fringe strings, 5*li.* 15*s* 11*d* ; to Mr. Sherwin for his journey to London to present these bookes, 3*li.* 2*s.*'

Vol. III, p. 342, note 5.—These books were bought by the Curators of the Bodleian with the Library money. They were not a special purchase by the University, and therefore there is no entry about them in the University accounts. It was different with the large accessions of Oriental MSS. which were added to the Library in 1691–92. *Comp. Vicecanc.* for 1691–92 : 'for Dr. Pococke's Oriental MSS., 800*li.* ; for carriage of the said bookes to the Library and to the person that brought the Jewish whipp, 12*s* ; to Dr. Huntingdon for Oriental MSS., 752*li.* 10*s* ; to Dr. Hyde for Oriental MSS., 50*li.*' *Ibid.* for 1692–93, 'to Dr. Edwards due to him for Dr. Huntington's Oriental MSS., 366*li.* 8*s* 8*d.*' The figures in Mr. Macray's *Annals of the Bodleian* are therefore much under the truth. *Comp. Vicecanc.* for 1690–91, 'to Mr. ⟨David⟩ Logan for his booke containing a description of the University of Cambridge, 3*li.* 4*s* 6*d.*'—These large purchases perhaps explain the unwillingness of the authorities to buy from Wood at this time, see vol. iii, p. 404.—An earlier purchase may be noted here : *Comp. Vicecanc.* for 1683–84, 'to Sir Timothy Tyrrell for Oriental MSS., 50*li.*'

Vol. III, p. 358, l. 24.—The Rev. J. T. Fowler corrects this. Read 'pillow-beere,' i. e. pillow-case.

Vol. III, p. 387, l. 1.—*Comp. Vicecanc.* for 1691–92, 'charges in discovering and apprehending of White very notorious for severall burglaries in the University, 10*li.* ; to two messingers sent to Stafford on the same occasion, 3*li.* 6*s* 6*d.*'

Vol. III, p. 390, l. 26.—*Comp. Vicecanc.* for 1691–92, 'to the ringers at St. Marie's for the victory at sea, 5*s.*'

Vol. III, p. 394, note 2.—In Twyne's time this belief was current ; the following lines are found in Twyne XXII. p. 440 :—

> 'En tibi crux vel Avis, nunc accipe quam tibi mavis :
> Utraque poena gravis, sed foemina pessima quavis,'

with the note—'to a man condemned to be hanged, whom a wench Avis would have begged for her husband ; and he chose rather to be hanged.'

Vol. III, p. 394, l. 3 from foot.—*Comp. Vicecanc.* for 1692–93, 'to Mr. Loggan the University engraver, 5*li.*,' paid, after 4 Oct. 1692, ? to his executors. The statutable fee was 1*li.* per annum, and it had latterly been paid once in five years.

Vol. III, p. 394, last line. Michael Burghers, frequently called Burgess, was at this time in constant employment in the University, and now succeeded Loggan as 'the University engraver.' *Comp. Vicecanc.* for 1685–86, 'paid Mr. Burgesse for ingraving plates for Dr. Morison's 2d. volume, 2*li.* 11*s.*' *Ibid.* for 1686–87, 'paid Mr. Burgess for ingraving plates for Dr. Morrison 2d. volume, 9*li.* 17*s* 6*d.*' *Ibid.* for 1687–88, 'to Michael Burghers for engraving 4 plates for Dr. Morison's booke, 10*li.* 13*s.*' *Ibid.* for 1688–89, 'to Mr. Burghers for engraving 10 plates for Dr. Morison's booke, 27*li.* 18*s.*' *Ibid.* for 1689–90, 'to Mr. Burghers for engraving one copper-plate for plants, 2*li.* 18*s.*' *Ibid.* for 1691–92, 'to Mr. Burghers for 5 plates and cutts for Dr. Hyde's booke, 8*li.* 12*s*; to Mr. Burghers the ingraver for cutts for Dr. Wallis booke, 7*li.* 11*s.*' *Ibid.* for 1692–93, 'to Mr. Burghers for cutts for Dr. Wallis his booke, 38*li.* 6*s.*' *Ibid.* for 1693–94, 'to Mr. Burghers, the University engraver, 38*li.* 18*s* 2*d.*' *Ibid.* for 1694–95, 'to Mr. Burgher the engraver for cutts for Dr. Wallis's booke and for the Almanack, 33*li.* 5*s* 2*d.*'

Vol. III, p. 399, l. 14. Her goods were (nominally) forfeited to the University. *Comp. Vicecanc.* for 1691–92, 'recept. pro bonis Eliz. Simmons, felonis de se, 1*s.*'

Vol. III, p. 405, l. 5.—*Comp. Vicecanc.* for 1692–93, 'to the ringers at St. Marie's, Oct. 21, 1692, 5*s.*'

Vol. III, p. 415, l. 12 from foot.—*Comp. Vicecanc.* for 1692–93, 'to the ringers at St. Marie's upon the king's inauguration day, 5*s.*'

Vol. III, p. 426, l. 22.—*Comp. Vicecanc.* for 1692–93, 'to Mr. Addison, bursar of Queen's College, for the carriage of the bishop of Lincoln's books given to the University, 23*li.*' See Macray's *Annals of the Bodleian*, p. 157. Dr. Barlow had also bequeathed a piece of plate: *Comp. Vicecanc.* for 1691–92, 'given to him that brought the bishop of Lincoln's plate, 1*s.*'—The 'other' books would include the large collections of Oriental MSS., *supra*, p. 83.—The shelving was paid for by the University. *Comp. Vicecanc.* for 1692–93: 'to Young, the smith, for worke at St. Marie's, *the Library*, and Physick Garden, 33*li.* 7*s*; the mason's bill for worke at St. Marie's, and *the Library*, 3*li.* 13*s*; the carpenter's bill for worke at *the Library*, Schools, and St. Marie's, 95*li.* 16*s* 8*d*; the plumber's bill for worke at the Musaeum, *Library*, Physick Garden, 52*li.* 2*s* 4*d*; to Roger Judge for 760 foot of bords used in the Library, 4*li.* 15*s.*'

Vol. III, p. 427, note 4.—*Comp. Vicecanc.* for 1692–93, 'to the music for their performance at the Act and other times, 7*li.* 10*s*; to Mr. Estwick for entertaining the music, 6*li.* 5*s.*'

Vol. III, p. 449, l. 9.—Edward Prince; see Ogle's *Royal Letters to Oxford*, p. 321.

Vol. III, p. 471, l. 6 from foot.—A large amount of building took place at the Physic Garden 1692–96. *Comp. Vicecanc.* for 1692–93, 'to Robinson the mason for worke done at the Physick Garden, 39*li.* 5*s* 9*d*; to the plaisterer similiter, 15*li.* 1*s* 9*d*; the carpenter's bill for work done at the Physick Garden, 42*li.* 15*s* 5*d.*' *Ibid.* for 1693–94, 'to Young the smith for worke at the Physick Garden, 14*li.*; to Robinson the mason for worke at the Physick Garden, 122*li.* 8*s* 11*d.*' *Ibid.* for 1694–95, 'to Mr. Vanderstene, carver, for worke done at the Physick Garden, 26*li.* 10*s*; to Robinson the mason for worke at the Physick Garden, printing-house and St. Marie's, 54*li.* 8*s* 1*d*; to ⟨George⟩ Smith the carpenter for worke done at the Physick Garden, the printing-house, and St. Marie's, 56*li*. 9*s* 7*d*; to the plaisterer for worke at the printing-house and Physick Garden, 13*li*. 7*s*; to the painters for worke done in the Physick Garden, 11*li*. 7*s* 6*d*.' *Ibid*. for 1695–96, ' to the mason for worke at the Physick Garden, 33*li*. 13*s* 7*d*; to John Vandersteen, carver, for cutting the earle of Danby's statue and for other worke at the Physick Garden, 7*li*. 12*s*.'

Vol. III, p. 477, l. 31.—*Comp. Vicecanc.* for 1694–95, 'paid the charges of the delegates that went to London with the addresse to his Majestie, 94*li*. 15*s* 4*d*; for the bookes then presented, 26*li*. 5*s* 7*d*.'

Vol. III, p. 479, l. 3 from foot.—The town-clerkship was the subject of further litigation, Samuel Thurston being finally confirmed in the office in 1700, and Job Slatford ejected. See Ogle's *Royal Letters to Oxford*, pp. 317–325.

Vol. III, p. 489, l. 4 from foot.— *Comp. Vicecanc.* for 1695–96, ' to the musick upon a Thanksgiving day, 5*li*. 17*s*.'

Vol. III, p. 490, l. 11.—A note by Wood, in MS. Rawl. J. (fol.) 13, fol. 26, states more fully the information given—' 25 Sept. 1695, met with Mr. Harbin[1], a non-juror, at Dr. Charlot's and he told me he had seen a book of John Skelton's which I mention not ⟨in the *Athenae*⟩ and therein saith he was bred in Cambridge—quaere. Harbin, a nonjurer, somtimes chaplain to the bishop of Ely, in grey cloathes.' Perhaps George Harbin, B.A. Eman., 1686.

Vol. III, p. 495, l. 8 from foot.—*Comp. Vicecanc.* for 1695–96, ' payd severall bills for the entertainment of his Majestie and the duke of Ormond our Chancellor in Nov. 1695, 499*li*. 19*s*; for severall things lost at the entertainment of his Majestie, 1*li*. 10*s*.'

Vol. III, p. 495, l. 5 from foot.—*Comp. Vicecanc.* for 1695–96, ' to the Stamp Office for degrees conferred upon the nobilitie and gentry when the King and our Chancellor were last at Oxford, 18*li*. 2*s*.'

Vol. III, p. 501, l. 14.—*Comp. Vicecanc.* for 1695–96, ' to Frogley the joyner for worke done in the Musaeum and for wainscott and shelves for Mr. Wood's books, 31*li*. 4*s* 2*d*; to Thompson the bookbinder for binding of Statute Books ⟨? issued to persons matriculating⟩ and severall of Mr. Wood's bookes for the Musaeum, 16*li*. 16*s* 10*d*.' *Ibid.* for 1696–97, ' to Mr. Lloyd for taking a Catalogue of Mr. Wood's bookes given to the Musaeum, 6*li*. 12*s*.'

1 ' Harvey' corr. to ' Harbin.'

CATALOGUE

OF

THE MS. AUTHORITIES USED BY WOOD

IN HIS TREATISES ON OXFORD

AND CITED BY HIM IN HIS NOTES.

————+ +————

1. Aim and sources of this Catalogue.

THIS Catalogue seeks to identify, and to give the exact modern reference to, every MS. cited by Wood in his Annals of the University of Oxford as edited by Gutch and his Antiquities of the City of Oxford as edited by myself. In the great majority of instances this has been done: but many MSS. are described by Wood so vaguely that identification has proved impossible.

Wood's printed works are thus cited:—

Hist. = Historia et Antiquitates Univ. Oxon., 1674.

Ath. = Athenae Oxonienses, 1691–92.

Coll. or *Colleges* = The History and Antiquities of the Colleges and Halls in . . . . Oxford, edit. John Gutch, 1786.

Fasti = Appendix . . . . containing Fasti Oxonienses, edit. Gutch, 1790.

Annals = The History and Antiquities of the University of Oxford, edit. Gutch, 1792–96.

City = Survey of the Antiquities of the City of Oxford, edit. Andrew Clark, 1889–90.

Life = The Life and Times of Anthony Wood, edit. Clark, 1891–94.

————————

O. C. = [Edward Bernard's] 1697 Catal. MSS. Angl. et Hibern.

Wood himself, in a treatise (*O. C.* 8561), now bound up with others in Wood MS. E. 4 (see *Life*, ii. 301), has a substantial contribution towards a Catalogue of this kind. I have tried to get the modern references for all the MSS. described there, and have added notices of all MSS. on the same subjects which I have seen referred to in the many MS. volumes of Collections by Wood perused by me during the last seven years. I have taken pains also to collect the quaint old marks by which Twyne, Langbaine, and Wood distinguished their own MS. volumes and volumes in the University Archives. These marks have been little known, and consequently references by them have so far been useless to scholars.

2. Arrangement of the Catalogue.

The documents and MSS. described are arranged under the following heads :—

  I. *Ecclesiastical*, comprising muniments and registers of—
    1. Religious Houses, paragraphs 3–57.
    2. Bishops' Sees, par. 58–65.
    3. Oxford city parishes, par. 66–80.
    4. Miscellanea, par. 81–84.
 II. *Academical*, comprising muniments and registers of—
    1. the University of Oxford, par. 85–130.
    2. the Colleges of Oxford, par. 131–151.
    3. Miscellanea, par. 152, 153.
III. *Civil*, comprising muniments and registers of—
    1. the national Record Offices, par. 154–170.
    2. the archives of the City of Oxford, par. 171–190.
    3. private owners, par. 191–194.
 IV. *Collections by Antiquaries*, having special reference to Oxford, par. 195–258.
  V. *Anthony Wood's Collections*, par. 259–280.
 VI. *Authors*, par. 281–518.
VII. *Anonymi and Miscellanea*, par. 519–526.

I. ECCLESIASTICAL RECORDS.

Muniments, etc., of Religious Houses.

3. Abingdon Abbey.

(i) *Liber vel registrum coenobii Abendonensis* : MS. Cotton Claud. C. 9. It begins *Mons Abendone* ; is 'a fair large folio, written temp. Henr. III.'

Printed (along with the next volume) in Rolls Series, 1858.

(ii) *Alter liber sive registrum*; MS. Cotton Claud. B. 6.   It begins, imperfectly, —*lam inhabitantibus*; 'a very fair large folio, excellently written in a large hand tempore Ric. I.'   It belonged once to lord Fenton [Thomas Erskine, viscount Fenton in 1615, afterwards earl of Kelly, obiit 1639].

Printed in Rolls Series, 1858.

Both volumes are frequently distinctly cited in *Annals, Colleges, City*: but occasionally the reference leaves it uncertain which volume is intended.   Brian Twyne's excerpts, especially from (i), are found in Twyne XXII and XXIV; Richard James' excerpts in MS. Ric. James, vol. 8 and vol. 24; Wood also apparently had '*Collections from Abingdon Abbey book*' (see *City*, i. 571), but I have not come across them.

(iii) *The third register* contained 'pleas, grants, dimissions, et alia negotia' of the abbey; was 'divided into *particulae*'; and was shown by — Bury of Culham to Twyne, who made excerpts from it (Twyne XXII. 155, 183–188, 335).

Wood cites it several times in *Annals, Fasti, City*; but only from Twyne's notes.   Wood never saw the MS. itself, nor ascertained what had become of it.

(iv) *Rotulus chronicularis coenobii Abendonensis*, in parchment, containing a short account of the foundation of the abbey, a list of abbots to Peter de Hanney (1361), with some notes intermixed concerning the affairs of the abbey.   The beginning was 'imperfect through time and use'; the first words decipherable were *sicut . . . careret consortio . . . apud Sewkesham convocato*.   At the end of the roll was a statement that it was compiled from 'the landbook' of the monastery, from the martyrology, from the white book composed by abbot John Glostinevyle, and Thomas Marcham's chronicle.

Wood cites this roll frequently in *Annals, Fasti, City*; but I have nowhere found any statement of where he found it.   Wood's excerpts from this 'rotular chronicle' are found in Wood MS. D. 11 (i), pp. 65–72: these excerpts are cited in *City*, i. 327.

(v) *Chronica Abendoniae in bibl. publ. Cantab.*, init. 'Anno a plenitudine temporis': Cambr. Univ. library, Dd. ii. 5.

Cited occasionally in *Annals*, e.g. i. 221, 233, 267; but it was known to Wood only through the excerpts of Twyne (Twyne XXI. 237, XXIV. 616), and Richard James (MS. Ric. James 17, p. 78).

(vi) Miscellaneous papers relating to Abingdon Abbey, in MS. Cotton Jul. A. 9; MS. Cotton Aug. 2; Claud. B. 6 and C. 9; Vitell. A. 13.

(vii) *Excerptiones Simonis de primis fundatoribus coenobii Abendoniae*, et de abbatibus Abendoniae, quae etiam bona quaeve mala fecerint; MS. Cotton Vitell. A. 13 nu. 6.

(viii) A leiger-book in Christ's Hospital in Abingdon, written by

Francis Little, sometimes mayor of Abingdon, 20 Sept. 1627.—
Excerpts from this are found in Wood MS. D. 11 (i), p. 73.

Twyne XXII. 372 cites 'a small parchment roll of Mr. Little of
Abingdon.'

(ix) Twyne III. 493–8 cites a parchment-roll 'in the hands of
Mr. Carpenter of Oxford,' which contained 'Computa omnium
. . . terrarum et tenementorum' of the Abbey.—Wood cites this
from Twyne's excerpt, in *City*, ii. 36.

(x) *Alius rotulus abbatum*, cited in *Annals*, i. 131, I cannot identify.

(xi) Wood's *Catalogue of the abbots of Abingdon*, among the Fulman
MSS. in C.C.C. Oxon.

4. Alberbury Priory.

Papers in All Souls College treasury: see C. T. Martin's Catalogue
of the Archives of All Souls (1877).

5. Barnwell Priory.

(i) Richard James (MS. Ric. James 17, p. 138) has excerpts from
a *Registrum Barnwellense* MS. 'in the hands of Robert Hagar.'

(ii) He has also (MS. Ric. James 7, p. 23) excerpts from an
Arundel MS., *Annales prioratus de Barnwell* (Christ to Henry III).

(iii) *Processus monasterii Bernwellensis* de visitatione Univ. Cantab.
per episcopum Ely, 1431: Twyne XXII. 66–70: copied from MS.
Cotton Faust. C. 3 fol. 153 and a MS. in the State Papers Office.

6. Brackley Hospital.

Excerpts from 'liber Hospitalis de Brackley' in Magd. Coll.
archives are found in Wood MS. D. 18 (*O. C.* 8563), and are cited
in *City*, i. 527, *Life*, ii. 34.

7. Bruton Abbey.

Chronicon sive Annales monasterii de Bruton, com. Somerset: MS.
Cotton Otho A. 4.   See Twyne XXI. 10, Twyne XXIV. 8–13.

Cited several times in *Annals*, *Fasti*, *City*.   Wood several times
gives the name as **Brinton**, as I suppose from misreading in Twyne's
vague handwriting the spelling Bruiton.   There seems also confusion
between the references to this MS. and the Burton annals.

8. Burton Abbey.

Annales monasterii Burton super Trent in com. Stafford: MS.
Cotton Vespas. E. 3. See Twyne VII. 346, XXI. 10, 15, 76.
Printed in Rolls Series (*Annales Monastici*, I), 1864.

Cited frequently in *Annals*: but see par. 7.

Richard James' excerpts, made while the MS. was still in lord Paget's hands, are found in MS. Ric. James 10, pp. 82–86 and MS. Ric. James 25, p. 163. Wood's excerpts from it are found in MS. Bodl. 594.

These annals were printed by William Fulman, Oxford 1684. Wood cites this edition as 'Annals of Burton which I have,' *Annals*, i. 257.

9. Canterbury, S. Augustine's Abbey.

(i) *Liber vel registrum monasterii beati Augustini Cantuar.*: in the Exchequer at Westminster. Twyne XXIV. 244, 245.

Cited in *Annals*, i. 398, 419.

(ii) *Cartulary*: MS. Cotton Faust. A. 1.

(iii) *The 'Red book' of Canterbury*: MS. Cotton Claud. D. 10.

(iv) Twyne XXI. 179 cites *Antiquum registrum Sti. Augustini Cantuar.* 'quod habuit Mr. Johannes Harus.'

(v) MS. Ric. James 8, p. 164 cites a *register of S. Augustine's Canterbury* in Thomas Allen's library.

(vi) Twyne XXI. 407 cites *Thomae de Thanet* (vixit 1272) *matricula* scil. de variis chartis, libertatibus ac privilegiis et possessionibus monasterii S. Augustini Cantuar.: init.— 'In nomine domini nostri Jesu Christi notum sit omnibus tam praesentibus quam posteris quod ego Adhelbertus,' &c. This MS. was given by John Twyne of Canterbury (Brian Twyne's grandfather) to Thomas Smyth, high-customer of London; and was afterwards in the hands of Richard James of C. C. C. Oxford: a thick 4to with a red cover.

(vii) *Chronicon monasterii S. Augustini* ab adventu Augustini ad annum 1406: MS. Cotton Vitell. E. 14: transcribed by Arthur Agard from a Trin. Coll. Cambr. MS.

(viii) MS. Ric. James 8, p. 289 has excerpts from (Sprott's, or Thorne's) *Vitae abbatum S. Augustini Cantuar.*: MS. Cotton Tiber. A. 9, foll. 105–180.

(ix) William Lambard's Collections *ex annalibus ecclesiae S. Augustini Cantuar. incerti authoris*: MS. Cotton Vespas. A. 5.

(x) Wood in Wood MS. E. 4 refers to MS. Cotton Vitell. D. 9, a MS. since destroyed in the Cottonian fire.

(xi) MS. Ric. James 17, p. 9 has excerpts from *Annales S. Augustini Cantuar.*: MS. Corp. Chr. Cambr. 301.

10. Canterbury Cathedral.

Known to Wood only through Twyne's notes or through communications from William Somner.

(i) Registrum ecclesiae Cantuarensis de rebus extra Cantium : cited in *City*, ii. 276, 282, 283, *Colleges*, p. 651.

(ii) Registrum in domo consistorii eccles. Cantuar.: cited in *Annals*, i. 482.

(iii) Twyne II. 286–337 has excerpts from a 'Registrum Cantuar. in le audit house of the church of Canterbury, titul. *Oxon*.'

11. Cirencester Abbey.

(i) *Liber Cirencestriae* : see Leland's Itinerar. vol. ii. Cited in *Fasti*, p. 5 and *City*, ii. 162.

Wood knew it only from some excerpts made by Henry Jackson, which he himself had (Wood MS. D. 18): it is these that are alluded to in *City*, ii. 162, note 2.

12. Croyland Abbey.

(i) *Historia coenobii Croylandiensis* vel Crowlandensis per Ingulphum et Petrum Blesensem et alios continuata ad tempora Henrici VII: MS. Cotton Otho B. 13 (a MS. destroyed in the fire). See Hardy, Descriptive Catalogue, ii. 58, 128.

Ric. James has excerpts, MS. Ric. James 18, p. 79, from *Chronicon Ingulphi* in the Cottonian library, p. 82, from the *continuator Ingulphi*, p. 100, from *Historia Croyland. de tempore Ric. I.*

(ii) MS. Digb. 42 contains excerpts from Croyland Chronicles about Oxford and Cambridge.

12*. Dorchester Abbey : *Life*, i. 278.

13. Dunstable Priory.

Chronicon sive annales Dunstapliae: MS. Cotton Tiber. A. 10 fol. 5–59: printed 1864 in Rolls Series (*Annales Monastici*, vol. ii). See Twyne XXIII. 641.

Cited frequently in *Annals*.

Ric. James has excerpts from it MS. Ric. James 10, pp. 133–136.

14. Durham Abbey and Cathedral.

Twyne, as on the foundation of C. C. C. Oxon, inveighs against Durham (Twyne II. 34 b) :—' O thou ungratefull Durrham that hast no monument or writinge left of Richard Foxe our founder.' It may serve to show the thoroughness with which Wood used up the hints supplied by Twyne if we note that he turns to account (*City*, i. 533) even this expression of feeling.

(i) [Simeon[1] of Durham's] *de exordio et progressu ecclesiae cathedralis . . . Dunelm.*

Found in various recensions, in MS. Cotton Faust. A. 5, foll. 24–96,

---

[1] Wood cites this as Turgot's : *Annals*, i. 29.

Vespas. A. 6, foll. 62–91, Titus A. 2, foll. 5–86, and in MS. Laud Misc. 700 (*O. C.* 1579) and 748 (*O. C.* 1339). Printed in Twysden's *Decem Scriptores* 1652, and in Rolls Series (1882).

Twyne's excerpts, from the Cottonian MSS., are found in Twyne XXIV. 53–57, Twyne XXIII. 497, Twyne XXI. 117, and in Wood MS. D. 32, p. 307.

MS. Laud H. 76, i. e. *O. C.* 1339, is cited in *City*, ii. 22, 266.

(ii) Turgot's *Historia ecclesiae Dunelmensis.*

MS. Cotton Titus A. 2 and Vespas. A. 6.

Printed in Twysden, as above.

The frequent citations of *Hist. eccles. Dunelm.* in *Hist., Annals, Coll.,* probably refer vaguely to (i) and (ii), and also to (iii) and (iv). Also *Acta episc. Dunelm.* cited in *Coll.* p. 38.

(iii) Gaufridus, sacrista de Coldingham, *de statu ecclesiae Dunelm.*: MS. Cotton Titus A. 2, fol. 69; MS. Laud Misc. 700 (*O. C.* 1579,) fol. 82 ᵛ. Twyne XXIII. 497. Printed, with the following, in the Surtees Society's series 1839, from other MSS.

The Cottonian MS. is cited in *City*, ii. 264: the Laud MS. (MS. Laud L. 53 = *O. C.* 1579) is cited in *City*, ii. 264, 266, 267, &c.

(iv) Robertus de Greystanes, *continuatio status ecclesiae Dunelm.*: MS. Cotton Titus A. 2; MS. Laud Misc. 700 (*O. C.* 1579). See Twyne XXIII. 497.

(v) Reginaldus, monachus Dunelm., *de virtute et miraculis Cuthberti*: MS. Cotton Claud. D. 4, foll. 88–113: Twyne XXIV, 53.

(vi) Twyne XXI. 700 cites a *Liber MS. de statu eccles. Dunelm.* which was once in the possession of Dr. ⟨John⟩ Dee.

(vii) *Registrum diversarum litterarum de officio cancellariatus monachorum Dunelm. quondam Roberti de Longchester*: excerpts from it are found in Twyne II. 32–34, Twyne III. 573.

Cited in *Annals*, i. 426, 430, *City*, ii. 67.

Is this MS. Cotton Faust. A. 6, foll. 1–111?

(viii) *Variae epistolae de rebus ecclesiae Dunelm.*: cited in Twyne XXIV. 322 as in the hands of Robert Hegge of C. C. C. Oxon.

Cited in *City*, ii. 269.

(ix) *Reliquiae eccles. Dunelm.*: MS. Digb. 41.

(x) *Reliquiae eccles. Dunelm.*: excerpts from it in MS. Ric. James 2, part 2, pp. 129–131, who says it was in Robert Hegge's possession.— Cp. 'The legend of S. Cuthbert, with the antiquities of the church of Durham,' Lond. 1663 [1].

(xi) Wood in Wood MS. E. 4 refers to '*A discription of the antient monuments, rites and customes belonging to the monasticall church of Durham*, before the suppression; written 1597 [2]': printed in no. 15 in

---

[1] Wood's copy is Wood 216 (1).   [2] '1593,' in the Surtees volume.

the Surtees Society's publications. 'The ancient rites and monuments of the monastical and cathedral church of Durham . . .' published by John Davies of Kidwelly[1], Lond. 1672, pp. 164, was an edition, with considerable liberties, of the same MS.

(xii) *De antiquitate monasterii Dunelm.*: MS. Cotton Claud. D. 4. Cited in *Annals*, i. 154.

(xiii) *Registrum primum decani et capituli Dunelm.* Cited in *Hist.* ii. 71, *Coll.* p. 76.

(xiv) Twyne II. 34 cites *Repertorium quoddam* in the office of the dean and chapter of Durham.

15. Ely Cathedral.

(i) *History of Ely Church*, viz. de temporibus monachorum Ely, de temporibus episcoporum, &c.; init., 'Cum animadverterem excellentiam Eliensis ecclesiae'; MS. Laud Misc. 647.

Probably the MS. referred to in *Annals*, i. 65, 93.

(ii) *Episcoporum Eliensium historia*: MS. Laud Misc. 698.

(iii) *Registrum alterum de prioratu et episcopatu Eliensi*: incipit a tempore Edwardi I: initium 2^{di} folii 'A nostre seniour le roy et a son conseil,' &c.

Lent to Brian Twyne by Christopher Lacy, Twyne III. 457; and contained 'several things of Cambridge worth the noting.'

Cited in *Annals*, i. 93.

Wood never saw the volume: but has notes referring to MS. Cotton Domit. A. 15 fol. 7; MS. Cotton Titus A. 1 foll. 1–62; and MS. Cotton Vespas. A. 6 foll. 92–137, as possibly containing the same matter.

(iv) *Historia insulae Eliensis*: MS. Ric. James 10, pp. 148–155.

16. Evesham.

(i) *Chronicle*: made use of by John Leland. Cited in *City*, ii. 296.

(ii) Thomas Winchcombe's *Antiquities of Evesham Abbey*: cited in *City*, ii. 260: I assume, only from Leland.

---

[1] Wood's copy in Wood 216 (2), in which he says 'John Davis was not the author.' On the back of the title-page he writes:—'The private note of Dr. Thomas Barlow of Qu. Coll. concerning this book runs thus:—liber hic omnino apochryphus, μυσαρᾶς et legendae putidae plurimum, verae historiae (praxi et cultu monachorum superstitioso exceptis) parum habet adeo ut mirari subit inscitiam ejus qui edidit et negligentiam (veritati et ecclesiae Anglicanae damnosam) ejus qui praelo permisit.'

17. Eynsham Abbey.

(i) *Registrum chartarum et munimentorum* in Christ Church Treasury:
no. 341 in G. W. Kitchin's *Cat. of Ch. Ch. MSS.* (Oxford, 1867).

(ii) *Registrum alterum* in Ch. Ch. Treasury; no. 342 in Kitchin's
Cat.; containing inquisitions, terriers, and rentalls of the Abbey lands.

Twyne consulted both volumes by leave of Philip King, auditor of
Ch. Ch., Twyne II. 43, 44; Richard James also saw them (MS. Ric.
James 8, p. 6). Wood sometimes cites the former volume definitely
(e. g. 'liber magnus Einsham' in *City*, i. 406); but often it is not
plain from his reference which of the two is intended.

(iii) *Notae Einsham*, otherwise entitled *Collectiones ex libro Einsham*.

This is a volume of excerpts by Wood, Wood MS. D. 11 (2), pp. 1–29
being from (i), pp. 30, 31 being from (ii); (i) is also excerpted from
in Wood MS. C. 2, p. 1. Wood frequently refers to this volume, by
both titles, in *City*.

(iv) Survey of Eynsham Abbey lands in the Augmentations Court—
cited in *City*, i. 524.

A transcript (as I suppose) of this is now in MS. Tanner 416 fol.
101, having formerly been fol. 127 in an older volume.

(v) Wood's drawing of the ruins of Eynsham, in Wood MS. E. 1:
reproduced in *Life*, i. 228.

18. Glastonbury Abbey.

(i) *Glastonbury leiger-book* 'Secretum Abbatis'; once an Arundel
MS.; afterwards Ralph Sheldon's of Beoly: now MS. ab Ant. Wood, 1
(*O. C.* 8589). *Life*, iii. 342.

MS. Ric. James 26, p. 68 has some excerpts from it while still an
Arundel MS.

(ii) William of Malmsbury's *Antiquitates coenobii Glastoniensis:*
Twyne VII. 314, Twyne XXI. 829.

Cited frequently in *Annals*.

Wood (Wood MS. E. 4) confesses that he 'never saw this book:
onlie spoke from Twyn of him.' Twyne may have used MS. Cotton
Tiber. A. 5. There are also MSS. of it in Trin. Coll. Cambr. (referred
to by Gutch, *Annals*, i. 135).

(iii) Adam de Domerham's *Continuatio historiae coenobii Glastoniensis:*
Twyne XXI. 829.

The MS. is in Trin. Coll. Cambr. and was printed by Hearne in
1727.

(iv) Johannes, monachus Glaston., *de antiquitate ecclesiae Glaston.:*
MS. Bodl. 854 (*O. C.* 2613). Initium prologi 'de antiquitate vetuste

ecclesie beate Marie Glaston.': initium operis (on p. 7 of MS.) 'Universis patribus et fratribus suis in monasterio Glaston.'

Cited occasionally in *Annals*.

On p. 251 of this MS. Wood was delighted to find the writer speaking 'of King Alfred and his doings at Oxford—that, concilio . . . sancti Neoti abbatis, scholas publicas variarum artium apud Oxonias primus instituit.' Richard James has excerpts from it in MS. Ric. James 2, part 1, page 131 and in MS. Ric. James 25, p. 24. Old press-marks are MS. G. 2. 15 Th., MS. sup. Art. D. 14, MS. Arch. F. 14.

(v) MS. Ric. James 8, p. 29, cites *liber Glaston.*, 'in custodia Mri Kingman.'

(vi) MS. Laud Misc. 750 (*O. C.* 912) is *Chronicon Angliae Glas-toniense.*

19. Gloucester: S. Peter's Abbey.

(i) *Liber . . . de prima fundatione monasterii S. Petri Glouc.*: MS. Queen's Coll. Oxford, no. 367 in Coxe's Catal., formerly belonging to Henry Jackson: printed from this MS. in Rolls Series 1863. Another copy is MS. Cotton Domit. VIII, wrongly identified by Wood (*Life*, i. 460, note 1) with Jackson's MS.

Cited in *Annals, Fasti, Colleges, City*.

Henry Jackson's excerpts from it are found in Wood MS. D. 18; Brian Twyne's, in Twyne XXIV. 59, 60, 592, 602, 605; Richard James', in MS. Ric. James 8, p. 51.

(ii) *Liber de fundatione ecclesiae Glocestrensis*: cited in *City*, ii. 250, as a Cotton MS., perhaps Domit. VIII.

(iii) *Memoriale ecclesiae Gloucestriensis compendiarium*: Wood MS. B. 1 (*O. C.* 8572). Written, or at least transcribed, in 1608: 'Antonii à Vuood Oxon. A.D. 1661' on fly-leaf: printed, except the last 4 pp., in Dugdale's *Monasticon*.

(iv) *Chronica* ab origine gigantum in insula Albion olim habitantium quae nunc Anglia dicitur usque ad tempus regis Ric. II: et consequerentur *de abbatissis et abbatibus monasterii S. Petri Gloucestriae,* a tempore Osrici regis . . . usque ad regimen domini Walteri Froucestre abbatis: MS. in the hands of Henry Jackson, 'a preserver and lover of antiquities.' Excerpts in Twyne XXIII. 673, XXIV. 602.

Cited, from Twyne, in *Annals*, i. 42.

20. Godstow Abbey.

(i) *Liber vel registrum chartarum coenobii Godstow*: in the Exchequer: composed in 1404, at the expense of Alicia de Eaton, 'commonialis.'

Twyne's excerpts from it are in Twyne XXIV. 232–243 : Richard James also has excerpts from it in MS. Ric. James 23, p. 44. Wood knew it, I think, only from these excerpts : he cites it freely in *City* and occasionally in *Annals*, as Registrum Godstow, Registrum Godstow Latinè, Liber Godstow, Godstow book, &c.

(ii) *Register of Charters . . . of Godstow, in English.*

This was owned by Sir James Ware, afterwards by Henry Hyde, 2nd Earl of Clarendon, and is now MS. Rawl. B. 408—at the beginning is now pasted a rude drawing of Godstow nunnery, taken by Wood in 1666 (*Life*, i. 346).

Twyne has notices of this volume in Twyne XXI. 199, 245, 366 ; but I am not sure that he had actually seen it. Wood has excerpts (professedly) from it in Wood MS. D. 11 (1), pp. 50–56 ; but they were in fact transcribed from bishop Robert Sanderson's excerpts, and these, in their turn, from Randall Catherall's (*Life*, ii. 355). An edition of this for the Early English Text Society is one of my overdue promises.

Cited frequently in *City* as Registrum Godstow Anglicè, English register of Godstow, &c.

(iii) In S. John's College Archives is a volume of extracts from the deeds relating to Godstow in the possession of the College.

21. Haghmon Abbey.

Register, 'in Dame Margaret Barker's hands.'
Cited in *City*, i. 240.

22. Hyde Abbey (juxta Winton).

(i) *Chronicon vel Annales monasterii de Hyde* : MS. in Shirburn Castle North Library 24. g. 9 ; printed in Rolls Series, 1866.

This was known to Twyne, but possibly only through John Stowe's transcript (now MS. Lansdowne 717) ; Twyne's excerpts are found in Twyne VII. 314 ; Twyne XXI. 15. Wood was most anxious to discover it, because of its unhesitating ascription of Oxford University to Alfred, but failed.

(ii) *Registrum chartarum abbatiae de Hyda* : MS. Cotton Domit. A. 14, foll. 22 sqq. Searched by Wood.

(iii) *Chronicon monasterii de Hyda*, ab anno 1035 ad Edwardum III, per Henricum Bowser : MS. Cotton Vitell. F. 2, no. 7.

23. Kirkstall Abbey.

Liber sive registrum coenobii Kirkstallensis : 'qui quidem liber reponitur in le Dutchy,' i. e. of Lancaster, office : in the Public Records Office.

Cited in *Annals*, i. 241.

Known to Wood only from Twyne XXIII. 444, 494.

24. Kirkstede Abbey.

Liber sive registrum chartarum et privilegiorum coenobii de Kirkstede, co. Lincoln.

Known to Wood only by Twyne's excerpts; Twyne III. 501; Twyne XXI. 835; Twyne XXIV. 663, 664.

25. Lanercost.

Richard James, MS. Ric. James 10, p. 79, cites *Chronicon de Lanercost*, and p. 81, *breve Chronicon ante librum histor. canonici de Lanercost.*

26. Lanthony cell, near Gloucester.

(i) An old *liber rapsodicus* (i.e. miscellany) belonging to Lanthony, in the possession of Henry Parry, of C. C. C. Oxon. Excerpts from this are found in MS. Ric. James 26, p. 147 and in Twyne XXII. 188, 419.

(ii) An old MS. *Rationale* of Lanthony, in C. C. C. Oxon library, containing a prayer for S. Frideswyde's day, is noticed in Twyne XXI. 833.

Cited in *City*, ii. 137.

See no. 192 in Coxe's Cat. of C. C. C. Oxon MSS.

27. Lewes.

(i) Twyne XXI. 375 cites *Liber niger prioratus S. Pancratis de Lewes*, composed 1444 at the instance of Robert Amcell.

(ii) Richard James cites *Registrum prioratus S. Pancratis de Lewes;* MS. Ric. James 8, p. 103.

28. Lichfield Cathedral.

(i) *Liber albus* ecclesiae cathedralis Lichfeildiensis penes regestrarium decani et capituli ibidem : cited by Twyne in his *Catalogus Cancellariorum* p. 19 (i.e. Twyne XIX).

(ii) *Chronicon ecclesiae Lichfeildiensis* : MS. Cotton Vesp. E. 16. Twyne XXII. 366. Perhaps that cited in *Colleges*, p. 354.

(iii), (iv) MS. e Mus. 204 (*O. C.* 3555) : MS. Bodl. 204—*Life*, ii. 175, note 1.

(v) *Historia ecclesiae Lichfeldensis* : formerly in Dr. Thomas Barlow's possession : *Life*, ii. 175.

29. Lincoln Cathedral.

Known to Wood only from Twyne's and Sanderson's notes.

(i) *Registrum Linc. Ecclesiae* : Twyne II. 18ᵛ, 19.

(ii) *Libellus de chartis pensionum* apud Lincoln. MS.
Cited in *City*, i. 145.

(iii) In a volume of Collections by Dr. Robert Sanderson (*Life*, ii.
354), foll. 709, 718, 735, 736, Wood found excerpts 'ex libris et
chartis ecclesiae Lincoln.'
Cited in *City*, ii. 54.

30. Littlemore Priory.

(i) *Muniments of Littlemore Priory*, in the Christ Church treasury,
are cited several times in *City*.

(ii) *Muniments of Littlemore Priory*, in Wood's own hands, are
cited in *Colleges*, p. 654. These documents, 48 in number, are now
in the Bodleian ; see W. H. Turner's Calendar of Charters and Rolls,
p. 292. Wood communicated them to Dugdale, who in the *Monasticon*
confused Littlemore by Sandford in com. Oxon. with the priory of
Sandford in Berks.

31. Malmsbury Abbey.

(i) *Liber vel registrum coenobii Malmsburiensis* : in the Exchequer
at Westminster.
Cited in *Fasti*, p. 8.
Excerpts from it in Twyne XXIV. 244 : MS. Ric. James 23, p. 57.
Printed in Rolls Series, 1879.

(ii) *Register*, in Wood's possession.
Bought from Wood for the Bodleian in 1690 : now MS. ab Ant.
Wood 5.

(iii) Richard James (MS. Ric. James 8, p. 67) cites a *Registrum
Malmsbury*, written circ. 1250, ' in the hands of Mr. Warneford.'

(iv) *Collections from Malmsbury book*, by Henry Jackson, are found
in Wood MS. D. 18.

(v) Wood MS. D. 8 (*O. C.* 8538) belonged to this abbey : *Life*, ii. 200.

32. Merton Priory, co. Surrey.

(i) *Liber vel registrum*, MS. Laud Misc. 723 ; see Twyne XXII. 392.
Cited in *City*, i. 77.

(ii) *Another copy of the said register* : MS. Cotton Cleop. C. 7.
Excerpts from this are found in MS. Ric. James 24, p. 107.

33. Osney Abbey.

(i) *Chartae, evidentiae, &c.* ; in Christ Church treasury.
Cited *passim* in *City* and occasionally in *Annals* and *Fasti*.

Twyne's excerpts from these are found in Twyne XXIII. pp. 67–106. Wood's excerpts are in Wood MS. D. 2, pp. 480–586 (*Life*, ii. 112).

(ii) *Charters*, &c. in the Bodleian.

Six large volumes, containing 468 charters, formerly in Wood's possession ; see W. H. Turner's Calendar, p. 315.

Cited occasionally in *Fasti* and *City*.

(iii) *Rentalls* of Osney Abbey, 'for single years, not bound together, but separate ; many of them fragmentary' ; in Ch. Ch. treasury : Twyne XXII. 353.

Cited *passim* in *Annals* and *City*.

Some excerpts by Twyne from Osney rentalls are found in a MS. at C. C. C. Oxon (no. 280 in Coxe's Cat., at fol. 97). These excerpts have been transcribed by Wood in MS. Bodl. 594, foll. 186ᵛ–189ᵛ.

Wood's excerpts from these rentalls are found in Wood MS. D. 2, pp. 417–479 ; and the dated accounts he excerpts from range from 1259 to 1498. It is possible that the frequent citations in *Annals* (e.g. ii. 731, 735, &c.) of early rentalls of Osney as 'in manibus authoris' refer only to these excerpts and not to the originals : they seem too early for the papers noted in (v).

(iv) *A parchment book of Osney rentalls*, 1463 (?)–1479 ; in Christ Church treasury.

Cited occasionally in *City*.

Wood has excerpts from it in Wood MS. D. 2, pp. 587–592.

(v) *A book of Osney rentalls*, 1445–1481 ; Wood MS. F. 10. It contains either the *Rentale Osney* or the *Computus Collectoris Osney*, or both, for several years between these limits : see *Life*, ii. 114.

(vi) *A rentall of Osney for* 1498 : Wood MS. F. 15.

Cited in *City*, ii. 189.

(vii) *Registrum munimentorum de terris, potissime in rure*, in Ch. Ch. treasury, no. 343 in Kitchin's Catalogue : given by Sir Robert Cotton to Ch. Ch. in exchange for the Burton Annals (par. 8, *supra*) : init. 'Memorandum quod Robertus de Olleyo et Rogerus de Ivereyo.' See Twyne XXII. 339 ; Twyne IV. 301 ; Twyne II. 132.

This Cartulary is frequently cited in *Annals* and *City*, as Registrum Osney in thesaurario (*or* chartario, *or* domo capitulari) Aedis Christi. Some few references barely as 'Osney book' or 'leiger-book of Osney' are ambiguous between this volume and the next [1].

Richard James has excerpts from this MS. in MS. Ric. James 6, p. 53. Wood has some excerpts from it at the beginning of Wood MS. C. 2 and at p. 147 of Wood MS. D. 18 : see also (ix).

---

[1] similarly, Wood notes in Wood MS. E. 4 (*O. C.* 8561), p. 125, that in MS. Cotton Julius C. 6 are 'notes out of Osney book,' but does not say which 'book.'

(viii) *Registrum munimentorum de terris tam in Oxon. quam in rure:*
MS. Cotton Vitell. E. 15, destroyed in the fire: see Twyne IV. 429.

Cited frequently in *City, Annals, Fasti*, as Registrum (or liber)
Osney in bibl. Cotton. Some references are ambiguous, see (vii).

Twyne's excerpts from this volume are found in Twyne XXII.
285–291; Twyne XXIII. 107, 109, &c. Wood's excerpts from it are
at p. 360 of Wood MS. D. 2.

(ix) Wood's *Collections from Ousney Register* (from Osney book,
&c.) are cited by him in *City*, i. 220, 272, &c.

These are found in Wood MS. D. 2, pp. 360–404, partly from the
Cottonian cartulary, but partly also (I imagine) from the Ch. Ch.
cartulary. The references to his 'Collections from Ousney register
in sheets' (*City*, i. 331), 'the last Collections ex libro Osney' (*City*,
i. 352) may belong here, or may imply unbound papers, now
dispersed or destroyed.

(x) Wood, quoting Twyne, says that 'Osney register is also in
Mr. Fanshawe's office in Scaccario ex parte memoratoris regis.'

This refers, I suppose, to the cartulary now in the Public Records
Office, the first 60 folios of which are in English. An edition of
the English portion is one of my overdue promises to the Early
English Text Society.

Wood has excerpts 'out of the English leiger-book of the abbey of
Osney' in Wood MS. D. 11 (1), pp. 89, 90. In *City*, ii. 181, he cites
'Osney English register that I have,' meaning presumably only these
excerpts.

(xi) *Thomas Wyke's Chronicle of Osney*: MS. Cotton Tiberius
A. 9: printed, 1869, in the Rolls Series (*Annales Monastici*, vol. iv).

'Chronicon vel Annales Osney: initium "Anno ab incarnatione
Domini 1065 obiit Edvardus rex Anglorum et successit dux
Haraldus"; continuatur per authorem ad annum 1292; postea per
alium ad annum 1318': see Twyne XXI. 751; Twyne XXII. 79.

Cited constantly in *Annals* and *City*. In *Annals*, i. 397, 398,
&c., the *Continuator chronici Wykes* is separately cited.

Richard James has excerpts from this in MS. Ric. James 26, p. 177.
Twyne's excerpts are in Twyne XXII. 79–87. Wood's excerpts
from it are in Wood MS. D. 2, pp. 359, 360; Wood MS. D. 18,
p. 135; MS. Bodl. 594 (towards the end).

(xii) *Annales Osney*: MS. Cotton Vitell. A. 14.

This was afterwards printed as Wyke's Chronicle: and *now* has
that name; but Wood's *Wyke* is the preceding volume. Printed in
Rolls Series in the same volume as the preceding.

Wood's citations of the Osney Chronicle, e.g. *City*, i. 331, 396,
&c. are often ambiguous between this and the former volume.

(xiii) Twyne XXI. 751 cites a 'Chronicon incerti authoris ad chron. T. Wyke, incipiens a prophetiis Merlin.'

(xiv) Twyne XXII. 292 cites a *Chronicon coenobii Osneyensis* in suburbiis Oxon., two leaves, from the conquest to 1179, written by a monk of that abbey, init. 'Anno ab incarnatione Dni MLXV obiit Edwardus, rex Anglorum,' &c.; prefixed to the Cottonian Cartulary of Osney, MS. Cotton Vitell. E. 15. See Hardy's *Descriptive Catalogue*, ii. 416.

I cannot find that Wood ever saw it.

(xv) Twyne XXI. 532 cites *Chronicae Osney fragmentum* per quendam anonymum canonicum ejusdem loci, quam Mr. Thomas Allen invenit in bibliotheca Henrici Ferrers apud Baddisley in com. Warwic. armigeri, post mortem 1633[1]: and adds 'videtur scriptum per Thomam Wyke.'

This is cited, but only from Twyne's excerpt, in *Annals* and *City*. Certain vague citations ('ille alter anon. Ousney,' &c.) possibly belong to this.

Wood never saw the MS., but imagined it might be MS. Digb. 168 or MS. Cotton Titus A. 14.

(xvi) Chronicon de eventibus ab adventu Normannorum in Angliam usque ad Johannem regem, scriptum per canonicum Osney: MS. Cotton Galba A. 7, fol. 100. See Hardy's *Descriptive Catalogue*, iii. 37.

(xvii) *Rationale Osney*, cited in *City*, ii. 220, as if in Ch. Ch. treasury.

In MS. Ric. James 26, p. 160 is an excerpt from a Liber rationalis Osneiae; and in the same volume p. 159 is an excerpt from 'MS. vetus de offic. Osney.'

(xviii) *Series abbatum* coenobii Osney a prima fundatione ad annum 1403, per quendam canonicum Osney: Twyne XXIII. 107, 108.

I have not identified it: it is possibly that cited in *Annals*, ii. 753; *City*, ii. 210, 211 sqq.

(xix) *Series altera abbatum* a prima fundatione ad Johannem Walton qui fuit postea Archiepiscopus Dublin.: Twyne XXI. 265.

I have not identified it.

(xx) *Catalogus abbatum Osney*, per anonymum: penes quondam ⟨John Bridges⟩ episcopum Oxon.

Wood knew it only from Twyne's excerpts. He cites it as 'anon. Ousney' in *City*, i. 435, ii. 202, 204, &c. It is possibly the volume cited in *Annals*, i. 329, ii. 760.

(xxi) Wood in *City*, i. 321, refers to *Wyke's Catalogue of the abbots of Osney*. Wood in MS. Rawl. D. 1268 (in a note printed by

[1] the date is wrong; as Wood notes, 'obiit Allenus 1632.'

Thomas Hearne at the end of Liber Niger Scaccarii) mentions 'the Acts of the abbates of Osney that Leland speaks of, of Wike's writing.'

(xxii) *Tabulae Osney*, referred to by Wood as cited in ⊤, and in Twyne XXII. 141. These contained notes about the foundation of the several orders of monks and friars and, under the year 1300, a notice of Piers Gaveston. Wood never saw the original.

(xxiii) *Notes of the foundation of Osney*, 'per anonymum': Wood MS. F. 31.

34. Oxford: S. Frideswyde's Priory.

(i) *Muniments of S. Frideswyde's Priory* in Christ Church treasury; 'variae chartae, munimenta, rentalia putrida.'

Cited freely in *Annals* and *City*.

Twyne consulted these at Christmas-tide 1622, by the kindness of Leonard Hutten, Treasurer of Christ Church; and the excerpts he made are in Twyne XXIII. 67–106. Wood's excerpts are in Wood MS. D. 2, pp. 32, 480–586.

(ii) *Charters &c. of S. Frideswyde's Priory* in the Bodleian: see W. H. Turner's Calendar of Charters and Rolls (Oxford, 1878), pp. 300 sqq. These were formerly in Wood's possession, and are cited in *Annals*, i. 48, *Fasti*, p. 23.

(iii) *Liber vel registrum magnum chartarum &c.*, folio. in Christ Church treasury (no. 340 in G. W. Kitchin's *Cat. Codd. Aedis Xti*), written temp. Ric. II.

Cited frequently in *Annals*, *Fasti*, *City*, under various titles, such as Liber magnus, Registrum magnum (or majus), the great leiger-book, &c.

Twyne's excerpts from this volume are found in Twyne II. 120–122; Twyne III. 93–115; Twyne XXII. 242–263, 298, 369; Twyne XXIII. 63–66, 569, &c. Richard James has some excerpts in MS. Ric. James 6, p. 38. For Wood's excerpts, see (v).

This volume is being edited for the Oxford Historical Society (along with the second cartulary) by the Rev. S. R. Wigram.

(iv) *Registrum parvum vel antiquum*, in C. C. C. Oxon. (no. 160 in Coxe's Catalogue), written temp. Edw. I. It belonged to Thomas Allen, who gave it to Brian Twyne, and Twyne gave it to his college.

Cited freely in *Annals* and *City*, under several titles, such as Liber parvus, Liber antiquus, old or little register, little register, &c.

Twyne's excerpts from it are found in Twyne II. 4, 281, 282, 473; Twyne XXII. 306, 307, 332–335. Richard James has excerpts from it in MS. Ric. James 26, pp. 137–147, 155. For Wood's excerpts see (v).

(v) Wood's *Collectanea ex libro S. Frideswydae.*

These are in Wood MS. C. 2, pp. 2–73 (from the larger or Christ Church cartulary), pp. 76–112 from the older or Corpus Christi cartulary). A few excerpts from the larger cartulary are found also in Wood MS. D. 11 (i), pp. 91, 92.

Cited frequently in *City.*

(vi) Wood's *Contenta parvi libri S. Frideswydae.*

This is an abstract of the Corpus Christi cartulary, extending to 127 pages; old mark **F** (for Frideswyde); press-mark Wood MS. C. 4.

It is cited in *City* very frequently by its mark **F**: sometimes by its title; and is probably the volume meant by 'liber extractorum ex parvo libro S. Frideswide' (*City*, i. 130), 'collect. ex parvo libro S. Frideswydae' (*City*, i. 75).

(vii) Wood, in *City*, ii. 144, cites *S. Frideswyde's English register*, as being in his own possession. I know nothing of it.

(viii) Twyne XXII. 353 cites a 'rentale S. Frideswydae,' of date 20 Sept. 1517 which he saw (in 1622) in the hands of Mr. ⟨Thomas⟩ Flaxney, registrar ⟨to the bp. of Oxford⟩. Wood cites this in *City*, ii. 37.

(ix) *Survey of S. Frideswyde's lands*, 1524. The original in the Augmentations Court is cited in *City*, i. 73, ii. 178; a copy in the possession of Brome Whorwood of Holton co. Oxon. is cited in *Annals*, ii. 768.

(x) *Lives of S. Frideswyde.*

(*a*) *Philippus*, prior coenobii S. Frideswydae (1180), *de miraculis S. Frideswydae virginis*, MS. Digb. A. 177. See Twyne XXI. 13, 491. Hardy's *Descriptive Catalogue*, i. 459–463.

Cited frequently in *Annals* and *City.*

Wood's excerpts from this are found [1] in MS. Ballard 70, p. 36.

(*b*) *Vita et miracula S. Frideswydae virginis Oxon.*, initium prologi 'de vita et virtutibus beatissimae,' initium vitae 'anno itaque ab incarnatione Dni nostri Jhu Christi': in a MS. collection of lives of Saints given to Jesus College Oxford by Sir John Prise.

Wood cites this volume [2] several times in *Annals* (e.g. i. 31) and *City* (e.g. ii. 42, 59, &c.). But he knew it only from Twyne's excerpt in Twyne XXII. 89–92 (*Life*, ii. 221).

(*c*) Wood mentions another life of S. Frideswyde as found at p. 33 of **F**, but the volume so marked I have failed to identify.

(*d*) A life of S. Frideswyde is found in a Balliol College MS.; no. 228 in Coxe's Catalogue.

---

[1] wrongly said to be in MS. Bodl. 594 in *Life*, i. 321.   in *City*, i. 244; and not (as the note there suggests) Jeffrey Monmouth.

[2] this is probably the volume cited

35. Oxford: Canterbury College.

(i) *Statutes of the College*; cited by Wood (no doubt from Twyne's notes from the archiepiscopal registers of Canterbury) in *City*, ii. 285.

Twyne XXIV. 111 has *Statuta aulae Cantuar. in Univ. Oxon.*; init. 'Simon permissione divina Cant. arch.'; and the beginning of the last chapter of them is 'quia aulam praedictam de bonis archiepiscopatus et nostris.' Twyne V. 309–320 has *Statuta Coll. Cant. per Gulielmum Courtney*.

(ii) Wood in *City*, ii. 288, cites an *Inventory of Goods in the College*, and *Computi gardianorum Collegii*: no doubt from some paper of Twyne's, but I failed to find it in my search through the Twyne volumes. The *Computi* for 1395–97 were printed in 1881 from the originals in the Chapter archives at Canterbury.

(iii) Foundation charter of the College; in Wood MS. F. 29 A.: *Life*, ii. 435.

36. Oxford: S. George's College in the Castle.

(i) *Statuta Collegii S. Georgii infra castrum Oxon.*: initium 'Noverint universi quod quotiens sacerdos scholaris.'

The original MS. formerly given by Thomas Allen to Brian Twyne, and by Twyne to Corpus Christi College, is now in the Bodleian (MS. Rawl. Statutes 34).

A transcript, by Twyne, is found at pp. 522–533 of Wood MS. D. 32. This copy is cited by Wood in *City*, ii. 63, 64, 184.

Wood's excerpts from the transcript are found in MS. Ballard 70 (*olim* 20), pp. 23–25, 88, 89.

(ii) *Notes of the foundation of S. George's in the Castle*, 'per anonymum': in Wood MS. F. 31.

37. Oxford: Gloucester College.

(i) *Liber statutorum Collegii Glocestrensis*, or *Statuta aulae Glo-cestrensis*, is cited by Wood in *City*, ii. 248, 259; but I have not succeeded in tracing it.

(ii) MS. Cotton Tiber. E. 4 has papers about the foundation and endowment of Gloucester College: Twyne XXI. 238. Wood discovered that Reynerus in his 'Apostolatus Benedictinorum in Anglia' had drawn a great deal from this volume, and has a note in Wood MS. E. 4, 'I shall make much use of it' in the second edition of *Hist. et Antiq. Oxon*.

38. Oxford: S. Mary's College (Canons Regular).

(i) *Statutes of S. Mary's College near North Gate, Oxford*: init. prologi 'Incipiunt statuta Collegii beatae Mariae Canonicorum Regu-larium.'

The original MS. was given by Thomas Allen to Brian Twyne, and by Twyne to Corpus Christi College (so Wood says, in Wood MS. E. 4); now MS. Rawl. Statutes 34.

Twyne's transcript is found at pp. 503–519 of Wood MS. D. 32. Cited in *City*, ii. 231, 239.

Wood's excerpts from the transcript are found in MS. Ballard 70, pp. 85–87.

(ii) *Inventory of goods there*, 1541.

Wood MS. D. 32, pp. 550–552; printed in *City*, ii. 531.

39. Oxford: S. Bartholomew's Hospital.

(i) *Muniments*, in Oriel College treasury.

Cited several times in *City*.

Wood has excerpts from these in Wood MS. F. 28, foll. 57–61 : and cites them in *City*, ii. 265.

(ii) *Leiger-book of muniments* belonging to S. Bartholomew's Hospital, ordered to be written 1521 : in Oriel College treasury.

Excerpts from it are found in Wood MS. C. 1, p. 69.

40. Oxford: S. John Baptist's Hospital.

(i) *Munimenta, chartae, &c. Hospitalis S. Johannis Bapt.* : in Magdalen College treasury.

Cited in *Annals, Colleges, City*.

Wood's excerpts from these are found in Wood MS. D. 2, pp. 161–229; and he cites these ' Collect. ex archivis Coll. Magd.' in *City*, ii. 154.

(ii) *Rentalia Hospitalis S. Joh. Bapt.* : in Magd. Coll. treasury: Twyne XXIII. 127.

Cited *passim* in *City*.

Wood's excerpts from these 'rentalls' are found in Wood MS. D. 2, pp. 228–229, 230–243. The dated accounts range from 1294 (22 Edw. I) to 1546 (38 Hen. VIII), Wood not separating the Hospital from the College records.

(iii) *Liber vel registrum chartarum* . . . *Hosp. S. Jo. Bapt.*, in Magd. Coll. ; see Twyne XXI. 159, 183; written about 1280. See 4th Report of Hist. MSS. Comm. p. 460 : *City*, ii. 533.

Cited frequently in *City* under different titles, e.g. Liber continens extract. evid. Hosp. S. Jo. Bapt. in arch. Coll. Magd.; Liber. Coll. Magd.; Liber (*or* Registrum) evident. Hosp. S. Jo. Bapt.

Wood's excerpts from it are found in Wood MS. D. 11 (i), pp. 2–27; and he cites these ' Collectanea ex registro S. Jo. Bapt. Hosp.' in *City* (e. g. i. 409).

41. Oxford : miscellaneous notices.

(i) De aedibus religiosis in Oxon. Anglicè. This was a paper written, probably, 'per quendam scholarem Oxon. tempore Edwardi VI. vel Mariae.'

It was sent by Henry Jackson to Twyne, whose transcript is found in Twyne XXI. 204—'Hawles, abbayes, and friers houses dissolved in King Henry his time in Oxford.'

Cited in *City*, ii. 185.

(ii) In MS. Wood F. 12 (*O. C.* 8474), in Latin and not in Wood's hand, are a short life of S. Frideswyde, excerpts from the C. C. C. cartulary of S. Frideswyde's, and brief notes about Rewley Abbey, Sandford Priory, Thame Abbey, Studley Priory, Abingdon Abbey, Dorchester Abbey, Godstow Abbey, Bruer[n]e Abbey.

(iii) William Wyrley : *Fundationes domorum religiosorum*, a fragment, containing notes about S. Frideswyde's, S. George's in the Castle, and Osney, apparently from the cartularies at Christ Church, partly in Wood MS. F. 16 (*O. C.* 8478), partly in Wood MS. F. 31.

42. Pershore Abbey.

Historia Coenobii Pershoriensis : Twyne III. 246 : in the Public Records Office.

Cited in *Annals*, i. 262 : known to Wood only from Twyne.

43. Ramsey Abbey.

(i) *Cartulary*, in the Public Records Office : printed in Rolls Series, 1884 : not cited by Wood.

(ii) *Registrum diversarum rerum* touching the estates of the abbey : MS. Cotton Vespas. A. 18, foll. 92–101.

Wood has an excerpt from 'Liber Ramsey' in MS. Ballard 46, p. 117 : is it from this MS. or the next?

(iii) *Registrum chartarum* abbatiae de Ramsey, by Robert Dodeford : MS. Cotton Vespas. E. 2. Wood searched this for any notice of Gloucester College, but found none.

(iv) *Nomina et gesta abbatum* : MS. Cotton Vespas. A. 18, foll. 113ᵛ–146.

(v) *Chronicon coenobii Ramseyensis* : MS. Cotton Otho D. 8 ; see Twyne XXIV. 58. It noticed the great conflict of 1354.

(vi) *Chronicon Ramsey*, in Bodl. as MS. Jesus Coll. Oxon, 88 : formerly in Wood's possession ; printed in the Rolls Series, 1886.

Excerpts from it are found in Wood MS. D. 18, foll. 171–177.

44. Reading Abbey.

(i) *Leiger-book*, in the hands of Dr. Edward Bernard, a large quarto or a little folio.

Wood has excerpts from it in Wood MS. D. 2, p. 357, relating to the grant by Peter the son of Herbert to Reading Abbey of a court and garden in Oxford and the advowson of the Church of S. John Baptist situate in that court, and the confirmation (dated 20 June, 1255) of the grant by Reginald son of Peter son of Herbert.

(ii) *Liber Redyng* in the hands of Sir John Davys of Pangborne, co. Berks.

Wood has excerpts from it, relating to the same matter, in Wood MS. D. 2, p. 358.

(iii), (iv) MS. Cotton Domit. A. 3 and MS. Cotton Vespas. E. 5.
Wood found there nothing about S. John Bapt. Church, Oxford.

(v) Richard James has excerpts from *MS. Reading*, MS. Ric. James 25, p. 149.

45. Rochester Cathedral.

(i) *Liber vel registrum* ecclesiae S. Andreae Roffensis : MS. Cotton Vespas. A. 22, foll. 63, 128, &c. : 'fragments of a cartulary,' see Twyne XXIV. 76.

John, prior of Rochester, there licenses Roger Staplehurst and John Ealding, monks O. S. B., to study at Oxford.

(ii) *Annales Roffensis ecclesiae* : MS. Cotton Vitell. E. 14, foll. 242, 264. It has something about Walter de Merton.

(iii) *Chronicon Roffensis ecclesiae* usque ad finem Edwardi I ; by Edmund de Hadenham, a monk of Rochester; among William Lambard's collections in MS. Cotton Vespas. A. 6, foll. 53–56. Something there about Walter de Merton.

(iv) MS. Ric. James 18, p. 145 has an excerpt from *Annales Roff.*, 9 Edw. II to 20 Edw. III.

46. S. Alban's Abbey.

(i) *Magnus liber de origine et processu Monasterii S. Albani*, MS. Cotton Claud. E. 4 : see par. 443 (i), 455, 503.

Cited in *Annals* and *Fasti*.

Printed, from MS. Royal 14 C, in Rolls Series, 1867.

(ii) *Gesta Johannis Whethamsted*, abbatis S. Albani : MS. Cotton Claud. D. 1.

Referred to in *City*, ii. 260.

Printed, from MS. Arundel 3, in Rolls Series, 1867.

(iii) *Gesta paucula Johannis &c.* ; MS. Cotton Otho B. 4.

Cited in *City*, ii. 257, 258.

(iv) Wood in Wood MS. D. 18 (*O. C.* 8563), fol. 113 has excerpts ex registro S. Albani in bibl. Cotton. ; and there are similar excerpts in MS. Ric. James 8, p. 119. See MS. Cotton Julius D. 3, Tiber. E. 6, Nero D. 1, Otho D. 3.

Wood's excerpts are cited in *City*, ii. 262.

46*. Salisbury Cathedral : *Life*, iii. 400.

47. Sandford Preceptory.

(i) *Registrum continens transcripta cartarum de terris* of the Knights Templar in Sandford, co. Oxon.; MS. ab Ant. Wood, num. 10; bought from Wood in 1690.

Cited in *Annals*, ii. 735.

(ii) *Rentale terrarum* of the Templars in Sandford and Littlemore, co. Oxon.; no. 320 in Coxe's Cat. Codd. C.C.C. Oxon.

48. Sherborne Priory.

Liber monasterii de Shireburne dio. Sarum : MS. Cotton Faust. A. 2, foll. 23–90 ; see Twyne XXIV. 231.

49. Studley Priory.

(i) ' *Rentalls*,' formerly in the archives of the City of Oxford, but now missing.   Wood knew them only from Twyne's notes.

They are frequently cited in *City*.   One of them is cited individually several times, e.g. *City*, i. 75 ' rotulus pergamen. de computo receptoris priorissae de Stodley.'

(ii) *Liber sive registrum chartarum . . . de Stodley in com. Oxon.* : formerly in Thomas Allen's library, where it was seen and excerpted from by Twyne ; Twyne XXIII. 409 ; Twyne XXIV. 642–661.

Cited frequently in *City*.

(iii) Wood's *Collections out of Stodley nunnery book* are cited by him in *City*, i. 578 : but I have seen no trace of them.   At most they would be only a transcript of Twyne's notes, since there is no evidence that Wood had ever seen the original.

50. Tewkesbury Abbey.

(i) *Annales monasterii de Theoksbury*, MS. Cotton Cleop. A. 7 : printed, 1864, in Rolls Series (*Annales Monast.* vol. i).

Excerpts from it in MS. Ric. James 17, p. 163.

(ii) *Chronicon Tewkesbury* ab anno 1066 ad 1268 ; initium ' Anno MLXVI obiit Edwardus, rex Anglorum.'

Cited in *Annals*, i. 190.

In John Theyer's library (*Life*, ii. 143).

51. Thame Abbey.

(i) *Chartae, &c.* of the abbey of S. Mary's Thame, in Ch. Ch. treasury.

Excerpts from these are found in Wood MS. D. 11 (1), pp. 85–88, and in Wood MS. F. 32 (*O. C.* 8494).

(ii) *Charters*, in the Bodleian, formerly belonging to Wood.
See W. H. Turner's Calendar of Charters, p. 314.

52. Westminster Abbey.

(i) Richard Sporley, monk of Westminster, *de fundatione &c. ecclesiae Westmon.*, written 1450: MS. Cotton Claud. A. 8.

(ii) Richard Sporley, *de praepositis . . . ecclesiae Westm.*: ibidem.

53. Winchcombe Abbey.

(i) Richard Kederminster's *Renovatio privilegiorum, &c. monasterii . . . de Winchelcomba.* See Twyne II. 190; liber Epist. FF. epist. 20; Twyne XXIV. 552.

Cited in *Annals*, ii. 21, *City*, ii. 430.

(*a*) One copy of this is MS. Dodsworth 65.

(*b*) Another copy was in the hands of Samuel Fell, Canon (afterwards Dean) of Christ Church, from which Twyne made excerpts (Twyne XXIV. 533–538).

Wood, I think, never saw the MS., and the statement (*Life*, ii. 253) that it passed to Dr. John Fell is probably conjectural.

(*c*) Sir William Morton's copy (*Life*, ii. 87) perished in the great fire of London.

(ii) *Catalogue of abbots*, Twyne XXIV. 533.

(iii) *Annales* (vel Historia) *de Winchelcumba* (Christ to 1205): MS. Cotton Tiber. E. 4.

Cited occasionally in *Annals*.

54. Winchester Cathedral.

(i) *Chronicon ecclesiae Wintoniensis*, Christ to 1277: MS. Cotton Domit. A. 13: printed, 1865, in Rolls Series (*Annales Monast.* vol. iii): see Twyne XXI. 5.

Perhaps the MS. cited in *Annals*, i. 112.

Wood was disappointed at finding there 'no mention of King Alfred's doings at Oxford.' At the end of MS. Bodl. 594 Wood has some excerpts 'ex vetusto chron. Winton. ecclesiae'; and in MS. Ric. James 18, p. 27 are excerpts from 'Chron. Winton.'—possibly from this MS.

(ii) *Annales Winton.*, Christ to Henry II; MS. Cotton Vitell. A. 17. Examined by Wood: but 'nothing therin to my purpose.'

(iii) *Annales Winton.*, Christ to Henry III: MS. Cotton Galba A. 15.

(iv) Twyne XXIV. 54 cited a volume (among the Cottonian MSS.) *Antiquitates ecclesiae Wynton.*: principium 'Ab origine mundi ii^M. iiii^o. iiii^{xx}. x annis Brutus venit in terram hanc.' It came down to Henry V.

Wood knew it only from Twyne's notes, but he perhaps cites it in *Annals*, ii. 819, 820.

55. York Cathedral.

MS. Tanner 416 contains, at fol. 17, excerpts from registers at York; at fol. 20, excerpts from a register (1427–1509) of the dean and chapter of York; at fol 38^v, excerpts from another register (1543–1572). These notes have been stolen from Wood MS. E. 3 (*O. C.* 8567) where they were foll. 55, 57, 50^v: cp. no. 53 with no. 75 in the Catalogue of MSS. in Gutch's Wood's *Annals*, vol. i.

Wood cites *York notes*, in *City*, ii. 273, *Fasti*, p. 19; perhaps referring to these papers.

56. York: S. Leonard's Hospital.

Liber vel registrum chartarum Hosp. S. Leon. in Ebor.: MS. Cotton Nero D. 3, num. 1: see Twyne XXIV. 76.

Cited in *Annals*, ii. 767.

57. York: S. Mary's Abbey.

Stephanus Wythybiensis *de fundatione monast. S. Mar. Ebor.*, with continuation by others, and a catalogue of abbots and priors: MS. Bodl. 39. See Twyne XXI. 273.

Wood cites the Cat. of Abbots in *Hist.* i. 65.

EPISCOPAL REGISTERS.

58. Registers of the see of Canterbury.

These are kept at Lambeth Palace: see H. J. Todd's *Catalogue of the MSS. . . . at Lambeth Palace*, Lond., 1812. They are frequently cited by Wood in *Hist., Annals, Colleges, Fasti, City*; but there is no evidence that Wood ever saw the originals. I give therefore the references to the excerpts in Twyne, which Wood made use of. Twyne in 1626 'had warrant of my Lord Grace of Canterbury' (George Abbot) to peruse the registers, from Peckham's to Parker's inclusive, 'and to transcribe thence what he saw fitt at Mr. John Drake's house in Paulle's Chayne neere Doctors Commons, London': so a note, in Twyne's hand, now found in Wood MS. E. 4.

(i) *Registrum Johannis Peckham*, from June 1279 to 1292, 249 folios. Excerpts in Twyne II. 188; Twyne VII. 373–375; Twyne XXIV. 153–169, 280.

(ii) *Registrum Roberti Winchelsey,* 1294–1313, 343 folios. Excerpts in Twyne II. 188 b; Twyne XXIV. 89–92, 95–96.

(iii) *Registrum Gualteri Reynolds,* 1314–1326, 314 folios. Twyne II. 189 b, 238–244; Twyne VII. 391–393; Twyne XXIV. 92–95, 103, 147–152.

(iv) *Registrum Simonis Islip,* 1349–1366, 346 folios. Twyne II. 188 b, 239 b, 240; Twyne XII. 19–30; Twyne XXIV. 110–112, 152.

(v) *Registrum Simonis de Langham,* 1366–1368, 144 folios. Twyne II. 189; Twyne XXIV. 97–103.

(vi) *Registrum Gulielmi Wittlesey,* 1369–1374, 172 folios. Twyne II. 189; Twyne XXIV. 103–105.

(vii) *Registrum Simonis de Sudbury,* 1375–1381, 150 folios. Twyne II. 189; Twyne III. 201–211; Twyne XXIV. 125–126.

(viii) *Registrum Gulielmi Courtney,* 1381–1396; in two parts, pars prima, 361 folios; pars secunda is bound in one volume with the registers of Bourchier (161 folios), Morton (256 folios), and Deane. Twyne II. 189 b, 248–270; Twyne XXI. 105–109.

(ix) *Registrum Thomae Arundel,* 1396–1413; in two parts, pars prima, 561 folios, pars secunda, 204 folios. Twyne II. 189–190; Twyne VII. 53–60, 79–80; Twyne XXIV. 112–125, 140–146.

(x) *Registrum Henrici Chicheley,* 1414–1443; in two parts, pars prima, 490 folios, pars secunda, 411 folios. Twyne II. 190; Twyne XXIV. 126–133, 152.

(xi) *Registrum Johannis Stafford,* 1443–1452, 202 folios, bound in one volume (of 347 folios), with the next Register. Twyne II. 190 b; Twyne XXIV. 134–136.

(xii) *Registrum Johannis Kempe,* 1452–1453, 138 folios, bound with the preceding in one volume, where it begins on fol. 210. Twyne XXIV. 135.

(xiii) *Registrum Thomae Bourchier,* 1454–1486, 161 folios, part of a volume which contains Courtney, and the two following. Twyne XXIV. 109, 136.

(xiv) *Registrum Johannis Morton,* 1486–1499, 256 folios; see the preceding. Twyne XXIV. 109, 136.

(xv) *Registrum Henrici Deane,* 1501, bound in one volume with Courtney and the two preceding. Twyne XXIV. 109.

(xvi) *Registrum Gulielmi Warham,* 1504–1532, 425 folios.

(xvii) *Registrum Thomae Cranmer,* 1533–1553, 434 folios. Twyne XXIV. 137–138.

(xviii) *Registrum Reginaldi Pole,* 1556–1558, 82 folios. Twyne XXIV. 138–139.

(xix) *Registrum Matthaei Parker,* 1559–1575; in two parts, pars prima, 411 folios, pars secunda, 132 folios.

59. Registers of the see of Lincoln.

Wood cites these freely, sometimes as 'Registrum,' sometimes as 'Memoranda' or 'Liber memorand.' in *Hist., Annals, Fasti, City;* but he never saw the originals and quoted only from Twyne's excerpts. Twyne was at Lincoln, examining the registers, in 1617, and at least once afterwards; Twyne II. 27 b.

(i) *Registrum Hugonis Wells,* 1209; Twyne II. 27 a; Twyne III. 260.

(ii) *Registrum Oliveri Sutton,* 1280; Twyne II. 1, 23 b, 24, 27 b, 28 a; Twyne III. 221–223, 259; Twyne XII. 2, 7, 160.

(iii) *Registrum Johannis D'alderby,* 1300; Twyne II. 3, 15 a, 16 a, 23 b, 27 b, 28 a; Twyne III. 35, 215–217; Twyne VII. 161, 163, 260, 353, 376; Twyne XII. 13.

(iv) *Registrum Henrici Burwash* or Burgesh, 1320; Twyne II. 5 b, 18 b, 23, 27 b, 28 b.

(v) *Registrum Thomae le Bec,* 1341; Twyne II. 13.

(vi) *Registrum Johannis Gyncwell* or Synwell, 1347; Twyne II. 7 b–12, 15 a; Twyne III. 45; Twyne V. 137–147.

(vii) *Registrum Henrici Beaufort,* 1398; Twyne II. 14 b; Twyne III. 41.

(viii) *Registrum Philippi de Repingdon,* 1405; Twyne II. 13 a, 15 b, 18 a, 22 a; Twyne VII. 95–97; Twyne XII. 31.

(ix) *Registrum Gulielmi Alnewick,* 1436; Twyne II. 16 a; Twyne III. 275–277.

(x) *Registrum Gulielmi Smyth,* 1495; Twyne II. 13 a.

(xi) *Registrum Johannis Longland,* 1521.

60. Registers of the see of Bath and Wells.

Excerpts from these, in Wood's handwriting, are found in MS. Tanner 416, foll. 63 sqq. These used to be Wood MS. E. 3 (*O. C.* 8567), foll. 90 sqq., but were stolen from the Ashmolean.

One of these excerpts, from the register of bp. Rad. de Salopia (1329–1364), is cited in *Fasti,* p. 19.

61. Registers of the see of Carlisle.

In Wood MS. B. 14. (*O. C.* 8587), foll. 104 sqq., not in Wood's hand, are excerpts from the register of bp. John Halton (1293–1318).

62. Registers of the see of Lichfield.

Wood in Wood MS. E. 4 notes that he made use of the Register of bp. Roger Northburge (1322–1359) to determine the Chancellor of Oxford in the year 1333.

Twyne XXI. 280 has an excerpt from the *Institut. MS.* of bp. Roger de Westham (1245–1256).

63. Registers of the see of Oxford.

Referred to in *City*, ii. 13. Archives of the see are referred to also in *City*, ii. 3, *Colleges*, p. 630.

64. Registers of the see of Winchester.

Referred to in *Annals*, ii. 120. Wood never had access to them, and the solitary references he makes to them are due probably to some correspondent.

(i) Excerpts from the register of bp. John de Pontissara (1282–1305) are found in MS. Tanner 416, fol. 62ᵛ; formerly in Wood MS. E. 3 (*O. C.* 8567), fol. 89ᵛ—whence they were stolen.

(ii) The register of bp. Henry Woodstock (1405–1446) is cited in *Annals*, i. 249.

65. Registers of the see of York.

In MS. Tanner 416, fol. 1 (but torn out from—*O. C.* 8567—Wood MS. E. 3, where they began on fol. 31) are excerpts from the registers of the see of York; the names of the archbishops whose registers are cited will be found at no. 75 in the Catalogue of MSS. prefixed to Gutch's Wood's *Annals*.

These excerpts are in Wood's handwriting, but I am certain that they have been copied from some collection of notes (possibly Dodsworth's) and not from the originals.

Wood cites *York Notes* and *Notes from York Registers* in *Fasti*, *Colleges*, *Annals*, *Life*.

Registrum Nevile is dated in *Colleges*, p. 146; *reg. Rotherham*, ibid. p. 147; *reg. le Zouche*, ibid. p. 145: *reg. Kempe*, ibid. p. 265.

Muniments and Records of the Oxford Parish Churches.

66. All Saints Church.

(i) *Evidentiae, chartae*, &c. in archivis ecclesiae Omnium Sanctorum.

(ii) *Churchwardens' accounts*, rentals of parish property.

Cited in *City*, i. 124, 146. Wood's excerpts are found in Wood MS. D. 2, pp. 323–335. The accounts cited range from 1356 to 1569.

(iii) *Register of baptisms, marriages, and burials*. Wood's excerpts are found in Wood MS. D. 5, pp. 48, 51, 92, 95, and in MS. Tanner 454, fol. 144.

67. S. Aldate's Church.

(i) *Munimenta, evidentiae,* &c.; (ii) *computi guardianorum.*
Cited in *Colleges*, p. 422; *Annals*, ii. 772. Twyne's excerpts are found in Twyne XXIV. 250; Wood's in Wood MS. D. 2, pp. 67–69.

(iii) *Register.* Wood's excerpts are found in Wood MS. D. 5, pp. 60, 64, 66–68.

68. S. Clement's Church.

Register. Wood's excerpts are in Wood MS. D. 5, p. 8.

69. S. Ebbe's Church.

(i) *Evidentiae, munimenta,* &c.; (ii) *computi guardianorum.*
See *Life*, ii. 345, 450. Twyne has some excerpts in Twyne XXIII. 675; Wood, in Wood MS. D. 2, pp. 342–346.

(iii) *Register.* Wood's excerpts are in Wood MS. D. 5, p. 16, and MS. Tanner 456, fol. 58.

70. S. Giles' Church.

(i) *Accounts of the parish*: see *Life*, ii. 477: Wood's excerpts, ranging between 1492 and 1664, are in Wood MS. D. 2, pp. 348–353.
Cited in *Annals*, ii. 306.

(ii) *Register.* Wood's excerpts are in Wood MS. D. 5, pp. 70, 71, 73.

71. Holywell (S. Cross') Church.

Register. Wood's excerpts are in Wood MS. D. 5, pp. 9, 10, 12. Cited in *Life*, ii. 254.

72. S. John Baptist Church.

(i) *Register*, drawn up by Wood; see *Life*, i. 446; Wood MS. E. 33, MS. Rawl. B. 402 a.

(ii) Description of the parish in 1424; a paper in Merton College archives: cited frequently in *City*.

(iii) Description of, in 1662, by Wood; Wood MS. E. 33. Printed in *Life*, i. 447.

(iv) John Gurgany's register; *Life*, i. 130.

(v) John Wilton's register; *Life*, i. 446.

(vi) Matthew Jellyman's register; *Life*, i. 183.

73. S. Martin's (Carfax) Church.

(i) *Evidentiae, munimenta,* &c.; (ii) *churchwardens' accounts.*
Wood's excerpts are in Wood MS. D. 2, pp. 48–50.

(iii) *Register.* Cited in *Annals*, ii. 164. Wood's excerpts are in Wood MS. D. 5, pp. 29, 36, 39, 98; MS. Tanner 456, fol. 46.

74. S. Mary Magdalen Church.

(i) *Evidentiae, munimenta, &c.*; (ii) *churchwardens' accounts.*
Cited in *Fasti*, p. 39. Twyne has excerpts in Twyne XXIV. 255;
Wood, in Wood MS. D. 2, pp. 298–304. The accounts quoted
begin about 1509.

(iii) *Register.* See *Life*, ii. 131. Wood has excerpts in Wood MS.
D. 5, pp. 19–21, 28; MS. Tanner 456, fol. 66.

75. S. Mary the Virgin Church.

(i) *Munimenta lacerata*; (ii) *computi guardianorum.*
Cited in *Annals, Fasti, City.* See *Life*, i. 489. Wood has excerpts
in Wood MS. D. 3, pp. 250 sqq., the accounts quoted ranging from
1461 to 1623. All the earlier accounts of the church seem now lost.

(iii) *Register.* Wood's excerpts are in Wood MS. D. 5, pp. 75, 76,
87–89; *Life*, ii. 476.

(iv) Wood cites his 'Collections from S. Mary's Church writings'
in *City*, i. 86, 98, &c., referring to Wood MS. D. 3, as noticed *supra*.

76. S. Michael's at North-Gate Church.

(i) *Evidentiae, munimenta, &c.*; (ii) *churchwardens' accounts, &c.*
Cited several times in *City*. Twyne's excerpts are found in Twyne
XXIII. 507–510; Wood's in Wood MS. D. 2, pp. 35–43. The
accounts quoted range from 1403 to 1547.

(iii) *Register.* Wood's excerpts are found in Wood MS. D. 5,
pp. 53, 58, 59; MS. Tanner 454, fol. 143; MS. Tanner 456, fol. 64.

(iv) Wood cites his collections from the archives of this church in
City, i. 69, 227; referring to Wood MS. D. 2, as noticed *supra*.

77. S. Peter's in-the-Baily Church.

(i) *Munimenta, &c.*; (ii) *computi guardianorum.*
Cited several times in *City*. Twyne's excerpts are found in Twyne
XXIII. 577; Wood's, in Wood MS. C. 1, pp. 75 sqq. The accounts
quoted range from 1338 to 1547.

(iii) *Register.* Wood's excerpts are in Wood MS. D. 5, p. 14; MS.
Tanner 456, fol. 57; *Life*, ii. 387.

78. S. Peter's in-the-East Church.

(i) *Evidentiae, &c.*; (ii) *churchwardens' accounts.*
Cited in *City*. Twyne's excerpts are found in Twyne XXIII. 579;
Wood's in Wood MS. D. 2, pp. 44–47.

(iii) *Register.* Wood's excerpts are in Wood MS. D. 5, pp. 1, 7;
MS. Tanner 456, fol. 59 b.

79. S. Thomas' Church.

(i) *Churchwardens' accounts*; see *Life*, ii. 452.

(ii) *Register*. Wood's excerpts are in Wood MS. D. 5, pp. 38, 45; MS. Tanner 456, fol. 52.

(iii) *List of benefactors*, 1612–1651; Wood MS. F. 28, fol. 318.

80. Histories, &c. of the Oxford parish Churches.

(i) *Brian Twyne's*; see Twyne III, Twyne XVIII, Wood MS. F. 29 A.

(ii) *Anthony Wood's*; Wood MS. F. 29 A; printed in *City*, ii. 14–117.

(iii) Wood has notes on the Oxford churches in Wood MS. F. 31, fol. 91.

MISCELLANEA.

81. Miscellanea Ecclesiastica Oxon.

(i) In Wood MS. F. 28, fol. 200 are excerpts from 'a register in Nicholas Horsman's hands.'

Cited in *City*, ii. 52 ('Horsman's writings'), 68: *Colleges*, p. 264 ('a register in the keeping of the bishop of Oxford's registrar'). See *Life*, ii. 121.

(ii) In MS. Bodl. 594, foll. 193–196, among papers of Wood, are excerpts (but not in Wood's handwriting) from the registers of the Oxford Office of Wills; and in the same MS. fol. 232 excerpts from a 'register of wills, 1544–1550, in Mr. Cooper's Office.'

(iii) Papers about the archdeaconry of Oxford:—

(*a*) Taxationes ecclesiarum &c. in archidiaconatibus Oxon., Bucks, &c. 1291: Wood MS. C. 3 (*O. C.* 8525).

(*b*) Value of the yearly revenues of the archdeaconry of Oxon, 1534; Wood MS. F. 11 (*O. C.* 8473, art. 2).

(*c*) Registrum de decimis regis . . . infra archidiaconatum Oxon.: MS. Rawl. C. 910 (*O. C.* 8473, art. 1). See *Life*, ii. 212, notes 3, 4.

(*d*) Wood's Catalogue of Archdeacons of Oxford: Wood MS. E. 3 (*O. C.* 8567).

(iv) *Liber sive recorda primitiarum et decimarum*, 26 Henry VIII, 1534, concernentium valores collegiorum in utraque Universitate; Twyne XXI. 701, 802 a, 803–815.

Cited frequently in *City* ii, but only from Twyne.

(v) *Survey of the Colleges*, &c., 37 Henry VIII, 1545.

See Scargill-Bird's Guide to the Public Record Office (1891), p. 327.

Miscellaneous ecclesiastical records.

82. (i) *Valuation records.*

(*a*) Liber taxationum ecclesiarum in diocesi Lyncoln., 1209. See Twyne II. 19 a; Twyne VII. 345; Twyne XII. 159. The volume contained also several papal bulls, and a list of religious houses in the archdeaconry of Oxford. Wood's excerpts from it (via Twyne) are found in Wood MS. C. 3.

Cited in *Annals*, i. 250; *City*, ii. 45.

(*b*) Twyne in Twyne XXII. 137 has excerpts from 'Taxatio ecclesiarum Anglicarum, ex quodam MS^to. Mri. Roberti Bowyer, clerici Parliamenti.'

(ii) *Records of General Councils.*

(*a*) Concilium Basiliense : see Twyne XXI. 304, 324 ; Twyne XXII. 400.

Acta in concilio Basiliensi, Balliol College Library, MSS. nos. 166 A, 164, 165 B, 165 A, in Coxe's Cat. Codd. Ball. They were originally in the library of Durham (now Trinity) College : Twyne XXIII. 651, 659, 727, 732 ; Twyne II. 142 ; Twyne XXII. 400. Twyne in Twyne XXIII. 645–649 gives an abstract of their contents. Richard James has excerpts from them in MS. Ric. James 2, part 1, p. 55 and MS. Ric. James 22, p. 1.

Cited occasionally in *Annals, City.*

Acta quaedam gentis Anglicanae in concilio Basiliensi quae in corpore conciliorum non extant, MS. ; Twyne II. 142, 143 from MS. Digb. 66 (*O. C.* 1667); see par. 406.

(*b*) Concilium Constantiense.

Disceptatio in concilio Constantiensi super dignitate et magnitudine regnorum Britannici et Gallici, habita ab utriusque oratoribus et legatis, edita a Roberto Wingfield equite, circ. 1513. Printed[1] at Louvain 1517. Twyne XXI. 251, 324, 762 ; Twyne XXIII. 727.

Cited in *Hist.* i. 207.

Acta quaedam in Concilio Constantiensi : Twyne XXIII. 641 ; see MS. Cotton Nero E. 5 and Cleop. E. 2.

Protestatio dominorum Anglicorum in concilio Constantiensi : MS. Ric. James 10, p. 169.

(*c*) Concilium Pisanum.

Res gestae in concilio Pisano : Twyne XXIII. 727.

83. (iii) *Books about Religious Orders, &c.*

(*a*) Regular Canons.

Forma capituli generalis Regularium Canonicorum ordinis S. Augustini provinciae Angliae, at Osney 1499 : MS. ab Ant. Wood 21 (*O. C.* 8609).

(*b*) Benedictines.

Constitutiones ordinis Benedicti : MS. Cotton Claud. E. 4. Cited in

---

[1] Twyne, however, in Twyne XXI. 251, cites a MS. treatise in the Royal Library at S. James', London, which was not included in the printed copy.

Annals, i. 68, 240, ii. 734.   Cited also as 'Tractatus de praerogativis et dignitatibus ordinem monasticum concernentibus' in *Annals*, i. 30, 73, &c.

Constitutiones ordinis S. Benedicti factae Abendoniae, 1279: MS. Cotton Faust. A. 2, foll. 93–97 ; see Twyne XXIV. 231.

Constitutiones Benedicti XII pro monachis Benedictinis : cited by Twyne in Twyne XXIV. 323–328, from a MS. belonging to Robert Hegge : cp. MS. Cotton Faust. A. 6, foll. 112–142.

Rules, statutes, &c. of the Order of S. Benedict: MS. ab Ant. Wood 23 (*O. C.* 8611).   Perhaps cited in *City*, ii. 239.

Thomas Woodhop (alias *White*), *Collections about English Benedictines* 1540–1645 : Wood MS. B. 6 (*O. C.* 8577): see *Life*, ii. 321.

Thomas Vincent (alias *Vincent Sadler*), *Catalogue of English Bene-dictines* : MS. perhaps in Ralph Sheldon's hands in 1675 : *Life*, ii. 321.

(*c*) Carthusians.

Statuta et consuetudines ordinis Carthusiani temp. Ric. II : MS. ab Ant. Wood 14 (*O. C.* 8602).

(*d*) Cistercians.

Constitutiones quaedam Cisterciensium nigri ordinis Oxon. : Twyne XXII. 192 : no. 35 in Coxe's Cat. Codd. Coll. Jesu Oxon.

Cited in *Annals*, i. 191.

Nomina abbatiarum ordinis Cistercii : MS. Digb. 11 (*O. C.* 1612), fol. 128^{v}.

Cited in *City*, ii. 304.

(*e*) Black Friars.

Rotulus continens Acta fratrum Praedicatorum et magistrorum Univ. Oxon., 1311 : MS. Digb. 234 (*O. C.* 1835).   Printed in *Collectanea*, vol. ii (Oxf. Hist. Soc. 1890).   Twyne's transcript of it is found in Twyne III. 297–352 ; Langbaine's transcript in Wood MS. D. 18 (*O. C.* 8563).   See also Twyne XXI. 108, 109, 750.

Cited frequently in *Annals*, *Fasti*.

Ordinarium sacrarum caeremoniarum fratrum Praedicatorum : cited by Twyne XXII. 37 : as M. 8. 11. Theol. in 4° in the Bodleian.

Martyrologium fratrum Praedicatorum Oxon., cited by Wood with a reference to ¶ p. 27.

(*f*) Grey Friars.

Registrum fratrum Minorum London. de fundatione et monumentis ecclesiae fratrum Minorum London. : MS. Cotton Vitell. F. 12.   Printed in Rolls Series (*Monumenta Franciscana*) 1858.

Cited frequently in *City*, ii. 345, 368, &c.

Fragmentum historiae fratrum Minorum in Anglia, MS. : cited in *City*, ii. 348, 362, 365, &c.   This is possibly the treatise of Eccleston : see *infra*, under Eccleston.

(*g*) White Friars.

De privilegiis papalibus fratrum ordinis Carmelitarum : a MS. belonging to Dr. Edward Lapworth : known to Wood only from Twyne XXII. 397. The book was mutilated at the beginning : on fol. 12 was a (mutilated) papal bull, dated S. Peter's Rome 1448, against Johannes de Poliaco and his tenets, and in favour of the Preaching, Minorite, Austin, and Carmelite friars, directing that the University of Paris should condemn heretical opinions as often as required by the 'magister generalis et provincialis minister' of these orders.

De origine fratrum . . . de Carmelo : MS. Laud Misc. 722 (*O. C.* 1174), fol. 113.

Cited in *City*, ii. 432.

(*h*) General.

Twyne II. 34 cites a *Tractatus de origine monachatus cum aliis de statu monachali* which he found in the chapter (?) library at Durham.

MS. Ric. James 20, p. 1 and 31 at the end cites *Improperium cujusdam in monachos* : MS. Bodl. 561 (*O. C.* 2345).

84. (iv) *Books about various monasteries, &c.*

(*a*) *De fundatione quorundam coenobiorum in Anglia* : Twyne XXI. 234. Wood knew it only from Twyne, who found it at the end of 'Canones calendarii fratris Johannis Somer cum tabulis ejus ad meridiem Oxon. inter lib. A.' Wood assumes that it had been in Thomas Allen's library.

(*b*) *Cartae de monasteriis*, in the possession of Brian Twyne : excerpts from them are found in MS. Ric. James 21, p. 124.

(*c*) *Catalogus monasteriorum quondam in Anglia*, collected from Camden and other authors : Wood MS. D. 32, foll. 227–359. A treatise in English, originally paged as a separate treatise pp. 1–46, and then the paging discontinued, by an unknown hand : belonged to Brian Twyne.

(*d*) *Papers about the suppression of monasteries in England* : MS. Cotton Cleop. E. 4. There are excerpts from them in MS. Ric. James 8, p. 254.

Cited in *Annals*, ii. 64.

(*e*) *Register of the English College at Douay.*

Cited in *Hist.* ii. 220 ; no doubt from information supplied by letter.

(*f*) *Litterae pertinentes ad monasterium beatae Mariae de Becco Helvini* Rothomagensis diocesis in Normannia : init. 'Post obitum bonae memoriae domini Petri quondam abbatis.' Excerpts from this volume are found in MS. Ric. James 21, pp. 115–124 and in Twyne XXI. 272, 690, and Twyne XXII. 166 : and it is said to be in

C.C.C. library Oxford. Wood entitles it 'res gestae quorundam abbatum monasterii,' &c., and cites it (from Twyne) in *City*, ii. 255. I have not traced the MS.

(*g*) A book of evidences in the hands of Elias Ashmole.

Cited in *Hist.* i. 133.

(*h*) Twyne II. 32 a cites a MS. *Liber provincialis de sedibus archiepiscopalibus et episcopalibus mundi* which he found in Durham library bound up with other treatises, e. g. 'excerpta quaedam de expositione abbatis Joachim super Esayam ubi aperit de onere Babilonis.'

(*i*) Twyne XXI. 379 cites a *Catalogus rotularis episcoporum Ossoriensium*: init.—'Anno Dni. MCII obiit rev. pater Foelix Odullane'; which he saw in the hands of Peter Hooker of C.C.C. Oxford. It had a notice of John Bale.

(*j*) *Copies of papal bulls directed to English church dignitaries*: two volumes folio, written in a modern Italian hand: MS. ab Ant. Wood 11 et 11* (*O. C.* 8599), *Life*, iii. 343.

(*k*) *Works of Pope Innocent III*: MS. ab Ant. Wood 4 (*O. C.* 8592), *Life*, iii. 343.

(*l*) *De superstitione Pharisaeorum*: init. 'Ab uno de monachis amatore cleri'; in the same volume as the Cottonian Tryvytlam (par. 486): excerpts in Twyne XXIV. 304, 305. In Wood MS. E. 4 (*O. C.* 8561) a slip at p. 21, Wood notes, from Twyne, 'it is all against the Mendicants, the writer defending the cause of the University and Monks against the Friars.'

Cited in *Annals*, i. 78.

(*m*) *De gestis et ritibus cleri Cambrensis*: init. operis sive prologi ad opus 'Reverendo patri ac domino S., Dei gratia, Cantuar. archiepiscopo': MS. in Magd. Coll. library. Excerpts in Twyne XXII. 93, 163 c.

Cited, from Twyne, in *Annals*, i. 176.

See Henry Wharton's *Anglia Sacra*, ii. p. 521: MS. no. 255 (32) in Coxe's Cat. of MSS. of C.C.C. Oxford.

(*n*) *De defensione ecclesiae Rothomagensis*: MS. in bibl. Coll. S. Benedicti (Corp. Chr.) Cambr. Excerpts in MS. Ric. James 17, p. 49: Twyne III. 439; Twyne XXIV. 616.

Cited in *Annals*, i. 91, 393.

(*o*) *Calendarium vetus domus S. Thomae martyris juxta Stafford*: excerpt in Twyne XXI. 250.

Cited, from Twyne only, in *City*, ii. 230.

(*p*) *A justification of the Minister's petition*: MS. Bodl. 124, p. 59 (*O. C.* 1987), *olim* MS. Bodl. B. 3. 3. Made use of under the year 1579 (*Annals*, ii. 197).

Muniments and Registers of the University of Oxford.

85. Muniments of the University of Oxford.

These are kept in the Lower Room of the Archives in the Tower of the 1618 Schools, under the custody of the Keeper of the Archives. They comprise charters, letters patent, writs, Acts of Parliament, indentures, leases, &c. If the arrangement which prevailed in Wood's time still holds, they are deposited in four sets of drawers and boxes.

I. *North Press*; three boxes [1] A, B, C.

Wood cites these (for distinction's sake) as pyx. α, pyx. β, pyx. γ, in *Hist., Annals*.

II. *East Press*: a set of drawers in a press on the east side of the room, numbered A–Y; and cited by these letters by Wood in *Hist., Annals, Colleges, Fasti, City* :—'pyx. A,' 'pyx. B,' 'pyx. Y,' &c.

In Twyne XI. pp. 1–83, is a Calendar of these documents. His enumeration there gives only A–I, K i, K ii, L i, L ii, M, N, O.

III. *West Press*: a set of drawers in a press on the west side of the room, numbered A–S; and cited [2] by Wood in *Hist., Annals* (for distinction's sake) as 'pyx. AA,' 'pyx. BB,' &c. See *Hist.* ii. 408.

In Twyne's time they perhaps numbered only A–I, K–P; and were, when he first began to deal with the archives, deposited in the Old Congregation House at S. Mary's 'in archivis venerabilis domus Congregationis.' Lists of the documents contained in them, with transcripts and excerpts, are found in Twyne I :—

pyx. A, at pp. 1–10, 122–123, 279–282.   pyx. I, at pp. 81–72, 304–306.
  „ B, „ „ 11–27, 283–287.   „ K, „ „ 73–74, 307.
  „ C, „ „ 27, 287–289.   „ L, „ „ 74–78, 308.
  „ D, „ „ 27–30, 289–291.   „ M, „ „ 78–88, 309–312.
  „ E, „ „ 31–41, 292–293.   „ N, „ „ 89–100, 313–318.
  „ F, „ „ 41–53, 294–298.   „ O, „ „ 101–110, 319–322.
  „ G, „ „ 54–56, 299–300.   „ P, „ „ 127–134, 323–326.
  „ H, „ „ 56–60, 301–303.

IV. Long boxes, numbered 1–26, cited by Wood sometimes as 'pyx. long. num. 2,' &c., sometimes as 'L. B. 26,' i.e. Long Box 26, &c.: e.g. *Annals*, ii. 23, 845, &c.

In Twyne's time they numbered only 1–23, with 'a square black box'; and were originally kept in the Old Congregation House.

---

[1] 'pyxis' is used for a box or a drawer; 'abacus' for a press containing a set of drawers.

[2] single documents are cited sometimes by the box they are in, sometimes by their title: e.g. 'Liber MS. (membran.) continens chartam Dominae Margaretae de fundatione lecturae suae' may also appear as 'in pyxide A A in Turri Scholarum.'

Lists of the documents contained in them are given in Twyne I:—
Long Boxes 1–19, at pp. 110–120, 135; Long Boxes 1–23, (another
draft) at pp. 327–330; a square black box, at p. 135.

86. The transference of these documents (nos. III and IV, *supra*)
from the Old Congregation House to the Lower Archives Room in the
Schools Tower seems to have been begun by Twyne in Nov. 1640
(Twyne XXIV. 519; and in vol. ii of Collectanea Twyne et Langbaine[1]), but to have been completed only after the surrender of Oxford
(1646), under his successor Dr. Gerard Langbaine. In the mean-
time they had been in considerable danger, and had suffered some
slight loss, as appears from this note by Langbaine in Twyne I. 278 :—

'Memorandum that from the latter end of October 1643 till the
surrender of Oxford (June the 24th 1646), this place being a garrison
of the king's, the Old Congregation house was employed to lay match
in. About the time of the surrender the key of it was given up (by
one . . . Broad, as I was informed) to Mr. [Matthew] Crosse, the squire
bedle in Law, but I could not procure the sight of it before Sept.
1647, and then I discovered that severall panes, in the presse of
evidences where the Universitye's records lay, had been broken, and
was affrayed that many of them might be imbesil'd; but afterwards, in
February 1648 [i.e. ⁸⁄₉], taking a particular survey of all the severall
boxes and writeings in each box, I missed only these fower :—

(1) B. 36—extracta e registris et libris Universitatis concerning the
vintners. This may be supplyed, and so the losse not great.

(2) D. 22—Henry Milward's lease of Beefhall for 40 years, dated 26
Martii, 41 Eliz., anno 1599. This lease is expired and another in
being, and so not of any use.

(3) I. 6—confirmatio privilegiorum ac libertatum Univ. Oxon. per
Oliverum Sutton, episc. Lincoln., ac loci diocesanum (nominatim vero
constitutionis illius provincialis factae in concilio Rading prid. Cal. Aug.
anno 1279), dat. Oxon. xi Cal. Septembr., pontificatus ejus anno
primo [22 Aug. 1281]. The copy of this is extant here above [i.e. in
Twyne I] page 66.

(4) K. 2—vetus quoddam inventarium de bonis Thomae de
Hamme, bibliopolae et stationarii (ut videtur), anno Dom. 1353[2].'

87. According to the universal Oxford practice of triply safe-guarding
things, these muniments, both in their old location and in their new,
were secured by the keys of three officials, whose joint presence was
necessary to obtain admission to them. This is shown in a note by
Twyne (Twyne I. 274) :—

'Keys of the *Abacus* in the Congregation House; the uppermost lock,

---

[1] see par. 243.

[2] this date is astonishingly early; 1353.

but Twyne twice over gives the figures
1353.

the Junior Proctor's keye; the second, the Senior Proctor's; the two lowermost, Mr. Vicechancellor's, the lowermost of all beinge an hollowe key, the other solide.

' The *Abacus* or presse in the west side of *Camera turris Scholarum;* the two uppermost locks the Vice-chancellor's key servinge to both lockes: this key hangeth with the middle key of the mathematicall chest. The two lowermost locks the Proctors' keyes; the Senior Proctor's on the right hand and it hangeth on a loope in the great bunch, marked X; the Junior's on the left hand—the Junior Proctor's key hath a small peice of parchment tied to the bowe thereof, it is in a bunch of five keyes tied together.'

88. Official Calendar of the University Muniments.

The Senior Proctor has in his custody a Calendar of the muniments, entitled 'List of Documents in the custody of the Keeper of the Archives.' A duplicate copy, formerly in the custody of the Vice-chancellor, is now deposited in the Archives. This Calendar was drawn up in 1664[1], under the supervision of Dr. John Wallis (Custos Archivorum 1658–1703), and has been continued to 1720, under the supervision of Wallis's successor, Bernard Gardiner (Custos 1703–1726). It contains a revision of Twyne's Calendars[2], and, in addition, useful lists of the University statute-books, registers, &c. which will presently be described.

89. Indenture Books of the University.

The earliest of these now preserved in the archives seems to be that beginning 1659 and going down to 1732.

90. Account-books of the University of Oxford.

Computus Vice-cancellarii.

At the end of each year of office the Vice-chancellor presented a statement of his receipts and payments for the University during the year, to a delegacy, who scrutinized the items and allowed or rejected them. This statement was, as a rule, written out three times; one copy remained with the outgoing Vice-chancellor himself (and hence in the College muniment-chests some rolls of Vice-chancellor's accounts

---

[1] *Computus Vicecancellarii* for 1664–65 :—'for transcribing of two bookes in which are inserted the particulars of deeds and antiquities gathered by Dr. Wallis, 6s 9d.' Wood was employed in this work; *Life,* ii. pp. 11, 12. The original *Repertorium Chartarum* in Dr. Wallis's handwriting is preserved in the Archives.

[2] Calendar of the muniments *in archivis domus Congregationis,* in Twyne I; Calendar of the muniments *in Turri Scholarum,* Twyne XI. pp. 1–83: a transcript of Twyne's Calendar is Univ. Oxon. Arch. North West Press 33.

are found, deposited there by a former head, e.g. Fitzherbert Adams at Lincoln College), one copy was placed in the archives (and of these several are there preserved), one was entered into a large folio book[1]. The earliest of these books of Vice-chancellor's accounts are as follows : —

(i) *Liber vetus Computi Vicecancellarii*, beginning[2] with the accounts of Walter Wright, Vice-chancellor 1547–1549, and coming down (with a few omissions) to 1666.

(ii) *Computi Vicecancellarii, vol. II*, 1667–1697 : old press-mark *Arch. Univ. Oxon.* **Ar.**

(iii) *Computi Vicecancellarii*, 1697–1735.

91. The Vice-chancellor's Accounts for the Schools.

The building of the New Schools in 1618 introduced yearly statements of moneys received and paid out on their account. These were at first written at the unoccupied beginning of the *Liber Vetus Comp. Vicecanc.*, where the Schools' Accounts for 1621–1655 are found. Beginning in 1656, it became the practice to write them immediately after the *Computus Vicecanc.* for the year.

92. The Vice-chancellor's Accounts for the Theatre.

Following the precedent of the Schools, the building of the Sheldonian introduced a new yearly account. It seems to have been archbishop Gilbert Sheldon's intention to give a sum of 1000*li.* for the building, to be spent under the direction of Dr. John Fell, and at the end of the Vice-chancellor's Accounts for 1663–64 is Fell's account[3] of his expenditure, viz. 151*li.* 12*s* from 7 July to 19 Sept. 1664, out of 200*li.* paid by Sheldon as a first instalment of his 1000*li.* At the end of the Vice-chancellor's Accounts for 1664–65 is Fell's account of his expenditure from 19 Sept. 1664 to 20 Sept. 1665, viz. 412*li.* 8*s* 5*d* : to which this note is added, ' Whereas my Lord's Grace of Canterbury hath been pleased to take upon himselfe the whole charge of building the Theater, it was thought fitt not to continue this accompt any further.' After the Theatre had been handed over to the University, the yearly account of its funds was resumed and appended to the Vicechancellor's Accounts for the Schools. This begins in 1671.

93. The Proctors' Accounts.

The Proctors rendered yearly an account of the sums received and spent by them on behalf of the University. These accounts were

---

[1] many excerpts from the two first *Lib. Comp. Vicecanc.* will be found in Appendix II, *supra* : pp. 51–85.

[2] i.e. chronologically : in the book they come at the end.

[3] see *supra*, p. 68.

deposited in the form of a roll for each year, and also entered into a folio book.

(i) Rolls of Proctors' accounts are found for the years 1464, 1469, 1471-4, 1477-9, 1481, 1482, 1488, 1492, 1494, 1496, 1561.

(ii) The earliest book of Proctors' accounts begins with the year 1564 and is continued (with a very few omissions) to 1787. The entries are, for the most part, meagre and formal.—A '*Catalogue of Proctors*, as far as they can be gathered out of the Registers,' is prefixed, beginning in 1262 and brought down by various hands to 1758.

Cited in *Fasti*, 109, 112.

94. Accounts of the University Chest.

This was an actual chest, secured by five locks, in which were stored the money and other valuables of the University. It was instituted by decree of Convocation 17 Dec. 1545, and deposited in the Treasury of Univ. Coll.

(i) The first volume of these accounts extends from 1545 to 1668: press-mark *Arch. Univ. Oxon.* **Aw.** Title, added recently, 'Rationarium Academicum sive registrum omnium e cistâ publicâ extractorum et in eandem inductorum ab anno 1545.' *Incipit*, 'Liber status bonorum Universitatis Oxon. post horrendum commissum furtum in quo crux magna Universitatis, thuribula, candalabra argentea, pecunia, ac pignora in cistis existentia, ceteraque omnia Universitatis jocalia, auferebantur per quosdam Joannem Stamshewe et Robertum Raunce, ejusdem facinoris perpetratores; de quibus bonis pauca quaedam restituta sunt.'

(ii) The second volume, following a new plan of balancing, extends from 1668 to 1756.

95. Fee-books of the University.

The following seem to be the earliest of these:—

(i) *Liber Feodalis*, 1608-1620, a record of fees paid (according to one conjecture) by undergraduates 'answering under bachelor,' see Wood's *Life*, i. 175, Clark's *Reg. Univ. Oxon.* II. i. 24.

(ii) *Liber Feodorum*, 1618-165$\frac{3}{9}$, a record of fees paid on taking all degrees. This may very likely prove to be of use for checking the record of admission to degrees in the Registers of Congregation.

(iii) Register of fees paid for dispensations and graces, 1609-1614; preserved in the South Press of the Archives. See Clark's *Reg. Univ. Oxon.* II. i. 224.

96. Statute-books of the University.

(i) A folio volume of statutes, formerly in the custody of the Vice-chancellor for the time being. See Anstey's *Munimenta Academica*, p. ix.

Old mark **A** ; old title *Liber Vice-cancellarii* ; by both of which it is freely cited by Wood in his published works and in his MSS.

Anstey, *l. c.*, has printed all the earlier matter in this and the other old statute-books; but there is needed a volume giving the alterations of and additions to the statutes from the date where Anstey stops to the publication of the Laudian Code of 1636. The printed volume of the Laudian Code and the printed *Corpus Statutorum* (1768) took the place of this MS. statute-book as the official copy passed on by the retiring Vice-chancellor to his successor, and then the MS. was placed in the archives: press-mark *Arch. Univ. Oxon.* **A**. The same thing happened with the Proctors' copies of the statutes.

Twyne's excerpts from *Liber Vice-cancellarii A* are found in Twyne I. 124–126, 165–185; Twyne XXII. 389, 391; Twyne XXIV. 413, 422 Wood's excerpts from it are found in MS. Bodl. 594, foll. 177–180 and in an unpaged paper at the end of that MS.

(ii) A folio volume of statutes, formerly in the custody of the Senior (or Southern) Proctor for the time being. See Anstey's *Mun. Acad.* p. xiii.

Old mark **B** ; old title *Liber procuratoris senioris*: press-mark *Arch. Univ. Oxon.* **B**.

Twyne's excerpts from it are found in Twyne I. 124–126, 186, 187, 197–294; Twyne IV. 415–427.

In this volume is found ⟨*Francis*⟩ *Babington's Catalogue of Proctors*, mentioned in *Fasti*, p. 35, and frequently cited in that work.

(iii) A folio volume of statutes, formerly in the custody of the Junior (or Northern) Proctor for the time being. See Anstey's *Mun. Acad.* p. xiv.

Old mark **C** ; old title *Liber procuratoris junioris*; press-mark *Arch. Univ. Oxon.* **C**.

Twyne's excerpts from it are found in Twyne I. 124–6, 189.

(iv) A volume of statutes among the Cottonian MSS. in the British Museum Library. See Anstey's *Mun. Acad.* p. xvii. It is a codification of the statutes in the three preceding volumes, made about the reign of Henry VI. See Twyne XII. 31 ; Twyne XXI. 711.

Old mark **C C** by which it is freely cited in *Annals*; press-mark MS. Cotton Claudius D. 8, foll. 1–108.

(v) A folio volume of statutes, formerly belonging to Thomas Allen, of Gloucester Hall. See Anstey's *Mun. Acad.* p. xvi.

Old mark **D**, by which it is frequently cited by Wood ; press-mark MS. Bodl. 337.

It is a transcript of statutes from B and C ; on parchment, 98 folios, but foll. 86–98 are blank. A list of contents is found at foll. 83–85. See Twyne I. 124–126, 231–234. Wood notes :—'There was an ancient Calendar before it, as appears in Twyne XXII. 405, but there is none now' (1674): the MS. looks as though a gathering or two were missing at the beginning.—At the beginning is now inserted a tract of 6 folios of a later writing, paper, entitled 'Index rubricarum omnium privilegiorum Univ. Oxon. a tempore regis Henrici tertii usque ad annum tricesimum quartum Eliz. reginae': this has nothing to do with the volume, but belongs to a volume of 180 folios.

Outside, under a transparent horn-covering, is the title of the volume, 'Liber diversorum privilegiorum statutorum et rerum memorabilium almae Univ. Oxon.' Inside the binding is the malediction :—' Liber negotiorum Universitatis Oxon. : qui male tractando me spoliaverit vel ab Academia alienaverit, anathema sit, nisi emendaverit.'

(vi) A folio volume of Statutes, drawn up for or by George Darrell of All Souls, Junior Proctor in 1604. See Anstey, *Mun. Acad.* p. xii.

Old mark **E**, by which it is occasionally cited by Wood. Its present (1893) press-mark is Bodleian Libr. **MS. Top. Oxon. b. 5** : but it was formerly known as being in Arch. Bodl. E. It contains folios *a* to *d*, 1–150 ; but foll. 103–116 and foll. 146–149 are blank.

This volume represents a noteworthy endeavour to codify the statutes of the University, and was made use of in drawing up the Laudian Code (*Annals*, ii. 387). In the earlier part of the book are a few marginal notes and titles and inserted slips, some in the copyist's hand, some in another hand (possibly Darrell's), some by Brian Twyne, and one by William Smith (on fol. 31 b 'ita testor Will. Smith, Coll. Univ. Socius, July 24, A. D. 1699 ').

The following are its chief heads :—

(*a*) *The old statutes of the University* transcribed from Libri Statutorum A, B, C, as above, foll. 1–77. The rubrics of A are found at foll. 117–119 a ; of B, at foll. 119 b–121 a ; and of C, at foll. 121–123— transcribed in 1604.

(*b*) *Statuta Edwardina*, the statutes made by Edward VI's Commissioners, 1549 (*Annals*, ii. 95, 100); foll. 78–83. The preface (added by Twyne on fol. 77 b) begins 'Edwardus sextus, Dei gratia,' &c.; the first chapter of the statutes begins 'Deum timete, regem honorate.' See Twyne VII. 143 ; Twyne XVII. 23, 27 ; Twyne XX. On fol. 82 b we have the provisions for the supply of disputants, in which the colleges are grouped in the following sets, (1) Ch. Ch. and Magd. Coll., (2) New Coll. and Alls., (3) Corp., Mert., and ' Aula de

Aulburne' (i. e. S. Alb. H.), (4) Oriel, Bras., Queen's; (5) S. Mary H., Hart H., and ' Collegium Barnardinum,' (6) Linc., Ball., Exet., Univ.

(*c*) *Statuta Reginaldi Pole, Cardinalis*, Statutes made by the Visitors appointed by Cardinal Pole, 1556 (*Annals*, i. 130, 132); foll. 83–86. See Twyne XVII. 29.

(*d*) *Statutes and decrees made during Elizabeth's reign*, foll. 91–102. These are drawn from the later additions in A, B, C (see Anstey, *Mun. Acad.* p. xiii) and from the Registers of Convocation.

One section of these, beginning on fol. 98, had the specific name of *Nova Statuta*, see *infra*, p. 130.

(*e*) An old Calendar for the University; foll. 130–131.

(*f*) A catalogue of Chancellors and Proctors, 1268–1357, 1505–1604; foll. 132, 133.

(*g*) Miscellaneous papers; form of indenture for privileged persons, fol. 87; composition between the University and City, 17 Eliz., 1575, foll. 88–91; forms of oaths and of graces in the University, foll. 142–145.

(*h*) Tables of contents, of foll. 1–102 on foll. 124–129; a subject-index, on foll. 135–141.

(vii) A large quarto volume of statutes, in the University Archives, known as Twyne XX.

Old mark **B+** vel **F**, by which Wood occasionally cites it in his MSS.

It is a transcript of statutes, chiefly from B. *supra*, by Dr. Thomas James, with large additions by Brian Twyne, and contains 522 pages. It was made use of in drawing up the Laudian code, *Hist.* i. 338, *Annals*, ii. 386, 387. A note at the beginning of it, detailing these facts, is dated and signed ' Maii 12, 1704, William Smith.' Langbaine's description of it is—' Transcripta statutorum Univ. Oxon., ex antiquis statutorum libris eorumque exemplaribus, necnon authenticis registris quotquot jam supersunt, ab antiquissimis repetita temporibus usque ad annum Dni 16— continuata.'

It was originally intended to mark this volume **Lib. Stat. F** in continuation of the series of Statute-books; but this idea was abandoned, and F was used to begin the Letter-books.

(viii) A large quarto volume of statutes supplementary to the preceding, in the University Archives, lettered **T. J.**; press-mark Univ. Oxon. Arch. North East press 26.

Its title explains its contents :—' Liber novorum statutorum in quo continentur statuta omnia quae in Convocatione vel in Congregatione edita ac sancita fuerunt a tempore Edvardi VI usque ad annum 1599.' William Smith notes at the beginning :—

(1) ' Dr. Thomas James' Collection of Statutes from the reign of

Edward VI downwards till King James' time with some ancienter statutes towards the end of the Collection; containing 163 pages: (2) other Collections out of the University charters and Statute-books relating to privileges, presentations ⟨to degrees⟩, &c.; 97 pages. These loose sheets or papers were collected and disposed into order and rebound, A.D. 1704.'

The contents are (1) Statutes of Edward VI's Commissioners, pp. 1–28; (2) Statutes of Cardinal Pole's Visitors, pp. 29–53; (3) Statutes collected out of the Registers of Convocation and Congregation, pp. 54–127; (4) Statuta pro scholaribus scripta in fine libri statutorum procuratoris senioris, et vocantur *Nova Statuta,* pp. 144–153.

(ix) *Authenticus Liber Statutorum,* the authoritative MS. of the Laudian code, in the University Archives; reproduced in *The Laudian Code of Statutes* (1636) edited by Dr. John Griffiths 1888, where see pp. xi, xii, xxix of the preface by Mr. C. L. Shadwell.

The fair copy was written by William Ball; the payments for it being as follows :— 1636, 'to William Ball for writeing the authentike copy of the University statutes and inserting the additions into the Vice-chancellor's booke and the beedles' booke, 20*li*.,' 1637, 'to William Ball, by the allowance of the delegates, for his further satisfaction for the writeing of the University statutes, 13*li*. 6*s* 8*d*'—so in the *Comput. Vicecanc.*

This volume was lost for a time. In Twyne XVII. pp. 117–118 is a note that the Authenticus Liber Statutorum was lost in July 1648, but restored in 1661 by Lord Chancellor Hyde, having been secured by Dr. Gilbert Sheldon.

In MS. Bodl. 594 at fol. 213 is a paper (pp. 1–18), entitled 'Historia de statutis Univ. Oxon.' A note by Twyne is found at fol. 222, which states that this paper was written by him as a preface for 'the new statute-book,' and sent to Brian Duppa, Dean of Ch. Ch., but that Duppa kept the original and sent back this copy, which Twyne thinks is in Duppa's own handwriting. The 'Praefatio ad Lectorem' actually adopted in the Laudian code is different, and shorter.

(x) *Statuta Aularia,* statutes made by the University for the government of the Halls.

(a) An early copy of these is found in a volume (MS. Rawl. Statutes 34), formerly belonging to Thomas Allen. The title is :—

'Ordinationes et statuta edita per dominos cancellarios hujus almae Universitatis nostrae . . . ad hilaritatem et profectum scolarium aularium undecem in eadem.'

The first rubric is 'statuta de deo ab aularibus colendo'; and the colophon at the end of the last section is 'Istud opus quod Box explicit.'

(*b*) Brian Twyne's transcript of these statutes is found in Wood MS. D. 32, pp. 534–549.

(*c*) A late copy of Statuta Aularia is found in *Arch. Univ. Oxon.* **D. 28**, along with the records of admission of various principals : see Clark's *Reg. Univ. Oxon.* II. i. 289.

In the Laudian code the *Statuta Aularia* form one of the divisions of the Appendix Statutorum : see Dr. Griffiths' edition (1888), pp. 267–285.

(xi) *Statuta Edwardina* : see pp. 128, 130, *supra*.

The original whence Darrell derived his transcript is not certainly known. Richard James (MS. Ric. James 6, pp. 99, 100) says ' Edwardi statuta habentur in registro Orealensi,' and is followed by Twyne in a marginal note to Darrell and in Twyne XX : but in Twyne XVII. 27 it is said ' de originali non constat.' The volume to which Ric. James alludes may very probably be MS. Rawl. Statutes 45 ; see no. 15485 in Mr. Madan's new Summary Catalogue of MSS. in the Bodleian.

(xii) *Statuta Cardinalis Pole* ; see pp. 129, 130, *supra*. Where the original of these is reposed seems unknown.

(xiii) Dr. Richard Zouch (see *Annals*, ii. 387) was employed[1] to draft a code of Statutes preliminary to the Laudian code. A transcript of his collections ' de privilegiis Academiae Oxon.' is found in the archives of S. John's College : see fourth report of Hist. MSS. Commission ; see *Life*, ii. 7.

(xiv) Dr. Peter Turner[2] of Merton College (*Annals*, ii. 387) was similarly employed : he made similar collections ($16\frac{38}{48}$) which were seen by Twyne and are cited by him in Twyne XXIII. p. 765.

97. The old University Calendar.

The old University calendar stated the days on which the University celebrated special *diriges* and masses, which were left open for lectures and disputations, on which began and ended term, &c. See it printed in Anstey, *Mun. Acad.* pp. cxxxix–cl.

This calendar is found in nearly all the statute-books.

(i) The calendar in Lib. Stat. A is cited in *Fasti*, p. 18.

(ii) The calendar in Lib. Stat. B is cited in *Colleges*, p. 650.

(iii) The calendar in Lib. Stat. C is cited in *Fasti*, p. 18.

(iv) Lib. Stat. D has lost its calendar : see *supra*, p. 128.

(v) Lib. Stat. E has the calendar at foll. 130, 131.

(vi) The calendar of a primer of Sarum, 8 leaves, printed circ. 1505, formerly belonging to a bedell, afterwards to Wood, now in Bodl.

---

[1] *Comp. Vicecanc.* for 1630–31 :— ' to divers scribes that Dr. Zouch im- ployed in writeing of statutes, 2*li.* 10*s.*'

[2] some MS. notes in Dr. Peter Turner's hand are found in Wood MS. F. 31 : *Life*, i. 189, note 2.

(8vo. Rawl. 662), has the Academic items written in it by a contemporary hand.   This is cited by Wood, *Fasti*, p. 18, *Colleges*, p. 650.

98. Letter-books of the University.

(i) In the Cottonian library is a fragment of what seems to be the earliest known letter-book of the University; press-mark MS. Cotton Faustina C. vii.

This contains letters from Henry IV and V, Humphrey duke of Gloucester, &c.   They touch chiefly on the controversies about religion, and have many references to John Wycliffe.   Wood says that there are many things there not noted in his *Hist. et Antiq.*   See Twyne II. foll. 205–228; Twyne XXII. p. 204.   Twyne suggests that it was perhaps written by Robert de Paterna.

Cited several times in *Annals, Fasti, Colleges.*

(ii) MS. Corp. Coll. Cambr. 423 is a collection of letters, of the time of Edward IV, to and from the University of Oxford, formerly belonging to William Warham, Chancellor of Oxford 1506–1532.

Cited in *Annals*, ii. 778.

(iii) The old letter-book of the University, containing letters &c. from 1422 to 1503; see Anstey, *Mun. Acad.* p. xvii, Boase, *Reg. Univ. Oxon.* i. p. vi.

Old mark **F**; old title '*Liber Epistolarum F*,' or '*Registrum Farley F*,' or '*Reg. Farley*,' by all of which it is cited frequently by Wood.   Press-mark *Arch. Univ. Oxon.* **F**.

The title Farley is given to it because transcribed by John Farley (Boase, *l. c.* p. 32).   Twyne's excerpts from it are found in Twyne XXI. 467–472 and in Wood MS. D. 32, pp. 384–389.

(iv) The second letter-book of the University, containing letters &c. from 1508 to 1597.

Old mark **FF**; old title *Liber Epistolarum FF*; by both of which it is frequently cited by Wood.   Press-mark MS. Bodl. 282.

It contains 222 letters, chiefly in Latin, but some in English. Some are addressed to Archbishop Warham, Cardinal Wolsey, Sir Thomas More.   There are 154 leaves, but foll. 137, 140–154 are blank.   A folio extra numerum at the beginning contains forms of citation.

The old press-mark was Bodl. Arch. A. 166, and it is sometimes cited as 'Register of the University of Oxon, of the acts that passed under King Henry VIII,' e.g. in Twyne II. foll. 229–233.   Richard James' excerpts from it are found in MS. Ric. James 12, pp. 30–47.

(v) In the Cottonian library are found several single letters of the University: e.g. MS. Cotton Faust. A. v, fol. 2, a letter to pope

John XXII; MS. Cotton Vitell. E. x. foll. 121–133; MS. Cotton Vespas. F. xiii. foll. 50–52; MS. Cotton Titus B. i. foll. 356–7, a letter to Thomas Cromwell.

Excerpts from these are found in Twyne II. 192, 200.

(vi) From MSS. in various College libraries are cited letters of the University of Oxford, e.g. a 'liber sermonum' in bibl. Coll. Ball. (MS. Ball. Coll. 149, fol. 220) has two letters, cited in *Fasti*, p. 15: a MS. in Magd. Coll. libr. (MS. Magd. Coll. 53, fol. 317) is similarly cited in *Annals*, i. 533.

(vii) MS. Digby 188, fol. 47 (*O. C.* 1789), has a letter of the University of Oxford.

Cited in *Annals*, i. 533.

(viii) MS. Lambeth O. 12, no. 221 in Todd's Catalogue, contains several letters of the University.

Cited in *Fasti*, p. 23; *Annals*, i. 408.

(ix) Twyne II. fol. 42 cites 'Epistolae aliquot Univ. Oxon. contra fratres quattuor ordinum mendicantium,' which Mr. ⟨Richard⟩ James had 'in certaine old loose leafes MS.,' written circ. Henr. IV.

99. Registers of Congregation and Convocation.

These are folio volumes preserved in the University Archives, and are known, and for the most part are cited, by the marks given below in each case. In Twyne's time and in Wood's time some of the later volumes had not yet received their marks; and these were then cited by the date of their first entry. See Boase, *Reg. Univ. Oxon.* I. pp. v, vi, and Clark, *ibid.* II. i. pp. x, xi. Wood's form of citation is either by the mark only, i.e. Aa, or by the mark with Register prefixed, i.e. Reg. Aa; &c.

(i) **Aa**; register of Congregations[1] from 4 Dec. 1448 to 19 Nov. 1463, with a few acts of 1444 on fol. 24. See Twyne XXI. 476. Wood has excerpts from it in Wood MS. D. 3, pp. 1–10.

(ii) **G**; register of Congregations (with a few acts of Convocation) from June 1505 to 27 Nov. 1517. The letter **G** is the old Archive mark in sequence to the Liber Epistolarum. Wood has excerpts from it in Wood MS. D. 3, pp. 11–19.

(iii) **H**; register of Congregations from June 1518 to May 1535. Wood's excerpts are in Wood MS. D. 3, pp. 21–23.

(iv) **I**; register of Congregations from May 1535 to 1563.

[1] the Papal Archives at the Vatican, now being calendared for the Public Records, supply, in petitions of the University to the Pope on his succession, many lists of Oxford graduates earlier than those found in the extant University sources. Mr. W. H. Bliss reports also that in the papers of Urban V (1362–1370) he has found 'Rolls of graduates of Oxford and Cambridge.'

Wood's excerpts are in Wood MS. D. 3, pp. 35–46; and in MS. Bodl. 594, pp. 1–16.   See Twyne XXI. 164.

(v) **KK**; register of Congregations and Convocations from 12 Apr. 1564 to 9 Apr. 1582.   At the end are two letters dated 11 and 12 Oct. 1586.   Wood's excerpts are in Wood MS. D. 3, pp. 47–54.

(vi) **L**; Register of Congregations and Convocations from 28 Apr. 1582 to 5 Apr. 1595. Wood's excerpts are in Wood MS. D. 3, pp. 55–59.

(vii) **M**; Register of Congregations and Convocations from 30 Apr. 1595 to 22 July 1606.   Wood's excerpts are in Wood MS. D. 3, pp. 60–62.

Ma is the register of Convocations, written from the recto end of the book.

Mb is the register of Congregations, written from the verso end.

(viii) **⋊**; register of Congregations from 22 Oct. 1606 to 26 Aug. 1611.   The mark for it is a K turned round ; and I have therefore, for convenience, referred to it as **K** (**reversed**): and so in similar cases.

(ix) **Sa**; register of Congregations from 10 Oct. 1611 to 4 July 1622.

(x) **O**; register of Congregations from 10 Oct. 1622 to Hilary Term 16$\frac{29}{30}$.

Wood notes :—'After Egg-Saturday ⟨162$\frac{8}{9}$⟩ John French was elected Registrar, and he not understanding the way or manner ⟨of keeping the register⟩, hath committed many faults and omitted many things in the latter end' of the volume.   See Clark's *Reg. Univ. Oxon.* II. i. 249 et iii. 6.

(xi) **P**; register of Congregations from 17 Apr. 1630 to July 1634. See Clark, *l. c.* II. iii. 6.

Care must be taken with the mark P, to distinguish this volume (Reg. P) from the Matriculation-book marked by the same letter (Lib. Matric. P).

(xii) **Q**; register of Congregations from 10 Oct. 1634 to 13 July 1647.

(xiii) **Qa**; register of Congregations from 11 Oct. 1647 to 27 July 1659.   Wood has a few excerpts from it in MS. Bodl. 594, pp. 16, 23.

(xiv) **Qb**; register of Congregations from 10 Oct. 1659 to 17 July 1669.

(xv) **Bd**; register of Congregations from 11 Oct. 1669 to 14 July 1680.   Wood has excerpts from it in MS. Bodl. 594, pp. 67–89.

(xvi) **Be**; register of Congregations from 1680 to 1692.   Wood has excerpts from it in MS. Bodl. 594, pp. 92–97.

(xvii) **Bf**; register of Congregations from 1692 to 1703.

(xviii) **K**; register of Convocations from 13 Dec. 1606 to 18 Oct. 1615.

(xix) **N**; register of Convocations from 25 Nov. 1615 to 24 July 1628.

(xx) **R**; register of Convocations from 27 Nov. 1628 to 10 Nov. 1640.

(xxi) The acts of Convocation from Nov. 1640 to July 1642 are lost. See *Life*, i. 51.

(xxii) **S b**; register of Convocations from 11 July 1642 to 5 Aug. 1647. This is sometimes cited as **Reg. Convoc. S.**, e. g. in *Annals*, ii. 446, *Life*, i. 58.

(xxiii) **T**; register of Convocations from 23 Oct. 1647 to 6 Sept. 1659. Wood's excerpts are found in MS. Bodl. 594, pp. 17–23. See *Life*, ii. 91.

(xxiv) **Ta**; register of Convocations from 8 Oct. 1659 to 3 July 1671. Wood's excerpts are in MS. Bodl. 594, pp. 25–64.

(xxv) **Tb**; register of Convocations from 31 Aug. 1671 to 1683. Wood's excerpts are in MS. Bodl. 594, pp. 65, 66.

(xxvi) **Bb**; register of Convocations from 1683 to 1693.

(xxvii) **Bc**; register of Convocations from 1693 to 1703.

100. Wood's excerpts from the registers of Congregation.

The registers of Congregation contain all the ordinary degree-entries. In making preparations for the *Athenae Oxonienses*, the book for which Wood did really original work, Wood was at great pains to draw up lists of graduates at every stage of the degree-system. His Collections were long the only accessible source for information about degrees prior to 1659; but they are now superseded by the Oxf. Hist. Society's *Register of the University*, and Joseph Foster's splendid achievement, the *Alumni Oxonienses*, the former following the chronological order and still in progress, the latter arranged alphabetically and, to our great good fortune, complete.

Wood's degree-collections are arranged in the following sets :—

(i) Admissions to teach in Grammar and Rhetoric, $150\frac{8}{9}$–1568 ; Wood MS. E. 5 (*O. C.* 8511).

(ii) Admissions to B. Mus. and D. Mus., 1504–1669; Wood MS. E. 5.

(iii) Admissions to B.A., 1505–$169\frac{9}{4}$; Wood MS. E. 6. Cited in *Life*, ii. 542.

(iv) Determinations of B.A.s $151\frac{8}{9}$–$16\frac{79}{80}$; Wood MS. F. 14. Cited in *City*, ii. 254, note 1, *Life*, ii. 401.

(v) Licences to M.A., 1505–1691; Wood MS. E. 29. Cited *Life*, ii. 99, iii. 35.

(vi) Inceptions in all faculties [1], 1502–1680; Wood MS. F. 13. Cited as *Catalogus inceptorum* in *City*, ii. 9; *Life*, ii. 334.

(vii) Admissions to B. Can. L., 1505–1535, and to B.C.L. (or LL.B., as it was often called), 1505–1691; Wood MS. E. 7. Wood writes, under the year 1536, 'Nota quod nulli supplicatores pro gradu baccal. juris canonici hoc anno occurrunt: causa est quia monasteria dissoluta erant.'

(viii) Licences to D. Can. L., 1505–1531, and to D.C.L. (or LL.D.), 1505–168$\frac{8}{9}$; Wood MS. E. 7. Cited *Life*, ii. 99.

(ix) Admissions to B. Med., 1505–169$\frac{0}{1}$; Wood MS. E. 8.

(x) Licences to D. Med., 1508–1688; Wood MS. E. 8.

(xi) Admissions 'ad opponendum in S. Theologia,' 1505–1539; Wood MS. E. 9.

(xii) Admissions to B.D. (or S.T.B.), 1505–1690; Wood MS. E. 9. Cited *Life*, i. 476.

(xiii) Licences to D.D. (or S.T.P.), 1505–1690; Wood MS. E. 9.

101. Matriculation-books.

Preserved in the Archives of the University: see Clark's *Reg. Univ. Oxon.* II. i. pp. viii, ix.

(i) *Liber Matriculae* **P**, a folio volume, containing lists of members in 1565, and in 1572, followed by a register of matriculations beginning about 1572 and going down to 1615.

(ii) *Liber Matriculae* **PP**, a folio volume containing matriculations 1615–1647, entitled 'Registrum sive Liber matriculationis omnium personarum tam studentium quam servientium aut ministrorum eorundem omniumque aliarum privilegiatarum personarum juribus sive libertatibus Univ. Oxon. quocunque titulo sive praetextu utentium.'

(iii) *Liber Matriculae* **W**, a quarto volume, containing matriculations 164$\frac{8}{9}$–1662. For the history of this volume, see *Life*, i. 150, iii. 202.

(iv) *Liber Matriculae* **A g**; matriculations 1662–1693. *Comp. Vicecanc. pro Scholis* for 1662–63:—'to Mr. ⟨Samuel⟩ Clarke ⟨bedell⟩ for a matriculation booke bought by him, 9s.'

(v) *Liber Matriculae*, **A z**; matriculations 1693–1709.

<hr>

[1] there were several earlier lists of this kind which Wood may have used; e.g. *Registrum Comitiorum ab anno* 1565 *ad annum* 1616, (i. e. a Catalogue of all Doctors and Masters that 'went out' in that period); MS. Arch. Seld. *supra* 98, no. 2. At a later period the University began to keep a separate Register of Degrees: there is in the Archives a 'Register of all admitted to any degree, 1694–1731.'

102. Wood's excerpts from the Matriculation-books.

These are found in Wood MS. D. 1, Wood MS. E. 5, MS. Rawl. C. 910, Wood MS. F. 31, fol. 114 b (at fol. 197 of the same MS. are excerpts *not* by Wood). Cited in *Life*, ii. 273, 398, &c.

Other excerpts from the Matriculation-books.

Several volumes of this nature are found in the Archives. It will be enough to mention: *Arch. Univ. Oxon.* **Ah**, an index to Liber Matric. W and to part of Liber Matric. Ag. 164$\frac{5}{9}$–1667 ; *Arch. Univ. Oxon.* **Ak**, copies of matriculations, 1691–1699.

103. Subscription-books at matriculation.

See Clark's *Reg. Univ. Oxon.* II. i. pp. vi, vii.
 (i) *Subscription-book* **Ab** ; 1581–1615.
 (ii) *Subscription-book* **Ac** (*olim* **X**) ; 1615–1638.
 (iii) *Subscription-book* **Ad** ; 1650–1660.
 (iv) *Subscription-book* **Ae** ; 1660–1693.
 (v) *Subscription-book* **Af** ; 1694–1714.

104. Subscription-books at graduation.

See Clark's *Reg. Univ. Oxon.* II. i. 47.
 (i) *Subscription-book* **An** ; 1660–1670.
 (ii) *Subscription-book* **At** ; 1670–1695.
 (iii) *Subscription-book* **Ao** ; 1695–1706.

105. Books of subscriptions to the Act of Uniformity.

See *Life*, i. 453. The successive volumes of these, from the imposition of this Test, are preserved in the Archives. The first is from 1662 to 1807 ; press-mark *Arch. Univ. Oxon.* **Be.** *Comp. Vicecanc.* for 1661–62 :—'to John Barnes for a paper booke for subscriptions to the Act of Uniformity, 8*s* 6*d*.'

106. Liber Niger Procuratorum.

The Proctors' Black Book or 'Liber nebulonum' was a register in which the Proctors noted the severer penalties[1] imposed by them, whether fine, rustication, or expulsion. The earliest Liber Niger extant begins in 1630 ; one copy of it is in the custody of the Senior Proctor, another in the custody of the Solicitor to the University. Wood's sentence was entered in it in 1693 ; see *Life*, iii. 438.

---

[1] *Life*, i. 46, ii. 97, iii. 68.

<h1 align="center">107. Bedells' books.</h1>

(i) *Antiquus liber Bedellorum Univ. Oxon.* This is cited several times in *Annals, Fasti, City.* It existed in at least three copies.

(*A*) A copy, formerly in Wood's possession, afterwards in Thomas Hearne's (see no. 15411 in Mr. Madan's new Summary Catalogue), now in the Bodleian, press-mark 8vo Rawl. 662. This consists of four portions :—

(*a*) A printed calendar, 8 leaves, belonging to a primer of Sarum, of date circ. 1505, with MS. entries relating to University disputations, lectures, &c. See *supra,* pp. 131, 132.

(*b*) A MS. portion follows, 30 leaves : pp. 1–7 are blank : p. 8 is a later copy of p. 9 (substituting 'Henry VIII and Anne' for 'Henry VIII and Katherine'); pp. 9–36 give an account, written circ. 1515, of the masses, diriges, and other anniversary services of the University, which are found briefly stated in the Calendar in Anstey's *Mun. Acad.* : the beginning is 'hodie, hoc est in vigilia Sti Martini episcopi, orandum est pro omnibus benefactoribus'; tables of fees follow; pp. 37–39 are blank ; pp. 40, 41 contain the music[1] ('tenor' and 'contra-tenor') for (I suppose) the bedells' formulae at the Schools; pp. 42–45, in a considerably later hand than the preceding parts, resembling that on p. 8, give the formulae at the creation at the Act, &c. ; pp. 46–60 are blank.

(*c*) A printed treatise, part of the Primer, follows :—'Fratris Hieronymi Savanorolae, expositio in [quosdam] Psalmos.'

(*d*) At the end are 2 leaves of MS., being notes about fees.

Mr. Madan re-discovered this MS. in January 1893.—Note that the *Calendarium missarum* (see *Life,* i. 325) for Jan.–Feb. in MS. Bodl. 594, pp. 190–191, agrees so closely with pp. 11–14 of 8vo Rawl. 662 as to make it probable that Wood obtained this MS. from John Longford, after making that excerpt from it.

(*B*) A copy, written circ. Henr. VII, was in Thomas Allen's hands. A transcript of this, formerly belonging to Twyne, is found in Wood MS. D. 32, pp. 553–568. This contains practically the same matter as 8vo Rawl. 662, but there are slight differences, which show that the Allen MS. was not this identical book.

(*C*) A copy, also written circ. Henry VII, in the possession of Dr. (? Richard) James. A collation of this is added by Twyne in his transcript of the Allen MS. Slight differences show that the

---

[1] Wood, in *Life,* i. 223, note 1, speaks of 'the song of the bedells in Oxon.' I am inclined to think that this is the scurrilous poem on the four bedells and their wives, found in MS. Tanner 306, fol. 302, and in several printed collections.

James MS., although containing substantially the same matter, was independent certainly of Allen's copy and perhaps of 8vo Rawl. 662 : see Twyne's note in Wood MS. D. 32, p. 395.

(ii) *John Bell's Collections* (Esquire Bedell of Arts and Medicine, 1605–1638); *Life*, iii. 44. This volume contains :—

(1) Exercitia praestanda pro baccalaureatu in Medicina, et pro doctoratu in medicina ; (2) ordo collegiorum ut suo loco concionentur in pleno termino ; (3) an extract of certaine decrees of Convocation, 3 Aug. 1590, that concern the increase of learning and good government of the University of Oxford; (4) Catalogue of High Stewards of the University from 1555, with several matters taken out of the registers concerning the election of High Stewards ; (5) the order of the solemnity of the creation of Thomas Egerton, lord Ellesmere, to be Chancellor of the Universitie, 1610; (6) elections of the squire- and yeomen-bedells[1], commencing from 1540; (7) Catalogues of Chancellors (1505–1630), Vicechancellors (1565–1635), Proctors (1505–1635); (8) Catalogue of Inceptors, 1505–1642; (9) the names of physicians admitted *ad incipiendum* ⟨i. e. M.D⟩ and *ad lecturam Aphorismi Hippocratis* ⟨i. e. M.B.⟩ and *ad practicandum*[2]; (10) an account of laying the first stone of the Arts library over the proscholium, 16 July[3] 1610; (11) an account of laying the first stone of Wadham College (31 July 1610), and the New Schools; (12) the controversy between the University and City[4] decided at Whitehall 22 June 1612.

This volume is now[5] in the Archives; press-mark *Univ. Oxon. Arch.* **A1.**

(iii) *Matthew Crosse's book* (Esquire Bedell of Law, 1618–1648); this is, I suppose, the volume **Am** now bound with **A1.**

(iv) *John Thimble's book* (Esquire Bedell of Divinity, 1615–1641). On the first leaf is written ' John Thimble's book 6 May 1615.' It contains regulations for, and notices of, University sermons, and elections of officers ; it is kept in the South Press in the Archives; an 8vo volume.

(v) *Henry Jacob's book* (Esquire Bedell of Divinity, 1641–1648), containing lists of inceptors, 1565–1647, is in MS. Rawl. C. 876.

108. Records of Curia Seneschalli.

The court of the Steward of the University had formerly jurisdiction

---

[1] Clark's *Reg. Univ. Oxon.* II. i. p. 257.

[2] *ibid.* p. 123.

[3] Wood, following Twyne, gave the date as 19 July, *Hist.* ii. 91; then, following this authority, changed it to

16 July, *Annals*, ii. 936.

[4] *Annals*, ii. 308.

[5] bound with it is another treatise of like sort, formerly *Univ. Oxon. Arch.* **Am**, containing collections 1505–1641.

in cases of homicide. Several bundles of papers in connexion with this court and cases tried in it are found in the Archives of the University. The trials are of the years 1562, 1614, 1634.

109. Records of the Leet-Court of the University.

Presentments of the leets, court-rolls, summonses, and other papers for the years 1573, 1575, 1593, 1596, 1597, 1601, 1602, 1635-38, 1651, are found in the Archives. 'Rolls of the view of frankpledge of the University' 1636, are cited in *City*, i. 434.

110. Registers of the Vice-chancellor's Court.

The Court of the Chancellor (Curia Cancellarii), or, as it has long been more familiarly called, *the Vice-chancellor's Court*, was the ordinary court of law for the trial of cases in which members of the University were concerned. The registers of the proceedings in this court, some threescore and ten folio volumes, are preserved in the Archives of the University. In Wood's time the earlier volumes were called *Registra*, but the later ones *Libri Actorum*. They are now usually cited by mention of the years which they cover, but formerly by their distinctive letters or marks. Wood cites the volumes either by their letters only, e. g. Aaa, or with Registrum prefixed, e. g. Reg. Aaa.

(i) **Aaa**; Registrum Curiae Cancellarii 1434–1469.

See Anstey (*Mun. Acad.* p. xviii), who has printed a large portion of it. Wood's excerpts from it are found in Wood MS. D. 3, pp. 63–126 and in MS. Bodl. 594, pp. 173–176.

(ii) **Ɑ**; Reg. Cur. Canc. 1498–1505. The mark is a D turned backwards, and therefore for convenience it is cited in the notes to *City*, as **D (reversed)**. In his MSS. Wood often carelessly writes the symbol as **Δ**, and in a few places in the notes to *City*, it has been, by an oversight, called **Reg. Delta**. Wood's excerpts are in Wood MS. D. 3, pp. 131–149.

(iii) **Ⅎ**, i. e. **F (reversed)**; Reg. Cur. Canc. 1506–1514.

Wood's excerpts are in Wood MS. D. 3, pp. 153–174.

(iv) **ᗺ**, i. e. **B (reversed)**, or (formerly) **EEE**; Reg. Cur. Canc. 1527–1543.

Wood's excerpts are in Wood MS. D. 3, pp. 177–202.

(v) **GG**; Reg. Cur. Canc. 1545–1555.

See Clark's *Reg. Univ. Oxon.* II. i. p. xii. Wood's excerpts are in Wood MS. D. 3, pp. 203–229.

(vi) **HH**; Reg. Cur. Canc. 1558 to 1560; cited sometimes as *Registrum* **HH**, sometimes as *Liber Actorum* **HH**.

(vii)	*Liber Actorum*	**A**,	1561–66.
(viii)	,,	**B**,	1566–78.
(ix)	,,		1577–78[1].
(x)	,,	**Bb**,	1578–80.
(xi)	,,		1578–80[1].
(xii)	,,	**C**,	1578–82.
(xiii)	,,	**D**,	1580–84.
(xiv)	,,	**E**,	1584–85.
(xv)	,,		1585–95[1].
(xvi)	,,	**F**,	1585–87.
(xvii)	,,	**G**,	1587–88.
(xviii)	,,	**H**,	1588–89.
(xix)	,,	**I**,	1589–90.
(xx)	,,	**K**,	1590–91.
(xxi)	,,	**L**,	1591–92.
(xxii)	,,	**Kk**,	1593–94.
(xxiii)	,,	⍦,	1594.
(xxiv)	,,	⊖,	1594–96.
(xxv)	*Reg. Cur. Canc.*	1596–97.	
(xxvi)	,,	,,	,, 1596–1604.
(xxvii)	,,	,,	,, 1597–1600.
(xxviii)	,,	,,	,, 1600–3.
(xxix)	,,	,,	,, 1604–7.
(xxx)	,,	,,	,, 1608–11[2].
(xxxi)	,,	,,	,, 1611–15.
(xxxii)	,,	,,	,, 1615–18.
(xxxiii)	,,	,,	,, 1618–22.
(xxxiv)	,,	,,	,, 1622–23[3].
(xxxv)	,,	,,	,, 1623–25.
(xxxvi)	,,	,,	,, 1625–28[4].
(xxxvii)	,,	,,	,, 1633–36.
(xxxviii)	,,	,,	,, 1636–39.
(xxxix)	,,	,,	,, 1638–40.
(xl)	,,	,,	,, 1640–41.
(xli)	,,	,,	,, 1644–45.
(xlii)	,,	,,	,, 1644–52.

[1] i.e. subsequent to the binding of the first set of books, and lettering them, papers belonging to these years have been sorted and bound up.

[2] in *Annals*, ii. 299, Wood cites 'Liber Actorum Curiae Cancellariae, 5 Feb. 160⅞ to 13 Dec. 1611.' I have not found any trace of it, but I hardly think that it can be lost.

[3] this volume is cited by Twyne in Twyne XIV. 45.

[4] this volume is cited by Twyne in Twyne XIV. 187.

(xliii)	*Reg. Cur. Canc.*			1652–53.
(xliv)	,,	,,	,,	1654–57.
(xlv)	,,	,,	,,	1659–62.
(xlvi)	,,	,,	,,	1662–66.
(xlvii)	,,	,,	,,	1669–76.
(xlviii)	,,	,,	,,	1677–79.
(xlix)	,,	,,	,,	1679–84.
(l)	,,	,,	,,	1684–85[1].
(li)	,,	,,	,,	1685–91.
(lii)	,,	,,	,,	1692–98.
(liii)	,,	,,	,,	1698–1706.

111. Books of depositions in the Vice-chancellor's Court.

The depositions of witnesses in cases before the court are bound in volumes as follows:—(i) 1566–1578; (ii) 1578–84; (iii) 1584–92; (iv) 1605–18; (v) 1619–27; (vi) 1627–44; (vii) 1641–42.

112. Testamentary books of the Vice-chancellor's Court.

The Curia Cancellarii from early times had jurisdiction in the probate and administration of the wills of *scholares* and *personae privilegiatae*; see the preface to John Griffiths' *Index to wills proved in the Court of the Chancellor of the Univ. of Oxford* . . . Oxford 1862. The earlier documents of this kind are entered in the registers of the court; the volume GG alone containing some 470 wills or testamentary documents (a few of which have eluded Dr. Griffiths' search and are not noted in his index).

About 1840, under the care of Dr. Philip Bliss, then Keeper of the Archives, the original testamentary papers, so far as then found in the Archives, were bound up into four series :—

(i) *Wills*, arranged alphabetically, in 15 volumes ;
(ii) *Inventories*, in 11 volumes ;
(iii) *Administration-bonds*, in 8 volumes ; and
(iv) *Accounts*, in two volumes.

113. Books and Papers connected with the degree system or ceremonies.

(i) *Liber creationis Magistrorum* secundum usum Oxon., MS. Coll. Magd. ; Twyne's excerpts from it are found in Wood MS. D. 32, p. 579. Twyne afterwards noted that 'this MS. was lost when the MSS. of Magd. Coll. were newly bound.' See however MS. Magd. Coll. 38, fol. 32. Wood entitles the MS. 'Modus incipiendi.'

---

[1] in the South Press in the Lower Room.

(ii) *Disputationes et suppositiones quorundam Inceptorum* in Univ. Oxon., written circ. Ric. II; *init.* 'Quaestio ad quam respondebat Thomas Bradeley'; MS. Corp. Oxon. 116. Twyne's excerpts, Twyne XXIV. 261, 282. Cited in *Annals*, ii. 724, 725.

(iii) *Forma disputationis in Theologia* in publicis scholis Oxon.; MS. Lambeth 221, fol. 262; formerly belonging to lord Lumley. Cited in *Annals*, i. 563.

(iv) *De exercitiis theologorum*; Twyne II. fol. 147 b, Twyne XXIV. 282.

(v) Twyne's notes of his argument in a controversy 'for the seniorship of the Act at Oxford A.D. 1618, between Daniel Hollyday of C. C. C. and Robert Kinge of Ch. Ch. (who claymed it as being a bishop's sun); delegates—for Hollyday, Brian Twyne of C. C. C., John Bally of St. John's, —for Kinge, Dr. ⟨Edward⟩ James, Dr. ⟨Richard⟩ Kilby: it was argued in Dr. William Goodwyn's lodginge, the deane of Ch. Ch. and Vicechancellor.' Twyne II. foll. 69, 70.

(vi) *Liber admissionum ad studiendum Jure Civili*, $16\frac{69}{70}$–$171\frac{0}{1}$, in Arch. Univ. Oxon.; press-mark **A u**.

(vii) *Registrum admissorum ad regendum*, 1634–1705.
Preserved in the Archives. See Clark's *Reg. Univ. Oxon.* II. i. 88.

(viii) Very precise notes as to the proceedings in the *Vespers* and the *Act*[1] are found in ⊖ ⊖ fol. 405ᵛ, 406ᵛ: see par. 200. See also about the Act, Twyne XXI. 349; Twyne XXII. 437, and ⊕✝ 145 (see p. 211 *infra*).

114. Exercises (in their College and in the Schools of the University) performed by candidates for degrees.

A complete set of these for the seventeenth century may one day be pieced together from the papers of Oxford students. As a beginning towards it I note the following:—

For M.A.—Brian Twyne's 'lectiones solennes': par. 254 (iii) — speeches of *Terrae filii* at the Act, *Life*, ii. 266, iii. p. vii.

As Regent Master.—Oratio Ricardi James cum inciperet moderari in Augustiniensibus: MS. Ric. James 13, pp. 145–151. See Clark's *Reg. Univ. Oxon.* II. i. 74.
— Lectiones in Musica, *Life*, iii. p. vii.

For B.D.—Oppositio Ric. James in Schola Theologica, to Moore Fortune (B.D. 1621) on the thesis *An papistae juste accusantur idolatriae?*—MS. Ric. James 13, p. 256. See Clark's *Reg. Univ. Oxon.* II. i. 133.

---

[1] a minute description of the Act in the eighteenth century is found in Thomas Hearne's Diaries, vol. 175, pp. 117 sqq.

Miscellaneous.

— Gerard Langbaine's Oratio habita in aula Reginensi 1625 : on
the theme 'Infantes sumus et senes videmur' : MS. Langb. 14
(at the end).

— Gerard Langbaine's Oratio in aula habita cum Suetonium pro
more praelegerem 25 Jan. 163$\frac{2}{3}$: MS. Langb. 17, p. 3.

115. Narratives, &c., about their office by ex-officers.

(i) *Gesta cancellariatus Laud* ; see *Life*, ii. 214 : cited very frequently
in *Annals* and in *City*.   Printed in Wharton's *Remains of Laud*.

(ii) *Robert Pinke's narrative of his Vicechancellorship*; see *Life*,
i. 133 : cited frequently in *Annals*.   Excerpts from this are found in
MS. Ballard 70.

(iii) *Speeches of William Strode*, Public Orator 1629–1644 ; see
MS. Corp. Oxon. 301 fol. 129.

116. Books and papers connected with the Visitations of the University.

(i) Henry VIII's (Thomas Cromwell's) Visitation ; Twyne II. 202 ;
Twyne VII. 112, 113.

(ii) Edward VI's Visitation [1] ; Twyne VII. 139–146.

(iii) Queen Mary's (Cardinal Pole's) Visitation ; Twyne VII. 147–
155.

Excerpts from Dr. ⟨William⟩ Gager's papers about it are found in
Twyne VII. 155–157.   Articuli interrogatorii in (Cardinal Pole's) Visit.
Acad. Oxon.; Twyne II. 84.

(iv) Queen Elizabeth's Visitation ; Twyne VII. 158.

(v) Archbishop Laud's projected Visitation ; Twyne VII : see par.
222.

(vi) The Parliamentary Visitations, 1647–1659: see the list of
authorities in *Life*, i. pp. 141–144.

Especial prominence must be given to the *Register of the Visitors*,
MS. e Mus. 77 in Bodl., printed by Professor M. Burrows for the
Camden Society (1881).   Cited frequently in *Annals*, and *Fasti*.—
This register is however incomplete, and has to be supplemented
in many points by the original orders issued by the Visitors, found
among the papers given to Wood, when he was writing his *Historia*,
by Dr. Gilbert Sheldon and Dr. Thomas Barlow, now known as
Wood MS. F. 35.   This volume contains some autograph letters by

[1] the proceedings of these Commissioners at Magd. Coll. are noted in MS.
Corp. Chr. Cambr. 127, artt. 21–28.

Dr. Samuel Fell, and diaries of the Visitation by John Newton, Thomas Barlow, and others.

(vii) Charles II's Visitation, 1660: see *Life*, i. 325, 324 note 6.

A copy of the commission issued for this Visitation, and some other papers relating to it, are found in Wood MS. F. 35.

The Minutes of the Commissioners' meetings are in a volume in the University Archives, entitled 'Acts of the Commissioners of Charles II, Sept. 1660—24 July 1662.'

117. Royal and other Visits.

(i) Miles Windsor's account of Queen Elizabeth's first visit [1], 1566, is found in Twyne XXI. 792–800.

(ii) Twyne's collections, Twyne XVII. 147 sqq. These comprise, (1) adventus Ricardi III, 1483; (2) Henry VIII, Queen Katherine, and Wolsey; (3) Queen Elizabeth, 1556 Aug. and Sept., pp. 153–167; (4) Count Alasko; (5) Queen Elizabeth, 1592 [2], pp. 174–180; (6) James I, 1605 [3] Aug. 3, pp. 181–186; (7) Charles I, 1638, pp. 187–203. Twyne has entitled this paper 'Enterteynments.' On p. 209 of this volume Wood had begun an account of Charles II's visit, 1663; but left off abruptly, no doubt that he might begin a similar volume of his own.—For other accounts of Queen Elizabeth's visit in 1592 and King James' in 1605, see Patrick papers vol. 34 and Baker MS. 3, foll. 441–452, in Cambr. Univ. library; Cat. of MSS. of Cambr. Univ. libr. vol. v, pp. 180, 446.

(iii) Wood's Collections, Charles II to William III, 1661–1695; MS. Wood D. 19 (3). These have been printed in their places chronologically in *Life*, e.g. i. 412, &c. He entitled his volume (after Twyne) 'Entertainments and solemnities.'

118. Some Royal Charters.

(i) *King Henry VIII's Charter* to the Univ. of Oxf., 1511, Wood in 1674 found 'in the hands of Dr. John Lloyd, principall of Jesus College, written in a velum book. Dr. John Williams his predicessor had it and left it behind him when Vice-chancellor (i.e. in 1605); and so hath continued in his successors' hands ever since.'

(ii) *Charta Carolina.* A volume in the Archives, press-mark 'North-West Press 28,' contains a transcript of Charles I's great charter (see

---

[1] see other papers reprinted in Plummer's *Elizabethan Oxford* (Oxf. Hist. Soc.), 1886.

[2] Elizabeth's speech on this visit is found in MS. Cotton Faust. C. vii.

foll. 210–214.

[3] James' speech *in Comitiis* on this occasion is found in Twyne II. fol. 89, and Wood MS. D. 32, p. 351.

Annals, ii. 402) and some other papers. The volume was once marked **CC**.

119. Books relating to the Halls.

(i) *Statuta Aularia*; see *supra*, p. 13.

(ii) *Admissiones principalium Aularum*, a volume in the University Archives, press-mark **D 28**; see Clark's *Reg. Univ. Oxon.* II. i. p. 289.

(iii) *Visitationes Aularum*, four volumes in the University Archives, press-marks **D24–D27**, containing notes of the dues &c. in the Halls about 1650.

(iv) *Catalogues of the old halls*:—

(*a*) Simon Parrett's (or Perrott's) Catalogue; *City*, i. 637.

(*b*) John Rouse's Catalogue; *City*, i. 638.

(*c*) William Standish's Catalogue; *City*, i. 635, 651. Cited frequently in *City*, e.g. i. 293, 303, &c.

(*d*) Thomas Key's Catalogue; *City*, i. 517.

(*e*) Miles Windsor's Catalogue; *Arch. Univ. Oxon.*, press-mark North-West Press no. 27.

(*f*) Brian Twyne's Catalogues; Twyne XXI. 44, 45 b, 149–151; Wood MS. D. 32, pp. 619–626.

(*g*) Anthony Wood's Catalogues; found in Wood MS. F. 29 A, foll. 136, 49, 130; cited in *City*, i. 82 ('Catalogus noster Aularum'); printed in *City*, i. 506, 509, 512.

(v) *Catalogue of the principals of the old halls*; Wood's Catalogue, cited in *City*, i. 124, 146, &c., found in Wood MS. D. 7 (1), is printed in *City*, i. 586–606.

Michael Woodward's notes towards such a Catalogue are found in Wood MS. F. 28, and printed in *City*, i. 606–609.

120. The Market.

(i) *De mercatu*, a treatise by Twyne; see Twyne XVI.

(ii) The evidence of witnesses, Apr. 1582, to determine whether the Vicechancellor or Proctors should appoint the clerks of the market; Twyne II. foll. 51–56. See Clark's *Reg. Univ. Oxon.* II. i. 252.

(iii) Dr. John Delaber's collections *de mercatu*, are found in Twyne II. foll. 59–63, with the note 'Mr. George Bayly sometimes fellow of C.C.C. gave me these notes long ago and as I remember he told me that he had them of Dr. Dalober whose kinswoman he married.'

(iv) *Books of the Clerks of the Market*. These are found in the University Archives, some twelve small volumes, for the periods 15 Nov. 1617 to 30 Apr. 1645, and 24 Aug. 1653 to 5 May 1658.

See Rev. O. Ogle's account of the Oxford Market in Oxf. Hist. Soc. *Collectanea*, vol. ii.

121. Books and Papers relating to the Bodleian.

(i) Copies of deeds connected with the Library, Twyne II. 104 sqq.

(ii) Collections by Twyne for the history of the Library, Twyne VI. 161–173.

(iii) Account of the laying the first stone of the Bodleian by Dr. John King, Dean of Ch. Ch. and Vice-chancellor, at 10.30 A.M. on 19 July 1610; Twyne XXI. 285. See *supra* p. 139, note 3.

(iv) *Statuta Bibliothecae Bodleianae* : initium praefationis ' Quando-quidem in hoc rerum humanarum curriculo'; written in English by Sir Thomas Bodley and put into Latin by Dr. John Budden of Gloucester Hall (*Annals*, ii. 926); what was probably Twyne's copy of these is found inserted after page 568 in Wood MS. D. 32. It is followed by a list of benefactors to the Library.

Another copy, followed by a Catalogue of books in the Library, in two volumes, marked **AAA**, drawn up for the Vice-chancellor's use, is found in the Archives.

(v) *Account-books of the Bodleian.*

(*a*) Bodleian accounts 1613–1676; a quarto book in vellum binding; the accounts for each year signed by the Curators present at the audit; preserved in the archives of the Library. A duplicate copy is in the University Archives, press-mark **Ax**.

(*b*) Bodleian accounts, 1676–1813 ; a folio book bound in leather; signed as before; preserved in duplicate in the archives of the Library.

(*c*) Bodleian accounts, 1653–1659; a quarto book in leather binding; preserved in the archives of the Library.

(vi) A note of what happened at the Visitation of 1613, with complaints about the loss or misplacing of 3 MSS. and the shifting of books, is found in Twyne II. foll. 108–112.

(vii) *Libri Benefactorum bibl. Bodl.*

These volumes are preserved in the Library, two large vellum books, entitled ' Registrum donationum quibus ampliata est Bibliotheca Bodleiana'; vol. i. 1600–1688, vol. ii. 1693–1791.

The first volume begins with the benefaction of Thomas Sackvile lord Buckhurst, the Chancellor, and up to page 91, col. 1 med., is *printed*; the last printed entry being a donation of Robert Barker, the King's printer, in 1604. The MS. continuation goes on to p. 428, concluding with the gifts in 1688 of Dr. Thomas Marshall, and Charles Hatton (brother to Christopher lord Hatton). There are also at the end unpaged some blank leaves and eight leaves of index.

The second volume begins with catalogues of the MSS. of Edward Pocock and Robert Huntingdon added in 1693, and ends at p. 216 with a notice of a subscription in 1789-91 to buy early editions. The second half of the volume is blank.—The register seems to have many gaps.

Twyne's excerpts from the first of these volumes are found in Twyne II. fol. 107. Other excerpts are found in a paper bound up with Wood MS. D. 11.

(viii) *Libri Admissorum in bibl. Bodl.*

(1) Liber Admissorum, 1610-1676 (1692); see Macray's *Annals of the Bodleian*, p. 459 note; Clark's *Reg. Univ. Oxon.* II. i. 262. This MS. was *olim* MS. Bodl. 766: *Life*, i. 258.

(2) Thomas James, MS. 'Catalogue of books in the Bodleian,' has at the beginning[1] a list of 19 foreigners admitted to the Bodleian, 'Anno 1604, mense April—' press-mark **MS. Bodl. 510.**

(3) Liber Admissorum (peregrinorum), 1682-1833; Macray, *l. c.*

(4) Extranei nobiles et generosi, admitted 1602-1666; Wood MS. E. 5. Some other notes by Wood to the same effect are found in Wood MS. F. 31, foll. 108 sqq.

Cited in *Life*, ii. 265 as *Cat. studentium in bibl. Bodl.*

(5) The first draft of Dr. Thomas James' Catalogue of admissions to the Bodleian, extending to over 100 pp., is now in MS. Rawl. D, *olim* 1290, *nunc* 912.

122. Sir Henry Savile's Foundation.

(i) *Statutes for the Geometry and Astronomy professors*, given by the founder 10 Aug. 1619 and approved by the University 16 Aug. 1619, beginning 'In nomine gloriosissimae et individuae Trinitatis,' are found in Reg. Convoc. N, foll. 261 sqq.—A transcript of them, not by Wood, is found in Wood MS. B. 14 (*O.C.* 8587), foll. 97-103.

(ii) Twyne's notes of the inaugural lectures, by Savile on 12 July 1620 and by Henry Briggs on 8 Jan. 162$\frac{0}{1}$, are found in Twyne XXI. 818, 838: see *Annals*, ii. 334.

123. The Schools.

(i) *Rotulus computi . . . supervisoris fabricae Scholae Theologicae*, 1453. Cited in *Annals*, ii. 777, and there said to be in the Treasury of Univ. Coll.

(ii) A lamentable account of the shameful maltreatment of the Schools in Edward VI's time is found in Twyne XXI. 215.

---

[1] there is also a note that James Atwood, a Worcestershire gentleman, gave 22*s* to the New Schools.

(iii) *Liber computi de receptis et expensis pro fabrica Scholarum*, 1557, in the University Archives, press-mark South Press 7. Cited in *Annals*, ii. 763.

(iv) *Book of Benefactors to the building of the New Schools.*

This is a large folio in vellum, preserved in the archives of the Bodleian, lettered on the back 'Regist. Aedif. Public.,' and entitled 'Nomina et cognomina eorum qui ad construendam Novarum Scholarum fabricam vel pecunias numeratas vel aliud aliquod munificentiae genus subministrarunt.' The first 98 pages are written on; quite a third of the volume is blank; there is an index at the end.

Wood has excerpts from this, dating from 1612 to 1616, in a paper bound up with Wood MS. D. 11; see *Life*, i. 78, note 6.

(v) The Vice-chancellor's *Accounts for the Schools*; *supra*, p. 125.

(vi) Register of Examinations, giving the names of Candidates and of the Examiner who took them in the examination. The first volume[1] extends from 1638 to 1669, press-mark *Univ. Oxon. Arch. Ap*: the second volume is 1693–1706.

124. The Physic Garden.

Twyne's note of the ceremony of laying the foundation-stone of the Physic Garden, 25 July 1621, is found in Twyne XXI. 838.

125. The Sheldonian (The Theatre).

(i) An account of the moneys laid out in building the Theatre at Oxford by archbishop Sheldon; MS. Bodl. 898: see *supra*, p. 68. This gives a detailed account of every penny laid out, and to whom the payments were made.

(ii) The Vice-chancellor's Accounts for the Theatre: see *supra*, p. 125.

126. The Ashmolean.

Narrative of the opening, &c., of the Ashmolean; Wood MS. F. 31, fol. 141; printed in *Life*, iii. 54.

127. Lists of Officials and Servants of the University.

(i) *Catalogus Cancellariorum, &c.; Fasti Oxonienses*: lists[2] of the Chancellors, Vice-chancellors, Proctors, &c.

---

[1] Proctors' accounts for 1638–39:— 'pro registro ad excipienda nomina examinatorum et candidatorum, 3s 6d.'

[2] numerous papers of this kind exist in MSS. other than those cited here, e. g. by Thomas Walker, in MS. Univ. Coll. 128. See also *supra*, pp. 126, 127, 139.

(1) Miles Windsor's, 1220–1616; Wood MS. F. 27.

(2) Brian Twyne's, 883–1642; Twyne XIX; 883–1626, Wood MS. F. 27.

(3) Anthony Wood's:—(*a*) the Latin version, printed in *Historia et Antiquitates*, 1674; (*b*) the English version, in MS. in Wood MS. F. 2; printed in *Athenae Oxon.* 1691, 1692, and in *Fasti* (by Gutch). Cited frequently in *City*, e. g. i. 173; ii. 269, &c.

(ii) Catalogues by Wood, (*a*) of *Wardens of the chests*, 1510–1519; (*b*) of *Registrars*, 1508–1659; (*c*) of *Bedells*, 1508–1634; are found in Wood MS. E. 5. Some notes by Wood about the Bedells are in Wood MS. E. 4 (*O. C.* 8561), on a slip attached to p. 161.

128. Miscellaneous Lists.

(i) *Names of 'privileged persons'*; in 1384, to the number of 145, Twyne IV. 199; in 1410. Twyne IV. 70.

(ii) Names of bishops, &c., educated at Oxford, collected by Twyne; Twyne II. foll. 123–125; Wood MS. D. 32, pp. 476–482.

(iii) Names of benefactors of Oxford University, notes by Twyne; Wood MS. D. 32, pp. 461–2.

(iv) Names of the Doctors and M.A.'s in every College in Oxford in 1616; Wood MS. B. 14 (*O. C.* 8587), pp. 111 sqq.

(v) Lists of students serving in the King's army, 1641–3; see *Life*, i. 105.

129. Estimations of the number of Students of the University.

(i) In 1592, at Queen Elizabeth's second visit; Twyne XXI. 513 (from Symmachus Lambithensis). Twyne notes that the list for Cambridge (*ib.* p. 511) is swollen by the inclusion of 'poor scholars,' while in the Oxford list are given only those on the foundation.

(ii) In 1605; Twyne II. fol. 80; at King James' visit.

(iii) In 1611; Twyne XXI. 513—'the number of the students of the University of Oxon, as it was delivered to Prince Henry at his request by Dr. Thomas Shingleton, then Vice-chancellor of Oxford, anno 1611, 20 Augusti.'

(iv) In 1612; Twyne XXI. 514; 'an exact account of the whole number of scholars and students in the University of Oxford taken 1612 in the long vacation.' Printed, from MS. Tanner 338, fol. 28, in [Rev. John Walker's] *Oxoniana*, ii. 247.

Tables of Members of the Colleges and Halls.

1605		1611		1612	
Ch. Ch. .	309	Ch. Ch.	214	Queen's .	267
Magd. C.	220	Magd. C.	211	Magd. C.	246
Bras.	180	Exet.	188	Ch. Ch. .	240
Exet.	165	Bras.	178	Bras.	227
Queen's	130	Queen's	150	Exet.	206
New C.	126	Ball.	123	Magd. H.	161
S. John's	107	New C.	122	Broadg. H.	131
Ball.	96	Broadg. H.	112	New C.	130
Oriel .	90	S. John's	111	S. John's	128
Magd. H.	90	Linc.	101	Ball.	127
Alls.	71	Trin. .	97	Trin.	116
Trin.	70	Magd. H.	90	Linc.	109
Mert. .	70	Corp. .	85	Corp.	94
S. Alb. H.	66	Alls.	77	Alls.	93
Corp.	65	Gloc. H.	74	Mert.	93
Univ. .	60	Mert.	73	Jes. C.	91
S. Mary H.	56	Univ.	69	Oriel	79
Linc. .	54	Oriel	64	Univ. .	72
Gloc. H.	54	Jes. C.	62	Hart H. .	71
Jes. C.	50	Hart H.	62	Gloc. H. .	62
Hart H.	46	S. Alb. H.	46	S. Alb. H.	52
Broadg. H.	40	S. Edm. H. .	42	S. Mary H.	48
S. Edm. H.	38	S. Mary H.	38	S. Edm. H.	47
N. I. H.	1	N. I. H. .	20	N. I. H.	30
in Colleges .	1863	in Colleges .	1925	in Colleges .	2328
in Halls . .	391	in Halls . .	484	in Halls . .	602
Total	2254	Total	2409	Total	2930

130. Miscellanea.

(i) *Planctus Univ. Oxon. contra laicos*, tempore magni conflictus, 1354⅚; MS. Bodl. 859. Excerpts in MS. Ric. James 19, p. 148; Twyne XXI. 634.

Cited in *Annals*, i. 459.

(ii) *Errorum Oxon. et Paris. collectio et condemnatio*, MS. Magd. Coll. 217, fol. 4.

Cited in *Hist.* i. pp. 125, 127.

(iii) *Historiola Univ. Oxon.*; this is only the preface to Statute-books A, B, C, CC: see *supra*, p. 127. A transcript of it is found in MS. Corp. Cambr. 340, fol. 188.

(iv) *Apology for the government of Oxford University against Henry VIII*; written by a Regent Master [? Richard Jones, B.C.L. of New Coll.] in 1597; Wood MS. D. 18 (*O. C.* 8559).

(v) *Sigilli Univ. Oxon. descriptio*; Twyne III. 304; Twyne XXII. 349.

(vi) Paper about a theft of University plate, &c., 154¾; cited in *Annals*, ii. 73, and there said to be in Wood's own possession. See *supra*, p. 126.

(vii) *The migration* (1333) *to Stamford*. Brian Twyne in 1617 visited Stamford to collect what evidence he could on the spot: his notes taken there are found in Twyne II. 131; Twyne XXII. 152.

(viii) Miscellaneous speeches and papers by Oxford men, 1623–1686: Wood MS. D. 19 (2) (*O. C.* 8565).

(ix) Miscellaneous papers about the University: Wood MS. D. 18 (*O. C.* 8563); Wood MS. F. 27.

(x) Notes on the University and its leading men, 1642–1660: in Wood MS. F. 31: printed in *Life*.

(xi) Collection of speeches, letters and other matters relating to the University of Oxford, temp. Jac. II et Car. I: formed by Richard Saunders of Oriel: see *Life*, i. 116, 382 note 3.

(xii) MS. Cotton Cleopatra F. 1 (papers on the Ecclesiastical power). Cited in *Annals*, i. 531.

(xiii) Twyne IV. 243 speaks of a 'fasciculus variarum chartarum concernent. Oxon. quas mutuo mihi tradidit Dns Robertus Cotton.'

(xiv) Twyne VII. 81–83 has excerpts from 'chartae solutae' in Sir R. Cotton's library, one of them being a bull of pope Boniface VIII.

(xv) The earl of Dorset's letter to the University. Cited in *Annals*, ii. 289: lost in the volume Wood MS. F. 31 (*O. C.* 8493).

(xvi) Sextus liber decretalium, per Bonifacium VIII ad Acad. Oxon. missus: MS. e Mus. 60 (*O. C.* 3648): *Life*, ii. 204.

(xvii) Epistola papae Johannis XXII ad Acad. Oxon. 1 Nov. 1317: MS. Cotton Faust. A. 5. Cited in *Annals* i. 394, ii. 823.

(xviii) *De theologicis Quaestionibus*, liber chartaceus: at the end was written 'Articuli subscripti fuerunt reprobati tanquam erronei a magistris theologiae Oxon.'; apparently MS. no. 284 in Coxe's Cat. of Mert. Coll. MSS. Excerpt in Twyne XXI. 766. Cited, from Twyne, in *Annals*, i. 385.

(xix) Twyne, in Wood MS. D. 32, p. 221, has a note about the glass in the east window of the Old Congregation House.

131. All Souls College.

(i) *Muniments in the Treasury*. Chartae, evidentiae, munimenta, &c., in the upper chamber of the Tower over the common gate, which chamber is called ‘the Treasury.’

Excerpts from these are found in Wood MS. D. 2, pp. 137–146; *Life*, ii. 75. The documents cited by Wood are chiefly about the site of the College and lands and tenements in Oxford: the drawer in which they were contained was marked ‘pyx. Oxon.’

There is a printed Calendar of these documents—‘Catalogue of the Archives . . . of All Souls,’ by C. T. Martin, 1877.

(ii) *Account-books*. Certain old books of accounts in the lower chamber of the Tower over the common gate: cited in *Coll.* p. 260.

(iii) *Indenture-book*. An old parchment register beginning 1443, containing compositions, indentures, acquittances, obligations, letters, &c.

Excerpts from this volume are found in Wood MS. D. 2, pp. 147–150.

(iv) *Statutes-book*.

Excerpts from the ‘liber Statutorum’ are found in Wood MS. F. 28, foll. 144, 145.

(v) *Registers*.

The ‘Registrum Antiquum’ is cited in *Coll.* p. 262.

(vi) *Catalogue of fellows*, from the foundation to 1660, begun by Robert Hovenden (Warden from 1571 to 1613). In Twyne II, at the end of the life of Chichley. Wood had a transcript of it.

(vii) *Life of the founder*, written by R[obert] H[ovenden].

‘Henrici Chichleii . . . vita, 29 Decembr. 1574 conscripta: *initium* “Henricus Chichleius in pago prope Northampton quod Higham-ferris nuncupatur” &c.’ The original is in the custody of the Warden of All Souls; there are transcripts in Twyne II. fol. 177, and Wood MS. F. 28, fol. 140. This MS. was followed by Arthur Duck in his ‘Vita Henrici Chichele,’ Oxon. 1617.

132. Balliol College.

See 4th Report of Hist. MSS. Commission, p. 442.

(i) *Muniments*. Chartae, evidentiae, &c. kept ‘in a room on the south side of the Chapel’ in Wood’s time; *Life*, ii. 45.

Wood’s excerpts from these are found in Wood MS. D. 2, pp. 107–122, 274–277.

(ii) *Statutes of the Foundress*.

'Statuta Devorgillae de Balliol: *initium* "Devorgulla de Galweda, domina de Balliol, dilectis," &c.'

(iii) *Statutes of the Somerville foundation.*

'Statuta domini Philippi Somervylle: *initium* "In nomine sanctissimae et individuae Trinitatis," &c.'

(iv) *Will of John Snell*, proved Aug. 1679.

This is found in Wood MS. F. 28, fol. 41 : other papers about Balliol are found, ibid. foll. 44–51.

(v) *Register.*

'Registrum actorum,' beginning 1520; imperfect till 1556 ; afterwards good.

(vi) *Admissions-book*, 1636–1681.

(vii) *Catalogue of Fellows*, 1502–1682, compiled by Nicholas Crouche, senior fellow. This is found in Wood MS. F. 28, foll. 54–61. Another draft is in MS. Tanner 456, foll. 79 sqq.

(viii) *Catalogue of Masters of Arts*, 1607–1642, compiled from the buttery-books, by Nicholas Crouche. In Wood MS. F. 28, foll. 53–55.

(ix) *List of Benefactors.*

This is a very interesting document, drawn up (by some Romanist fellow expecting expulsion) at the accession of Elizabeth and entered into the College register, that the memory of those for whom the College was bound to pray might not be forgotten. Nicholas Crouche's transcript of it, made Apr. 1685, is found in Wood MS. F. 28, foll. 36–39. There is a similar list, made at the same time and under the same circumstances, in the Old Register of Lincoln College.

(x) *Bursar's accounts.*

The accounts (1649–1689) of Nicholas Crouche, together with his private accounts and a scanty diary, are found in a MS. in Ball. Coll. (no. 355 in Coxe's Cat.).

(xi) *Henry Savage's Balliofergus.*

Printed in 1668 : but Wood had had earlier access to it in Dr. Savage's MS. copy, which was composed in 1661 ; see MS. Ball. Coll. 255 in Coxe's Cat., also MS. Barlow 2 in the Bodleian.

Cited frequently in *City* as Historia Balliol., Balliofergus, &c.

133. Brasenose College.

(i) *Muniments in the Treasury.* Twyne in 1624 consulted these in the rooms of Dr. Samuel Radcliffe, principal; Twyne XXIII. 126. Wood cites them several times, but always with a reference to Twyne's excerpts, showing that he himself never had access to them.

(ii) *Cartulary.* 'Leiger-book of the evidences and muniments' of Brasenose College, compiled by Dr. Thomas Yates (principal 1660–1681)—see Twyne XXIII. 126 b.

Excerpts from this are found in Wood MS. D. 2, pp. 290–296.

(iii) *Catalogue of Fellows.* Some notes towards such a Catalogue are found in Wood MS. F. 28, foll. 162–165.

(iv) *Register.*

The old register begins in 1543; Wood MS. F. 28, fol. 162.

134. Christ Church.

See Scargill-Bird's Guide to the Public Records Office (1891), p. 226.

(i) *Muniments in the Treasury.*

Relating especially to the properties which came to the College from S. Frideswyde's and Osney: see *Life*, ii. 118, 114.

Excerpts thence are found in Twyne III. 21; and in Wood MS. D. 2. In Wood's time they were arranged in drawers by parishes, e. g. 'pix. S. Aldati,' *City*, i. 156, 'pyx. B. Mar. Virg.,' *Annals*, ii. 733.

(ii) *Statutes of Cardinal College.*

Statuta cardinalis Wolsey, *initium* 'Thomas miseratione divina tituli S. Caeciliae' &c., *finis* 'data in aedibus nostris prope West-monasterium 1º mensis Julii anno dni quingentesimo 27º, T. Carl^{lis}. Ebor.'

One copy was in the inner treasury of Christ Church (see no. 339 in Kitchin's Cat. of Ch. Ch. Muniments, folio, 122 fol.); another copy, 31 leaves in vellum, with Wolsey's arms and seal at the end, 'in the office of *pellis exitus* in the exchequer of the receipt of the King's treasury at Westminster' (Twyne XXII. 127, 150); another in the Palace Treasury at Westminster (Twyne XXIV. 492–495); another in the Brit. Mus. Libr. MS. Cotton Titus F. 3, foll. 2–90. Richard James, MS. Ric. James 7, p. 89 cites a copy which was lent to him in 1628 by William Boswell.

(iii) *Cardinal Wolsey's book* is cited in *City*, ii. 178: but what it is I do not know, unless an archiepiscopal register at York.

(iv) *Statutes of Henry VIII's College.*

See Twyne XXIV. 493; no. 344 in Kitchin's Cat. of Ch. Ch. Muniments.

(v) *Admissions-Register.*

'Registrum electionum et admissionum alumnorum et aliquorum canonicorum,' begun by Thomas Randolph on 12 March 15$\frac{48}{50}$. At the beginning are noted some students of 1546–1548. From 154$\frac{7}{8}$ to 1568 it is fairly continuous; there is a gap from 1568 to 1581; it is brought down to 1619.

Wood made a transcript of this, now in Wood MS. F. 28, foll. 171 b–175: he found it in the hands of John Willis, then Chapter-clerk.

(vi) *Catalogue of Westminster Students.*

Wood found a 'Catalogue of Students bred in Westminster and preferred to Christ Church in Oxon and Trinity College in Cambridge,' beginning in 1565, in the custody of the Dean of Christ Church; he made a transcript of it, brought down to 1689, now in Wood MS. F. 28, fol. 194 (170).

(vii) *Register of burials in Christ Church*, beginning 16—. See *Life*, i. 47, note 3.

(viii) Note of the monasteries suppressed to provide for the foundation of Cardinal Wolsey's College ; in Brit. Mus. Libr. MS. Cotton Cleop. E. iv, fol. 276 ; in Bodl. Libr. MS. Dodsworth 26, fol. 23.

(ix) Note of the lands assigned by Henry VIII to his Cathedral Church in Oxford, 1 Oct. 1546 : Wood MS. F. 28, foll. 176, 177.

(x) *Fabric-rolls of Christ Church.*

'Liber computi pro aedificatione Collegii Cardinalis': Twyne found this in the possession of — Poore of Blechingdon, and made excerpts from it, Twyne XXI. pp. 350–357. Hearne copied Twyne's excerpts (now MS. Tanner 338, fol. 422), which Gutch printed in *Collect. Curiosa*, i. 204. Of the original I know nothing.

(xi), (xii) *Collections of Leonard Hutten or Richard Washbourne.*

Wood MS. C. 7 (*O. C.* 8541), a volume strongly bound in black leather, formerly owned by 'John Towman' or 'Tawman,' and 'Willem Godfary,' and used as a copy-book. It contains at one end a series of orders by the governing-body of Christ Church from 1549 onwards: e.g. on 2 December 1554 it was ordered that henceforth the College should not contribute to the expenses of acting plays except 20*s* each for two comedies and 40*s* each for two tragedies, one play to be in Latin and one in Greek. At the other end is a short Latin account of Christ Church—*init.*—'Ecclesia Cathedralis Christi Oxon. ex fundatione regis Henrici 8[i], Anglice, the cathedrall church,' &c.—followed by a list of bishops of Oxford (to Richard Corbet), and of deans of Christ Church (to Samuel Fell) and of canons under their respective stalls.

Cited in *City*, ii. 4, as *Catalogus Decanorum Aedis Christi* : cited frequently in *City* as *Catalogus canonicorum Aedis Christi quem habui a magistro Washbourne.*

Wood MS. C. 8 (*O. C.* 8542) contains lists of members, and records of elections of office-bearers and students (1547–1619). The earlier lists are very full, giving not only the academical members, but the *pueri musici, ministri, operarii, beadmen, &c.* Wood has made some notes and additions.

These two volumes bear the initials R. W. : and I have no doubt that these are for Richard Washbourne, who was appointed chaplain of Ch. Ch. in Sept. 1665 (Wood MS. F. 28, fol. 172 b): see *City*, i. 161, ii. 7, 8, &c. An envelope inserted in C. 7 bears the address, 'to his honoured freind Mr. Richard Washbourne at his chamber in Christ Church.' On the binding of C. 8 is a (wrong, as I take it) note 'Richard Watson's chaplain of Ch. Ch. his hand'; and I think that the 1697 Catalogue in assigning them to 'Richard Watkins,' mistook this note.

Wood attributed these collections to Leonard Hutten: see *City*, ii. 5, note 2.

For other similar collections by Leonard Hutten, see par. 203.

135. Corpus Christi College.

See 2nd Report of Hist. MSS. Comm. p. 126.

(i) *Muniments in the Treasury.*

They were contained in bundles in drawers (marked A. 4, E. 8, &c.) ; Twyne's excerpts from them are found in Twyne II. 156; Twyne XXIII. 663-671 ; Twyne XXIV. 329. Wood's citations of these documents are always accompanied by a reference to Twyne, from which it may be safely concluded that he never had access to the originals.

(ii) *Cartulary.*

Registrum chartarum primum, marked A. 1, containing transcripts of the deeds about the site of the College, &c.: referred to as 'Reg. A. 1.'

Excerpts from this are found in Wood MS. D. 2, pp. 609-617: see *Life*, ii. 122.

(iii) *Statutes*: in Bodl. Libr. MS. Laud Misc. 621. Richard James has excerpts from these, MS. Ric. James 17, p. 168.

(iv) *Lease-book*: cited in Twyne XXIII. 668.

(v) *Register.*

Registrum electionum praesidum et sociorum et alumnorum, 1517-1660.

(vi) *Catalogue of Fellows.*

Collected from College documents by Robert Hegge, with corrections and additions by William Fulman: printed in Dr. Fowler's *History of Corpus Christi College.*

(vii) *Lives of the Founder.*

(*a*) Thomas Greenway's (President 1562-1568) 'Vita Ricardi Fox . . . breviter descripta: *initium* "Richardus Foxus, familia satis splendida," &c.,' MS. no. 280 in Coxe's Cat.: see Dr. Fowler, *l. c.* p. 123.

(*b*) Brian Twyne, according to Wood, had 'written of the founder's life'; but Wood 'could never see nor hear of it'; whence he inferred that it had perished in the fire (see par. 214).

(viii) Twyne's MSS. contain a number of papers and notes referring to events at C. C. C. in his own time, e. g. Twyne II. fol. 151 b, 'formula citationis ad electionem praesidis C. C. C. Oxon.'

136. Exeter College.

See 2nd Report of Hist. MSS. Comm. p. 127.

(i) *Muniments.*

Cartae, evidentiae, &c. ; kept, in Wood's time, in a lower room on the north side of the College. Wood had exceptionally free access to these documents, *Life*, ii. 44. His excerpts from them are found in Wood MS. D. 2, pp. 71–94.

(ii) *Accounts.*

Rotuli computorum rectorum Coll. Exon. Wood's excerpts from these, ranging from 1329 to 1531, are found in Wood MS. D. 2, pp. 318-322.

(iii) *Statutes-book.*

Statuta Stapledon ; Statuta Petreana ; Liber Statutorum Coll. Exon. Wood's excerpts are found in Wood MS. D. 2, pp. 314, 315.

(iv) *Registers.*

(*a*) *Registrum primum*, 1539–1619, containing notices of elections of fellows and other acts of the society. See Boase, *Reg. Coll. Exon.* (edit. 1), p. 35.

Wood's excerpts from this volume are found in Wood MS. D. 2, pp. 306–313.

(*b*) *Registrum secundum*, 1619–1737.

(v) *Cautions-books.*

These contain 'the names of all those that are admitted fellow-commoners, sojourners or commoners, battlers, servitors.' The first book extends from 1629 to 1686 ; the second from 1686–1743.

[Wood uses the term *Bursar's books* for these : but the title *Liber Bursarii* is now confined to a volume of directions for the bursar, which was compiled in 1636.]

(vi) *Catalogue of Rectors, Fellows, and Benefactors.*

Compiled in 1574 by Robert Newton and William Wyott, then Rector and Sub-rector.

Wood's excerpts from this volume are found in Wood MS. D. 2, pp. 95-105 ; and also *ibid.* at p. 316, where it is called 'Liber Benefactorum Coll. Exon.'—The original is now lost (2nd Rep. Hist. MSS. Comm. p. 127), and the volume now in the College archives is only a transcript.

(vii) List of contributors to the new buildings (1672) between the gate and the chapel : Wood MS. D. 2, p. 356.

(viii) *Rotulus membranaceus de Aula S. Stephani* : cited in *City*, i. 113, 115.

(ix) *Cartulary* : a large folio volume, begun in 1631, containing transcripts of evidences.

137. Gloucester Hall.

(i) *Statuta Aulae Glocestriensis*, facta (ut videtur) 1560: Twyne XXI. 206.

Cited in *Coll.* p. 639: but only from Twyne's excerpt, Wood having never seen the original.

(ii) *Liber Aulae Glocestriensis*, 1630: see 2nd Rep. of Hist. MSS. Comm. p. 143.

(iii) *Papers relating to Gloucester Hall*: Wood MS. F. 38, foll. 310–315 (386–395 in another foliation).

138. Hart Hall.

(i) *Papers relating to Hart Hall*: Wood MS. F. 28, foll. 256–259 (310–318).

(ii) Gerard Langbaine's notes about Hart Hall, from the archives of Exeter College; Wood MS. F. 28, foll. 260–264 (319–323).

(iii) I may take this opportunity of noting that in lord Macclesfield's library at Shirburn Castle (unbound MSS., bundle 3) is 'An account of the Universities and Halls and particularly of the University of Oxford and of Hart Hall, with respect to the pretensions of Exeter Colledge: by Richard Newton, D.D.,' fol., 31 pages.

139. Jesus College.

See 2nd Rep. of Hist. MSS. Comm. p. 130.

(i) *Variae chartae, munimenta, evidentiae* in the College treasury. Cited in *Coll.* p. 569.

(ii) *Statutes.*

(iii) *Registrum compositionum* benefactores concernentium: fol.

(iv) *Registrum electionum sociorum et scholarium*, 1602–1633. Cited *Life*, ii. 221.

(v) *Bursar's accounts*: vol. i. 1631–1650; vol. ii. 1650–1660; vol. iii. 1660–1686.

(vi) *Buttery-books.*

(vii) *Life of Francis Mansel*, principal 1630–1648: Wood MS. F. 30 (*O. C.* 8492): privately printed in 1858 and attributed to Sir Leoline Jenkins.

Cited in *Life*, iii. 162.

(viii) *Life of Sir Leoline Jenkins*, principal 1661–1672: MS. Aubrey 6, fol. 25 a.

(ix) *Account of the foundation of Jesus College*; notes on benefactors, on MSS. in Jes. Coll. library; by 'anonymus'; Wood MS. F. 31 at fol. 145. Wood has jotted a few notes on it.

(x) Owen Wynne's Collections about Jesus College, cited by Gutch in *Coll.* p. 570 and said to be in All Souls library: see nos. 216, 222, 240, 264 in Coxe's Catal. Codd. Coll. Om. Anim.

See 2nd Report of Hist. MSS. Commission, p. 130.

(i) *Muniments* 'in the upper chamber of the Tower over the common gate.'

Cited in *Annals, Colleges, City*.

Twyne's excerpts from these are found in Twyne XXIV. 251–253 : Wood's excerpts, in Wood MS. D. 2, pp. 51–66.

The Rev. Octavius Ogle has drawn up a MS. Calendar of these documents (240 folios) and, in 1893, presented it to the College. The deeds range from the thirteenth century.

(ii) *Account-books.* The earliest extant of the yearly 'computi' are now bound up into eight volumes :—

Vol. I, containing the years 1456, 1476–1478, 1489, 1492, 1495 1503, 1514: vol. II, 1488, 1505–1510: vol. III, 1512, 1513, 1515, 1517, 1520, 1521, 1524, 152 : vol. IV, 1526–1530, 1532, 1535, 1538: vol. V, 1539, 1541, 1543, 1544, 1546, 1548–1550, 1559, 1560: vol. VI, 1561, 1566, 1568, 1571, 1573–1577, 1580: vol. VII, 1581–1590 : vol. VIII, 1591–1600.

The 'computi' of later years are mostly in single thin folio volumes, one for each year.

(iii) *Statutes*, given by Thomas Rotherham, bishop of Lincoln, 11 Feb. $14\frac{79}{80}$.

The original, with the bishop's signature, is preserved in the College archives. The copy printed in ' Statutes of the Colleges of Oxford,' 1853, is faulty in minor points.

(iv) *Registers.*

(*a*) *Registrum vetus*, begun about 1470: contains elections and resignations of rectors and fellows, and other acts of the society : see *Life*, ii. 121.

Cited in *Colleges* and *City*.

Twyne's excerpts from it are found in Twyne XXII. 325.

(*b*) *Registrum medium*, begun on 1 June 1577.

Wood's excerpts from it are found in Wood MS. F. 28, fol. 133.

(*c*) *Registrum novum*, that now in use.

(v) *Composition with Edmund Audley, bishop of Sarum.*

(*a*) One copy is in the archives of the College.

(*b*) Another copy was given to the Bodleian by Thomas Barlow: now MS. Barlow 50 : cited in *Colleges*, p. 239.

(vi) *Catalogue of fellows.*

(*a*) A list of fellows, begun 20 Feb. $151\frac{8}{9}$ and continued to 1650, is found in the *Reg. vetus* at fol. 165.

(*b*) Wood's list, 1436–1681, is found in Wood MS. F. 28, foll. 126–137.

(vii) *Brevis annotatio de fundatoribus et benefactoribus*, drawn up by Robert Parkinson at the accession of Elizabeth (see par. 132, § ix), is found in *Reg. vetus* at fol. 125 ᵛ.

(viii) *Cartulary.*

(*a*) A cartulary, drawn up in 1474, is found at the beginning of the *Registrum vetus.*

(*b*) A transcript, with some additions, of this, by William Vesey (fellow 1703–1755), is preserved in College in a MS. called *Exemplificatio cartarum.*

(ix) *Catalogue of MSS.*[1] *in the Library*, 1474, is found in the *Registrum vetus.*

(x) *Admission-books*, of undergraduates.

(*a*) 11 Feb. 167⅔—27 March 1740.

(*b*) From 31 Oct. 1733.

(*c*) From 6 Nov. 1829.

(xi) *Caution-books.*

Only one seems preserved: *Catalogus fidejubentium*, May 1622—Aug. 1649. It shows the deficiency of the University Matriculation-register at that time.

(xii) *Buttery-books.*

(xiii) *Stone's verses on the founder.*

Metrificatio super versus Richardi Flemmyng, quondam episcopi Lyncoln., by . . . Stoone, a Carthusian monk: cited in *Colleges*, p. 236.

(*a*) MS. Bodl. 496, *olim* MS. 4° A. 14 Art. : from which MS. Twyne cites them in MS. Arch. Seld. supra 79, p. 289 : MS. Ric. James 19, p. 149.

(*b*) At p. 132 'of an old MS. in a bookseller's shop near Temple-barre' Twyne found a copy with lines not in the Bodl. MS., which he cites in Twyne XXIII. 643.

141. S. Mary Magdalen College.

See 4th report of Hist. MSS. Comm. p. 458 and 8th Report, p. 262.

(i) *Muniments* in a Tower on the north side of the outer chapel. Cited in *Colleges, Annals, Fasti.*

Twyne's excerpts, made in March 1632, are found in Twyne III. 638. Wood has a list of some papers there, made in July 1675, in Wood MS. F. 28, foll. 154–157. Wood's excerpts from the muniments of S. John Bapt. Hospital there; see par. 40.

---

[1] the very first on the list is now in the Rawlinson MSS. in the Bodleian.

Wood cites his *Collect. ex Arch. Coll. Magd.* in *City.*

(ii) *Rentalls* in the Treasury.

Cited in *City*, i. 68.

Wood's excerpts from these, see par. 40.   A rentall of 1661 is transcribed in Wood MS. F. 28, foll. 149–153.

(iii) *Liber Collegii Magd.*, cited in *City*, i. 130, 131: perhaps the same as the Cartulary of S. John Bapt. Hospital, see par. 40.

(iv) *Registers*, containing elections of fellows and demies, presentations to College livings, &c.

(*a*) Registrum vocat. per litteram 'A': Aug. 1480–1492.

Cited in *Annals, Fasti, Colleges.*

Wood's excerpts from this are found in Wood MS. D. 2, pp. 151–158.   See *Life*, iii. 456.

(*b*) Registrum secundum 'B': 1492–1538.

Cited in *Coll.* and *Fasti.*

(*c*) Registrum tertium ⟨ ? 'C'⟩: 25 July 1539—8 July 1614.

Cited in *Annals.*

(*d*) Registrum quartum ⟨ ? 'D'⟩: 1615—Wood's time.

(*e*) Registrum 'E.'

Cited in *Annals*, ii. 106, *Coll.* p. 316.

(v) *Statutes.*

(vi) *Book of Counterparts.*

Cited in *City*, i. 198.

(vii) *Cartulary.*

Twyne III. 638 gives excerpts 'out of a thick book of the abstracts of Magd. College evidences, beginning *Chalgrave cum pertinentiis.*'

(viii) *Accounts*, beginning 1543.

Cited in *Colleges, Annals.*

(ix) *Punishment-book of Magdalen College*, 1547—Wood's time. 'Registrum quoddam ab anno 1547, crastino die S. Johannis Baptistae ⟨25 June⟩, ad hodiernum diem; folio, in paper.   It chiefly containes the punishments of the fellows and scholars for faults committed, leave for them to be absent from the college, letters from Kings, Queens and Bishops of Winchester (their Visitors), with some elections of praesidents: in the hands of the president': so in Wood MS. E. 4.

(x) *Fabric-rolls of Magdalen College*, 1466–1472. 'Liber papyrus continens expensas structurae murorum vel clausurae collegii ab anno 6 Edwardi IV (1466) usque ad annum 12 Edwardi IV (1472); initio "haec sunt receptiones in pecunia numerata per me, magistrum Richardum Berne, de domino meo, domino Willielmo Weynfleto, Winton. episcopo ac fundatore nostri collegii," &c.   It contains 24 folios, in which it appears that the founder built at his own charge the wall that encompasses the college.   And therfore Roger Dodsworth in his collections of antiquities, followed by Dr. Thomas Fuller in his Book of Worthies (in com. Lanc.), is mistaken in saying that Anthony Molineaux, fellow of his house, doctorated in Divinity anno 1531, did build the said wall. But yet perhaps he did raise it higher by embatling it, quaere. There is also in the said book of expenses mention made that the founder built the common gate next the street: — which gate stood till Dr. Frewen's time ⟨President 1626–1644⟩, and then this that now stands next to Magdalen Hall was built in its place ': —so in Wood MS. E. 4. Wood adds: — 'I saw and perused it in hospitio praesidentis.'

(xi) *Narrative of the proceedings of James II's Commissioners*, by Wood: MS. Tanner 456*, foll. 21 sqq.: printed in *Life*, iii. 514.

(xii) *Catalogus praesidentium Coll. Magd.*, cited in *City*, i. 195, 198, 226. Apparently a volume of Collections by Wood: I have found no trace of it.

(xiii) Carmina in fenestris in magna camera praesidentis Coll. Magd. : Twyne XXI. 233.

(xiv) Proceedings in Magd. Coll., 1663 : MS. Tanner 338: *Life* i. 473.

141*. S. Mary Magdalen Hall.

(i) Papers about it, by Dr. Henry Wilkinson and others, in MS. Ballard 46.

(ii) Dispute about the right to nominate the principal : paper in Wood MS. D. 18: *Life*, iii. 456.

142. Merton College.

See 6th Rep. of Hist. MSS. Comm. p. 545.

(i) *Chartae, evidentiae* . . . in Thesaurario. They have been recently calendared for the College.

Cited *passim*, in *City, Coll., Annals, Fasti*.

Twyne's excerpts from these are found in Twyne III. 591–605; Twyne XXIII. 755–764. Wood's excerpts are found in Wood MS. F. 31, MS. Ballard 46, MS. Bodl. 594.

Wood cites his *Collect. ex archivis Coll. Mert.* in *City*, ii. 461.

(ii) *Rentalia, computus bursariorum*, &c. in Scaccario Coll. Mert.

Cited in *Colleges*, p. 654.

Wood's excerpts from these accounts, 1299–1435, giving the names of fellows who occur in them, are found in MS. Bodl. 594.

Wood cites his *Collect. ex computis Coll. Mert.* several times in *City*.

(iii) *Statutes* of Walter de Merton: see Twyne XXI. 197.

(*a*) A copy 'in the Library or Checquer.'

(*b*) A 'transcript in the Subwarden's hands, made at the charge of John Holder' (Brodrick's Memorials of Merton, p. 249).

Cited in *Annals*, several times.

Wood's excerpts from the Mert. Coll. statutes are found at the end of MS. Bodl. 594, in the portion with folios marked in pencil, foll. 152ᵛ–159. In Wood MS. E. 4 is this note :—'These statutes served for a pattern of those at Peterhouse in Cambridge, as is somewhere said.'

(iv) *Statuta Wyllyet pro portionistis* : cited in *City*, i. 183.

(v) *Registrum sive abstractum evidentiarum*, made in 1288. 'Habeat rubrum tegmen : et numerat fol. 36 : reponitur in cista oeconomica in scaccario' : so Wood MS. E. 4.

Cited in *Hist.* i. 134 : perhaps this is the volume cited in *Coll.* p. 655, *City*, i. 106.

(vi) '*Thin register in parchment* containing divers occurrences relating to the College temp. Edw. II, Ric. II, et Henr. IV, et alia ad Universitatem spectantia : init. "Ven. in Christo patri ac domino Simoni, Dei gratia Cantuar. arch." : continet pag. 38, et reponitur in cista oeconomica in scaccario : see Twyne XXII. 320, 322' : so in Wood MS. E. 4.

Perhaps that cited in *City*, i. 380, &c., ii. 462, &c.; *Coll.* p. 177; *Annals*, i. 426.

(vii) *Thin register in the Subwarden's hands* : cited in *City*, i. 382; probably one of the preceding ; Wood's citations being very vague.

(viii) *Registers of Merton College* : Registra actorum Societatis.

(*a*) Registrum primum, 1482–1567. See Twyne III. 611–613 ; Twyne XXII. 320; Twyne XXIV. 597.

Cited in *City, Coll., Fasti, Annals.*

(*b*) Registrum secundum, 21 Nov. 1567—Wood's time.

Cited in *City, Coll., Annals.*

Wood's excerpts from the Registers of Merton College are found at the end of MS. Bodl. 594, in the portion foliated in pencil, foll. 141–152 (extracted by him in 1658); also in MS. Ballard 46 ; also (from the second register) in Wood MS. F. 31, fol. 159 of the present but pag. 81 of the old numeration.

Wood cites his *Collect. ex registris Coll. Mert.* several times in *City.*

(ix) *Catalogues of Fellows of Merton College.*

(*a*) *Vetus Catalogus sociorum* : incip. 'Haec sunt nomina sociorum Collegii de Merton a prima fundatione' : brought down to 1589.—See Brodrick's Memorials of Merton College, p. vii.

Cited in *City, Annals, Coll.*

(*b*) *Catalogus alter sociorum* : incip. 'Gualterus de Merton, vir doctrina,' made in the wardenship of Henry Savile, and continued to Wood's time.—See Brodrick, *l. c.* p. ix.

Cited in *City*, i. 150.

(*c*) *Catalogus novus sociorum* : Brodrick, *l. c.* p. x.

(*d*) Wood's Catalogue, 1264–1455 : see Brodrick, *l. c.* p. xi.

This is found in Bodl., in MS. Ballard 46, pp. 1–22, with a transcript (MS. Ballard 46*) of a portion which is now in the Kilner Collection in Merton College.

Cited in *Life*, ii. 287; iii. 253 : cited (by Gutch) in *Fasti*, p. 48.

(x) Brian Twyne's Merton College Collections : Twyne III. 583–625.

(xi) Wood's Collections for Merton College were in a volume marked **Notae M.** (M. for Merton), which he cites frequently in *City* as **M.** or **m.**, e. g. *City*, i. 127, 128, 177, &c. : ii. 460, 461, &c.

(xii) Papers about Merton College in Sir Thomas Clayton's wardenship : MS. Rawl. B. 339 : see *Life*, i. 398.

(xiii) Wood's notes about his contemporaries in Merton College, 1642–1650 : MS. Tanner 436, MS. Rawl. D, *olim* 1290, *nunc* 912 ; printed in *Life*, i. 134–138.

143. New College.

See 2nd Report of Hist. MSS. Comm. p. 132.

(i) *Chartae, evidentiae*, &c. in the College Treasury.

Cited in *Fasti, Colleges.*

Wood has excerpts nominally from these, but in reality from the cartularies noted below, in Wood MS. D. 2, pp. 244–270.   He seems not to have had access to the muniments themselves.

Wood cites these *Collect. e Coll. Novo* in *City*, i. 77.

(ii) *Account-books of New College.*

(*a*) Bailiffs' rolls : (*b*) bursars' computi : (*c*) rent-rolls.

Cited in *City, Colleges, Annals.*

Wood's excerpts from these are found in Wood MS. D. 2, pp. 271–273, 280–288.

(iii) *Cartularies* of New College.

(*a*) *Registrum primum*[1]; the 'White book' : Twyne II. 78 : *Life*, ii. 82.

Cited frequently in *City*, under various titles, e. g. album registrum (*City*, i. 346, note 4, where 'nigro' possibly is an error), great white book of evidences (*City*, i. 360), albus liber (*City*, i. 40).

Wood's excerpts from it are found in Wood MS. D. 2, pp. 244–270.

(*b*) *Registrum secundum* ; cited in *City*, i. 171, 172.

Wood's excerpts from it are in Wood MS. D. 2, pp. 287, 288.

(*c*) *Liber niger*, containing transcripts of deeds about College property : 'a great black book,' Twyne II. 80.

(iv) *Statuta* : see *Life*, ii. 119.

Cited in *Coll.* p. 183.

Wood's excerpts are in Wood MS. D. 3, pp. 278, 279.

---

[1] the titles *Registrum primum* (*Coll.* pp. 177, 178, 676, *Annals*, i. 538), and *Registrum secundum* are ambiguous between these Cartularies and the Registers of the Acts of the College noticed below.

(v) *Catalogus sociorum* composed from the protocollons by Thomas Man (fellow 1615–1632), in the custody of the Warden.

Dr. Sewell, the present Warden, has compiled a complete register of the Wardens, Fellows, and Scholars.

(vi) *Protocol-books*, in several volumes, 1453–1495, 1496–1522, 1523–1546, 1547–1578, 1579–1610, &c. These are the records of the admission of the fellows and scholars of the College, attested by a notary-public.

(vii) *Liber seneschalli aulae.*

(viii) *Registra actorum societatis Coll. Novi.*

(*a*) Registrum primum, 1411–1475.

Wood's excerpts from it are in Wood MS. F. 28, fol. 111.

(*b*) Register beginning 1522.

Wood's excerpts from it are found in Wood MS. F. 28, fol. 110.

(ix) Papers about New College: Wood MS. F. 28, foll. 102–107.

(x) *Narrative of the building of New College*: cited in *Hist.* ii. 127, 130: *Colleges*, pp. 176, 177, 181, 182: said by Wood to be in the Bodleian. I cannot find it.

(xi) *Interments in New College Chapel*: Wood MS. F. 31, foll. 175 sqq.

(xii) *Lives of the Founder.*

(*a*) Thomas Chandler's *Vita Gulielmi Wykeham* in the custody of the Warden: see Twyne XXI. 683; Twyne XXII. 342. 'Distribuitur iste liber in varias collocutiones, et interlocutores in eodem sunt Panescius et Ferrandus: Harpesfeild hath collected much thence about William Wykeham in Historia Ecclesiastica saec. 14, cap. 20 '—so Wood in Wood MS. E. 4.

Cited in *Coll.* p. 176.

(*b*) Thomas Chandler's *Chronica et notae de vita &c. Gulielmi Wykeham*: MS. Cotton Titus A. 24: divided into seven collocutions. ' Dr. Marten [1] hath furnished himself with materialls from this book '— so in Wood MS. E. 4.

Cited in *Coll.* p. 177.

(*c*) ' *Historica narratio de ortu et sede natali Gulielmi Wykeham* simul et illius veteris quaestionis de genuino et gentili ejus nomine in gratiam Wykehamensium alumnorum explicatio: in nova bibliotheca eccles. Dunelm. erecta per Johannem Cosinum.'

(*d*) John London's ' scandalous report ' that Wykeham was a bastard: MS. Cotton Julius C. 6.

Cited in *Coll.* p. 171.

A note about this, by Wood, is found in Rawl. Letters 17, fol. 13.

(*e*) A long MS. Life of Wykeham is in MS. Tanner 102.

---

[1] Thomas Martyn's ' Historica descriptio complectens vitam ac res gestas Wicami,' Lond. 1597.

(xiii) *Michael Woodward's papers*, Warden 1658–1675.

(*a*) Notes [1] on the site, foundation, &c. of New College, in Wood MS. F. 28 : see *Life*, i. 459. Described and partly printed in *City*, i. 579–584. Woodward's diagram to illustrate these notes is now found in Wood 276 B. fol. 114ᵛ.

(*b*) Narratives of his progresses through the College estates : several little MSS. in the custody of the Warden, containing matters of much interest towards a knowledge of the social conditions of the seventeenth century.

144. Oriel College.

See 2nd Rep. Hist. MSS. Comm. p. 136.

(i) *Chartae, evidentiae* in the Treasury.

Cited frequently in *City, Coll., Annals, Fasti.*

Twyne's excerpts from them are found in Twyne IV. 148–150 : Twyne XXII. 347, 393 ; Twyne XXIII. 210–213. Wood's excerpts are found in Wood MS. C. 1, pp. 21–68, 70 ; Wood MS. F. 28, foll. 57–61. The documents were then arranged in drawers lettered A to X, and in drawers marked ' Biddle Hall,' ' Tackley's Inn,' ✠, &c.: ' pix. A ' is cited in *City*, i. 144, ' pix. W.' in *City*, i. 290 ; &c.— A Calendar of these muniments, by Mr. C. L. Shadwell, is being privately printed.

Wood marked the volume (now Wood MS. C. 1), containing his excerpts from these muniments by the letter **O** (for Oriel) ; and he cites it constantly by that letter in his notes to *City*, e. g. *City*, i. 92, 138, &c. ; *City*, ii. 23 (' Collect. ex arch. Coll. Oriel in O ').

(ii) *Treasurer's accounts*, 1411–1523, in a paper book.

Cited in *Fasti*, p. 65.

Excerpts from these are found in Wood MS. C. 1, pp. 70, 71.

(iii) *Liber Statutorum* : see Twyne XXII. 373.

Cited in *Annals, Colleges.* Now MS. Rawl. Statutes 45 ; see fol. 6 of C. L. Shadwell's *Oriel College Muniments.*

(iv) *Calendar*, prefixed to the Liber Statutorum, has some notes of deaths of members of the College : Twyne XXII. 393.

Cited in *Coll.* p. 125 ; *City*, ii. 16.

Excerpts from it are in Wood MS. C. 1, p. 1.

(v) *Cartularies.*

(*a*) Registrum vel transcriptio chartarum ; abstract of Oriel College evidences, by Mr. Henry Hawley, 1663 : at the end of the Liber Statutorum. Now MS. Lansdowne 386.

Cited frequently in *City, Annals*, under various titles, e. g. ' Oriel

---

[1] Wood cites these notes in *City*, i. 603, col. 2, as ' Winchester College notes.'

College leiger-book' (*City*, ii. 29), 'Summarium chartarum Coll. Oriel' (*Colleges*, p. 670).

Wood has excerpts from it in Wood MS. C. 1, pp. 1–16; cited in *City*, ii. 17 ('Collect. ex . . . indice munim. Coll. Oriel.').

(*b*) *Aliquis liber munimentorum* (quaere whether another Cartulary): excerpts thence in Wood MS. C. 1, p. 17.

(vi) *Registrum actorum societatis*; 'the Dean's register'; see Twyne XXII. 352.

Cited in *City, Annals, Fasti, Coll.*

Excerpts from this in Wood MS. C. 1, pp. 71, 72.

(vii) *Catalogue of Fellows.*

(*a*) Wood's, in Wood MS. F. 28, foll. 63^v–72, brought down to 1665.

(*b*) 'Mr. Henry Hawley hath a Catalogue more perfect then this'—so in Wood MS. E. 4.

(viii) Burials in Oriel College Chapel: Wood 16: *Life*, i. 210.

145. Pembroke College.

See 6th Rep. of Hist. MSS. Comm. p. 549.

(i) *Muniments*: cited in *Coll.* pp. 616, 617. Some excerpts from them are found in Wood MS. D. 2, pp. 621–624.

(ii) *Statutes*: a transcript in Wood MS. F. 28, foll. 246–255 (foll. 296–309 of another numeration).

(iii) *Bursar's books*, from 1650.

(iv) Papers about Pemb. Coll.; Wood MS. F. 28, foll. 241–245 (291–295): *Life*, i. 106. The list of Pembroke men in Charles I's service is printed in H. W. Chandler's *Five Court-rolls of Great Cressingham* (Lond. 1885), pp. 117, 118.

146. Queen's College.

See 2nd Rep. of Hist. MSS. Comm. p. 137: 4th Rep. p. 451; 6th Rep. p. 551.

(i) *Chartae, evidentiae* . . .; in Wood's time kept 'in a lower room on the south side of the common gate.'

Cited in *Coll., Annals, Fasti.*

Excerpts from them in Wood MS. D. 2, pp. 125–131.

(ii) *Account-books*, 1593–1613, 1623–1651, &c.

(iii) *Statutes* given by the Founder 10 Feb. 1341.

(*a*) 'A copy in the Tower of London': so in Wood MS. E. 4.

(*b*) MS. Cotton Claud. A. 4, foll. 57–80.

Cited in *Coll.* p. 139.

Excerpts thence in Wood MS. F. 28. fol. 92^v.

(iv) *Cartulary*: 'registrum magnum, or leiger-book, a large folio in paper: on fol. 1 is the charter of Edward II, giving licence to Robert Egglesfeld[1] to found a College'—so in Wood MS. E. 4.

Cited in *Coll.* p. 138.

(v) *Liber obitalis*, parchment, folio: containing notices of benefactors and their gifts: *Life*, ii. 435.

Cited in *Coll.*, several times.

Excerpts from it in Wood MS. F. 28, fol. 98. See MSS. Ashm. 826, 833.

(vi) *Registrum actorum societatis*, 1581 to Wood's time.

Cited in *Coll.* p. 662.

Excerpts from it in Wood MS. F 28, fol. 92.

(vii) *Catalogue of members*, in the custody of the Provost.

(*a*) An octavo MS., written circ. 1610 and continued by other hands.

(*b*) A large folio MS., in paper.

The contents of this Catalogue are given as follows:—

(1) Catalogus (imperfectus) sociorum.

(2) Catalogus thesaurariorum et camerariorum, to 1652.

(3) Catalogus (imperfectus) capellanorum, 1402–1635.

(4) Catalogus taberdorum vel pauperum puerorum, 1566–1636.

(5) Catalogus clericorum, 1588–1648.

(6) Catalogus pauperum puerorum servientium, 1588 (et antea)–1605.

(7) Catalogus Mag. Art., 1588, 1589,

(8) Catalogus Doctorum, 1588 (et antea)–1605.

(9) Scholares Grindalli, 1583–1599.

(10) Catalogus[2] studientium adm. in Coll., 1580–1642.

(viii) Wood has some notes towards a Catalogue of Provosts and Fellows in Wood MS. F. 28, foll. 95–97.

147. S. Edmund Hall.

(i) *List of matriculations*, 1572–1643, 1662–1693: transcribed from the University Matriculation-books, Wood MS. F. 28, foll. 266–279, 287–296: a very few notes are added in Wood's hand.

(ii) *List of admissions*, 1658–1684: transcribed from the buttery-books: Wood MS. F. 28, foll. 280–285. This list gives the day, month, and year of admission, and the aulary status of the person (servitor, semi-commoner[3], or gentleman-commoner).

---

[1] Wood gives *Ter fulgens boreale sidus* as anagram for 'Robert Eglesfeld' (Robertus Eaglensfieldus).

[2] Wood also speaks of 'Catalogus commensalium superioris et inferioris ordinis, battellariorum, et servientium ab anno 1581 ad hunc annum'; but he possibly means only this, with its continuation.

[3] this is, I suppose, a variant for 'battellar.'

(iii) *Papers relating to S. Edmund Hall*: Wood MS. F. 28, foll. 297–309; including inscriptions on 35 pieces of plate (1659–1677) sold, in March 16$\frac{79}{80}$, towards building a chapel; and a list of benefactors, 1659–1677.

(iv) *Andrew Allam's notes* about S. Edmund Hall, MS. Tanner 454, foll. 22, 142, &c. Several of them also are found in Wood's Almanacs and have been printed in *Life*. See *Life*, iii. 116.

148. S. John's College.

See 4th Report of Hist. MSS. Comm. p. 465.

(i) *Chartae, evidentiae,* &c., in the tower-chamber over the common gate.

Cited in *Coll.* pp. 535, 629.

Excerpts from them are found in Wood MS. D. 2, pp. 625–648.

(ii) *Statutes*: cited in *Coll.* p. 538.

(iii) *Registrum primum,* containing 'several matters of the foundation of the College, the election and resignation of presidents and fellows, gifts of benefactors, &c.'—so in Wood MS. F. 4.

Cited in *Coll.* p. 535.

Excerpts from it in Wood MS. D. 2, pp. 649–656. Wood no doubt means the *Register of Elections* 1564–1596, which contains a list of benefactors 1564–1618.

(iv) *Registers of acts of the Society.*

(*a*) 1557–   . ; (*b*) 1591–1624; (*c*) 1624–1667; (*d*) 1667–1691.

(v) *Catalogue*[1] *of fellows.*

(*a*) Christopher Wren's.

(*b*) Griffin Higgs[2]: now in Wood MS. F. 28, foll. 204–212 (244–252); having a few notes by Wood.

(vii) *Account-books,* beginning 1564.

(vii) Joseph Taylor's *Notes on S. John's College*: Wood MS. F. 28, foll. 215–221 (257–263): see *Life*, ii. 83.

(viii) Papers relating to S. John's College: Wood MS. F. 28, foll. 213, 214.

(ix) Griffin Higgs' *MS. Life of Sir Thomas White*: cited in *Coll.* p. 536: said by Wood (in the *Athenae*) to be in the custody of the President.

149. Trinity College.

See 2nd Report of Hist. MSS. Comm. p. 142.

---

[1] there is also, in the President's custody, a more modern catalogue by William Holmes (President 1728–1748).

[2] among the Wood Almanacs is a short diary, possibly by Griffin Higgs: see *Life*, i. 12, note 3.

(i) *Chartae, evidentiae, &c.*: cited in *Coll.* pp. 517, 518: excerpts from them in Wood MS. D. 2, pp. 618–620.

(ii) *Statutes*: cited in *Coll.* p. 519.

(iii) *Liber indenturarum.*

(*a*) Register 'A': 1556–1683; cited in *Coll.* p. 521.

(*b*) Register 'B': 1685–1748.

(iv) *Admission-book*, 1648–1737.

(v) *Bursar's accounts*, 1556–1669.

(vi) *Catalogue of fellows*: init. 'Alumni illi quos venerabilis vir Thomas cognomento Pope,' &c. first written by Ralph Kettle (President 1599–1643) and continued since his time by others.

(*a*) The original is in Trinity College: Wood's excerpts from it are found in Wood MS. F. 28, foll. 194–197.

(*b*) a copy of it, possibly the original scroll-copy, is now in Wood MS. F. 28, foll. 172–182 (old numeration).

(vii) *Catalogues of benefactors.*

(*a*) *Catalogue of benefactors to the library*: MS. in Trinity College: Thomas Allen is the first set down.

(*b*) *Catalogue of benefactors to the new building* (1665): vellum, a thin folio: MS. in Trinity College.

(*c*) *Catalogue of benefactors to the new quadrangle*: Wood MS. D. 11.

(*d*) *Catalogue of benefactors*: Wood MS. F. 28, fol. 183 (old numeration).

(viii) Arthur Charlet's *Nomenclator*, lists of members: *Life*, i. 158, note 1.

150. University College.

See 5th Rep. of Hist. MSS. Comm. p. 477.

(i) *Chartae, evidentiae, &c.* in the treasury over the common gate of the College: see Twyne II. 87.

Cited freely in *City, Annals, Coll., Fasti.*

Wood's excerpts from them are found in Wood MS. D. 2, pp. 1–32 (with some jottings by William Smith) and Wood MS. F. 28, foll. 11, 17.

(ii) *Rotuli et computi procuratorum*, ibid.

Cited frequently in *Annals, Fasti, Colleges.*

Wood's notes from them, in Wood MS. D. 2 (ut supra), are from accounts ranging from 1382–1545.

(iii) *Liber Statutorum Coll. Univ.*

Cited very frequently in *Annals, Colleges.*

Excerpts from it are found in Wood MS. F. 28, foll. 11ᵛ, 21, 27, 29, 33.

This MS. apparently contains the following sections, which Wood cited separately :—

(*a*) 'Copia ordinationum congregationis regentium et non-regentium executorum et procuratorum venerabilis viri magistri Willelmi de Dunelm., dat. 1292.'

Wood's transcript is in Wood MS. F. 28, fol. 22.

(*b*) Statuta sive ordinationes pro scholaribus magistri Willelmi de Dunelm.: *init.* 'Ad honorem Dei et virginis gloriosae,' dat. 3 July 1311.

See Twyne I. 68, 170; Twyne XXIII. 363.

(*c*) Statuta alia, data 1475.

A transcript of these is in Wood MS. F. 28, foll. 30*-32.

(*d*) *Rentale*, in libro Statutorum, p. 13: see Twyne XXIII. 363.

Cited in *City*, i. 107 ; *Annals*, ii. 757.

(*e*) *Cartulary*, at the end of the volume; cited *passim* in the first volume of *City*.

(iv) *Calendarium seu vetus rationale*: given to John Bancroft (Master 1609–1642) by Thomas Allen.

Cited in *Annals*, i. 113, *Coll.* pp. 37 sqq.

Wood knew it only from Twyne's excerpts (Twyne XXII. 404), and was told when he enquired for it that it was lost. Is no. 178 in Coxe's Cat. of Univ. Coll. MSS. a fragment of it?

(v) *Registrum actorum Societatis*, from 1509 onwards.

Begun by Ralph Hamsterly, Master 1509–1518; init. 'Registrum hoc Collegii Universitatis sive Magnae Aulae Universitatis ex fundatione Gulielmi Dunelm.'

Cited in *Hist.* ii. 62.

Excerpts from it in Wood MS. F. 28, foll. 7–10.

(vi) *List of members.*

At the end of 'a book of engrossments of leases' in the College treasury are 'the names of sundry scholars that have been of the College from 1573 to 1598'— so in Wood MS. E. 4— 'most are but surnames, but to those surnames which are the names of learned men Dr. John Browne, sometimes fellow, hath added their Christian names.'

(vii) Wood's *Catalogue of Fellows*, 1381–1654: Wood MS. F. 28, foll. 1–10, only partly in Wood's hand.

(viii) *List of benefactors*: Wood MS. F. 28, foll. 12–15.

(ix) *Inscriptions at Univ. Coll.*, Twyne's copies of, taken in 1624: Twyne XXII. 408–410.

(x) Richard Gascoigne's excerpts concerning William, archdeacon of Durham, from the chest of Roche Abbey in St. Marie's Round Tower in York; Twyne II. 180–182.

151. Wadham College.

See 5th Rep. Hist. MSS. Comm. p. 479.

(i) *Chartae, evidentiae,* &c. in the treasury.

Cited in *Coll.* p. 591.

Wood's excerpts from these are found in Wood MS. F. 28, foll. 227–229 (268–270).

(ii) *Statuta data per Dorotheam relictam Nicholai Wadhami fundatoris.*

(*a*) The original, under the seal of the foundress, is in the College treasury. 'These statutes, they say, were put into Latin by John Bond': so in Wood MS. E. 4: 'commentator upon Horace (quaere); died 1613.'

(*b*) A transcript in the Warden's hands.

(*c*) A transcript in the Subwarden's hands, 'given for his use by Alexander Huish, fellow.'

(iii) *Accounts of the expenses of building* the College, 1610–1613: in the College archives: cited by Gutch in *Colleges.* See T. G. Jackson's Wadham College (1893), p. 29.

(iv) Twyne XXI. p. 285 : 'ult. July 1610, 9 A. M., the first stone of Wadham College was laid by the Vice-chancellor and Dr. Rives of New College: Dr. Rives made a Latin speech in praise of the founders before, and after the choristers sang *Te Deum.* The mayor (Thomas Harris) was present.'

(v) *Registrum* : continens omnia decreta et acta privata et publica a tempore fundationis.

(vi) *Liber Coll. Wadh. de admissionibus guardianorum, sociorum, &c.,* a great folio, beginning 'In Dei nomine Amen, per praesens publicum instrumentum.'—This is **A.** in R. B. Gardiner's Registers of Wadham College, i. pp. xiv, xvi.

(vii) Catalogus Sociorum (in bibliotheca Collegii), inchoatus per quendam socium, continuatus per Nicholaum Lloyd ad 1672. This is, I suppose, **B.** in Gardiner, *l. c.*

(viii) Wood's *list of members.*

(*a*) Catalogue of fellows, 1613–1681: Wood MS. F. 28, foll. 232–237 (275–280).

(*b*) Catalogue of fellow-commoners and commoners : Wood MS. F. 28, fol. 225 (266)

(*c*) Catalogue of members, 1613–1693: Wood MS. F. 28, foll. 198 (238), fol. 241–245 (284–289).

(ix) *Register of burials* in Wadh. Coll. Chapel: Wood MS. D. 5, pp. 11 and 12* : *Life,* i. 126.

Miscellanea Academica.

152. Cambridge.

(i) Nicholas de Cantelupe's *Historia nigri codicis Univ. Cantab.*, *init.* 'Anno a mundi creatione 4321 inclitus rex Britonum Gurgent': see Twyne XXI. 24, 663; Twyne XXII. 23.

Cited in *Fasti*, 1, 4; *Annals*, i. 109.

(ii) *Brevis historia* per quendam neotericum: see Twyne XXI. 836. *Init.* 'Ab origine mundi MLXXXX annos Brutus venit': in MS. Bodl. 487, written by a late hand.

(iii) John Herrison's *Historiola de fundatoribus Univ. Cant.*, written about 1464: known to Wood only from Caius, lib. i. p. 44, and Fuller's History of Cambr. p. 82.

(iv) Dr. Samuel Ward's *Tractatus de gymnasii Cantab. antiquitate*, a Llanerch MS., see *Life*, iii. 383.

(v) Matthew Parker's *Historia brevis Acad. Cantab.*, at the end of the Lives of the Archbishops of Canterbury (edit. 1, anno 1572) in S. James' (the Royal) Library: see Twyne XXI. 669.

Cited in *Annals*, ii. 24 as a 'MS. in S. James' library.'

(vi) *Cambridge papal Bulls*: Twyne VII. pp. 132 sqq., 237, 241.

(vii) *Bulla qua Cantab. facta est universitas*: Twyne III. 236.

(viii) *Cantabrigiensis Universitatis institutio*: Twyne III. 438, 439; Twyne XXI. 9, 237, 673; Twyne XXIV. 281, 616.

(ix) Twyne II. fol. 82 notices 'Sir Robert Cotton's Saxon monument for the antiquity of Cambridge scholes and university, whereof notwithstanding here is found no mention but only of certain gilds and fraternities of tradesmen there.'

(x) Liber Domesday de Cantab.; Twyne III. 379; Twyne XXII. 281.

(xi) Rotulus, inquisitionis de burgo Cantab.; Twyne XXII. 373.

(xii) Elizabeth's 1561 charter to Cambridge; Twyne XXII. 36–43.

(xiii) Registrum Thomae Markaunt, Cantab.: Twyne II. 67: Twyne VII. 46.

Cited in *Annals*, i. 151, 363, 365.

(xiv) Matthew Stokys, bedellus Cantab.: Twyne XXII. 22.

Cited in *Fasti*, 1.

(xv) Matthew Parker's Cambridge Collections at the end of Lives of the Archbishops of Canterbury, edit. 1572, 'in St. James Library.'

(a) *Contenta chartarum Acad. Cantab.*: Twyne XXI. 650: cited in *Annals*, i. 151.

(b) *Catalogus cancellariorum, . . . doctorum, . . .* in Acad. Cantab.: Twyne XXI. 671; Twyne XXII. 1. Wood's excerpts from it are found in Wood MS. E. 3 (*O. C.* 8567), foll. 1–8.

(xvi) Catalogus diversorum registrorum Acad. Cant. ; Twyne XXI. 662, 665.

(xvii) Catalogue of books given to Cambr. Univ. library, 1574, by Matthew Parker, Twyne XXI. 672.

(xviii) Latin verses *de adventu regis* at Cambr. : Twyne II. fol. 185.

(xix) Mr. James Tabor registrary of Cambr., his certificate containing the University of Cambridge's power of licensing innkeepers, &c., July 3, 1639 : Twyne XVI. foll. 169–170.

(xx) Cambridge notes (Aug. 1635) about the exemption of the Universities from Metropolitan Visitation : Twyne VII. 227–262.

(xxi) *Catalogue of the provosts and fellows of King's College Cambridge* : see *Life*, iii. 35.

Wood's excerpts from this are found in Wood MS. E. 3 (*O. C.* 8567), foll. 9–26.   These excerpts are cited in *Coll.* p. 437.

153. Paris.

(i) Twyne II. 101–103 has a list of the colleges at Paris, and verses about the University of Paris.

(ii) *Statutes for the English nation* there, made 1251 : Wood MS. F. 27 : see *Life*, ii. 268.

Cited in *Annals*, i. 242.

III. CIVIL RECORDS.

Documents in the State offices in London.

154. The Public Records.

The Records in the Tower, the Rolls Office, the Exchequer, &c. are cited freely in all Wood's books. His knowledge of them was (for all practical purposes) due entirely to Twyne, though he may have used also Robert Hare's excerpts from them and Richard James' excerpts (MSS. Ric. James, nos. 7, 23, 24, and 25). On the occasions on which he visited the Tower, &c. (*Life*, ii. 109, 111, &c.) he seems to have done no more than 'verify his quotations' from Twyne. When, however, he came to work for the *Athenae*, he was thrown on his own resources, and his citations from the Wills Office, the Heralds Office, and the Prerogatives Office, seem taken at firsthand (*Life*, ii. 167, 243 ; iii. 163). I have, therefore, contented myself with indicating the general title of the records and giving the references to Twyne. A brief guide to the Public Records as they now are, with special reference to Oxford, would be a much greater boon to students, but it is one which I am quite unable to confer.

155. Records of the Tower of London.

(i) *Chartae antiquae,* excerpts in MS. Rich. James 24, p. 28.

(*a*) Chartae antiquae 'AA'; Twyne II. 40 a; Twyne XXII. 107.

(*b*) Chartae antiquae 'FF'; Twyne II. 40 a.

(*c*) Chartae antiquae 'NN'; Twyne II. 40 b.

(*d*) Chartae antiquae 'D'; Twyne II. 40 b; Twyne XXIII. 7. These last are cited not infrequently, e. g. *City,* i. 351, &c.

(ii) *Rotuli finium et fines ;* Twyne II. 39 b. The earliest cited seem to be 1204, *City,* i. 199; 1228, *City,* i. 152; 1230, *City,* i. 273.

(iii) *Oblata* or fine rolls; Twyne II. 40 a; Twyne XXII. 107.

(iv) *Rotuli Chartarum,* charter rolls; Twyne VII. 36; Twyne XXII. 40 a, b, 42 b, 46 a, b.

(v) *Rotuli parliamentarii,* Mr. Bowyer custos; Twyne XXIII. 50–56, 114, 117. Cited in *Annals,* i. 476.

(vi) *Rotuli patentes, litterae patentes,* patent rolls; Twyne II. 38 a, b, 40 b, 41, 42, 44 b, 45; Twyne VII. 33; Twyne XXII. 107–109; Twyne XXIII. 14, 15, 21, 44–46, 60, 114.

Cited frequently in *Annals, Coll., City,* &c. The earliest cited seem to be 1236, in *City,* i. 273; 1237, *City,* i. 241; 1244, *City,* i. 252.

(vii) *Rotuli,* Twyne XXIII. 2–4.

(viii) *Rotuli clausi,* close rolls; Twyne II. 47 a; Twyne VII. 32; Twyne XXII. 119; Twyne XXIII. 7.

Cited frequently in *Annals, Fasti, City.* The earliest cited seem to be 1326, in *City,* i. 2 9; 1331, *City,* i. 275.

(ix) *Rotuli Romani ;* Twyne VII. 395; Twyne XXII. 158.

Cited frequently in *Annals, Fasti.*

(x) *Rotuli hundredorum,* hundred rolls; Twyne XXIII. 111.

(xi) *Fasciculi eschaetorum;* Twyne II. 48 b; Twyne XXII. 327, 328; Twyne XXIII. 46, 48, 110. Cited frequently in *Annals, City.* The earliest cited seem to be 1267, in *City,* i. 274; 1305, *City,* i. 157.

(xii) *Fasciculi petitionum parliamentariarum ;* Twyne II. 42 a; Twyne XIV. 151; Twyne XXIII. 29, 30, 34, 40–43, 48, 49. Cited in *Annals, Fasti, Coll.*

(xiii) *Summonitiones ;* Twyne XXIII. 58, 59. Cited (1265) in *City,* ii. 160, 210; cited in *Annals,* i. 422.

(xiv) *Inquisitiones post mortem.*

(xv) *Inquisitiones ad quod damnum.* Cited (1303) in *City,* ii. 316.

(xvi) *Fasciculi inquisitionum ;* Twyne II. 45 a, b, 47 b, 48; Twyne XXII. 131; Twyne XXIII. 1, 13. Cited frequently in *Annals, City,* e. g. 1331 in *City,* i. 274.

(xvii) *Rotulus generalis inquisitionis comitatus et villae Oxon.* per hundreda captae anno 6 et 7 Edw. I, 1278; Twyne II. 47b; Twyne

XXII. 131–134; Twyne XXIII. 1. Cited *passim* in *Annals, Colleges, City*. This roll is also cited by its parts:—e. g.

(*a*) *Inquisitio hundredi de Bolendon*, Twyne II. 43; *City*, i. 335.

(*b*) *Inquisitio dominici domini regis de Woodstock*, Twyne II. 43; *City*, i. 474.

(*c*) *Inquisitio de hundredo extra portam borealem Oxon.*, Twyne II. 47 b.

(xviii) *Liber Parliamenti*. Cited in *Annals*, i. 330, 368.

(xix) *Brevia*. ' Bundellum Brevium (quaere an in Turri London. ?) cujus hic est character ♃,' Twyne XXII. 161. Cited in *Annals*, i. 345, in *City* (1294), i. 142.

(xx) *Fragmenta Hebraica*, Twyne XXIII. 32.

(xxi) *Placita parliamentaria*, Twyne XXIII. 50. Cited in *Annals*, i. 388.

(xxii) *Originalia*.

(xxiii) *Communiae*.

(xxiv) *Quo warranto*.

(xxv) *Pleas of the King's Bench*.

(xxvi) *Pleas of the Commons*.

156. Rolls Office—' in officio sive heteria Rotulorum, vel capella Rotulorum vel Domo Conversorum in vico Chancery Lane, London.'

(i) *Recorda, rotuli, registra*, ibidem; Twyne IV. 559, 589–594; Twyne VII. 139–142; Twyne XXII. 139, 145 b; Twyne XXIII. 23. Cited in *City*, ii. 388.

(ii) *Literae patentes*, ibidem; Twyne XXIII. 23; cited in *City*, ii. 178.

(iii) *Rotuli clausi*, ibidem; Twyne XXIII. 24–26, 28.

157. The Exchequer.

(i) *Rotuli, libri, chartae, repertoria, partes originales*, in officio vel heteria rememoratoris scaccarii ex parte domini Thesaurarii; ' sir Peter Osburne, sir John Osburne, custodes, in Ivy Lane; sir Thomas Fanshaw, K. B., was remembrancer of the King's exchequer, 1638.'—Twyne II. 48 a; Twyne IV. 579 b–583; Twyne XXIII. 6, 9, 16, 37, 38, 62.—Excerpts from documents in the Exchequer are found in MS. Ric. James 23, p. 116, &c.

(ii) *Libri irrotulamentorum, literarum patentium*, in officio vel heteria auditoris receptionum scaccarii; ' sir Robert Pye, auditor.'— Twyne IV. 500, 598, 599.

(iii) *Libri* in officio vel heteria receptionum scaccarii domini regis Westmonast.; ' Mr. Bradshaw custos.'—Twyne IV. 1, 617; Twyne XXII. 297.

Calendars and books in the office of Mr. Bradshaw in the treasury of the Exchequer; Twyne XIV. 190.

Libri, calendarii, rotuli, libri abbreviationum in thesaurario scaccarii ; 'Mr. Bradshaw custos.'—Twyne XXIV. 477, 487, 490, 491.

Liber abbreviationum de placitis coram rege—in the treasury of the Exchequer; Twyne XVI. fol. 12.

Rotuli in the old chapter-house at Westminster in the cloisters, 'Mr. Bradshaw custos'; Twyne XXII. 284, 297.

A booke or repertory of abstracts of records at large kept in the house within Westminster cloister; Twyne XIV. 65.

(iv) *Recorda regis* in thesaurario receptionum scaccarii sub custodia domini Thesaurarii; Twyne XIV. 69–82.

158. Alienations Office. See Twyne IV. 585.

159. Court of Augmentations at Westminster.

(i) *Fasciculi, rotuli, computi, libri, certificati,* ibidem repositi; Twyne IV. 559, 597; Twyne XXIII. 18, 19. Cited in *Annals, Colleges, City.*

(ii) *Liber indenturarum* et irrotulatorum, ibidem; Twyne XXII. 140. Cited in *Colleges*, p. 429.

(iii) Book of Survey of all College and Church lands, 1534; Twyne XXI. 803; Twyne XXIII. 19, 20, 36. Cited in *City*, ii. 23, 56: see *Annals*, ii. 60. See par. 81.

(iv) *Certificate ordering a survey of all chantry lands,* 1547. Cited in *City*, ii. 39.

160. Crown Office 'in Hospitio quondam Lincolniensi London.'
Variae chartae, ibidem: Twyne XXIII. 492.

161. Heralds' Office.

(i) Ralph Sheldon's *Collections out of the Heralds Office*, about the burials of noblemen, are found in Wood MS. B. 7, foll. 2–8.

(ii) Wood's *Collections from the Heralds Office* are found in Wood MS. B. 14 (*O. C.* 8585); Wood MS. B. 13; Wood MS. E. 5 (*O. C.* 8520); MS. Rawl. D. 857, fol. 53.

162. Palace Treasury at Westminster.

(i) *Variae chartae et munimenta* in officio sive heteria Thesaurarii palatii apud Westm.; Twyne III. 251.

(ii) *Repertorium recordorum*, ibidem; Twyne XXIV. 492–494, 497.

163. Papers Office at Whitehall.

Leave to search the office of papers of state was given to Twyne 30 May 1634, by Sir Francis Windebanke, Secretary of State; Twyne IV. 559, 601, 603.

Referred to in *Annals*, ii. 272.

164. Pellis Exitus.

Bullae papales et recorda sive registra in officio vel heteria vocato 'Pellis exitus' in scaccario recept. thesaur. regii apud Westmonasterium: Twyne XXI. 127, 139, 150.

Cited in *City*, ii. 289, 310.

165. Pipe Office at Westminster.

Rotuli, computus vicecomitum Oxon. et eschaetorum, indices sive tabulae, &c.: Twyne II. 39, 48; Twyne IV. 563 b–576 b; Twyne XXII. 330–332; Twyne XXIII. 11, 17, 35; Twyne XXIV. 291, 349.

Cited frequently in *Annals* and *City*. The earliest documents cited are 1161 (*City*, i. 471); 1174 (*City*, i. 272); 1227 (*City*, i. 268).

166. Prerogatives Office.

Wood's *Notes from the Prerogatives Office*, chiefly excerpts from wills there, are found in Wood MS. D. 11 and Wood MS. B. 13. See *Life*, iii. 163.

Cited in *City*, ii. 274, 385.

167. Star Chamber.

Registrum decretorum Camerae Stellatae apud Westmonasterium.
Cited in *Annals*, ii. 130.

168. Tallies Office.

Chartae variae in officio talliarum: Twyne XXII. 141.

169. Wills Office 'in the Deane's Yard of St. Paul.'

Excerpts from wills there are found in Wood MS. B. 13: *Life*, iii. 273.

170. Doomsday book.

(i) *Liber Domesday vel censualis*, made 20 Will. Conq., 1086; Twyne III. 379; IV. 447; XXI. 319; XXII. 280.

Constantly cited both in *City* and *Annals*.

(ii) *The little Domesday book* 'kept in the office of the receipt of the king's exchequer'; Twyne XXII. 280.

(iii) *Epitome libri de Domesday*, MSS. Cotton Julius C. 1, p. 9, Faustina C. 11, nu. 2.

(iv) *Transcript of Doomsday book* in the Arundel library.

(v) *Arthur Agard*: treatise on obscure words in Doomsday book, MS. Cotton Vitell. C. 9.

(vi) *Francis Tate*: on terms in Doomsday.

This treatise was in Ralph Sheldon's library. Some excerpts from it are found in Wood MS. C. 3, and a copy of the excerpts, in Wood's own hand, in Wood MS. F. 32 (*O. C.* 8594), fol. 120.

DOCUMENTS OF AND ABOUT THE CITY OF OXFORD.

171. Our knowledge of the Archives of the City of Oxford during the seventeenth century, when they were much more extensive than they are now[1], begins and ends with Brian Twyne, whose narrative of his researches in them is found in Twyne IV. 349 a–354, and whose excerpts from them occupy much space in Twyne IV, Twyne XXIII, and Twyne XXIV. Richard James, MS. Ric. James 26, p. 112, cites 'rolls in the City Archives,' but his citations are probably from his friend Twyne's notes: and all Anthony Wood's references are to Twyne's excerpts and not to the originals.

172. *A Catalogue of the Archives,* entitled 'Oxford City Records, Part I:—Volumes in alphabetical order; Part II:—Separate Documents in chronological order,' by F. Madan, M.A., was printed in 1887, 28 leaves fol.—Some notes on the City Records will be found in W. H. Turner's 'Records of the City of Oxford, 1509–1583,' Oxford, 1880. The more important of the charters, &c. have been recently transcribed and edited by the Rev. O. Ogle in his 'Royal Letters addressed to Oxford,' Oxford, 1892, pp. xii + 388.

173. The old municipal bounds ('the franchises') of Oxford.

Twyne IV. 391; Twyne XXI. 738: see Thorold Rogers' *Oxford City Documents* (Oxf. Hist. Soc. 1891), p. 300.—Twyne IV. 395–401 is an argument 'that all the isle of Osney and Rewley &c. are without the franchises of the towne of Oxford and suburbes thereof.' An early statement of these bounds is in Nicholas Bishop's *Collectanea,* fol. 319: see par. 199.

174. Length and Breadth of the City of Oxford.

Twyne XXI. 802 gives the measurements as taken by him in 1621. '*Length,* from Osney mill to the end of Bollshipton farm-house[2] in St. Clement's is 104 perches; *breadth,* from St. Giles Church to Fryar Bacon's study, 64 perches.' This seems intended for the utmost dimension of the City, including the suburbs: beyond the points mentioned the open country began.

175. Registers of the City of Oxford.

(i) *The Great White book of wills;* old mark **A.**
'Liber magnus albus in papyro testamentorum burgensium Oxon.';

---

[1] in the Town Archives at Bridgewater are several papers concerning Oxford, believed to have come from the Oxford City Archives.　　　[2] *City,* i. 283.

it contains also 'variae chartae, chyrographa, et indenturae'; it begins 1321 (14 Edward II) and comes down to 1667. Twyne's excerpts from it are found in Twyne XXIII. 142–153, and 510–552; and the names of those who have wills in it are found in Twyne IV. 336, 337. See also Twyne IV. 321; and Twyne XXIII. 142, 235, 236.

Wood had seen this book, but when he wished to consult it more thoroughly was refused permission: *Life*, ii. 480. It is freely cited, from Twyne's notes, in *City*, and occasionally in *Annals*.

It is still found in the City archives, and is now called 'The Old White Book,' or 'The Enrolment Book'; Madan, O. C. R. p. 7, col. 2.

(ii) *The Great Red book*; old mark **B**.

A 'great red book, transcribed about 1616, wherein are various charters'; it contained 460 pages. An index to its contents is given in Twyne IV. 333. Collections from it are found in Twyne II. fol. 10; Twyne XXIII. 140, 141, 371, 553; Twyne XXIV. 259.

Wood seems to cite this volume in *Colleges*, pp. 179, 181, 593, but with *three* 'red books' in the City archives his vague references cannot (without a thorough collation) be fixed with certainty.

This volume is probably still in the archives, and if an opportunity is had of collation with the Twyne excerpts it will perhaps be identified with one of the following :—

Enrolment Book, 1588–1690, for the enrolment of deeds, conveyances, &c.; Madan, O. C. R. p. 4.

Vellum Book I, 1650–1750, copies of City documents, charters, indentures, wills, benefactions, leases, &c.

Vellum Book II, 1630–1800, a similar book; Madan, O. C. R. p. 9.

(iii) *The Old Red book* : old mark **B**.

An 'old red book in quarto containing pleas of the Crown for the City of Oxford from 13 Edward I (1285) and a French treatise of pleas.'

Excerpts from this are found in Twyne IV. 1–12, 205, 357, 617; Twyne XXII. 277–280, 309–320; Twyne XXIV. 249. The beginning was 'Coram Salamone de Roff., Richardo de Boyland, &c., justic. itiner., in crastino S. Hilarii 13 Edw. I.'

Perhaps this is the volume cited in *Annals*, i. 171, 400, &c.; *Fasti*, pp. 14, 15; *City*, i. 339, 340, 379; ii. 16, 67 : but see *supra*, § ii.

(iv) *The Smaller Red book*: old mark **C**.

'Rubrus liber minor in pergameno, varias continens chartas et tractatus; in the beginning was the order of bringing in the Mayor of Oxon at his returne from taking his oath at London; it contained multa scitu digna both for the City and the University'—so Twyne IV. 321; Twyne XXIII. 560. A list, page by page, of its contents is given in Twyne IV. 321–332; on fol. 155 it had some deeds about S. Bartholomew's Hospital.

This book is said to be now missing from the City archives; Turner, Oxford City Records, pp. v, xiv. It might be worth while printing the contents as in Twyne, *l. c.*, in the hope of its being identified in some library of MSS.: cp. par. 199.

Collections from this volume are found in Twyne II. fol. 9 b; Twyne IV. 29, 30, 34, 134, 190, 210; Twyne XXII. 273–277; Twyne XXIII. 172, 560–572.

176. Books of Benefactors to the City of Oxford.

(i) An old quarto MS., where there is a picture of a crucifix and an old Calendar; old mark perhaps **E**. It had a list of the benefactors, for whose souls the City was to pray on the day of election of officers, up to 1480: and contained about 110 leaves. See Twyne IV. 203; Twyne XXIII. 133, 185.

It is, perhaps, the volume cited in *City*, i. 205, and ii. 36, 55. It is said to be missing now; Turner, City Records, pp. v, vi.

(ii) '*The small vellum book*,' now in the City archives, containing a form of thanksgiving for benefactors to the City, with details of their gifts, 1630–1823 (Madan, O. C. R. p. 3), seems to me to be the surviving member of a set of benefaction-registers.

(iii) *The city bidding-prayer*; Twyne IV. 317.

177. Town Council Books.

(i) *Town Council Book A* : Liber senatus concilii civitatis Oxon., continens acta senatus concilii. It contains proceedings in the Town Council, 21 Apr. 1520—30 Sept. 1592; Madan, O. C. R. p. 8.

Collections from it are found in Twyne IV. 267, 280; Twyne XXIII. 448–450, 457–459, 582–608, 661. It is cited freely, from Twyne's notes, in *City* and *Annals*.

(ii) *Town Council Book B*, 6 Oct. 1592—6 Nov. 1628.

(iii) *Town Council Book C*, 4 Dec. 1628—6 June 1664.

(iv) *Town Council Book D*, 30 Sept. 1663—17 July 1702.

These contemporary books, however, would not be accessible to Twyne or Wood.

178. Town Council Minute-books.

These contain minutes of proceedings at meetings of the Town Council, often referring to matters not copied into the Council Books *supra*; Madan, O. C. R. p. 8.

(i) 29 Feb. 15$\frac{87}{88}$—16 Sept. 1588, with a few notes 1588–1594.

(ii) 29 Sept. 1594—25 Sept. 1606.
(iii) 4 March 161⅝—22 Sept. 1634.
(iv) Sept. 1635—21 Sept. 1657.
(v) 29 Sept. 1657—14 Sept. 1668.
(vi) 29 Sept. 1681—30 Sept. 1701.
These, naturally, would not be accessible to Twyne or Wood.

179. Account-books of the City of Oxford.

(i) *Rotuli computus camerariorum*, in pyxide vel theca intitulata 'Accompts.' See Twyne XXII. 360, 361 ; Twyne XXIII. 181, 226–249.

Cited frequently in *City, Annals, Fasti.* The earlier documents in the series appear to be lost ; one of 1308 is cited in *City*, i. 253 ; one of 1321 is cited *ibid.* 426, &c.

Madan, O. C. R. p. 3, mentions as now in the City archives :—

(*a*) Audit of the accounts of the Chamberlains &c., 1553–1591, and 1591–1682.

(*b*) The accounts of the Common Chest of the City (custodes quinque clavium), 1555–1644, and 1644–1686, and 1686–1725.

(ii) *Rentalia Civitatis Oxon.*, see Twyne XXIII. 132. All the early documents of this sort seem now to be lost ; a rental of 1274 is cited in *City*, i. 312, with a reference to Twyne XXIII. 229 ; one of 1388 is cited in Twyne IV. 210.

180. Court-books of the City of Oxford.

(i) *Rotuli curiae maioris Oxon.* of an early date are excerpted in Twyne XXIII ; and are cited from Twyne's excerpts by Wood, e. g. a roll of 1275 in *City*, i. 492 ; one of 1289, *ibid.* 493 ; one of 1292, *ibid.* 488 ; one of 1321, *City*, ii. 279, &c. All these earlier records seem now to be lost. Madan, O. C. R. p. 6, gives the following as now in the City archives :—

Proceedings in the Mayor's Court, (1) 1527–1535; (2) 30 Apr. 1574—16 Sept. 1586; (3) 9 June 1592—19 Sept. 1597; (4) 3 Aug. 1636—8 Sept. 1638 ; (5) 5 Oct. 1638—25 Sept. 1640 ; (6) 11 May 1660—23 Sept. 1664—after which the series is continuous.

(ii) *Rotuli curiae Hustengorum Oxon.* ; collections thence are found in Twyne IV. 24, 152 ; Twyne XXIII. 134–138, 249–257, 259, 263–362, 368–382, 384, 406, 407 ; Twyne XXIV. 256–276. They are cited freely in *City*, and occasionally in *Fasti*.

The hustings' court dealt chiefly with business connected with the freemen of the City. A large number of volumes in the City archives relate to this court, and are thus tabulated by Madan, O. C. R. pp. 5, 13 :—

(*a*) Proceedings in the hustings' court, (1) 1530–1591 ; (2) 26 Apr. 1564—24 Oct. 1586 ; (3) 5 June 1592—8 Oct. 1595 ; (4) 8 Oct. 1636—24 Sept. 1638 ; (5) 8 Oct. 1638—5 Oct. 1640 : (6) 14 May 1660—26 Sept. 1664, after which the series is continuous.   Some earlier records of the court exist in separate documents, 1290–1292, 1340–1342, 1400.—It may be added that in the collection of Charters in the Bodleian are several documents connected with the hustings' court: see W. H. Turner's 'Catalogue of the Charters and Rolls in the Bodleian.'

(*b*) Lists of suitors (' sectatores ') in the hustings' court, (1) 1520–1591 ; (2) 1591–1613 ; (3) 1613–1639 ; (4) 1640–1663 ; (5) 1662–1698.

(*c*) Lists of actions brought in the hustings' court, (1) 1 Oct. 1662—29 Sept. 1668 ; (2) 16 Oct. 1668—29 Sept. 1675 ; (3) 2 Oct. 1675—26 Sept. 1694.

(iii) *Rotuli curiae ballivorum* ; excerpts in Twyne XXIII. 261, 382, 386.   A bailiffs' court roll of 1416 is cited in *City*, i. 96, from Twyne XXIII. 376.

(iv) *Rotuli curiae pedis pulverizati* : rolls of pie-powders' court are cited in Twyne XXIII. 442.

(v) *Rotuli coronatorum* : see Twyne IV. 39 ; Twyne XXIII. 154, 166.   Coroner's inquests of dates $129\frac{6}{7}$, $129\frac{7}{8}$, $\frac{1299}{1300}$, 1300, 1303, 1304, 1305, 1308, are still found in the City archives ; Madan, O. C. R. pp. 13, 14.   Coroner's inquests are cited freely by Wood, from Twyne's notes, in *Annals* and *City* : some of them being more ancient than any now extant ; e. g. an inquest of 1285 in *City*, i. 163, 528 ; and one of 1295, *ibid.* 198.   See Prof. Thorold Rogers' *Oxford City Documents* (Oxf. Hist. Soc.), 1891, p. 145.

(vi) *Rotuli recognitionum* : Twyne XXIII. 139.   Cited in *Annals*, i. 467.

All the early records of this class seem lost.   The recognizances now in the City archives date only from the Epiphany sessions of 1740 ; Madan, O. C. R. p. 7.

181. Miscellaneous legal documents of the City of Oxford.

(i) *Rotuli de visu franciplegii* ; Twyne XXIII. 383, 384, 444. Cited, of the year 1424, in *City* i. 298.

(ii) *Rotuli pipae* : Twyne XXIII. 441.

(iii) *Rotuli casus fortunae* : Twyne XXIII. 178.

(iv) *Fasciculus sessionum et goal. deliv.* ; cited, no doubt from Twyne's notes, in *Annals*, ii. 18.

(v) *Fasciculus praesentationum juratorum*: Twyne XXIII. 431, 435, 444. This is perhaps the source for the citation, of the year 1403, in *City*, i. 313 ; and, of the year 1406, *ibid*. 228, &c.

(vi) *Rotulus temptationis panis*: cited in *Fasti*, p. 20.

(vii) *Rotuli assisae panis et cervisiae*: cited in *Fasti*, pp. 22, 25.

(viii) *An obligation*: cited in *Fasti*, p. 28. I believe that all such references came directly from Twyne's notes.

(ix) *A book with inquisitions*: cited in *Fasti*, p. 14.

182. Writs, &c., relating to the City of Oxford.

Twyne XXIII. 403, 445, has excerpts from a *Fasciculus brevium*. Citations of these are made several times in *Annals, Colleges, Fasti*, and *City*.

A few writs of Edward I, II, III, Richard II, Henry VI, of dates 1305, 1320, 1321, 1322, 1328, 1330, &c., 1380, 1446, are still found in the City archives ; Madan, O. C. R. pp. 14, 15, 17, 19.

183. Pleas of the Crown relating to the City of Oxford.

(i) Those contained in a register (now lost) : *supra*, p. 181.

(ii) Those in 'the exchequer at Westminster' : Twyne IV. 1, 615, 617. Partly printed in Thorold Rogers' *Oxford City Documents* (O. H. S., 1891), pp. 194 sqq.

(iii) *Fasciculus placitorum coronae*, frisc. fort., &c., in archivis civitatis : Twyne XXIII. 446.

This is probably the source of the citations in *City*, i. 244; ii. 457, 461, 463.

184. Tax-books of the City of Oxford.

Twyne XXIII. 432, 435, 436, 464, has excerpts from a *Fasciculus de taxationibus* in the City archives. There are citations from documents of this kind in *Annals*, i. 362, &c.; and frequently in *City*, e. g. i. 95, 115, 118, &c. The tax of clerks' houses in Edward II's reign is cited with especial frequency in *Annals* and in *City*.

The old documents of this kind seem to be all lost. The earliest extant tax-books in the City archives are of date 1667–1670 and 1691–1694 ; Madan, O. C. R. p. 8.

185. Miscellaneous deeds of the City of Oxford.

(i) *Fasciculus chartarum de tenementis in diversis parochiis*: Twyne XXIII. 390–403.

Cited in *Colleges*, p. 249.

(ii) *Fasciculus diversarum chartarum de libertatibus*: cited in *Hist*. i. 134 (*City*, ii. 479).

(iii) *Fasciculus libertatum* : cited in *City*, ii. 301, with a reference to Twyne XXIII.

(iv) *Fasciculus variorum scriptorum* : cited in *City*, ii. 317.

(v) In Wood MS. D. 18 (*O. C.* 8563) are transcripts by Gerard Langbaine of several charters of the City. The same volume contains a number of miscellaneous papers about the City of Oxford.

186. Lease-books of the City of Oxford.

Twyne XXIII. 436 mentions a 'great book of counterpart leases' : and this is probably cited in *City*, i. 427.

Madan, O. C. R. p. 5, mentions the following ledger-books of leases granted by the City, as being now in the City archives, (1) 2 Sept. 1579—27 Sept. 1636; (2) 27 Sept. 1636—10 May 1675; (3) 1 Sept. 1675—16 Feb. 169$\frac{8}{9}$.

187. Documents about the jurisdiction of the City, especially in points in conflict with the privileges of the University.

(i) *Fasciculus qui inscribitur* The Qui dicunt *pro libertatibus* civitatis Oxon.; Twyne IV. 203.

(ii) *Fasciculus variarum chartarum* concernentium Universitatem Oxon.; Twyne XXIII. 452-5.

Cited in *Annals*, i. 485, and perhaps also *ibid.* 412, 418.

(iii) *Fasciculus chartarum de magno conflictu* : cited in *Annals*, i. 473.

(iv) *Chartae continentes varios articulos* contra Universitatem : cited in *Annals*, ii. 32, 35, 36, 53, 57.

(v) *Papers about controversies with the University*, 1391, &c. : cited in *Fasti*, pp. 33, 36.

(vi) *Sir William Morton's book ; Life*, ii. 277.

(vii) Madan, O. C. R. p. 8, notes as in the City archives :—

(*a*) Papers about disputes between the City and University.

(*b*) Copies of records, &c., about disputes between the University, 1086-1680 ; not seen by Twyne or Wood.

(*c*) Papers connected with the privileges of the University, 1575-1800.

(*d*) Copies of proceedings in the case Barbour *v.* Dodwell (see *Life*, ii. 381 sqq.).

188. Lists of persons connected with the City.

(i) *Catalogues of Mayors and Bailiffs.*

(*a*) *Brian Twyne's*, to 1648 (the last few years being by a later hand) ; Wood MS. F. 26 (*O. C.* 8502).

(*b*) *Anthony Wood's*, 1122-1695 ; Wood MS. D. 7 (5).

(*c*) Madan, O. C. R. p. 6, notices a catalogue of Mayors and Bailiffs, &c., 1528–1759, as now in the City archives.

(ii) *Lists of members of the Town Council*, 1520–1528, mentioned by Madan, O. C. R. p. 8, as in the City archives.

(iii) *Lists of Freemen of the City* ('Hanasters'), from 1520; Madan, *l. c.* p. 4.

(iv) *Lists of apprentices enrolled*, from 1514; *ibid.* p. 3.

189. Papers connected with the trade-gilds and trades of the City.

(i) Twyne has notes, in Twyne IV of barbers, p. 126; tailors, p. 277; glovers, p. 280; brewers, p. 289; mercers, p. 289; white-bakers, p. 290; butchers, p. 292; weavers and fullers, p. 293.—See also Twyne-Langb. I. par. 242; and Twyne-Langb. IV. par. 245.

(ii) Madan, O. C. R. p. 8, notes various records of the incorporated trades; *ibid.* p. 7, licences for setting up signs, from 1587; *ibid.* p. 5, licences issued to innholders, &c., from 1579.

(iii) *The tailors*: Twyne in Wood MS. D. 32, p. 594 gives a rough sketch of the arms of the tailors' company: Madan, O. C. R. p. 8, notes, as in the City archives, the accounts of the tailors' company, 1612–1699.

(iv) *The weavers*: an 'old book of the weavers' is cited in *City*, i. 496.

(v) *The glovers*: excerpts from papers of the glovers' corporation are found in Twyne XXIV. 250: 'writings of the glovers' are cited in *City*, ii. 111, 'MS. book in parchment of the glovers,' in *City*, ii. 112.

(vi) *The barbers*: the books and papers of this gild[1] are now deposited in the Bodleian; see Mr. Madan's new Summary Catalogue of MSS. in the Bodleian, nos. 31110–31127.

190. Miscellanea Civica.

(i) Account of the nobility and gentry buried in Oxford, 1643–1688; Wood MS. F. 4. Printed out in *Life*. Papers of the same kind are found in Wood MS. F. 31 and MS. Rawl. D, *olim* 1290, *nunc* 912: printed in *Life*.

(ii) Orders for cleansing and improving the streets of Oxford, 1633; Wood MS. F. 31.

(iii) Papers relating to the siege of Oxford, 1646: *Life*, i. 128.

(iv) Notes of coats of arms in Oxford; Wood MS. D. 19 (1); Wood MS. D. 4; Wood MS. F. 33.

(v) Wood's Collections for the City; Wood MS. F. 27.

[1] incorporated 1675; *Life*, ii. 328.

Deeds in private possession relating to private property.

191. The Cartulary of Boarstall Manor.

Consulted by Twyne, see Twyne II. 90 ; and by Wood, see *Life*, ii. 134.

Cited in *City*, ii. 454, 460 ; *Hist.* i. 118.

192. Deeds of Oliver Smyth, of Grandpont, mayor of Oxford in 1624.

Wood knew these only from Twyne's excerpts, in Twyne XXIII. 473–478 ; but cites them several times, e. g. in *Hist.* i. 171, 443 : *City*, i. 201, 298. Wood in *City*, i. 201, cites Mr. John Smith's writings, probably the same.

193. Cartulary of Sir Richard Feteplace.

This was a book containing various writings about lands at Newbury co. Berks, and at New Bridge, Bablockhythe, &c., and belonged at one time to Sir Richard Feteplace of Childrey in that county. It was lent to Twyne by . . . Spire, a bookseller. Wood knew it only from Twyne's excerpts, Twyne IV. 243 ; Twyne XXI. 800 ; Twyne XXII. 437.

It is cited as belonging to 'D. Ri. F., Bercher., militem' in *Annals*, i. 598 ; and apparently as 'liber coenobii de Newberry' in *City*, i. 158.

194. Deeds of various owners, partly cited only from Twyne's excerpts :—

(i) Liber munimentorum Thomae French, Twyne XXII. 337 a ; perhaps cited in *City*, i. 300, 304.

(ii) Mr. Philip French's writings ; cited in *City*, i. 300.

(iii) Sir William Morton's writings, cited in *City*, i. 201, ii. 396. Quaere whether different from par. 187 (vi) *supra*.

(iv) Francis Peacock's deeds ; cited in *City*, i. 338.

(v) The writings of William Randall of Milton Abbat co. Devon, Twyne XXII. 337 ; cited in *City*, i. 304.

(vi) Mr. . . . Walker's lease ; cited in *City*, i. 576.

(vii) Brome Whorwood's deeds ; cited in *City*, i. 338.

(viii) An old book of Mr. Fryar's ⟨i. e. Frere's⟩ leases, of Oxford, in the hands of Mr. Timothy Carter ; Twyne XXIII. 181.

(ix) Muniments of . . . Blakgrave of S Giles' parish Oxford : Twyne XXII. 428.

IV. COLLECTIONS BY ANTIQUARIES, HAVING SPECIAL REFERENCE TO OXFORD.

195. Minor Collections and Notes.

(i) *Thomas Barlow*, provost of Queen's College.

(*a*) Notes about Port Meadow: cited *City*, i. 58, note 2 [1]. Wood had excerpts from these under the window of his study (*City*, i. 313): these are now found in Wood MS. D. 18 (*O. C.* 8563) and are printed in *City*, i. 614.

(*b*) Notes about the dispute as to the church in which Christ Church men preaching before the University in their turns should preach (*Life*, ii. 274, 283): no. 37 in Wood. MS. F. 27 (*O. C.* 8489).

(*c*) Notes about the see of Oxford: cited *City*, ii. 3, 6, 7.

(*d*) Wood had access to Barlow's collection of MSS.: *Life*, ii. 174, 175.

(*e*) Wood addressed queries to Barlow: e. g. in MS. Rawl. D. 1268 (*Life*, ii. p. vii) Wood has a note 'remember to ask Mr. Barlow whether any one hath made any private [2] collections of Oxon or the shire.'

(ii) *John Fell*, dean of Christ Church.

(*a*) His additions to Wood's 'copy' in *Hist. et Antiq. Oxon.* (see *Life*, ii. 260). These are several times cited in *Annals* (e. g. ii. 449, 470, 477), where the sentences from this source are indicated by Gutch, following Wood's MS., by being enclosed in square brackets: *Life*, ii. 199, note 6.

(*b*) Wood had access to his collection of MSS. : *Life*, ii. 277.

(*c*) Wood addressed queries to him: *City*, i. 91, ii. 8.

(iii) *Nathaniel Greenwood*, of B. N. C.

Collection of inscriptions in Oxford and Oxfordshire churches: *Life*, ii. 267, note 5 : cited in *City*, ii. 271.

(iv) *White Kennet* in the last years of Wood's life collected for the *Athenae* lists of Cathedral dignitaries, &c. See *Life*, ii. 519; iii. 7, 39, 124.

(v) *John Lamphire*, principal of Hart Hall.

(*a*) In Wood MS. F. 27 (*O. C.* 8489), art. 36 is a paper by him: *Life*, iii. 262.

(*b*) Wood addressed queries to him: *City*, i. 46, note 6 (c).

---

[1] in this reference and in *City*, i. 45, note 8, 'Barton' is in error for 'Barlow'; the writing in these notes is sometimes very indistinct and requires outside knowledge of the facts to decipher it correctly.

[2] i.e. unprinted.

(vi) *Robert Sanderson*, bishop of Lincoln.

A folio volume of collections by him, containing 766 pages; and marked 'Cartae X': *Life*, ii. 354, 355.

(vii) *William Somner*, of Canterbury: *City*, ii. 276 ; *Life*, ii. 435.

(viii) *John Willis*, chapter-clerk of Christ Church.

(*a*) He had MS. collections about Ch. Ch., *City*, i. 40.

(*b*) He lent Wood MSS., *Life*, ii. 268.

(*c*) Wood addressed questions to him, *City*, i. 63.

(ix) *John Wilton*, chaplain of Merton College.

(*a*) Notes by him, *Life*, i. 446; ii. 38.

(*b*) Oral information by him, *Life*, ii. 5 ; *City*, i. 386, 493 ; *Annals*, ii. 107 (where the name is misprinted as ' Wilson ').

196. Andrew Allam's Collections.

Andrew Allam, vice-principal of S. Edmund Hall, died in June, 1685 (*Life*, iii. 144).   Wood acquired many of his books and papers (*Life*, iii. 167).   The following points deserve separate notice :—

(i) *Notes about authors and books*, especially contemporary, made to help Wood in his projected *Athenae*. A great number of these will be found dispersed throughout Wood MS. F. 46–50. They are easily recognisable by Allam's peculiar handwriting.

(ii) *Notes about contemporary Oxford events*: e. g. list of preachers (circ. 1676–1680) in the City and University of Oxford, with notes whether they did well (' be.' i. e. *bene*, ' opt.' *optime*) or ill, Wood MS. F. 48, foll. 1149–1157 ; notes about the contested election to the principalship of S. Edmund Hall, MS. Tanner 454, slip at fol. 22, foll. 142, &c.

(iii) *Diaries* : Allam, according to a common practice of the day, kept an interleaved almanac in which he noted incidents in Oxford, &c., as they occurred. Wood cut up some volumes of these, and pasted slips from them in his own Diaries, see *Life*, ii. 509. Many of these notes have been printed in *Life*.

(iv) *Letters by Allam to Wood*, sometimes signed with initials only (A. A.), Wood MS. F. 39, foll. 24–43.

(v) *Letters to Allam* by Richard Mulleneux, Godfrey Bosseville of Gunthwait, and others, are found in the Wood Collection of letters.

197. Thomas Allen's Collections.

The great library[1] of MSS. of Thomas Allen of Gloucester Hall, picked up by him at a time when the scattered treasures of monastic libraries were floating about the country, was searched for Oxford

---

[1] see Macray's *Annals of the Bodleian*, p. 23.

matters by Richard James and Brian Twyne. Allen himself was interested in matters of antiquity, and some stray notes of his have been preserved, partly autograph and partly in copy, by Twyne, Richard James, Langbaine.

(i) *Catalogue of Allen's MSS.*, by Brian Twyne : Wood MS. F. 26 (*O. C.* 8488) : see *Life*, i. 249.

(ii) *Collectiones variae ad rem antiquariam spectantes.* Cited in *Annals*, i. 393; *City*, ii. 249, 259, 260, 296.

These probably are the stray notes by, or copied from, Allen, found in Twyne II. 34 b; Twyne III. 29, 137, 239, 555; MS. Arch. Seld. supr. 79, pp. 149, 150, and at the end; in MS. Ric. James 21, p. 44 ; in MS. Wood E. 4 (*O. C.* 8561), p. 204. The verbal information by Allen referred to in *Annals*, ii. 107, is probably to be found in one of the Twyne references.

198. John Aubrey's Collections.

Wood and Aubrey first met in 1667, *Life*, ii. 116 ; and almost from the first corresponded with each other. I have little doubt that Wood received a good deal of information from Aubrey towards the biographical parts of the *Historia et Antiquitates*. When Wood planned the *Athenae* he urged Aubrey to jot down his recollections of men he had known. This Aubrey did, and after depositing them with Wood for a time, finally placed them in the Ashmolean (*Life*, ii. 508). Aubrey was also the person to whom Wood most frequently had recourse to answer questions about books or men. I have transcribed all the biographical portions of the Aubrey MSS. now in the Bodleian, in hopes one day of editing them. The marginal jottings and marks made by Wood in these MSS. show how closely he studied them.—In 1813 the Rev. John Walker and Philip Bliss published '[Letters written by Eminent Persons . . . and] Lives of Eminent Men by John Aubrey,' but the omissions are very numerous and the errors not a few.

The following MSS. are of most importance here :—

(i) *Lives, part i*: press-mark **MS. Aubr. 6.**

This volume was written by Aubrey in Feb. 16$\frac{79}{80}$; contains 122 leaves, chiefly folio, besides a few unfoliated slips ; in Aubrey's foliation it was marked foll. 1–86, but many papers were afterwards inserted, and foll. 4, 14, 31, and 35 were cut out. Cited in *Life*, iii. 162.

(ii) *Lives, part ii*: press-mark **MS. Aubr. 7.**

This is a mere fragment, only foll. 47 and 48 remaining of the volume as originally constituted; but the addition of notes (by Aubrey) written to supplement part i has brought its present number of leaves up to

21.   Aubrey has a note at the beginning, full of anger and bitterness at the mutilation of his MS. by Wood [1].

(iii) *Lives, part iii*; press-mark **MS. Aubr. 8.**

Written by Aubrey in 1681; contains 105 leaves, folio. It consists largely of notes supplementary to the lives in part i; but contains several additional lives, especially of English mathematicians.

Cited in *Life*, iii. 91.

(iv) *Life of Thomas Hobbes*; press-mark **MS. Aubr. 9.**

Written in Febr. $16\frac{78}{89}$; contains 55 leaves, quarto.

Cited in *Life*, ii. 508.

(v) *Collectio Geniturarum*; press-mark **MS. Aubr. 23.**

Written in 1677; contains 125 leaves; is a series of horoscopes, chiefly of contemporaries, with dates of birth and other biographical notes.

(vi) *Hypomnemata Antiquaria: liber A*; old mark (Aubrey's) $\hbar$; press-mark **MS. Aubr. 3.** Contains antiquarian notes of Wiltshire, 217 leaves. This was perused by Wood for its biographical matter, in Feb. $168\frac{5}{6}$. It has been printed, with some licence, in ' Wiltshire: the Topographical Collections of John Aubrey, corrected and enlarged by John Edward Jackson': Devizes 1862.—The companion volume 'Hypomnemata Antiquaria: liber[2] B' was lent to Aubrey's brother soon after it was placed in the Ashmolean, and never recovered— 'quod N. B.' (to use a favourite note of Aubrey's), when the question arises about lending books or MS. out of our great public libraries.

(vii), (viii) *The Natural History of Wiltshire*; **MS. Aubr. 1, 2.**

These volumes contain a good deal of biographical matter, and were perused by Wood. The substance of them was printed by John Britton in 1847.

(ix) *Miscellaneous papers*, **MS. Aubr. 21.** A folio volume, made up of scattered papers, some of them biographical.

(x) *Aubrey's letters to Wood.* The bulk of these is found in MS. Wood F. 39, foll. 116–452. But stray letters of this set are scattered throughout different volumes in the Wood and other Collections; e. g. Wood MS. F. 40, foll. 372, MS. Ballard 14, foll. 80–100, MS. Tanner 456, foll. 3, 14–21, 23, 27, 31–35, 40, 41, MS. Aubr. 13, foll. 2, 4, 8.

(xi), (xii) *Letters to Aubrey.* **MS. Aubr. 12,** letters from about 70 correspondents whose names run from A to N, among whom may be noticed William Browne (G. F., Gulielmus Fuscus), foll. 35, 41–50,

---

[1] in MS. Rawl. D. 727, foll. 93–96, are three lives by John Aubrey and in his writing, which some notes show to have been in Wood's possession. But as they are unfoliated, I doubt whether they are any portion of the prey mentioned here.

[2] Aubrey's MS.B. is cited in *City*, ii. 177.

and John Lydall, foll. 292–319, both of Trinity College, containing notices of events in Oxford during the Civil War period[1]. **MS. Aubr. 18**, letters from over 30 correspondents, P to Y, Anthony Wood's letters coming at foll. 361–372.

(xiii) His paper about certain antiquities at Woodstock: *Life*, i. 283.

(xiv) His notes about heraldic glass, &c., in Trinity College: *City*, ii. 272, 274.

199. Nicholas Bishop's Collections.

(i) *Collectanea Nic. Bishop*, continentia chartas et instrumenta de variis terris, ecclesiis, tenementis in Oxon.; written 1432. Now in Cambridge University Library, MS. Dd. xiv. 1 : 330 leaves.

Cited *passim* in *City*, and occasionally in *Annals*, *Colleges* : but Wood knew it only from the excerpts in Twyne, in whose time it was in the archives of the City of Oxford.

Twyne's collections from it are found in Twyne II. 87, 88 ; Twyne IV. 332, 391 ; Twyne XXI. 711–738 ; Twyne XXIII. 172–176, 410–430.

(ii) *Breve chronicon de regibus Angliae* : part ii of the same MS. Cited in *City*, ii. 291, *Annals*, i. 624 ; from Twyne IV. 332.

200. Thomas French's Collections.

(i) *Collectiones Mri. French, registrarii* : press-mark ' Arch. Univ. Oxon. North West Press 34.' Extracts from registers and charters of the University, 1523–1628 : 311 pages.

Cited in *Annals*, ii. 387.

(ii) *Transcript of charters, leases*, &c. affecting the University : a thick folio volume in the University archives, formerly marked ⊖–⊖

A note by William Smith (of Univ. Coll.) on a fly-leaf suggests that this is the volume cited in *Hist.* i. 338 : but I think it is rather the preceding volume.

201. William Fulman's Collections.

(i) Notes, observations and additions to Wood's *Hist. et Antiq. Oxon.* : Wood MS. D. 9 (*O. C.* 8540), part 1.

(ii) Letters from Fulman to Wood : Wood MS. D. 9, part 2. Cited, perhaps, as *Fulmaniana*, in *Life*, ii. 403.

(iii) Fulman's papers in C. C. C. Library, nos. 296–316 in Coxe's Cat. Codd. C. C. C. Oxon.

To these Wood had not access (see *Life*, iii. 408), except so far as Fulman himself communicated matters to him (*City*, ii. 13). Ful-

---

[1] see *Life*, i. 122, note 1.

man was a person whom Wood was in the habit of asking information from ('qu⟨aere⟩ Mr. Fulman,' *Annals*, ii. 164, note 3).

(iv) Catalogue of Fellows of C. C. C. Oxon : see par. 135 (vi).

202. Robert Hare's Collections.

Robert Hare was of Gonville College, Cambridge (MS. Cott. Faust. C. 3, fol. 432). Concerning his Oxford collections, Twyne naively remarks : ' He might have been larger for Oxon as he was for Cambridge, but the last was his mother and therefore he could do no less.' He was ' buried in Paul's church, in the body, toward the west end, with this epitaph on a flat stone :—

Hic jacet Robertus Hare, quondam clericus, thesaurarius, et scriptor rotulorum de receptis et exitibus thesaurarii Scaccarii, qui obiit senex 2º die Nov. anno 1611.'

(i) *Liber privilegiorum Oxon.* : in the University archives.

This is a collection of charters of privileges, &c., transcribed from the originals in the Tower of London. It is in Latin, folio, vellum, and contains an index of 10 leaves and 210 leaves of text ; was written in 1592 [1], and contains documents ranging from 15 Henry III (1231) to 18 Elizabeth (1576).

Cited *passim* in *Annals, Fasti*, &c., under various titles, as ' Harus,' ' Harus de privilegiis,' ' lib. Privileg.' &c.

Twyne gives an abstract of the contents of this volume in Twyne XXI. 387-390 : and indicates documents omitted in it in Twyne XXI. 466, 519–521 ; Twyne II. 29, col. 2 a ; Twyne XV. 15.

There are transcripts of this volume in the Bodleian, MS. Bodl. 906 (*O. C.* 2873), and MS. Rawl. Q. c. 12 ; and another in the archives of the University.

(ii) *Liber memorabilium Oxon.* : in the University archives.

This is a collection of matters relating to Oxford, transcribed from documents in the Tower of London and elsewhere. It is in Latin, folio, vellum, and contains an index of 10 leaves and 139 leaves of text : was written in 1592. The contents are arranged chronologically by king's reigns.

Cited frequently in *Annals, Fasti, City*, under various titles, e.g. ' Harus,' ' Hari Mem.,' ' Mem.,' ' liber Memorab.' Frequently the king's reign is added in the citation, e. g. Henry III (*City*, i. 240), Edward III (*City*, i. 275, 482), &c.

Twyne gives an abstract of its contents in Twyne XXI. 391-466. Excerpts from it are found in Twyne-Langb. 3 : see par. 244.

---

[1] on a fly-leaf are these lines :— Ad laudem Christi finis libro datur isti.
' Anno milleno quingento duodeno Spiritus authoris hinc gaudeat omnibus
Atque octageno domini dictamine pleno   horis.'

(iii) *De cartis et privilegiis Oxon.*: MS. Cotton Faust. C. VII. foll. 20 sqq., a large collection of papers about the University of Oxford; 'collectio, ut videtur, Roberti Hari.' See Twyne II. 187. Twyne in Twyne VII. 81–83 has notes from 'fragmentary notes in the Cottonian library apparently by R. Hare,' presumably extracted from this volume.

(iv) *Catalogus cancellariorum Oxon.*, 1231–1597: MS. Cotton Faust. C. VII. foll. 1–19.

Cited frequently in *Fasti*.

(v) *Novum registrum monumentorum Univ. Cantab.*: MS. Cotton Faust. C. III.

Contains papal indulgences, royal charters, petitions in parliament, foundations and endowments of Colleges, letters-patent, briefs, &c. from John to Richard II (1399). See Twyne XXII. 1, 3. Twyne has an index to the charters in it in Twyne XXII. 51–60.

Cited in *Annals*, i. 90; *City*, ii. 459.

(vi) *Catalogus cancellariorum Cantab.*: MS. Cotton Faust. C. III. foll. 79–100: see Twyne XXIII. 3.

Cited frequently in *Fasti*, in *City*, ii. 459, &c. It extends 'ab Amphibalo martyre (anno Christi 289) ad Robertum Cecill (A.D. 1604),' otherwise stated as 'from 800 years before Henry IV to 400 years after him.' Twyne says that 'This may be considered ψευδολό-γιον seu Florilegium mendaciorum Cantabrig.'

(vii) *De excidiis et reparationibus Cantab.*: in MS. Cotton Faust. C. III: see Twyne XXII. 21.

Cited in *Annals*, i. 90; *Fasti*, p. 5.

(viii) '*Censura sive responsio R. Hari* (vel alterius incerti authoris Cantabrigiensis) ad impugnationem Nicolai Harpesfeildii adversus Honorii papae bullam ad Cantabrigiam et historiam nigri codicis Cantabrigiensis: MS. Cotton' (Twyne XXII. 29–35). Perhaps MS. Cotton Faust. C. III. fol. 452.

(ix), (x) *Miscellaneous collections of Robert Hare*, two volumes: Gonville and Caius Library (nos. 55 and 56 in the 1697 *Cat. Codd. Angl. et Hib.*).

203. Leonard Hutten's Collections.

Dr. Leonard Hutten, Canon of Christ Church 1599–1632, made several collections towards the history of that foundation.

(i) *Of the antiquity of the University* written by way of letter to a friend: init. 'Sir, your two questions.'

Cited in *City*, i. 325, &c.; ii. 146.

There were several MSS. of this extant in Wood's time, *Life*, iii. 119. Wood had either a copy of this treatise or some notes collected from it, which he cites (*City*, ii. 139, 'MS. L. H.[1] penes me'; ii. 301, 'Collectiones[2] L. Hutten penes me'), but I have not found them among his papers.

Printed by Hearne in 1720; reprinted in Plummer's *Elizabethan Oxford*, pp. 37–104.

(ii) *Historia fundationum Ecclesiae Christi Oxon.*; una cum episcoporum, decanorum, et canonicorum ejusdem catalogo: init. 'Monasterium sive prioratus S. Frideswydae virginis fundatum est ab eadem Frideswyda filia Didaci vel Didani.'

Cited in *Hist.* ii. 257; *City*, ii. 5, 7; *Coll.* p. 434.

It was at one time in the hands of Dr. John Fell (Wood MS. E. 4).

(iii), (iv) *Catalogue of Bishops of Oxford, Deans and Canons of Christ Church*: Wood MS. C. 7 and C. 8: see par. 134 (xi).

Cited in *City*, ii. 5.

(v) *Collections concerning S. Frideswyde's priory and Christ Church.*

(*a*) In Twyne XXIV. 559–561 are 'Dr. [Leonard] Hutten's notes as it is thought,' *init.* 'The old priory of S. Frideswyde's,' &c.

(*b*) Twyne, *l. c.*, says 'I have seen a much larger copy in Mr. Edward Carpenter's hands, MS. which I read.'

(*c*) Barten Holyday had some papers of this sort by Hutten; *Life*, i. 386.

(vi) *Catalogue of the king's Professors of Divinity, Hebrew and Greek.*

Wood says, 'imperfect, but help'd me,' and refers to Twyne XXII. 145. I do not know where Wood saw them: the notices of the *lectores publici* in Wood MS. C. 8 (see par. 134. xi) are very fragmentary.

204. Matthew Hutton's Collections.

Matthew Hutton, B.D., Fellow of Brasenose, a Yorkshire man by birth, was for a long time an intimate acquaintance of Wood in Oxford; see especially *Life*, ii. 2, 134.

(i) *Collectiones monumentales* et fenestrales ex quibusdam ecclesiis et capellis in variis comitatibus Angliae.

Referred to in *City*, ii. 308, 339; *Life*, i. 387.

(*a*) *In the Bodleian Library.* Gutch (in *Colleges*, pp. 28, 292, &c.) cites frequently 'Hutton's Epitaphs, MS. in Bibl. Bodl.' This is no doubt[3] MS. Rawl. B. 397, made 1659–60, containing epitaphs &c., in Oxford and Oxfordshire.

---

[1] cp. the passage in Plummer, *l. c.* p. 46 (pag. 21 of Hearne's MS.).

[2] cp. the passage in Plummer, *l. c.*

p. 73 (pag. 83 of MS.).

[3] in the Catalogue of Rawl. MSS. it is attributed to *Michael* Hutton; but

(*b*) In the *British Museum Library*, among the Harleian MSS. : see Dict. Nat. Biogr.

(ii) Wood, in *City*, ii. 13, cites Hutton's Notes to Godwin's Bishops; and in *Colleges*, p. 128, Hutton's Notes on the bishops of Oxford. Are these now in Brit. Mus. Libr. ?

205. Henry Jackson's Collections.

(i) *Catalogue of books bequeathed by Dr. John Reynolds*, 1607, to the Bodleian, College libraries, and Oxford students : Wood MS. D. 10 (*O. C.* 8546). *Life*, i. 460.

The volume contains several autograph signatures of the recipients, chiefly of C. C. C., Queen's, and Magd. Coll. Most of the names are printed in *Annals*, ii. 293, 294.

(ii) *Vita Thomae Lupset* : Wood MS. F. 30 (*O. C.* 8492).

(iii) *Collectanea*, being excerpts from various cartularies, &c. : Wood MS. D. 18 (*O. C.* 8563) : *Life*, i. 460.

(iv) *Collections about John Claymund* : Wood MS. F. 30 (*O. C.* 8492).

(v) *Papers by Richard Hooker* (or copies of them) : *Life*, i. 442, note 2.

206. Richard James' Collections.

Richard James, of C. C. C., was a contemporary and friend of Brian Twyne. In MS. Ric. James 13, p. 237 are notes about his Russian journey, and *ib*. p. 300 are letters, verses about himself, and copies of his degree exercises. He died 28 Dec. 1638, in the house of Sir Robert Cotton, whom he had served as custodian of his great library.

(i) *Adversaria quaedam* ad rem antiquariam spectantia : Twyne III. 245, 438 ; Twyne XXIV. 616. These are notes partly communicated to Twyne by James himself, partly extracted by Twyne from James' *Collectanea* when in the hands of ' Mr. Greives [1] of C. C. C.' Twyne XXII. 171 has Richard James' notes about barges coming to Oxford.

(ii) *Collectanea*, in 43 volumes.

Marginal notes and jottings by Wood in several of these volumes show that they were perused by him. They are referred to in *Annals*, i. 257, 287, &c. ; *City*, ii. 250, 253. Thomas Tanner's Catalogue of them in *O.C.* pp. 258–263 is wofully defective : a good table of contents has been written in the fly-leaves of several of the volumes by a hand which I take to be William Smith's of Univ. Coll.

MS. Rawl. C. 254, fol. 27 (seven pages of ' Church Notes about Baronets ') attributed in the Catalogue to Matthew Hutton, seems to be a later writing by the same hand.

[1] Thomas Greaves : see Macray's *Annals of the Bodleian*, p. 148.

These *Collectanea* contain excerpts from an enormous number of MSS., perused by Richard James in the libraries of Oxford[1], Cambridge[2], and London[3], and in private libraries[4]. The excerpts relate chiefly to matters of history, especially ecclesiastical.

The following volumes seem to have had old marks :—

MS. Ric. James 24—old mark **A**.

MS. Ric. James 11—old mark **D**.

MS. Ric. James 22—old mark **E**.

207. Thomas James' Collections.

Thomas James, of New College, was the first Bodley's Librarian ; and was one of the pioneers who prepared the way for the Laudian Code of Statutes.

(i) *Transcripts of Statutes of the University* : Arch. Univ. Oxon. **Đ+** : see par. 96 (vii).

(ii) *Transcripts of Statutes of the University* : Arch. Univ. Oxon. **T. J.** : see par. 96 (viii).

(iii) *Catalogue of persons admitted to read in the Bodleian*, 1602-1609 : *Life*, ii. 483.

(*a*) The draft copy of this is in MS. Rawl. D, *olim* 1290, *nunc* 912 ; and perhaps belonged at one time to Wood (see *City*, ii. 31).

(*b*) The final copy is *olim* MS. Bodl. 310 : *Life*, ii. 483.

(iv) *Letter about Asser Menevensis*, addressed to Thomas Allen, init. ' Gentle Mr. Allen, Now at length I have here sent you.'

Twyne III. 225 (? the original); Twyne II. 75 (a copy). Wood's copy formerly in the lost Wood MS. F. 31 (*O. C.* 8493) is now in MS. Rawl. D, *olim* 1290, *nunc* 912, fol. 693 : see *Life*, ii. p. vii.

(v) ' *Ecloga* ' or ' Ecloga MSS.'

Cited in *Annals*, i. 386 ; *City*, ii. 161, and continually in Wood MS. E. 4.

[1] Bodleian, MS. Ric. James 2, 3, 6, 11, 15. 20, 21, 26, &c.; All S., MS. Ric. James 26 ; Ball., MS. Ric. James 11 ; Christ Church (cartularies), MS. Ric. James 6, 8 ; C. C. C. Oxf., MS. Ric. James 6, 8, 19, 20, 21, 26, 32 ; Exet., MS. Ric. James 19 ; Linc., MS. Ric. James 22 ; Magd. Coll., MS. Ric. James 2, 19, 22 ; Mert., MS. Ric. James 20, 21, 22 ; Oriel, MS. Ric. James 20 ; Queen's, MS. Ric. James 26 ; S. John's, MS. Ric. James 26 ; Univ., MS. Ric. James 26 ; &c., &c.

[2] Corpus Chr. Cambr., MS. Ric. James 17, 18; Pembr. Cambr and Trin. Cambr., MS. Ric. James 17.

[3] S. Paul's library, London, and the Exchequer, MS. Ric. James 23 ; Tower of London, Privy Council Register, &c., MS. Ric. James 24 ; the Royal Library, MS. Ric. James 25 ; Arundel library, MS. Ric. James 7.

[4] Thomas Allen's of Glouc. Hall, MS. Ric. James 6, 8 ; Sir Robert Cotton's, MS Ric. James 2, 7, 8, 10, 17, 18, 24, &c. ; Dr. Edward Lapworth's (several of whose MSS. passed afterwards into the Harleian MSS.), MS. Ric. James 8, 19, 31.

This is the printed book *Eclogae Oxonio-Cantabrigienses*, Lond. 1600. Wood's copy (containing only the Oxford portion) is Wood 513.

208. Thomas Key's Collections.

(i) *Collectiones et excerpta ad rem antiquariam spectantia,* maxime vero modo responsionis ad Londinensem de antiquitate Univ. Cantab. 1568: quondam in manibus Thomae Allen.

Wood cites this in *Hist.* ii. 179, 234; but knew it only from Twyne III. 373; Twyne XXIV. 632. It is also cited by the second part of the above description as 'Responsio imperfecta ad librum Londinensis vel Caii de antiquitate Univ. Cantab.'

(ii) *Assertio antiquitatis Acad. Oxon.*; no. 257, foll. 1–9 in Coxe's Cat. Codd. C. C. C. Oxon.

Printed in 1568. Another MS. copy is found in Arch. Univ. Oxon. North West Press 27 (Miles Windsor's Collections), pp. 257–284. At the end of it is a note by Wood, saying it is Key's autograph, and a note by William Smith questioning this. I have little doubt that this is the MS. from which Hearne reprinted the treatise in 1730.

(iii) Wood attributes to him a Catalogue of old halls in Oxford: see *City*, i. 651. I have found no trace of it.

209. Gerard Langbaine.

Dr. Gerard Langbaine was a worthy successor to Brian Twyne in the Keepership of the Archives. Oxford owes a very great debt to him for his care in preserving the Archives intact at the critical time of the Puritan occupation of Oxford, and for his zeal in securing for the Archives the volumes bequeathed by Twyne. Langbaine's labours also in arranging, cataloguing, and binding up the scattered papers in his charge were great and most praiseworthy.

210. *Collections in the University Archives.*

(i) *First series*: three volumes marked **GL vol. I**; **GL vol. II**; **GL vol. III.**

GL vol. I is a large folio volume containing copies of charters, privileges, &c., arranged chronologically, from Henry III downwards. It has this initial note 'Aug. 17, 1647, payed to Ralph Beckford by me Gerard Langbaine for the bindeing of this book twenty pence, for strings sixpence, in all two shillings and two pence.' The first part of the volume (and this a considerable part) is unpaged; the second part is paged 1–706 pp.

At the beginning of the volume are Langbaine's notes towards a list of the sheriffs of Oxon and Berks.

GL vol. II is a similar volume, from Henry IV downwards; and is paged 707–1441 pp., but many are blank. It has this initial note 'Aug. 20, 1647, payed to Ralph Beckford for the binding of this book 2 and 20 pence and for stringes sixepence by me Gerard Langbaine.'

These two volumes are founded on Hare's *Liber privilegiorum*, but contain much additional matter.

They were bound in black covers, with green strings (the roots of which still remain). The '*books with green strings*' are cited several times, e.g. in *City*, i. 191. They seem also to have been known as **G1, G2**; and also as $\underset{\text{L}}{\text{C}}$, i.e. a monogram for G.L.

GL vol. III is described by Langbaine himself as 'a large long book in folio every leaf being a whole sheet, marked GL, which I bound up, Jan. 1, 164$\frac{7}{8}$.' It extends to 536 folios; contains collections about the University of Oxford. Langbaine gives a synopsis of its contents in Twyne I. pp. 367–369: among them is an account, in 5 sheets, of the 'Actors' attyre at King James his beinge here in Oxon 1605,' transcribed from a paper in pix. P. fascic. 5 of the University archives.

GL in Turri scholarum is cited in *City*, ii. 5; see also *City*, ii. 63, 245.

(ii) *Second series*: in the University archives: six volumes, marked Twyne-Langbaine; see par. 241.

(iii) *Repertorii chartarum et munimentorum Univ. Oxon.* (prout nunc se habet, 1650) *methodus generalis*: press-mark Arch. Univ. Oxon. North West Press 33. This is a modification of Twyne's Calendar of the archives (see par. 216), to adapt it to the arrangement of Langbaine's time.

211. *Collections in the Bodleian Library.*

Twenty-one volumes of Langbaine's Adversaria, chiefly notes about and excerpts from MSS. in Oxford libraries, were placed in the Bodleian and are described in the 1697 Catal. MSS. on pp. 268–271. On the back of vol. 1 is a slip which states 'one volume, marked ♈ (Aries), was lost[1] by bishop Fell to whome it was lent[2], as also one or two folio volumes of lives of saints.'

I notice here only those volumes which have old marks, or are cited specially by Wood.

[1] I fancy that this volume came into Wood's possession, and is now Wood MS. donat. 7; see *infra*.

[2] 'Quod N. B.' again, see par. 198 (vi).

MS. Langb. 1 is marked **MS. C.**, where C is for 'Cant.' (i. e. Laud) MSS., which are largely noted in it; pp. 626.

MS. Langb. 4 is marked ♌, i. e. Leo, and contains, inter alia, excerpts from Digby MSS.; pp. 722.

MS. Langb. 5 is marked ♉, i. e. Taurus, and contains excerpts from MSS. in the Bodleian. Wood cites it sometimes as ♉ **Gl.**, to distinguish it from the Twyne volume with the same mark. This is probably the volume cited in *City*, ii. 258, 398, 407.

MS. Langb. 6 is marked **Ⅱ**, i. e. Gemini; and contains excerpts from MSS. in the Bodleian.

MS. Langb. 7 is marked ♋, i. e. Cancer. It contains notes about MSS. in the Bodleian and in the libraries of Magdalen, New, Queen's, Oriel colleges, pp. 518. At p. 393 is a copy of Thomas Allen's list of titles of Roger Bacon's works which were found among Allen's MSS.

MS. Langb. 8, pp. 468, and 10, pp. 546, are marked **C, D.** Possibly MS. Langb. 10 is the volume cited as *sched. gl. D* in *City*, i. 340.

MS. Langb. 12, pp. 504, is marked ♌, and contains excerpts from the episcopal registers of Lincoln, and from the registers of the University of Oxford. Cited in *Annals*, i. 373.

MS. Langb. 14, pp. 362, is marked **KKK** or **KK** and contains Langbaine's catalogue of books in his own 'study.' At the beginning is a note of the times when, and the persons to whom, he had lent books; this gives a number of names of strangers resident in Oxford during the siege (1644–46).

MS. Langb. 15, 350 pp., is marked **A-C** or **ᗺ**; and contains extracts from MSS., especially Laud MSS. It is cited frequently in Wood MS. E. 4 as **Ac Gl** or **Ac.** Cited in *City*, ii. 400.

MS. Langb. 16 is marked **A̶A̶C̶C̶**; and contains excerpts from Laud MSS.

MS. Langb. 18 is marked **Ɐa** or **Ɐb**, according as you read it from one end or the other. It contains excerpts from MSS., pp. 266 +114.

MS. Langb. 19, 606 pp., is marked **☉**; and is occasionally cited by Wood as **☉Gl.,** to distinguish it from the Twyne volume with the same mark.

212. *Collections in Wood's possession*, nine Langbaine volumes bequeathed by Wood to the Bodleian. These are described in the 1697 Catalogue nos. 8614–8622: see *Life*, i. 248, 249.

MS. Wood donat. 1, 3, 5, 6 are marked by Wood as *Fragmenta*

Langbainiana, voll. I–IV. Possibly MS. Wood donat. 3 is the volume cited as *Gl. sched.* 2, in *Annals*, ii. 164.

MS. Wood donat. 2, 9 are marked by Wood as *Adversaria Langbainiana*.

MS. Wood donat. 4 contains Langbaine's notes of MSS. in Ball. Coll. library, and is cited in *City*, ii. 213. The tract 'de origine Cisterciensium' found here is cited in *City*, ii. 292.

MS. Wood donat. 7, marked ♈, an 8vo volume, is cited in *City*, ii. 260, 269. It seems to be the volume alluded to in par. 211 (init.).

MS. Wood donat. 8 is marked PH.

Collections and papers in the Wood collection: see *Life*, i. 247, 248: in Wood 602 (a copy of Twyne's *Apologia*, Oxon. 1608, with a good many notes by Langbaine), Wood MS. D. 18, F. 27, F. 28, F. 32, F. 29 a.

Papers in Exeter College library: see no. 12 in Coxe's Cat. Codd. Coll. Exon.

Vague citations. Wood's references are sometimes so indistinct that it is impossible to say from them which series of Langbaine volumes he is citing. Again, there are several vague references (by **GL, Gl, gl**) presumably to collections by Langbaine: but possibly to Twyne III: see par. 218.

213. Thomas Neale's Collections.

Dialogus in adventum serenissimae reginae Elizabethae, 1566: init. 'Siccine chara tuis'—'together with the draughts[1] or images of the Colleges in Oxon with verses[2] under each of them describing the respective foundations of them.' *Annals*, ii. 159.

MS. Bodl. 13 (*O. C.* 3056): Twyne's transcript of the verses is in Twyne XXI. 779–791. The MS. has been reproduced in facsimile[3] by Mr. J. Guggenheim (Oxford 1882).

Wood was puzzled by such references as 'Chronographia sive origo collegiorum,' &c. (in Windsor's Europaei orbis academiae, p. 42); 'Tabula typographica Oxon.' (in Twyne XVII); 'A map of Oxford describing the Colleges and Halls with verses underwritten'—but these are probably vague descriptions of this MS. (Bodl. 13).

214. Brian Twyne's Collections.

Brian Twyne, the most industrious of antiquaries, was admitted on the foundation of Corpus Christi College, 13 Dec. 1594 (Fowler's

[1] the drawings were by John Bereblock; *Fasti*, p. 103.

[2] most recently reprinted in Plummer's *Elizabethan Oxford*, pp. 155–168.

[3] Plummer, *l. c.* p. xvii.

History of C. C. C., p. 393), became Keeper of the Archives (being the first to hold that office) in 1634 ; and died in June 1644.

He read and made large excerpts from the muniments and registers of the University and Colleges, the parish Churches, and the City of Oxford ; from MSS. in the Bodleian Library, the libraries of the Colleges of Oxford and Cambridge, of Thomas Allen, Sir Robert Cotton, and other private book-collectors ; the Public Record Offices ; the episcopal and chapter Archives of Canterbury, Lincoln, Durham ; &c.

At his death he bequeathed (see his will, *infra*) his MS. Collections to the Archives of the University and the Library of his College. But the great fire of October 1644 [see Wood's *Life*, i. 111] swept down upon the house where his books and papers lay, before his executor had disposed of them ; many were scattered abroad [1], and several lost altogether—see *Life*, i. 429. Those volumes of Twyne's Collections which Wood knew, and which I have been able to trace, are enumerated below.

Copy of Brian Twyne's Will, from a volume of wills in the Archives.

4to Julii 1644°. In the name of God, Amen. I Bryan Twyne, bachilor of devinytye and keeper of ye Archives of the University of Oxford, beinge weake in body but in perfect mynd and memory, doe commend my soule to the god of heaven from whence I receaved it and my body to the earth to bee interred in the chappell of Corpus Christi Colledge in Oxford ; for the estate which god hath blessed mee with my will is that out of my studdy of bookes I doe give to Corpus Christi Colledge all such bookes that they have not in their library ; for the executor of this my last will and testament I doe appoynt Richard Twyne my nephew ; I doe give unto one goodwife Carter that hath intended mee in my sicknes forty shillings ; I doe give likewise to the Universitye of Oxford all such bookes and writings whatsoever I have gathered or are in my possession concerninge them to bee delivered by my executor into the hands of doctor Pincke vicechancellor or Mr. John ffrench the Register of the Universitye to

---

[1] One example may be given. In Twyne XXIV 263 Twyne notices 'Summa Dumbleton philosophiae naturalis,' in folio, init. 'Plurimorum scribentium grati labores digni,' which had an inscription recording that it was given by William Aketon to Clare Hall, Cambridge. On this Langbaine notes, ' This book I saw in Mr. Twine's study after his death.' And then Wood takes up the story :—' But when that fier hapned in Oxon 1644 this book came into the earl of Lyndsey's hands who leaving it with Dr. Herbert Pelham of Magd. Coll. in Oxon he shewed it to me and hath now this year (anno 1662) given it to Magd. Coll. library—A. Wood.' See also p. 214, *infra*.

bee reposed and layde up in the archives for the use of that famous
body; I doe give William Carter, the son of goodwife Carter before-
mentioned, forty shillings; I doe give unto Rebecca Thomas, my
landrosse, thirty shillings; I doe give to Abell Parne, my landlord,
forty shillings; I doe give unto Mr. John ffrench, my freind, twenty
shillings. In witnes that this is my last will and testament I have
subscribed my name and doe desire the underwritten witnesses to
testifye this to bee my last will and Testament.

Ita est BRYAN TWYNE.

ROBERT NEWLIN.
ELI: WRENCH.
JOHN FFRENCH.
　　　Vera copia sub sigillo curiae
　　　　　per William Wells testem.

215. Twyne volumes in the Lower Room of the Archives.

These are 24 in number, nos. 1–19 being folios, nos. 20–24 quartos.
They were arranged and bound together under the direction of
Dr. Gerard Langbaine, Twyne's successor in the Keepership of the
Archives, who has supplied in most cases full lists of contents. The
short Latin description of each volume, which is given below, is also
by him. During Dr. Wallis's Keepership, who followed Langbaine,
the volumes passed through the hands, first, of Anthony Wood, and
afterwards of William Smith (Fellow of Univ. Coll. 1675–1705, Rector
of Melsonby, Yorks, 1704 till his death 19 Dec. 1735); both of whom
have written occasional notes in them[1]. Besides papers written by
Twyne himself, the volumes contain excerpts and transcripts made
for him by many hands, e. g. by John Pregion[2] (registrar of the
bishop) and Philip Pregion[3] at Lincoln, and by Horton Drayton[4]
(registrar of the archbishop) at Canterbury.

In what follows, only a brief description of each volume is given,
all the more important items having been elsewhere noted in connexion with the source from which they are taken or the subject
to which they relate.

216. Twyne I, a folio volume of 369 pages, many of which are
blank (e. g. 137–161, 255–270, 343–365). There are two notes
referring to the binding :—(*a*) In Langbaine's hand, 'payed to Roger

---

[1] e. g. some writing by Wood is found
in Twyne XVII. 209, written circ. 1664;
and a note by William Smith, dated
26 May 1699, is found in Twyne II.

[2] Twyne II. foll. 25 b, 27a.
[3] Twyne II. foll. 22, 23 a.
[4] Twyne II. foll. 286–337.

Smith for binding this book, 1*s*; added in blank paper, 2*d*'; (*b*) 'This volume the early leaves of which were much damaged was carefully repaired in the Long Vacation, 1888; T. V. B.'

The volume contains 'Excerpta ex archivis et statutis antiquis et Repertorium chartarum.'

Some of the component parts of the volume require separate mention, because of the old marks by which in Wood's MSS. they are generally cited, and which are not generally understood.

Twyne I. 1–136: *old mark* ✠.

Repertorium chartarum et munimentorum Univ. Oxon. in archivis domus Congregationis olim reconditorum, et excerpta inde—written out by Twyne in January 163�. The contents of 'boxes' A–O are given pp. 1–110, 122–123; and of box P, pp. 127–134; of 'long boxes' 1–12, pp. 110–120; of long boxes 13–19, and of a square black box, on p. 135. Pages 124–126 contain a notice of Statute-books A, B, C, D. A transcript of this in the Archives is marked *Univ. Oxon. Arch. North West Press* 33.

Twyne I. 165–189: *old mark* ✶.

Contenta in veteribus statutorum libris; originally paged separately, pp. 1–25. Pages 1–21 (i.e. 165–185 of the volume as it now is) give the heads of the chapters in Liber Vicecancellarii (Statute-book A).

Twyne I. 197–224; originally paged pp. 1–26 as a separate treatise; gives the heads of the chapters in 'Liber Procuratoris Australis *seu* Senioris' (Statute-book B).

Twyne I. 231–254: originally foliated, foll. 1–9, as a separate treatise; gives the heads of chapters of Statute-book D.

Twyne I. 279–341; paged originally pp. 1–63 as a separate treatise; contains an earlier draft of the Calendar of University muniments, which however supplements the other in some particulars. *Repertorium sive inventarium omnium chartarum . . .* in abaco domus Congregationis. The contents of boxes A–P are given pp. 1–48 (i.e. pp. 279–326); and of long boxes 1–23, pp. 52–55 (i.e. pp. 327–330 of the whole volume).

In this volume, p. 366, is a fragment belonging to the University register of wills :—'June 5, 1657, administration of the goods of Thomas Mayo, carpenter, a privileged person, was granted to Jocosa (Joyce) Steele, sister of Pleasance Mayo, the widow.'

The whole volume, and not the first part only, is often cited by the mark ✠ When carelessly written, ✗, this mark presents some possibility of confusion with ☉, i.e. Twyne 24. An index of names occurring in the volume is given in Wood MS. C. 5. The volume is frequently cited in *City*.

217. Twyne II, a folio volume of 339 folios, containing extracts from episcopal registers, &c. relating to Oxford.

Langbaine entitles it 'Farrago rerum Oxoniensium, ex variis registris et actis publicis magnam partem congesta, collectore B. Twyne.'

The old mark (assigned, I think, by Gerard Langbaine[1]) for the whole volume is ⊼ or ⊼; but the separate parts of which it has been made up had each their own mark, or title.

    foll. 1–12; ⊓, Lyncolne notes[2].
    foll. 13–14; ◁, ,, ,,
    foll. 15–18; ⅀, ,, ,,
    fol. 19; Ц, ,, ,,
    fol. 20; ◁, ,, ,,
    foll. 23–31; ⌐, ,, ,,
    foll. 32–33; O—O, Durham notes.
    fol. 34; ⌐O, ,, ,,
    fol. 34 b; ⌐□, ,, ,,

'Lincoln Notes,' therefore=Twyne II. foll. 1–31.

'Durham Notes,'=Twyne II. foll. 32–34 b.

Foll. 38–48 (?); ₵ = ex turri London. (But this mark perhaps includes foll. 38–179: it is perhaps a monogram for C. L. i. e. Civitas London.).

Foll. 170–173; ℒ = excerpta ex Nicholao Harpsfeldio, paged originally separately, pp. 1–8.

Wood generally cites this volume by the mark ⊼, which in the notes to *City* I have always turned into Twyne II. In the notes to *City*, there are several citations of a volume **A**, (e. g. *City*, i. 54, 94, ii. 399); the present volume is one of those which must be searched for these references[3], since possibly the **A** may be a careless writing of ⊼.

A minute summary of the contents of the volume is given in Wood MS. D. 18 (1), pp. 82–93.

218. Twyne III, a folio volume of 688 pages, containing excerpts, chiefly from deeds and other manuscripts, relating to Oxford.

---

[1] see the note at the end of Twyne E. N. 1, *infra*, par. 248.

[2] but to the mention of 'the great conflict,' 1354, in the Lincoln registers, Twyne adds here much matter from other sources.

[3] *City*, ii. 265, note 8, is an example; where, with a reference to A. 34, we have cited 'vetus MS. bibliothecae Dunelm.' Now in Twyne II. 34 we have an excerpt 'ex quodam tractatu ubi inscribitur de origine monachatus cum aliis de statu monachali in bibl. Dunelm. or else in some old booke in that place where the praebend showed me the foundation of Durham College in Oxon by Thomas Hatfield.'

Langbaine gives this summary of it ' Miscellanea varia, ut de ecclesiis Oxon., locis religiosis, sigillis, Wyclefo, actis Fratrum Praedicatorum, Cantabrigia, antiquitatibus Eliensibus, Abingdon, rebus ad religionem spectantibus, monumentis Coll. Merton, et aliis.'

The old mark for the whole volume is o✕o; and by this, hastily written as ✕, Wood usually cites it. But the parts of it had at one time been distinguished, partly by separate titles, partly by marks Ϛ 1–Ϛ 6. As regards these latter, I am not sure that they were imposed by Twyne, and it is not easy exactly to fix their limits. So far as I can determine, the following are the divisions of the volume :—

pp. 1–14, *Miscellanea quaedam, primo, de antiquis ecclesiis et parochiis Oxon.*, a Latin treatise. S. Aldate's on p. 1 ; S. Budoc's on p. 8 ; S. Clement's on p. 10 ; S. Benedict's on p. 13.

A later and fuller draft of this treatise, extending from S. Aldate's to S. Edward's Church (alphabetically), is found in Wood MS. F. 29 A, foll. 372–377.

pp. 15–18, ⟨? Miscellanea, quaedam, secundo?⟩ de religiosis locis Oxon.

pp. 457–516, Ϛ 1, de antiquitatibus Eliensibus, de monasterio et villa Abbendon.

pp. 19–115, Ϛ 2, ex archivis AEd. Xti, ex libro S. Frideswydae, &c.

pp. 373–453, Ϛ 3, de Cantabrigia.

pp. 121–285, Ϛ 4 ; de sigillis monasteriorum, pp. 121–127, with a drawing of the window with S. Frideswyde and her parents (*City*, ii. pp. 159, 160) ; collections to vindicate the antiquity of Oxford against Sir Robert Cotton, pp. 137–157 ; notes of Oxford history A. D. 1255 to 1269, pp. 163–175, &c.

pp. 563–640, Ϛ 5, ex archivis Coll. Univ., Mert. (pp. 583–625), et Magd. On p. 623 Twyne has a note of a prayer by ' Mr. Evans of St. Clements,' ' Lord, putt a milstone about the neck of our sins, and cast them into the bottome of the sea, till they cry plump againe, good Lord !'

pp. 517–539, Ϛ 6 ; excerpts from MSS. and printed books.

pp. 297–352, de actis Fratrum Praedicatorum A. D. 1311 ex rotulo pergameno Mri Thomae Allen (now MS. Digb. 234).

A minute summary of the contents of this volume is given in Wood MS. D. 18 (1), pp. 98–106.

219. Twyne IV, a folio volume of 710 pages, of which pp. 283–

288 seem missing, containing a mass of excerpts from the archives of the City of Oxford.

Langbaine describes it as 'Burgus Oxon. &c., placita coronae ibidem de tempore Edward I, excerpta maxime ex archivis civitatis Oxon. aut aliunde quae eo spectant.'

The old mark for the whole volume is ⊖, by which Wood usually cites it in his notes ; but, as in the preceding volumes, separate parts of it had at one time their own peculiar marks.

pp. 1-524, ⊖ ; excerpts from the City archives.

pp. 525-547, ⊋ ; (i.e. ℭ reversed) ; paged originally as a separate treatise pp. 1-21, being Twyne's 'A supplie of other charters and conclusions out of them tendinge to the disprovinge of the pretended charter of the restoration of the towne liberties after the great conflict.'

pp. 559-612, collections out of the Public Records.

pp. 615-end, Ↄ, i.e. ℭ inverted, paged originally as a separate treatise pp. 1-66, being *Placita coronae de burgo Oxon.*

Wood cites the volume frequently in *City*; and has a minute summary of its contents in Wood MS. D. 18 (1), pp. 110-120 b.

220. Twyne V, a folio volume of 424 pages, containing Twyne's collections concerning the controversies between the University and the City.

Langbaine describes it as ' Conflictus (et compositiones) varii Univ. Oxon. maxime cum burgensibus'; and he has put a table of its contents at p. 413.

The old title of the volume, by which Wood usually cites it, is **Liber conflictuum** or **Liber conflictuum et compositionum.**

Some parts of it were originally separate treatises with distinctive titles or marks.

pp. 79-86, **T** ; composition between the University and City 18 Edw. I.

pp. 169-172, a briefe discourse about the towne's offeringe uppon St. Scholastick's daye.

pp. 359-375, **Y**; the orders of the lordes of the counsell in king James his time with the grievances on both sides.

221. Twyne VI, a folio volume of 678 pages, containing Twyne's Collections about University buildings and property.

Langbaine describes its contents as 'Ecclesia beatae Mariae, campanae &c., pegmata ibidem ; bona et possessiones Universitatis Oxon. ;

bibliothecae; publici professores,' &c.; and gives a table of contents at p. 671.

Wood cites it frequently in *City* and has a summary of its contents in Wood MS. D. 18 (1), pp. 121–125.

The old mark of the volume is ☉. The chief sections in it are:—

pp. 15–30, St. Marie's church, and bells, and scaffoldes ⟨for the Act⟩; written 8 Dec. 1639.

pp. 43 sqq., de bonis Universitatis; including the Physic Garden, pp. 161–173, and Carfax conduit, pp. 179–207.

pp. 267–657, endowments and mortmains for the foundation of public lectures (i. e. professorships).

222. Twyne VII, a folio volume of 644 pages, containing Twyne's notes about Laud's projected metropolitical visitation of the University (1635) and the several royal visitations.

Langbaine has entitled it 'De Visitationibus Universitatis,' and added at pp. 621–633 a list of its contents. On the binding is this note:—' Oct. 6, 1646, reseved of D. Langbinge for the binding of this booke and ading papore to it, the some of 1*s* 6*d*, by me Ralph Beckford.'

Wood cites the volume by its title '**Liber Visitationum.**' The following are its chief contents:—(i) *Royal Visitations*:—

pp. 112, 113; Visitation of the University under Henry VIII.

pp. 139–146; Visitation under Edward VI.

pp. 147–157; Visitation under Queen Mary (Cardinal Pole).

pp. 158 sqq.; Visitation under Elizabeth.

(ii) *Metropolitical Visitation*, intended 1635–36:—

pp. 5–12, 'a supply of allegations' (by Twyne) 'for the exemption of the University from archiepiscopal and episcopal visitation.'

p. 19, paper 'delivered to Thomas Tempest of Lincoln's Inn' by Twyne, 'whom I entertayned for counsell in the matter of Visitation,' &c. On pp. 285–287 are Thomas Tempest's notes taken out of Twyne's notes.

pp. 219–222, 'Saturday, 27 Febr. 163$\frac{5}{8}$, conference with Sir John Lambe at his chamber in Doctors Commons concerning the exemption of the University from archiepiscopal and episcopal jurisdiction.'

p. 265, letters from Dr. Robert Pinke to Twyne concerning the Visitation.

p. 273, 14 June 1636, list of books taken up to Hampton Court.

223. Twyne VIII, a thin paper book folded vertically, with three pages of writing, giving references to the pages of the registers of Convocation and the Vice-chancellor's Court, from which the excerpts described below were taken.

'**II,** the mark of this book: An index belonging to another book marked ♈ containing a collection of such precedents out of our registers and act-books as were prepared for our hearing before the Lords in Parliament in answer to the articles of the towne which were presented by them against the University in the house of Lords, Jan. 15, 164⅖.'

This paper is sometimes called Twyne XXV, being kept at the end of the series on account of being unbound. The volume ♈ seems now unknown.

224. Twyne IX, a folio volume of 414 pages, containing Twyne's notes about controversies with the Town, 1632–1636.

Langbaine has entitled it ' Eristica seu controversiae cum oppidanis, maxime de visu franciplegii, earumque decisiones ' ; and has given a list of contents at pp. 7–11.

pp. 103–121 originally formed a separate treatise, marked ⊕, being 'an abstract of the present differences betwixt the Universitie and the Towne.' The whole volume is sometimes cited by this mark.

pp. 37–46 contain the University Under-Steward's (Unton Croke's) notes of the case for the University in one of these controversies.

225. Twyne X, a folio volume of 492 leaves, containing Twyne's Collections about the perquisites of the University.

Its contents, as enumerated by Langbaine in the title he has given the volume, are as follows :—' Vicorum custodia, &c., pp. 7–25 ; [the exemption of priviledged persons from taxation, pp. 41–43 ;] felonum bona et perquisita Universitatis, pp. 53–165 ; tolnetum purpresturae, pp. 217 sqq.; legata Universitati, p. 247 ; licentia eleemosynas petendi, p. 253 ; [licentia] carnes in 40ᵃ (quadragesima) edendi, p. 255 ; fines for forest-lands, &c., p. 263.' Langbaine has appended a detailed list of contents at pp. 485–487.

The old mark of the volume is ℞, or simply ℞, and Wood several times cites it thus ; but he more usually cites it by the old title, **de bonis felonum.**

Several sections of the volume were originally separate papers with separate pagination and marks :—

pp. 55–105, **notae R** ; paged pp. 1–33 : ' perquisita Univ., viz., bona et catalla felonum, thesaurus inventus, deodanda.'

pp. 111–139, Я, i. e. R inverted ; paged pp. 1–18, ' bona et catalla felonum, felonum de se, vclagatorum, fugitivorum, &c., deodanda—the Universitie's title to them with an answer to the towne's plea lately interposed for the clayme of them to the writt of Quo Warranto.'

pp. 141–165, Я, i. e. R reversed ; paged pp. 1–13, ' certain notes and observations upon the Towne's clayme of felons' and fugitives' goods, deodands, and the like, specified in their plea of Quo Warranto, 1635.'

pp. 167–211, ✛O✛ ; 'concerninge the Quo Warranto and the Towne's plea unto it.'

pp. 327–478, R R ; about toll, especially of grain in the market.

226. Twyne XI, a folio volume of 134 + 510 pages, containing especially Twyne's classified catalogue of the archives.

There is this note at the beginning :—'Octob. 3ᵈ, 1646, reseved of D. Lanbine for the binding of this booke and papore bound with it, 1*s* 6*d*, by me, Ralph Beckford.'

The volume contains two distinct treatises :—

(i) *Repertorium chartarum*, evidentiarum, chirographorum, aliorumque munimentorum *in abaco camerae Turris novarum Scholarum* repositorum : see *supra*, p. 122. This occupies pp. 1–83 of the first part of the volume.

(ii) *Repertorium chartarum* aliorumque munimentorum almae *Univ. Oxon.* quotquot in archivis ejusdem jam supersunt denuo recognitum et *in certas classes, locos et capita digestum*, unde facile quicquid in illis continetur depromi poterit.

This occupies pp. 109–134 of the first part, and the whole of the second part of the volume ; it classifies the whole of the documents in the archives, both those formerly in the Tower of the Schools and those formerly in the Old Congregation House.

227. Twyne XII, a folio volume of 328 pages.

Langbaine describes it as ' Confirmatio cancellarii ; officiarii Universitatis ; feodi.'

Its old mark, for the first part of the volume, was ⊕✛ ; but to this other treatises have been added.

pp. 1–80, ⊕✛ ; collections about the relations of the Chancellor of the University to the bishop of Lincoln, &c.

pp. 81–106; paged pp. 1–26, a transcript of the Elizabethan matriculation statute, and the Vice-chancellor's remembrancer.

pp. 111–120; paged pp. 1–10, a summary of the statutes about academical dress.

pp. 145–151; notes about the Vespers and Act.

228. Twyne XIII, a folio volume of 743 pages.

The old mark was possibly Π. It contains three treatises.

pp. 1–584, **de visu franciplegii** Univ. Oxon. et amerciamentis inde provenientibus analecta.

pp. 1–16 of this treatise contain 'notes for the University case,

1632, Mr. Edward Littleton (Recorder of London) being the University counsell.'

pp. 631–705, **notae E**; paged pp. 1–48, 'leet-court of the University down to these modern times.'

pp. 713–730, **notae D**; paged pp. 1–15; notes about Regent-Masters.

229. Twyne XIV, a folio volume of 456 pages.

Langbaine entitles it 'Cognitio placitorum, discommunicatio,' and has drawn up a list of its contents on six unpaged leaves at the beginning and on pp. 319, 320.

Wood cites it by its title, **Liber cognitionis placitorum.**

230. Twyne XV, a folio volume of 354 pages.

Langbaine's description of it indicates its contents :—'Chartae Universitatis earumque allocatio ; Charta Carolina ; inde et aliunde excerpta ; commissio ad pacem, excubiae nocturnae ; latio armorum ; proclamationes ; leges ad obligandos laicos ; bannitio, &c.; potestas Universitatis in his, &c.'

The old mark of the volume is ⊞ ; the old title is **Liber de chartis et privilegiis.**

231. Twyne XVI, a folio volume of 418 leaves, containing Twyne's Collections concerning the market.

Langbaine has described it as treating of 'Mercatus Oxon., clericus mercatus, merchandizatio per privilegiatos, regratarii, hostelarii, victualarii, vinetarii, pandoxatores, braciatores, pistores'; and has added a list of contents on foll. 404–418.

Wood often cites this volume by its title **Liber mercatus.** Much use has been made of it in Ogle's *Oxford Market* in Oxf. Hist. Soc. *Collectanea,* vol. ii.

232. Twyne XVII, a folio volume of 486 pages, containing Twyne's collections about codes of statutes and royal visits.

Langbaine has described it as treating 'de statutis Universitatis ; orders occasionall ; enterteynments ; juramentum vicecomitis, majoris, et burgensium ; jurisdictio spiritalis contra incontinentes, &c.; testamentorum probatio, &c.'; and has added a list of contents at pp. 471–477.

The old mark of the volume is ⊕ ; the old title, **Liber de statutis.** Wood cites it sometimes by the one, sometimes by the other. Wood gives a summary of its contents in Wood MS. 18 (1), pp. 93–96.

At **p. 147** begins what was originally a separate treatise, paged pp. 1–43, and entitled **Entertainments**. It is a collection of narratives of royal visits from 1483 (Richard III) to 1636 (Charles I).

233. Twyne XVIII, a folio volume of 520 pages, containing, (i) Twyne's collections about public buildings in Oxford; (ii) his excerpts from Leland about famous Oxonians.

Langbaine entitles it 'Aulae, scholae, bibliothecae; vici et plateae; ecclesiae parochiales Oxon.; viri celebres Oxonienses ex Lelando collectandi.'

It is made up of a number of separate treatises, which Wood cites by their titles. He has a summary of contents of the latter part of the volume, in Wood MS. D. 18 (1), pp. 126–131.

pp. 17–84, de antiquis scholarium aulis; with several notes added by William Smith. Wood cites this as '*in aulis B. T.*,' and the like; e.g. *City*, i. 315. Here also probably belong such references as 'B. T. in Aula Edmundi,' *City*, i. 85; 'Twyne, Catalogus de aulis,' *City*, i. 144; 'Twyne, additamenta ad aulas,' *City*, i. 185.

pp. 93–99, 111–142, de scholis et bibliotheca. Wood cites this as '*B. T. de scholis*,' and the like; e.g. *City*, i. 161, ii. 258.

pp. 153–242, de antiquis urbis locis, originally a separate treatise, paged pp. 1–66, is treated as two distinct articles :—

(i) De vicis et plateis, pp. 1–47 of the section, pp. 153–217 of the volume. Wood cites this as *Brian Twyne de vicis*, e.g. *City*, i. 229; or *B. T. de venellis*, e. g. *City*, i. 360; or the like. Here also probably belong such references as 'Twyne in Lumbard Lane,' *City*, i. 307; 'Twyne in voce Ousney,' *City*, i. 316.

(ii) De ecclesiis parochialibus Oxon., pp. 48–66 of the section, pp. 218–242 of the volume. The churches are arranged alphabetically from S. Aldate's (p. 218), S. Bennet's (p. 219) . . . to . . . All Saints (p. 234), S. Thomas (p. 237).

pp. 257–486, old mark **IL**, i. e. **IL** (Ioannes Leland); collections from Leland about famous Oxonians. Wood cites this frequently by the mark or the initials, e. g. *City*, i. 555, ii. 335, &c., but just as frequently as *Collect. ex Lelando per B. Twyne*, e.g. *City*, ii. 283, 327, &c.

234. Twyne XIX, a folio volume of 172 pages, containing Twyne's chronological list of Chancellors, Vicechancellors, Proctors, High Stewards, and Parliamentary Burgesses from 'Anno 883, S. Grimbald' to 'anno 1842, John Tolson.'

Its title is 'Br. Twyne: Fasti Oxonienses Cancellariorum et Proctorum.' A note inside the binding says 'this book consisting of tatterd and torn sheets was placed in order and bound up in the year 1704.'

Note that in Wood MS. F. 27, Wood had Twyne's first draft of this treatise ' Fasti Oxonienses,' brought down only to 1626.

Wood cites this work frequently as *Twyne's Catalogus Cancellariorum.*

235. Twyne XX, a large quarto volume of 522 pages, containing Thomas James' transcripts of the University Statutes with large additions by Twyne. See *supra*, pp. 129, 198.

The old mark of the volume is ✠. It was at one time also called **Liber Statutorum F.** It is occasionally cited, combining these, as ✠ vel **F.**

236. Twyne XXI, a quarto volume of 840 pages, containing a mass of citations about Oxford from printed books and MSS.

Langbaine has marked this volume as ' Antiquarii volumen 1um '; and Twyne XXII as 'Antiquarii Oxoniensis vol. 3um.' I conjecture that he reserved ' vol. 2um ' for the volume ♈, concerning which Twyne makes a note at the beginning of Twyne XXI, but which has never been found.

The old mark of Twyne XXI is ♀ or ♀, and by this Wood habitually cites it in his MSS. He has a minute summary of its contents in Wood MS. D. 18 (1), pp. 1–32 e.

A note at the beginning of the volume gives its history :—' Hunc librum ♀ Universitati Oxon. cum aliis manu propria scriptis ab authore legatum testamento, sed per incendium [1] illud miserabile direptum et aliquandiu desideratum, matri Academiae tandem vindicavit, restituit, et fratri [2] suo gemello ♉ conjunxit, Herbertus Pelham, D.LL.'

237. Twyne XXII, a quarto volume of 439 pages, containing Collections largely about Cambridge.

Langbaine marked it ' Liber Univ. Oxon. ex legato Br. Twine. Custodis Archivorum ; Antiquarii Oxoniensis vol. 3um.'

The old mark is ♉ or ♉ or ♉, and by this Wood cites it freely in his MSS. He has a minute summary of its contents in Wood MS. D. 18 (1), pp. 65–81 ; and an Index of names occurring in it in Wood MS. C. 5.

238. Twyne XXIII, a quarto volume of 780 pages, containing Collections about Oxford from the Public Records and other Muniment Rooms and from printed books and MSS.

---

[1] in Oct. 1644; Wood's *Life*, i. 429; cp. ibid. p. 111. See p. 203, *supra*.
[2] i. e. Twyne XXII. Note that Twyne XXI is the volume spoken of in Wood's *Life*, i. 429, note 4, which I could not then identify.

Langbaine has entitled the volume ' Collectiones ex Turri Londini ; praecipue ex archivis civitatis Oxon.'

Its history is very diverting. It was bequeathed by Twyne to the Archives of the University ; but laid hold of by a member of C. C. C. and placed in the archives of that College. When the fellows of C. C. C. were ejected by the Puritan Visitors in May—June 1648, one of them thought he could safely pass on the strayed volume to its intended destination, being soon to be out of the way of punishment by his College. Accordingly, having removed it and kept it quietly for a long time, he at last[1] sent it by another hand to Dr. Gerard Langbaine, who put it into the Archives, and held his tongue about the transaction until prescription entitled the volume to remain there. This history is set out in these two notes :

(i) At the beginning of Twyne XXII : '⊙ (est) nota sive character ulterius libri : this booke was by mistake after Mr. Twyne's death putt into the archives of Corpus Christi College ; and thence taken by I know not which of the old fellowes in the yeare 1647 or 1648.'

(ii) At the beginning of Twyne XXIII itself : 'A. d. xviii. Kalend. Maias anno Domini MDCLVII. Die et anno suprascriptis, librum hunc Collectaneorum per Mrm Brianum Twyne, Custodem Archivorum Universitatis Oxon., ex variis munimentis hinc inde congestum, diu multumque post obitum authoris et in eo munere predecessoris mei longe meritissimi frustra quaesitum, postliminio tandem reducem amici operâ (qui nomen suum reticeri mallet), per hominem mihi penitus ignotum transmissum, recepi ; et inter caeteros id genus ab eadem manu et in eundem finem, in usum scilicet Academiae (prout supremis tabulis cavit author), reposui, successoribus ejus meisque, Archivorum Custodibus qui olim erunt, deinceps tradendum.

GERARDUS LANGBAINIUS,

Custos Archivorum Universitatis Oxon.'

The old mark of the volume is ⊙, or, as it is generally written in haste, ⊙, or ⊙. By this Wood cites it freely in his MSS. Wood has a minute summary of its contents, in Wood MS. D. 18 (1), and an index of names found in it in Wood MS. C. 5.

Originally the volume consisted of two distinct treatises, each with its own mark and paging.

(i) pp. 1–684 = ⊙.

(ii) pp. 685–780 = ♯ ; paged pp. 1–78, containing :—pp. 690–723, i.e. 4–37, excerpts from Gascoigne's Theological Dictionary pars 1ma ; pp. 724–749, i.e. 38–63, excerpts from ibid. pars 2da ;

---

[1] this was in 1657. Was the man applying to the *Ars Kleptica* the maxim of the *Ars Poetica*—nonum prematur in annum ?

pp. 755–764, i. e. 69–78, excerpts from Merton College muniments ; on p. 765, notes about certain collections of Dr. [Peter] Turner of Mert. Coll., see p. 131, *supra*.

239. Twyne XXIV, a quarto volume of 733 pages, but pp. 671–733 are blank.

The title given to the volume by Langbaine is a sufficient clue to its contents :—'Excerpta e codicibus variis (tam manuscriptis quam impressis), registris et aliis monumentis publicis, quae ad Universitatem Oxon. quoquo modo spectare videntur.' Langbaine has prefixed an Index auctorum et librorum of the citations. It may be noted here that on pp. 443–466 are Twyne's Collections about South Bridge, and on pp. 467–473, about the highway between East Gate and Magdalen Bridge, showing that the Town is liable for the repair of them.

The old mark of the volume is ♀ : and by that Wood habitually cites it in his MSS. He has a minute summary of its contents in Wood MS. D. 18 (1), pp. 33–48 ; and an index of persons and places in it in Wood MS. C. 5.

240. Twyne XXV = Twyne VIII, q. v.

241. Twyne volumes in the Upper Room of the Archives.

These are six in number, folios. They are entitled 'Collectanea B. Twyne, Langbaine,' &c. This title is misleading, because by far the larger number of the papers are of Twyne's own writing or are transcripts made for him. The arrangement of the papers is not good, and the binding is subsequent to the time of Wood, who knew them and cites them as 'loose papers.' Many of the papers and extracts are duplicates of what are found in the previous series.

It is difficult to give a proper title to this series. The titles 'Collectiones,' 'Collectanea,' 'Adversaria,' 'Notae,' 'Libri Annotationum,' are all used by Wood in vague reference to the former series as well as to this, and as covering also the volumes in C. C. C. library and in Wood's possession. To use one of them here might therefore cause confusion. I propose to call the volumes 'Twyne-Langb.' as the simplest (though inaccurate) way of citing them. Note that the order in which I give the sections of each volume is a mere grouping of subject matter, and may have no reference to the sequence of papers in the volume. The volumes[1] are in great confusion and are innocent of foliation.

---

[1] the *Collectiones de processionibus* cited in *City*, ii. 136, are possibly somewhere in these volumes.

242. Twyne-Langb. 1. The chief contents are :—

(i) The statutes about matriculation and degrees, foll. 1–39.

(ii) Collections about the waterworks, the wharf, and the navigation of the river

(iii) Excerpts from pleas of the crown.

(iv) Proposed charters for the City. This is the paper ⅂ (i. e. F reversed), which goes with Twyne-Langb. 6 *infra*.

(v) Collections about alehousekeepers, bakers, brewers, butchers, carriers, cooks, graziers, innholders, maltsters, manciples, tailors, victuallers.

(vi) Exemptions, e. g. of College buildings from the saltpetre-diggers, of privileged persons from subsidies, &c.

(vii) Of the Sheriff's oath ; see Clark's *Reg. Univ. Oxon.* II. i. 313, 314.

(viii) *Viae, vici, nocumenta, purpresturae.*

Wood cites this paper, e. g. *City,* i. 61. He made excerpts from it (*Life* i. 385), now found in MS. Bodl. 594, foll. 181–182, which he cites ibid.

(ix) De viis, vicis, circuitu 5 milliarium, pavimentis.

(x) The leet or view of frankpledge.

243. Twyne-Langb. 2. The chief contents are :—

(i) *De cotagiis* sive tuguriolis, et casis sive 'cabbyns.'

Wood cites this paper, e. g. as ' Twyne's notes of cottages,' in *City,* i. 259.

(ii) De ludis scenicis (plays [1]).

(iii) Controversy about privileges, in 164$\frac{0}{1}$, between the University and City.

(iv) A similar controversy, in 1643, about taxation.

(v) Collections about the privileges of Cambridge University.

(vi) Lay Visitors for certain Colleges intended by the Commonwealth.

244. Twyne-Langb. 3. The chief contents are :—

(i) Collections from Hare's *Liber Memorabilium.*

(ii) Collections about proclamations, mulcts, by-laws ; the market, discommoning ; felons' goods, deodands, &c.

245. Twyne-Langb. 4. The chief contents are :—

(i) Collections about apothecaries, barbers, physicians, surgeons.

Wood cites this paper, as ' Twyne of surgeons,' *City,* i. 480.

---

[1] here I may note that the University authorities frequently paid small sums to companies on their tour, to stay away from Oxford, threatening them with imprisonment if they visited the town. *Comp. Vicecanc.* for 1621–22 : 'histrionibus regiis ut discederent ab Academia nec luderent, 20*s.*'

(ii) Collections about ale-licensing, victuallers, millers, chandlers, assize of weights and measures, the scavenger, &c.

(iii) Collections about stationers, parchment-sellers, &c.

(iv) Collections about carriers, coaches, post-horses.

(v) Collections about stonemasons, slaters, plasterers, carpenters, painters.

(vi) Collections about weavers, fullers, tailors, shoemakers, glovers, cappers ('birretarii').

(vii) Collections about liabilities for taxes, subsidies, war-contributions, &c.

(viii) Collections about liability to repair the City wall with its towers, and the City moat.

(ix) Collections de vicis et plateis, and of the scavenger.

(x) The right of the University to have a band of its own ('the University music') as distinct from the City band or waits ('the Town music').

(xi) S. Scholastica's day.

(xii) The 'praecinctus Universitatis' and the rights of the University within it.

(xiii) The night-watch, anno 1640 or $\frac{9}{1}$.

(xiv) Comparison of Cambridge privileges with those of Oxford.

(xv) Papers prepared with a view to obtaining the *Inspeximus* of 1635, i.e. the Charta Carolina.

246. Twyne-Langb. 5. Transcripts and abstracts of Royal Charters granted to the University, Henry IV–Charles I.

247. Twyne-Langb. 6. Papers about the University and City leets and amercements.

These papers were originally in separate bundles marked by letters **A, B,** ... to ... **Y. Z**, and Ɐ. ꓭ, Ɔ, ꓷ, Ǝ, (i.e. A, &c., reversed). The bundle ꓩ, which belongs here, is in Twyne-Langb. 1 *supra*.

These papers are cited by Wood as 'Twyne's notes, **A**, **Ɐ** (i.e. A reversed or inverted) B, C, &c.' *City*, i. 40, note 1 (c); which correct by this. 'Twyne's Notae S' are cited by him in *City*, i. 330, note 6.

248. Twyne volumes extra numerum in the Lower Room of the Archives.

Twyne E. N. I, a narrow folio of 52 leaves, paper, with a parchment cover cut from an old register, having inside of cover an extract by Gerard Langbaine from Twyne's will. On fol. 1ᵛ is its title in Twyne's hand, 'Br. Twyne—Index Extract[orum] ex variis libris et monumentis Universitatis Oxon.'   It is an alphabetical index of matters in Hare's Lib. Privel. and Lib. Memor. and in Lib. Vicecanc. A.

At the end is Langbaine's 'A note of such books, papers, or other muniments and records belonging to the University as were received by me Gerard Langbaine, Custos Archivorum, from Richard Twine, executor of Mr. Brian Twyne my predecessor at New Coll. in Mr. Vice-chancellor's lodgings in the presence of one Mr. Henderson, a Scottish man, July 13th 1644.'   Also notes by Langbaine of documents and registers lent by him out of the Archives, e. g. 11 Sept. 1646 'the originall indenture of the stationers of London for 200*li*. per annum to the University for forbearance of the printing of bibles &c.' lent to John Selden.

Twyne E. N. II, a folio, Magnae Chartae Carolinae pars posterior, anno regni 11°, 'conteining the explanations of the ancient priviledges with addition of new ones.'

Twyne volumes in Corpus Christi College.

249. (i) A folio volume; no. 280 in Coxe's Catalogue of C. C. C. MSS.   It contains Collections by Miles Windsor and Brian Twyne. Collections about Oxford occupy foll. 6–120.   Here are found the often-quoted *Tabella Rous* and other Catalogues of old halls, see *City*, i. 635, 637, 638; Shepreve's Verses on Claymond (fol. 204), see *City*, i. 288, 486.

The old mark is **ℬ** i. e. B. T. in a monogram.   It is very difficult to say whether such references as 'Collect. B. T. in C. C. C.' (*Colleges*, p. 382) are to this particular volume, or vaguely to the Twyne MSS. in C. C. C.   But this volume is plainly cited in *City*, ii. 440, note 8; and I think that most of Wood's references marked **ℬ**, or B. T., will be found to belong to it.

Wood's excerpts from this volume are found in MS. Bodl. 594, foll. 185–189, 199–210.

250. (ii) A folio volume, marked **B**; no. 255 in Coxe's Cat.   Wood describes it as 'a miscellany of Collections': a large part of it relates to Abingdon Abbey.   On foll. 200, 201 are 'Notitiae monasticae, scilicet, de fundatione monasteriorum, in Anglia collecta quaedam.'

This would be I suppose 'Liber annotationum B.'   At any rate Twyne's 'Liber annotationum A' is mentioned in Twyne XXI. 521, 534; has not been identified; and is supposed to have been destroyed.

251. (iii) A similar folio volume, marked **C**; no. 256 in Coxe's Cat.

Its contents deal largely with Christ Church in Canterbury.   On

foll. 196ᵛ–200 are 'Notae de fundatione monasteriorum variorum.'
Cited *City*, ii. 34.

Wood had 'Collect. ex libro annotationum C' (this volume,
perhaps), which he cites in *City*, i. 310, 335; but I have not found
them.

252. (iv) A folio volume of 'mathematical and astronomical observations'; no. 254 in Coxe's Cat.

(v)–(ix) Five 'little 8vo MSS.'; nos. 261–265 in Coxe's Cat. No.
263 on foll. 79–83 has 'tabula abbreviationum MSS. veterum,' and on
foll. 88–102 has excerpts 'ex libro statutorum Academiae Oxon.'

(x)–(xiii) Four small quarto volumes; nos. 257–260 in Coxe's Cat.
No. 257 contains many papers about Oxford during the reigns of
Mary, Elizabeth, James I. No. 258 contains Robert Talbot's 'Aurum
ex stercore.' No. 260 has on foll. 82–84 excerpts from the *Liber
bedellorum Oxon.*, then in Thomas Allen's possession.

253. Twyne volume among Selden's MSS.

'MS. arch. Seld. *supra* 79' is a volume by Twyne, described by Wood
(Wood MS. E. 4) as 'a rapsodie of various astronomical, astrological,
and mathematical matters.' It is a quarto of 295 pages, with unpaged
leaves at the beginning and the end.

The old mark of the volume is ℞. A note from it is printed in
City, i. 343, note 5. At the beginning of the volume is a Calendar
for 1605.

254. Twyne volumes formerly in Wood's possession.

(i) *Liber notarum F* a quarto volume, press mark Wood MS. D.
32; see *Life*, i. 429.

This volume is frequently cited by Wood as *Liber notarum F*;
also, e.g. *City*, i. 236, ii. 136, 234, &c. as *Liber notarum* simply;
also in *City*, ii. 414, as 'Twyne's Collect. in 4to which I have.'

The chief contents of this volume are :—

(*a*) Writers of Oxford, of Cambridge, and *dubii* (i.e. uncertain to
which University they belonged) before printing, pp. 135–155, 464–
475, 578.

(*b*) Catalogue of monasteries in England and Wales, chiefly from
Camden, pp. 227–359. Not by Twyne himself; the writer had
a good deal of local knowledge of Oxford, but yet makes some bad
mistakes. The Oxfordshire monasteries mentioned are—Eynsham
(p. 264, *olim* 38), Godstow (266), S. Frideswyde's and Osney (267),
Carmelite Friars (269), Durham and Gloucester Colleges (270),

Burcester, Thame, Preaching Friars (Oxford), Raylew (i. e. Rewley) (p. 271, *olim* 45).

(*c*) Lists of Cardinals and Bishops educated at Oxford and Cambridge, chiefly from Francis Godwin's English Bishops, pp. 476, 477.

(*d*) Twyne's excerpts from charters and MSS. pp. 188–218.

(*e*) Mirabilia Angliae, p. 457.

(*f*) Statutes of S. Mary's College Oxford, pp. 503–519 ; see *supra*, p. 106.

(*g*) Inventory (1541) of goods in S. Mary's Coll. pp. 550–552 ; see *supra*, p. 106.

(*h*) Statutes of S. George's College Oxford, pp. 522–533 ; see *supra*, p. 105.

(*i*) Statuta Aularia Univ. Oxon., pp. 534–549 ; see *supra*, p. 131.

(*k*) Liber antiquus bedellorum Oxon., pp. 553–568 ; see *supra*, p. 138.

(*l*) Statutes of the Bodleian, inserted after p. 568 ; see *supra*, p. 147.

(*m*) List of Merton College writers, pp. 485, 589.

(*n*) Catalogus veterum aularum, pp. 619–626 : see *supra*, p. 146.

Wood made excerpts from this MS., which he cites as *Collect. ex libro notarum* in *City*, ii. 196. They are found in MS. Bodl. 594, foll. 161–165 ; 'collections out of some Collections of Brian Twyne's of some monasteries in Oxon which he collected from *anonymus*.' There is a transcript of these excerpts, in the handwriting of Thomas Rawlins, in MS. Ballard 60, foll. 17–22.

(ii) *Liber secundus schediasticorum.* This is bound up, with the Liber notarum F just described, in Wood MS. D. 3². It consists of excerpts from authors, generally scored through, as though made use of elsewhere. Cited in *City*, ii. 146.

(iii) *Liber quartus schediasticorum*, now in Bodl. as MS. Jes. Coll. E. 30 ; see *Life*, i. 430. It contains notes on logic, physics, and Hebrew and Greek grammar. Foll. 82–95 contain antiquarian notes (in Wood's judgement 'worth little or nothing') ; foll. 156–286 'Catalogus librorum veteris bibliothecae C. C. C. Oxon.'; foll. 124–140 'lectiones solennes pro gradu Magistri in Artibus,' which may serve as a type of these exercises (see Clark's *Reg. Univ. Oxon.* II. i. 76).

(iv) *Liber duodecimus schediasticorum,* 'in a little octavo' ; now Wood MS. B. 11 ; see *Life*, i. 430.

(v)–(vii) Twyne's *Catalogue of Mayors of Oxford*; now Wood MS. F. 26 (*O. C.* 8502). In the same volume, bound up with this Catalogue, are unimportant notes by Twyne about authors and bishops (*O. C.* 8503, 8504).

(viii) Twyne's *Catalogus Cancellariorum &c. Oxon.* ; now Wood MS. F. 27 ; see *supra*, p. 214.

(ix) Twyne's *The Universitie's Musterings &c.* 1642–1643; now MS. Ballard 68; printed out in *Life*, i. pp. 53 sqq., 103.

(x) Twyne's *Miscellanea quaedam de antiquis ecclesiis civ. Oxon.;* now in Wood MS. F. 29 A, foll. 372–377. See *supra*, p. 117.

(xi) Twyne's *Catalogue of Thomas Allen's MSS.*; in Wood MS. F. 26 (*O. C.* 8488); see *supra*, p. 191.

(xii) Twyne's additions to Francis Godwin's *de praesulibus Angliae;* Wood MS. D. 21 A; *Life*, i. 247.

(xiii) Little scraps in Twyne's handwriting are found pasted in various MSS. of Wood's, e. g. in Wood MS. E. 4 (*O. C.* 8561), at p. 169 a note about early matriculation records, and (at the end) a note about the registers of the see of Canterbury: also in MSS. in other Collections (from the débris of Wood's papers), e. g. in MS. Tanner 454, slips in Twyne's hand are found at foll. 105, 132, 133.

255. Lost MSS. of Twyne's.

See the notice of Twyne in the *Athenae* and in *Life*, i. 429.

(i) *Liber annotationum A*; see *supra*, p. 219.

(ii) *Magnus liber annotationum*, ℣, folio; cited in Twyne XXI. 370, XXII. 105; the citations are to pp. 126, 127 of it.

(iii) Notes in a copy of Godwin's Catalogue of English bishops: *Life*, i. 75. Perhaps this is the 'interleaved copie' referred to in *Life*, iii. 35. In Wood MS. E. 4 (*O. C.* 8561), p. 96, Wood speaks of considerable additions made by Twyne to the life of Sylvester Giraldus in Godwin's Bishops.

256. Vague Citations of Twyne by Wood.

Wood's references to Twyne are occasionally so vague as to be of no practical use.

(i) He sometimes cites the Twyne Collections without giving a clue even as to whether they are in the Archives or in C. C. C.—e. g. *Hist.* ii. 60; *City*, i. 149, 202, 'in notis B. Twyne'; *Annals*, i. 393, 'Twyne's Adversaria MS.'; *Colleges*, 387, *City*, i. 77, ii. 288, &c. 'Twyne's Collectanea'; *City*, i. 86, 'Twyne's private notes' (where 'private' means only unpublished as opposed to the Apologia).

(ii) He sometimes refers only to the locality without specifying the volume; e. g. *City*, i. 304, 'Twyne's private notes in Arch. Acad.'; *City*, i. 413, 417, 'Twyne's Collectanea in Archivis Academiae'; *City*, i. 189, 'B. T. in bibliotheca C. C. C.'

(iii) His references are frequently ambiguous; e. g. *City*, i. 365, 'Liber annotationum,' which may refer to the MSS. in par. 250, 251, or to that in par. 254 (i); *City*, i. 175, &c., 'Twyne's Appendix,' which probably means the papers printed at the end of the Apologia [1], but may mean some papers in the Twyne-Langb. set, *supra*, par. 241.

257. Wood's debt to Brian Twyne.

The mere perusal of this Catalogue will draw forcibly the reader's attention to two points which have been much before me during its composition.

I. No doubt can possibly be entertained as to the reality and thoroughness of Wood's personal research into our antiquities. There are those many volumes of his excerpts from the registers of the University, the archives of several Colleges, the muniment-chests of Oxford parish churches, &c., the mere spectacle of whose number and bulk calls a blush to the cheeks of the modern student when he thinks how dwarfish his own Collections would appear in comparison.

II. On the other hand, it is plain also that, in the first composing of his treatises on the City and on the University of Oxford, Wood did little more than put together materials accumulated by Twyne. There are four things which show that we cannot state this second point too strongly :—

(*a*) There are those minute analyses and indexes made by Wood to the Twyne volumes (par. 216–239).

(*b*) There are extant the drafts of Twyne's Catalogues of Chancellors and Mayors which Wood incorporated into his own *Fasti* and *Catalogue of Mayors.*

(*c*) In the first draft of Wood's City treatise nearly every citation of a document is fortified by a reference also to the Collections of Twyne, indicating whence Wood obtained the quotation.

(*d*) To many of the originals which Wood cites he had never access. There is no record of his having been to Durham or Lincoln ; and the minuteness of his Diary renders it certain that such record would have been found, had he ever been there. It is on record that he was refused access to the archives of the City of Oxford (*Life*, ii. 480). The vagueness of his citations of several Thomas Allen MSS. and other MSS. shows that he had never seen them. And although it is true that at the time when the *Hist. et Antiq.* was going through the press, Wood's diaries record journeys to London and researches in the Cottonian and Royal Libraries, the Tower, &c.: yet this implies no more than the credit of verifying his references, and looking up in the originals passages formerly transcribed by Twyne.

It is right, therefore, that we should critically examine Wood's

---

[1] Wood 602 is Wood's copy of Twyne's *Antiq. Acad. Oxon. Apol.* Oxon. 1608, with a good many notes added by Gerard Langbaine and Wood.

attitude towards the older student. The facts of the case look ugly; but they admit, I am convinced, of satisfactory interpretation.

(*a*) Taking the draft of Wood's treatise on the University as prepared by himself for publication, e. g. in the *Hist. et Antiq.* printed in his own lifetime, we find an entire absence of acknowledgement of debt to Twyne's Collections; and the same is true, to a certain extent[1], of the *Annals*, &c., which he left in MS. ready for press. Yet we may say that there is hardly a single reference in these treatises which did not come, in the first instance, from Twyne.

(*b*) In the Catalogue of MSS. used by him for the *Hist. et Antiq.*, when he describes the MSS. of Twyne (Wood MS. E. 4, pp. 211–213), Wood cites only the Twyne volumes in C. C. C. Library and those in his own possession; but he gives no description of, and makes no allusion to, the thirty Twyne volumes in the University archives which formed so to speak the heaps of hewn stone and squared timber out of which he had constructed his own work.

But, these two facts notwithstanding, I am convinced, as the result of several years' work among the Wood papers, that he intended neither 'suggestio falsi' nor 'suppressio veri' as regards his debt to Twyne. His true attitude to Twyne I believe to be indicated by his manuscript copy of the *City* treatise, as edited by me, in which the citations of authorities are all accompanied by references to Twyne.

The reason why in his printed volume no such references are given is to be sought in the ideas of the time about original authorities. A passage from a MS. as quoted by Twyne was little thought of, the citation must be from the MS. itself. It was only when Twyne did not state his authority that he himself became an authority, and was cited as 'Mr. Twyne in his private notes,' 'Mr. Twyne's Collect. MS.' The idea of giving not only your citation, but also an acknowledgement of who helped you to it, had not yet come into being in Oxford, and, to judge by the complaints of some scholars of to-day, it is still 'an infant of days' whose existence is lightly disregarded.

The omission of a description of the Twyne Archive volumes in the Catalogue of MSS. stands on the same footing. Wood was writing a Catalogue of 'original' authorities, and these Twyne volumes were only transcripts. It was enough therefore to put down say 'Episcopal Registers at Lincoln' for the satisfaction of the reader, and to add in his own MS. for his private information, 'Twyne II.'

I have no wish to minimise Wood's debt to the incredible industry of Brian Twyne; the older antiquary's work is so little known that I have

---

[1] Gutch's editions of the *Annals*, &c. omit *some* of the references given by Wood in his MS., apparently because the editor did not know what MSS. were indicated by the symbols which Wood used.

pleasure in plucking some bays from Wood's garland to add them to that of Twyne; but it is right that Wood should be judged fairly, and according to the literary practice of his time.

This has not been always done. It is amazing to us to notice the extreme suspicion with which Wood was regarded in his own day and for some time after, and how the most sinister intentions were supposed to underlie even his most innocent and childish actions. In the *Athenae* the adoption of a phrase or two from a correspondent's letter of information was attributed to inveterate malice against this or that class of men. And similarly he was accused of appropriating to himself the collections of Twyne, Allam, and others, and lying about his debt. One characteristic example of this may be given.

William Smith, of University College (fellow 1675–1705), was a most diligent and painstaking worker in the archives of the University, and in those of his own College. He seems to have been taken up by Dr. John Wallis, Keeper of the Archives, to help him there, after Wallis' quarrel with Wood (*Life*, iii. 84); and imbibed, possibly from Wallis, a bitter animosity to Wood. In Twyne IV. p. 350 a, speaking of his researches in the City archives, Twyne says:—
'I gathered also out of antient deeds and chirographes there y[e] names, in forme of a Catalogue, of as many mayors and bayliffes, newe and old, as I could finde there.' On this Wood notes in the margin, opposite *Catalogue*, 'But where is it now?'; under which is written, very likely[1] by another hand, 'Burnt long since.' And then William Smith writes:—

'The question seems made in Mr. Wood's hand who very well could have answered it having it y[n] in his own possession and now bequeathed with other MS[ts]. to ye Universitie—vide Musaeum Vodianum[2]. The burning it was a fiction of his own to keep the world in ignorance to whose painfull studies he was beholden for the greatest part of his *History*, quoting everywhere the originalls for many things he borrowed at 2[d] hand from Mr. Twyne as may appear from his citing *Cartophylacium Civitatis Oxon.* for what he took out of no other than this very volume, Twyne IV, of which in his printed bookes he never makes mention, nor of Mr. Twyne's *Fasti Academici*, which he has, allmost *verbatim*, transcribed and published at the end of his *History*, &c.'

I know no better example of the manner in which animus against

---

[1] I have been at work on Wood MSS. for years, and familiar with his scrappy notes at all dates of his handwriting; and I am inclined to think that the words 'Burnt long since' are not by Wood. The fire of 1644 was matter of common knowledge, *Life*, i. 111, 429; *supra*, p. 214.

[2] i.e. 'Mr. Wood's study,' the room in the Ashmolean in which his bequest was stored, and where Twyne's *Catalogue of Mayors* was Wood MS. F. 26.

another perverts a man's judgement and seduces him into taking falsehood for truth. Wood had access to Twyne IV in July 1660 (*Life*, i. 326); it may very reasonably have been several years later (cp. *Life*, i. 429) before the stray Twyne MS. came into his hands; and what more natural, and *more suo*, than that on his *first* seeing Twyne IV Wood should put the query in the margin? But Smith *assumes that, before Wood saw Twyne IV, he had acquired Wood MS. F. 26. He *assumes* also that Wood was not only rogue but fool enough to bequeathe to the University a MS. which he had expressly stated to have been burnt and whose destruction was necessary to save his own credit. He *ignores* the facts (*a*) that Wood's *Catalogue of Mayors* is fuller and more accurate[1] than Twyne's, in consequence of his own careful work in College, &c., muniment-rooms, and (*b*) that in the *Athenae* Vol. II, published 1692, Wood makes express mention of Twyne's *Catalogue of Chancellors*, and (*c*) that Wood bequeathed his copy of it (in Wood MS. F. 27) to the University.

It is due also to Wood to state here the sense which is to be put upon his notice of Brian Twyne in the *Athenae*. Among Brian Twyne's papers there are few connected treatises on the History of the University. His Collections were in the main a mere mass of notes from many sources, gathered under heads in many cases, it is true, but never into a narrative or treatise. The chief exception was a treatise (now Twyne IX) about the then controversies between the City and the University. Wood in the *Athenae* mentions this particular treatise, and deplores that Twyne's other connected treatises on the History of the University had been lost; his words have no reference to the volumes of notes. He believed—whether *rightly* or not I cannot say, but, I am certain, *honestly*—that there had been such treatises[2] which he could have incorporated in his own work, and that they had been lost.

258. Miles Windsor's Collections.

'He was chosen, from Balliol College, Scholar of C. C. C. in 1556.'

(i) *Collectiones variae de Academia Oxon.*: two vols. quarto, nos.

---

[1] it is a characteristic of Wood's work that he was most diligent in strengthening his own immature work, and adding to what he found in Twyne, by his later researches. For example, having collected from College and other archives his volumes V. (Wood MS. D. 2), O. (Wood MS. C. 1), F. (Wood MS. C. 4), A. W. (Wood MS. C. 2), A. B. (Wood MS. D. 3), A. V. (Wood MS. D 11 [1]), the lost volume M., and others, Wood went over the whole of his *City* volume, and added references to them. A glance over the notes of my edition of it will show what an amount of time and trouble Wood expended in thus improving his earlier work by genuine later research.

[2] see for one instance of them, par. 135 (vii).

266 and 267 in Coxe's Cat. Codd. Coll. Corp. Chr. Oxon. See Twyne XXII. 399.

Windsor's Collections are frequently cited, under various titles ('Mr. Windsore's notes,' 'notae M. Windsore,' 'Collections of Mr. Windsore's,' &c.), e. g. in *City,* i. 58, 168, &c., *Annals,* ii. 224, 230, &c. These two volumes are no doubt the principal, if not the exclusive, source of these citations.

Wood had excerpts from Windsor's collections, which he called **W** (for 'Windsor'). These are frequently cited in *City,* both by the title 'Collect. ex M. Windesor,' 'Collect. ex M. W.' (*City* i. 54, 58, &c.) and by the mark **W** (*City,* i. 66, 114, &c.). These excerpts by Wood are now found in MS. Ballard 69 (*olim* 19), pp. 1–85.

Of these Windsor volumes Wood says 'all were of little use to me, having several frivolous and credulous matters in them.'

(ii) *Tabula calamitatum Oxon.,* 914–1387: no. 267 (fol. 151ᵛ–158) in Coxe's Cat. Codd. C. C. C.

(iii) *Catalogus Cancellariorum Oxon.* (et vicecancell.), 1220–1616: Wood MS. F. 27 (*O. C.* 8489).

(iv) *Collections,* containing notices of early printed books, a catalogue of old Oxford halls, &c.: Arch. Univ. Oxon. North West Press 27: old mark **Y**. This volume was formerly in Wood's possession (*Life,* i. 429), and is cited as in his hands in *City,* i. 496, *Annals,* ii. 747.

(v) Narrative of Elizabeth's 1566 visit to Oxford; Twyne XXI. 792–800.

(vi) No. 280 in Coxe's Cat. Cod. Corp. Chr. Oxon. (old mark **ᵬ**), contains papers by Windsor as well as by Twyne: see par. 249 (1).

In MS. Bodl. 594 fol. 185 is a transcript by Wood of a note of Windsor's from **ᵬ**.

(vii) Collections about Eton College: no. 267 (sub fin.) in Coxe's Cat. C. C. C.

(viii) *Europaei orbis Academiae,* Windsor's printed book (London 1590) with his MS. notes; no. 280 in Coxe's Cat. C. C. C. (foll. 22–27). Cited in *Annals,* ii. 839: *Hist.* ii. 138: *City,* i. 544, ii. 248.

(ix) Stray notes by Windsor, easily recognizable by the peculiar handwriting, are found pasted in various Twyne volumes; e. g. Twyne IV. 142, Twyne II. 101–103, 115ᵛ–118, 152.

(x) Windsor added a great many marginal notes in his copy of Londinensis' [i. e. Johannes Caius'] *de Antiquitate Cant. Acad.* Lond. 1568, and in Thomas Caius' *Assertio Antiq. Oxon.,* Lond. 1568, bound with it. This volume he bequeathed to the library of C. C. C. Oxford, from which (Thomas Hearne's note on fly-leaf) it was 'sold as a duplicate'! It is now 8° Rawl. 135, no. 15600 in Mr. Madan's Summary Catalogue.

V. ANTHONY WOOD'S COLLECTIONS.

259. Collections for his own life and the history of his times.

(i) *History of his family*: MS. Phillipps 7018: *Life*, i. 4, ii. 100, iii. 109, 468.

(ii) His *Autobiography*: MS. Harl. 5409, MS. Tanner 102 part 1: see *Life*, i. 1, 2.   Fully printed in *Life*.

MS. Rawl. D. 97 is a transcript of the Harleian MS.

(iii) His daily entries in his interleaved *Almanacs*, 1657–1695. Some slips belonging to these are found in Wood MS. F. 31 and in MS. Phillipps 7018.   Completely printed in *Life*.

MS. Rawl. D. 26 is a transcript by Dr. Richard Rawlinson of considerable portions of these.

Cited in *City*, i. 155, 386, &c.

(iv) His notes for the contemporary history of the University 1660-1681, MS. Tanner 102, part 2.   Some papers of this set are in Wood MS. F. 31, and in MS. Bodl. 594.   These have been practically printed out in *Life*.   For the same purpose he made excerpts from the newspapers, now in Wood MS. D. 18: *Life*, i. 14.

(v) His narratives of contemporary royal visits and other great functions: Wood MS. D. 19 (3) (*O. C.* 8566).   Some papers of this set are found in MS. Tanner 456.   Printed out in *Life*.

(vi) *Modius salium*: specimens of contemporary wit[1]: Wood MS. E. 32, written by Wood in 1674: some papers of the same sort are found at the end of Wood MS. F. 31.   Printed in 1751: see *Life*, i. 5, note 1.

(vii) His collection of contemporary Oxford satirical pieces in verse; Wood MS. E. 31; now lost, except that duplicates of a few pieces are found in MSS. Tanner 306 and 465.   *Life*, iii. p. vii.

(viii) His accounts of persons buried in Oxford in his time: Wood MS. F. 4 (*O. C.* 8466).   Printed out in *Life*.

(ix) Autobiographical notes by Wood are found in a great many of his printed books and in MSS. possessed by him: e. g. in an old Calendar in Wood MS. C. 12 are notes about his family (see *City*, i. 618).   Search has been made for these, and note taken of them in *Life*.

(x) Many slips with autobiographical jottings passed with Wood's 'private papers' into Thomas Tanner's hands and are found in MSS. Tanner 290, 338, &c.: a few slips of like kind are among the Ballard MSS. and Rawlinson MSS.

---

[1] many of them are old 'Joe Millers,' with contemporary names attached to them.

260. Letters addressed to Wood.

(i) Numbers of these are now in the Wood Collection of MSS., bound in seven folio volumes: they are very largely letters of information towards the *Athenae*.

Wood MS. F. 39 contains letters from about fifteen correspondents whose names begin with A. Those from Elias Ashmole occupy foll. 57–96.

Wood MS. F. 40 contains letters from about seventy correspondents whose names begin with B or C. Thomas Blount's letters occupy foll. 62–231; Arthur Crew's (of Magot-mill), foll. 409–419.

Wood MS. F. 41 contains letters from about twenty-five correspondents, D–F. Francis Hunt or Davenport's letters are foll. 18–37; Henry Dodwell's, foll. 56–62; Sir William Dugdale's, foll. 65–178; Edmund Elys' (often under initials E. E.), foll. 188–210; Nathaniel Freind's, foll. 248–264; and William Fulman's (see par. 201), foll. 267–387.

Wood MS. F. 42 contains letters from about seventy-five correspondents, G–K. Thomas Gore's letters are foll. 61–102; Thomas Guidott's, foll. 116–118, 122–124; George Hickes', foll. 192–198; William Hopkins', foll. 218–250; Matthew Hutton's, foll. 262–266; Sir Leoline Jenkins', foll. 298–302, 310; William Joyner's, foll. 322–326; White Kennet's, foll. 328–350.

Wood MS. F. 43 contains letters from about sixty correspondents, L–R. Nicholas Lloyd's letters are foll. 36–72; Increase Mather's, foll. 112–137; John Prince's, foll. 244–275; Richard Reeves', foll. 286–294; William Rogers', foll. 322–344.

Wood MS. F. 44 contains letters from over twenty correspondents, whose names begin with S. Ralph Sheldon's letters are foll. 18–204; Sir Edward Sherburne's, foll. 221–303; Thomas Smith's (Magd. C.), foll. 317–324; William Sprigg's, foll. 329–337.

Wood MS. F. 45 contains letters from over fifty correspondents, T–Z.

(ii) There are also numerous letters in other volumes of the Wood Collection:—

e. g. in Wood MS. F. 46, letters from over twenty correspondents, including White Kennet (foll. 239–249), Robert Plot, Increase Mather.

— in Wood MS. F. 49, letters from over twenty correspondents including John Aubrey, Thomas Gore, Nicholas Lloyd, Increase Mather.

— in Wood MS. F. 50, letters from about a dozen correspondents, including Francis Hunt or Davenport.

— in Wood MS. F. 51, letters from various correspondents, including John Aubrey, Arthur Charlett, Thomas Tanner.

(iii) There are letters addressed to Wood, also in other Collections:— e. g. in MS. Ballard 14, foll. 3–12, letters of Sir William Dugdale to Wood; foll. 13, 14 letters of Elias Ashmole to Wood; foll. 80–100 letters of John Aubrey to Wood.

— in MS. Smith 66, letters of Dr. Thomas Smith (of Magd. Coll.) to Wood.

— in MS. Tanner 456, letters of John Aubrey to Wood (see p. 192); and of Sir William Dugdale to Wood, foll. 10, 24–26.

— in MS. Rawl. D. 742, fol. 35, letter from Arthur Charlett.

—also in MSS. Ballard 9, 11, 17, 21, 27, 34, and 46.

261. Letters written by Wood.

(i) Drafts of letters written by Wood are found on the backs of many of the letters addressed to him in Wood MSS. F. 39–45.

(ii) Letters by Wood are found in MS. Ballard 14, foll. 21–26, 37: also in MSS. Ballard 9 and 15.

(iii) Letters by Wood to John Aubrey are found in MS. Tanner 456, foll. 12, 48; and to Ralph Sheldon, ibid. fol. 22. Also in MS. Tanner 24.

(iv) Letters by Wood to John Aubrey are found in MS. Aubrey 13 foll. 361–372.

(v) The collection 'Rawlinson Letters' in the Bodleian requires to be searched for this and the preceding head.

(vi) A large number of letters written by Wood to William Fulman are among the Fulman MSS. in C. C. C. Oxford.

(vii) Letters, probably now lost, formerly in the possession of Robert Dale, 'Richmond' herald, who died April 4, 1722: *Life*, i. p. 1, note 1.

(viii) MS. Ashm. 1131, fol. 281 : *Life*, ii. 248.

262. MS. of Wood's treatise on the University and Colleges: see *Life*, ii. 290, 291.

(i) The final copy, Wood MS. F. 1 and F. 2 (*O. C.* 8463, 8464). Printed, on the whole with great faithfulness and completeness, by John Gutch. Cited as *English History, English Copy or History*, &c. in *Life*, i. 313, &c., iii. 84.

(ii) An imperfect earlier copy: Wood MS. F. 38.

(iii) A still ruder copy, probably now destroyed, but some fragments of it possibly exist; see *Life*, ii. 162 note 5, 335.

(iv) A copy for the *Hist. et Antiq.* written out for press, which Wood refers to as the 'translator's copy' in *City*, ii. 32, no doubt destroyed. See however *City*, i. 530.

(v) Wood's printed copy of the *Historia et Antiquitates* (Wood 430) contains a large number of his MS. notes and corrections.

(vi) An index to *Hist. et Antiq.*: Wood MS. F. *olim* 37, *nunc* in F. 22.

263. MS. of Wood's treatise on the City.

(i) MS. Wood F. 29 A: mostly printed in *City*, i and ii and will be completed in *City*, iii: see *City*, i. 31. Some slips belonging to this volume are now in Wood MS. F. 31.

William Smith of Univ. Coll. has written several marginal notes in this treatise. These have been printed in *City*, i. 119 note 2, 120 note 11, 121 note 5, 122 note 5, 123 note 4, 133 note 3, 191 note 8, 225, note 1, 560 note 7; *City*, ii. 150, 153.

The transcripts of this MS. are noticed in *City*, i. 33, 34.

(ii) There seems to have been a Latin version of this treatise. Thus in *City*, i. 260, ' our Latin copy at the end of the discourse of churches '; i. 61, ' my Latin copy in the beginning of streets '; i. 66, 117, &c. ' Latin copy.'

264. Collections towards Wood's treatise on the City.

(i) Wood's early notes with a view to his ' Antiquities of the City of Oxford' are found in MS. Rawl. D. 1268; see *Life*, ii. p. vii. Most of them have been printed in *City*, and *Life*: e. g. in *City*, i. 575.

MS. Rawl. B. 176 is a transcript of them by Thomas Hearne.

(ii) Many notes and slips belonging to Wood's City treatise are found in MSS. Tanner 438, 456, and 456*.

(iii) Wood MS. C. 5 (*O. C.* 8528) contains indexes of persons and places to Wood's volumes designated by the marks A. V., F, O, V. These indexes were compiled by Wood with a view to furnishing references for his City treatise.

(iv) *Schedae*, or *Schedulae* [cited in contracted forms, *sched.* or *sced.*].

These are so constantly cited by Wood in the notes to *City* that I conclude they were papers (similar to those described in par. 266 (i)) containing notes preparatory to the City treatise. I can bring forward no proof of this conclusion, since I have found no trace of even a single one of these papers; but it seems highly probable. They may have been all destroyed by Wood himself or after his death.

There appear to have been two sets of these papers, one set indicated by letters, the other by Arabic numerals.

Sched. A (cited up to its 8th page), *City*, ii. 31; *Sched. B* (to 5th p.), ii. 9, 29, &c.; *Sched. C* (to 11th p.), i. 541, ii. 9, &c.; *Sched. D* (to p. 11), ii. 31, 234, &c.; *Sched. E*, ii. 31; *Sched*. . . [letter or figure dropped ?], ii. 174.

Sched. 1, in *City*, ii. 275; *Sched.* 3, ii. 174; *Sched.* 4 (cited up to 5th page), i. 383, &c.; *Sched.* 5, ii. 333; *Sched.* 6, i. 149; *Sched.* 7, ii. 28; *Sched.* 8, i. 97; *Sched.* 11, ii. 68; *Sched.* 15 (to 7th p.), i. 563; *Sched.* 16, i. 486; *Sched.* 18 (to 8th p.), ii. 232; *Sched.* 20 (to 9th p.), i. 543; *Sched.* 22, (to 8th p.), ii. 19; *Sched.* 23 (to 7th p.), i. 94; *Sched.* 24 (to 4th p.), i. 486; *Sched.* 25, ii. 22.

265.   MS. of Wood's Athenae.

(i) The copy for the i and ii volumes of the *Athenae*, printed in 1691 and 1692, has no doubt been destroyed, with the possible exception of a stray sheet or two.

(ii) The proof copy of these, which was left in Wood's hands (now Wood 431), is full of corrections and inserted slips placed there by Wood in preparation for his second edition. Most of these were incorporated in Jacob Tonson's 1721 edition, but with occasional awkwardness or imperfection.

(iii) At Wood's death he had in hand the copy for a third volume of (or 'Appendix' to) the *Athenae*. This passed into the hands of Thomas Tanner, and was finally published in the 1721 edition. The good faith of this edition was vehemently suspected by Thomas Hearne whose Diaries are full of severe strictures upon it. But careful inquiry has convinced me that, except for cutting out a few harsh reflections, the printed copy faithfully represented Wood's text. The original MS. was, it is to be feared, destroyed. See *Life of Nathaniel lord Crewe* in the Camden Society's Miscellany, (1894), p. 45.

266.   Wood's Collections towards the Athenae.

(i) One very extensive class of these consisted of biographical jottings, answers to queries, information sent by correspondents, &c. They were arranged in a methodical way on Wood's shelves in bundles, each paper marked in red ink with the letter or symbol of the bundle and its own number, and by these marks Wood cites them in his MSS. At Wood's death, many of these papers were no doubt lost and destroyed, but a good many can still be traced.

A. 1, 2, 6, 12, 16, 17, 29, 30, are in *Wood MS. F.* 46.   A. 3 is fol. 136, and A. 10 is fol. 133 of *Wood MS. F.* 45.   A. 15 is fol. 387 of *Wood MS. F.* 44; A. 26, fol. 16 of *Wood MS. F.* 45.

B. 4, 17, 20, 21 are in *Wood MS. F.* 46. B. 1 is fol. 298 of *Wood MS. F.* 43.

C. 2, 5, 9, 11, 12, 23 are in *Wood MS. F.* 46.   C. 25 is fol. 8 of *Wood MS. F.* 45; and C. 33 is fol. 329 of *Wood MS. F.* 43.

D. 2, 4–9, 11, 21, 22, 26, 43–45, 47 are in *Wood MS. F.* 46.

E. 3, 17, 24 are in *Wood MS. F.* 46. E. 13 is fol. 167 of *Wood MS. F.* 43; E. 16 is fol. 115 of *Wood MS. F.* 45; and E. 19 is fol. 284 of *Wood MS. F.* 43.

F. 3, 5, 9, 12, 18, 19, 20, 21–24, 27 are in *Wood MS. F.* 46. F. 20 is fol. 99 of *Wood MS. F.* 45.

G. 4, 7, 9, 17, 21, 23, 28–30 are in *Wood MS. F.* 46.

H. 1, 2, 5–11, 15–18, 22, 23, 25 are in *Wood MS. F.* 46.

I. 2, 4, 8, 9, 12, 15, 16, 19, 20, 22, 23, 25, 27, 33 are in *Wood MS. F.* 46. I. 35 is fol. 306 of *Wood MS. F.* 42.

J. 15 is cited in *Life*, ii. 173.

K. 1, 2, 4, 7, 8, 10–15, 18, 20, 22–24, 26–33, 35 are in *Wood MS. F.* 46.

L. 1–4, 6–19, 21–32, 34–48, are in *Wood MS. F.* 46.

M. 1, 2, 12, 13, 16–19, 25–28, are in *Wood MS. F.* 46. M. 9 is fol. 213 of *Wood MS. F.* 42; M. 10 is fol. 90 and M. 15 is fol. 243 of *Wood MS. F.* 45; and M. 20 is fol. 16 of *Wood MS. F.* 44.

N. 1–6, 8–10, 12–14, 16, 17, 22–25, 27–29, 32, 33, 35, 38, 39, are in *Wood MS. F.* 46. N. 21 is fol. 306 of *Wood MS. F.* 43, and N. 37 is fol. 41 of *Wood MS. F.* 45.

O. 1, 6, 12 are in *Wood MS. F.* 46. O. 16 is fol. 325 of *Wood MS. F.* 43.

P. 8, 10, 13, 15, 17, 19, 20, 25, 26 are in *Wood MS. F.* 46. P. 22 is fol. 315 of *Wood MS. F.* 43. P. 13 is cited in *Life*, ii. 265.

Q. 1, 3, 4, 15, 19, 21 are in *Wood MS. F.* 46. Q. 8 is fol. 9, 20 of *MS. Ballard* 14; Q. 16 is fol. 322 of *Wood MS. F.* 42.

R. I have found none of. R. 3 is cited in *Life*, iii. 28.

S. 2, 3, 11, 12, 14, 18, 19 are in *Wood MS. F.* 46. S. 6 is cited in *Life*, iii. 88.

T. 4, 8, 10, 11, 12, 18 are in *Wood MS. F.* 46. T. 20 is fol. 97 of *Wood MS. F.* 45.

V. 7–10, 12, 13, 20, 21 are in *Wood MS. F.* 46.

W. I have found none of.

X. 2, 12 are in *Wood MS. F.* 46. X. 6 is fol. 322 of *Wood MS. F.* 43; X. 8, fol. 37 of *Wood MS. F.* 45; and X. 16 is fol. 315 of *Wood MS. F.* 44.

Y. 1, 8, 19 are in *Wood MS. F.* 46; Y. 2 is cited in *Life*, iii. 261.

Z. 2 is in *Wood MS. F.* 46. Z. 7 is fol. 227 of *Wood MS. F.* 43; Z. 9, fol. 300 of *Wood MS. F.* 44; Z. 12, fol. 64 of *Wood MS. F.* 45; Z. 15, fol. 29 of *Wood MS. F.* 45; and Z. 17, fol. 209 of *Wood MS. F.* 43. Z. 8 is cited in *Life*, iii. 322.

AA. 1–31, 33–36 ; BB. 1–42 ; CC. 1–32, 34–37 ; EE. 1–30, 32–44 ; FF. 1–19, 22–24 ; GG. 1–25 ; HH. 1–33 ; II. 1–33 are in *Wood MS. F.* 47. EE. 31 is fol. 29 of *Wood MS. F.* 43.

KK. 2–24, 26–30 ; LL. 1–34 ; MM. 1–25 ; NN. 1–12, 14–32 ; OO. 1–30 ; PP. 1–14, 16–35 ; RR. 1–3, 5, 30, 32 ; SS. 1–18, 20–33 are in *Wood MS. F.* 48.

I believe that this series (AA, &c.) was at one time complete on to ZZ, and that FFF *infra* is a survival of a third series. There are a good many references to the two-letter series of notes in *Life*, e. g. :—

AA. 34 is cited in *Life*, iii. 19 ; DD. 14, in ii. 272 note 4 ; FF. 35 in iii. 25, and FF. 43 in iii. 19 ; HH. 13 in ii. 258, and HH. 27 in iii. 26 ; MM. 1, in iii. 105, 106 : NN. 19, in iii. 124 ; OO. 1, in ii. 561, OO. 8 in ii. 298, iii. 137, and OO. 18 in iii. 24 ; QQ. 31 in iii. 209, 218.

FFF. 1, 4, 12, 18 are in *Wood MS. F.* 48.

✝ 4, 15 are in *Wood MS. F.* 46.   ✝ 2 is fol. 255 of *Wood MS. F.* 42 : ✝ 3 is fol. 184 of *Wood MS. F.* 43 ; ✝ 7 is fol. 186 of *Wood MS. F.* 43 ; ✝ 8 is fol. 319 of *Wood MS. F.* 44 ; ✝ 9 is fol. 87 of *Wood MS. F.* 45 : ✝ 12 is fol. 192 of *Wood MS. F.* 43.

‡ 3, 11, 18 are in *Wood MS. F.* 46. ‡ 8 is fol. 110 of *Wood MS. F.* 43.

3, 4, 11, 12 are in *Wood MS. F.* 46. # 8 is fol. 101, and # 15 is fol. 163 of *Wood MS. F.* 43. # 3 is cited in *Life*, iii. 352.

♀ 14, 15, 18 are in *Wood MS. F.* 46. ♀ 2 is fol. 44 of *Wood MS. F.* 45 ; ♀ 6 is fol. 180 of *Wood MS. F.* 43 ; ♀ 8 is fol. 62 of *Wood MS. F.* 41 ; ♀ xi[1] is fol. 303 of *Wood MS. F.* 44 ; ♀ 13 is fol. 52 of *Wood MS. F.* 45.

⊕ 2 is fol. 94 of *Wood MS. F.* 43 ; ⊕ 4 is fol. 205, and ⊕ 7 is fol. 25 of *Wood MS. F.* 45, and ⊕ 9 is fol. 113 of *Wood MS. F.* 43. ⊕ 11 is cited in *City*, ii. 177 note 3.

(ii) The following MS. volumes consist of notes made by Wood solely or partly for purposes of the *Athenae* :—

Wood MS. F. 7—Collections of genealogies of bishops and writers ; *Life*, ii. 364.

Wood MS. F. 30 (*O. C.* 8492)—a Collection of lives.

Wood MS. D. 4, and D. 7 (2)—excerpts about writers from printed books, collections of epitaphs, &c.

Wood MS. E. 4 (*O. C.* 8560)—collections of lives and biographical notes.

---

[1] Wood usually writes xi instead of 11, for clearness' sake, to avoid confusion with ii.

Wood MS. E. 3 (*O. C.* 8567), *Wood MS. B.* 14 (*O. C.* 8587), and MS. Tanner 416—collections about deans and canons of various Cathedral churches.

(iii) MS. Tanner 454 contains many scattered notes by Wood towards the *Athenae.*

MS. Rawl. D. *olim* 1290 *nunc* 912, also contains many scattered notes for the *Athenae.* Here are lists of bishops (1572) &c. stolen from *O. C.* 8569 (Wood MS. D. 21 A).

(iv) A very large number of the printed books in the Wood Collection have on their title-pages and fly-leaves notes by him with a view to the *Athenae.*

(v) Wood compiled an index to the terminal lists of books published in London ('Term Catalogues,' *Life*, i. 15): Wood MS. F. 36 (*O. C.* 8498).

267. Wood's Lives of English musicians.

Notes for the lives of the English musicians, with catalogues of their works: probably suggested by the *Athenae*: Wood MS. D. 19 (4) (*O. C.* 8568).

268. Wood's Catalogues of printed books and MSS.
Compiled or arranged chiefly for the *Athenae.*

(i) *MS. Catalogues of books and pamphlets* found by Wood in the libraries of Oxford students, booksellers, &c.

Catalogue 1 (pp. 424)—*O. C.* 8530[1], now in Wood MS. E. 10: of the books of Henry Foulis and Dr. Thomas Marshall of Linc. Coll. Ralph Sheldon of Beoly, and Richard Davis the bookseller, *Life*, i. 178 note 5, 316, ii. 321.

Catalogue 2 (pp. 307)—*O. C.* 8531, now in Wood MS. E. 2 : *Life*, ii. 519 note 4. Cited in *Life*, i. 385, ii. 97, &c.

Catalogue 3 (pp. 100)—*O. C.* 8532, now in Wood MS. E. 2 : of Wood's own books : *Life*, ii. 519.

Catalogue 4 (pp. 140)—*O. C.* 8533, now in Wood MS. E. 2, of Andrew Allam's books and of books in various shops : *Life*, ii. 519 note 4, iii. 9.

Catalogue 5 (pp. 236)—*O. C.* 8534, now in Wood MS. E. 2 : of Arthur Charlet's books, and books in the Bodleian and Jesus College Library : *Life*, ii. 361, iii. 195, 307.

Catalogue 6 (pp. 80)—*O. C.* 8535, now in Wood MS. E. 4 ; of Thomas Barlow's printed books, and books in the Bodleian ; *Life*, iii. 405.

---

[1] in this volume are Wood's notes out of Fuller's *History of Cambridge.*

Catalogue 7 (pp. 150)—*O. C.* 8536, now in Wood MS. E. 4 : catalogue of plays in Nicholas Cox's shop : *Life*, iii. 119.

(ii) *MS. Catalogues of plays.*

(*a*) Catalogue of plays in the hands of Gerard Langbaine and Nicholas Cox = *Catalogue* 7, supra.

(*b*) Catalogue of plays in the hands successively of John Horne, John Houghton. . . . Hearne[1], and Ralph Sheldon; now Wood MS. D. 18 : *Life*, iii. 119.

(iii) *Catalogue of writers on Heraldry,* O. C. 8570, Wood MS. E. 3 ; *Life*, ii. 140.

(iv) *MS. Catalogues* of *MSS.*

(*a*) Catalogue of Dr. Thomas Barlow's MSS.; now lost : *Life*, ii. 174.

(*b*) Catalogue of Ralph Sheldon's MSS.: Wood MS. D. 6 : see *Life*, ii. 321 ; iii. 103.

(*c*) Catalogue of MSS. cited in the *Hist. et Antiq.,* O. C. 8561, now in Wood MS. E. 4 : *Life*, ii. 301.

This seems to be the volume cited in *City,* i. 54, as *Catalogus novus scriptorum* : and as *Catalogus MSS.* in *City,* i. 233, ii. 309. See also *Annals,* ii. 52, 136.

(v) *Printed catalogues, arranged and annotated by Wood* for purposes of the *Athenae* :—

(*a*) The series of Catalogues nos. 1–68, and the continuation and supplements to them : Wood E. 20–23 : *Life*, i. 19.

(*b*) A number of similar Catalogues : *Life*, i. 19.

(*c*) Similar catalogues of plays : Wood E. 28 : *Life*, i. 19, 20.

269. Wood's Collections for Merton College.

For some time before his death Wood had been engaged in collecting materials for a history of Merton College, his own College (see *Life,* iii. 181): and at the time of his death papers of this kind were supposed to be in his hands (*Life*, iii. 501). No connected papers of this sort have come to light : all that we have are scanty and, for the most part, fragmentary notes.

Wood cites or mentions separately :-

(i) his *Collect. ex archivis Coll. Merton.*

(ii) his *Collect. ex computis Coll. Merton.*

(iii) his excerpts from the statutes of Merton College.

(iv) his *Collect. ex registris Coll. Merton.*

(v) his Catalogue of fellows of Merton College : see for these par. 142.

[1] ? James Herne : *Life*, iii. 143.

Some of these collections he had arranged in a volume [1], which he called **M** (for 'Merton'), which is continually cited in *City* as **M**, **Notae M**, or **m**. The 'disjecta membra' of this are probably seen in Wood's Merton College slips in Wood MS. F. 31, MS. Bodl. 594, MS. Ballard 46, MS. Tanner 456.

Collections by Wood about Merton College are said to be in the Archives of that College and in the Kilner collection there: but I have not seen these nor any detailed account of them.

270. Wood's Collections about Schools in England.

(i) Wood seems at one time to have contemplated an historical account of the endowed and grammar schools in England.

School Notes was the title he gave to his Collections under this head. This volume was *O. C.* 8518; but was misused in the Ashmolean, and is now partly in Wood MS. D. 11 (4), and partly in Wood MS. D. 4. Wood also cited the volume by the symbol ⛨.

(ii) *Monumental inscriptions in Eton College Chapel*; Wood MS. B. 12 (*O. C.* 8583): *Life*, i. 400.

Catalogue of the provosts and fellows of Eton College: Wood MS. B. 12 (*O. C.* 8583).

(iii) *Carmina et orationes scholarium . . . Winton.*, with other papers referring to Winchester College; Wood MS. D. 13 (*O. C.* 8545); *Life*, ii. 180.

271. Wood's Collections for the County of Oxford.

See *Life*, i. 5, 215, &c.

(i) *Monumental inscriptions in Oxfordshire churches*, taken by Wood in 1656 and 1657: Wood MS. B. 15 (*O. C.* 8586).

(ii) *Arms and epitaphs in Oxfordshire churches &c.*: Wood MS. D. 4 (*O. C.* 8518); and in Wood MS. F. 31.

(iii) *Arms and epitaphs in Oxfordshire churches*: Wood MS. E. 1 (*O. C.* 8505): 307 folios in the new paging, 278 in the old.

Wood cites his 'Church notes of Tackley' in *City*, ii. 175.

(iv) *Collections relating to the antiquities of several towns and villages in Oxfordshire*: Wood MS. F. 12 (*O. C.* 8474), now bound up with F. 21.

(v) *Notes about Oxfordshire gentry, arms in Oxfordshire houses*, &c.; Wood MS. F. 33 (*O. C.* 8495); Wood MS. D. 19 (1) (*O. C.* 8564).

(vi) Richard Lee's *Visitation of Oxfordshire*, 1574, from the original

[1] the slips differ in size, some being 4to, others 12mo. Was there one volume 4to called **M**, and another 12mo called **m**?

in the Heralds' Office: Wood MS. D. 7 (4) (*O. C.* 8522).   Printed by
W. H. Turner for the Harleian Society, 1871.

Cited in *Coll.* p. 353.

(vii) *Oxfordshire coats of arms, taken by Lee,* 1574 : Wood MS. D.
14 (*O. C.* 8548).

Cited in *Coll.* p. 324.

(viii) *Inscriptions in Oxfordshire Churches* : Wood MS. C. 10 ; see
Life, i. 215 ; ii. 364, 376.

272. Wood's Collections for the County of Berks.

Wood MS. F 32, art. 32 (*O. C.* 8494): historical notes about
several towns and villages in Berks.

Wood MS. D. 4, and D. 11 (3) (*O. C.* 8518 (part 2) and 8517):
epitaphs, &c. in Berkshire churches.

273. Notes by Wood in printed books.

Besides those which have been noted under previous heads, a few
books with notes by Wood remain to be noticed.

(*a*) Wood MS. D. 21 (A) is Francis Godwin's Latin 'de praesulibus
Angliae commentarius,' Lond. 1616 : *Life,* i. 247.   In this Wood has
several notes, both marginal and on inserted slips.

Cited as *additamenta ad Godwinum* in *City,* ii. 13 ; *Notae ad Godwinum*
in *City,* i. 158, *Coll., Fasti.*

(*b*) Wood MS. D. 21 (B) is Godwin's English 'A catalogue of the
bishops of England,' Lond. 1615.   In this Wood has a few notes.

Cited in *City,* ii. 5.

(*c*) Vindication of the historiographer of . . . Oxon : Lond. 1693,
Wood 614(7), had notes by Wood : *Life,* iii. 419.

274. Stray notes by Wood.

A considerable number of scraps in Wood's handwriting are dispersed about the volumes of the Ballard, Rawlinson, and Tanner
collections : and a few have been bought of late years by the Bodleian :
see the indexes to the Catalogues of Rawlinson MSS. A, B, C, D, of
Tanner MSS., and Mr. Madan's new Summary Catalogue of MSS. in
the Bodleian.

275. Lost MSS. or notes by Wood.

(*a*) *Notae ad Pitsaeum,* insertions by Wood in his copy of that
writer's 'de Scriptoribus Angliae' : *Life,* i. 247.   Frequently cited in
City.

(*b*) *Catalogus praesidentium Coll. Magd.* : see par. 141, § xii.   Cited
occasionally in *City.*

(*c*) Wood MS. E. 31 : *Life*, i. 8.

(*d*) Wood MS. *olim* F. 31 : *Life*, i. 8.

276. Vague citations by Wood of his own Collections[1].

Wood's references to his own Collections are sometimes so vague that the papers intended cannot be identified, and sometimes it cannot even be guessed whether they are extant.

(i) He refers merely to their origin :— *Collect. ex bibl. Cotton.*, *City*, ii. 275.

(ii) To their place in his study :—*Collect. sub fenestra ex bibl. C. C. C.*, *City*, ii. 399 ; a brief 'under my window,' *City*, i. 242. See *Life*, ii. 129, 133.

(iii) To their contents : 'my paper *de antiquis scolis*,' *City*, i. 157 ; and the like.

277. Miscellaneous.

(i) *Folio book of monuments* : cited in *City*, ii. 173. The folio pages giving inscriptions in various Oxford churches in Wood F. 29 A are perhaps a portion of this.

(ii) Wood's notes sent to Sir William Dugdale in view of his *Baronage of England* : Wood MS. D. 20 : *Life*, i. 146 ; ii. 336, 434.

(iii) Wood's Collection of pedigrees : Wood MS. F. 33.

(iv) Wood's chronological list of writers on English history to 1602, pp. 142 : MS. Ballard 71.

(v) Sir Christopher Wren's report on Salisbury Cathedral : Wood MS. B. 14 : *Life*, ii. 275. A better copy of this report is in MS. Aubrey 21.

(vi) Wood's transcript of Sir Thomas Browne's account of Norwich Cathedral : Wood MS. B. 14 : *Life*, iii. 9.

(vii) Henry (Hyde, second) earl of Clarendon's account of Winchester Cathedral : in Wood MS. F. 33 : *Life*, iii. 73.

(viii) Inscriptions, &c. at Winchester : Wood MS. D. 4 ; *Life*, iii. 134.

278. Wood's MSS. cited by titles.

In his papers Wood frequently cites his MSS. by titles, more or less descriptive of their contents. These can readily be found in this Catalogue by referring to the head for their subject matter : e. g. *Collect. ex libro S. Frid.* is to be looked for in par. 34 ; *Collect. e reg. Coll. Mert.*, in par. 142 ; *Notae Einsham*, in par. 17 ; *Catalogus Inceptorum*, in par. 100 ; &c. The following are some of the more frequent or more difficult of these references :—

[1] on some occasions Wood was unable afterwards to make out his own citations: see one instance in *Life*, ii. 372, 'Catalogue of pamphlets,' and note 4.

(i) *'Almanacs'* : *Life*, i. 10.

(ii) *Appendix* : e. g. (*a*) *City*, i. 81, 91, &c. ('in appendice'); (*b*) *City*, i. 128 ('appendix domuum'); (*c*) *City*, i. 226 ('Latin appendix aularum'). These refer to several collections in connexion with his City treatise : (*a*) and (*b*) e. g. to the paper printed in *City*, i. 512–529, and (*c*) to that in *City*, i. 586.

(iii) *Black book* : not identified : cited in *Life*, i. 313, 316, &c. *Book of libells MS.* : Wood MS. E. 31 : *Life*, i. 380, 440, &c.

(iv) *Catalogues* : of books, *Life*, i. 18 ; of graduates, par. 100 ; of Chancellors, par. 127 ; of Halls, par. 119 ; of names, see § vi *infra*.

Catalogus Praecentorum sc. eccles. Cathedralis Lincoln. : cited in *Life*, iii. 10, is at the end of *O. C.* 8567, Wood MS. E. 3. *Catal. Decanorum*, sc. of Worcester, cited in *Life*, iii. 67, is in *O. C.* 8587, Wood MS. B. 14 or in Wood MS. E. 3 (see *Life*, iii. 137).

(v) *Collections.*

Collect. ex libro annotat. C. : see par. 251.

Collect. Devon. : Wood MS. D. 7 (3) : *Life*, i. 182 note 5.

Collections out of Dugdale : cited in *City*, ii. 226 : perhaps now lost.

Collections from *Mercurius Aulicus* : cited in *Life*, ii. 13 : perhaps now lost.

Collections from Sir Thomas More's life : cited in *City*, ii. 283 : perhaps now lost.

Collections concerning old Clarendon : *Life*, i. 335.

Collect. ex registris : cited in *City*, ii. 402 ; perhaps Wood MS. D. 3.

(vi) *Encaenia papers* : *Life*, i. 16 ; ii. 248.

English History : par. 262 (i).

Entertainments : Wood MS. D. 19 (3) : par. 117.

(vii) *Gazette* : *Life*, i. 15.

(viii) *Index.*

Wood's 'indexes' were perhaps slips of paper on which Wood wrote down brief notes under heads for future use. Probably most of them were destroyed at Wood's death, if not before, by himself (*Life*, iii. 498).

Index pro anno . . . is cited in *City*, i. 142, 340, &c. I think that MS. Tanner 102 part 2, is a survivor of this series.

Index pro Carmelitis (*City*, i. 445); *Index pro Fratribus Minoribus* (*City*, ii. 391); *Index pro Collegio Cantuar.* (*City*, ii. 283), would be collections for chap. 31 of the City treatise ; as *Index pro temporal government* (*City*, i. 154), for chap. 33 ; and *Index pro Castello* (*City*, i. 272, &c.), for chap. 14.

Index of papers, a series of notes for the *Athenae* and *Fasti*. Cited in *Life*, iii. 19 : probably now lost.

Index to his Almanacs, *Life*, iii. 107 : MS. Tanner 430.

Index nominum. Here, I imagine, Wood took an old Oxford family-name (Kepeharme, e. g.) and wrote down under it notes about the different persons of that family. Some leaves of this kind are found in Wood MS. F. 29 A. foll. 360–363. *Index nominum* is cited in *City*, i. 125, &c., *Catalogus nominum* in *City*, ii. 209.

(ix) *Libells MS.* : 'Libells and Songs' : Wood MS. E. 31 : *Life*, ii. 44, 90, 300, &c.

(x) *News* : see *Life*, i. 14.

(xi) *Notae.*

Notae ad Godwinum : par. 273.

Notes out of Hobs' Leviathan : cited in *City*, i. 84, *Life*, ii. 472 ; in Wood MS. D. 11.

Notes from Norwich register : cited in *Life*, ii. 305 : Wood MS. E. 3 or B. 14.

Notes from Sir Henry S. George ; probably now lost, unless they be the paper noticed in *Life*, ii. 268 note 1.

Notae ad Pits : par. 275.

School Notes : par. 270.

Notes from Convocation : Convocation Notes ; Notes from registers of Convocation, &c. : MS. Bodl. 594.

Notes from Dr. Plot's book : cited in *Life*, ii. 359 : probably now lost.

Notes from Fuller's *Cambridge* : see *supra* p. 235 note.

Notes from Brook : par. 317.

(xii) *Obital book* : Wood MS. F. 4 : par. 190.

(xiii) *Oxoniensia*, almost always the papers in Wood 276 A (*Life*, i. 489 ; ii. 85, &c.) ; but occasionally the pamphlets in Wood 512, sqq. (*Life*, ii. 239), or those in Wood 423 (*Life*, iii. 322, 324).

Oxford papers : Wood 276 A : *Life*, ii. 299.

Oxfordshire monuments : Wood MS. E. 1 : *Life*, iii. 225.

(xiv) *Russet book* : 'book with russet cover' : not identified : cited in *Life*, i. 312, 313.

(xv) *Sheldrake* : not identified : cited in *Life*, i. 313 ; ii. 338, &c.

(xvi) *Solemnities* : Wood MS. D. 19 (3) : par. 117.

(xvii) *Term Catalogues* : *Life*, i. 15.

279. Wood MSS. cited by letters and symbols.

A.B. : for A. Bosco (*Life*, i. 23) : cited frequently in *City*, and occasionally in *Annals*. This is **Wood MS. D. 3**, *O. C.* 8514.

A.V. : for A. Vuood (*Life* i. 23) : cited freely in *City*. This is **Wood MS. D. 11 (1)**, *O. C.* 8517. In some cases, from the similarity of the monograms, references to this MS. may have been confused with the next.

A.W.: for A. Wood (*Life*, i. 23): cited freely in *City*. This is **Wood MS. C. 2**, *O. C.* 8516. See preceding notice.

C (with a stroke); see *infra* ₵.

Cunei **V**: see *infra*, under V.

F.: for Frideswyde's: cited *passim* in *City*. This is **Wood MS. C. 4**; *O. C.* 8526.

F. (broken); see *infra*, **ϯ**.

M.: for Merton; often cited in *City*, now lost or dispersed: see par. 269.

O.: for Oriel: cited *passim* in *City*. This is **Wood MS. C. 1**; *O. C.* 8515.

V.: perhaps for Vvood; cited on almost every page of *City*, being perhaps the most important volume of Wood's Collections. This is **Wood MS. D. 2**; *O. C.* 8513.

Cunei **V** was a volume of considerable size, being cited up to its 210th page (*City* i. 490). It is not **V** of Wood's collection, nor **Ꝧ** of Langbaine's: I am unable to identify it.

W: for [Miles] W[indsor]: cited frequently in *City*. This is MS. Ballard 69, pp. 1–85: see par. 258.

{ **A1, A2,** &c. to **Z1, Z2,** &c.
{ **A A1, A A2,** &c. to **Z Z1, Z Z2,** &c.
{ **A A A1, A A A2,** &c.

These were collections for the *Athenae*, see par. 266.

ÆB = A. B. *supra.*

Ʌ/ = A. V. *supra.*

ᴀ/ᴡ = A. W. *supra.*

⛉ = **Wood MS. D. 7 (2)**: *O. C.* 8519: being notes about authors and books, especially from the library of Ralph Sheldon. Cited *Life*, i. 431.

⛉ = **Wood MS. D. 11 (4)** + part of **Wood MS. D. 4** (*O. C.* 8518): being Wood's 'School Notes.' Cited *Life*, ii. 13.

⛉ = **Wood MS. E. 5** (*O. C.* 8520) + part of **Wood MS. E. 4**: being collections from the Heralds' office. Cited *Life*, i. 282, 385, &c.

ϯ, **ǂ**, **#**, **⚲**, **Ⴔ** are marks of *Athenae* Collections: see par. 266.

₵ (cited as 'C with a stroke,' *City* i. 77; ii. 275, &c.), contained notes of MSS. chiefly in the Cottonian library, but also in Lambeth library, and in Corpus Christi (St. Bennet's) College, Cambridge. It was a volume of moderate size, being cited up to its 52nd page. In Wood MS. E. 4, when describing MS. Cotton Domit. A. 14, Registrum chartarum abbatiae de Hida, Wood notes that he found there no notice of the University being without North Gate, and writes in the margin 'No; so I say in ₵ 32'; and again, speaking of the Cottonian cartulary of Abingdon, he says 'in my Cat. of MSS. in bibl. Cotton extracted from the Cat. of MSS. which is in bibl. Cotton in folio,' and gives the reference ' ₵ quaere': so that these places suggest that ₵ was of his composing. On the other hand, Wood never visited C. C. C. Cambr.—I have found no trace of it. It is cited constantly in the Catalogue of MSS., Wood MS. E. 4 (*O. C.* 8561).

⊤ (cited as 'F (broken)' in *City*, i. 58, ii. 161, &c) was a volume of considerable size, being cited up to its 174th page. In Wood MS. E. 4, p. 147 is this expression: 'see also of Neot in my collections thence ⟨i. e. from the MS. he is there speaking of⟩, ⊤ 25, 26': from which ⊤ would appear to be collections by Wood himself.

♡ cited in *City*, ii. 150, contained excerpts from Dugdale's Monasticon. I cannot say whether it was by Wood or not.

280. Table of press-marks of Wood's MSS. and MS. notes.

I give here a table of the present press-marks of those MS. papers of Wood's writing or collecting, which are mentioned in this work, adding (where there is any) the running-number in the 1697 Catalogue, which alone gives a fixed notation in the Euripus of changing press-marks and the Chaos Regained which has resulted from jumbling one MS. into another. Also, in the case of the more important MSS. only, the nature of the contents is indicated. The smaller volumes, 12mo and 8vo size, are in the B and C sets; the 4to volumes, in the D and E sets; and the folios in the F set. In each case the paragraphs in the present Catalogue in which the MSS. are referred to, or the pages in the *Life*, are given.

Wood	*O. C.*
B 1	8572 : par. 19.
B 2	8573 : *Life*, i. 182.
B 3	8574 : *Life*, i. 426.
B 4	8575 : *Life*, ii. 321 ; iii. 295.
B 5	8576 : *Life*, i. 199.
B 6	8577 : par. 83.
B 7 .	8578 : par. 161, 464 (ii).
B 8	8579 : *Life*, i. 182 : iii. 102.
B 9 .	8580 : *Life*, iii. 102.
B 10 .	8581 : *Life*, iii. 102.
B 11 .	8582 : par. 254 (iv).

Wood   O. C.

B 12 . 8583: par. 270, 367, 390.

B 13 . 8584: par. 161, 166, 169.

B 14 . { 8585: par. 161, 277,—notes from Heralds' Office.
        { 8587: par. 61, 122, 128, 266, 277, 278 (xi), 464 (ii).

B 15   8586: par. 271—Oxfordshire Collections.

C 1   8515:   par. 39, 77, 144—Collections from Oriel muniments.

C 2 . 8516: par. 17, 33 (vii), 34 (v)—S. Frideswyde's Collections.

C 3   8525: par. 81, 82, 170.

C 4 . 8526: par. 34 (vi)—S. Frideswyde's Collections.

C 5 . 8527: par. 216, 237–239, 264.

C 6   8539: *Life*, i. 182.

C 7 . 8541: par. 134 (xi).

C 8   8542: par. 134 (xi).

C 9   8549: *Life*, i. 182.

C 10   8550: par. 271, 464 (ii).

C 11 . 8551: par. 464 (ii).

C 12 . 8571: par. 259.

C 53 . *Life*, i. 7.

D 1 . 8512: par. 102.

D 2 . 8513:   par. 33, 34, 40, 44, 66–78, 131–150, 457 (i). Collections from College muniments.

D 3   8514:   par. 75, 99, 110, 143—Collections from University registers.

D 4   8518[1] (part 2): par. 190, 266, 270, 272, 277.

D 5 . 8524:   par. 66–79—Collections from Oxford parish registers.

D 6 . 8528: par. 268, 464 (i).

D 7 (1)   8529: par. 119.

D 7 (2)   8519: 266 (ii), 464 (i)—Collections about Oxford writers.

D 7 (3)   8521: par. 278 (v).

D 7 (4)   8522: par. 271.

D 7 (5)   8523: par. 188.

D 8 . 8538: par. 31.

D 9 . 8540: par. 201, 443 (ii).

D 10 . 8546: par. 205.

D 11 (1)   8517 (part 1): par. 3 (iv and viii), 20, 33 (x), 40, 51.

D 11 (2)   8517 (part 2): par. 17.

D 11 (3)   8517 (part 3): par. 272; *Life*, ii. 352, 404–414.

---

[1] and fractions of other volumes.

Wood	*O. C.*
D 11 (4)	8518[1] : par 121 (vii), 123, 166, 270.
D 12 .	8544 : *Life*, ii. 505.
D 13 .	8545 : par. 270, 358.
D 14	{ 8547. 8548 : par. 271.
D 15	8522 : par. 464 (ii).
D 16 .	8555 : *Life*, i. 24.
D 17	8566.
D 18[2]	8537[2] : par. 217–221, 232, 233, 236–239, 259 (iv), 268, 464 (i). 8557. 8559 : par. 130 (iv). 8563 : par. 6, 11, 19, 31, 33 (vii), 46, 83, 130 (ix), 141*, 185, 195, 205, 489 (ii).
D 19 (1)	8564 : par. 190, 271.
D 19 (2)	8565 : par. 130 (viii) : *Life*, i. 437, ii. 180, 436, iii. 313.
D 19 (3)	8566 : par. 117, 259.
D 19 (4)	8568 : par. 267.
D 20 .	par. 277.
D 21 A	8569 : par. 254 (xii), 266 (iii), 273.
D 21 B :	par. 273.
D 32 :	par. 14 (i), 36, 38, 84, 96 (x), 98, 107, 113, 119, 121, 128, 254, 308, 411, 414, 432—Collections by Twyne.
E 1 .	8505 : par. 271—Oxfordshire Collections.
E 2	8531 : par. 268. 8532 : par. 268. 8533 : par. 268. 8534 : par. 268.
E 3	{ 8567 : par. 55, 60, 64, 65, 81, 152 (xv and xxi), 266, 278 (iv and xi). 8570 : par. 268 (iii).
E 4	8535 : par. 268 (i). 8536 : par. 268 (i). 8554 : *Life*, ii. 545. 8560 : par. 266 (ii), 379 (v), 390. 8561 : par. 1, 127, 268 (iv)—Catalogue of MSS. used in *Hist. et Antiq.*
E 5	{ 8511 : par. 100, 102, 121 (viii), 127. 8520 : par. 161.

---

[1] part of *O. C.* 8518 with parts of other volumes.

[2] and parts of other volumes.

Wood			*O. C.*
E 6 .			8506 : par. 100.
E 7 .			8508 : par. 100.
E 8 .			8509 : par. 100.
E 9 .			8510 : par. 100.
E 10		.	8530 : par. 268.
E 11			
E 12	.	.	8553 : *Life*, iii. 104.

E 20—E 23 : par. 268.
E 28 : par. 268.

| E 29 | . | . | 8507 : par. 100. |

E 30 : *Life*, i. 8.
E 31 : par. 259—the missing volume of Oxford satires (verse).
E 32 : par. 259—the book of Oxford jests.
E 33 : par. 72.

F 1, 2			8463, 8464 : par. 262—the treatise on the University and Colleges.
F 3 .			8465 : par. 464 (ii) : *Life*, iii. 106.
F 4 .	.		8466 : par. 190, 259.
F 5 .	.	.	8467 : *Life*, iii. 102.
F 6 .	.	.	8468 : *Life*, iii. 102.
F 7	.		8469 : par. 266, 464 (i).
F 8 .	.		8470 : par. 304.
F 9 .	.	.	8471 : par. 306.
F 10 (with F 15)			8472 : par. 33 (v).
F 11	.	.	8473 : par. 81.
F 12 (with F 21)			8474 : par. 41, 271.
F 13	.	..	8475 : par. 100.
F 14	.		8476 : par. 100.
F 15	.	.	8477 : par. 33 (vi).
F 16	.	.	8478 : par. 41.
F 17 (with F 21)			8479.
F 18 (with F 11)			8480 : *Life*, iii. 102.
F 19 (with F 21)			8481.
F 20 (with F 21)			8482.
F 21	.	.	8483 : par. 364.
F 22		.	8484[1] : *Life*, i. 351 ; ii. 54, 59, 179, 436, 533, 534.
F 23 (with F 21)			8485 : *Life*, ii. 118.
F 24 (with F 21)			8486.
F 25	.	.	8487 : par. 349.

[1] other papers are put instead of the lost treatise.

Wood	*O. C.*
F 26 .	8488 : par. 188, 197, 254 (xi).
F 27	8489 : par. 130, 153, 190, 195, 234, 258 : *Life*, i. 310.
F 28 .	8490 : par. 39, 79, 81, 119, 131–151—Collections about the Colleges.
F 29 A	8491 : par. 80, 119, 218, 254 (x), 263, 277 : the treatise on the City.
F 29 B, F 29 C *Life*, i. 8.	
F 30 (with F 32)	8492 : par. 139, 205, 266, 373 (viii), 466.
olim F 31 . .	8493 : missing : par. 130 (xv), 207 : *Life*, ii. 53.
F 31[1] [*Life*, i. 8] : par. 36, 41, 80, 102, 126, 130, 139, 142, 143 (xi), 190, 259, 263, 269, 271, 478.	
F 32 . .	8494 : par. 51, 170, 272.
F 33 .	8495 : par. 190, 271, 277 (iii et vii), 464 (ii) : *Life*, i. 209.
F 34 (with F 32)	8496 : *Life*, i. 243 ; ii. 165.
F 35 . .	8497 : par. 116, 433 : *Life*, i. 142.
F 36 (with F 22)	8498 : par. 266.
F 37 (with F 22)	8499 : par. 262.
olim F 38 . .	8500, *nunc* Wood 430.
olim F 39 . .	8501, *nunc* Wood 431.
olim F 40 [*nunc* in F 26] 8502 : par. 188, 254 (v).	
olim F 41 [*nunc* in F 26] 8503 : par. 254 (vi).	
olim F 42 [*nunc* in F 26] 8504 : par. 254 (vii).	
F 38 : par. 262.	
F 39 : par. 196, 198 (x), 260, 261.	
F 40 : par. 198 (x), 260, 261.	
F 41 : par. 260, 261.	
F 42 : par. 260, 261, 266.	
F 43 : par. 260, 261, 266.	
F 44 : par. 260, 261, 266.	
F 45 : par. 260, 261, 266.	
F 46 : par. 196, 260, 266.	
F 47 : par. 196, 266.	
F 48 : par. 196, 266.	
F 49 : par. 196, 260.	
F 50 : par. 196, 260.	
F 51 : par. 260 : *Life*, i. 9.	

---

[1] a composite volume, recently made up of fragments of other MSS. : *Life*, i. 291.

Wood Almanacs with interleaved diary, 39 vols.: par. 259.

Wood MS. 127: *O. C.* 8589: *Life*, i. 77.

Wood 16: par. 144 (viii): *Life*, i. 249.
Wood 276 A.: par. 278 (xiii).
Wood 276 B.: par. 143 (xiii): *Life*, i. 450; ii. 148.
Wood 276 C.: *Life*, i. 469.
Wood 365 (12): *Life*, i. 184.
Wood 418: *Life*, i. 146.
Wood 419: *Life*, ii. 7, 16, 345.
Wood 430: par. 262.
Wood 431: par. 265.
Wood 436: *Life* i. 182.
Wood 460: *Life*, i. 426.
Wood 602: par. 212, 256.
Wood 614 (7): par. 273.

MS. Wood donat. 1–9: (*O. C.* 8614–8622): par. 212.

	O. C.
MS. empt. ab Wood 1	8589: par. 18.
2	8590: *Life*, ii. 486; iii. 343.
3	8591.
4	8592: par. 84 (*k*).
5	8593: par. 31.
6	8594.
7	8595.
8	8596: *Life*, iii. 343.
9	8597.
10	8598: par. 47.
11	8599: par. 84 (*i*).
11*	8599: par. 84 (*i*).
12	8600: *Life*, iii. 343.
13	8601: *Life*, iii. 343.
14	8602: par. 83.
15	8603: *Life*, iii. 343.
16	8604.
17	8605.
18	8606.
19	8607: *Life*, iii. 343.
20	8608.

O. C.

MS. empt. ab Wood 21 8609 : par. 83.

22 8610.

23 8611 : par. 83.

24 8612.

25 8613.

MS. Ashm. 1131 : par. 261.

MS. Aubrey 9 : *Life*, ii. 291.

MS. Aubrey 13 : par. 198 (x and xi), 261.

MS. Ballard 9 : par. 260, 261.

11 : par. 260.

14 : par. 198 (x), 260, 261.

15 : par. 261.

17 : par. 260.

21 : par. 260.

27 : par. 260.

34 : par. 260.

46 : par. 43, 141*, 142, 260, 269.

46* : par. 142 (ix).

68 : *O. C.* 8558 : par. 254 (ix).

69 : par. 258, 279.

70 : par. 34 (x), 36, 38, 115, 317, 331, 404 (iii), 411, 457 (v).

71 : par. 277.

MS. Bodl. 594 : *O. C.* 8562 : par. 8, 33 (iii and xi), 54, 81, 96 (i and ix), 99 (iv and xiii–xvi and xxiii–xxv), 107, 110, 142, 242, 249, 254, 259, 269, 294 (xvi)— a mass of notes by Wood, including excerpts from Convocation Registers.

MS. Harl. 5409 : par. 259.

MS. Jes. Coll. 30 : par. 254 (iii).

31 : *Life*, i. 430 note 2.

32 : *Life*, i. 23, 430 note 2.

88 : par. 43.

MS. Phillipps 7018 : par. 259.

MS. Rawl.[1] B 8 : *Life*, i. 209.

B 402 a : par. 72.

C 910. *O. C.* 8473 : par. 81, 102.

---

[1] note that Mr. Macray in the Rawlinson Catalogues occasionally errs in ascribing papers to 'Wood's hand,' which are not :—e.g. Rawl. D. 317, fol. 177 ('list of carriers to Oxford'), fol. 201 ('payments to the marshall of the beggars').

MS. Rawl. D 742 : par. 260.

D 807 : *Life*, i. 350, 477.

D 857 : par. 161.

D 1268 : par. 33 (xxi), 195, 264.

D *olim* 1290[1] *nunc* 912 : par. 121 (viii), 142 (xiii), 190, 207, 266 (iii).

Rawl. Letters : par. 261.

Rawl. Letters 17 : par. 143 (xii).

8vo Rawl. 662 : par. 97, 107.

MS. Sancroft 135 : *Life*, iii. 159.

MS. Thomas Smith 66 : par. 260.

MS. Tanner 24 : par. 261.

102 part i : par. 259.

102 part ii : par. 259.

290 : par. 259.

306 : par. 259.

338 : *Life*, ii. 40, 310 : par. 141 (xiv), 259.

416 : *O. C.* 8567 : par. 55, 60, 64, 65, 266.

436 : par. 142 (xiii).

438 : par. 264.

454 : par. 66, 76, 147, 196, 254 (xiii), 266 (iii).

456 : par. 69, 73–79, 132, 198 (x), 259, 260, 261, 264, 269.

456* : par. 142 (xi), 264.

465 : par. 259.

VI. AUTHORS.

281. Abbo, Floriacensis.

De vita et passione S. Edmundi regis : cited in Twyne XXII. 573–576, from a MS. in Thomas Allen's library.   Probably MS. Digb. 109 (*O. C.* 1710), of which MS. Fairfax 12 seems to contain a portion.

Cited in *Annals*, i. 120.

282. Ailredus, Rievallensis abbas.

(i) *Vita S. Edwardi regis et confessoris* : MS. Laud. Misc. 668 (*O. C.* 1052) : MS. Digb. 59 (*O. C.* 1660) : MS. Cotton Vitell. C. 12. —Printed in Twysden's Decem Scriptores.   Wood's excerpts from it are in MS. Bodl. 594.

(ii) *Genealogia regum Angliae* : MS. Digb. 19 ; MS. Cotton Cleop. B. 3.   Printed (partly) in Twysden's Decem Scriptores.

Cited in *Annals*, i. 42.

---

[1] a most important MS., cited *passim* in *Life*: no. 13678 in Mr. Madan's Summary Catalogue.

Portions of this treatise are mentioned by Wood under separate titles :—

(*a*) History of David, King of Scots : MS. Cotton, Vespas. B. XI foll. 106–112ᵛ : MS. Laud. Misc. 1052.

Cited in MS. Ric. James 22, p. 113, from a MS. in Magd. Coll.

(*b*) History of England to the time of Henry II : MS. Cotton Cleop. B 3, Julius A 11.

Cited in *Annals*, i. 40.

(*c*) De regibus Aluredo, Edwardo, Ethelstano, . . . sibi invicem succedentibus : MS. Laud. Misc. 668.

283. Albericus, Philippus—see Twyne XXII. 403.

Wood found a MS. volume of his Collections among Thomas Barlow's MSS. This contained a treatise [Aubrey Mantuan's] *de casu animae*, cited in *Colleges*, p. 387.

284. Albertus—see Twyne XXI. 23, 202, 218.

285. Alfredus, rex.

(i) Translatio Historiae . . . Bedae : MS. Cambridge University Library Kk. iii. 18.

Printed by Abraham Wheloc in 1643.

(ii) Translation of Paulus Orosius' History of the World : MS. Bodl. 180 (*O. C.* 2079).

(iii) Translation of Boetius' *de consolatione Philosophiae* : MS. Junius 12 (*O. C.* 5124).

(iv) *Praefatio in pastorale Gregorii papae.* MS. Hatton 20 (*O. C.* 4113). Excerpts from it in MS. Ric. James 10, p. 181. Printed by Matthew Parker in 1574 : reprinted Lugd. Bat. 1597.

(v) In MS. Ric. James 6, pp. 68, 69, a 'Liber Alfredi' is cited as among Thomas Allen's MSS. : probably now in the Cottonian library.

(vi) ' *Decreta judiciorum,* idiomate Saxonico scripta, qui liber ad nos injuria temporum non pervenit ' : so William Lambard in preface to his *Archaionomia* (1568).

Cited in *Hist.* i. 15.

(vii) Wood in MS. E. 4 (*O. C.* 8561), p. 7 gives (from Twyne XXI. 240, 267, Twyne XXIV. 340) 'King Alfred's arms ' i. e. 'azure, a cross couped or.'

286. Robertus Anglicus : cited in *City*, i. 54.

(i) *Commentarii in sphaeram Johannis de Sacro Bosco* (*O. C.* 1649) MS. Digb. 48. Twyne II. 95, 96 ; Twyne XXI. 144.

(ii) Translation into Latin from Arabic of Alkindus 'de judiciis ';
MS. Digb. 91 (*O. C.* 1692).   The MS. is largely in Thomas Allen's
handwriting.

287.   Aristoteles.

Secretum secretorum ad Alexandrum magnum : MS. Digb. 228 (*O. C.*
1829): possibly the same as a MS. formerly in the hands of Dr.
John Dee.   See Twyne XXI. 23 ; XXII. 431 sqq.

Perhaps cited in *Annals,* i. 40.

288.   Richard (Fitzralph), Armachanus.

Sermo . . . archiepiscopi Armachani, Avinionae Nov. 8, 1397 : MS.
Bodl. 144 (*O. C.* 1914): MS. Bodl. 158 (*O. C.* 1997): MS. Bodl. 865
(*O. C.* 2737).   Twyne's excerpts in Wood MS. D. 32, p. 207 ; Ric.
James' in MS. Ric. James 21, p. 64.

Cited several times in *Annals, City* ; under title ' de mendicitate (*or*
paupertate) Christi.'

289.   Thomas Arundel.

Provincial Constitutions : MS. Cotton Vitell. A. 1.
Cited in *Colleges,* p. 652.

290.   John Ashendon, or Eschendon, or Escuidus.

Prognosticationes pro annis 1345, 1349, 1357, et 1365 : MS. Digb.
176 (*O. C.* 1777).   Twyne's excerpts are in MS. arch. Seld. supra 79
(*O. C.* 3467), pp. 91–131, Twyne XXII. 235, 236.

Cited in *Annals,* i. 450, 479, 491.

291.   William Asketell.

Cited in *Annals,* i. 27 : but only from Leland.

292.   Asser, Menevensis.

(i) *de vita regis Alfredi.*

(*a*) the copy cited by Leland (tom. 4, pp. 111, 112), which mentions
Oxon : see Twyne XVIII. p. 325.

(*b*) MS. Cotton Otho A. 12 ; formerly in lord Lumley's library :
see Twyne II. 75, III. 226, 254. ' This Asser mentions nothing of
Oxon.'   This was ' the same that Matthew Parker published, Lond.
1573 : vide Usserius *de primordiis eccles. Britan.* p. 342.'

(*c*) William Camden's edition, Frankfort 1603, containing the Oxford
passage.   See par. 207 (iv).   A letter by Twyne to Camden about
this edition is found in MS. Cotton Julius C. 5, dated Feb. 24, 162⅖ :
see also, in Twyne XXII. 385–387, a note of a conversation with
Camden about it, Feb. 18, 162⅘ (printed in *Annals,* i. 22–24).

(ii) *The Annals of Asser Menevensis*, 596–914 A. D., transcribed by John Joscelin (from MS. Trin. Coll. Cambr. R. 7. 28) : MS. Cotton Vitell. foll. 154–175. 'Not a word of Oxford in it.'

Printed by Thomas Gale (from the Cambr. MS.) 1691.

293. John Bacon *vel* Baconthorpe.

Speculum ordinis fratrum beatae Mariae de Monte Carmeli : MS. Laud. Misc. 722 (*O. C.* 1174), fol. 118.   Twyne XXI. 710.

294. Roger Bacon.

See Twyne XXI. 203, 207, 208, 219 : MS. Langb. 4, p. 540, MS. Langb. 7, pp. 381, 389. Wood MS. E. 4 (*O. C.* 8561), p. 25, mentions a 'Catalogue of the MSS. of Bacon' which he received 'from Mr. ⟨? Obadiah⟩ Walker'; this I have not found among his papers. He notices also there, and in *Annals*, i. 343, the difficulties found in drawing up a list of Bacon's works, especially from the fact that 'some bear several titles.' Thomas Allen's list of titles of Bacon's works among the MSS. owned by him is found in MS. Langb. 7, p. 393.—See Little's *Grey Friars in Oxford* (O. H. S., 1892), pp. 195–210. I give here only a classified statement of Wood's notes on Bacon's works as found in Wood MS. E. 4 (*O. C.* 8561), pp. 25–30; it is abundantly plain that Wood was in a great fog about them, and had not worked through the MSS. himself.

(i) *Computus naturalium* : init. 'Omnia tempus habent et suis spatiis transeunt' : cited by Twyne in MS. arch. Seld. supra 79, p. 150 ; probably from MS. no. 48 in Coxe's Cat. of Univ. Coll. MSS.

(ii) *In meteora* : MS. Digb. 190 (*O. C.* 1791).

(iii) **Opus Majus** : Twyne XXIV. 37, 38.

Praeambulum ad opus majus et minus in fine summae sive operis, Twyne XXIV. 25, 33–36, 39 : collections thence Twyne XXI. 96, 106.

Cited in *Annals*, i. 334.

(A) *Pars prima Operis Majoris* : init. 'Sapientiae perfecta consideratio consistit in duobus' : MS. Digb. 235 : Twyne II. 157 a, XXI. 96, 106.

With this Wood identified MS. Cotton Julius D. 5, p. 15, *De utilitate Scientiarum* ad Clementem papam, ubi agit de quattuor veritatis offendiculis : Twyne XXIV. 18–25.

Cited in *Annals*, i. 286, 334, 335, &c.

(B) *Pars secunda Operis Majoris* : init. 'Relegatis igitur 4 causis totius humani erroris' : MS. Cotton Julius D. 5, p. 136 : Twyne II. 157 a.

(C) *Pars tertia Operis Majoris*: init. 'Declarato igitur quod una est sapientia perfecta quae sacris literis continetur' MS. Cotton Julius D. 5, p. 149; called 'opus tertium' in Twyne XXIV. 25, 'tertia pars' in Twyne XXIV. 37, 38.

Cited in *Annals*, i. 200, 335.

(D) *Pars quarta Operis Majoris*: init. 'Manifesto quod multae praeclarae radices sapientiae dependent ex potestate linguarum': Twyne II. 157 a, XXIV. 14.

Wood notes that the fourth part in MS. Cotton Julius D. 5 is 'far different from' the fourth part in MS. Digb. 235.

This 'Pars quarta' is found also in MS. e Mus. 155 (*O. C.* 3705), p. 185.

To this part belong several treatises cited separately by Wood:—

(*a*) Excerpts from Bacon, partly *ex libro de Scientia*: MS. Cotton Julius F. 7, fol. 175–200.

(*b*) *De mathematicis*: MS. Cotton Tiber. C. 5: Twyne XXII. 435. Cited in *Annals*, i. 200.

(*c*) *De potestate mathematicae in scientiis* MS. Cotton Tiber. C. 5, foll. 49–119: MS. e Mus. 155: Twyne XXIV. 14.

(*d*) *De laudibus mathematices*: MS. Digb. 218 (*O. C.* 1819): Twyne in MS. arch. Seld. supra 79, p. 6.

(*e*) *De commendatione Aristotelis mathematicae*: MS. Lambeth V. 7, (*nunc* MS. Lamb. 200, art. 1).

(E) *Pars quinta Operis Majoris*: init. 'Praepositis radicibus sapientiae tam divinae quam humanae,' &c.

To this part belongs the treatise cited separately by Wood:—

De perspectivis: MSS. Digb. 77 and 91 (*O. C.* 1678 and 1692): MS. Bodl. 874 (*O. C.* 2932): Twyne XXI. 113, 208.

Cited in *Annals*, i. 290.

(iv) **Opus Minus.**

Cited frequently in *Annals*, but only from excerpts in Twyne. Wood notes, from Twyne, that it was addressed to pope Clement IV, and that the *incipit* of the work was 'Quattuor sunt consideranda circa sapientiam': Twyne XXIV. 13, 14, 26–33, 207. Twyne seems generally to cite a Cottonian MS. but in MS. arch. Seld. supra 79, p. 90, he cites a MS. of the Opus Minus 'formerly belonging to John Dee.' According to J. S. Brewer the one MS. of the Opus Minus is MS. Digb. 218.

The *Preamble to the Opus Majus et Minus*, init. 'Sanctissimo patri, domino Clementi, summo pontifici,' is often cited, e. g. by Twyne in

Twyne XXIV. 25, 33, 39, and in MS. arch. Seld. supra 79, pp. 168–170: and by Richard James in MS. Ric. James 2, part 2, pp. 120–130 (from MS. Arch. A. 68, i. e. MS. Bodl. 211=*O. C.* 2927).

Cited, I suppose, as 'Letter to Clement IV prefixed to the Opus Minus' in Twyne XXI. 218, and in *Annals*, i. 284; and as 'Letter of Bacon in the Opus Minus' in Twyne XXI. 146.

The *Epilogue to the Opus Minus* is cited in Twyne XXIV. 30.

Two treatises separately cited seem to be parts of this Opus minus :—

(*a*) *De erratis theologorum*, MS. no. 43 in Thomas Allen's library (see *O. C.* 8488, Wood MS. F. 26, p. 4), the subsequent history of which Wood was unable to trace: probably identical with *Tractatus de peccatis theologorum sui temporis*, cited in Twyne XXIV. 38, from (Wood assumed) a Cottonian MS.

Cited in *Annals*, i. 210, *Hist.* ii. 61.

(*b*) *De rerum generationibus*, cited in Twyne XXIV. 39, from a Cottonian MS.

(v) **Opus Tertium** : sive Summa ad Clementem IV, papam, in quo tanguntur omnes radices sapientiae : MS. Cotton Tiber. C. 5, foll. 1–48 : Twyne XXIV. 25, 37, 38. Wood is in a mist about this, identifying it now with the Pars tertia Operis Majoris and now with the Opus Minus. Another MS. of the Opus tertium is MS. e Mus. 155 : and a transcript of this is MS. no. 49 in Coxe's Cat. of Univ. Coll. MSS.

Cited in *Annals*, i. 286, *Coll.* p. 39.

(vi) *De speculis comburentibus* : MS. Cotton Tiber. B. 5 : Twyne XXI. 202.

(vii) **Compendium Philosophiae** : Brewer's Baconi Opera Inedita, pp. xlix–liv, Little's Grey Friars, p. 202.

Of this treatise three portions are found mentioned in Wood's notes :—

(*a*) *Compendium studii philosophiae* ⟨Wood writes 'theologiae'⟩ in quo ostenditur quid impediat sapientiam et quid promoveat ad eandem: MS. Cotton Tiber. C. 5, foll. 120–155 : Twyne XXII. 228.

(*b*) *Grammatica Graeca* : cited in MS. Ric. James 26, p. 156, as being ' propria Rogeri Baconi manu scripta : in C. C. C. Oxon library :[1] quondam apud Brianum Twynum' : see also Twyne XXI. 649.

---

[1] no. 148 in Coxe's Cat. of MSS. of C. C. C. Oxford.

A transcript of the treatise is MS. no. 47 in Coxe's Cat. of Univ. Coll. MSS.

(*c*) *Communia Naturalium* : init. 'Postquam tradidi grammaticam secundum linguas diversas' : MS. Digb. 70 (*O. C.* 1671): Twyne in Twyne XXI. 218, XXIV. 15–17, and in MS. arch. Seld. supra 79, pp. 165–167. Wood seems to speak also of a copy among the Cottonian MSS.

Cited in *Annals*, i. 284.

(viii) **Compendium studii theologiae.**

Cited by Twyne XXII. 228 from a MS. in Thomas Allen's library, and in Twyne XXII. 233, from MS. Bodl. C. 4 : 'Quarta pars' of it is cited by Twyne in MS. arch. Seld. supra 79, pp. 42–75. and 78–86. The MS. of this was in the possession of Dr. John Prideaux and is now MS. Reg. F. 7 : there was accessible to Twyne and Wood a transcript of it in MS. no. 47 in Coxe's Cat. of Univ. Coll. MSS.

Cited in *Annals*, i. 196, 200, 241.

(ix) *Breve Breviarium* : init. 'Breve breviarium breviter abbreviatum sufficit' : MS. Digb. 119 (*O. C.* 1720) and in MS. e Mus. 155.   This treatise is also attributed to Johannes de Sacro Bosco : MS. Langb. 5, p. 266.

Cited in *Annals*, i. 338.

(x) *Epistolae*, and miscellaneous tracts : MS. Cotton Julius D. 5, foll. 150–165.

(xi) *De retardanda senectute* : MS. no. 31 in Thomas Allen's library : cp. MS. e Mus. 155, pp. 591–637.

(xii) *Glossae in 'Secretum Secretorum' Aristotelis* : MS. no. 149 in Coxe's Cat. of MSS. of C. C. C. Oxford.   Cited, apparently from a MS. in C. C. C. library, by Richard James in MS. Ric. James 11, p. 248 : by Twyne, in Twyne XXI. 12, XXII. 431 ; by Langbaine, in MS. Langb. 15, p. 281, and in MS. Wood donat. 7, p. 80.   See *Life*, ii. 199.

Cited in *Annals*, i. 39.

(xiii) *Calendarium* : MS. Cotton Vespas. A. 2, foll. 2–10.

(xiv) *De anima et operibus ejus* : init. ' de anima secundum se ipsum in praecedentibus dictum est ' : 'in MS. Cotton in his book that hath the four parts of the Opus Majus' ⟨ ? MS. Cotton Julius D. 5, see § iii, *supra*⟩ : Twyne II. 157 a.

(xv) *De impedimentis scientiae* : MS. Cotton Galba A. 8, num. 1 : MS. Ric. James 10, p. 44, Twyne III. 246.

(xvi) Wood had Collections from Bacon, which he cites in *City*, ii. 194: now in MS. Bodl. 594 (*O. C.* 8562). He also refers to his 'Collections from Roger Bacon ex libro C. ⟨see par. 251⟩ in bibl. C. C. C,' but these I have not found.

295. Geoffrey Baker: see *City*, ii. 225.

Chronicon: MS. Bodl. 761: excerpts in MS. Ric. James 19, p. 100. Referred to in *Annals*, i. 267.

296. John Bale: see Twyne XXI. 302, 379: Wood MS. E. 4, (*O. C.* 8561), pp. 32, 33.

(i) *Collectiones*: MS. Cotton Titus D. 10: Bale's autograph.
Cited in *Annals*, i. 542: *City*, ii. 415.
(ii) *De scriptoribus Angliae*: MS. arch. Seld. supra 64 (*O. C.* 3452). Edited by Dr. R. L. Poole in the Clarendon Press *Anecdota* series.
(iii) *Catalogus discipulorum Wiclevi*: MS. e Mus. 86 (*O. C.* 3629) fol. 54^v: Bale's autograph.
Cited in *Annals*, i. 491.
(iv) *Catalogus Scriptorum*: MS. Cotton Vitell. D. 4. num. 9: *Catalogus Scriptorum pro vera religione*, ibid. num. 1 et 2.

297. John Barton, 'medicus.'

Novum symbolum contra . . . . . *Lollardos*: MS. Bodl. 117 (*O. C.* 1979). See Twyne II. 235^v; MS. Ric. James 21, p. 67.

298. Robert Baston, 'Carmelita': *City*, ii. 437.

Rythmus de guerra Scotiae, et de aliis: MS. Cotton Titus A. 20, fol. 68; Claud. D. 5, fol. 182. See Hardy's Descriptive Catalogue, iii. 366.

299. Beda.

(i) *Historia ecclesiastica gentis Anglorum.*
Cited in *City*, *Hist.*: but from a printed copy.
See § iv *infra*. There are numerous MSS. in the Bodleian: MS. Ric. James 11, pp. 194–202, notices one which contains more than the printed text, MS. Th. B. 11. 9 (MS. Bodl. 712=*O. C.* 2519), foll. 1–88.
(ii) *Chronica de adventu Anglorum* in Britanniam secundum Bedam, A.D. 449–1066.
MS. Bodl. 712 (*O. C.* 2619): see Twyne XXI. 135, 188, 190, 532, 582.

Cited in *Annals, City*, as 'Chronicon[1] (*or* MS.) quod falso inscribitur Bedae.'

Chronicon de adventu Normannorum in Angliam, A.D. 1066– 269: ibid.

Cited as 'Continuator Bedae' frequently in *Annals, City.* See Hardy's Descriptive Catalogue, iii. 174.

(iii) *Glossarium Saxonicum Bedae*, repertum Oxoniae 1572 ; MS. Cotton Vitell. C. 9.

Cited in *Annals*, i. 10.

Wood notes that it was 'made use of' by Abraham Wheloc 'when he published' Cambr. 1643, 'his Calvinisticall notes on Bede (simple notes, rather) to derogate from his work': Wood MS. E. 4 (*O. C.* 8561) p. 35.

(iv) Twyne, in Twyne III. 179–185, gives an *Epilogium de vita eximii doctoris Bedae*, which he found at the end of a MS. of Bede's Hist. Eccles., the oldest MS. of that work which Twyne ever saw. The MS. belonged to James Ussher[2], archbishop of Armagh, who lent it to Twyne in 1640[3] 'when the archbishop was at Oxford all the long vacation.'

(v) Twyne XXI. 24 has excerpts 'ex libro antiquo de nativitate et conversatione Bedae apud Dunelm.'

(vi) 'Bede's' verses *de horis, momentis, &c.* incip.

'Addita lux luci cum quarta parte diei,'

are cited by Twyne in MS. arch. Seld. supra 79, p. 186, and in Twyne XXIV. 80–83, probably from MS. Digb. 88 foll. 84–88.

(vii) *Vita et mors Bedae*, per anonymum: MS. sometimes in Thomas Allen's library.

Cited in *Colleges*, p. 61.

Probably MS. Digb. 59 (*O. C.* 1660).

300. Beleth.

(i) Collectanea ex libro Beleth : MS. Bodl. 57 (*O. C.* 2004).

(ii) Speculum ecclesiae ex Beleth, et aliis collectum : MS. Cotton Tiber. B. 13. Cp. MS. Bodl. 196 (*O. C.* 1897).

---

[1] incipit : 'Ut sciatur origo causae quare Willelmus bastard,' &c.

[2] MS. Laud Misc. 243 (*O. C.* 1301), a twelfth century MS. of Bede's *Hist. Eccl.*, formerly Ussher's, answers this description.

[3] Twyne III. 511 notices another MS. which he then saw : 'A MS. booke or transcript of a late hand in folio, bound in yellow leather, to which there is this note *e MS. bibl. Thuani no.* 91 : which coppie I borrowed of my Lord Primate of Ireland when he was here in Oxon in the longe vacation 1640—the title of the first treatise there is this "incipit de poenitentiali Theodori." Of another treatise he notes that it was 'transcribed *e MS. bibl. Thuani no.* 43 in folio anno 1637.'

(iii) MS. rapsodicus ex libro Beleth, penes quondam Henricum Jackson, socium C. C. C. Oxon: Twyne XXI. 280.

(iv) Wood notes a John Bileth in Pits (see no. 76 in Coxe's Cat. of Oriel MSS.); a Michael Belet, tempore regis Johannis, Twyne IV. 259[v], 270[v]; and a Michael Belet, founder of Wroxton priory, in Dugdale's Monasticon: Wood MS. E. 4 (*O. C.* 8561), p. 37.

301. Johannes Belluacensis.

No. 178 in Coxe's Cat. MSS. Coll. S. Joh. Oxon., fol. 362.

302. Sir Peter Besill: *City*, ii. 323, 340.

Testamentum: Twyne XXII. 372.

303. Michael Blancpaine, or Cornubiensis.

(i) *Poems and epistles in verse*: initium prologi 'solus et sapientia desudant in certamine,' init. carminum 'Intravit clausam quicunque paludibus urbem': MS. Cotton Vespas. D. 5.   Twyne's excerpts are in Twyne XXI. 289, 747–749; Richard James', in MS. Ric. James 10, p. 175.

Cited several times in *Annals*, e.g. i. 72, ii. 16.

(ii) *Tractatus metricus contra magistrum Henricum Abryncensem*: MS. Cotton Titus A. 20.   Noticed by Twyne in Twyne XXI. 5, 289.

Cited in *Annals*, i. 52, 207.

304. Robert Blofield.

' *Viri illustres ecclesiae restauratae*: The renowned divines of the late reformed tymes . . . 1560–1672': Wood MS. F. 8 (*O. C.* 8470). Wood notes that the book is a compilation 'from printed authors, and little or nothing therein but what was known before.'

305. Boetius.

(i) *De disciplina scholarium*: MS. Digb. 190 (*O. C.* 1791): see *Life*, ii. 199.

Cited in *Annals*, i. 20, 24.

(ii) William Whetley's Commentarii in tractatum Boetii de disciplina scholastica: MS. Coll. Exon. no. 38 in Coxe's Catalogue: MS. Coll. Merton[1].   See Twyne XXII. 298.

Cited in *Annals*, i. 53, 59, &c.

---

[1] I can find no Merton Coll. MS. of him: MS. Corp. Oxon, no. 255 in Coxe's Cat., has some excerpts from him.

306. Edmund Bolton.

Hypercritica : Wood MS. F. 9 (*O. C.* 8471) : *Life*, iii. 431.
Printed by Anthony Hall : Oxford, 1722.

307. Bonaventura.

Sermo . . . in textum ⟨Prov. ix. 1⟩ 'Sapientia aedificavit sibi
domum'; MS. Digb. 33 (*O. C.* 1634), foll. 16–30.   See Twyne XXI.
148.
Cited in *Annals*, i. 27, 57.

308. William Boolde, monachus Cantuariensis, 1468.

Liber : MS. O. I. 4 Med. (MS. Bodl. 648 = *O. C.* 2291).
Cited in MS. Ric. James 11, p. 149; and by Twyne in MS. Wood
D. 32, p. 301.

309. Johannes Bostonus, Buriensis.

(i) *Catalogus major*, mentioned by Pits, p. 299, in margine.
(ii) *Catalogus minor scriptorum*, quem Mr. Thomas Allen mutuo
accepit a Mro Ricardo James : princ. 'Omnis divina scriptura in
duobus testamentis continetur,' &c. : Twyne XXII. 403, 406.

This was shown by Allen to Twyne, who (Twyne XXI. 406)
copied from it a list of 195 houses in which Boston saw MSS.,
including Osney, S. Frideswyde's, Eynsham, Abingdon, Thame,
Reading.
Cited in *Annals*, i. 174, &c.; *City*, ii. 379.

(iii) A copy was supposed to be among the MSS. of Thomas
Barlow from the library of Archbishop Ussher : see *Life*, iii. 35, and
Wood MS. E. 4 (*O. C.* 8561) p. 38, where Wood notes 'Dr. Thomas
Marshall concludes that Dr. Thomas Barlow must needs have this
book : see Dr. Thomas James' *Manuductio*, p. 135.'

(iv) A copy in Thomas Gale's possession from the library of Sir
Thomas Twysden : *Life*, iii. 35.

(v) In Wood MS. E. 4 (*O. C.* 8561), p. 99, speaking of the *Architrenius* of John de Hauteville, Wood says that 'it is divided into 9
books, dedicated to Walter de Constantiis, bishop of Lincoln circ.
1183 ; ascribed wrongly by Bostonus Buriensis (in his *Catalogus
Minor*) to Johannes Sarisburiensis.   Bostonus says he saw a copy in
the library of the monastery of St. Edmund's Bury, and also at the
monastery of Ingarston in Essex.'—Ibid. p. 11, Wood says :—' This
author' ⟨? Walter de Monmouth⟩ 'hath writ but two books according to Boston's little catalogue or imperfect : vide Notas ad Pits,
p. 352.'

310. William Botoner or Worcester (Wyrcester): see Twyne XXI. 77.

(i) *Stellae verificatae*: MS. Laud Misc. 674 (*O. C.* 504), *olim* Laud B. 32.

Cited in *City*, ii. 377.

(ii) MS. Ric. James 6, p. 88, cites a MS. of William Wyrcester as being in Thomas Allen's library.

311. William Bourne.

Prognosticatio trium annorum: Twyne XXI. 370.

312. Henry Bracton.

De legibus et consuetudinibus Anglicanis: MS. Bodl. 170 (*O. C.* 2419).

Cited in *Annals*, and *City*, but from the printed copies: Hardy's Descriptive Catalogue, iii. 173.

313. Simon Bredon, or Biridanus.

(i) *Theorica planetarum*: MS. Digb. 93 (*O. C.* 1694): Twyne XXII. 324, XXIII. 106.

(ii) *Tractatus theoriae planetarum*: MS. Digb. 48 (*O. C.* 1649).

314. Brekinsaw, or Breconson.

(i) De vera differentia regiae potestatis et ecclesiasticae: Twyne XXI. 349.

Cited in *City*, ii. 34.

(ii) Wood cites a printed book without author's name ('Opus eximium de vera differentia,' &c., Lond. 1534, 4to), which had on fol. 52ᵛ the statement that William the conqueror gave to Battle Abbey 'ecclesiam Sti Olavi in Oxon,' in error for 'Exon': Wood MS. E. 4 (*O. C.* 8561), a slip at p. 41.

315. John Britton.

De legibus Angliae: cited in *Annals*, i. 197: from some printed copy.

316. John Brompton, abbot of Jervaux.

Historia Angliae: MS. Cotton Tiber. C. 13. Twyne has excerpts from it in Twyne III. 247, XXIV. 1–7 ; Richard James, in MS. Ric. James 10, pp. 95–102. Twyne and James (MS. Ric. James 10, p. 99) seem to say that this copy had marginal notes by Cardinal Wolsey. Printed in Twysden's Decem Scriptores, 1652.

Cited in *Annals*, i. 9, 13, 33, sometimes as *Brompton's Chronicle*, sometimes as *Chronicle of Jorevall*.

Richard James in MS. Ric. James 17, p. 14, has excerpts from the
Corpus Cambr. MS. (no. 96) of this author. Wood, in MS. E. 4
(*O. C.* 8561), p. 40, refers to Selden's 'de scriptoribus nuper editis,'
pp. 36, 38, 39, on the question of the authorship; and cites 'ultimo
Maii 1436 commissio ad benedicendum abbatem de Jorevall noviter
electum,' from York notes, sched. 3, p. 11, and Mr. Fulman's notes,
p. 36.

317. Ralph Brooke, 'York' herald.

Wood has some excerpts from his corrections of Camden's 1594
Britannia ('Discoverie of certaine errours,' publ. 1596) in MS. Ballard
70, p. 38, which he cites as *Notes from Brook* or *Collections out of
Brooks* in *City*, i. 272, 277, 278.

318. Thomas Buckley, or Bulkley.

Libel of various people in Oxford : MS. Tanner 465, fol. 105 : see
Life, iii. p. vii.
Cited in *Annals*, ii. 164.

319. Edmund Bunney.

'A defence of his labour in the work of the ministry, written by
him Jan. 20, 160⅔ : MS.' — Wood gives no indication where he
found this.

320. Robert Burhill.

Britannia Scholastica : MS. e Mus. 132 (*O. C.* 3507). See Twyne
XXII. 153.
Cited in *Annals*, i. 114, *City*, i. 547.

321. Walter Burley.

(i) *Abbreviatio problematum Aristotelis* : MS. no. 65 in Coxe's Cat.
of Magd. Coll. MSS. ; MS. Digb. 77 ; MS. Digb. 153. See Twyne
XXI. 125, XXII. 101.
Cited in *Annals*, i. 18, *City*, i. 50, 349.
(ii) *Super literalem sensum Porphyrii* : MS. no. 47 in Coxe's Cat.
of Magd. Coll. MSS.
Cited in *Annals*, i. 514.

322. Richard de Bury, Dunelmensis.

Philobiblon : MS. no. 232 in Coxe's Cat. of C. C. C. Oxford MSS.
Cited in *Annals*, *City* : no doubt from a printed edition.

323. William Butler.

MS. no. 68, fol. 202 in Coxe's Cat. of Mert. Coll. MSS.
Cited in *Annals*, i. 396.

324. Lewis Caerlyon.

Observationes eclipsium anno Xti 1482 : cited by Twyne, from
a MS. in the hands of Dr. John Bainbridge, in MS. arch. Seld. supra
79, pp. 87–89.

325. Johannes Caius, Cantabrigiensis.

Annotationes ex primo libro Antiquitatis Cantabrigiae : Twyne
XXI. 489.

326. Petrus de Calo.

Legendae : MS. in York library, Twyne XXI. 105.
Cited in *Fasti*, p. 12, but only from Twyne.

327. William Camden.

In Twyne XXII. 385–387 Twyne has a note of a conversation
with Camden, Feb. 18, 162⅔, in which Camden promised to appoint
him Camden Professor at Oxford in succession to Degory Wheare [1],
and urged him to persevere in his studies.

(i) Letters of learned men to Camden: MS. Cotton Julius C. 5.
Printed by Thomas Smith in 1691.
Cited in *Hist.* i. 9.

(ii) *Pedigrees and coats of arms* : MS. formerly in Sir Henry
St. George's hands ('Garter' King of Arms, died 1644): *Life*,
ii. 268.

(iii) *Annales regis Jacobi* : MS. Trin. Coll. Cambr.   Printed by
Thomas Smith in 1691 in 'Camdeni . . . epistolae.'

(iv) Note by Camden in MS. Cotton Titus B. 8.
Cited in *Annals*, ii. 330.

328. Edmund Campion.

(i) *History of Ireland* : MS. Cotton Vitell. F. 9.   Printed by Sir
James Ware, 1633.   Twyne XXI. 192–195 cites Campion's autograph
copy 'in the hands of Dr. Chenell, Oxford' (John Cheynell, M.D.
(C. C. C.), died 1613).

(ii) 'Life of Edmund Campion,' in English verse, MS. Laud
Misc. 755 (*O. C.* 1034).   Wood says of it—'a simple thing ; I could
get nothing out of it' :   Wood MS. E. 4 (*O. C.* 8561), p. 48.

---

[1] Wheare outlived both Camden and Twyne.

329. Gervase of Canterbury (Dorobernensis).

(i) *Chronicon* a Stephano ad Ricardum I [The greater chronicle: printed in Rolls Series 1879]: MS. Cotton Vespas. B. 19, foll. 21–194. Excerpts from it in Twyne XXI. 237, 383; MS. Ric. James 10, pp. 1–12, 29–31. Ric. James has also excerpts from the Trin. Coll. Cambr. MS. (R. 4. 11) in MS. Ric. James 17, p. 51.

Cited in *Annals*, i. 135, 154 (from MS. Ff. 1. 29 in Cambr. Univ. Libr.).

(ii) *Gesta regum* [The smaller chronicle: printed in Rolls Series 1880]: MS. Corp. Cambr. 438, art. 4.

(iii) *Actus Pontificum*: MS. Corp. Cambr. 438, art. 5. Excerpts from it in MS. Ric. James 17, p. 104. Printed in Twysden's Decem Scriptores, 1652.

Cited in *Annals*, i. 156.

330. Robertus Canutus.

De connubio Jacob: MS. Laud Misc. 725: MS. no. 167 in Coxe's Cat. of Ball. Coll. MSS.

Cited in *Hist.* i. 48; *City*, ii. 161.

331. John Capgrave.

(i) *Epistola dedicatoria Humfredo duci Gloverniae*, quae praefigitur postillae super Genesim per Johannem Capgrave: MS. no. 32 in Coxe's Cat. of Oriel Coll. MSS.

Cited in *Annals*, ii. 916, 917; *City*, ii. 446, 459.

(ii) *Vitae sanctorum*: MS. Cotton Otho D. 9. Twyne has excerpts in MS. arch. Seld. supra 79, p. 155; Richard James, in MS. Ric. James 2, part 2, pp. 1–21; Wood has excerpts from Capgrave's *Historiae sanctorum Angliae* in MS. Ballard 70, p. 32, which he cites in *City*, i. 278:—cited no doubt from the printed edition (*Nova Legenda Angliae*, by Wynkyn de Worde, 1516).

332. John Case, M.D.

De Academia or *Apologia Academiarum*: cited by Twyne in Twyne XXIII. 499, from a copy which he saw in the earl of Dorset's [? Edward Sackville, fourth earl] 'study' at Knoll. See also MS. 321 in Coxe's Cat. of C. C. C. Oxon MSS., which is perhaps William Fulman's copy.

333. Roger de Cestria.

Polycraticon seu *Polychronicon*: MS. Cotton Jul. E. 8. fol. 181.

334. Osbertus de Clara.

(i) *Vita . . . S. Edburgae*: cited by Twyne in Twyne XXI. 752, XXII. 150 from a MS. in Thomas Allen's library. See, perhaps, MS. Laud Misc. 714 (*O. C.* 1547).

Cited in *Annals*, i. 41.

(ii) *Epistolae*: MS. Cotton Vitell. A. 17, foll. 17ᵛ–163ᵛ. Printed in 1846: Hardy's Descriptive Catalogue, i. 642.

335. Clemens V, pope.

Constitutiones: Twyne XXI. 3, 5, 122, 176: MS. Langbaine 12, pp. 65, 66: MS. no. 13 fol. 223ᵛ in Coxe's Cat. of Mert. Coll. MSS., and no. 70, fol. 36 in Coxe's Cat. of C. C. C. Oxon. MSS.

Cited in *Hist.* i. 156.

336. Richard Clifford, bishop of London.

His will, cited in *Colleges*, p. 651, from Twyne XXIV. 588. Twyne had it from Edmund Lynolde, rector of Heling near Grimsby, co. Linc.

337. William de Conchis, or Shelley: Twyne XXI. 21.

(i) No. 95 in Coxe's Cat. of C. C. C. Oxon. MSS.

(ii) Bale, cent. 13, cap. 30, cites a MS. at Oriel College, which cannot now be found.

338. Constantius, Lugdunensis.

Vita S. Germani: MS. Bodl. 793 (*O. C.* 2641).
Cited in *Annals*, i. 26.

339. Bartholomew de Cotton.

(i) *Chronicon*: de regibus Anglicis Dacis et Normannis liber secundus [Hardy, Descriptive Catalogue, iii. 260]: MS. Cotton Nero C. 5, foll. 160–251. Twyne XXII. 331. Printed in Rolls Series, 1859.

Cited frequently in *Annals*, and in *City*, i. 235.

(ii) *De archiepiscopis et episcopis Angliae*: MS. Cotton Nero C. 5, foll. 252–280. Twyne XXII. 332. Printed in Rolls Series, 1859.

340. Walter de Coventry.

(i) *Memoriale*: Ric. James in MS. Ric. James 17, p. 18, has excerpts from MS. Corp. Cambr. 175, art. 8. Another MS. is MS. Cotton Vitell. E. 13. Printed in Rolls Series, 1872.

(ii) *Chronicon Britonum* [see Stubbs' edit. of the *Memoriale* in Rolls

Series, i. p. xxvi]. Cited in Twyne XXII. 104, from a MS. in the possession of Edward James (ob. 1616): which afterwards became MS. Bodl. 355 (*O. C.* 2444). MS. Ric. James 21, p. 56, has excerpts apparently from this MS.

Cited in *City*, i. 236, 237.

341. Nicholas Cratzer, or Kratcher.

(i) A note by him at the end of *de compositione horologeorum*, MS. no. 152 in Coxe's Cat. of C. C. C. Oxon. MSS.; Twyne XXI. 125, 296, 832.

Cited in *Hist.* i. 247, ii. 35.

(ii) *Canones Horoptri*: MS. no. 152, C. C. C., *ut supra*; MS. Bodl. 504 (*O. C.* 2168).

Cited in *City*, i. 546, 547.

(iii) Twyne in MS. arch. Seld. supra 79, p. 187, cites a MS. formerly belonging to Nicholas Kratzer, which had been in Dr. John Dee's library and passed thence into Thomas Allen's.

342. Henry Cromp, or Crump.

De monasteriis: known to Wood only from the references in Sir James Ware (see Hardy's Descriptive Catalogue, iii. p. 132), and Dugdale's Monasticon.

343. Roger of Croyland.

' Concerning the life of Thomas à Becket,' a MS. found by Wood in the hands of Dr. Thomas Barlow. See MS. e Mus. 133 (*O. C.* 3512).

344. William Darrell.

MS. Cotton Vesp. A. 5, fol. 88 a.

345. Davenant.

Chronicle from Richard I to Henry V: 'MS. C. 62 in bibl. Coll. S. Joh. :' see no. 209, fol. 38^v in Coxe's Cat. of MSS. of S. John's, Oxford.

346. John Dee: *Life*, i. 308.

(i) *Discourse for the reformation of the vulgar calendar*, addressed to Queen Elizabeth: see MS. no. 254, fol. 141 in Coxe's Cat. of MSS. of C. C. C. Oxon.

Known to Wood only from ' p. 23 of Twyne's mathematical collections in C. C. C. library ' and Twyne XXII. 324.

(ii) *Vita et gesta Johannis Dee* ad 1592 : MS. Cotton Vitell. C. 7.

(iii) Twyne has excerpts from several MSS. which were formerly in his possession : e. g.—

(*a*) Twyne XXI. 832, a MS. of John Dee now in the library of C. C. C. Oxford.

(*b*) MSS. formerly belonging to him, seen by Twyne in a London bookseller's shop—Twyne XXII. 430, 'incertus author de ortu et origine episcopatus Worcestr. et Wynton.,' written temp. Henr. VI: Twyne XXI. 700, a MS. 'de statu ecclesiae Dunelm.'

(*c*) MSS. of Dee's which passed into Allen's library :—Twyne in MS. arch. Seld. supra 79, pp. 90, 155 (Roger Bacon's *Opus minus*); ibid. p. 171 (Petrus Peregrinus Maricurtensis *de magnete*); ibid. pp. 177–179 (rabbi Moyses *de venenis*); ibid. p. 187 (a MS. of Nicholas Kratzer's).

347. Richard of Devizes (Divisiensis).

(i) *Historia Angliae* : MS. C. C. C. Cant. 339 (num. 1); MS. Cotton Domit. A. 13.

(ii) *De rebus gestis Ricardi I* : MS. C. C. C. Cant. 339 (2); MS. Cotton Domit. A. 18, foll. 70–87 ; Twyne XXIII. 115. In MS. Ric. James 17, p. 35, are excerpts from the Corp. Cambr. MS. Printed in 1838 by Rev. Joseph Stevenson.

348. Radulphus de Diceto.

(i) *Abbreviatio Chronicorum* : MS. Cotton Claud. E. 3, foll. 8–60^v, Twyne XXIV. 65, 67, 68, 77, 79. Printed in Twysden's Scriptores Decem, 1652 : in Rolls Series, 1876.

Cited in *Annals*, i. 122.

(ii) *Ymagines historiarum* : MS. Cotton Claud. E. 3, foll. 60^v–151, MS. Cotton Otho D. 7. Excerpts in MS. Ric. James 10, pp. 139–142. Richard James in MS. Ric. James 25, p. 155, cites a 'MS. in S. Paul's library' : see MS. Lambeth 8.

(iii) *Epistola* R. de Duceto ad Walterum de contemptu mundi : init. 'exemplar autem epistolae de contemptu mundi' : Twyne XXIV. 60–62 (from a Cottonian MS.).

Cited in *Annals*, i. 143.

(iv) *Continuator Radulphi de Diceto* : MS. Cotton Claud. E. 3, fol. 152 [ab anno 1199 ad 1272] ; Twyne XXIV. 67–68.

Cited in *Annals*, i. 276 ; *Fasti*, p. 33.

349. Roger Dodsworth : *Life*, ii. 265, 266.

(i) *Collections*, in Bodleian.
Cited *Coll.*, p. 46.

(ii) *Collections*: Wood MS. F. 25 (*O. C.* 8487).

(iii) In Wood MS. E. 4 (*O. C.* 8561) Wood has on a slip at p. 67 these notes :—

(*a*) Dodsworth ⧌ fol. 14 a 'inquisitio de hundredo extra portam borealem Oxon.'

(*b*) ' M. 78 : Richard Flemmyng borne as it seems at Croston in Yorkshire.'

350. Simeon of Durham.

(i) *De exordio . . . ecclesiae . . . Dunelm.* : par. 14 (i).

(ii) *Chronicon ab adventu Saxonum ad annum* 1119 : MS. Cotton Calig. A. 8, foll. 25–40 : an abridgement of (i) : see Hardy's Descriptive Catalogue, ii. 137.

(iii) *Historia Anglorum post obitum Bedae* : MS. Bodl. 521 (*O. C.* 2182) : a redaction of (i).

Cited in *Annals*, i. 119.

(iv) *Historia Regum* : printed in Twysden's Decem scriptores, 1652, and in Rolls Series, 1885, from MS. Corp. Cambr. 139 (7).

351. Thomas Eccleston.

(i) *De primo adventu Fratrum Minorum in Anglia* :—

(*a*) MS. in York Cathedral library : ' seen and perused' by Wood, *Life*, ii. 203, note 3 (but possibly only in a transcript). Printed in Rolls Series (Monumenta Franciscana I), 1858.

Cited in *Annals*, i. 210 ; *City*, ii. 348, &c.

(*b*) MS. Cotton Nero A. 9 + a fragment (apparently of the same MS.) at Lamport hall. This fragment has been printed in Rolls Series (Monum. Francisc. II), 1882.

Cited in *Annals*, i. 210 ; *City*, ii. 347.

(*c*) Leland (tom. 4, Collect. p. 226, tom. 2, p. 296), cited a copy which he saw ' in the Queen's library at Granta Gerviorum.' Possibly MS. Phillipps 3119 (foll. 71–80) : *Life*, ii. 203, note 3. See Twyne XXII. 142.

(*d*) Leland (tom. 4, p. 206 ; Twyne XVIII. p. 385) saw a copy in the Grey Friars' library at Oxford.

(*e*) Wood had the loan of a copy which he lent to Francis Davenport (or S. Clara), *Life*, ii. 203. Was this the York MS. or a transcript of it ?—It is not, in the abstract, impossible that it may have been the Lamport MS. : the Isham family frequented Oxford—only a little later the sons of Sir Justinian Isham were at Christ Church, and he himself died in Oxford, 1675 : *Life*, ii. 309.

(ii) Wood's excerpts from Eccleston are found in Wood MS. D. 18, pp. 151 sqq.

352. King Edward VI's Journal.

Liber regis Edwardi propria manu scriptus: MS. Ric. James 10, p. 32.

353. Thomas de Elmham, prior of Lenton temp. Henr. V.

Annales Britonum, Saxonum, et Anglorum usque ad tempora Ricardi II cum indictionibus: MS. Cotton Claud. E. 4, incip. 'Terreni Deus imperii fit ab altitonante': verses thence in Twyne XXI. 214, which Wood thought 'worth the setting down.'

354. Richard de Elye.

Dialogus de scaccario: cited by Twyne XXIII. 502 b, 504, from a MS. 'in the earl of Dorset's study.' Other copies are MS. Cotton Cleop. A. 16; MS. Laud Misc. 654 (*O. C.* 650). Wood notes 'it goes under the name of Gervasius Tylburiensis, but written by Richard Ely, Lord Treasurer [temp. Henr. II], as 't is said.' It is now attributed to Richard Fitz-nigel, bp. of London 1189–1198: Hardy's Descriptive Catalogue, ii. 411.

355. Jacobus Eremita.

Sophilogium: cited in Twyne XXI. 319, from a MS. in S. Paul's library, London. It had something about the University of Paris.

356. Alexander Essebiensis.

Epitome historiae Britannicae: MS. Corpus Cambr. 138.
Cited, I assume, from Ric. James' notes only, in *Annals*, i. 39.

357. Nicholas Fakenham, S. T. P. Oxon., de ordine Fratrum Minorum.

Determinatio . . . . facta Oxon. Nov. 5, 1395, de scismate inter Bonifacium papam et Benedictum anti-papam: init. 'Reverendi Magistri ac Domini, cum ex lege naturae,' &c., excerpts by Twyne, in Twyne XXII. 223, from a MS. 'formerly in the library of Exeter Cathedral.' See MS. Harl. 3768, fol. 128.
Cited, solely from Twyne's excerpt, in *Annals*, i. 535.

358. John Favour, fellow of New College.

Orationes et Carmina: in Wood MS. D. 13 (*O. C.* 8545): *Life*, ii. 180.

359. John Felton, vicar of S. Mary Magdalen, Oxford.

(i) *Abstractum libri Perae Peregrini*: MS. no. 109 in Coxe's Cat. of S. John's Coll., Oxford MSS.
Cited in *City*, i. 359.

(ii) *Sermones dominicales*: cited in MS. Ric. James 21, p. 89, from MS. F. 1. 11 Th. (*O. C.* 2090 = MS. Bodl. 187).

(iii) MS. Corp. Cambr. 360.

360. John Fisher, bishop of Rochester.

Oration at Cambridge before Henry VIII: init. 'Etsi nullis unquam verbis': Twyne XXII. 28 a.

361. Flete.

Fleta, seu commentarius juris Anglicani: MS. Cotton Julius B. 8; edited by John Selden in 1647. Excerpts in MS. Ric. James 10, p. 160.

Cited in *City*, i. 473.

362. Florilegus *vel* Flores Historiarum: see par. 508.

Ascribed to 'Matthew of Westminster,' from MS. Cotton Claud. E. 8. Printed by Matthew Parker in 1567, and again in 1570. Printed in Rolls Series, 1890 sqq.

Cited frequently in *Annals* and *City*.

Excerpts by Twyne are found in Wood MS. D. 32, pp. 194, 211: and in Twyne XXI. 223.

Of the numerous MSS. of it [Hardy, Descriptive Catalogue, iii. 313], Wood definitely refers to three:—

(*a*) MS. in S. James' library (MS. Reg. 14 C. 6): cited in Twyne XXI. 580, 627, 628.

Cited expressly in *City*, i. 233.

(*b*) MS. Cotton Nero D. 2.

(*c*) John Aubrey's MS., sent by him to Wood, to be given to the Bodleian; now MS. e Mus. 149 (*O. C.* 3659).

363. William Forrest.

(i) *Life of Queen Catherine* (of Aragon): MS. ab Wood 2: *Life*, ii. 486.

Cited in *Annals*, ii. 46, 115.

(ii) *History of Joseph: Life*, ii. 485, 486, note 1.

364. Henry Foulis, of Lincoln College.

(i) Account of sermons preached before the Long Parliament, 1640–1648: Wood MS. F. 21 (*O. C.* 8479).

(ii) Wood's Catalogue of pamphlets in his possession: see par. 268 (i).

Cited in *Life*, i. 308.

365. John Free, or Phree.

Cosmographia Mundi: MS. no. 124 in Coxe's Cat. of Ball. Coll. MSS.: Twyne XXI. 285.

Cited in *Annals*, i. 12 ; *Hist.* ii. 76.

366. Nathaniel Friend, of Westerleigh, co. Glouc.

Survey, or Notes of Antiquity, concerning Bristol: Life, iii. 174, 175 : a 4to MS. in English.

Wood notes that he made use of it in the ' Catalogue of High Stewards ' (in *Fasti*).

367. Thomas Frith : *Life*, ii. 224, note 6.

(i) *Catalogus . . . decanorum . . . capellae . . . S. Georgii . . . Windsore*, drawn up in 1618 (and brought down to 1625) by Frith ' ex archivis ejusdem capellae ' : a MS. in Dr. Thomas Barlow's hands, now MS. no. 284 in Coxe's Cat. of MSS. of Queen's Coll. Oxford : Frith's autograph. Wood notes ' Frith was formerly fellow of All Souls : a usefull and also a necessary man in ordering the affaires of the said College of S. Georg . . . I have his will,' Wood MS. E. 4 (*O. C.* 8561), p. 85.

(ii) Wood's transcript of this Catalogue : Wood MS. B. 12.

Cited in *Coll.* p. 316.

368. Thomas Gardiner, monk of Westminster, temp. Henr. VIII.

Flowers of England, or a brief abstract of the English story : MS. Cotton Otho C. 6.

369. Thomas Gascoigne.

(i) *Lexicon Theologicum* sive *Liber de veritatibus* ex S. Scriptura et scriptis sanctorum et doctorum collectis, partes 2 : nos. 117, 118 in Coxe's Cat. of Linc. Coll. MSS.

Excerpts from it in Robert Sanderson's Collections (*Life*, ii. 355); in MS. Ric. James 18, p. 48 ; in Twyne XXI. 196, 197, Twyne XXIII. 493, 690–723 (from part i) and 724–729 (from part ii).

Wood notes (Wood MS. E. 4, *O. C.* 8561, p. 88) that by his will[1] Gascoigne gave this book, written in paper, to Sion College, with orders to have it transcribed on parchment, and carefully to preserve both copies : ' but this book in parchment, written in two volumes in folio, came[2] tempore Jacobi I into Lincoln College Library.'

Cited frequently in *Hist., Annals, Fasti, Coll.*

---

[1] in Reg. Aaa, p. 166 : cited in Twyne XXIII. 493 : printed in Anstey, *Mun. Acad.* p. 671.

[2] Wood's authority is Dr. Gerard Langbaine's MS. Collections, e. g. MS. Wood donat. 3, p. 61.

Excerpts from it were printed by Thomas Hearne at the end of Walter Hemingford, 1731 ; and by Thorold Rogers, 1881.

(ii) *Fragmenta*: in quibus plura sunt de Roberto Grostest.   Twyne XXII. 148 speaks of them as formerly in Thomas Allen's library: Richard James speaks of them as in the hands of Henry Fowler (*Life*, iii. 343).

Cited in *Annals*, i. 249.

(iii) Note by him about Grostest, at the end of Grostest's *de cura pastorali*: MS. Bodl. 312, foll. 117, 172ᵛ. See Twyne XXI. 145, Wood's *Analecta Grostest* (infra, p. 275), pp. 16, 17.

Cited in *Annals*, i. 249.

(iv) Note by him about the death of Wycliffe : in Ivo Carnotensis, MS. Cotton Otho A. 14 (1).   Twyne XXIII. 17.

Cited in *Annals*, i. 512.

(v) Notes about the miracles of S. Bridget : MS. Cotton Otho A. 14.

Cited in *Hist.* ii. 107.

(vi) Note about pope Nicholas V in MS. G. 8. 8 (i. e. MS. Bodl. 312), p. 119.   Twyne XXII. 373 (2).

(vii) Note on the beheading of archbishop Scroop : MS. Auct. D. 4, 5 (*O. C.* 1878).

(viii) Note on Richard Fishacre, in MS. no. 43 in Coxe's Cat. of Oriel MSS.

Cited in *City*, ii. 339.

(ix) Note in Isidore's Etymology, MS. no. 64 in Coxe's Cat. of Linc. Coll. MSS.: MS. Ric. James 22, p. 160.

(x) Note in a copy of Rationale divinorum secundum Gulielmum presented by him to Linc. Coll.: MS. Ric. James 22, p. 159.

(xi) Note at the beginning of a copy of the Summa Alex. de Hales : MS. Ric. James 21, p. 13.

(xii) Note about S. Edmund of Canterbury in MS. no. 235 in Coxe's Cat. of Ball. MSS.: see par. 526, § vi (*f*).

370. Charles Gibbs, fellow of Merton.

Speech spoken at Merton College to the Prince Palatine, 162— : init.: ' Ignosce importunitati nostrae (serenissime princeps) si te jam ab istiusmodi salutationibus calentem,' &c.

371. Frater Gilbertus.

Sermones : MS. Bodl. 542 (*O. C.* 2607): Twyne XXIV. 281 : MS. Ric. James 29, p. 72.

Cited in *Annals*, i. 469.

372. Gildas, Badonicus vel sapiens.

De gestis Britonum: MS. Cotton Vitell. A. 6.

Printed in 1568: Hardy's Descriptive Catalogue, i. 134. Wood notes that the work of Nennius is frequently cited as Gildas.

In *Annals*, i. 11, 25, &c., he cites a MS. of Gildas in the Bodl.; this is MS. Bodl. 163 (3) (*O. C.* 2016), a Nennius MS.; see Hardy's Descr. Cat. i. 324.

373. Sylvester Giraldus.

I omit those works to which no allusion is made by Wood: Ric. James has excerpts from many of them.

(i) *Distinctiones, libri quatuor*, init. (according to Pits) ' Nunc ad ea quae contra naturae,' &c.: MS. formerly of Henry Parry of C. C. C. Oxon, now MS. Cotton Tiber. B. 13 (1). Excerpts from it in Twyne XXII. 163 e, 164, 229; MS. Ric. James 2, part 1, pp. 11–44.

Cited frequently in *Annals*, e. g. i. 11, 52, &c., ii. 724.

(ii) *Epistolae*, quibus titulus ' Symbolum electorum ad capitulum Herefordiense ': MS. Cotton Cleopatra D. 5, fol. 98 ; Twyne XXII. 293. Ric. James in MS. Ric. James 17, p. 7, and 18, p. 133, has excerpts from the Cambridge MS. (MS. Trin. Coll. Cambr. R. 7. 11), from which the Symbolum Electorum is printed in Rolls Series, 1861.

Cited frequently in *Annals*, e. g. i. 63, ii. 817.

(iii) *Retractationes*: MS. Cotton Domit. A. 1, fol. 135^v. Twyne speaks of a MS. in S. James' Library London : Twyne XXII. 150.

(iv) *Catalogus librorum* ab ipso Giraldo compositorum : MS. Cotton Domit. A. 1, fol. 136^v. Printed, as also the Retractationes, in Rolls Series, 1861.

(v) *De rebus a se gestis* : MS. Cotton Tiber. B. 13, art. 2. Excerpts in Twyne XXII. 164, 190 ; MS. Ric. James 2, part 2, p. 45. Printed in Rolls Series, 1861.

Cited frequently in *Annals*, e. g. i. 58, 64, &c., ii. 766.

(vi) *Vita Galfridi Plantagenet*, archiepisc. Ebor.; MS. C. C. C. Cambr. 390. Excerpts in Twyne XXIV. 617 ; MS. Ric. James 17, p. 61.

Printed in Rolls Series, 1873.

(vii) *Speculum ecclesiae*: MS. Cotton Tiber. B. 13, art 3.

Printed in Rolls Series, 1873.

Cited in *Annals*, i. 52, 191.

(viii) Wood's *Collectanea de Giraldo* are found in Wood MS. F. 30 (*O. C.* 8492).

374. Nicholas of Gloucester.

Chronicon ab initio mundi ad annum 838 : MS. Cotton Calig. A. 3, foll. 12–145^v.

375. Robert of Gloucester.

Metrical Chronicle of England. Printed in Rolls Series, 1887. Wood notices two MSS. of it :—

(i) MS. Cotton Calig. A. 11, foll. 1–163. This Cottonian copy is noticed in Twyne V. 55 ; MS. Ric. James 18, p. 69.

(ii) MS. Digby 205 (*O. C.* 1806), formerly Thomas Allen's.

Cited frequently in *Annals, City.*

376. Godefridus, prior of S. Swithun's Winchester.

Veruss : MS. Cotton Vitell. A. 12, foll. 111–114 ; MSS. Digb. 65 and 112, fol. 120^v (*O. C.* 1666, 1713).

377. Godfrey Goodman

(i) *Historia sui temporis*, bibl. Bodl. : *Life*, ii. 169.

(ii) *Answer to Sir Anthony Weldon's book* against the character of King James : MS. e Mus. 50 (*O. C.* 3603).

Cited in *Annals*, ii. 330.

(iii) In Wood MS. E. 4 (*O. C.* 8561), p. 91, Wood notes 'Some letters of his I have seen and made use of. As his notes have done me some curtesie : so shal I by that which followes, to his memory.'

378. Thomas (or John) Gray : claruit 1217.

Historia sive Scala chronicon, Gallice : Twyne XXI. 669.

379. Robert Grosseteste : Twyne XXI. 95, 106, 133, 145, 262 ; Twyne XXII. 224 ; Twyne XXIV. 24 : see *Life*, ii. 174.

(i) *Epistolae* : MS. Bodl. 312, fol. 126 ; MS. Corp. Cambr. 453, &c. Printed in Rolls Series, 1861. Excerpts in Twyne II. 143^v, 149 ; Twyne XXI. 262 ; Twyne XXII. 373 ; Twyne XXIV. 96 a ; MS. Ric. James 2, part 2, pp. 23–56.

Cited frequently in *Annals, Fasti, City.*

(ii) *Constitutiones* rectoribus ecclesiarum . . . ad rem religionis in Oxon. spectantes : MS. Cotton Nero D. 2 (see Twyne III. 517–525), and MS. Barlow 49 (*O. C.* 6375).

(iii) Two verses on his name : MS. Wood F. 26 (*O. C.* 8488), p. 38.

(iv) *Vita Roberti Grosthed*, by Richard, monk of Bardney : MS. Cotton Otho C. 16 : init. Lincolniensis apex, praesul sacrate Wilelme. ' Written in verse to William Smyth, bishop of Lincoln 1503 : sed fabulosa multa inseruit author, tanto viro non satis congruentia ' : Wood MS. E. 4 (*O. C.* 8561), p. 34.

Cited in *Annals*, i. 198.

Partly printed by Henry Wharton in *Anglia Sacra*, vol. ii : Hardy's Descriptive Catalogue, iii. 130.

(v) Wood's *Analecta de vita et scriptis Roberti Grosthead*, 17 leaves, are now in Wood MS. E. 4 (*O. C.* 8560, art. 1).

380. Thomas Habington (Habendon).

(i) *Antiquities of Worcester Cathedral : Life*, ii. 277.
Wood followed this in stating that bishop Thomas Peverell was buried in the Carmelite Church at Oxford, *Hist.* i. 104; *City*, ii. 430.

(ii) In Wood MS. E. 4 (*O. C.* 8561), p. 98, Wood says 'see notes of his *Antiquities of the County*, that ⟨? i. e. the notes⟩ I have : he hath not written of all the countie but of most part.' Thomas Habington's Worcestershire Collections are found among Lord Herbert's MS. Collections in Jesus College library, see Coxe's Cat.

381. Thomas de Hanney.

Twyne XXI. 648 has an excerpt from an old MS. in the Bodleian : —'Grammatica Thomae de Hanneya quae dicitur *Memoriale Juniorum*': see MS. Auct. F. 3, 9 (*O. C.* 3581), p. 189.

382. John de Hanvyle or Hauteville.

(i) *Architrenius*: MS. Cotton Vespas. B. 13 : MSS. Digb. 64, and 157. Twyne's excerpts are in Twyne XXI. 642; Ric. James has excerpts from a MS. of it in Thomas Allen's library in MS. Ric. James 22, p. 53. See MS. Digb. 64, fol. 52.
Cited in *Annals* and *City*.
Printed in 1517 : Hardy's Descriptive Catalogue, ii. 447.

(ii) *Scholia in Architrenium*, written by Hugh Legate, a monk of S. Alban's temp. Henr. IV, Twyne XXI. 642. See MS. Digb. 64, fol. 108.
Cited in *Annals*, i. 12 ; *City*, ii. 259 : but only from Twyne.

383. John Harding.

Metrical Chronicle: MS. arch. Seld. B. 10 (*O. C.* 3356). Twyne has a note of it in Wood MS. D. 32, p. 317.
Cited in *Annals*, i. 6.

384. Nicholas Harpsfield.

(i) *Treatise concerning marriage*: MS. no. 311 in Coxe's Cat. of New Coll. MSS.: see *Life*, ii. 213.
Cited in *Annals*, ii. 45.

(ii) 'Impugnatio contra bullam Honorii Papae I ad Cantabrigiam : MS.'—see Twyne XXII. 29.

(iii) Wood notes that of his *Historia Anglicana Ecclesiastica,* printed at Douay in 1622 :—

(*a*) Harpsfield's autograph copy is MS. Cotton Vitell. C. 9, num. 12.

(*b*) A transcript of it is MS. Lambeth 53 and 54.

Cited in *Annals* and *City.*

(iv) *Historia haeresis Wicliffianae,* published with (iii), is in MS. in MS. Lambeth 140, foll. 1–98.

(v) Wood assigns to him a Chronicle in Latin verse 'a diluvio Noe ad annum 1559': MS. Cotton Vitell. C. 9, num. 13; but this is by John Harpsfield.

(vi) Twyne has collections about William of Wykeham from Harpsfield in Twyne II. foll. 170–173.

385. Robert Hegge, of C. C. C. Oxford.

(i) Catalogue of Fellows of C. C. C.: par. 135 (vi).

Cited in *City,* i. 541, 544.

(ii) Book of the Cylinder in C. C. C.: MS. no. 40 in Coxe's Cat. of C. C. C. Oxford MSS.

Cited in *City,* i. 546.

(iii) In MS. Ric. James 2, part 2, pp. 129–131 there is cited as in his hands or by him *Reliquiae in ecclesia Dunelmensi,* see p. 93.

(iv) *History of S. Cuthbert,* printed after his death in 1663.

Cited in *City,* i. 546.

(v) *Monumental inscriptions* in Cambridge and elsewhere : MS. 430 in the supplement to Coxe's Cat. of MSS. of C. C. C. Oxford.

383. Walter Hemingford or Gisburne.

Chronicon: MS. no. 53, fol. 253 in Coxe's Cat. of Magd. Coll. MSS.: Twyne XXII. 93. Richard James in MS. Ric. James 21, p. 49 cites a Merton Coll. MS. Printed by Thomas Gale in 1691.

387. Henricus rex IV.

Epistola ad papam Benedictum XIII anno 1403 : Twyne XXII. 411 from a Cottonian MS.

Cited, from Twyne, in *Hist.* i. 201.

388. Lord Herbert of Cherbury.

Materials for the life of Henry VIII: MSS. nos. 71 and 72 in Coxe's Cat. of MSS. of Jes. Coll. Oxford.

Cited in *Annals,* ii. 17.

389. John Herd, M.D.

Historia Anglicana, carmine heroico : MS. Cotton Julius C. 2.

390. Peter Heylyn.

(i) *Diary*, MS.

Wood's excerpts from this are found in Wood MS. E. 4 (*O. C.* 8560).

Cited in *Annals*, ii. 136, 338, &c.

(ii) ' Dr. Thomas Barlow hath Heylyn's *Continuation* to Godwin ' ⟨de praesulibus Angliae⟩ : so a note at the beginning of Wood MS. D. 21.

(iii) *Catalogue of the Deans and Canons of Westminster.*

Wood's transcript of this is in Wood MS. B. 12, pp. 144–175.

391. Ranulph Higden.

(i) *Polichronicon* seu Polycraticon.

Cited by Twyne in Twyne XXI. 229, 583 ; XXIII. 122 ; MS. arch. Seld. *supra* 79, p. 153 ; and in Wood MS. D. 32, p. 192. Printed in Rolls Series, 1865. There are numerous MSS. of this work in the Bodleian, but Wood cites it generally with reference to a Balliol College MS. (no. 235 in Coxe's Cat.), e. g. in *Annals*, i. 491, ii. 738 ; *City*, i. 289, ii. 291. Ric. James also, in MS. Ric. James 11, p. 159, cites the Balliol MS.

(ii) In a copy of Higden formerly in Thomas Allen's library were marginal notes (de Grimbaldo, Twyne XXI. 21, 22 ; de Adulpho patre Alfredi, Twyne XXI. 22): see Twyne XXI. 25, and MS. Langb. 15, p. 51. See MS. Digb. 201 (*O. C.* 1802).

Cited in *Annals*, ii. 106, 819.

392. John Holbroke, astronomus.

Tabulae Cantabrigienses : Twyne II. 92b, 93a, 143 ; Twyne XXI. 53.

393. Robert Holcot.

Commentarii in librum Sapientiae : excerpt in MS. Ric. James 21, p. 47, from a Merton MS.—see nos. 112, 161, 162 in Coxe's Cat. of Mert. Coll. MSS., also MS. Bodl. 279 (*O. C.* 2241).

Cited in *Annals*, i. 406.

394. John Hooker (Vowell *alias* Hooker).

(i) *Description of the City of Exeter* : MS. Ashm. 762 (*O. C.* 7421, 8079, being twice catalogued).

Cited, indirectly, in *City*, i. 234.

(ii) *Catalogue of bishops of Exeter.*
Cited in *Coll.* p. 384; *Annals*, i. 412.

395. Huguitio, Pisanus.

Derivationes magnae: MS. Bodl. 376 (*O. C.* 2486): Twyne XXII. 305.
Cited in *City*, i. 484.

396. John Joscelin.

Wood notes, in Wood MS. E. 4 (*O. C.* 8561), p. 114, that 'he wrot, as 'tis supposed, [Matthew Parker's] *de Antiquitate Britannicae ecclesiae* [1572], quaere Dr. Thomas Marshall: Dr. Thomas Barlow hath a note of John Joscelin before the *Antiq. Britan.* which he hath, quaere.'

(i) *Opuscula*: MS. Cotton Nero C. 3.

(ii) *Historia ecclesiastica regni Angliae* et vitae archiepiscoporum Cantuar.: MS. Cotton Vitell. E. 14, Vitell. D. 7.

(iii) *The Annals of England*, composed from above twenty MSS.: MS. Cotton Vitell. E. 14.

397. Henry Knighton.

Cronica, or *Historia eventuum in Anglia*: MS. Cotton Tiber. C. 7, Claud. E. 3. Excerpts in Twyne II. 278–281: XXIV. 68–71, 72–75; and in MS. Ric. James 10, pp. 34–44, 156, 164, 165. Printed in Twysden's Decem Scriptores, 1652; and in Rolls Series, 1889.
Cited frequently in *Annals*.

398. William Lambard.

Collections: MS. Cotton Vespas. A. 5.

399. Pierre de Langtoft.

Historia Bruti, in French verse: MS. Cotton Julius A. 5. Printed in Rolls Series, 1866.

400. Stephen Langton.

Expositio super Ecclesiasticum: MS. no. 20 in Coxe's Cat. of Ball. Coll. MSS.; no. 24 of Exet. Coll. MSS. and no. 239, foll. 14 of the MSS. at C. C. C. Oxford. Wood specially refers to fol. 201 of the Balliol MS. for Langton's censure on monks 'qui *decretistas* se dici cupiebant.'

401. Thomas Lanton.

Twyne XXI. 624 has an excerpt from 'Fragm. MS. incerti authoris nisi forte fuerit Thomas Lanton, Carmelita.'
Cited, from Twyne only, in *Annals*, i. 450. See p. 308.

402. John Lawerne.

Lecturae: MS. Bodl. 607 (*O. C.* 2508): Twyne XXI. 175, 178.

403. Layamon, or Laghamon.

Historia Britonum: MS. Cotton Calig. A. 9: excerpts in MS. Ric.
James 10, p. 52.

Printed in 1847: Hardy's Descriptive Catalogue, i. 353.

404. John Leland.

A careful new edition of this writer seems a distinct want in English
antiquities.

Wood notes, Wood MS. E. 4 (*O. C.* 8561), p. 124: 'Many eminent
antiquaries have made use of these his Collections; of which some
have acknowledged so, and some not.   Bale made great use of them,
but to no other end (as Pits saith) onlie to deforme them.   Camden
made us of them, but acknowledges them not: see Ralph Brooks,
York herald.'

(i) *Collectiones* or *Collectanea*: 4 vols., Leland's autograph: (*O. C.*[1]
5102–5105), MS. Top. gen. C. 1–4.   See *Life*, i. 222.

The four volumes are cited frequently in *Annals* and *City*, and
occasionally in *Fasti*.   Vol. iv is sometimes cited by its special title
'*de scriptoribus Angliae*,' e. g. in *City*, ii. 291, 292.

Vol. iv was printed by Anthony Hall in 1709 as *Commentarii de
scriptoribus Britanniae*: vols. i–iii were printed by Hearne as *De
rebus Britannicis Collectanea* in six vols., 1715.

(ii) Twyne's excerpts from Leland's *Collectanea*, vol. iv: see par.
233.

(iii) Excerpts by Wood from Leland's *Collectanea* are found in MS.
Ballard 70 (*olim* 20), foll. 1–15: but these can be only a fraction of his
excerpts.   Not only does he cite his excerpts up to fol. 17 (*City*, ii. 282,
note 9), but he cites them under an extraordinary variety of titles:—

(*a*) Collections from Leland 'under the window,' in *City*, i. 61, ii.
339, &c.: Collect. ex Lelando 'sub fenestra sched. 3,' in *City*, ii. 161,
222, &c.

(*b*) Collections from Leland, 'in 8vo,' in *City*, i. 234.

(*c*) Collect. 'ex primo tomo Lelandi,' in *City*, i. 234; 'ex quarto
tomo,' in *City*, ii. 296.

(*d*) Collect. ex Lelando 'prima schedula,' in *City*, i. 388, ii. 250, &c.

(iv) MS. Bodl. 353 (*olim* MS. Bodl. 372, *olim* MS. F. 11. 18 N.E.)
O. C.[2] 5106, is a transcript of some Collections by Leland, from

---

[1] they occur twice in the numeration, being also *O. C.* 3117–3120.

[2] numbered also, in duplicate, *O. C.* 2495.

a MS. (Leland's autograph) in the hands of Sir Henry St. George: see *City*, i. 641.

(v) Collectiones ex antiquissimis authoribus desumptae quae ad Britanniam spectant: Leland's autograph: MS. Cotton Julius C. 6.

(vi) *Itineraria in Anglia*: (now) 8 volumes, Leland's autograph: (*O. C.*[1] 5107–5112*), MS. Top. gen. E. 8–15.

In Wood's time they were four volumes, of which vol. i is cited in *Annals* and *Colleges*; vol. ii, repeatedly in *City*, and in *Annals*, i. 46; vol. iii, possibly in *Coll.* p. 273; vol. iv, frequently in *City*, ii, and possibly in *Coll.* p. 307.

Printed by Thomas Hearne in 9 volumes, 1710–1712.

(vii) A fragment of the Itineraries is in MS. Cotton Vespas. F. 9.

(viii) Wood had *Collections out of Leland's Itinerary*, which he cites in *City*, i. 272, ii. 223: but I have found no trace of them except some insignificant fragments in, I think, a Tanner MS.

(ix) Transcripts of the *Itineraries* :—

(*a*) William Burton's, MS. Bodl. 470 (*olim* MS. F. 11. 13 N. E.), O. C. 2490; and MS. Gough Gen. Top. 2.   See Hearne's Collections (O. H. S. 1889), iii. 18.

(*b*) John Stowe's, MS. Tanner 464, said to be the best.

(*c*) Browne Willis's, MS. Top. gen. C. 5, bought by the Bodleian in 1883.

(x) A MS. of Leland's in the hands of Purefoy of Wadley: *Life*, ii. 264, note.

(xi) In Twyne XXII. 167 there seems to be cited a MS. of Leland's *de Alphredo* in Thomas Allen's library.

405. Leo, Hebraeus.

Twyne II. 336; XXII. 235.   Wood MS. F. 26 (*O. C.* 8488), p. 9, no. 9 in the Catalogue of Thomas Allen's MSS.: see MS. Digb. 176 (*O. C.* 1777).

406. William Linwood, or Lyndwood.

Fragmentum MS. protestationum . . . ex parte regis et nationis Anglicanae in concilio Basiliensi anno 1433: MS. Digb. 66 (*O. C.* 1667): Twyne XXI. 304.   See par. 82 (ii).

407. Robert de Losinga, bp. of Hereford.

Liber . . . de annis domini: excerpts in Twyne XXII. 371 from MS. V. 1. 8 Jur. (i. e. MS. Auct. F. 3. 14 = *O. C.* 2372).

See Hardy's Descriptive Catalogue, ii. 75.

---

[1] also *O. C.* 3121–3123.

408. Lucianus.

De laude Cestriae: MS. Bodl. 672: excerpts in MS. Ric. James 2, part 2, p. 189.

409. John Lydgate.

Wood notes in Wood MS. E. 4 (*O. C.* 8561), p. 125:—'A false author: his books not allowed by act of parliament 34 et 35 Henr. VIII (Twyne XXI. 526); of great account with *Londinensis*; confuted by Twyne in his *Apologia.*' Excerpts in MS. Ric. James 19, p. 116; 21, p. 146, and (from a C. C. C. Oxford MS.) 26, p. 152.

Cited in *Hist.* i. 41.

410. Henry Lyte.

Wood notes that his 'brother Kit' had a copy of Lyte's Herball; see *Athenae.*

(i) '*The mysticall Oxon of Oxfourde*: a true and most auntiente recorde of the originall of Oxfourde and all Britayne'; (or, under a second title) · Certaine breif conjecturall notes touching the originall of the Universitie of Oxon and also of all Britaine called Albania and Calydonia Sylva; by Henry Lyte of Lyte's-cary, Sept. 16, 1592, sometimes a student of Oxon'; a paper found in Twyne II. foll. 162–169.

Twyne's note about it is (Twyne XXII. 417, 418): 'Here are pretty fancies which may be of some use as occasion shall serve by way of reply for Oxon against the farre-fett antiquities of Cambridge.' This note Wood, *more suo*, has taken bodily into the *Athenae.* The paper was given by Miles Windsor, a little before his death, to Twyne.

The paper contains only some dull sixteenth-century etymologies, to which we would not apply the term 'pretty fancies.'

(ii) '*Recordes of the true originall of the noble Britaynes* that sprange of the remaynes of the Troians, taken out of oblivion's treasurie, by Henry Lyte of Lyte's-carie, 1592 '; a paper found in Twyne II. foll. 160, 161.

Of the same stamp as the preceding.

411. William of Malmsbury.

Although referring to MSS. of this author, Wood for the most part used the early editions. Thus in MS. Ballard 70, p. 37, are excerpts by Wood from the Frankfort 1601 edition of Malmsbury. Cited in *City,* i. 235, 241.

(i) *De gestis pontificum Anglorum*: MS. Bodl. 357 (*O. C.* 2452): MS. Laud Misc. 598 (*O. C.* 1475). Twyne has some excerpts in Wood MS. D. 32, p. 210. Printed in Rolls Series, 1870.

Cited in *Annals,* i. 120.

(ii) *Gesta regum Anglorum*, cited also as *De regibus Angliae* or *Gesta Anglorum*: MS. Laud Misc. 548 (*O. C.* 1377): MS. Bodl. 712 (*O. C.* 2619). Excerpts from the 'Bodley' MS. are found in MS. Ric. James 11, p. 203. Printed in Rolls Series, 1887.

Cited in *Annals*, i. 39, 41, &c.

(iii) *De antiquitate coenobii Glastoniensis*: par. 18 (ii).

(iv) Abbreviatio Gulielmi Malmesbury de gestis Haymonis de imperatoribus: excerpts by Langbaine in MS. Wood donat. 2, p. 29 from MS. no. 125, fol. 86ᵛ in Coxe's Cat. of Ball. Coll. MSS.

Cited in *Annals*, i. 135.

412. John Mandwith, astronomer.

Tabulae: Twyne II. 92 b, 93 b.

413. Walter Mape.

(i) *De nugis curialium*: MS. Bodl. 851 (*O. C.* 3041): a transcript in MS. Ric. James 14, pp. 81–136, and in MS. Ric. James 31. Excerpts in Twyne XXI. 69, 241, 243, 262; Twyne XXII. 293. Printed (Camden Society), 1850.

Cited frequently in *Annals, City*.

(ii) *Apocalypsis*: MS. Ric. James 14, pp. 136–146, MS. Ric. James 19, p. 186 (from a MS. in the hands of Dr. Edward Lapworth).

(iii) *Dicta Goliardi*: a transcript in MS. Ric. James 32, from a MS. of Dr. Edward Lapworth (now MS. Harl. 978).

414. Marianus Scotus.

(i) MS. Bodl. 297 (*O. C.* 2468): excerpts in MS. Ric. James 11, pp. 218, 220, and by Twyne in Wood MS. D. 32, p. 360, as a MS. 'given to him under the name of Marianus Scotus.' It is really a copy of Florence of Worcester: Hardy's Descriptive Catalogue, ii. 46.

Cited in *Annals*, and *City*, ii. 247.

(ii) This Chronicle is continued to 1131 in MS. Bodl. 297: Hardy, *l. c.* p. 181.

Cited as 'a nameless Chronicle at the end of Marianus Scotus' in *Annals*, i. 136.

415. Adam de Marisco.

Epistolae: MS. Cotton Vitell. C. 8. Excerpts in Twyne III. 361–364; XXI. 208, 209, 262, 263, 314; XXII. 294, 296; XXIV. 24. Printed in Rolls Series (Monum. Francisc. vol. i), 1858.

Cited freely in *Annals, Fasti, Coll., City.*

416. Henry de Marleburgh.

Chronica, excerpta de medulla diversorum chronicorum a Christo ad annum 1421 : MS. Cotton Vitell. E. 5.

417. William Masters.

Oratio . . . coram Elizabetha regina at Cambridge, 5 Aug. 1564 : seen by Twyne in 'the earl of Dorset's study at Knoll,' Twyne XXIII. 499.
Cited, from Twyne only, in *Annals,* i. 99.

418. Nicholas Maurice.

A disputation, in 1583 : cited in *Annals,* ii. 216, as in Wood's possession.   I have not found it.

419. Galfredus de Meldis, astronomus.

Prognosticationes de conjunctione Saturni et Jovis . . . 1325 : MS. Digb. 176 (*O. C.* 1777) : Twyne XXII. 235.
Cited in *Hist.* i. 172.

420. John Merick, bishop of Sodor.

Litterae : MS. Cotton Julius F. 10.

421. William Merle.

Regulae ad futuram aeris temperiem : MS. Digby 176 : excerpts by Twyne in MS. arch. Seld. *supra* 79, p. 162, and in Twyne XXII. 105, 235.
Cited in *City,* i. 52.

422. Ambrose Merlin.

(i) *Vaticinia* : MSS. in Thomas Allen's library : excerpts in Twyne XXI. 147, 243, 264 (vaticinium de fractione cornuum super muros Oxon.), 277, 313, 757.   See MSS. Digby 28, 98, and 196 (*O. C.* 1629, 1699, 1797), and MSS. Bodl. 91 and 623 (*O. C.* 1891, 2157)
Cited, from Twyne, in *City,* i. 233, 234.
(ii) *Commentatores Merlini.*
Twyne XXI. 277, 288, 313; XXIII. 122.

423 John Mirfield (Marfield).

Breviarium Bartholomei : a large folio treating of medicine, temp. Henr. VI : a MS. in Pembroke College (see 6th Rep. of Hist, MSS.

Comm. p. 550): excerpts in Twyne II. 96 b, XXII. 374, being lent to him by Mr. Thomas Clayton, Master of Pembroke.

Cited, but only from Twyne, in *Annals*, ii. 715.

424. Jeffrey Monmouth.

Historia Britonum: excerpts by Twyne in Wood MS. D. 32, pp. 189, 216.

Cited generally from the printed copy, as e. g. in *City*, i. 56, 233, 238: but MS. copies are also vaguely cited:—

(*a*) A MS. in S. Paul's library (*City*, i. 233).

(*b*) A MS. in the Bodleian (*City*, i. 233); where there are, of course, several MSS. of this author.

(*c*) A MS. in New Coll. library, no. 276 in Coxe's Cat. of New Coll. MSS. (*City*, i. 233).

425. William de Monte, or de Montibus.

(i) *Numerale*, init. 'Deus unus est, contra': MS. Cotton Vespas. E. 10; Twyne XXI. 30; XXII. 136, 165; XXIII. 32, 42.

Cited in *Fasti*, p. 8.

(ii) *De tropis*: also in MS. Cotton Vespas. E. 10.

(iii) *Summa*: cited in MS. Ric. James 21, p. 108 from a Corpus (Oxford) MS., no. 360 in Coxe's Cat.

426. Robertus Montensis.

Chronicon, or *Supplementum ad Chronicon Sigeberti*, A.D. 1013–1210: MS. Cotton Domit. 8, foll. 70ᵛ–82: MS. Bodl. 212 (*O. C.* 2041): MS. Cotton Julius B. 10. Excerpts in Twyne II. 25 b; XXI. 778; XXII. 239; XXIV. 77–80. Often printed from 1513 onwards.

Twyne in one place cites MS. Cotton Claud. E. 8, foll. 1–60 as Montensis, but that is Diceto: see par. 348.

427. Sir Thomas More.

(i) More's *Epistola ad Acad. Oxon.* (printed 1633): Twyne II. fol. 144.

(ii) More's *Life of Richard III* (printed 1651): cited in *Coll.* p. 383: *City*, i. 531, 532.

(iii) Life of Sir Thomas More: Twyne XXI. 325.

(iv) William Roper's Life of Sir Thomas More: MS. Bodl. 966 (*O. C.* 3303).

Cited in *City*, i. 511.

(v) Life of Sir Thomas More, in Wood's hands, cited in *City*, i. 511, is, I suppose, a printed book, perhaps Wood 289 (John Hoddeson's *Vita*, Lond. 1662).

428. Daniel de Morley, or de Merlac.

De natura inferiorum et superiorum, libri duo : MS. in C. C. C. Oxford : Twyne XXI. 6, 283. Twyne's excerpts are in MS. no. 268 (fol. 166ᵛ) in Coxe's Cat. of MSS. of C. C. C. Oxon.

Cited in *Annals*, i. 168, 281.

Wood notes in Wood MS. E. 4 (*O. C.* 8561), p. 137 :—'Dedicated to John of Oxford, bishop of Norwich. The book itself I have not quoted, only the preface to it : but since my seing it in C. C. C. library Oxon, I heare by Dr. ⟨Edward⟩ Pocok that the said preface is toren out by some vile and envious person. In the initiall letter of the said preface was the picture of a doctor, with a book laying before him, and certaine auditors with gownes on that seemed attentively to heare him.' The book seems now to have gone from C. C. C. altogether.

429. Adam de Murimuth.

MS. no. 53 in Coxe's Cat. of Magd. Coll. MSS. ; MS. Cotton Claud. E. 8. Excerpts by Richard James in MS. Ric. James 10, p. 159, and 19, p. 3 ; and by Langbaine in MS. Langb. 6, pp. 263, 266. Printed in Rolls Series, 1889.

Cited in *Annals*, i. 392.

430. Johannes de Muris.

Tractatus de conjunctione Saturni et Jovis, 1345 : MSS. 5 and 61 among Thomas Allen's MSS. : excerpts in Twyne XXII. 235. MSS. Digb. 97 and 176 (*O. C.* 1698, 1777).

431. Alexander de Neckam.

(i) *Super Cantica*, libri sex, quorum primus totus est in laude Beatae Mariae Virginis : MS. Bodl. 356 (*O. C.* 2716) : excerpts in Twyne XXIII. 658, and by Langbaine in MS. Wood donat. 7, p. 127.

Cited, *de laude beatae Virginis*, in *Annals*, i. 190.

(ii) *De naturis rerum* : MS. no. 245 in Coxe's Cat. of MSS. of C. C. C. Oxford. Excerpts in MS. Ric. James 26, p. 165. Printed in Rolls Series, 1863.

Cited in *Annals*, i. 27.

(iii) *De sapientia divina* : printed with (ii).

Cited in *Annals*, i. 12.

432. Nennius, Bangoriensis.

Historia Britonum : excerpts by Twyne in MS. Wood D. 32, pp. 312, 350. The following MSS. are mentioned by Wood in MS. Wood E. 4 (*O. C.* 8561), p. 146 :—

(*a*) MS. Cotton Vespas. D. 21 : 'a very old copy, containing more than other copies.'

(*b*) MS. Bodl. 163 (*O. C.* 2016) : 'a copie, which though it seems to be antient, yet many things therin seeme to contradict other authors.'

Cited in *Annals*, i. 11, 25.

Excerpts from the copy in MS. Corp. Cambr. 101 are in MS. Ric. James 18, p. 50.

In Twyne XXII. 414 Twyne says that Richard James showed him in Jesus College library [1] a large folio MS. of Nennius Britannicus : init. 'in principio confecisset deus informem materiem' : 'explicit liber qui dicitur Ymago Mundi.' Twyne has excerpts from this MS. in MS. arch. Seld. supra 79, p. 163.

433. John Newton, of Brasenose College.

(i) *History of the Parliamentary Visitation*, 1648 : Wood MS. F. 35, fol. 178 : *Life*, i. 142.

(ii) He is probably the 'Mr. Newton' cited in *City*, i. 292, note 4.

434. Nigellus, monk of Rewley.

In Twyne XXII. 106 Twyne mentions 'a book containing extracts from Liber Nigelli, fratris de Regali Loco in surburbiis Oxon. formerly in the possession of Robert Stevyns, Scoti, in vico Regali apud West-monasterium degentis ; which Robert said he was descended from Herbert Stevyns, steward of Rewley Abbey.' The *incipit* of the book was 'Notandum secundum collectiones quas primordialiter.'

Cited, but only from Twyne, in *Annals*, i. 148 ; *City*, ii. 82.

435. Ralph Niger.

Chronicon a condito mundo : MS. Cotton Cleop. C. 10, foll. 1–55 : excerpts in MS. Ric. James 7, p. 231, and 10, p. 79 ; and in Twyne XXI. 304. Ric. James in MS. Ric. James 26, p. 2, cites MS. 4⁰ Th. A. 21 (MS. Bodl. 101 = *O. C.* 1948).

Cited in *Annals*, i. 161.

436. Lawrence Noell.

(i) Collectanea ex chronicis Gregorii Caerguent [Hardy's Descriptive Catalogue, iii. 214] : MS. Cotton Vespas. A. 5.

(ii) Collections out of the registers of Worcester and Gloucester : also in Vespas. A. 5.

(iii) *Collectanea* : MS. Cotton Vitell. D. 7 ; Domit. A. 18, fol. 49.

[1] apparently not now in Jes. Coll. library.

437. William Noy.

Collect. de chartis regiis concernentibus prohibitiones regias : Twyne XXII. 382.

438. William Occam : Twyne XXI. 754.

Dialogi inter magistrum et discipulum : MS. 69 in Coxe's Cat. of MSS. of S. John's Oxford.

Cited, from the printed copies, in *Annals,* i. 307, 320.

439. Walter de Odington, or Evesham.

(i) De planetarum domibus : Twyne II. 92 b.

(ii) Tabulae astronomicae : Twyne II. 92 a, b, 94.

(iii) Rectificatio de motu octavae sphaerae : MS. Laud Misc. 674 (*O. C.* 504).

(iv) Liber vel tractatus de aetate mundi : cited frequently by Ashenden in his *Summa.*

(v) Observations of the fixed stars.

(vi) Tabulae latitudinum planetarum : MSS. Digb. 72 and 97 (*O. C.* 1673, 1698).

(vii) Tractatus qui dicitur *Icosedron* : MS. Digb. 119 (*O. C.* 1720).

440. John Orum.

Lectura super Apocalypsim : MS. Bodl. 859 (*O. C.* 2722).
Cited in *Hist.* ii. 62.

441. Johannes de Oxenedes.

Annales ab adventu Saxonum: MS. Cotton Nero D. 2, foll. 214–234.
Printed in Rolls Series, 1859.

442. William Packington (or Pachenton).

Chronicon : known to Wood only from Leland Collect. tom. 1, p. 657 : it gave 29 June as the day of the beheading of Piers Gaveston ; *City,* ii. 322.

443. Matthew Paris : Twyne XXI. 697.

(i) *De origine et processu monasterii S. Albani* : MS. Cotton Claud. E. 4 : begun by Matthew Paris, continued by William Rishanger, and by Thomas Walsingham : Twyne III. 247, XXI. 690 : MS. Ric. James 10, pp. 103–117, 166.   Printed in Rolls Series, 1867.

(ii) *Historia Major,* or Chronica Major, or Flores Historiarum : MS. Cotton Nero D. 5, foll. 1–293, MSS. Corp. Cambr. 26 and 16,

MS. Reg. 14 C. vii, fol. 157. Excerpts in Twyne XXI. 10, 78, 144, 627, 630 ; MS. Ric. James 10, pp. 16–29 and 18, p. 117. Printed in 1571 by Matthew Parker: and by William Wats in 1640: and in Rolls Series, 1872 sqq.

Cited, from the printed copy, frequently in *Annals* and *City* : cited also as a ' MS. in S. James's Library ' (i. e. MS. Reg. 14 C. vii) in *Annals*, i. 127, 803, from Twyne, who noted, in Twyne XXI. 816, that it ' differs much from the printed copy.'   Twyne's strictures on Wats' edition are found in Twyne XXII. 535 ; and William Fulman's strictures in Wood MS. D. 9, p. 11.

(iii) *Historia Minor*, or Historia Anglorum : MS. Reg. 14 C. vii, foll. 9–156^v : printed from that MS. in Rolls Series, 1866.

444. Reginald Peacock.

(i) *Abbreviarium* : cited in Twyne II. 236 as a MS. in bibl. Bodl. In MS. Ric. James 21, p. 63 are excerpts from MS. Bodl. 117 (*O. C.* 1979).

Cited, from Twyne, in *Annals*, i. 604.

(ii) MS. Ric. James 14, pp. 49–79 is Peacock's *Donet*.

445. Martinus Polonus.

MS. no. 122 in Coxe's Cat. of Mert. Coll. MSS.: MS. Bodl. 355 (cited in MS. Ric. James 10, p. 81).

Printed from 1559 onwards.

446. Richard de Pophis.

Summa secundum stilum curiae Romanae : MS. no. 55 in Coxe's Cat. of MSS. of C. C. C. Oxon.   Cited, from this MS., in Ric. James 21, p. 110 : Twyne XXII. 165.

Cited in *Annals*, i. 620.

447. Edmund Powell.

Tractatus contra Lutherum : Twyne XXI. 481 (printed in 1523).

Cited in *Hist.* ii. 108.

448. William Reade.

(i) *Vitae archiepisc. Cantuar.*: MS. Cotton Julius B. 3: Twyne XXI. 147.

Cited in *Annals*, i. 475 ; *City*, ii. 283.

(ii) *Brevis historia a condito mundo* : MS. Cotton Julius B. 3 : Twyne XXI. 147.

(iii) *De vitis pontificum Romanorum* : MS. Cotton Julius B. 3 : cited in Twyne XXII. 402 as a MS. in Thomas Allen's library.

(iv) *Tabulae Oxonienses* : Twyne II. 92 b, 93 a, 95 b, 96, 143 a. See in Macray's Catalogue of Digby MSS.

(v) *Canones*, in explanation of the Tabulae : Twyne II. 92 b, 94 b.

(vi) *Prognosticationes* : MS. Digb. 176 (*O. C.* 1777). Cited in *Annals*, i. 450, 479.

(vii) Part of his will : Twyne XXIV. 107.

449. Ralph Remmington.

Annales : Twyne III. 438, 439 ; XXI. 237.

450. William de Remmington.

Sermo in synodo apud Eboracum, 1573, in illud thema *Luceat lux vestra coram hominibus* : cited in Twyne XXIII. 116 as no. 8 among Thomas Allen's 4° MSS.

Cited, from Twyne, in *Fasti*, p. 29.

451. Reymundus.

Opus majus Reymundi Galfredi de rebus astrologicis : init. 'In Dei nomine Amen : incipit Raymundus,' &c. It at one time belonged to Edward Kelly, and was seen by Twyne 'in the earl of Dorset's study at Knoll' (Twyne XXIII. 499).

452. Richard, prior of Hexham.

Historia de gestis regis Stephani : MS. Corp. Cambr. 139, art. 3 : excerpts from that MS. in MS. Ric. James 17, p. 96 : Twyne XXIV. 618. Printed in Twysden's Decem Scriptores, 1652.

Cited in *Annals*, i. 63.

453. Richard Ringsted (Rynsted).

Lectura super parabolas Salamonis : MS. Bodl. 829 (*O. C.* 2720). Cited in *City*, ii. 261, from Twyne XXII. 241.

454. Thomas Risdon.

(i) *Survey of Devonshire* : *Life*, i. 182 note 5, 508.

(ii) Wood's notes from Risdon are in Wood MS. D. 7 (3) (*O. C.* 8521), and are possibly the Collect. Devon. cited in *City*, i. 389. Wood took from Risdon the statement that 'David Tolley was borne at Kingsbridge' (*Hist.* ii. 360).

455. William Rishanger.

(i) Continuation of the book *de origine et processu monasterii S. Albani*, A.D. 1259–1272: MS. Cotton Claud. E. 4: Twyne XXI. 690, MS. Ric. James 10, pp. 169, 170. Printed in Rolls Series. See par. 46 (i).

Cited in *Annals*, i. 266, 267.

(ii) *Chronicon*: MS. Cotton Claud. D. 6, fol. 97, Faust. B. 9: Twyne XXI. 16 b, 176, 456. Printed (Camden Society), 1840.

456. Daniel Rogers.

In Wood MS. E. 4 (*O. C.* 8561), a slip at p. 170, and p. 186, Wood has notes for his life, which he afterwards embodied in the *Athenae*.

(i) 'A book of the Greek language of his composure in Archivis bibl. Bodl.': Wood MS. E. 4, p. 186: but this is perhaps only a misdescription of MS. Auct. D. 3. 19, a Greek MS. formerly *owned* by him.

(ii) Verses printed in Ralph Agas' 1578 map of Oxford.

Cited in *Annals*, i. 16; *City*, i. 44, &c.

(iii) *Antiquae de Britannia observationes*: MS. Cotton Titus F. 10.

457. John Rous, or Rossus: Twyne XVIII. 481.

'A person he was more industrious than judicious': Wood's note in Wood MS. E. 4 (*O. C.* 8561), p. 191.

(i) *Historia de regibus Angliae*: MS. Cotton Vespas. A. 12. Printed by Thomas Hearne in 1716.

Cited *passim* in *City, Annals, Colleges*.

(*a*) William Lambarde's Collections from it are found in MS. Cotton Vespas. A. 5.

(*b*) Richard James', in MS. Ric. James 7, p. 197.

(*c*) Brian Twyne's, in Twyne XXI. 93, 98–103, 238; VII. 314; XXII. 349, 350.

(*d*) Anthony Wood's, in Wood MS. D. 2, pp. 406–409.

(ii) *Rotulus membranaceus de comitibus Warwic*. Printed by Thomas Hearne in 1729.

Cited in *Annals*, i. 114; ii. 222.

Two MSS. of this are alluded to:—

(*a*) One which Twyne (Twyne XXI. 623) found 'penes Robertum Arden de Parkhall, com. Warw.' In Twyne XXII. 238, Twyne wrote down some verses which occurred at the end of it, and Wood printed these, solely from Twyne, in *Hist.* ii. 77. On a slip inserted at p. 189 in Wood MS. E. 4 (*O. C.* 8561), Wood says of this roll:—

'Upon the dorse of which roll is written an account of the originall name of England, a catalogue of popes, the names of the bishops of Worcester, and severall genealogies of various earles of England: armes also and pictures of severall earles of Warwick and other nobles.'

(*b*) In Wood MS. E. 4 (*O. C.* 8561), p. 190, Wood mentions a copy which he found in the hands of Sir William Dugdale 'written in a book'; and he there notes down from it some emendations of the text of the verses.

(iii) *Liber de vita et gestis Richardi Beauchamp*, comitis Warwic.: MS. Cotton Julius E. 4, fol. 201.

(iv) *De Academiis*: cited in Twyne XXI. 47.

(v) *Tabella aularum*: found in an excerpt in MS. no. 270, fol. 51^v of Coxe's Cat. of C. C. C. Oxford, and in Robert Plot's transcript of Sir Henry St. George's fragment of Leland, i. e. MS. Bodl. 353: see *City*, i. 641. Printed in *City*, i. 638–641.

Cited *passim* in *City, Annals, Colleges.*

Wood's transcript of it is in MS. Ballard 70.

458. Thomas Rudborn, monk of S. Swithun's, Winchester.

(i) *Chronicon*: MS. Cotton Nero A. 17: Twyne XXI. 16 b. Wood notes, Wood MS. E. 4 (*O. C.* 8561), p. 185:—'he speaketh of Grimbald and Neot, but there is nothing of Oxon in it.'

Cited in *Annals*, i. 339. In *Annals*, i. 112, it is cited as in Lambeth library: but MS. Lamb. 183 is Rudborn's *Historia Major.*

(ii) In Wood MS. E. 4 (*O. C.* 8561), is this note:—
'*Historia Major*' (of Rudborn) 'est in bibliotheca S. Benedicti' (i.e. C. C. C. Cambr.) 'se ₵ 57.'

459. Johannes Sarisburiensis.

Policraticus sive *De nugis curialium*: Ric. James has excerpts from a MS. in S. Paul's library, in MS. Ric. James 23, p. 31. In Wood MS. E. 4 (*O. C.* 8561), p. 135, Wood notes that he saw a copy of *De nugis curialium,* 'printed beyond seas in an old black character' in the hands of John Wilton (*Life*, ii. 38).

460. Michael Scot.

Liber introductorius ad astrologiam: MS. Bodl. 266 (*O. C.* 2466). Cited in *Annals*, i. 287.

461. Senatus Bravonius.

Epistolae: MS. Bodl. 633 (*O. C.* 1966). Excerpts in MS. Ric. James 2, part 2, pp. 179–187; Twyne XXI. 240.

Cited in *Annals*, i. 75, 177.

462. Serlo.

MS. Ric. James 15, foll. 73ᵛ–176.

463. Richard Shann.

Book of Memories, MS.: *Life*, ii. 295. Wood had excerpts in Wood MS. D. 18, which are printed in *Life*, ii. 302–304.

Cited in *Annals*, ii. 279.

464. Ralph Sheldon.

In his house at Weston, near Long Compton in Warwickshire, Sheldon had a considerable collection of MSS.[1], chiefly genealogical and heraldic, the greater part of which are now in the College of Arms (*Life*, iii. 115). He had also a considerable library of printed books. Several of his MSS. and books came into Wood's possession: *Life*, iii. 102–105.

(i) *Wood's Collections from Sheldon's books and MSS.* may be thus summarized :—

(a) *Notes of Sheldon's books*: Wood MS. D. 7 (2) (*O. C.* 8519): excerpts from books in this collection. Frequently referred to in Wood's various notes. It is sometimes cited as *Collect. Sheldon*.

(b) *Catalogue of plays in Sheldon's library*: in Wood MS. D. 18.

(c) *Catalogue of MSS. in Sheldon's library*: Wood MS. D. 6 (*O. C.* 8528).

(d) *Collections of genealogies* made from this library: Wood MS. F. 7 (*O. C.* 8469): *Life*, ii. 364.

(e) *Notes of parchment-rolls* in this library: Wood MS. D. 6 (*O. C.* 8528).

(ii) *Sheldon's own Collections* may be thus summarized :—

(a) *Catalogue of MSS. in his possession*: Wood MS. B. 7 (*O. C.* 8578), foll. 11–22.

(b) Notes of his travels in France and Italy: Wood MS. B. 14, fol. 50; *Life*, ii. 181.

(c) *Church notes*: collections of epitaphs, &c. from various churches in England: Wood MSS. C. 10 and C. 11 (*O. C.* 8550, 8551).

---

[1] one of them is cited in *City*, i. 271, note 4. 'Sheldon's Chest,' containing pedigrees, is cited in *Colleges*, p. 306.

(*d*) *A book of pedigrees* : Wood MS. F. 3 (*O. C.* 8465).

(*e*) *Miscellanea* : collections from MSS. : Wood MS. D. 15 (*O. C.* 8552).

(*f*) Transcript of a MS. of lord Brudenell's, about peers and knights temp. Edw. II : Wood MS. F. 33 (*O. C.* 8495).

(*g*) *Common-place book* : cited in *City*, ii. 44.

(*h*) *Liber Collectionum* : cited in *City*, ii. 56, and perhaps in *Coll.* p. 145.

465. William Shepesheved (Schepseved).

Chronicon : MS. Cotton Faust. B. 6, foll. 69–91.

466. John Shepreve (Schepreve).

Life of John Claymond in Latin hexameters : MSS. nos. 257, 266 (foll. 234–244), 280, 302 in Coxe's Cat. of MSS. of C. C. C. Oxford. A transcript of it, by Henry Jackson, is in Wood MS. F. 30 (*O. C.* 8492).

Cited in *Coll.* p. 359, and frequently in *City*.

467. Henry de Silegrave.

Chronicon : MS. Cotton Cleop. A. 12. Printed (Caxton Society), 1844.

468. Walter Skirlaw.

De generatione et corruptione : MS. in Durham library.
Cited in *Coll.* p. 46.

469. John Somour (Somer).

(i) *Chronicon* : init. : 'Dani interfecti in Anglia' : MS. Cotton Domit. A. 2 : see Little's Grey Friars, p. 245.

(ii) *Calendarium* ad meridiem Univ. Oxon. : MS. Cotton Vespas. E. 7 and Faust. A. 2 : MS. Digb. 5 (*O. C.* 1606), fol. 73. Twyne XXI. 234.

Cited in *City*, ii. 377.

(iii) *Castigationes Calendarii.*
Cited in *Annals*, i. 341.

470. John Stafford (Strafford).

Versus de regibus Angliae et eorum gestis : MS. Cotton Titus A. 19.

471. Gilbertus de Stone, Canon of Wells.

Epistolae : MS. Bodl. 859 (*O. C.* 2722) : excerpts in Twyne II. 126 a; III. 245 ; XXI. 634 ; and in MS. Ric. James 19, p. 127.

Cited in *Annals*, i. 470.

472. John de Stratford, archbishop of Canterbury.

Constitutio provincialis : MS. Digb. 81 (*O. C.* 1682) : MS. Cotton Otho A. 16.

473. Thomas Swan.

Epistola ad Gulielmum Swan, Oxon., ex Aula Graeca Londini : MS. Cotton Cleop. C. 4, fol. 142ᵛ. The Cottonian Catalogue (1802) puts it as 'Epistola . . . scripta Oxonii in aula Graeca.'

474. William Swanne.

Bullae, litterae, processus Curiae Romanae de rebus ad ecclesiam Anglicanam et Acad. Oxon. spectantibus : MS. arch. Seld. B. *olim* 21 *nunc* 23 (*O. C.* 3351) : MS. Cotton Cleop. C. 6.

475. Roger Swinset.

De insolubilibus : MS. Bodl. 676 (*O. C.* 2593).
Cited in *Annals.* i. 419.

476. Robert Talbot.

(i) Annotationes in Antonini Itinerarium : MS. Cotton Julius F. 11 : MS. e Mus. 199 (*O. C.* 3709).

(ii) *Aurum ex stercore* : init. 'Certe non est rarum quod barbari stili,' &c. : 4° MS. in Thomas Allen's library : MS. no. 258 in Coxe's Cat. of MSS. in C. C. C. Oxford. See Twyne XXI. 363.

Excerpts by Wood are found in MS. Ballard 70, pp. 45, 46. One of the lines in it is :—

'Oxoniam multi veniunt redeunt quoque stulti.'

Cited frequently in *Annals.*

Bound up with this in the Corp. MS. is John Twyne's 'Observations from Humanity authors.'

477. Thomas Talbot.

Analecta : MS. Cotton Vespas. D. 17.
Cited in *Hist.* ii. 346.

478. . . . Taverner.

History of the family of Taverner : now in Wood MS. F. 31 : see also *Life,* i. 50.

479. Johannes de Taxter.

Chronicon : MS. Cotton Julius A. 1, foll. 2–42. Hardy's Descriptive Catalogue, iii. 167.

480. Thomas de Teukesbury.

Quatuor principalia Musicae : MS. Digb. 90 (*O. C.* 1691).
Cited in *Annals*, ii. 722 ; *City*, ii. 377.

481. Themistius.

(i) *Commentarii in Aristot. de Coelo et Mundo* : see 'Catal. MSS. Coll. Ball.' pp. 113, 123 ⟨perhaps MS. Wood donat. 4 : see par. 212⟩.
But in Coxe's Cat. of Ball. Coll. MSS., MS. no. 195 is given as Commentarii super Aristot. libros *de anima*.

(ii) Turned into Latin by William de Morebecka, see Twyne XXIV. 263 ; Cat. of Allen's MSS. (*O. C.* 8488), p. 5, num. 51.
Cited in *Annals*, i. 279.

In Coxe's Cat. of Ball. Coll. MSS. no. 99 is William de Morbeka's Latin version of *Simplicius*, comment. super Aristot. de Coelo et Mundo.

482. Francis Thynne.

(i) *Collections of Antiquities* : MS. Cotton Cleop. C. 3, fol. 62.
(ii) *Miscellanies of the Treasury* written to Thomas lord Buckhurst anno 1599 : seen by Twyne 'in the earl of Dorset's study at Knoll' : Twyne XXIII. 502 b.
(iii) *Vitae archiepiscoporum Cantuar.*
Cited in Twyne's *Apologia* p. 116 ; Twyne XXI. 13. Wood's excerpts from these lives are found in MS. Bodl. 594.

483. . . . Tilley.

History and antiquities of England, Anglicè : cited by Twyne in Wood MS. D. 32, p. 322, Twyne IV. 448.
Cited, from Twyne only, in *Annals*, i. 126, 128.

484. Nicholas Trivet.

Annales regum Angliae :—

(*a*) MS. no. 256 in Coxe's Cat. of Merton Coll. MSS. Excerpts from this by Ric. James are found in MS. Ric. James 19, p. 49 ; 22, p. 30 ; by Twyne, in Twyne II. 174, XXII. 343 ; and by Wood in MS. Bodl. 594 (cited in *City*, ii. 325).
Cited frequently in *Annals, Fasti, City*.
(*b*) Wood notes in Wood MS. E. 4 (*O. C.* 8561), p. 207, that the copy published at Paris in 1668 by Lucas Acherius was from a MS. belonging to Emericus Bigot, and that 'it differs from the Merton copy in many things.'
(*c*) MS. Arundel 220.
(*d*) MS. Cotton Nero D. 10, Otho D. 8.

485. John de Trokelowe.

Annales A.D. 1307–1323: MS. Cotton Claud. D. 6, fol. 192.
Printed in Rolls Series, 1866.

486. Friar Tryvytlam.

De laude Univ. Oxon. : init. 'Ad te nunc habeo verbum, O civitas.'
Cited in *Annals*, i. 78, 491.

(*a*) There was a copy in the Cottonian library: 'a narrow long
book in a hand of King Henry VI his time: it has much for the
Minorite Friars and against the endowed religious, viz. Benedictines
and Cistercians': so Wood in Wood MS. E. 4, p. 207, from Twyne.
Excerpts from this Cottonian MS. are found in Twyne XXIV. 219–
304; and in MS. Ric. James 7, pp. 85–88.

(*b*) Printed by Hearne, in 1729, from a MS. of Roger Gale.

487. Simon de Tunstede.

De musica : MS. Digb. 90 (*O. C.* 1691): MS. Bodl. 515 (*O. C.*
2185).
Cited in *Hist.* ii. 722 ; *City*, ii. 377.

488. John Twyne.

(i) *Collections*, in C. C. C. library, given by his grandson Brian
Twyne, including 'Observations on Humanity authors': MS. no.
258, fol. 69 in Coxe's Cat. of MSS. of C. C. C. Oxon.

(ii) His epitaph ; Twyne XXI. 625 ; MS. no. 256, fol. 63 in Coxe's
Cat., *ut supra*.

489. John of Tynemouth.

(i) *Historia Aurea* : MS. Bodl. 240 (*O. C.* 2469).
This MS. is cited under great varieties of title and of attributions
of authorship :—

(*a*) *Historia Aurea* is cited in *Annals*, i. 121, 203, 510, &c.
(*b*) *Golden History*, in *City*, i. 233, 244, &c.
(*c*) *Abbreviationes Historiae Aureae*, in *Fasti*, p. 31.
(*d*) *Chronicon Tynmouth*, in *Annals*, i. 362 ; *City*, ii. 161, 249.
(*e*) *John Tynmouth*, in *City*, i. 234, 255.
(*f*) *Johannes Anglicus*, in *City*, i. 233, 255.
(*g*) *Johannes Eboracensis*, in *City*, i. 233.

Wood refers for this MS. to Twyne II. 34 ; IV. 172 ; XXI. 293,
313, 586; and to MS. Wood donat. 4, p. 2.   Richard James has
excerpts 'ex historia Johannis Anglici' in MS. Ric. James 2, part 1,

pp. 56–83. In Wood MS. E. 4 (*O. C.* 8561), pp. 204, 205, Wood has a number of jottings on the question of the authorship.

(ii) *Vita . . . Oswini*: MS. in 16mo. formerly in Brian Twyne's possession: init. 'Antiquorum incuria modernorum diligentiam in multis conatibus cogit deficere': see MS. no. 134 in Coxe's Cat. of C. C. C. Oxford MSS.

Excerpts from this MS. by Henry Jackson, are found in Wood MS. D. 18 (*O. C.* 8563), fol. 162.

490. John Tyssington.

(i) *Confessio* adversus Wycliffe: MS. Bodl. 703 (*O. C.* 2766): MS. e Mus. 86 (*O. C.* 3629). Twyne XXI. 106, XXII. 323.

(ii) *Scutum fidei Catholicae* adversus Wycliffe: Twyne XXI. 501.

491. Richard de Ullerstone.

Defensorium dotationis ecclesiae, finit. Oxoniae 1401; MS. formerly in Salisbury library. Cited in Twyne XXII. 402: cited, as being in Twyne's possession, in MS. Ric. James 22, p. 144.

Cited, from Twyne only, in *Annals*, i. 373.

492. Radulphus de Ulmonte.

Disquisito de modo unionis ecclesiae: init. 'In nomine patris et filii' &c.—altogether for Benedict and against Boniface: Twyne XXIII. 652.

493. Nicholas Upton.

De coloribus armorum: MS. Cotton Nero C. 3. Cited in *Annals*, i. 141.

494. Augustine Vincent.

Catalogues of Knights, &c.: *Life*, iii. 102.

495. John Vincent.

Catalogues of Knights, &c.: *Life*, iii. 102.

496. Petrus de Vineis.

Epistolae: MS. Bodl. 816 (*O. C.* 2686), contains more than the printed copy: MS. Ric. James 2, part 2, pp. 57–64; Twyne XXI. 357; Langbaine in MS. Wood donat. 7, p. 87.

Cited frequently in *Annals*.

497. Galfridus Vinesauf, or Anglicus.

Poetria de artificio elocutionis: MSS. Digb. 64 and 104 (*O. C.* 1665, 1705): MS. Laud Misc. 707 (*O. C.* 850). Twyne XXI. 644; XXII. 103, 420.

498. ... Vitellio.

Perspectivae magistri Vitellionis, Poloni; initium libri 'Veritatis amatori, fratri Willelmo de Morbeka': a MS. formerly belonging to John Dee, seen by Twyne, who thought it three hundred years old. —Printed at Nürnberg, 1535.

Cited in *Annals*, i. 279.

499. John Waldby.

Expositio in symbolum Apostolorum.

(*a*) 'Lately in the library of John Theyer.' See MS. Reg. 7 E. ii and 8 C. i.

(*b*) Cited in *Annals*, i. 54, as in Lambeth library.

(*c*) MS. Laud Misc. 296 (*O. C.* 1159).

500. Roger Walden.

(i) *Historia*, ab initio mundi ad annum 1249 : MS. Cotton Julius B. 13.

(ii) Epitome Historiae Rogeri Walden : in MS. Cotton Faust. B. 9. Twyne XXI. 182.

Cited in *Colleges*, p. 74.

501. Thomas Walden.

(i) *Fasciculus Zizaniorum* Johannis Wiclevi : MS. e Mus. 86 (*O. C.* 3629). Twyne XXI. 114; XXII. 141. Printed in Rolls Series, 1858. Cited in *Annals, Fasti.*

(ii) *Doctrinale antiquitatum fidei* ecclesiae Catholicae : MSS. Bodl. 261, 262 (*O. C.* 2436, 2437). Twyne XXI. 487, 493, 497 : XXII. 141.

(iii) *De sacramentis*, MS.

Cited in *Fasti*, p. 18 : *City*, ii. 383, 406.

502. John de Wallingford.

Chronicon : MS. Cotton Julius D. 7, art. 6. Excerpts in MS. Ric. James 18, p. 104. Printed by Thomas Gale in 1691.

503. Thomas de Walsingham.

(i) Continuation of de origine et processu monasterii S. Albani : MS. Cotton Claud. E. 4 : Twyne XXI. 690. See par. 46 (i).

Cited in *Annals* i. 158, 388, 398.

(ii) *Deflorationes ex historia majore Thomae Walsingham* : cited in Twyne XVI. 588.

Cited in *Annals*, i. 544, 545.

(iii) *Ypodigma Neustriae* : cited by Twyne in MS. Wood D. 32, pp. 190, 215. Printed in Rolls Series, 1876.

504. John Walter.

Canones Tabularum : MS. Laud Misc. 674 (*O. C.* 504) : Twyne II. 93[v], 94.

505. William Warham.

A roll containing his ' inthronization.'

(*a*) MS. Bodl. Rolls 8 (*O. C.* 2968), a *printed* paper.

(*b*) MS. Bodl. 966 (*O. C.* 3033), probably a transcript of (*a*). See Twyne XXII. 189.

506. Roger Wendover.

Chronicon or *Flores Historiarum* : MS. Cotton Otho B. 5. Twyne XXII. 62–65.   Printed in Rolls Series, 1886.

Cited in *Annals, City*.

507. Thomas Werkworth.

Tractatus Sphaerae : MS. Digb. 97, fol. 143 (*O. C.* 1698).   Twyne II. 92.

508. Matthew of Westminster : same as **Florilegus**, par. 362.

Flores Historiarum : printed by Matthew Parker, Lond. 1570. Printed in Rolls Series, 1890.

Cited in *Annals*, i. 182.

(*a*) A MS. in S. James' library (*nunc* MS. Reg. 14 C. 6) is cited in *City*, i. 237.

(*b*) MS. e Mus. 149 : see par. 362.

(*c*) MS. Laud Misc. 572.

(*d*) MS. no. 37 in Coxe's Cat. of All Souls Coll. MSS. : excerpts from this MS. in MS. Ric. James 26, p. 91.

509. William Wey.

Itinerarium ad Terram Sanctam : MS. Bodl. 565 (*O. C.* 2351) : MS. Langb. 5, p. 452.

510. John de Whethampstead.

(i) *De historiis et historiographis* : MS. Cotton Nero C. 6.   Twyne XXI. 24.

Cited in *Annals*, i. 62.

(ii) *Granarium* [Johannis de ' loco-frumenti '] : excerpts thence in MS. Ric. James 23, p. 88 ; 26, p. 32.

(iii) MS. Ric. James 21, p. 43 has the inscription *Fratribus Oxoniae* printed in *City*, ii. 258.

511. Robert Whitinton.

MS. Bodl. 523 (*O. C.* 2199): Twyne XXI. 318.
Cited in *Hist.* ii. 722.

512. Wulstanus.

Vita S. Swithuni : MS. Auct. F. 2. 14 (*O. C.* 2567): Twyne XXI. 270.
Cited in *City*, ii. 44.

513. John Wycliffe.

(i) *Determinatio de Dominio* : MS. Bodl. 703 (*O. C.* 276, art. 6). Twyne XXI. 501 ; MS. Ric. James 3, p. 262.

(ii) *Trialogus* : Twyne XXI. 445, 494, 499, 500, 592 ; XXII. 284, 321, 322 : MS. Ric. James 3, p. 268.
Cited in *Annals*, i. 485, *City*, ii. 383, 406.

(iii) *Articuli Wiclefi* : Twyne XXI. 765. MS. Ric. James 3, p. 323 cites MS. Bodl. 540 (*O. C.* 2262).

(iv) *Processus contra illum in causa Coll. Cantuar.* in Univ. Oxon.: in Twyne II. 286–337, extracted from a register (in the ' audit-house ' at Canterbury) titul. *Oxon.*
Cited in *City*, ii. 283.

514. William de Wycumbe, prior of Lanthony.

Vita . . . Roberti de Betun, episc. Heref. Partly printed in Henry Wharton's Anglia Sacra, vol. ii.

(*a*) MS. Ric. James 17, p. 141 has excerpts probably from MS. Cotton Julius X. foll. 2–28.

(*b*) Wood had a copy (Wood MS. F. 30 = *O. C.* 8492), for whose source see *Life*, ii. 268.
Cited in *Annals*, i. 136, 141.

515. William Wydeforde (Wodeford).

(i) *Determinationes contra Wyclefum* : MSS. Bodl. 303 and 703 (*O. C.* 2224, 2766). Twyne XXI. 500, 502 ; MS. Langb. 5, p. 433.

(ii) *Defensorium contra Armachanum* : MS. no. 75 in Coxe's Cat. of Magd. Coll. MSS. Twyne III. 245 ; XXII. 103 b ; XXIV. 346 ; MS. Ric. James 19, p. 57.
Cited frequently in *Annals, Colleges, City.*

(iii) Rationes et motiva ac reprobationes XLV articulorum Johannis Wyklef et Johannis IIus : MS. Bodl. 825 (*O. C.* 2714): Twyne XXII. 825.

(iv) Responsiones contra mag. J. Wyclyf et Lollardos : MS. Bodl. 703 (*O. C.* 2766) : Twyne XXII. 323.
Cited in *Annals*, i. 493, 512 ; *City*, ii. 369.

(v) *Contra Trialogum Wiclefi* : MS. e Mus. 86 (*O. C.* 3629, art. 39). Cited in *Annals*, i. 195; *City*, ii. 364.

516. Nigellus Wyreker.

Wood notes in Wood MS. E. 4 (*O. C.* 8561), p. 230, that Dr. Thomas James in a letter (1624) to Mr. Calandrine ⟨Caesar Calendrinus⟩ stated 'Nigellus Wyrcker was long since printed and not to be had': and that John Nicolls in his Pilgrimage [Lond. 1581] 'familiarly quotes it as if it were printed.'

Printed at Cologne in 1449.

Speculum Brunelli or *Speculum Stultorum.*

Cited in *Annals*, i. 164.

MS. Cotton Julius A. 7, Cleop. B. 3, Vitell. D. 11 (art. 4), Titus A. 20: MS. Digb. 27. Copies, redacted from several MSS., in MS. Ric. James 15, pp. 146–162 and 15, foll. 1–73.

517. Peter de Yckham.

Chronologia (or *Genealogia*) a Bruto ad Edwardum I.

Cited in *Annals*, i. 91, 394; *City*, ii. 383, 391, 407.

(*a*) MS. Laud Misc. 730 (*O. C.* 1401).

(*b*) Twyne XXI. 237 cites a MS. 'in bibl. publ. Cantab.,' and copies a note prefixed to it.

(*c*) Twyne cites also a MS. in Corp. Cambr. (nos. 194, 339, 427 : see Hardy's Descriptive Catalogue, iii. 271).

(*d*) At the end of one copy, 'In anno 1320 sic scribitur : Hoc anno de studio Grantbrugge facta est universitas, sicut est Oxon., per curiam Romanam.'

(*e*) Twyne XXIII. 65, 75, XXIV. 65 cites also the Cottonian MS., Domit. A. 3 (foll. 1–38).

Wood also refers to Twyne XXIV. 281, 616, 669; Twyne XXI. 438, 439; and MS. Langb. 15, p. 52.

518. Roger Young (Infans).

Computus ... in quinque libros divisus : MS. Digb. 40 (*O. C.* 1641).

VII. ANONYMI AND MISCELLANEA.

519. 'Anonymi.'

(i) *De primis philosophis* : init. primi capitis ' Philosophantes famosi fuerunt Caldaei ' : a MS. in Merton College library. Excerpts from it are in MS. Ric. James 21, p. 37 ; Twyne XXI. 760.

Cited in *Annals*, i. 211.

(ii) *De inventione horarum planetarum*, Anglicè: excerpt in Twyne (place of MS. not stated) XXI. 305.

Cited in *Annals*, i. 79.

(iii) Tractatus metricus, qui sic incipit,

'Quis dabit capiti pelagus aquarum':

in the same volume as the Cottonian Tryvytlam (see par. 486): Twyne XXIV. 304.

(iv) *Conciones diversae*: init. 'Contigit anno domini 1235': MS. in S. Paul's library, London : excerpt in Twyne XXI. 319.

Cited in *Annals*, i. 359.

(v) *De Simone de Glovernia* qui legebat theologiam apud Oxon. : see Dugdale's Cat. of MSS. at the end of his Hist. Eccles. S. Pauli and Twyne XXIII. 91.

(vi) *De Wiclefo*: in MS. Bodl. 117 (*O. C.* 1979), *olim* MS. Bodl. A. 21. The volume contained also Augustinus de dignitate conditionis humanae, Johannis de Bethlem epistolae. Excerpt in Twyne II. 235–237.

Cited in *Annals*, i. 491, 510.

(vii) *Conciones Latinae Anglicanis dictionibus intermixtae*: init. 'Nunc dies salutis 2º ad Corinthios viº': MS. Bodl. 649 (*O. C.* 2293). Excerpt in Twyne XXI. 620.

Cited in *Annals*, i. 564.

(viii) *A fragment, anon.* : source not stated: in Twyne XXI. 629. Cited, from Twyne, in *Annals*, i. 121.

(ix) *Tractatus de studiis philosophorum*, in a very old hand, belonging to Dr. Edward James, bound up with Quaestiones Johannis Pecham contra Gulielmum de Sancto Amore de paupertate Christi (init. Pecham 'Quis dabit capiti meo aquam') and Roger Conwey pro defensione 4 ordinum Mendicantium adversus Armachanum, &c. : excerpts in Twyne XXI. 319 ; XXII. 102. It contained notices of places (e. g. Paris) where philosophy was studied.

Cited, from Twyne, in *Annals*, i. 49, 70, &c. MS. no. 182 in Coxe's Cat. of MSS. of C. C. C. Oxon seems to fit this description.

(x) *Anon., continens varia*: excerpt, about George Neville's feast, 1452, in Twyne XXII. 437.

Cited in *Annals*, i. 598. Wood thought it was in the same MS. as the Cartulary of Sir Richard Feteplace (see par. 193).

(xi) *Dialogus inter quaerentem et solventem* : MS. in Magd. Coll. library. Excerpts from it in Twyne XXII. 163ᵛ, MS. Ric. James 2, part 3, p. 146. Wood notes in Wood MS. E. 4 (*O. C.* 8561), p. 17 :—'It is proved thence that Sylvester Giraldus did frequent Oxford.'

(xii) *Speculum Laicorum*: init. praef. 'In Christo sibi dilecto quondam conscholari,' init. libri ' Abstinentiae 3-plex est species.' MS. Bodl. 474 (*O. C.* 2000). Excerpts in MS. Ric. James 21, pp. 56, 59; Twyne XXII. 103 d, 148; MS. Langb. 19, p. 605.

Cited in *Annals*, i. 53, 357, &c. In *Annals*, i. 202, it is said to have been in the Grey Friars' library, Oxford.

(xiii) A book containing fabulous narratives, &c.: init. of one treatise ' Templum Domini sanctum est '; init. of another treatise in it 'Utrum a sphaeris coelestibus continue mutabilibus': it belonged originally to the cell of Lanthony near Gloucester, and in 1617 to Henry Parry of C. C. C.; afterwards to C. C. C. library. Excerpts in Twyne XXII. 162, 163. Perhaps the same as § xix and § xxiii *infra*.

Cited in *Annals*, i. 161; *City*, ii.

(xiv) *De modo praedicandi et quattuor ejus causis*: written circ. Henr. IV vel V, bound up with Palladius de re rustica, Vitruvius de architectura, Vegetius de re militari, in a MS. belonging to Robert Hegge of C. C. C. Excerpt in Twyne XXIV. 317–321.

Cited, from Twyne, in *Annals*, i. 181.

(xv) *Anon.*: MS. Bodl. 487 (*O. C.* 2067), *olim* MS. Bodl. C. 2. 6. Excerpt in MS. Langb. 5, p. 286.

Cited in *Annals*, i. 570.

(xvi) *Carmina cujusdam socii de Merton*: prefixed to Quaestiones Magistri Dumbleton in Merton College library (MS. no. 306 in Coxe's Cat.). Excerpts by Twyne in Wood MS. D. 32, p. 574 and in Twyne XXI. 637, 760.

Cited in *Annals*, i. 469.

(xvii) *De scriptoribus Angliae*: a MS. in the hands of William Crowe: *Life*, ii. 333, note 1.

Cited in *Hist.* ii. 195.

(xviii) *Sermones examinatorii*: a MS. in Lambeth library: see ¢ 55.

(xix) *Liber de mirabilibus mundi*: a MS. in the hands of Henry Parry of C. C. C.: see § xxiii *infra*.

Cited in *City*, ii. 75.

(xx) *Glossarium Latinum*: MS. no. 155 or 227 in Coxe's Cat. of Ball. Coll. MSS.

Cited in *City*, i. 484.

(xxi) *Anon.*: MS. Cotton Nero D. 2, fol. 85.

Cited in *Annals*, i. 46.

(xxii) MS. Bodl. 859 (*O. C.* 2722), *olim* inter Codd. Med.[1] num. 123.

Cited in *Fasti*, p. 37.

---

[1] the MSS. cited as ' Med.' in Wood's time seem to have been those in *O. C.* nos. 2600–2724: MSS. super D. 1 Art.

(xxiii) *Fragmenta narrationum*, written about the time of Thomas of Canterbury : a MS. in C. C. C. Oxford : excerpts in MS. Ric. James 26, p. 28 and at the end of MS. Ric. James 31.   Hence came the legend of the bread at Osney, *City*, ii. 203.   Cited in *City*, ii. 203, as having formerly belonged to Henry Parry of C. C. C.   Perhaps not different from § xix *supra*, and § xiii *supra*.

(xxiv) *Anon.* : MS. in Magd. Coll. library, containing notes of events in and near Oxford, and especially at Osney.

Cited in *Annals*, i. 187, 224.

(xxv) Several 'Anon. MS.,' very vaguely cited, may here be lumped together :—

MS. antiquus : mentioned in Wood MS. E. 4 (*O. C.* 8561), p. 19, where Wood adds, ' but I have forgot where it is and what more to say of it.'

Anonymus, on Henry VIII's divorce : cited in *Annals*, ii. 45.

Anon. MS., formerly in Thomas Allen's library : cited in *Annals*, i. 442.

Anon. MS., in Linc. Coll. library : cited in *City*, ii. 384.

Anon. MS., in bibl. Cotton : cited in *City*, ii. 292.

Vetus scriptor in . . . library : cited in *City*, ii. 299, note 7.

Anon. MS. penes I. T. : cited in *City*, ii. 351.

MS. formerly in Grey Friars' library, Oxford : cited in *City*, ii. 364.

Anon. contra Johannem Wellys : referred to in *City*, ii. 260.

Anon. at the end of Somer's Calendar (see par. 469) : cited in *City*, ii. 260.

520. Annales, &c. : see also **Chronica**, par. 522.

(i) *Annales a Bruto ad Edwardum I* : MS. Cotton Julius D. 4, foll. 2–124.   Excerpts in Twyne XXIV. 55, 57.

Cited in *Annals*, i. 121, 123, 124, 316; *City*, ii. 250.

(ii) *Annals*, quorum author de suo nomine sic graphicè scribit :—

' Guido de Cremo Jo et hannes sit anathema,' &c. : cited in Twyne XXII. 94 as a MS. in Magd. Coll. library.

(iii) *De origine gigantum insulam Albion primo inhabitantium* : init. ' De origine gigantum ' : no. 33 on p. 3 of Cat. of Thomas Allen's MSS. (Wood MS. F. 26 = *O. C.* 8488).

(iv) *De primis hujus Albionis insulae inhabitatoribus*, et de Bruto et Britanniae regibus sibi succedentibus : init. : 'A principio mundi ⟨anno⟩ iii.^{M} ix.^{c} erat in Graecia quidam rex potentissimus.' Excerpt in Twyne XXII. 403 from a MS. in Thomas Allen's library. The narrative was brought down to A. D. 1367 : MS. Cotton Jul. B. 3, fol. 49^{v}.

MS. no. 200, foll. 40–56 in Coxe's Cat. of Magd. Coll. MSS. seems to be the same piece.

(v) *De origine et rebus gestis Britonum* : MS. no. 72 in Coxe's Cat. of Magd. Coll. MSS.: Hardy's Descriptive Cat. ii. 472. Excerpts in Twyne XXII. 92.

Cited, from Twyne, in *Annals*, i. 43, 121 ; *City*, i. 56, 234.

(vi) *Compendium Historicum de regibus Anglo-Saxonicis* : cited in Twyne XXIV. 49. Possibly MS. Cotton Domit. A. 8, foll. 1–10.

(vii) *Rotulus de genealogia regum Angliae et ducum Normannorum* usque ad Henricum VI : a MS. in Twyne's possession. Excerpts in Twyne XXII. 220.

Cited in *Annals*.

(viii) *Tractatus historiae rerum Anglicarum*, excerpt. e Granario Johannis Whethampsted, MS. Bodl. 4° A. 16 (MS. Bodl. 585 = *O. C.* 2357). Excerpt in Twyne XXIII. 124.

(ix) *De rebus gestis Edwardi III* : init.[1] operis 'Edwardus, filius Edwardi, post Conquestum tertius, adolescens circiter quindecim annorum' : MS. no. 69 in Coxe's Cat. of Magd. Coll. MSS. Excerpts in Twyne XXI. 487 ; XXII. 93 ; and in MS. Ric. James 19, p. 16. It contained an account of the 'Great Conflict' in Oxford, 1354.

(x) *Genealogia regum Angliae* : MS. in manibus Episcopi Oxon. (John Bridges). It contained something about Cambridge. Excerpts in Twyne XXI. 264, 317 ; XXII. 317, 838.

Cited in *Annals*, i. 33, 37, 43 ; *City*, i. 235.

In Twyne XXI. 264 is a description of the MS., a folio volume, containing several authors (e. g. 'Speculum Theologiae' Johannis Methensis), in the hands of the bishop of Oxford at Stanton-Harcourt. The first piece was a tract about 'res ludicrae' (e. g. the form of the Cherubim); the second about ' res genealogica et quattuor summa imperia' from Adam to the Assyrian empire (init.: 'considerans historiae sacrae prolixitatem') ; the third, a chronicle from Adam to Henry VI of England (init. praef.: 'Cuilibet principi congruum utile et honestum ').

521. Calendarium.

(i) *Calendarium vetus* in quo obitus variorum abbatum, monachorum, nobilium, &c. : MS. Cotton Vitell. A. 8.

(ii) *Old MS. Calendar* in Mert. Coll. library 'in libro bestiario moralizato.' It contained a list of members of the College (including Robert Gilbert, the Warden), who were with Henry V in Normandy :

---

[1] Wood notes that this *incipit* is identical with that of Walter Hemmingford's Chronicle (MS. no. 53, fol. 253, in Coxe's Cat. of Magd. Coll. MSS.).

MS. no. 249, fol. 76 in Coxe's Cat. of Mert. Coll. MSS.   Excerpts in Twyne XXI. 761.

(iii) *Calendar*, prefixed to a breviary : MS. Wood C. 12 : see *City*, i. 618.

(iv) *Calendar* : MS. ab Wood 19 : *Life*, iii. 342.

(v) *De correctione Calendarii* ex Rogero Bacon e libro ad Clementem papam : MS. Laud Misc. 674 (*O. C.* 504).   Excerpt in MS. Langb. 15, p. 42.

522.   Chronica : see also Annales par. 520 and Historiae, par. 523.

Many of these are unidentified.   The reason is that in most cases the source of the citation is Twyne, and Twyne states that between the time of his first extracting his notes of them from MSS. in the Bodleian and his subsequent making use of them, there had been a ' shifting ' in the Bodleian which rendered it impossible for him to find the MSS. again.   The difficulty is perhaps the less deplorable because it is probable that these ' Chronica incertorum authorum ' contained little except ' some proof more for Brute ' or ' Alfred's gests at Oxon.'

(i) *Chronica de Anglia* : MS. Cotton Vitell. C. 8, foll. 16–17ᵛ.   Excerpt in Twyne XXII. 293.

Cited in *Annals*, i. 118, 119.

(ii) *Chronicorum manipulus* : init. ' de adventu S. Augustini et conversione Anglorum ad fidem ' : place not stated.   Excerpt in Twyne XXI. 113.   It had a note about Robert Grostest.

(iii) *Chronicon antiquum*, quod sic incipit ' Anno ab incarnatione MLXVI. Willelmus Conquestor dux Normanniae venit in Angliam.' Excerpt in Twyne XXI. 134.

(iv) *Chronicon de tempore Henrici III* : init. ' Anno gratiae 1259, Rex Anglorum, Henricus ' : MS. Cotton Claud. E. 3.   Excerpts in Twyne XXIV. 71, 72.

(v) *Chronicon* : init. ' Anglia quattuor partes habet ' : carried down, by a second writer, to A. D. 1546.   It mentioned King Alfred's founding of Oxford.   Excerpt in Twyne XXI. 222.

Cited in *Annals*, i. 37, 127.

(vi) *Chronicon rotulare*, of date about 1447 ; ' in archivis bibl. Bodl.' Excerpts in Twyne XXI. 216, 221 ; XXIV. 55, de insurrectione laicorum [1354].

(vii) *Chronicon* : init. ' Anno XLII Octaviani Augusti ' and going down to Boniface VIII : in bibl. Bodl.   Excerpts in Twyne XXII. 245 ; MS. Langb. 15, pp. 83–85.

Cited in *Hist.* i. 66.

(viii) *Chronicon rotulare*, Anglicè, in parchment, init. 'King Samuel' (of the Britons), going down to 1485 : MS. in the possession of ⟨Peter⟩ Hooker of C. C. C. Excerpt in Twyne XXI. 253.

(ix) *Chronicon* : init. 'In diebus sanctissimi regis Edwardi confessoris anno ejus penultimo' : Magd. Coll. library ⟨MS. no. 199 in Coxe's Cat.⟩. Excerpts in Twyne XXII. 79.

Cited in *Annals*, i. 145.

(x) *Chronicle of England* from Brute to end of Henry V : MS. Hatton 53 (*O. C.* 4112). Wood refers for it to MS. Langb. 15, pp. 75, 88 : see also *Life*, ii. 231.

(xi) *Chronicon*, Britannicè : MS. (formerly of Humphrey Lhuyd, afterwards of lord Lumley) in S. James' library.

Excerpts in Twyne XXI. 649 : 'initium ejus prae vetustate legere non possum.'

Cited in *City*, i. 238, 239.

(xii) *Chronicle* in French, in Twyne's possession : title 'Cy coññence vne petyt tretiz de la Brut abbregge' : init. operis 'Deuant la natiuite nre seignoʳ Jhu Crist M. CC. ans.' Excerpt in Twyne XXIV. 630.

(xiii) *A brief Chronicle* from Brute to Edward I, in French : MS. ab Wood 8 (*O. C.* 8596).

(xiv) *Chronicon rerum Anglicarum*, from 1066 : MS. Langb. 15, p. 51. See MS. no. 200, fol. 57 in Coxe's Cat. of Magd. Coll. MSS.

(xv) *Chronicon*, 1042–1275 : MS. Langb. 15, p. 76.

(xvi) *Chronicon incerti* : MS. in All Souls Coll. library. Excerpt in MS. Ric. James 26, p. 70 (about the slaughter of the Danes, 1002).

(xvii) *Chronicon anon. de gestis Anglorum et Normannorum :* a Bodleian MS.

Excerpt in MS. Ric. James 11, p. 9 (about Robert Pulleyn at Oxford).

(xviii) *Chronicle by a monk of S. Alban's* : MS. Bodl. 462 (*O. C.* 2454). Excerpt in MS. Ric. James 11, pp. 40–98 (about Edward — ejecting scholars at Oxford).

(xix) *Chronicon* vel Historia *pertinens ad eccles. Wigorn.*

Excerpt in Twyne XXI. 238.

Cited in *City*, ii. 250.

(xx) *Chronicon Britannorum Shirburni* : MS. no. 78 in Coxe's Cat. of MSS. of S. John's Oxford.

(xxi) Twyne XXI. 277 cites a MS. in bibl. Bodl. in 16mo., to which is prefixed a Roman Calendar, and there follow fragments of various chronicles.

(xxii) Twyne XXI. 176 cites a Chronicon incerti authoris (nisi est Gul. Rishanger) : in bibl. Bodl.

(xxiii) *A little Chronicle of England*: MS. belonging to Henry Jackson.   Excerpt in Twyne XXIV. 229.

(xxiv) *Chronicon rotulare*, in libraria B. Twyne.

Cited in *City*, ii. 311, 328.

523. Historiae: see also Chronica par. 522.

(i) *Historia Saxonico-Latina* a primis Britanniae incolis ad tempora Edwardi Confessoris perducta: init. ' Britannia insula habet in longitudine 800 miliaria': MS. Cotton Domit. 8.   Excerpts in Twyne XXIV. 49-52, 58-59.

Cited in *Annals*, i. 10, 38, &c.

(ii) *Historia de regibus Angliae* a Saxonum adventu usque ad tempora Edward II, 1328: init. 'Saxones patientius agentes.' Excerpt in MS. Langb. 15, p. 10.

(iii) *Historia* sive chronicon *de rebus in Anglia gestis*.   Excerpt in Twyne XXI. 624.   Described the death of lord James Douglas in Spain 'Contra quinque Saracenos solus dimicans quinque localibus vulneribus ab ipsis est occisus sed et ipsos occidit, teste fratre Thoma de Lantoné, Carmelita, qui pro tunc saecularis sub suo ducatu in exercitu Christianorum ut potuit laboravit.'

Cited in *Annals*, i. 450.   See p. 278, par. 401.

524. Notae.

(i) *Nota*, at the end of a MS. (press-mark S. 5. Art.) in Jesus College library: in Twyne XXI. 176.   It gave the story about Oxford students begging, *City*, i. 511, 512.   Cited also in *Annals*, i. 620.   Wood 'looked after this, anno 1667 or 68, and could not find it': Wood MS. E. 4 (*O. C.* 8561), p. 11.

(ii) *Nota*, at the end of a MS. (entitled ' Algorismus in prosa') in Mert. Coll. library: in Twyne XXI. 761 ; XXII. 163.

Cited in *Annals*, i. 57.

(iii) *Nota*, in a Merton Coll. MS., about Duns Scotus: in MS. Ric. James 21, p. 42.

(iv) *Nota*, in a MS. formerly belonging to the cell of Lanthony, afterwards to Henry Parry of C. C. C. (init. 'Utrum a sphaeris coelestibus continue mutabilibus'): in Twyne XXII. 163.   See par. 519 (xiii).

(v) *Notae* vel variae observationes de Wicliffo et Lollardis : init. 'In Universitate Oxon. surrexit': MS. Bodl. 117 (*O. C.* 1759). Excerpts in Twyne II. 235-237.

Cited in *Annals*, i. 491.

(vi) *Notae* incerti authoris, at the end of Walter Burley 'super literalem sensum Porphyrii' in Magd. Coll. library ⟨MS. no. 47 in Coxe's Cat.⟩ : in Twyne XXII. 101.

Cited in *Annals*, i. 514.

(vii) *Note* by Edmund Bonner in Wood's copy of Rufinus' Latin version of Eusebius' Eccles. Hist., edit. Basil. 1528. This copy is not now in the Bodleian.

Cited in *Hist.* ii. 322, and in *Athenae.*

(viii) *Note* in a Ball. Coll. MS. ⟨MS. no. 124 in Coxe's Cat.⟩.

Cited in *Hist.* ii. 346, note (*e*).

(ix) *Note* in the beginning of a Magd. Coll. MS.

Cited in *Fasti*, p. 39.

(x) *Note* at the end of MS. Bodl. 718 (*O. C.* 2632), *olim* MS. Med. 33.

Cited in *Fasti*, p. 65.

(xi) *Note* at the end of MS. Bodl. Rolls 10, *olim* in bibl. Bodl. Arch. A. 180.

Cited in *Hist.* ii. 76.

(xii) *Note* in a Ball. Coll. MS.

Cited in *Hist.* ii. 77.

(xiii) *Note* in a Magd. Coll. MS. ⟨MS. no. 65 in Coxe's Cat.⟩.

Cited in *Hist.* ii. 346.

(xiv) *Note* in an Oriel Coll. MS. ⟨MS. no. 26 in Coxe's Cat.⟩ : *City*, ii. 226.

(xv) *Note* in an Oriel Coll. MS. : in MS. Ric. James 11, p. 132.

Cited in *Annals*, i. 54, note 203.

(xvi) *Note* in a Jesus Coll. MS.

Cited in *City*, ii. 293, note 2.

(xvii) *Note* in a New Coll. MS.

Cited in *City*, ii. 321, 336.

(xviii) *Notes* in a C. C. C. MS. (formerly in Exeter Cathedral library).

Cited in *City*, ii. 321, 336, 453.

(xix) *Note* in a Bodleian MS. of Augustine's ' Civitas Dei ' : MS. Bodl. 198 (*O. C.* 1907).

Cited in *City*, ii. 381.

(xx) Twyne XXI. 710 cites a note prefixed to an English exposition of the Lord's prayer in metre in a Bodleian MS.

(xxi) Twyne XXII. 118 cites a note about Segrym Hall (*City*, i. 564) which he saw in a MS. copy of Aristotle's Organon (formerly belonging to Merton College), in a bookseller's shop in London.

(xxii) Twyne XXI. 647 has copies of the inscriptions under the four principal rivers of England on the conduit in Somerset-House yard, London. That under the Thames (' Me penes imperium,' &c.) is cited in *City*, i. 431.

525. Vaticinia.

(i) Ambrose Merlin's *Vaticinia* : par. 422 *supra*.

(ii) In Twyne XXI. 491 are notes from a MS. belonging to . . .
Mason, having predictions in English verse. Init. vaticiniorum
Calapii :—

> 'The sea is weighty and high
> It waxeth and vanisheth :'

init. vaticiniorum Johannis Bridlington :—

> 'Beware of the fleshy flea
> Which will worry the white swan.'

(iii) Twyne, in Wood MS. D. 32, p. 301 quotes Bridlington's
'prophetiae'; among them :—

> 'Taurus cornutus ex patris germine Brutus.'

Cited in *City*, i. 233 note 6.

526. Vitae.

(i) *Lives of the Saints* : MS. Bodl. 779 (*O. C.* 2567): in process
of publication by the Early English Text Society.
Cited in *City*, i. 234, note 5, 324.

(ii) *De vita* et nobilitate et martyrio *SS. Albani et Amphibali* :
init. 'Julius Caesar, primus Romanorum imperator': MS. Bodl. 585
(*O. C.* 2357).

(iii) MS. Ric. James 19, p. 1 has excerpts from the Magd. Coll.
MS. ⟨MS. no. 53 in Coxe's Cat.⟩ *De passione S. Albani* : Hardy's
Descriptive Catalogue, i. 4.

(iv) *Vita Johannis de Beverlaco*, per incertum authorem qui floruit
1373 : init. 'Antiquioribus Brytonum sola illa patria vocabatur Deira':
transcript in Twyne XXII. 134–141 : original not stated.
Cited in *Annals*, i. 27.

(v) The inscription about John of Beverley in Sarum Old Library
window is copied in MS. Ric. James 11, pp. 238, 239.
Cited in *City*, i. 86.

(vi) *S. Edmund Rich.*
(*a*) *Certificatorium de vita B. Edmundi* . . . per Eustachium
monachum : Twyne XXII. 142.
Cited in *Annals*, ii. 738; *City*, ii. 100.
See MS. no. 154, p. 375, in Coxe's Cat. of MSS. of C.C.C.
Oxon.

(*b*) MS. Cotton Julius D. 6, foll. 123–157. Hardy's Descriptive Catalogue, iii. 87. Wood says (Wood MS. E. 4=*O. C.* 8561, p. 80) that he took his account of S. Edmund partly from this MS.

(*c*) Life, ascribed to his brother Robert Rich: MS. Cotton Cleop. B. 1, foll. 24–32. Hardy's Descr. Cat. iii. 87, 90.

Cited in *Annals*, i. 193.

(*d*) MS. Cotton Faust. B. 1, foll. 179–184: Hardy, iii. 90.

(*e*) MS. Lambeth 135, fol. 118 (*olim* Lambeth C. 1): Hardy, iii. 89.

(*f*) Life, by Albertus of Prusia. Thomas Gascoigne (in MS. no. 235 of Coxe's Cat. of Ball. MSS., in a marginal note to 'Polychronicon lib. 7, cap. 37 in the life of S. Edmund') 'saith that Albertus, archbishop of Prusia, wrot a book de canonizatione S. Edmundi *et est in bibliotheca Collegii Oriel*': Wood MS. E. 4 (*O. C.* 8561), p. 80.

(*g*) *Vita beati Edmundi*, ... in manibus magistri Obadiah Walker: init. prologi 'Ad honorem salvatoris Domini' et operis 'Beatus igitur Edmundus.'

This would seem to be the same as MS. Fell 1, vol. iv. pp. 1–44, in the Bodleian: Hardy's Descr. Cat. iii. 91.

(*h*) MS. Cotton Vitell. C. 12, foll. 280ᵛ–290.

(*i*) *Life* in MS. Ric. James 18, p. 172.

(vii) *De vita S. Francisci*: init. 'Vir erat in civitate Assissii': MS. no. 202 in Coxe's Cat. of MSS. of C. C. C. Oxon. See Twyne XXI. 273, 305.

(viii) MS. Life of S. Gilebert de Sempringham: MS. Digb. 36 (*O. C.* 1637); MS. Cotton Cleop. B. 1, foll. 33–168.

Cited in *Fasti*, p. 10.

(ix) *Vita S. Grimbaldi*: ⌐ p. 19.

'Grimbaldi vita MS.' is cited in *Annals*, i. 38, 39, 45, 46; ii. 819, without 'nearer definition.' See MS. Cotton Tiber. E. 1, fol. 205: Hardy's Descr. Cat. i. 555.

(x) Twyne XXII. 228 cites MS. Digb. 165 (*O. C.* 1766), *Vita S. Hugonis*, episc. Linc.: Hardy's Descr. Cat. ii. 542.

(xi) *S. Neot.*

Wood refers to ⌐ pp. 25, 26; Twyne II. 24 a; III. 239; XXI. 829: MS. Wood donat. 6, p. 2.

(*a*) *Vita*, by William, abbot of Croyland: init. 'Cum universarum essentialis': MS. Cotton Claud. A. 5. foll. 145ᵛ–160ᵛ. Wood says, Wood MS. E. 4 (*O. C.* 8561), p. 147:—'There is no mention of Alfred's gests at Oxon: which note.'

(*b*) *Vita, cum miraculis*, by William de Ramsey : MS. Bodl. 535 (*O. C.* 2254).   Excerpt in Twyne XXI. 270.

(*c*) The Life from which Leland made excerpts : see Leland, Collect. vol. iii. p. 11.

Cited in *Annals*, i. 33, 43.

In MS. Bodl. 353 (*olim* 379) is a Life said to be transcribed from a MS. of Leland's (see par. 404, § iv).

(xii) In MS. Ric. James 26, pp. 130–136 is a life of S. Oswin, transcribed from a MS. in Twyne's possession : init. ' Oswynus regis Deyrorum Osryci filius.'

(xiii) In Twyne XXII. 50 is a transcript of a paper prefixed by Henry Jackson to Stapleton's De tribus Thomis. It consists of 11 stanzas in English, of three-lines each, with the Latin refrain to each :—

> Gaude, gaude, Thoma :
> De quo canit Ecclesia.

Cited in *City*, ii. 114.

(xiv) *Vita S. Wlganii* : init. ' Gloriosus confessor Christi S. Wolganius ' : MS. Bodl. 852 (*O. C.* 2611).

Cited in *City*, ii. 44.

(xv) *Life of William Whittingham* : in Wood MS. E. 4 (*O. C.* 8560) : see *Life*, i. 302.

ADDENDUM.

Wood's paper G. 10 for the *Athenae* (*supra* p. 233, line 7) is MS. Aubr. 8, foll. 69 sqq., ' An apparatus for the lives of our English mathematical writers ' by John Aubrey, 1690.

INDEX I

OLD MARKS OF OXFORD MSS. BY LETTERS AND SYMBOLS.

Arch. = in the archives of the University; City = in the archives of the City; Langb. = a volume by Gerard Langbaine; Twyne = a volume by Brian Twyne, &c.

LETTER	COLLECTION	PAGE
D27	Arch.	146
D28	,,	146
D (reversed)	,,	140
D (reversed)	Twyne	218
DD	Wood	234
E	Arch.	141
E	Bodleian	128
E	City	181
E	Twyne	218
E	Wood	233
E (reversed)	Twyne	218
EE	Wood	234
EEE	Arch.	140
F	Arch.	132
F	Arch.	141
F	Twyne	129
F	Twyne	220
F	Wood	233
F (reversed)	Arch.	140
F (reversed)	Twyne	217
F (broken)	—	243
FF	Bodleian	132
FF	Wood	234
FFF	Wood	234
G	Arch.	133
G	Arch.	141
G	Wood	233
GG	Arch.	140
GG	Wood	234
GL	Langb.	199
H	Arch.	133
H	Arch.	141
H	Twyne	218
H	Wood	233
HH	Arch.	140
HH	Wood	234
I	Arch.	133
I	Arch.	141
I	Twyne	218
I	Wood	233
I (with a flourish)	Arch.	141
II	Wood	234
I.L	Twyne	213
J	Wood	233
K	Arch.	135
K	Arch.	141
K	Twyne	218
K	Wood	233
K (reversed)	Arch.	134
KK	Arch.	134
KK	Wood	234
Kk	Arch.	141
L	Arch.	134
L	Arch.	141
L	Twyne	218
L	Wood	233
LL	Wood	234
M	Arch.	134
M	Twyne	218
M	Wood	165
M	Wood	233

LETTER	COLLECTION	PAGE
Ma	Arch.	134
Mb	Arch.	134
MM	Wood	234
N	Arch.	135
N	Twyne	218
N	Wood	233
N	Wood	234
O	Arch.	134
O	Twyne	218
O	Wood	167
O	Wood	233
O (with a dot)	Langb.	201
O (with a dot)	Twyne	209
OO	Wood	234
P	Arch.	134
P	Arch.	136
P	Twyne	218
P	Wood	233
PP	Arch.	136
PP	Wood	234
Q	Arch.	134
Q	Twyne	218
Q	Wood	233
Qa	Arch.	134
Qb	Arch.	134
QQ	Wood	234
R	Arch.	135
R	Twyne	218
R	Wood	233
R (inverted)	Twyne	210
R (reversed)	Twyne	210
RR	Twyne	211
RR	Wood	234
S	Twyne	218
S	Wood	233
Sa	Arch.	134
Sb	Arch.	135
SS	Wood	234
T	Arch.	135
T	Twyne	208
T	Twyne	218
T	Wood	233
Ta	Arch.	135
Tb	Arch.	135
T.J	Arch.	129
V	Twyne	218
V	Wood	242
V	Wood	233
W	Arch.	136
W	Twyne	218
W	Wood	227
X	Arch.	137
X	Twyne	218
X	Wood	233
Y	Arch.	226
Y	Twyne	208
Y	Twyne	218
Y	Wood	233
Z	Twyne	218
Z	Wood	233

[The following symbols seem to be distorted letters or combinations of letters.]

[The following symbols seem borrowed from astronomy.]

[The following are heraldic.]

SYMBOL	COLLECTION	PAGE
[symbol]	Wood	242
[symbol]	Wood	242
[symbol]	Wood	242

[There are also the following.]

SYMBOL	COLLECTION	PAGE
[symbol]	Twyne	211
[symbol]	Twyne	212
[symbol]	Langb.	201
[symbol]	Twyne	206
[symbol]	Twyne	206
[symbol]	Twyne	214
[symbol]	Twyne	206

SYMBOL	COLLECTION	PAGE
[symbol]	Twyne	206
[symbol]	Twyne	206
[symbol]	Twyne	206
[symbol]	Wood	234
[symbol]	Wood	234
[symbol]	Wood	234
[symbol]	Twyne	215
[symbol]	Wood	234
[symbol]	Twyne	220
[symbol]	Twyne	205
[symbol]	Twyne	216
[symbol]	Twyne	214

INDEX II

THE END.

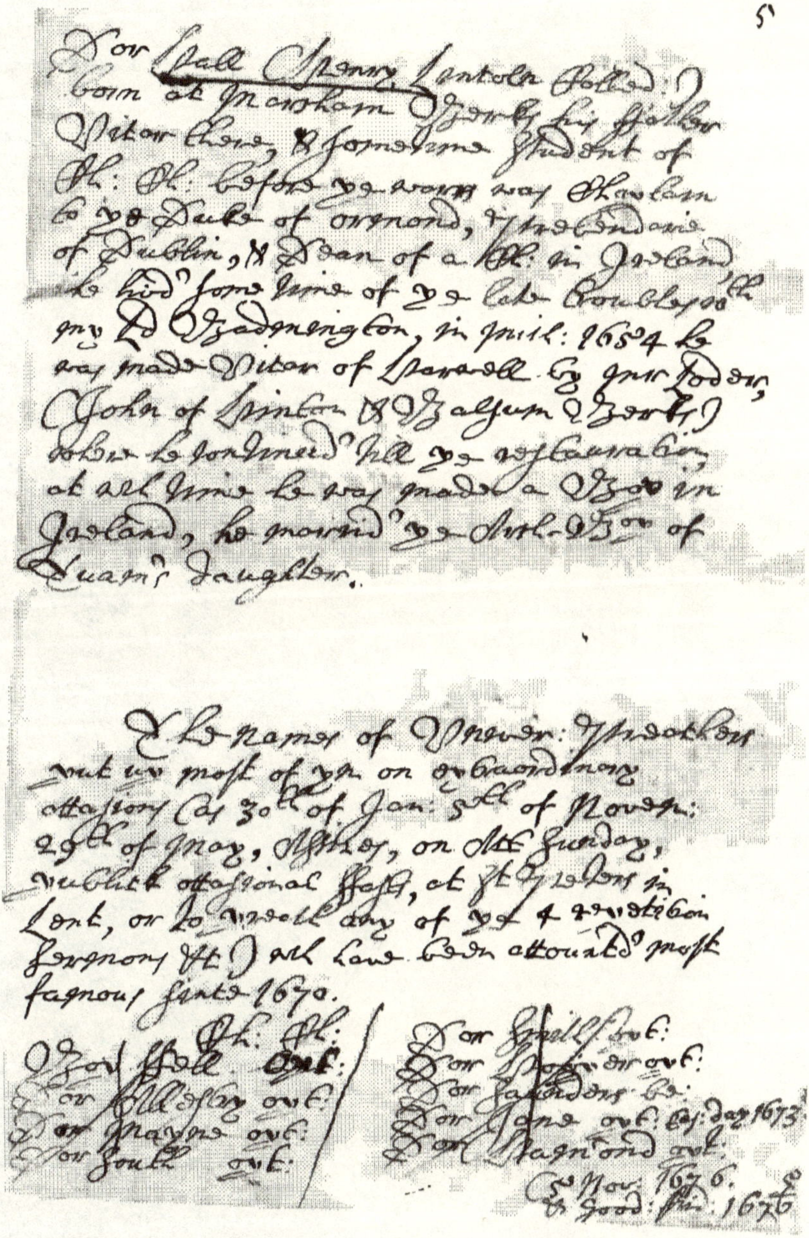

PLATE I.

ANDREW ALLAM'S WRITING.

Wood MS. F 48, fol. 1149.

Sr William Davenant, ^Knight^ Poet Laureate.

4

† AV Antiq: Oxon:

Was borne in ~~about the end~~ of February, baptized 3 of March A.D: 1605 ... street in the City of Oxford, at the Crowne Taverne. His father was ^John Davenant^ a Vintner there, a very grave and discreat Citizen: his mother was a very beautifull woman, & of a very good witt and of conversation extremely agreable. They had 3 sons viz. Robert, ... Davenant ... William, & Nicholas [an Attorney.] ... Robert his brother of Westkington ... & two handsome daughters, one m: to Gabriel Bridges B.D. of C.C. Coll: benefic'd in the Vale of White horse, another to Dr Sherburne minister of Pembridge in Herefsh: & a Canon of yt Church. Mr William Shakespeare was wont to goe into Warwickshire once a yeare, & did comonly in his journey lye at this howse in Oxon: where he was exceedingly respected. ~~I have ...~~

~~... Mr Shakespeare haveing given him a hundred kisses ...~~ Wm would sometimes when he was pleasant over a glasse of wine with his most intimate friends e.g. Sam: Butler [author of Hudibras] &c say, that it seemed to him that he writt with the very spirit that Shakespeare, and was ^seen^ contentedended enough to be thought his Son: he would tell them the story as above. ~~...~~

He went to schoole at Oxon to Mr Sylvester, Charles ...

, sic ... I . O . O Leave here was drawne from ...

Robert was a Fellow of St Johns Coll: in Oxon: then [parson?] to yt George of West... ...ington by Sr Jo: Suckling ... ...ngton by Sr Jo: Davenant whose Chaplaine he was.

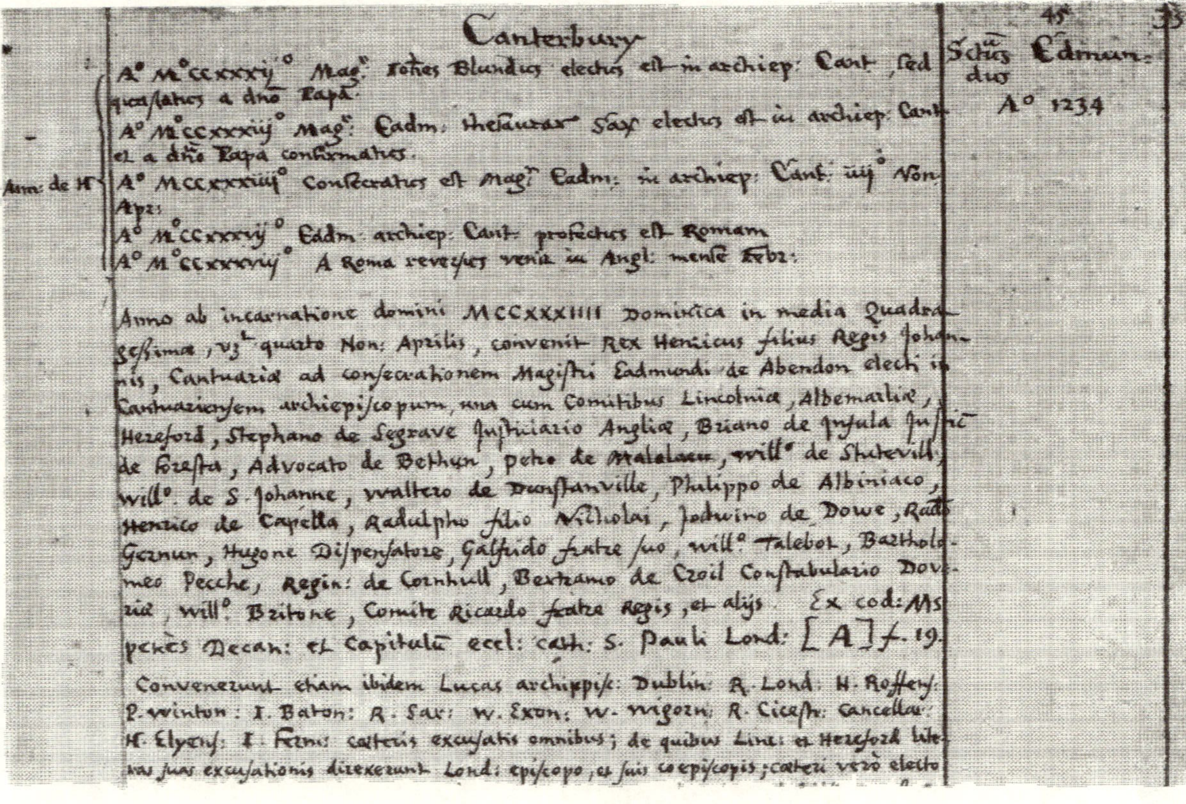

Canterbury

45 33

Sctūs Edmun-dus

A° 1234

Anno de H

A° M°ccxxxij° Mag. Iohes Blundus electus est in archiep: Cant: sed vacatus a dño Papa.

A° M°ccxxxij° Mag. Eadm: thesaurar Sar electus est in archiep: Cant et a dño Papa confirmatus.

A° M°ccxxxiiij° Consecratus est Magr Eadm: in archiep: Cant: iiij° Non: Apr:

A° M°ccxxxvj° Eadm archiep: Cant: profectus est Romam

A° M°ccxxxvij° A Roma reversus venit in Angl: mense Febr:

Anno ab incarnatione domini MCCXXXIIII Dominica in media Quadragesima, vz° quarto Non: Aprilis, convenit Rex Henricus filius Regis Johannis, Cantuaria ad consecrationem Magistri Edmundi de Abendon electi in Cantuariensem archiepiscopum, una cum Comitibus Lincolnia, Albemarlie, Hereford, Stephano de Segrave Justiciario Anglia, Briano de Jnsula justic de foresta, Advocato de Bethun, petro de Malalacu, willo de Shtevill, willo de S. Johanne, waltero de Dunstanville, Philippo de Albiniaco, Henrico de Capella, Radulpho filio Nicholai, Jodwino de Dowe, Rad Gernun, Hugone Dispensatore, Galfrido fratre suo, willo Talebot, Bartholomeo Pecche, Regin: de Cornhull, Bertramo de Croil Constabulario Dovrie, willo Britone, Comite Ricardo fratre Regis, et alijs.   Ex cod: Ms penes Decan: et Capitulu eccl: cath: S. Pauli Lond: [A] f. 19.

Convenerunt etiam ibidem Lucas archiepisc: Dublin: R. Lond: H. Roffen: P. winton: I. Baton: R. Sar: W. Exon: W. wigorn: R. Cicestr: Cancellar: H. Elyens: I. Fernn: cæteris excusatis omnibus; de quibus Linc: et Hereford literas suas excusationis direxerunt Lond: episcopo, et suis coepiscopis; cæteri verò electo

PLATE III.

SIR WILLIAM DUGDALE'S WRITING.

Wood MS. D 12, p. 33.

[Dugdale's writing is sometimes mistaken for Wood's.]

Epitaph made by a certaine Scholer
on m.r Allen of Glouc. hall, 1632.

Thomas Allen of Gloster Hall,
By that place known to great and small,
Ended in half an houre and lesse
Ninety yeares and nine Months progresse.
To Trinity College Librarie
He left his Bookes and laft Astrologie
Where they him layd with night solemnity
Untill the day of all celebrity
His furred coate of mickle fame,
Sir Kenelme Digbyes gift by name,
To Doctor Kettle be bequeathed
To lappe him warme while as he breathed
His wary watch he did bestow
On Mistris Anian as J trow.
On Doctor Tolson all the rest
With John his man to be his guest.

To Mr Benj. Jhonson on
his staple of niews first
presented.

* *
*

Sir if my robe and garbe were richly worth
The dainger of a statute comming forth
Were I of man of law or law maker
Or man of Courte to be an undertaker
For judgement would I then comm in and say
The manye honours of your staple play.
But being nothing so I dare not haile
The mightie floates of ignorance whoe saile
With winde and tide, their Sires as stories till
In our tieth Harries time crownd Skeltone Nell

Senex liberatus a peccato p[er] oratorem s[anctu]m Andreæ.

Miles silentium sibi loco pœniæ injunctum servans.

Quidam in episc[op]atu Lyncolñ cu[m] concubina
morbus reptus q[uem] dictus ou[...] q[uia] voluit
abstinere.

De Hudone ep[iscop]o Hyldernensi de Alemania
damnato. — Hoc narravit frater Johes
studens Oxon in domo fr[at]rum de
Hyldernensi vir fideli qui eundem
ep[iscopu]m frequenter vidit.   2'7.6.

De confess[i]one cujusdam meretricis p. S.
Narcisum. ex vita S. Narcissi ep[iscop]i.

2.º S. Chrysanthus convertit puellam Dariam.
ex vita Chrysanthi et Dariæ.   2'8.6.

De S. Thoma Cant: quam
              castus erat.
    et devotus.

Mater diabolus corpus X[rist]i veneravit.   28.y.

Cogitationes de peccatis nobis n[on] placentes
    non sunt ex diabolo. Ex vitis patrum.

Quo[modo] ep[iscopu]s parisiensis matrem paup[er]culam
    agnoscere noluit.

Simile de scholare, quem pudebat propr[iam]
    matrem qui p[at]rem male tractavit. a demone
suffocatus.

Leo puer septennis rogavit p[at]rem ut eleem[osynam]
faceret, quo mediante ad aurum ferret. —

2.º quidam præpositus prævidebit [...] in purgatorio
    per hic y duos annos.   2'9.6.

2.do peccator restitutus papæ Alexandr[o], qui
    ei dedit annulum suæ instantiæ ut quotidie
respiciat, cogitando se morituram.

Quot quidam parochiani in Saxonia duxerunt
    choream in cœmeterio prohibente sacerdote.

Qu[omodo] detestanda sit propria voluntas. exemplum
    ex vitam Alberti fratrum minorum spiritualium.

                                Deo gratias laus

A note of certayne motions
for ye Library by me moued at
ye visitation of ye same
A° 1613. 8° Nouembris.

D' Singleton Vicecan.
D' Abbotts Regius Professor
Theologiæ
D' Kilby Hebr. Lector
D' Perin Græce Lector
D' Budden iuris civilis
professor Regius
cum alijs quamplurimis

Imprimis yt enquiry be made of some MS. writings are wantinge
in ye Library, and haue beene there heretofore

Amongest wrytings are 2 Chronicles Lat. in 8° bounde
in old parchment, wth paper leaues, wch usually were
kept loose in ye closet vppon ye left side of ye Library,
as then it was.

The beginninge of ye one is this, de Britannia olim dicta
Britannia maior. of wch I haue made mention lib. 2.
Antiq: Oxon. p. 185. § 176. in these wordes. Et Antiquus
Anonymus in Oxoniensi Bibliotheca cui titulus est de Britannia
olim dicta Britannia Maior, qui Aluredum scholas publicas
apud Oxoniam instituisse, ac multis privilegijs communiuisse
scribit.

The beginninge of ye other I haue not taken, but it may
be knowen by this sentence, wch I haue also copied out
of him lib: Antiq: Oxon. 2. § 190. p. 192. Athe Rex de-
uotus monasterium fundauit, cuius suos sextifariè diuisit,
scilicet jam primum pauperibus, 2a fundationibus Ecclesiaru
3a scholaribus apud Oxoniam, quartam luminibus Ecclesie, 5a prelatura,
6a operarijs et artificibus.

There is wantinge also another antient MS. genealogy
of ye kinges of Englande whose beginninge I haue
not taken, but it may be knowen by this sentence. Cui
successit Gutro Danus et Paganus qui a Rege Alfredo postea
factus est christianus, et ab isto Gutro translatum est regnum
orientaliū Anglorū ad Reges Westsaxonū.

A cis- charwellia in|Trans- charwelliam S. Clementis, per pontem è saxo
eleganti constructum, et   arcubus lapideis, quibus fluuius de
charwell subrotabitur, sustentatum atq suffultum, transitur. qui à fluuio
quem sic excipit, pons charwellensis; à collegio cui adiacet, Magdalanensis;
à parte quam respicit orientalis; à mole, paruus, ad discrimen alterius
illius praegrandis scilicet pontis ad Australem urbis partem (de quo postea) nuncupatur; tametsi, si de illius dimensionibus agatur, non adeo paruus quidem,
immò reuera magnus, grandisq pons dici mereatur et tàm spatiosus quam
spatiosus dici mereatur. Sunt, qui non adeo vetustum esse perhibent; qui
nec fundationem Hospitalis S Joannis, annos abhinc prae quadringentos, nec
chartam Henrici primi ad Canonicos Fridesuidenses multò antea, viz: anno
Christi 1122, ubi duarum hidarū terras desuper pontem orientalem oxon
cū flimitibus suis meminit, animo complexi sunt. Sed et Ethelredus
multò anti ante Conquestum, Anglias Rex et egregius ille coenobij S. Fridesui-
deq Oxenia restitutor, in charta sua confirmatoria circa annū d̄ millesimū
quartum, in limitibus de Bottis, Coula, et Hedynden, quas illi monasterio
concessit, istius pontis meminit saxonicis hisce verbis meminit, yare iij
hideland ymere into Couslt fro charwell brigge and lonze ye strems on
yat ryche wt haklingcroft &c: ita codex Fridesuidensis.

Calena nomen urbis existimavit aliud Plinium scripsit li. 2.8. [...] Italia.

1. Ait: Cum in Tuscia sit sedes delubro formo[...], Calena germano [...]num, Italia.
   [...]bis ob id a Senatu legatis [...], Caesareum [...]rat [...] transtulit. Item
   Britannia [...]misse quod fecerit, et Calenam denominasse quod [...]

2. dicit, Antiquo nomine mutato. Item Plinius locu[m] commendaus suis, [...] Italia.
   illa Monument[...] Graeca chari[...]m, [...] athana, [...], [...] nichil [...]

3. Nationum et Animalium [...] Regiones in sua Geographia Calena [...] Italia.
   alia [...]get varias [...] Habet et Calena in sua Monasterio Calena magni [...] Italia.

4. Romanum appellarit. [...] quod [...] appellari. In Thessalia [...]
   in Anglia Civitas esse creditur, quam [...] [...] Scotorum. Scotia vel [...]

5. Latine [...]vit Romana, in eandem videt[...] [...] Monumentis multis [...]
   [...] lectione [...] Scientiarum [...]

6. Literaria [...]; tam [...], quam [...] [...] florebat et [...]ibus Chr[...] A. Italia.
   Calena in Anglia Scotia est, ubi Antiq[...]ima floruit Calena etiam meminit

7. Academia, omnium disciplinarum [...] florentissima [...] tempore [...]bonorum Scholae Caledo[...]
   Lelandi [...] [...]: Inde [...] literis [...] hoc tempore [...] manserit, quas loci
   amoenitati [...] Authores Calenam transtulerint, [...] alius[...] Literas
   [...] sedibus restiterit. Dum Academiae Catalogum ad Calcem Francisci

8. [...] et Academia Glass[...] [...] hic habet Vedla: Scotorum[...] secundo Italia.
   Calena [...] Doctor[...]. Achaii Pi[...]io [...] aniato in A[...]one Britan.

<h1 style="text-align:center">Oxford Historical Society.</h1>

<h2 style="text-align:center">PUBLICATIONS.</h2>

1884.

1. **Register of the University of Oxford.** Vol. I. (1449–63; 1505–71), edited by the Rev. C. W. BOASE, M.A., pp. xxviii + 364. (Price to the public, without discount, and prepaid, 16s.)

2. **Remarks and Collections of Thomas Hearne.** Vol. I. (4 July 1705—19 March 1707), edited by C. E. DOBLE, M.A., pp. viii + 404. (16s.)

1884–85.

3. **The Early History of Oxford (727–1100), preceded by a sketch of the Mythical Origin of the City and University.** By JAMES PARKER, M.A. With three illustrations, pp. xxxii + 420. (20s.)

1885.

4. **Memorials of Merton College, with biographical notices of the Wardens and Fellows.** By the Hon. GEO. C. BRODRICK, Warden of Merton College. With one illustration, pp. xx + 416. (16s., to members of Merton 12s.)

5. **Collectanea, 1st series,** edited by C. R. L. FLETCHER, M.A. (Contents :—*a.* Letters relating to Oxford in the XIVth Century, edited by H. H. Henson; *b.* Catalogue of the Library of Oriel College in the XIVth Century, edited by C. L. Shadwell; *c.* Daily ledger of John Dorne, bookseller in Oxford, 1520, edited by F. Madan; *d.* All Souls College *versus* Lady Jane Stafford, 1587, edited by C. R. L. Fletcher; *e.* Account Book of James Wilding, Undergraduate of Merton College, 1682–88, edited by E. G. Duff; *f.* Dr. Wallis's Letter against Maidwell, 1700, edited by T. W. Jackson.) With two illustrations, pp. viii + 358. (16s.)

1886.

6. **Magdalen College and King James II, 1686–88.** A series of documents collected and edited by the Rev. J. R. BLOXAM, D.D., with additions, pp. lii + 292. (16s., to members of Magdalen 12s.)

7. **Hearne's Collections** [as No. 2 above]. Vol. II. (20 Mar. 1707—22 May 1710), pp. viii + 480. (16s.)

8. **Elizabethan Oxford.** Reprints of rare tracts. Edited by the Rev. C. PLUMMER, M.A. (Contents:—*a.* Nicolai Fierberti Oxoniensis Academiæ descriptio, 1602; *b.* Leonard Hutton on the Antiquities

of Oxford; *c*. Queen Elizabeth at Oxford, 1566 [pieces by J. Bereblock, Thomas Nele, Nich. Robinson, and Rich. Stephens, with appendices]; *d*. Queen Elizabeth at Oxford, 1592, by Philip Stringer; *e*. Apollinis et Musarum Eidyllia per Joannem Sandford, 1592), pp. xxxii+316. (10*s*.)

1887.

9. **Letters of Richard Radcliffe and John James, of Queen's College, Oxford, 1749–83**: edited by MARGARET EVANS, with a pedigree, pp. xxxvi+306. (15*s*., to members of Queen's 10*s*. 6*d*.)

10. **Register of the University of Oxford, Vol. II (1571–1622), part 1. Introductions.** Edited by the Rev. ANDREW CLARK, M.A., pp. xxxii+468. (18*s*.)

1887–8.

11. **Do. Part 2. Matriculations and Subscriptions.** Edited by the Rev. ANDREW CLARK, M.A., pp. xvi+424. (18*s*.)

1888.

12. **Do. Part 3. Degrees.** Edited by the Rev. ANDREW CLARK, M.A., pp. viii+448. (17*s*.)

13. **Hearne's Collections** [as No. 2 above]. Vol. III. (25 May 1710—14 December, 1712), pp. iv+518. (16*s*.)

1889.

14. **Register of the University of Oxford, Vol. II, Part 4. Index.** Edited by the Rev. ANDREW CLARK, M.A., pp. viii+468. (17*s*.)

15. **Wood's History of the City of Oxford.** *New Edition.* By the Rev. ANDREW CLARK, M.A. Vol. I. The City and Suburbs. With three Maps and several Diagrams, pp. xii+660. (25*s*., to citizens of Oxford 20*s*.; the two Maps of old Oxford separately, not folded, 1*s*. 6*d*., to citizens 1*s*.)

1890.

16. **Collectanea, 2nd series**, edited by Professor MONTAGU BURROWS. (Contents:—*a*. The Oxford Market, by O. Ogle; *b*. The University of Oxford in the Twelfth Century, by T. E. Holland; *c*. The Friars Preachers of the University, edited by H. Rashdall; *d*. Notes on the Jews in Oxford, by A. Neubauer; *e*. Linacre's Catalogue of Grocyn's Books, followed by a Memoir of Grocyn, by the Editor; *f*. Table-Talk and Papers of Bishop Hough, 1703–1743, edited by W. D. Macray; *g*. Extracts from the 'Gentleman's Magazine' relating to Oxford, 1731–1800, by F. J. Haverfield. Appendix: Corrections and Additions to Collectanea,

Vol. I. (Day-book of John Dorne, Bookseller at Oxford, A.D. 1520, by F. Madan, including 'A Half-century of Notes' on Dorne, by Henry Bradshaw.) With one diagram, pp. xii + 518. (16*s*.)

17. **Wood's History of the City of Oxford** [as No. 15 above]. Vol. II. Churches and Religious Houses. With Map and Diagram, pp. xii + 550. (20*s*., to citizens of Oxford 16*s*.; Map of Oxford in 1440, separately, not folded, 9*d*., to citizens 6*d*.)

1890-91.

18. **Oxford City Documents**, financial and judicial, 1268-1665. Selected and edited by J. E. THOROLD ROGERS, late Drummond Professor of Political Economy in the University of Oxford. pp. viii + 440 (+ 2 loose leaves for vols. 6 and 16). (12*s*.)

1891.

19. **The Life and Times of Anthony Wood, antiquary, of Oxford, 1632-1695, described by Himself.** Collected from his Diaries and other Papers, by the Rev. ANDREW CLARK, M.A. Vol. I. 1632-1663. With seven illustrations. pp. xvi + 520. (20*s*.)

20. **The Grey Friars in Oxford.** Part I, A History of the Convent; Part II, Biographical Notices of the Friars, together with Appendices of original documents. By ANDREW G. LITTLE, M.A., pp. xvi + 372. (16*s*.)

1892.

21. **The Life and Times of Anthony Wood** [as No. 19]. Vol. II. 1664-1681. With ten illustrations. pp. xxviii + 576. (20*s*.)

22. **Reminiscences of Oxford, by Oxford men, 1559-1850.** Selected and edited by LILIAN M. QUILLER COUCH, pp. xvi + 430. (17*s*., to members of the University 10*s*. 6*d*.)

1892-93.

23. **Index to Wills proved and Administrations granted in the Court of the Archdeacon of Berks, 1508-1652.** Edited by W. P. W. PHILLIMORE, M.A. (Issued in conjunction with the British Record Society.) pp. viii + 200. (10*s*.)

1893.

24. **Three Oxfordshire Parishes. A History of Kidlington, Yarnton and Begbroke.** By Mrs. BRYAN STAPLETON. With a coloured map and 2 sheet-pedigrees, pp. xx + 400. (17*s*., to residents in the three villages 10*s*.)

25. **The History of Corpus Christi College, with Lists of its Members.** By THOMAS FOWLER, D.D., President of the College. With three illustrations. pp. xvi + 482. (20s., to members of Corpus 12s. 6d.)

1894.

26. **The Life and Times of Anthony Wood** [as No. 19]. Vol. III. 168½–1695. With three illustrations. pp. xxxii + 548. (21s.)

27. **The Register of Exeter College, Oxford,** with a history of the College, and illustrations. By the Rev. C. W. BOASE, M.A. Third edition, enlarged. pp. [8] + clxxxiv + 400. (*Presented to the Society by the author:* 15s., to members of the College 10s.)

28. **The Cartulary of the Monastery of St. Frideswide at Oxford.** Edited by the Rev. S. R. WIGRAM, M.A. With illustrations. Vol. I. General and City Charters. pp. xvi + 503 + six pages (loose) of corrections to Vol. XXIV. (21s.)

1895.

29. **The Early Oxford Press, a bibliography of printing and publishing at Oxford, '1468'–1640.** With notes, appendixes and illustrations. By FALCONER MADAN, M.A. pp. xii + 366. (Separate copies can be obtained only from the Clarendon Press, price 18s. The Society can only supply it in sets.)

Forthcoming Publication.

1895.

30. **The Life and Times of Anthony Wood** [as No. 19]. Vol. IV: Addenda. With illustrations. pp. xii + 322.

The 5th (and last) vol. of CLARK's edition of *Wood's Life and Times,* the 3rd (and last) vol. of the same Editor's *Wood's History of the City of Oxford,* the 2nd vol. of the *Cartulary of St. Frideswide's* edited by the Rev. S. R. WIGRAM, the 4th vol. of *Hearne's Diaries* edited by C. E. DOBLE, Esq., the *Place Names of the diocese of Oxford, Collectanea* III, edited by Prof. M. Burrows, and other volumes are in active preparation.

A full description of the Society's work and objects can be obtained by application to any of the Committee residing at Oxford (P. LYTTELTON GELL, Esq.. Headington Hill; FALCONER MADAN, Esq. (*Hon. Treasurer*), 90 Banbury Road; the Rev. the PROVOST OF QUEEN'S COLLEGE (Dr. MAGRATH); and C. L. SHADWELL, Esq., Frewin Hall, Oxford). The annual subscription is one guinea, and the published volumes as a set can be obtained by new members at one-fourth the published price (i.e. 10s. 6d. a year).

Jan., 1895.